BISMARCK

AND THE DEVELOPMENT OF GERMANY

VOLUME I

The Period of Unification, 1815–1871

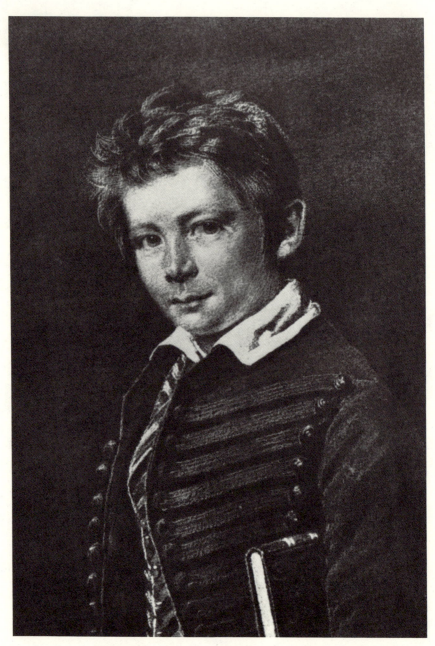

BISMARCK AT AGE ELEVEN, 1826 (PORTRAIT BY FRANZ KRÜGER).

BISMARCK

AND THE DEVELOPMENT OF GERMANY

VOLUME I

The Period of Unification, 1815–1871

Otto Pflanze

PRINCETON UNIVERSITY PRESS

PRINCETON, NEW JERSEY

✠

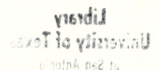

Bismarck and the Development of Germany

VOL. 1: THE PERIOD OF UNIFICATION, 1815–1871

VOL. 2: THE PERIOD OF CONSOLIDATION, 1871–1880

VOL. 3: THE PERIOD OF FORTIFICATION, 1880–1898

✠ ✠ ✠

Copyright © 1990 by Princeton University Press
Published by Princeton University Press, 41 William Street,
Princeton, New Jersey 08540
In the United Kingdom: Princeton University Press, Oxford
All Rights Reserved

Library of Congress Cataloging-in-Publication Data

Pflanze, Otto.
Bismarck and the development of Germany / Otto Pflanze. — [2nd ed.]
p. cm.
Previously published in 1963 in one volume.
Contents: v. 1. The period of unification, 1815–1871.
ISBN 0-691-05587-4 (v. 1)
1. Bismarck, Otto, Fürst von, 1815–1866. 2. Germany—History—1815–1866.
3. Germany—History—1866–1871. I. Title.

DD218.P44 1990   943'.07—dc20   89–11004   CIP

This book has been composed in Linotron Goudy

Maps on pages 22 and 317 by R. L. Williams

Princeton University Press books are printed
on acid-free paper, and meet the guidelines for
permanence and durability of the Committee on
Production Guidelines for Book Longevity
of the Council on Library Resources

Printed in the United States of America by
Princeton University Press, Princeton, New Jersey

1   3   5   7   9   10   8   6   4   2

✤ CONTENTS ✤

Book Four: *The Years of Fulfillment, 1867–1871*

✣ PREFACE ✣
To the First Edition

THE CAREER of a historical personality, observed Wilhelm Dilthey, is marked by reciprocating influences. In his early years such an individual is molded by forces the course of whose development he himself later helps to determine. Because of this interaction the biographer of Schleiermacher was compelled to broaden his subject to include the intellectual history of a whole epoch. What was true of Schleiermacher, the theologian, is also true of Bismarck, the statesman. The customary biographical form cannot capture the significance of a political figure of his stature. As important as the man himself were the many forces—social, political, intellectual, and institutional—which shaped his environment and with which he dealt.

This work is concerned with the interaction between these forces and the will of a political genius. It is a study of the effect of one man of extraordinary talent upon the historical process. Hence the more personal and anecdotal aspects of Bismarck's life are included only where they indicate attitudes or affected policy and events. The purpose is to expose the elements of thought and outlook which determined his political aims, the techniques of strategy by which he strove for their achievement, and the ultimate consequences of both for German political development.

Usually the period of German unification has been studied from the standpoint of foreign affairs. Such an orientation gives to the year 1871 the appearance of an end rather than a beginning. This book seeks to relate the story of diplomatic maneuver, war, and victory to the greater problem of Germany's internal political growth. The concentration is upon the internal consequences of both domestic and foreign policy and events. Seen from this viewpoint, the period of unification was one of revolution and reconstruction which established the character of German political attitudes and institutions until recent times. The subsequent period of consolidation, including the domestic history of the North German Confederation, has been reserved for a sequel volume.

During the years of research consumed by this project I incurred personal debts of many kinds. By far the greatest is that owed to Hajo Holborn of Yale University. It was he who more than a decade ago first pointed out to me the need for a fresh approach to the Bismarck problem. Without his advice, support, and encouragement along the way this volume would never have been completed. I am also deeply grateful to Herbert Kaplan and Theodore Hamerow, who read the entire manuscript and were responsible for many improvements; to Walter Steiner, my research assistant, for his patient help on many boring tasks; to Lawrence Steefel for graciously permitting me to profit from the manuscript of his work on the war of 1870; to Frank Rodgers and the library staff of the University of Illinois for much technical assistance; and to my wife, Hertha Haberlander Pflanze, whose keen literary sense pruned away many stylistic errors. In 1951–1952 I was aided by a research grant from the American Council of Learned Societies and during 1955–1957 by a United States government grant under the Fulbright act for research in Germany. The Universities of Massachusetts and Illinois also provided financial assistance. To the history department of the University of Minnesota I am particularly indebted for the recognition accorded the manuscript.

OTTO PFLANZE
Minneapolis
March 1, 1962

To the Second Edition and Sequel Volumes

THE GENESIS of this work has been long and arduous. At the outset it was not my intention to write a multivolume work, much less spend most of my working years on the project. When I went to graduate school in 1940, Germany was the world's greatest problem. How things got to be that way was a key question for those who entered graduate training at that time. I had the good fortune, furthermore, to come under the guidance of Hajo Holborn, one of the ablest historians of his generation. The dissertation I wrote on the development of the imperial administration in the Bismarck era proved to be too arid for my taste. In the course of it I developed an interest in Bismarck as a political tactician. But as my work on this topic progressed, I saw how impossible it was to separate that aspect from the whole complex of his thought and action. With Holborn's encouragement I broadened the investigation to include the entire man. My purpose then and thereafter was not to write a biography, of which there were already many, but to seek a better explanation of Bismarck's place in and his effect upon what he called "the stream of time."

Originally I thought of the work as a single volume. In the winter of 1958–1959 I fell ill and, during long months in the hospital at Urbana, Illinois, I had cause to meditate about my own mortality. I decided to terminate the book in 1871, not 1890. Health restored, I finished my final draft in the summer of 1961; publication followed in 1963. Having learned how to write history, I presumed that I could complete the second volume while on academic leave in 1966–1967. During that year I began to see that a new departure in German historiography, described in the introduction to this work, promised to yield much new and relevant information, particularly on economic and social history. As in all uprisings there were excesses, which one cannot ignore—if only to disagree. And yet the stream of usable information steadily widened. It soon became evident that I would have to write a new edition of the published volume, if only to provide a better footing for its sequel. Fortunately the theme and structure of the first volume enabled me to accommodate the new material without distortion.

During 1966–1967 I also concluded, coincidentally, that the traditional note-card system was inadequate for my task and invented another, which compelled me to retrace a lot of ground in the sources. During my next leave (1970–1971) I recognized the psychological basis for most of Bismarck's health problems, which added a significant new dimension to the entire project. Although I had a full draft by the end of 1975, I could not consider it complete without the opportunity to mine the archives at Merseburg and Potsdam in the German Democratic Republic. That opportunity finally came in 1976. The wealth of material that I uncovered there in the spring and summer of that year required a revision of the text, a task that was not completed until 1981. Although a rewarding experience, editing the *American Historical Review* (1976–1985) was a far greater distraction than I had anticipated. My subsequent appointment as Charles P. Stevenson, Jr. Professor of History at Bard College (1986 to the present) gave me the opportunity to finish what, I now realized, had become a three-volume work.

Those familiar with the volume published in 1963 will find that the general theme and structure are unaltered in the new edition. But new chapters and sections have been added, and no chapter has been republished unchanged. Sometimes the changes are cosmetic; usually they are substantial. No bibliography has been attempted for either this or the sequel volumes. The Bismarck literature is mountainous—and well nigh insurmountable. And yet the introduction and voluminous notes (sometimes of bibliographical character) do provide a guide to the works I found important.

The successive stages in the development of this work are demarcated by grants from American and West German foundations that freed me from academic obligations at critical times and provided for extended periods of research, reflection, and composition: Fellowship, John Simon Guggenheim Memorial Foundation, 1966–1967 (West Germany); Member, Institute for Advanced Study, 1970–1971 (Princeton); Fellowship, National Endowment for the Humanities, 1975–1976 (Minneapolis); Fellowship, International Research and Exchanges Board, 1976 (Merseburg, Potsdam); Member, Historisches Kolleg im Stiftverband für die Deutsche Wissenschaft, 1980–1981 (Munich); and Award, Fritz Thyssen Stiftung, 1986 (Munich). The years at the Institute for Advanced Study and the Historisches Kolleg were most important to me because of the logistic support those institutions provided, the scholarly contacts I made, and the intellectual inspiration I received. To the Historisches Kolleg, founded in 1980 to further the completion of opera magna by senior scholars, I am particularly indebted. My continuing relationship to that institution, to the eminent scholars of its Kuratorium, and to its ever helpful administrative staff (specifically, Georg Kalmer and Elisabeth Müller-Luckner) has been one of the most gratifying experiences of my life.

I am also thankful to my profession for providing me with the support required to write this work—to the foundations that awarded grants, to the scholars who supported my applications, and to all those (especially my family, to whom the sequel volumes are dedicated) who kept faith as the years passed and the manuscript grew. I owe much to five perceptive critics—Ronald Ross, Mark Lytle, Lamar Cecil, John Alden Nichols, and Ivo Lambi—who read the manuscript in 1987–1988 and offered many detailed corrections and suggestions. Through their efforts the text was greatly improved. In the final months (early 1989) I depended especially on Ross, a gifted, learned, and generous critic able to see blemishes that escaped me.

I wish also to thank Christina von Seggern for reading and criticizing an early draft of the manuscript; Thomas Kohut and Fred Weinstein, who provided important psychological insights; Klaus Bade for valuable advice and assistance at critical moments; Allan Palmer for his generous response to an inquiry; and John Röhl for access to the Eulenburg papers. Other scholars who helped are mentioned at appropriate places in the text. On my many stays in Germany over the years Rolf and Gelia Creutz added significantly to my understanding of the country and its people. Their generous hospitality enabled me on many occasions to desert the paper trails for Alpine paths—a refreshing diversion.

I am indebted also to many students whose seminar papers and discussions helped me focus my researches, and to research assistants on two continents who performed numerous tedious but necessary tasks. The assistants are too numerous to list, but I wish to express my gratitude in particular to Robert Berdahl, Donald Mattheisen, Stephen Lyders, Deborah Hertz, Rosemary Orthmann, Katrine Pflanze, Jutta Scott, Mechthild Clara Albus, Helmut Preuss, Wolfgang Smolka, James Brophy, and Lawrence Turner. To the archivists (universally and unfailingly helpful) of the many collections I consulted in the United States, the German Democratic Republic, and Federal Republic of Germany I extend my thanks—likewise to Fürstin Ann Mari von Bismarck and Graf Leopold von Bismarck for their gracious reception of me at Friedrichsruh in 1981 and for the access accorded me to the family archive. Finally, I am indebted to former colleagues in the Department of History at the University of Minnesota for sixteen years (1961–1977) of scholarly fellowship and to my new colleagues at Bard College whose friendly and good-humored reception eased the final months of hard labor on the manuscript.

Annandale-on-Hudson, New York,
in May 1989

✦ ABBREVIATIONS ✦
Used in the Footnotes

APP   Historische Reichskommission. *Die Auswärtige Politik Preussens, 1858–1871* (vols. 1–6, 8–10, Berlin, 1932–1939).

AWB   Heinrich von Poschinger, ed., *Aktenstücke zur Wirtschaftspolitik des Fürsten Bismarcks* (2 vols., Berlin, 1890).

BFA   Bismarck Family Archive (Friedrichsruh).

BGB   *Bundes-Gesetzblatt des Norddeutschen Bundes* (1867–1871).

BP   Heinrich von Poschinger, ed., *Fürst Bismarck und die Parlamentarier* (2d ed., 3 vols., Breslau, 1894–1896).

BR   Horst Kohl, ed., *Die politischen Reden des Fürsten Bismarck* (14 vols., Stuttgart, 1892–1905).

DPO   Heinrich Ritter von Srbik, ed., *Quellen zur deutschen Politik Österreichs, 1859–1866* (5 vols., Oldenburg, 1934–1938).

DZA   Das Zentralarchiv der Deutschen Demokratischen Republik (Potsdam and Merseburg).

GSA   Geheimes Staatsarchiv der Stiftung Preussischer Kulturbesitz (Berlin-Dahlem).

GSP   *Gesetzsammlung für die königlich preussischen Staaten* (Berlin, 1851ff.).

GW   Herman von Petersdorff and others, eds., *Bismarck: Die gesammelten Werke* (15 vols., Berlin, 1923–1933).

HW   Julius Heyderhoff and Paul Wentzcke, eds., *Deutscher Liberalismus im Zeitalter Bismarcks: Eine politische Briefsammlung* (2 vols., Bonn, 1925–1927).

OD   Ministère des Affaires Étrangère, *Les origines diplomatiques de la guerre de 1870/71: Recueil de documents officiels* (29 vols., Paris, 1910–1932).

RKN   Hermann Oncken, ed., *Die Rheinpolitik Kaiser Napoleons III. von 1863 bis 1870 und der Ursprung des Krieges von 1870/71* (3 vols., Berlin, 1926).

SBHA   *Stenographische Berichte über die Verhandlungen des Landtages: Haus der Abgeordneten.*

SBHH   *Stenographische Berichte über die Verhandlungen des Landtages: Herrenhaus.*

SBR   *Stenographische Berichte über die Verhandlungen des Reichstages.*

SEG   Heinrich Schulthess, ed., *Europäischer Geschichtskalender* (81 vols., Nördlingen and München, 1860–1940).

To All Volumes

ITH the exception of Napoleon and Hitler, no figure in modern European history has attracted as much interest as Otto von Bismarck. Since the first serious studies of the man and his career appeared eight decades ago, the size of the bibliography has reached staggering proportions. Still the stream of books and articles continues with no sign of abatement. Bismarck and national unification have as great a fascination for Germans as do Lincoln and the Civil War for Americans.

To foreigners as well, the personality and achievements of the master of *Realpolitik* have a magnetic attraction. His political career of more than half a century is one of the longest in the annals of statecraft. For nearly three decades of that time he was the dominant figure in German and European politics. Unexplored nooks and crannies, even whole rooms, are still being discovered in the edifice of his career. The wide range of his interests, the complexity of his mind, and his skill at political invention and maneuver have made the subject difficult to exhaust. The most important reason for continued interest, however, is the ongoing need to reassess Germany's past in view of its critical role in the disruption of the European political order in the first half of the twentieth century. Reviewing the "German catastrophë" in 1945, Friedrich Meinecke, the Nestor of German historians, wrote in sadness, "The staggering course of the first, and, still more, of the second world war no longer permits the question to be ignored whether the seeds of later evil were not already present in the Bismarck Reich."[1]

The Bismarck Problem, 1945–1961

Leading historians have never ceased to seek answers to the question Meinecke raised.[2] No other issue has aroused such intense, even impassioned,

[1] Friedrich Meinecke, *Die deutsche Katastrophe* (Wiesbaden, 1946), 26, translated as *The German Catastrophe: Reflections and Recollections* (Cambridge, Mass., 1950).

[2] The works discussed here are confined to those published in West Germany that are significant because they either influenced or typified the dominant trends in the Western interpretation of the Bismarck era since 1945. Readers interested in the East German perspective, which tends to be homologous and of little interpretative impact on the West, should consult Andreas Dorpalen, *German History in Marxist Perspective: The East German Approach* (Detroit, 1985). For an East German perspective on West German historiography see Gerhard Lozek and others, eds., *Unbewältigte Vergangenheit: Kritik der bürgerlichen Geschichtsschreibung in der BRD* (3d ed., Berlin, 1977).

interest among scholars in postwar Germany. For fifteen years the replies were mostly negative. In 1946 S. A. Kaehler set the tone by denouncing as "legend," "prejudice," and "propaganda" the view that any connection existed between Frederick the Great, Bismarck, and Hitler. Without taking the opposite viewpoint, Franz Schnabel questioned the wisdom of the solution that Bismarck provided for the problem of German unity. A more lasting solution, he argued, would have been a federal union of central Europe along lines advocated at the time by the publicist Constantin Frantz. By forcing Austria out of Germany in 1866, Bismarck prepared the way for the disintegration of the Habsburg monarchy and hence the ultimate isolation and decline of Germany itself. Gerhard Ritter and Wilhelm Schüssler were quick to rebut this "surprising thesis." The pressure of German nationalism, they asserted, was "irresistible"; the German people would have accepted no solution to the German question other than the one Bismarck devised. In reply, the Austrian historian Heinrich Ritter von Srbik reiterated once more his lifelong defense of the concept of a united central Europe.[3]

Ritter, Schnabel, and Schüssler agreed, nevertheless, that Bismarck was the last master of the art of eighteenth century "cabinet diplomacy" in an age increasingly dominated by national passions and crusading ideologies. According to Ritter, "Bismarck had nothing to do with the nationalism of the nineteenth and twentieth centuries and its blind fanaticism. One cannot possibly stress that fact sharply enough." Schnabel was equally emphatic, maintaining that Bismarck "had nothing in common with the dictators of the nationalistic period" and was completely devoid of that "*moderne Vaterländerei*" typical of the new national patriotism. "Bismarck was not at all a man of national or popular ideas," wrote Schüssler, but "a man of state and the reason of state . . . a man of pure *Staatsräson.*"[4]

This was also the position of Hans Rothfels, who denied that the Bismarckian Reich could validly be called a "national state." He believed this description applicable only to the western, not the eastern frontier, which included

---

[3] S. A. Kaehler, *Vorurteile und Tatsachen* (Hameln, 1949), 27–35; Franz Schnabel, "Bismarck und die Nationen," *La Nouvelle Clio*, 1–2 (1949–1950), 87–102, also in *Europa und der Nationalismus: Bericht über das III. internationale Historiker-Treffen in Speyer—17. bis 20. Oktober 1949* (Baden-Baden, 1950), 91–108; Gerhard Ritter, "Grossdeutsch und Kleindeutsch im 19. Jahrhundert," in Walther Hubatsch, ed., *Schicksalswege deutscher Vergangenheit: Festschrift für Siegfried A. Kaehler* (Düsseldorf, 1950), 177–201, and "Das Bismarckproblem," *Merkur*, 4 (1950), 657–676; Wilhelm Schüssler, "Noch einmal: Bismarck und die Nationen," *La Nouvelle Clio*, 1–2 (1949–1950), 432–455, and *Um das Geschichtsbild* (Gladbeck, 1953), 102–122; Heinrich Ritter von Srbik, "Die Bismarck-Kontroverse," *Wort und Wahrheit*, 5 (1950), 918–931.

[4] Gerhard Ritter, *Europa und die deutsche Frage* (Munich, 1948), 69–108, and "Bismarckproblem," 673, *Staatskunst und Kriegshandwerk: Das Problem des "Militarismus" in Deutschland* (Munich, 1954), vol. 1, 302–329; Franz Schnabel, "Bismarck und die klassische Diplomatie," *Aussenpolitik*, 3 (1952), 635–642, and "Das Problem Bismarck," *Hochland*, 42 (1949), 8–9; Schüssler, *Geschichtsbild*, 120–121.

many Poles and excluded millions of Germans. He quoted with approval the view of British historian Sir Lewis Namier that "German aggressive nationalism derives from the much belauded Frankfurt Parliament rather than from Bismarck and 'Prussianism.' " Although Bismarck was often criticized for having created the German state in defiance of the dominant ideas of his age, this was in Rothfels's opinion his greatest virtue. He is significant for our times precisely because he was alien to his own century and sought to disarm and confine those revolutionary forces that have since threatened our destruction. In a general survey of the Bismarck era, Walter Bussmann saw in Rothfels' writings the most penetrating analysis of the subject.[5]

On the other hand, two lifelong students of Bismarck's career, Arnold Oskar Meyer and Otto Becker, persisted in identifying him as a German patriot whose primary aim had always been national unification. To them the national character of the Second Reich was self-evident. In this they followed the views of two earlier historians, Heinrich Friedjung and Erich Brandenburg, both of whom saw evidences of national purpose very early in Bismarck's life. Another older school believed that he began as a Prussian patriot and made the transition to German nationalism fairly late. Richard Fester chose the year 1865, Erich Marcks 1866, Erich Eyck 1867. Wilhelm Mommsen argued that Bismarck had no other purpose than the establishment of Prussian hegemony over northern Germany and that the small-German Reich was the consequence of French imperialism. Its founder was an adherent of the national state only "in a very limited sense."[6]

Only upon one point was there near unanimity: postwar German scholars rejected the interpretations of both Eyck and Meyer, authors of detailed scholarly biographies of Bismarck. Completed during the Second World War, the two works are widely divergent in viewpoint. An émigré from the Hitler

[5] Hans Rothfels, *Bismarck und der Osten* (Leipzig, 1934), "Bismarck und die Nationalitätenfragen des Ostens," *Ostraum, Preussentum und Reichsgedanke in Königsberger historische Forschungen*, 7 (Leipzig, 1935), "Bismarck und das neunzehnte Jahrhundert," in Hubatsch, ed., *Schicksalswege*, 233–248, *Bismarck und der Staat* (Stuttgart, 1954), xvii–xlviii, "Zeitgeschichtliche Betrachtungen zum Problem der Realpolitik," in Richard Dietrich and Gerhard Oestreich, eds., *Forschungen zu Staat und Verfassung: Festgabe für Fritz Hartung* (Berlin, 1958), 526–529, and "Problems of a Bismarck Biography," *Review of Politics*, 9 (1947), 362–380; Lewis Namier, *1848: The Revolution of the Intellectuals*, in *Proceedings of the British Academy*, 30 (1944); Walter Bussmann, *Das Zeitalter Bismarcks* in Otto Brandt, Arnold Oskar Meyer, and Leo Just, eds., *Handbuch der deutschen Geschichte* (3rd ed., Constance, 1956), vol. 3/II, p. 247.

[6] Arnold Oskar Meyer, *Bismarck: Der Mensch und der Staatsmann* (Stuttgart, 1949); Otto Becker, *Bismarcks Ringen um Deutschlands Gestaltung* (Heidelberg, 1958); Heinrich Friedjung, *Der Kampf um die Vorherrschaft in Deutschland, 1859 bis 1866* (10th ed., Stuttgart, 1916), vol. 1, 141; Erich Brandenburg, *Die Reichsgründung* (2d ed., Leipzig, 1922), vol. 2, 30–35, 78–79; Richard Fester, "Biarritz: Eine Bismarck-Studie," *Deutsche Rundschau*, 113 (1902), 236; Erich Marcks, *Der Aufstieg des Reiches* (Stuttgart, 1936), 2, 274–275; Erich Eyck, *Bismarck: Leben und Werk* (Zurich, 1941–1944), vol. 2, 367; Wilhelm Mommsen, *Bismarck: Ein politisches Lebensbild* (Munich, 1959), 167–168.

regime, Eyck wrote from the standpoint of the nineteenth century liberal opposition. While marveling at Bismarck's genius, Eyck criticized his actions at
almost every turn of his career. Meyer's view, on the other hand, was that of
a conservative German nationalist, to whom Bismarck was the apex of German political achievement. German reactions to these works were markedly
different in tone and temper. Eyck's interpretation aroused a sharp, even irritated, response; the "old-fashioned," "outmoded" view of Meyer was generally treated with tolerance.[7]

Most postwar German scholars were equally adamant in repudiating the
view of Bismarck commonly held abroad: that of the "iron chancellor" or
"man of blood and iron." Schüssler, Otto Vossler, Leonhard von Muralt, and
Gustav Rein emphatically stressed that Bismarck, in stark contrast to Hitler,
was moved by a sense of ethical responsibility, grounded in an intense religious faith and earnest submission to a personal, all-powerful God. This inner
piety preserved him from the "demonism of power."[8] In an important work
Ritter strove to cleanse Bismarck's reputation from the taint of militarism.
Contrary to Moltke, the chancellor was opposed to "preventive war." During
the conflicts of 1864, 1866, and 1870, he insisted upon the primacy of diplomatic over military strategy. His "greatest service," Schüssler declared, was
the erection of "firm barriers" against demands of the generals for the priority
of military over political policy in wartime.[9]

With but few exceptions, German scholars of the immediate postwar era
rejected the view that there was any direct relationship between the Bismarckian and Hitlerian Reichs.[10] Later Meinecke himself appeared to retreat

---

[7] Rothfels, "Problems," 362–380; Schüssler, Geschichtsbild, 101–102, 142–143; Schnabel,
"Problem," 406; Ritter, "Bismarckproblem," 659ff.; Emil Franzel, "Das Bismarck Bild in unserer
Zeit," Neues Abendland, 5, (1950), 223–230; Wilhelm Mommsen, "Der Kampf um das Bismarck-
Bild," Universitas, 5 (1950), 273–280; Leonhard von Muralt, Bismarcks Verantwortlichkeit (Göt-
tingen, 1955), 218–220; Maximilian von Hagen, "Das Bismarckbild der Gegenwart," Zeitschrift
für Politik, 6 (1959), 79–83; Joachim H. Knoll, "Werk und Methode des Historikers Erich Eyck,"
Neue deutsche Hefte, pt. 64 (1959), 729–736.

[8] Schüssler, Geschichtsbild, 139; Otto Vossler, "Bismarcks Ethos," Historische Zeitschrift, 171
(1951), 263–292; Muralt, Verantwortlichkeit, 65–140; Gustav Adolf Rein, Die Revolution in der
Politik Bismarcks (Göttingen, 1957), 307–354. In 1943, however, Rein wrote of Hitler as "the
rescuer and benefactor of Europe." Europa und das Reich (Essen, 1943), 87.

[9] Ritter, Staatskunst, vol. 1, 238–329; Schüssler, Geschichtsbild, 80; also Muralt, Verantwortlichkeit, 34.

[10] See the compendia of Lothar Gall, ed., Das Bismarck-Problem in der Geschichtsschreibung nach
1945 (Cologne, 1971), and Hans Hallmann, ed., Revision des Bismarckbildes: Die Diskussion der
deutschen Fachhistoriker 1945–1955 (Darmstadt, 1972); and also the critical evaluation by Friedhelm Grützner, Die Politik Bismarcks 1862 bis 1871 in der deutschen Geschichtsschreibung: Eine kritische historiographische Betrachtung (Frankfurt a. M., 1986). Notable exceptions to the general
trend were the articles by Karl Buchheim, Alfred von Martin, Johann Albrecht von Rantzau,
and Walter Hofer translated in Hans Kohn, ed., German History: Some New German Views (London, 1954) 44–64, 94–107, 157–174, 187–205, Werner Richter, "Das Bild Bismarcks," Neue
Rundschau, 63 (1952), 43–63, and the neglected article of Herbert Michaelis, "Königgrätz: Eine

from his position of 1945. The Bismarckian *Machtstaat*, he concluded, was a geopolitical necessity for Germany. In the late 1950s Ritter even detected an upsurge of "Bismarck veneration." Bernhard Knauss wrote of a "certain tendency to repopularize Bismarck" by picturing him as the George Washington of German history; and Wilhelm Mommsen rejoiced over the development of a "much more positive judgment" of Bismarck, while cautioning against "too much of a good thing."[11] Comfort was found in the fact that the first German chancellor was not highly regarded by Nazi ideologists. Conservative historians were inclined to trace the origins of the Nazi revolution to the breakdown of the old aristocratic society and bureaucratic state under the impact of liberal and democratic ideas and emergence of the masses as a factor in politics. There was a tendency to see these ideas and movements as importations from abroad, foreign influences of cancerous effect on the sound organism of German society. It was assumed that the German Reich created by Bismarck and overturned in the revolution of 1918 was essentially a healthy institution, whose destruction eliminated the most effective obstacle to the rise of totalitarianism.[12]

The Bismarck Problem since 1961

Even as the first edition of this volume was in the process of publication (1961–1963) a revolution began in the interpretation of German history that

---

geschichtliche Wende," *Die Welt als Geschichte*, 12 (1952), 177–202. See also the remarkable work of Heinrich Heffter, *Die deutsche Selbstverwaltung im 19. Jahrhundert: Geschichte der Ideen und Institutionen* (Stuttgart, 1950), whose scope is considerably greater than its title. The criticism of Robert Saitschick, a Swiss literator, was one-sided and missed the mark; see his *Bismarck und das Schicksal des deutschen Volkes: Zur Psychologie und Geschichte der deutschen Frage* (Basel, 1949). Ludwig Dehio, editor of the *Historische Zeitschrift*, censured government policy and public temperament in the period of William II, but only by implication did his criticism extend to Bismarck and his work; see his *Deutschland und die Weltpolitik im 20. Jahrhundert* (Munich, 1955), translated as *Germany and World Politics in the Twentieth Century* (New York, 1959).

[11] Friedrich Meinecke, "Irrwege in unserer Geschichte?" *Der Monat*, 2 (1949–1950), 3–6, and the replies of Hajo Holborn and Geoffrey Barraclough, pp. 531–538, the former translated in Kohn, *New German Views*, 206–212; Ritter, "Bismarckproblem," 658; Bernhard Knauss, "Neue Beiträge zum Bismarckbild," *Politische Studien*, 10 (1959), 266–267; Wilhelm Mommsen, "Der Kampf um das Bismarck Bild," *Neue Politische Literatur*, 4 (1959), 210. Typical of the trend toward rehabilitation were the popular biography by Ludwig Reimers, *Bismarck* (2 vols., Munich, 1956–1957), the diplomatic "textbook" of Friedrich Haselmayr, *Diplomatische Geschichte des zweiten Reichs von 1871–1918* (3 vols., Munich, 1955–1957), the dramatized story of the dismissal by Richard Sexau, *Kaiser oder Kanzler* (5th ed., Berlin, 194?), and the similar, though not uncritical, work of Rudolf Baumgardt, *Bismarck: Licht und Schatten eines Genies* (Munich, 1951).

[12] Rothfels, "Bismarck und das neunzehnte Jahrhundert," 236ff.; Ritter, *Deutsche Frage*, 41ff. This was also the general tendency of Muralt, *Verantwortlichkeit* (187–217) and Rein, *Revolution in der Politik Bismarcks*. For an account of the historiographical environment that nurtured authors of the immediate postwar era see Bernd Faulenbach, *Ideologie des deutschen Weges: Die deutsche Geschichte in der Historiographie zwischen Kaiserreich und Nationalsozialismus* (Munich, 1980).

has profoundly changed the prevailing opinion of German historians concerning Bismarck and his works. Retirement and death had begun to thin the ranks of the generation that was born and educated in imperial Germany and never overcame a nostalgia for its political order and values. The multiplication of German universities and historical institutes in the postwar years, moreover, created a large number of new professorships, more than the dwindling old professoriate could dominate. The younger generation of scholars that now came to prominence was less interested in those problems associated with nationalism, national identity, and the "national state" that had absorbed their predecessors. Instead they turned their attention to problems of economic and social history that the older generation had tended to neglect.

The hallmark of the new historiography is a belief in the primacy of economic and social over political history. The decisive force in history is not the state, as earlier Prussian and German historians had believed, but society itself, specifically the economic changes that determine the course of social evolution, the growth of new social classes and interests, and the reactionary strategies and structures with which the traditional social and political order defended its hegemony against the rising tide of change and dissent.[13]

The transition did not occur without controversy. In 1961 the Hamburg scholar Fritz Fischer published in his *Griff nach der Weltmacht* an indictment of German foreign policy in the First World War that reopened the issue of German "war guilt" in 1914, a question that Weimar historians had answered in the negative. By implying that domestic concerns (private business interests and fear of socialism) had dictated foreign policy under Wilhelm II, Fischer called into question the "primacy of foreign policy" (*Primat der Aussenpolitik*), the traditional justification for monarchical authority in Prussia-Germany and the entire social-political order on which it was based. But he also shocked his colleagues in the historical profession by implying that a connection—indeed continuity—existed between Germany's objectives in the First and Second World Wars. Both implications have affected historians' interpretations and judgments of Bismarck and his influence upon German historical development.[14]

[13] Georg Iggers, ed., *New Directions in European Historiography* (Middletown, 1984) and *The Social History of Politics: Critical Perspectives in West German Historical Writing since 1945* (Dover, 1985); Richard Evans, "From Hitler to Bismarck; 'Third Reich' and Kaiserreich in Recent Historiography," *Historical Journal*, 26 (1983), 485–497, 999–1020; Hans Ulrich Wehler, "Historiography in Germany Today," in Jürgen Habermas, ed., *Observations on "The Spiritual Situation of the Age"* (Cambridge, Mass., 1984), 221–259.

[14] Fritz Fischer, *Griff nach der Weltmacht* (Düsseldorf, 1961), translated as *Germany's Aims in the First World War* (New York, 1967), and *Krieg der Illusionen* (Düsseldorf, 1969), translated as *War of Illusions* (London, 1974). On the "Fischer affair" see particularly John Moses, *The Politics of Illusion: The Fischer Controversy in German Historiography* (London, 1975), but also Immanuel Geiss, "Die Fischer-Kontroverse: Ein kritischer Beitrag zum Verhältnis zwischen Historiographie und Politik in der Bundesrepublik," *Studien über Geschichte und Geschichtswissenschaft* (Frankfurt

The search for continuity in German history and the effect of social change and conflict upon foreign policy led historians inevitably backward from the era of Wilhelm II to Bismarck. In the late Weimar period Eckart Kehr had already pointed in this direction in a work that traced the influence of ship-builders and armament makers on Germany's decision to build the high seas fleet that, more than any other factor, influenced Britain to join the Triple Entente. By publishing Kehr's essays under a provocative title, *Primat der Innenpolitik*, Hans-Ulrich Wehler proclaimed what became, in effect, the manifesto of a new generation of German scholars determined to overturn the German historiographical tradition.[15]

The discussions about "continuity or discontinuity" and "primacy of domestic or foreign policy" in modern German history have resuscitated a related problem, that of Germany's "special path" (*Sonderweg*). Is the German disaster of the twentieth century owed to her digression from an otherwise common European experience and tradition? The question is itself pejorative, of course, for it presumes that the countries of western Europe and North America were better equipped by their institutions and traditions to cope with mass democracy and totalitarian movements than were those of central Europe. Curiously this discussion has been conducted without reference to, and seemingly in ignorance of, its earlier history (described in the original introduction to this work). During the imperial and Weimar eras it was the common assumption of German historians that the divergence began in the late eighteenth century with the abandonment by Germany (in the philosophy of German idealism) of what had been a common European tradition of enlightened rationalism and natural law. Historians differed only in whether they judged Germany's uniqueness in a positive or negative light, with the former position predominating.[16]

Since the 1960s German historians have carried on this discussion exclusively in terms of social-political history. This time the negative view—that

---

a. M., 1972), 108–198, and A. Sywottek, "Die Fischer-Kontroverse," in Immanuel Geiss and Bernd Jürgen Wendt, eds., *Deutschland in der Weltpolitik des 19. und 20. Jahrhunderts* (Düsseldorf, 1973), 19–47; and Volker Berghahn, "Die Fischer-Kontroverse—15 Jahre danach," *Geschichte und Gesellschaft*, 6 (1980), 403–419.

[15] Eckart Kehr, *Schlachtflottenbau und Parteipolitik 1894–1901* (Berlin, 1930), translated as *Battleship Building and Party Politics in Germany, 1894–1901* (Chicago, 1975); Hans-Ulrich Wehler, ed., *Der Primat der Innenpolitik* (Berlin, 1965; 3d ed., 1976), translated as Eckart Kehr, *Economic Interest, Militarism, and Foreign Policy: Essays on German History* (Berkeley, 1977).

[16] The *Sonderweg* thesis in its earlier form pervaded German historical literature in the nineteenth and early twentieth centuries. The classic statements on the problem are Ernst Troeltsch, "The Ideas of Natural Law and Humanity in World Politics," in Otto Gierke, ed., *Natural Law and the Theory of Society, 1500–1800* (Cambridge, Eng., 1934), vol. 1, 201–222; and Hajo Holborn, "Der deutsche Idealismus in sozialgeschichtlicher Beleuchtung," *Historische Zeitschrift*, 174 (1952), 359–384, translated as "German Idealism in the Light of Social History," in *Germany and Europe: Historical Essays* (New York, 1970), 1–32. See also Faulenbach, *Ideologie des deutschen Weges*, especially pp. 6–13.

Germany's special path was an unfortunate detour on the road to "modernity"—has prevailed. The digression arose from the rapid pace of German industrialization in 1850–1873, the creation of a new elite based on banking and industrial wealth, its union with the old elite of agrarian landowners, and the continued power and influence of an autocratic, military, and bureaucratic state that primarily served the material and social interests of both elites.[17]

Naturally this historiographical trend raised doubts in many minds about the usefulness of biography as a form of historical knowledge. Should not the study of class and mass behavior have priority over the study of individual conduct? Is there any room left in history even for a "world-historical figure" of Hegelian dimensions? An early response to these questions came from Helmut Böhme, for whom Prussia's victory over Austria in the struggle for dominance over the Zollverein in 1860–1865 was more decisive for Germany's future than her military victory over Austria in 1866. In Böhme's account Rudolf Delbrück, the architect of Prussian economic policy, looms nearly as large as Bismarck, whose appointment in 1862 is asserted to have produced "no caesura" in Prussia's progress toward hegemony in Germany. The small-German unification of Germany arose, Böhme believes, more from Prussia's defense against the Austrian plan for an economic union of central Europe under Habsburg leadership than from Bismarck's plans for the expansion of Prussian power in Germany. By uniting Germany's agrarian and industrial elites, the protective tariff of 1879 constituted a "refounding of the German Reich"—an event that in Böhme's calculus rivals, indeed exceeds, in importance Germany's military victory over France and the establishment of the German Empire in 1870–1871.[18]

[17] See particularly Hans-Ulrich Wehler, *Das deutsche Kaiserreich, 1871–1918* (Göttingen, 1973), translated as *The German Empire, 1871–1918* (Dover, 1985) and Fritz Fischer, *Bündnis der Eliten* (Düsseldorf, 1979), translated as *From Kaiserreich to Third Reich, Elements of Continuity in German History, 1871–1945* (London, 1986). The English edition of Wehler's work contains in the notes and bibliographies extensive references to other contributions to the discussion on the "special path" and the related issues of continuity-discontinuity, and primacy of domestic or foreign policy. The character of the current debate on these issues and its connection with West German politics have been described by Richard J. Evans, "The New Nationalism and the Old History: Perspectives on the West German *Historikerstreit*," *Journal of Modern History*, 59 (December 1987), 761–797.

[18] Helmut Böhme, *Deutschlands Weg zur Grossmacht: Studien zum Verhältnis von Wirtschaft und Staat während der Reichsgründungszeit 1848–1881* (Cologne and Berlin, 1966), 15–17, 120–191, and 411–586, and "Politik und Ökonomie in der Reichsgründungs- und späten Bismarckzeit," in Michael Stürmer, ed., *Das kaiserliche Deutschland 1870–1918* (Düsseldorf, 1970), 26–50. For critiques of Böhme's position see Otto Pflanze, "Another Crisis among German Historians? Helmut Böhme's *Deutschlands Weg zur Grossmacht*," *Journal of Modern History*, 40 (1968), 118–129, and Hans-Ulrich Wehler, "Sozio-ökonomie und Politik in der Geschichte des Kaiserreichs," *Krisenherde des Kaiserreichs, 1871–1918: Studien zur deutschen Sozial- und Verfassungsgeschichte* (2d ed., Göttingen, 1979), 342–370.

Böhme's case for the importance of 1879 has had some impact on historians, but this cannot be said of his argument for the greater significance of 1865 over 1866. The hundredth anniversary of the era of unification produced a spate of articles and books distinguished more by new (and not so new) opinions than by new factual information.[19] But these publications did reveal a general agreement that historically Königgrätz was far more significant than Sedan. The events of 1866 had revolutionary consequences: the expulsion of Austria from Germany and Italy; the internal reorganization of the Habsburg Empire; the unification of northern Germany under Prussian hegemony; the reconstruction of the balance of power; and the encouragement given to nationalist aspirations everywhere in Europe. By comparison the events of 1870–1871, long celebrated by patriots as the glorious climax of German history, were now seen as anticlimactic. They merely completed, inevitably so, what had been begun four years earlier.[20]

The structural analysis of German social history in the nineteenth century has produced a strange paradox. On the one hand, its view of the course of German history in the period 1806–1933 is highly deterministic and depersonalized. The route to the Nazi assumption of power is a one-way street—no side streets, no alleys, and no turn-arounds. On the other hand, Bismarck's personal role in that process is curiously magnified. Contemporary "social science"–oriented historians regard Bismarck's "technique of domination" (Herrschaftstechnik)—illustrated by four models (negative integration, Sammlungspolitik, Bonapartism, and social imperialism)—as a work of genius responsible for merging the old Prussian-German aristocracy with the new entrepreneurial elite of industrial capitalism, thereby perpetuating an outmoded social and political order beyond its natural time of decay and demise. Bismarck's tactical genius, it is believed, consolidated a social-political structure that endured well into the twentieth century and prevented Germany's evolution into a democratic social and political order that could have withstood the

---

[19] Wolfgang von Groote and Ursula von Gersdorff, eds., Entscheidung 1866: Der Krieg zwischen Österreich und Preussen (Stuttgart, 1966) and Entscheidung 1870: Der deutsch-französische Krieg (Stuttgart, 1970); Adam Wandruszka, Schicksalsjahr 1866 (Graz, 1966); Helmut Böhme, ed., Probleme der Reichsgründungszeit 1848–1879 (Cologne, 1968); Richard Dietrich, ed., Europa und der Norddeutsche Bund (Berlin, 1968); Stürmer, ed., Das kaiserliche Deutschland 1870–1918; Karl Otmar von Aretin, "1866, ein Entscheidungsjahr der europäischen Geschichte," Fritz Kallenberg, "Die Vorgeschichte des Krieges von 1870–71," and Andreas Hillgruber, "Die Reichsgründung und das europäische Gleichgewicht," all in Institut für staatsbürgerliche Bildung in Rheinland-Pfalz, ed., Die Reichsgründung von 1871 im Urteil der Gegenwart: Versuch einer kritischen Bilanz (Mainz, no date); Theodor Schieder and Ernst Deuerlein, eds., Reichsgründung 1870–71: Tatsachen, Kontroversen, Interpretationen (Stuttgart, 1970); Ernst Deuerlein, ed., Die Gründung des Deutschen Reiches 1870–71 in Augenzeugenberichten (Düsseldorf, 1970); Eberhard Kolb, Der Kriegsausbruch von 1870: Politische Entscheidungsprozesse und Verantwortlichkeiten in der Julikrise 1870 (Göttingen, 1970); and Gall, Das Bismarck-Problem.

[20] Grützner, Politik Bismarcks, 80.

assault of political extremists of the left and right in an age of mass politics. Such an order, it is tacitly assumed, would have had a better chance of avoiding the German and European catastrophe of the twentieth century.[21]

Ironically this depiction of Bismarck resembles, except for the models, that of his admirers and hagiographers among earlier generations of historians—from Heinrich von Sybel, Erich Marcks, and Arnold Oskar Meyer to Hans Rothfels and Wilhelm Mommsen. Although they differ on whether Bismarck's works were good or bad for Germany, both schools of historiography—the old, political school and the new, economic-social school—are equally impressed by his skill as a manipulator of the historical process. German historians still look upon Bismarck and his career as the key to modern German history.[22]

Obviously it was premature to place Bismarck biography on the list of en-

[21] Wehler, *Das deutsche Kaiserreich, Bismarck und der Imperialismus* (Cologne, 1969), and *Krisenherde des Kaiserreichs*. For the debate on Wehler's position see Thomas Nipperdey, "Wehlers Kaiserreich: Eine kritische Auseinandersetzung," *Geschichte und Gesellschaft*, 1 (1975), 539–560, and *Gesellschaft, Kultur, Theorie* (Göttingen, 1976), 360–389; Hans-Ulrich Wehler, "Kritik und kritische Antikritik," in his *Krisenherde des Kaiserreichs*; and Otto Pflanze, "Bismarck's Herrschaftstechnik als Problem der gegenwärtigen Historiographie," *Historische Zeitschrift*, 234 (1982), 561–599, republished in *Schriften des Historischen Kollegs: Vorträge*, no. 2 (Munich, 1982).

[22] Recently the "new orthodoxy" has come under attack by two young English scholars. David Blackbourn and Geoff Eley, *Mythen deutscher Geschichtsschreibung: Die gescheiterte bürgerliche Revolution von 1848* (Frankfurt a. M., 1980), enlarged and translated in *The Peculiarities of German History: Bourgeois Society and Politics in Nineteenth-Century Germany* (Oxford, 1984). German scholars, they charge, know too little about the British model that is their standard of comparison for what went wrong in Germany; otherwise they would have seen that Germany, no less than Great Britain, actually experienced a bourgeois revolution "from below" in the nineteenth century. A "hegemony of the middle class" resulted from the acceptance of bourgeois standards and values in the society at large. What really matters in history, these historians argue, is what occurs among the masses of the population rather than among the elites that rule them.

The German reception of this work has been generally negative—most notably: Hans-Ulrich Wehler, " 'Deutscher Sonderweg': Kontroverse um eine vermeintliche Legende," Eley's reply and Wehler's rebuttal, and H. A. Winkler, "Der deutsche Sonderweg: Eine Nachlese," *Merkur*, 35 (1981), 478–487, 758–760, 793–804; Dieter Langewiesche, "Entmythologisierung des 'deutschen Sonderweges' oder auf dem Wege zu neuen Mythen," *Archiv für Sozialgeschichte*, 21 (1981), 86–111; Jürgen Kocka, "Der 'deutsche Sonderweg' in der Diskussion," *German Studies Review*, 5 (1982), 365–379. Kocka found "a little bit of gold mixed with a whole lot of sand."

The Blackbourn–Eley volume is an unfortunate by-product of their separate researches into the grass-roots politics of the German middle class. (The search for grass roots ought not to end with the discovery of straw men.) They belong to an English tradition of "history from below" that, no doubt, has something significant to contribute to German history. See Richard J. Evans, "Introduction: Wilhelm II's Germany and the Historians," in Richard J. Evans, ed., *Society and Politics in Wilhelmine Germany, 1888–1918* (London, 1978), 11–39, and Robert G. Moeller, "The Kaiserreich Recast? Continuity and Change in Modern German Historiography," *Journal of Social History*, 17 (1984), 655–683. Still, the genre is hardly unknown in German historiography (for example, the writings of Kocka, Gerhard A. Ritter, and many others, including the historians of *Alltagsgeschichte*). And the study of mass behavior can only supplement, never supplant, the study of elites.

dangered species. Indeed, the 1980s have already produced two major scholarly studies of the man—by Lothar Gall and Ernst Engelberg—one from each
side of the wall that separates East from West Germany.[23] Both books demonstrate the continuing fascination of the era of unification for scholars; Gall
devotes more than 60 percent, Engelberg the whole of his volume to the period up to 1871, which included only nine of Bismarck's twenty-eight years
in power. These nine dramatic years are, nevertheless, a touchstone for historical judgments concerning Bismarck's impact on German history. Despite
their differing ideological orientations, Gall and Engelberg are alike in their
belief that Bismarck, the pragmatist, had no choice (either in 1866 or 1870–
1871) but to make common cause with the liberal-national movement by
uniting Germany. For twenty years, according to Gall, Bismarck's actual aim
was the creation of an Austro-Prussian "condominium" over central Europe,
but "circumstances" eventually swept him into a more radical solution. To
believe that the alternatives he considered were actual choices is to credit
him with a freedom that he did not possess. The structure created in 1866–
1867 lacked—because it was not a national state—the "stabilizing and integrating factor" that could satisfy the expectations of a steadily widening circle
of the German public.[24] In Engelberg's interpretation Bismarck had to yield
to "bourgeois demands" lest he drive the bourgeoisie "leftward into the revolutionary camp." Bismarck did what "the cunning of history" demanded of
him by executing "from above" the bourgeois revolution that, according to
Marx, was the necessary prelude to a proletarian revolution "from below."[25]

A Discourse on Method

"Even a single historian, working at a single subject for a certain length of
time, finds when he tries to reopen an old question that the question has
changed."[26] This axiom by R. G. Collingwood contains a lot of truth, but it
is not universal. The question of Bismarck's impact on German and European
history is as valid and important today as it was in 1945. What has changed
is not the question but the answers. As the older generation of German scholars gave way to the younger, the predominant judgment shifted from positive
to negative. Succinctly stated, Bismarck-the-good-genius (Rothfels, Ritter)
gave ground, first, to Bismarck-the-bad-genius (Wehler) and, then, to Bis-
marck-the-diminished-genius (Gall, Engelberg). To this author none of these
positions does justice to the subject. How he differs from them should become

[23] Lothar Gall, *Bismarck: Der weisse Revolutionär* (Frankfurt a. M., 1980), translated as *Bismarck: The White Revolutionary* (2 vols., London, 1986); Ernst Engelberg, *Bismarck: Urpreusse
und Reichsgründer* (Berlin, 1985).

[24] Gall, *Bismarck*, 146–147, 307–339, 403ff.

[25] Engelberg, *Bismarck*, 438, 448, 453–454, 568, 571, 588, 619–621, 694–700.

[26] R. G. Collingwood, *The Idea of History* (Oxford, 1946), p. 248.

evident as the work unfolds. Impatient readers who like to know how the story ends before it begins may wish to peek at the final chapter of the third volume, where the author presents his conclusions. Impatient or not, most readers will still want to know how the author came to his final assessment. The following reflections on problems of nomenclature, categorization, and interpretation should assist them in understanding the text.

Three decades of fresh research have provided a wealth of new information on the German experience in the nineteenth century, particularly on economic and social development in relation to both domestic and foreign affairs. Because this is an ongoing, by no means finished discussion, the incorporation of these findings has often been difficult. In the present state of social history, for example, the definition of "class" remains a perplexing problem. What was so clear to Marx and Engels, and still is to orthodox Marxists, has grown ambiguous. The terms "working class," "proletariat," "middle class," "bourgeoisie," "petty bourgeoisie," and the like become increasingly questionable the more we learn from empirical studies about the character and complexity of the interest groups those terms are intended to represent. And yet all historical terms tend to become ambiguous with time and use, forcing those who would write with precision to attempt their redefinition. Historical usage, inevitably variable and changing, is constantly at odds with analytical precision. Those who invent new categories in their search for precision tend to return—unconsciously so, it would seem—to the older, traditional terms, no doubt because they are convenient and comfortable, like old shoes. The traditional terms are, furthermore, unavoidable if we are to understand how people once saw themselves and others in social terms. The categories they used (for example, *Arbeiterstand, Bauernstand, Mittelstand, Bürgertum, Adelsstand*) show how they perceived their society to be organized—perceptions that may not coincide with those derived today from quantitative and analytical evidence. Yet the lenses through which people once looked at their social world influenced, even guided, their actions.

The kind of analytical precision preferred by many historians today is often the enemy of effective, communicative English. In a work of this magnitude terms that are strange to most readers cannot be continually used without frequent repetition of definitions that interrupt the flow of the narrative or clutter the footnotes. Historians, as one philosopher of science observed, cannot be expected to write in the language of science. A historian writing in English about German history, furthermore, must translate German terms in ways that will not only communicate their meanings to English readers but also suggest unmistakably the German originals to scholars familiar with the literature. Sometimes only the original German word suffices (as in the case of *Mittelstand*), for the concept, being outside our historical experience, has no equivalent in our language. In general, I have preferred historical to analytical terms; the latter have been introduced only where greater precision seemed necessary. If the result is inconsistent, I plead guilty.

In the preface to the first edition I wrote that "the more personal and anecdotal aspects of Bismarck's life are included only where they indicate attitudes or affected policy and events." As work on the sequel volume progressed, it became apparent that Bismarck's personal life—particularly his physical and psychological condition—was more intimately connected with his political behavior than has been supposed. Hence an exploration of the psychological dimension of his personality became necessary. And yet no attempt has been made here to furnish the kind of in-depth psychoanalytic study of Bismarck that will satisfy "psychohistorians." Psychoanalytically informed readers will, nevertheless, find many new clues with which to arrive at their own interpretations of this complex man.

The author belongs to neither of the two schools identified by the binary phrase *Primat der Aussen- oder Innenpolitik*. In modern political history, as in contemporary politics, domestic and foreign affairs are never fully autonomous spheres. Neither has been totally dominant over the other in German history. The reality is one of continuing interaction and interdependence, with foreign affairs tending toward predominance in some periods (1858–1871), domestic affairs in others (1871–1887). Nor is it true that political power is merely a function of economic power, either in domestic or foreign affairs. This is a Marxist myth obviously contradicted by the history of every modern nation. The influence of general and group economic and social interests is apparent in the conduct of governments and political parties, but the limitations of that influence are also evident.

Both international and domestic politics have a dynamic character that tends to create semiautonomous systems within which the power struggle is conducted. The requirements of that struggle often transcend those of material interest and ideological commitment. Within each system—the party system in parliamentary politics and the state system in international politics— the participating units become functions of one another, owing to the necessities imposed by competitive interaction. History seen purely from the standpoint of the social- and interest-group conditioning of political action is likely to neglect this systems aspect of political behavior, which can not only produce unlikely alliances but also compel the most irreconcilable interests constantly to take each other into account. In the game of politics even deadly rivals become partners in hostility—each forced to modify his conduct according to his perception of the ambitions and vital needs of the other.

Nor are general ideas and ideologies merely a reflection of class interests. Although their arguments tend to serve the material wants of specific social groups, they can assume a life of their own, independent of their origins, because of the universal terms in which they are couched. Intellectual orientations that unite or divide a people cannot be dismissed as excess baggage, to be loaded and unloaded from the train of class interests at every crossing of the dialectic. They can be a critical part of the machinery that propels us. This is particularly true in the age of general literacy that began in the early nineteenth century. That previous generations of German historians placed too great an emphasis upon intellectual history in their search for an understanding of the past may be true. But that is no justification for ignoring the subject now that we have a broader perspective. Truth, as Hegel informed us, is only to be found in the whole.

A historian confronted with a problem of explanation on the scale attempted in these volumes must concern himself, then, not only with fundamental economic, social, and intellectual movements, but also with the ever fluctuating relationships between states and between political parties in the semiautonomous systems of international and parliamentary politics. In addition, he must describe the personalities whose character traits—insight or stupidity, tactics or whims, calculations or miscalculations—influenced the course of German and European affairs. Nor is it possible to leave out of such a history the record of discrete events that mark man's progress from stage to stage in the unending contest for power and influence. Analyses of mass behavior, valuable though they are, will never displace an accounting of the actions of those whom talent or chance has put in charge, if only briefly, of the wheels and levers that influence the course of human affairs.

History is the record of the unceasing interaction between freedom and necessity, between the creative power of individuals and groups of individuals with common purposes and the seemingly inexorable movement of "historical forces" that are nothing more than the trends and institutions that develop from the cumulative thoughts and labors of millions of individuals over long stretches of time. To discover the nature of that interaction is the principal task of all who are engaged in what Dilthey called "the human studies"— whether as philosophers, historians, social scientists, or literary artists. We shall see that Bismarck himself was aware of the problem.

BOOK ONE

The Years of Preparation,

1815–1858

One cannot possibly make history,
although one can always learn from it how
one should lead the political life of a great people
in accordance with their development
and their historical destiny.

—*Bismarck in 1892*

✠

CHAPTER ONE

The Stream of Time

T HE STREAM of time flows inexorably along. By plunging my hand into it, I am merely doing my duty. I do not expect thereby to change its course." This was the thought with which Bismarck began his career in the Prussian foreign service in 1851.[1] Four decades later, his view was still the same. To his many visitors in Friedrichsruh he was fond of saying: "Man can neither create nor direct the stream of time. He can only travel upon it and steer with more or less skill and experience; he can suffer shipwreck and go aground and also arrive in safe harbors."[2] His political career was one of the most effective of all time. Yet he felt to the end comparatively helpless before the push of historical forces. Only by examining the character of those forces can one understand his course and destination. What was the stream of time upon which Bismarck embarked?

In the early nineteenth century the currents of historical evolution in Europe were many and swift. The great cultural synthesis of the Enlightenment was in dissolution. Under the influence of economic change and laissez-faire doctrine, corporatism lost ground to capitalistic individualism, status society to class society, rationalism to romanticism, subjective to objective idealism. New centers of political orientation appeared in liberalism, conservatism, nationalism, and socialism. Everywhere people grappled for new principles in which to believe and new forms of organization with which to contain the growing complexities of modern life. Like the Atlantic nations, Germany was affected by the movement of these many forces. But here they appeared in a different order and strength, and tended to flow in different channels. Through Bismarck, furthermore, they were to be molded and transformed, their relationships split apart and recombined. The power with which he accomplished this was that of the Prussian state.

The Prussian State

Prussia was largely the creation of a series of long-lived, energetic, and talented rulers. The character of both the state and its subjects was determined by the effort to create under difficult circumstances a power capable of assert-

[1] GW, XIV, 249.
[2] GW, XIII, 558. For other similar remarks see GW, XI, 46; XIII, 304, 468; XIV, 751–752, 879–880.

ing itself in European politics. The land was poor, sparse in resources and population, and without easily defensible frontiers. Security and growth alike required a standing army large in proportion to the population. Once created, this force was also useful for the suppression of feudal liberty within the state. During the same half-century that saw the triumph of absolutism in France and its defeat in England, Elector Friedrich Wilhelm I (1640–1688) suppressed the feudal estates in his major possessions. Whatever possibility there might have been for their development into modern representative institutions vanished. Officials of the monarchy, appointed to collect new taxes and provision troops, assumed the function of building up the country's economy. In a country possessing little commerce and urban life the state was compelled, if the financial burden of the army was to be borne, to play a positive role in raising the productive capacity and living standard of the population. During the century after 1640 the power and influence of the bureaucracy penetrated every aspect of Prussian society.

The character of this bureaucracy was long influenced by its origins. It became a rigorously trained and disciplined instrument for the transmission of royal authority. Until the end of the reign of Frederick the Great (1740–1786) the king was the sole executive, acting through state secretaries whose function was not to formulate policy but to execute it. The system discouraged individual initiative and rewarded conformity. As early as the eighteenth century, university training and state examinations were required of officials; advancement came not through patronage but service. Dishonesty, disobedience, and independent action were punished. The employment of retired generals and disabled or overaged soldiers infused habits of military discipline.

The character of Prussia's army and bureaucracy influenced the mentality of its people. In an age of mercenary forces the army was more closely identified with the population in Prussia than it was in other countries. Although many foreigners served in all ranks, the officer corps was drawn largely from the Prussian nobility, foot soldiers from the peasantry. Hence the spirit of "cadaver obedience" (Kadavergehorsamkeit) drilled into the army carried over into the civilian population. The bureaucracy had a similar influence. Low-ranking officials—those most frequently in contact with the public—were retired soldiers, whose harshness of tone and authoritarian manner became typical of Prussian officialdom. The influence of army and bureaucracy upon the popular mind was all the greater because they lacked competition. No other institutions limited their impact upon public consciousness. The day of big business lay in the distant future. Far from being a rival, the Lutheran church was actually part of the state administration. In Luther's view the prince was ordained by God to maintain order in an evil world, to protect the Christian few from the majority. Luther was aware of the corrupting nature of power and considered the state a worldly institution. But he denied the right of popular resistance against tyrannical, even pagan, rulers. By abandoning its administration to the state, he made the church a vital prop of princely authority. Since the state assumed the functions of education and social welfare, the church was restricted to the propagation of faith.

With the growth of an administrative structure the state came to be regarded as an institution distinct from the person of the monarch. Hence Frederick the Great spoke of himself as "the first servant of the state." By refusing to intervene in matters of private law, he furthered the independence of the judiciary. Thus he founded the important tradition that, if absolute, the Prussian government ought not to be arbitrary. Those who wielded power were themselves subject to the laws of the state and the natural norms of justice. This was the beginning of the German concept of the *Rechtsstaat*, the state governed by the rule of law. After Frederick the Great monarchical absolutism evolved into bureaucratic absolutism. Although the final power resided with the king, the actual administration of government migrated into the hands of ministers. In military matters a similar migration of function was evident. During peacetime military affairs were routinely administered by high officers acting under the king's authority. Even in wartime Frederick's successors assumed only nominal command of the army.

Socially the Prussian system was an alliance between the monarchy and Junker aristocracy. Even as he subjected them to his authority, the Great Elector made important concessions to the nobles in local affairs. In Brandenburg and Prussia they were permitted to enserf the peasants on their estates. They were largely exempt from taxation, and commoners were forbidden to purchase noble estates. Rural Prussia was governed by royal agents (*Landräte*) nominated by the county nobility, though responsible only to Berlin. On the latifundia Junker landlords retained the feudal right to govern peasants and burghers. They were "kings in miniature," exploiting their powers of local government for their own economic advantage. In the eighteenth century they became the reservoir from which the Hohenzollern staffed the positions of command in both army and bureaucracy. Feudal vassalage was converted into the obligation and privilege of serving in the army officer corps. Although commoners were not totally excluded, their number was held to about 12 percent of the whole, and they were restricted to the less desirable branches. Under Frederick the Great aristocrats were given a virtual monopoly of the upper ranks of the state service. Without luck and exceptional talent burghers had little chance of advancement to the highest posts.

The Prussian system, it has been argued, did not differ essentially from that of the rest of Europe in the eighteenth century.[3] If not in kind, it did differ in

[3] Gerhard Ritter, *Die deutsche Frage* (Munich, 1948), pp. 21ff.; Fritz Hartung, *Deutsche Verfassungsgeschichte vom 15. Jahrhundert bis zur Gegenwart* (5th ed., Stuttgart, 1950), pp. 104ff. The best assessment of the Prussian social and political order in this era is Robert Berdahl, *The Politics of the Prussian Nobility: The Development of a Conservative Ideology, 1770–1848* (Princeton, 1988).

quality, which is the significant point. Enlightened despotism was a farce in
Russia, a failure in Austria, and untried in France. In the Prussia of Frederick
the Great it was a brilliant success. No other country possessed the same requisite combination of a genius-ruler, malleable population, and cooperative
nobility. In France the nobles had been stripped of all but property and social
prestige. But in Prussia they retained their traditional military and political
functions. On every level they were integrated into the state apparatus. Thus
was born what will be called here the "Prussian establishment," an interlocking combination of social, political, military, bureaucratic, religious, and monarchical institutions that dominated Prussian, and ultimately German, society and government into the twentieth century.

In an era of "cabinet diplomacy" and dynastic wars, the Hohenzollern rulers were not remarkably aggressive. Geography involved them, often involuntarily, in wars initiated by the great powers. Their territorial gains were not
made by an all-conquering army, but by skillful maneuver, timely investment
of force, and the ability and fortune to emerge on the winning side. There
was but one highly important exception: the surprise attack on Austria and
conquest of Silesia in 1740. To retain the prize Frederick the Great was compelled to fight three hard wars, the last of which brought him to the brink of
defeat. Far from convincing him of the value of aggressive war, this experience taught Frederick the value of a rational and limited foreign policy based
on the actual needs of the state and the European equilibrium.[4] For posterity,
however, the lesson was different. His talent and his success aroused the popular imagination and gave to his one great Machiavellian deed an enduring
aura of respectability.[5] By contrast, the foreign policy of French absolutism
ended in serious defeats and financial catastrophe. Through Frederick the
Great the Prussian military tradition acquired an offensive edge that not even
the debacle of 1806 could dull. Bismarck was to be its heir.

Moral Legitimation

Ultimately German idealism gave to Prussian absolutism, a revolutionary creation of the Hohenzollern dynasty, its moral legitimation. This philosophy
developed during an era of exceptional intellectual and cultural creativity in
Germany that lasted more than a half-century (1770–1830). In the age of

---

But see also Hans Rosenberg, *Bureaucracy, Aristocracy, and Autocracy: The Prussian Experience,
1660–1815* (Cambridge, Mass., 1958).

[4] Gerhard Ritter, *Staatskunst und Kriegshandwerk: Das Problem des "Militarismus" in Deutschland*
(Munich, 1954–1968), vol. 1, 25ff.

[5] On the Frederician tradition and its connection with the development of German nationalism see Alexander Scharff, *Der Gedanke der preussischen Vorherrschaft in den Anfängen der
deutschen Einheitsbewegung* (Bonn, 1929), and Paul Joachimsen, *Vom deutschen Volk zum
deutschen Staat* (3d ed., Göttingen, 1956), 35–36.

Kant and Hegel, Goethe and Schiller, Mozart and Beethoven, the Germans made their greatest contribution to European and world culture. In the fields of philosophy and literature German "idealists" departed from the Enlightenment in search of new insights and forms of expression. Dissatisfied with the limits of rationalism, they sought a deeper understanding of man, society, and history. Characteristic of the movement was an intense humanism, a vital absorption in problems of individual growth and self-development. Although primarily of lower middle class origin, its participants were an intellectual elite uncommitted to any class interest. For the most part they were nonpolitical. Although they valued freedom, what they had in mind was chiefly freedom of the human spirit, the capacity of man to realize his highest ideals, rather than the social and political freedoms of citizens.

The word *Libertät* made its debut in the German language as an expression of the corporate rights of princes against the emperor rather than of the natural rights of man. The progress of the princes toward absolutism within their principalities was but an extension of their struggle for autonomy within the Holy Roman Empire. In this way the German idea of freedom became associated with political authority, an association that long endured.[6] This binary relationship is also evident in the thought of Immanuel Kant, usually regarded as the intellectual father of German liberalism. His belief in the progress of reason, man as an end and not a means, the supremacy of law, and the ideal of popular sovereignty brought the German political tradition close to that of western Europe. And yet his rigorous ethics of duty, when coupled with his acceptance of the absolute state as a practical—though temporary—necessity, reinforced the Prussian tradition of obedience to authority.[7] Although Kant had a powerful influence on many educated Germans, his transcendental idealism was soon challenged by the absolute idealism of Georg Wilhelm Friedrich Hegel, who ultimately had the greater impact on German thought.

The ground was prepared for Hegel by Johann Gottfried von Herder, who rebelled against the Enlightenment's atomistic view of man and society by stressing the organic individuality of national cultures. Each nation, he taught, possesses a unique character determined by its folk spirit (*Volksgeist*) and the peculiarities of its historical growth. What applied to national cultures, others realized, could also be said of the state. As a traditional institution constructed by many generations, it too was an organism endowed with individuality. As such it also had the power and right of self-realization. In exercising that right, the state asserted its freedom. Like humans, the state was believed to possess a spiritual essence and moral worth. Hence Hegel could describe it as "the vessel of the world spirit [*Weltgeist*]," "the divine idea

⁶ Leonard Krieger, *The German Idea of Freedom* (Boston, 1957), 3ff.; Fritz Valjavec, *Die Entstehung der politischen Strömungen in Deutschland, 1770–1815* (Munich, 1951), 40.

⁷ Krieger, *German Idea*, 86–125; Wilhelm Metzger, *Gesellschaft, Recht, und Staat in der Ethik des deutschen Idealismus* (Heidelberg, 1917), 45–110.

as it exists on earth," and "the actually existing, realized moral life." "Christ died not only for men," declared the philosopher Adam Müller, "but also for states."[8] In their search for a new religious orientation, German idealists "changed the arena of ethical and spiritual decisions in human history." The state replaced the church as the repository of moral values. In western Europe morality continued to reside in the Christian faith and the ethical norms of natural law, but in German idealism it came to be identified with the state and the ruling power.[9] What Hohenzollern rulers (and contemporary German monarchs) had created in the interest of dynastic politics was apotheosized by German philosophers, whose works became the textbooks from which generations of nineteenth-century German students obtained their views of the world.

Its historicist viewpoint enabled German idealism also to explain and legitimate the changes that came to Germany as a result of the wars of 1792–1815. In a few years the conquest of Germany by France; the reconstruction accomplished by Napoleon assisted by German collaborators; the reforms in Prussia following its catastrophic defeat by Napoleon in 1806; and the decisions reached at the Congress of Vienna fundamentally altered the German political map. The Holy Roman Empire was swept away, its frontiers redrawn; the number of sovereignties was reduced from several hundred to thirty-nine; the ecclesiastical principalities disappeared, and all but four free cities lost their independence. The enlarged states that survived this massacre were confronted with problems of integration whose resolution required reforms. The reconstruction of the German map and reforms introduced for the consolidation of the surviving states tended to dissolve the hard crust of tradition and thereby expedite further change during the "restoration" era that followed.

Economic and Social Change

As monarchical absolutism and subsequently German idealism reached fruition, Germany was already in the early stages of permutations that ultimately transformed its economic and social life. After centuries of relative stability (except for losses suffered during the Thirty Years War) the German population began to expand in the late eighteenth century. In the first period for which trustworthy statistics are available (1817 to 1848) the number of people living in the area of the future German Reich increased from 25,009,000 to

[8] G.W.F. Hegel, *The Philosophy of History* (New York, 1944), 38–39; Jakob Baxa, ed., *Adam Müller: Die Elemente der Staatskunst* (Jena, 1922), vol. 2, 178–195. On Müller see Jakob Baxa, *Einführung in die romantische Staatswissenschaft* (Jena, 1931).

[9] Hajo Holborn, "Der deutsche Idealismus in sozialgeschichtlicher Beleuchtung," *Historische Zeitschrift*, 174 (1952), 359–384; Ernst Troeltsch, "The Ideas of Natural Law and Humanity in World Politics," in Otto Gierke, eds., *Natural Law and the Theory of Society, 1500–1800* (Cambridge, Eng., 1934), vol. 1, 201–222.

34,847,000. The highest rate of growth (beginning at 1.44 percent and descending to 1.30 percent annually) came in the first eight years. Although the reasons for this growth are disputed, some conclusions are justified. In the late eighteenth century the number and severity of epidemics declined and likewise the death rate. This was accompanied or followed by several linked conditions that favored a rapid expansion in the birthrate: agrarian prosperity in the late eighteenth century; increases in the acreage tilled and food supplied; a shortage of labor encouraging larger families; abolition of serfdom and legal restrictions on marriage; a reduction in the power of the guilds; and greater freedom of occupation (*Gewerbefreiheit*). More employment and greater personal freedom led to the creation of thousands of new households. Women married younger, increasing their childbearing years. Marriages delayed by the Napoleonic wars were consummated after 1815, producing a baby boom in the postwar years. The greatest increases in population came in the agrarian northeast and eventually in the urban centers of Rhineland-Westphalia, Saxony, the Main-Rhine region, and the northern seacoast. After 1826 the first wave of fecundity tapered off in the wake of economic difficulties.[10]

The long period of prosperity in the late eighteenth century was followed by wide fluctuations in the fortunes of European agriculture. During 1801–1817 grain markets were disturbed by overproduction, falling prices, some poor harvests, war, and Napoleon's continental system. In Germany a period of recovery began in 1811 but tapered off in 1817. Three bumper harvests in 1819, 1820, and 1821 filled granaries and depressed prices. By 1825 the price of grain in the interior of Germany was 23 percent under that of 1817. The result was "poverty, lamentation, and despair." In Prussia many peasant farmers, unable to meet their payments under the emancipation land settlement, were compelled to sell land. But neither did the estate owners fare well. A majority was forced by excessive indebtedness and falling land values to liquidate their holdings, which often passed into bourgeois hands. Many (including Bismarck) survived only with the help of friends and relatives. Not until the 1830s did grain prices finally begin to recover and resume their upward climb, a trend that lasted thirty years.[11]

The growth in population, though ultimately beneficial to agriculture, cre-

[10] Walther G. Hoffmann, *Das Wachstum der deutchen Wirtschaft seit der Mitte des 19. Jahrhunderts* (Berlin, 1965), 172–173; G. Mackenroth, *Bevölkerungslehre* (Berlin, 1953), 412ff.; Wolfgang Köllmann, "Bevölkerungsgeschichte 1800–1970," in Hermann Aubin and Wolfgang Zorn, eds., *Handbuch der deutschen Wirtschafts- und Sozialgeschichte* (Stuttgart, 1976), vol. 2, 9–15; Wilhelm Abel, *Agrarkrisen und Agrarkonjunktur* (2d ed., Hamburg, 1966), 188–204; Ernst Klein; *Geschichte der deutschen Landwirtschaft im Industriezeitalter* (Wiesbaden, 1973), 26–34. For a summary of debate on population growth and its causes see Peter Marschalck, *Bevölkerungsgeschichte Deutschlands im 19. und 20. Jahrhundert* (Frankfurt a. M., 1984), 14ff., 128–131.

[11] Klein, *Landwirtschaft im Industriezeitalter*, 49–52; Abel, *Agrarkrisen und Agrarkonjuntur*, 205–225.

ated new problems for German society. Despite increasing emigration (487,000 between 1831 and 1848), the new millions outstripped available opportunities for employment. Adverse conditions in agriculture depressed business activity in an economy still overwhelmingly agrarian. Although manufacturing made some progress during the late eighteenth century, it was hampered by the ensuing war and depression and by lack of capital. In the 1820s Germany was overpopulated, judged not by food supply but by the available means of livelihood.[12] Eventually industrialization provided succor, but the first surge did not arrive until the mid-1830s. Prussia's creation of a German customs union (Zollverein) during 1818–1834 expedited trade and led to some expansion in textile manufacture. Railway construction, begun in 1835, reached a preliminary climax in 1846, encouraging the production of coal, iron ore, pig iron, machinery, and allied industries. Even so, Germany in 1848 was still a generation behind Britain and Belgium in industrialization.[13] During the 1830s employment provided by early industrialization did not suffice to relieve pauperism among the thousands who migrated to the city slums in search of a livelihood.

The Napoleonic wars and Prussian reforms, fluctuations in the agrarian economy, early population growth and latent industrialization, mass poverty and social distress—these conditions had their effect on the structure of German society in the pre-March era. In rural areas abandonment of legal restraints on the sale of noble estates and growth in the export trade accelerated the shift from subsistence to capitalistic agriculture. To survive financially, estate owners were compelled to adopt many of the rationalized practices of businessmen. Those who made that transition expanded their latifundia at the cost of small farmers, enlarging the body of day laborers, many of whom became wage earners. In growing urban centers a new industrial elite began to rival the old merchant elite in wealth and status, although not yet in numbers.[14]

The power structure of traditional society—based economically on agricul-

---

[12] Wolfram Fischer, Jochen Krengel, and Jutta Wietog, eds., *Sozialgechichtliches Arbeitsbuch I: Materialien zur Statistik des Deutschen Bundes 1815–1870* (Munich, 1982), 34; Abel, *Agrarkrisen und Agrarkonjuntur*, 226–242, and *Massenarmut und Hungerkrisen im vorindustriellen Deutschland* (Göttingen, 1972); W. Conze, "Vom Pöbel zum 'Proletariat'," in Hans-Ulrich Wehler, ed., *Moderne deutsche Sozialgeschichte* (Cologne, 1966), 111–136; Nicholas Bullock and James Read, *The Movement for Housing Reform in Germany and France, 1840–1914* (Cambridge, Eng., 1985), 17–25.

[13] Friedrich-Wilhelm Henning, *Die Industrialisierung in Deutschland 1800 bis 1914* (Paderborn, 1979), 111–155.

[14] Friedrich Zunkel, *Der rheinisch-westfälische Unternehmer 1834–1979* (Cologne, 1962); Jürgen Kocka, *Unternehmer in der deutschen Industrialisierung* (Göttingen, 1975) and *Lohnarbeit und Klassenbildung, Arbeiter und Arbeiterbewegung in Deutschland, 1800–1875* (Berlin, 1985); Shulamit Volkov, *The Rise of Popular Antimodernism in Germany: The Urban Master Artisans, 1873–1896* (Princeton, 1978), 123ff.

ture, socially on agrarian landlords, and politically on bureaucratic absolut-ism—remained intact and dominant. But yeast had been added to the dough; changes were in prospect, praised by some, deplored by others. And so it was only natural that Germans began to search for new ideas and philosophical systems with which to reverse (romantic conservatism), contain (realistic conservatism and moderate liberalism), or promote (radical liberalism and Utopian socialism) the processes of social change. What they found depended on their interests as well as their convictions. For many Germans nationalism supplied the moral cement needed to reunite a society in which traditional bonds were dissolving and new ideological frictions appearing.[15] It also pro-vided an ideal goal that served the practical ends of new material forces gen-erated by industrial capitalism. Having tasted the fruits of the Zollverein, German businessmen began to consider what additional gains might be achieved through political unity—for example, uniform weights and mea-sures, common coinage and currency, centralized banking and credit, and common codes of patent and commercial law.

Varieties of German Liberalism

Germany did not have a liberal "movement" in the genuine sense of the word until the 1840s. Not until the industrial revolution first began to affect the traditional social structure could a popular force develop to challenge, in some degree, existing arrangements of society and government. Meanwhile, liber-alism was largely monopolized by intellectuals and progressive bureaucrats. The former sought to explicate it in the form of political philosophy; the latter, to give it practical effect in statecraft.

Although variations on the theme of liberalism were infinite, three clusters are evident: bureaucratic, moderate, and radical liberalism. Only radical lib-eralism, the weakest of the three, found the link between traditional authority and human freedom incompatible and chose the latter. To bureaucratic lib-erals came the first opportunity to enact liberal ideas into reality. In the Prus-sian reforms after 1807 Baron vom Stein and his associates sought to convert "subjects" into "citizens" by granting greater freedom in economic and social life and participation in local and regional government. In order to liberate Prussia and Germany from French rule, they wished to arouse in the citizen a sense of identification with the state and willingness to sacrifice for it. But they did not seek a fundamental transformation of society and government. Neither Stein nor Prince Karl von Hardenberg perceived a basic contradic-tion between monarchical authority and popular liberties. What they sought

[15] Robert Berdahl, "New Thoughts on German Nationalism," *American Historical Review*, 77 (1972), 65–80.

was an integral union of the two. Their aim was not to overturn the existing order but to modernize it.[16]

What the reformers achieved reflected not only their limited objectives but also the resistance of affected interests. Although freed from serfdom, peasants remained in economic servitude. Commoners received the legal right to acquire noble estates, but those who did so tended to adopt rather than change the social and political attitudes of the aristocracy. The power of the gentry in rural government remained unbroken. Although burghers were given a voice in urban government, no channel was constructed through which to make their will and interests understood in the central government. Universal military service and a popular militia remained without their natural complement in universal suffrage and an elected parliament. Talent and achievement were made the basis of officer selection, but the officer corps remained in actual fact the monopoly of the aristocracy. Although promised, a constitution was never granted, and the government remained absolute both in theory and practice. The individual received greater economic and social freedom, but the masses retained the habits of obedience and subservience typical of the old regime.[17]

Although the Prussian reforms demonstrated that an aristocratic bureaucracy was not impervious to liberal ideas, they also revealed that to a certain extent these ideas were compatible with the essential structure of the Prussian state and society. From the standpoint of what was to come, the greatest significance of the reforms was to initiate a process of compromise and modernization by which the old order either preempted or appropriated the program of popular liberalism. Although halted for a time on the political plane after 1815, this process continued on the economic one. By adopting free trade within Prussia in 1818 and extending it to most of Germany through the Zollverein, the Berlin government began the absorption of economic liberalism. All of these reforms preserved the tradition that the bureaucratic state was the only source of political initiative in Prussian society. Political change, it appeared, was best achieved not against the state, but through it.

Moderate liberals were torn between faith and doubt in the capacity of existing monarchies to provide room for popular liberties. Hence they were in constant quest of philosophical systems and governmental structures capable of containing both extremes toward which they were attracted. The ways they chose depended upon their particular political experiences and whether the means of harmonization were found in rationalist or organic thought.

---

[16] Krieger, German Idea, 139–165.

[17] See Walter Simon, The Failure of the Prussian Reform Movement, 1807–1819 (Ithaca, 1955); Franz Schnabel, Deutsche Geschichte im neunzehnten Jahrhundert (Freiburg i. Br., 1949–1959), vol. 1, 316–478; Heinrich Heffter, Die deutsche Selbstverwaltung im 19. Jahrhundert: Geschichte der Ideen und Institutionen (Stuttgart, 1950), 84–136; Ernst Rudolf Huber, Deutsche Verfassungsgeschichte seit 1789 (Stuttgart, 1956), vol. 1, 95–113.

Proximity to France gave southwestern liberals greater interest in the natural-law concepts of the Enlightenment. Most did not, however, accept the concept of popular sovereignty from across the Rhine and found their ideal instead in the "mixed constitutions" of Baden, Württemberg, and Bavaria, which combined an autocratic executive with a popular legislature. The "classical liberals" of the north, on the other hand, were nurtured on organic theory and rejected natural law. Following Hegel, they deified the state and wanted representation only in corporate form.[18]

Moderate liberalism became the typical political philosophy of the German "middle estate" (*Mittelstand*). This was the term by which the middle strata of German society (as determined by wealth, income, occupation, and status) identified themselves. Among them were an educated elite of professional persons (professors, lawyers, and jurists), big and small businessmen (bankers, manufacturers, merchants), lesser state officials, shopkeepers, artisans, and self-sufficient farmers. Except for the officials, they shared a sense of autonomy born of financial independence, distrust of those who stood above and below them in the social scale, and the conviction that theirs was the "general estate" (*allgemeiner Stand*) destined to lead the nation toward modernity. No common organization, much less political party, bound them together— merely a general conviction that their status group was the repository of enlightened thought and civic virtue, that the values they shared ought to guide the conduct of public affairs, and that the inevitable progress of reason guaranteed their ultimate implementation. During the restoration era they were exasperated by the censorship, political chicanery, and oppressiveness of Prussia's "bureaucratic absolutism." In the parliaments of the German medium states equipped with constitutions and in the provincial diets and city councils of Prussia the *Mittelständler* found but limited opportunity to translate their ideas into action. Not until the revolution of 1848 was it clear how widely they differed when it came to drafting concrete political programs and purposes.[19]

Distrustful of both *Adelsstand* and *Arbeiterstand*, members of the *Mittelstand* rejected the bureaucratic absolutism that protected the power and status of the former and the institutions of popular sovereignty that would open the door to political power for the latter. To fill the void that remained between aristocratic privilege and popular rule they turned to the concept of the

[18] Krieger, *German Idea*, 229–252, 278–322; Jacques Droz, *Le libéralisme Rhénan, 1815–1848* (Paris, 1940), 425–455.

[19] Herbert Obenaus, *Anfänge des Parlamentarismus in Preussen bis 1848: Handbuch der Geschichte des deutschen Parlamentarismus* (Düsseldorf, 1984); see also the essays by Gerhard A. Ritter, Herbert Obenaus, Hans Boldt, and Hartwig Brandt in Gerhard A. Ritter, ed., *Gesellschaft, Parlament und Regierung: Zur Geschichte des Parlamentarismus in Deutschland* (Düsseldorf, 1974), and Reinhart Koselleck, *Preussen zwischen Reform und Revolution: Allgemeines Landrecht, Verwaltung, und soziale Bewegung von 1791 bis 1848* (Stuttgart, 1967).

Rechtsstaat, which placed both monarch and subject under the rule of law. This became the most popular word in the lexicon of German liberalism. Although those who used the term meant different things by it, *Rechtsstaat* never lost its original function of reconciling authority and freedom. For all their dissatisfaction with the authoritarian states of the restoration period, moderate liberals were unwilling to sacrifice the state's power to act for what they considered to be the common good, to direct economic growth into the channels they desired, and to preserve public order in times of economic distress and social unrest. Moderate liberals had far more in common with bureaucratic than with radical liberals.[20]

Brought to life by the French Revolution, German radical liberalism was after 1815 a vague and inchoate movement within the *Burschenschaften*, fraternal organizations founded to perpetuate the popular spirit of the war against Napoleon. The Karlsbad decrees of 1819 caused many students to turn away from politics. Under the leadership of Karl Follen, a radical minority came to believe in the necessity of a democratic, unitarian republic to be achieved by revolutionary means. The radical *Burschenschaftler* remained, nevertheless, a small and ineffectual group, which finally dissolved after the revolution of 1830. During the next two decades the radical tradition was kept alive by the "young Germans" and "young Hegelians." They shared a burning desire to translate abstract ideals of human freedom into practical action. But they were composed of isolated literati and intellectuals on the fringe of German society. Many, like Heinrich Heine, Ludwig Börne, and Karl Marx, were abroad in exile. No more than the moderates did they represent a genuine popular force.

The Paris revolution of 1830 produced in some minor German states a brief flurry of revolutionary activity, whose aftermath can be seen in the Hambach festival of 1832 and an attempted coup in Frankfurt am Main in 1833. The 1840s were marked by new violence, beginning with an uprising of impoverished Silesian weavers in 1844 and climaxed by Berlin's "potato revolution" of April 1847. During the three intervening years Germany, like much of Europe, suffered an agricultural catastrophe; poor grain harvests were coupled with a blight that ruined the potato crop. The price of food rose astronomically—potatoes (the poor man's staple), rye, and wheat by an average of more than 100 percent. Hunger, disease, and death stalked the rural villages and lower class districts of the cities. Continued railway construction kept the mining, iron, and machine industries prosperous, but the absorption of purchasing power by increased food prices was soon felt in consumer industries.[21]

[20] Krieger, *German Idea*, 252–261; James Sheehan, *German Liberalism in the Nineteenth Century* (Chicago, 1978), 19–48; Reimund Asanger, *Beiträge zur Lehre vom Rechtsstaat im neunzehnten Jahrhundert* (Bochum, 1938), 11–25.

[21] Fischer, Krengel, and Wietog, eds., *Sozialgeschichtliches Arbeitsbuch*, vol. 1, 62–80, 180;

During the summer of 1847 the crisis eased owing to the prospect of a good harvest, but its traumatic effect lingered.

In the larger towns radical agitators fed upon the social discontent of artisans and factory workers. Opposition deputies from many parliaments met periodically to discuss programs and tactics. Organizations were formed for political as well as social purposes. In many regions and among many interest groups there was unwonted activity. But for what ends? How solid was the liberal front? Did its ideals actually have the loyalty and understanding of the rioters and demonstrators who occasionally poured into the streets? These were vital questions that only the test of revolution could answer.

Varieties of Conservatism

Faced with the challenge of liberalism, the aristocratic order was compelled to seek an ideological defense for powers and privileges previously taken for granted. As in the case of liberalism, the variations of conservative thought were many. But two clusters stand out: those of romantic and realistic conservatism.

The starting point for romantic conservatism was Edmund Burke's view of the social contract as an indissoluble partnership, embracing successive generations—not merely the living but also the dead and unborn. "Each contract of each particular state," he wrote in *Reflections on the Revolution in France*, "is but a clause in the great primeval contract of eternal society." The true law of nature, conservative philosophers maintained, was not based upon rational norms but upon historical development. The valid structure of German society and government was a corporate one inherited from the Middle Ages, not the atomized society of liberalism or the centralized government of absolutism. State and society were integrally joined in a living body, whose members were estates and corporations working together for the welfare and continued vitality of the whole. Romantic conservatives idealized the feudal system with its contractual rights, services, and dependencies. Whereas rationalists had completed the divorce of theology from political theory begun by Machiavelli, ultraconservatives accomplished their remarriage. The traditional institutions of society were God's handiwork and to do them violence was akin to blasphemy. If the state was a vital organism, then it was, like all living beings, a creation of the divinity. The state had not been created by men for the mere negative purpose of warding off evil; it had been instituted by God for the improvement of man's moral virtue.[22]

Theodore S. Hamerow, *Restoration, Revolution, Reaction: Economics and Politics in Germany, 1815–1871* (Princeton, 1958), 3ff., 75ff.

[22] Schnabel, *Deutsche Geschichte*, vol. 1, 194ff.; Valjavec, *Strömungen*, 255ff.; Klaus Epstein, *The Genesis of German Conservatism* (Princeton, 1966); and Sigmund Neumann, *Die Stufen des*

Like liberals, however, conservatives had an ambivalent attitude toward the state. Although the absolute state had absorbed the independent political rights of the nobility, its monarch was still the apex of the aristocratic pyramid and its power the bulwark of the traditional order against the rising pressure of new social interests. Hence romantic conservatives were faced with the problem of reconciling the feudal system they admired with the absolute state that was its natural foe.

The philosophy of Karl Ludwig von Haller provided a solution. Haller maintained that the natural and therefore God-ordained condition of man was not equality and personal autonomy but inequality and dependence, the stronger over the weaker. The microcosm of society was the family. As the father rules over wife and children, so the master governs his servants, the landowner his peasants, the teacher his pupils, the leader his followers, and the prince his subjects. The entire social fabric was woven from such dependent relationships based upon mutual duty and service more than force. The prince alone was independent, subject only to God. The state he ruled was simply the highest in a pyramid of contractual relationships, which were matters of private, not public law. Haller's denial of public law was, in effect, a rejection of the modern state itself.[23]

The models for Haller's system were the patrician order of his native Berne and the patriarchal governments of the smaller principalities in Germany. But his most devoted following appeared in Prussia, for whose "military state" he had less sympathy. Two influential noblemen, Ludwig and Leopold von Gerlach, formed the "Christian-Germanic circle" to study and propagate Haller's doctrine. In his *Restauration der Staatswissenschaft* they found an arsenal of ideas with which to defend the aristocratic order against absolutism and bureaucratic liberalism. Ludwig objected, however, to Haller's "deistic-naturalism," maintaining that legitimate monarchs governed by the grace of God, not by the right of the stronger. As the ruling caste, the nobility followed the dictates of divine will, not of natural law. The patrimonial state was a "Christian state"; its constitution, the ten commandments.[24]

In the Stein–Hardenberg period an aristocratic opposition developed in Prussia for the first time since the seventeenth century—dedicated to the defense of specific aristocratic rights rather than general human rights. Its power

preussischen Konservatismus: Historische Studien, vol. 190 (Berlin, 1930); Reinhold Aris, *History of Political Thought in Germany from 1789 to 1815* (London, 1936), 251–265, 288–319.

[23] Johannes Haller, *Restauration der Staatswissenschaft oder Theorie des natürlich-geselligen Zustands* (6 vols., Winthur, 1816–1834); Wilhelm Hans von Sonntag, *Die Staatsauffassung Carl Ludwig v. Hallers* (Jena, 1929); Ewald Reinhard, *Karl Ludwig von Haller, der "Restaurator der Staatswissenschaft"* (Münster, 1933).

[24] On the views of the Gerlachs see Hans Joachim Schoeps, *Das andere Preussen* (2d ed., Honnef, 1957), 11–92, and Helmut Diwald, ed., *Von der Revolution zum Norddeutschen Bund: Politik und Ideengut der preussischen Hochkonservativen, 1848–1866; Aus dem Nachlass von Ernst Ludwig von Gerlach; Erster Teil: Tagebuch 1848–1866* (Göttingen, 1970), 9–77.

and its chance rested upon influence rather than numbers. The brothers Gerlach were close friends and advisers of the crown prince. When the latter ascended the throne in 1840 as Friedrich Wilhelm IV, Leopold, a general, became his personal adjutant, and Ludwig, a career official, was appointed president of the superior court of appeals in Magdeburg. In accord with romantic doctrine Friedrich Wilhelm finally summoned an estates general, the ill-fated United Diet of 1847. Except for the attempt to restore the *Ständestaat* of earlier times, romantic conservatives tended to avoid political change. Law was regarded as the expression of God's will. To "make" rather than "find" it was to violate the divine order.[25]

Realistic conservatives found Haller's rejection of the modern state a denial of reality and sought a doctrine more in harmony with the facts of political life. Ultimately one appeared in the philosophy of Friedrich Julius Stahl. A converted Bavarian Jew, Stahl was given a professorial chair at the University of Berlin by Friedrich Wilhelm IV. In search of a way to harmonize unity and diversity in the world and to find absolute values in the flux of history, Stahl found his solution in the concept of personality. The "highest principle of the world" was a personal, creative being, the single source of all diversification and change. With this concept he was able to draw a parallel between the universe and the state. The supreme being expressed the unity of the world, the state that of its subjects. In monarchical systems the prince personified the state. The personal relationship between sovereign and subject was as necessary as that between God and man. Following Luther, Stahl believed the state was instituted by God to maintain order in a sinful world. To this end power was properly concentrated in the hands of the prince and not decentralized in a feudal hierarchy. In the Lutheran tradition he allowed only the rights of protest and passive resistance against tyranny.[26]

No more than the romantic conservatives was Stahl an absolutist. Though rejecting the organic theory as such, he believed in the necessity of an assembly of estates. By *Stände*, however, he meant the existing occupational groups into which society was "naturally" divided, not the medieval corporations of which romanticists fantasized. In 1848 he was willing to include even the urban proletariat.[27] The powers of the assembly were to be purely "moral" and

[25] Schnabel, *Deutsche Geschichte*, vol. 2, 32; vol. 4, 486. Actually the influence of the Gerlachs upon Friedrich Wilhelm IV was limited. The king was convinced that, as a divine-right monarch, he possessed insights not given to other mortals. Herman von Petersdorff, *König Friedrich Wilhelm der Vierte* (Stuttgart, 1900), 1ff., 35ff., 60ff.

[26] Friedrich Julius Stahl, *Die Philosophie des Rechts* (1st ed., 3 vols., 1830–1837). On Stahl see particularly Gerhard Masur, *Friedrich Julius Stahl: Geschichte seines Lebens* (Berlin, 1930); also Schnabel, *Deutsche Geschichte*, 4, 539–547, Erich Kaufmann, *Studien zur Staatslehre des monarchischen Prinzips* (Leipzig, 1906), and Herbert Marcuse, *Reason and Revolution: Hegel and the Rise of Social Theory* (2d ed., New York, 1954), 360–374.

[27] Friedrich Julius Stahl, *Die Revolution und die constitutionelle Monarchie* (2d ed., Berlin, 1849), 58–59; Bernhard Michniewicz, *Stahl und Bismarck* (Berlin, 1913), 101.

"consultative." Having no control over the executive and no firm financial authority, it was to act merely as a "watchman" to guarantee the supremacy of law.[28] Later he realistically accepted the wider powers granted to the Prussian legislature under the constitution of January 31, 1850. During the 1850s Stahl argued for representation only by the "higher classes"; that is, landowners and industrialists, with the former predominant.[29] Ultimately his conception, rather than Haller's, became the foundation of conservative thought in nineteenth-century Prussia. After 1848 it enabled conservatives to reconcile themselves to constitutionalism. But it also paved the way for their eventual acceptance of the Bismarckian Reich.

Crosscurrents of Nationalism

In Western civilization the idea of the nation has been reached from two directions. Among Atlantic peoples the molding force was that of the state. Here awareness of nationality developed from a common political allegiance and experience. But in central and eastern Europe the awareness of nationality preceded and even helped create the nation-state. Here national consciousness grew out of the chrysalis of unique cultures. This difference in historical timing and direction drove another of those divisive wedges into the center of European civilization. The Atlantic peoples have tended to regard nationality as a matter of subjective will—*un plébiscite de tous les jours* in the extreme formulation of Ernest Renan. But east of the Rhine nationality came to be determined by such objective factors as language, folkways, and ethnic origin. After the appearance of social Darwinism in the late nineteenth century it also became a matter of "blood" and racial stock.[30]

As Friedrich Meinecke demonstrated in a classic study, the idea of German nationalism was born within the cosmopolitan sentiment of the eighteenth century, from which it gradually separated.[31] By emphasizing the individuality of national cultures, Herder's concept of the *Volksgeist* helped to awaken national consciousness not only in Germany but also throughout central and eastern Europe. At the same time it accentuated that individuality by encouraging German authors to abandon the slavish imitation of French literary and intellectual models. The great outpouring of literary and philosophical

[28] Friedrich Julius Stahl, *Das monarchische Prinzip* (Heidelberg, 1845), 25–26.

[29] Friedrich Julius Stahl, *Philosophie des Rechts* (3d ed., Heidelberg, 1854–1856), vol. 3, 317–334, 389ff., 443–449; Michniewicz, *Stahl und Bismarck*, 101–107.

[30] Jacques Droz, "Concept français et concept allemand de l'idee de nationalité," in *Europa und der Nationalismus: Bericht über das 3. internationale Historiker-Treffen in Speyer—17. bis 20. Oktober 1949* (Baden-Baden, 1950), and Hans Rothfels, "Grundsätzliches zum Problem der Nationalität," in *Zeitgeschichtliche Betrachtungen: Vorträge und Aufsätze* (Göttingen, 1959).

[31] Friedrich Meinecke, *Weltbürgertum und Nationalstaat: Studien zur Genesis des deutschen Nationalstaates* (5th ed., Munich and Berlin, 1919); see also Joachimsen, *Vom deutschen Volk zum deutschen Staat*.

effort known as German idealism provided a new and richer content to German culture, which made Herder's concept all the more meaningful to educated people. From a mere recognition of the individuality of the German spirit, German intellectuals proceeded to the assertion of its superiority. "Every people has had its day in history," Schiller declared, "but the day of the German is the harvest of all time."[32] The conviction grew that German culture had a world mission to perform. The cosmopolitan universalism of the Enlightenment gave way to the nationalistic universalism of the emerging "age of ideology."[33]

In the beginning, nevertheless, this attitude was nonbiological, even nonpolitical. It did not mean national exclusiveness. In Herder's view civilization was many-sided; the efflorescence of all national cultures could but enrich the whole. Among German idealists the growing conviction of Germany's national mission actually signified a retreat from politics, rather than a politicizing of cultural ideas. In a period of French military domination they found a haven in the empire of the spirit. Here they felt a sense of superiority as the heirs and synthesizers of what was best in the Nordic and classical traditions.

In other minds, however, the French imperium soon produced a nationalistic reaction of political significance. The overthrow of the republic and the substitution of Napoleonic absolutism disillusioned those who had accepted the cosmopolitan message of the revolution as a fulfillment of the Age of Reason. The defeat of Prussia and the completion of the French conquest of Germany aroused in some Germans a fiery national sentiment like that which had inspired the French after 1789. For the first time the cry was raised for a closer political union of the German nation. As we have seen, however, the galvanizing energy for the war of liberation came from the Prussian bureaucracy rather than from a spontaneous popular movement. Through social, political, and military reforms liberal officials sought to generate the same kind of national power that had enabled the French to conquer most of Europe.

Initially the idea of German national unity appeared to be as great a threat to conservative interests as was liberal egalitarianism. Although Haller had largely ignored the question of the nation, his followers found it increasingly difficult to do so. Ultimately they adapted the concept of the *Volksgeist* to their own purposes. The true content of the German spirit, they argued, was the historic form of the nation: that is, political multiplicity rather than unity. Traditionally Germany was a collection of principalities ruled by legitimate princes headed by the Habsburg dynasty. The wars of the French Revolution and Napoleon had destroyed the Holy Roman Empire and with it many sovereignties. And yet much of the German tradition remained alive in

[32] Quoted in Schnabel, *Deutsche Geschichte*, vol. 1, 289.
[33] *Ibid.*, 283–315.

the German Confederation. Thirty-nine principalities remained, and kings, dukes, and grand dukes still sat on their thrones. Friedrich Wilhelm IV even toyed with the romantic notion of restoring the imperial crown to the Habsburgs.[34]

Cultural nationalism was not the only form of the national idea in Germany. Within the larger German states the growth of monarchical power had produced in the eighteenth century a "state nationalism" based on common dynastic allegiance and political experience. In Prussia the penetrating power and activity of the monarchy made the population acutely aware of the state in their daily lives. Service in the wars of Frederick the Great generated feelings of patriotic loyalty to both state and dynasty in the officer corps and Junker caste. Frederick sought to inculcate in them an "*esprit de corps et de nation.*" Although he demanded from ordinary subjects little more than hard work and obedience, this same national patriotism blossomed in some degree among the masses as well. The talent and fame of the philosopher-king and the glory of his victories were persuasive. They gave to many Prussians feelings of patriotic pride and, even in the absence of political rights, a sense of identification with and participation in a powerful national community.[35]

After 1815 the homogeneity of the Prussian nation was disrupted by the incorporation of the Rhineland. More urban than the rest of Prussia, the area possessed a larger business class, fewer landed noblemen, and more peasant freeholders. Its inhabitants were predominantly Catholic, initially more favorable to Austria than Prussia. Under the French imperium they had acquired the Napoleonic code, the French system of communal government, and the idea of free enterprise. With some success the Rhinelanders resisted the efforts of the Berlin government to impose the Prussian legal, political, and even social structure upon the west. But after 1840 Rhenish particularism began to dissolve. A new leadership appeared, composed of moderate liberals willing to collaborate with the regime. The best way to protect Rhenish interests, they maintained, was to work for a constitutional government in Berlin; they favored German unity under Prussian hegemony with a Hohenzollern Kaiser.[36] In combination with Prussia's militaristic tradition, state nationalism was a potentially disruptive force. Its inherent chauvinism was reinforced by the romantic view of the state as an organism requiring growth for self-realization and possessing an individuality that could only be developed in conflict with other states.

[34] Meinecke, *Weltbürgertum*, 223ff.; Schoeps, *Das andere Preussen*, 76ff.

[35] Meinecke, *Weltbürgertum*, pp. 30ff.; Gerhard Ritter, *Friedrich der Grosse* (2d ed., Leipzig, 1942), 199; Ernst Rudolf Huber, "Der preussische Staatspatriotismus im Zeitalter Friedrichs des Grossen," *Zeitschrift für die gesamte Staatswissenschaft*, 103 (1943), 430–468. See also the famous passages in *Dichtung und Wahrheit* (Books 2 and 7) in which Goethe described the influence of Frederick upon Germany as a whole.

[36] See Droz, *Le libéralisme Rhénan*.

In southern Germany, state nationalism took yet another form. Although the middle states—Baden, Württemberg, and Bavaria—were in varying degrees the artificial creation of Napoleonic statesmanship and the Congress of Vienna, all three succeeded after 1815 in building a sense of national identity. In Bavaria the task was easiest, for the Wittelsbach dynasty was Germany's oldest ruling house and the Bavarian *Stamm*, alone among the ancient German tribes, had retained through the centuries a degree of political homogeneity. Under Count Maximilian von Montgelas integration of the new territories, acquired with the help of Napoleon and retained at the Congress of Vienna, was accomplished through the methods of enlightened despotism. But in Baden and Württemberg it was achieved by the grant of constitutions providing for popular representation. Here an association developed between liberalism and state nationalism.[37]

Liberalism and German nationalism were in the beginning natural allies in the common struggle against particularism and reaction. As has been shown, however, German liberalism was not a single, but a divided, movement. Upon these divisions German nationalism acted as a welcome synthetic force. In the *Burschenschaften* it provided a new solution for the problem of combining authority and freedom. Among radicals it seemed to offer a convenient "moral lever" with which to set the masses in motion in the interest of democratic ideals.[38] Whatever their disagreements on political theory and program, moreover, moderates and radicals could at least agree on the necessity of German unification. In his *Briefwechsel zweier Deutschen* of 1831 Paul Pfizer analyzed this common bond, but pointed to a residual difference of prophetic significance. The moderate liberal of Pfizer's essay argued that Germany must be "first united and then free," the radical that freedom was the prerequisite of unity.[39]

Whatever their views on alternative paths toward freedom and unity, moderate and radical alike were attracted by the prospect of national power. German liberalism had its birth as a political force in a period of national humiliation. It was a child of the war of liberation, and the crucial issue of its earliest years was national independence more than freedom. Pride of intellectual achievement was not enough to appease indefinitely the growing national ego. The conviction developed that without political unity the cultural mission of the German *Volksgeist* could never be fully achieved. To many, Prussian leadership appeared indispensable for the achievement of German unity. Under Stein and Hardenberg Prussia had taken the lead in seeking the regeneration and liberation of the German nation. The territorial settlement

[37] Erich Brandenburg, *Die Reichsgründung* (2d ed., Leipzig, 1922), vol. 1, 43–45.

[38] Krieger, *German Idea*, 263, 329; R. Hinton Thomas, *Liberalism, Nationalism, and the German Intellectuals, 1822–1847* (Cambridge, Eng., 1951), 124ff.

[39] In *Deutsche Literaturdenkmale des 18. und 19. Jahrhunderts* (Berlin, 1911), vol. 144, 270–271.

North Sea

Baltic Sea

Jutland

Kolding

Düppel
Flensburg
Dannevirke
Kiel
Holstein
Lübeck
La.
Mecklenburg

Königsberg
East P.

West P.

Pomerania

Oldenburg
Hamburg
Bremen
Hanover
Hanover
Westphalia
Prussia
Cologne
Aachen
Rhineland
Koblenz
Nassau
Hesse
Palatinate
Baden-Baden

Br.
An.
Göttingen
Kassel
El.
Hesse
Gotha
Ducal
Frankfurt
Darmstadt
Thuringian
States
Karlsruhe
Stuttgart
Württemberg
Baden
Sigmaringen

Schönhausen
Potsdam
Berlin
Brandenburg
Elbe
Oder
Dresden
Erfurt
Saxony

Posen

Silesia

Bohemia

Olmütz

Moravia

Bavaria

Munich

Salzburg
Gastein
Carinthia

Empire of Austria

Vienna
Danube
Buda
Pest

Hungary

Tyrol

Lombardy
(Lost 1859)

Venetia
(Lost 1866)

Carniola

Rhone

Rhine

Visula

GERMANY
1815-1866

German Confederation
of 1815

Br. Brunswick
An. Anhalt
La. Lauenburg

French
Boundary
Changes

Luxemburg
Moselle
Prussia
Trier
Palatinate
Tholey
Saarlouis
Boundary of 1814
Landau
France
Metz
Rhine
Boundary of 1815

of 1815 had left Prussia more German in population than Austria. By organizing the Zollverein, Prussia started Germany on the path toward economic unity. In the European crisis of 1840 her army appeared to be the chief bulwark against foreign attack. Although unprepared to demand the exclusion of Austria, liberal nationalists began to regard Prussia as the natural nucleus of a future German union. They longed for her liberalization, but the reality was reaction. Hence they took refuge in the Hegelian myth of her liberality. In the "ideology of Prussianism" the Frederician state became the haven of spiritual freedom and intellectual cultivation. The assignment of a "national mission" to Prussia reinforced the traditional synthesis of freedom and authority in German thought.[40]

The Revolution of 1848

The propulsion behind the German revolution of March 1848 was not the liberal-national movement. Not doctrines or principles but specific grievances and general feelings of social injustice were the source of revolutionary discontent. Three successive years of crop failures, starvation, declining trade, and unemployment had left bitter memories that a good harvest and renewed business activity in late 1847 could not erase. Still, Germany would have had no revolution in March 1848 but for the February uprising in Paris and the revolutionary mood it produced in western and central Europe. News that the masses had taken to the streets in Paris, Budapest, Prague, and Vienna produced a like reaction in Berlin and other German cities.

And yet liberalism had become the conventional language of protest, and through its terminology, often imperfectly understood, the dissatisfied gave voice to their resentments. In 1847 Prussia's United Diet had provided liberal businessmen with the opportunity to voice their demands. Summoned by Friedrich Wilhelm IV, the diet, representing Prussia's provincial estates, had denied his request for railway construction credits unless he fulfilled his predecessor's promise of a constitution for Prussia. A year later, these moderate liberals were boosted into power by the kind of revolutionary violence they eschewed.[41] In Berlin an incohesive cabinet, composed of liberal businessmen (Ludolf Camphausen and David Hansemann) and "old Prussian" noblemen,

---

[40] See Scharff, Gedanke der preussischen Vorherrschaft; Droz, Le libéralisme Rhénan, 250ff.; Heffter, Selbstverwaltung, 254; and Hans Rosenberg, Rudolf Haym und die Anfänge des klassischen Liberalismus: Beihefte der Historischen Zeitschrift, 31 (Munich, 1933), 90ff.

[41] No attempt is made here to recapitulate the story of the revolution of 1848 as a whole. Of interest to this work are those events that involved or affected Bismarck and his career. On the revolution see Rudolf Stadelmann, Soziale und politische Geschichte der Revolution von 1848 (Munich, 1948); Hamerow, Restoration, Revolution, Reaction; Veit Valentin, Geschichte der deutschen Revolution (2 vols., Berlin, 1930–1931); and particularly Manfred Botzenhart, Deutscher Parlamentarismus in der Revolutionszeit 1848–1850: Handbuch der Geschichte des deutschen Parlamentarismus (Düsseldorf, 1977).

had the task of mediating between the Prussian national assembly, elected by universal and equal male suffrage, and the king, backed by a loyal officer corps and an obedient army. The task of mediation became steadily more difficult, as the assembly drifted to the left under the leadership of radical liberals and the king listened increasingly to a "camarilla" of reactionary officials and generals. In Frankfurt am Main a revolutionary parliament, elected to draft the constitution for a united Germany, was compelled to maneuver between the state governments, which they did not wish to liquidate, and the wishes of radical liberals, who wanted a more far-reaching revolution. Ultimately the spirit of compromise prevailed. The final draft provided for a federal structure with a monarchical head and a parliament elected by universal male suffrage. Essentially, however, the structure was one of mixed powers, for the cabinet was to be appointed by the Kaiser and its "responsibility" was undefined.

While the deputies debated, the foundation beneath them crumbled. Throughout most of Germany the revolutionary enthusiasm of March evaporated with astonishing speed. Burghers were shocked by the vigor with which artisans and workers manned the barricades and by the social goals they voiced. The lower social strata, moreover, were disappointed by the inadequate social program of the *Mittelstand* liberals whom they had boosted into power. During the summer and autumn renewed fighting occurred in Berlin, Baden, and Frankfurt. Faced with renewed unrest among the urban lower classes, the moderates turned increasingly to the right for support. But suddenly this prop too was removed. At the end of October the remaining moderates in the Berlin cabinet were turned out of office, and a reactionary cabinet under Count Friedrich von Brandenburg was appointed. The army disarmed the citizen guard without incident. The Prussian national assembly was removed from the capital and dissolved on December 5, 1848. As a last act of defiance, the deputies called upon the public to refuse taxes to the reactionary government. But the response was weak.

Having discarded the moderates, the monarchy appropriated their program by promulgating on December 5 a constitution with many liberal features. By this act the crown returned to the Stein–Hardenberg tradition of bureaucratic liberalism. But this time the reform had its origin in the strategy of a reactionary government, not in the genuine convictions of liberal state officials. On May 30, 1849, a second decree substituted for equal suffrage the famous three-class suffrage law, which divided and weighted votes according to income. The voters chose, furthermore, an electoral college, which selected the deputies. Other conservative features were added in the "constitutional charter" of January 31, 1850. Even so, the final result was a constitutional monarchy of mixed powers not unlike what the moderates had long advocated. Out of lumber burglarized from the liberal program the Prussian crown constructed a constitutional facade behind which the old order remained essentially intact.

Even before the restoration of monarchical authority in Prussia the cooperation between Berlin and Frankfurt had been limited. Although Friedrich Wilhelm IV had promised the merger of Prussia into a united Germany and the Frankfurt constitution provided for Prussia's dismemberment, neither the moderates of the Prussian cabinet nor the radicals who dominated the assembly were willing to abandon the Prussian state. Their Prussian patriotism competed with their German nationalism. But the radicals also hoped to make good in the Prussian constitution what they had sacrificed in the German one. By refusing the imperial crown offered by the Frankfurt Parliament in April 1849, Friedrich Wilhelm merely completed the withdrawal begun by the liberals themselves.

In Frankfurt the consequence of this refusal was the collapse of the moderate-radical alliance. While the moderates departed for home, the radical minority chose to resist. In Bavaria, Württemberg, and the Rhineland demonstrations occurred, but only in Dresden and the Palatinate did serious fighting develop. It was suppressed by the Prussian army assisted by the popular militia. For the most part the fate of the Frankfurt Parliament and its constitution met with general apathy; the popular movement had long since recoiled from its initial support. On all fronts and levels the revolutionary synthesis had dissolved.

In spite of its defeat the Frankfurt Parliament brought into focus for the first time some major problems of German nationalism. Like revolutionists everywhere, German liberals were dazzled by the prospect of power. The prevailing mood in Frankfurt is evident in Friedrich Dahlmann's famous words: "The path of power is the only one that will satisfy and satiate the swelling desire for freedom (*Freiheitstrieb*), because it is not merely freedom that the German has in mind. For the most part it is the power that he has hitherto lacked for which he lusts."[42] During the first months of the revolution the drive for power expressed itself in the demand for war against Russia and Denmark. Some genuinely believed that Russia was a threat to the German revolution, but others, like Max and Friedrich von Gagern, desired war in order to give "the highly charged nation . . . an object for its hostility; only by this means is unification possible."[43] When the Russians did not attack, the liberals found a better issue and easier target in Denmark, which since 1846 had been attempting to incorporate Schleswig. The Prussian army was commissioned for the attack, but in September 1848 it withdrew before the threat of British intervention. This failure, which the Frankfurt Parliament was impotent to prevent, left a livid mark on the liberal soul.

The chauvinism inherent in the national idea was also evident in the attitude of the revolutionists toward neighboring peoples. Like nationalists ev-

---

[42] Quoted in Friedrich Meinecke, *Die Idee der Staatsräson in der neueren Geschichte* (Munich, 1924), 493.

[43] Quoted in Lewis B. Namier, *The Revolution of the Intellectuals* (London, 1948), 54.

erywhere in 1848, the Germans started with the assumption that self-determination was a general human right valid for all peoples. Within weeks, however, they commenced to deny to the Poles, Danes, and Czechs what they demanded for themselves. Nevertheless, the Frankfurt Parliament ended by accepting realistic frontiers for the nation-state they planned.

All future problems of German unification were foreshadowed in the debates. Was Austria to be included or excluded? If inclusion was the choice, did this mean the whole of the Habsburg Empire or merely its German segment? The former solution would have defeated the whole concept of national unity, while the latter raised a difficult question: how could the German segment be built into two sovereignties, Austrian and German, without creating insoluble problems for one or both? Upon these issues the deputies soon divided, for and against Austria's inclusion, into two parties: the "great-Germanists" and "small-Germanists." In the end the majority decided for the small-German solution. By this act they deliberately excluded part of the German cultural nation and established the future frontiers of the German state.

The inroads of the Prussian government on the liberal program did not cease with her conversion into a constitutional monarchy. After rejecting the "pig crown" offered by the Frankfurt Parliament, Friedrich Wilhelm IV, counseled by Josef Maria von Radowitz, proposed a federal union of small-Germany under a conservative constitution. Although excluded from the federation, Austria would have been joined to it on a higher level, the "German union," which would have guaranteed the frontiers of the entire Habsburg Empire. Rather than impose this solution, Friedrich Wilhelm sought the approval of Germany's rulers, the Prussian Landtag, and a new German parliament, which met in Erfurt. While princes and parliaments deliberated and delayed, the opportunity slipped away. In August 1849 the Austrian government succeeded, with the aid of Russian troops, in crushing the Hungarian revolt. Fully recovered from the ordeal of revolution, Vienna could again look after her interests in Germany.[44]

Prince Schwarzenberg, the new prime minister, was in no mood to surrender the paramount position that Austria had for centuries enjoyed in Germany. He was determined, in fact, not only to revive the German Confederation, defunct since the revolution, but also to strengthen Habsburg primacy in that body. Once the domestic crisis ended in Austria, he summoned the lesser states in Germany to return to the diet in Frankfurt and demanded the inclusion of the entire Habsburg Empire in the federation. In January 1850, furthermore, the Austrian government proposed a customs union between the empire and the German Zollverein. This scheme, drafted by the new Minister of Commerce Ludwig Bruck, would have united central

[44] On the crisis leading to Olmütz see Friedrich Meinecke, *Radowitz und die deutsche Revolution* (Berlin, 1913), 233ff.

Europe in a common market of 70 million people protected by tariffs from outside competition. By entering the Zollverein and increasing Austria's weight in the German Confederation, Schwarzenberg and Bruck expected to establish conclusively the leadership of Vienna throughout the region from the North Sea to the Adriatic and the lower Danube. Prussia would have been reduced to the status of a second-rate power.[45]

During 1850 friction between Austria and Prussia steadily increased as both strove to gain support from the lesser states. In November both claimed the right to send troops into the principality of Hesse-Kassel to quell a disturbance. The armies of Austria and Prussia mobilized. At Bronzell near Fulda there was a skirmish on November 8. Germany wavered on the brink of civil war. In the end peace was preserved, and neither power gained its real objectives. Under pressure from ultraconservatives Friedrich Wilhelm dismissed Radowitz and abandoned the German union plan. The new cabinet, led by Otto von Manteuffel, demanded in its place parity for Prussia with Austria in the government of the confederation. Prussia, however, was unprepared for war, and the government was divided and confused. From Russia came admonitions against breach of the peace.[46] At Olmütz on November 29, 1850, Friedrich Wilhelm agreed to permit confederate occupation of Hesse-Kassel and to demobilize the Prussian army. In return the Austrians promised to discuss confederate reform at a conference in Dresden. No agreement was reached there, and in the summer of 1849 the confederation was restored unchanged.

Although both powers were frustrated in their political objectives, Prussia's defeat was the greater, and for two decades the "shame of Olmütz" rankled patriotic Prussians. Yet Berlin soon gained revenge, although it was not generally recognized as such, by defeating Bruck's scheme for a customs union. Under the skilled leadership of the Prussian official Rudolf Delbrück, Berlin outtrumped Vienna by insisting on low tariffs that would have been ruinous for Austria's infant industries. In 1852 Prussia secured its economic interests in northern Germany through a customs treaty with Hanover and then threatened to abandon the Zollverein if the lesser states would not accept its renewal on Prussian terms. The commercial advantages of the Zollverein were such that none of the lesser states dared to refuse. In 1853, the Zollverein was renewed for twelve years, with Austria again excluded. Vienna had to be satisfied with a treaty that delayed negotiations on the Bruck plan until after 1860.

Outwardly Germany appeared to have survived the cataclysm of 1848 un-

[45] Helmut Böhme, *Deutschlands Weg zur Grossmacht: Studien zum Verhältnis von Wirtschaft und Staat während der Reichsgründungszeit, 1848–1881* (Cologne, 1966), 19ff.

[46] For Russia's part in the Olmütz crisis see Willy Andreas, *Die russische Diplomatie und die Politik Friedrich Wilhelms IV. von Preussen: Abhandlungen der preussischen Akademie der Wissenschaften*, Jahrgang 1926, *Philosophisch-Historische Klasse*, no. 6 (Berlin, 1927), 45ff.

changed. Beneath the surface, however, changes of great significance were under way in political outlook and relationships. The age of romanticism was fast being replaced by that of realism and materialism.

Drift toward Realism

The mid–nineteenth century was a watershed between the great ages of philosophy and science. Abstract speculation gave way to empirical research, metaphysical systems to scientific theories. In the universities students deserted the lecture halls of the philosophers for those of the historians. The romantic style was superseded in art by impressionism and in literature by realism. In politics faith in the supremacy of principle began to yield to a belief that the great issues are decided by political coercion and military might.

To romantic conservatives the conflicting forces in European politics were opposed principles, not interests. As a matter of dogma they believed that the three great eastern monarchies had but a single cause: the maintenance of conservative order against France, the home of Jacobinism and Bonapartism, and against the forces of liberal and national subversion everywhere. But after 1849 motives of self-interest, never entirely absent from European politics, began to dominate. In Germany the conflicting plans of Radowitz and Schwarzenberg brought the dual powers close to conflict. In 1854–1856 the Crimean War shattered beyond repair the fragile structure of the Holy Alliance. Instead of aiding Russia against England and France, Austria, while officially neutral, actually sided with the western powers. Schwarzenberg's successor, Count Karl von Buol-Schauenstein, prided himself on having accomplished "nothing less" than a revolution in Austrian foreign relations. But he had done more than that. He had inaugurated a new era in diplomacy in which the interests of power were to take precedence over the principle of conservative solidarity.[47]

This development in the sphere of practical politics had been foreshadowed by several decades in German political thought. Hegel accomplished the moral legitimation of power politics by identifying the rational with the real. Because history proceeded according to God's "idea," there could be no distinction (contrary to enlightened thought) between the state as it was and the state as it ought to be. Unlike the rationalists, Hegel recognized no conflict in statecraft between the egoistic pursuit of power and the demands of universal law and morality. War was not an absolute evil, but a logical necessity.[48]

[47] See Gavin B. Henderson, "The Diplomatic Revolution of 1854," *American Historical Review*, 43 (1937), 22–50, and S. A. Kaehler, "Realpolitik zur Zeit des Krimkrieges—Eine Säkularbetrachtung," *Historische Zeitschrift*, 174 (1952), 436–445.

[48] Meinecke, *Staatsräson*, 427–460; Hermann Heller, *Hegel und der nationale Machtstaatsge-*

In organic theory German conservatives found a similar means of legitimizing power politics. The historical school was never able to accept the political quietism of romantic conservatism. The most essential characteristic of an organism, they argued, was that of growth and development. Being itself the product of change, organic existence could have no permanence. The state-personality, moreover, could achieve self-realization only through conflict. Hence Adam Müller maintained that the power struggle could not be judged from the standpoint of personal morality. The wars of the eighteenth century had their origin not in the caprice of rulers and cabinets, but in "an inner pressure toward vital growth stemming from the push of past generations and completely unapparent to the present."[49] Although critical of wars fought for total domination at the cost of the European community (for example, the Napoleonic wars), Müller's philosophy was tantamount to a moral approbation of war as such.[50]

With the passing of the great age of philosophy the concept of the organic power-state was perpetuated in German thought by the historians. Although he rejected Hegelian metaphysics, Leopold Ranke also viewed the state as a spiritual force whose vitality and individuality were determined by its "idea." The shaping of this innate idea, however, did not occur in isolation, but in conflict with the ideas of other states. Hence war was not a scourge, but the final and necessary test of the moral and spiritual fiber of the state. And yet Ranke persisted from the beginning to the end of his long, prolific career as a historian in the search for the connecting links between the individual (whether person or state) and the general. But in this he was unique among contemporary German historians whose focus was on German, not universal history; their ideal was the Prussian military state, to which they attributed a national mission.[51]

Before 1848 German liberals had relied primarily upon the force of idealism to achieve their goals. The tide of liberalism, they believed, would inevitably sweep over the cracking seawall of the Metternich system. Through the failure of 1848, however, their trust in the power of principle suffered a terrible blow from which it never fully recovered. The collapse of their hopes had varying effects upon the lives and views of the participants. Many radicals, like Carl Schurz, emigrated to lands where their ideals had already been realized; some, like Wilhelm Liebknecht and Ferdinand Lassalle, gravitated

---

danke in Deutschland (Berlin, 1921), 57ff.; and Franz Rosenzweig, Hegel und der Staat (2 vols., Munich, 1920).

[49] Quoted in Meinecke, Weltbürgertum, 141.

[50] Müller, Elemente der Staatskunst, vol. 1, 80–81; Schnabel, Deutsche Geschichte, vol. 1, 312–315.

[51] Theodore H. von Laue, Leopold Ranke: The Formative Years (Princeton, 1950), 80, 86; Heller, Machtstaatsgedanke, 147–155; and particularly Leonard Krieger, Ranke: The Meaning of History (Chicago, 1977).

into socialism; others, like Johann Karl Rodbertus and Lothar Bucher, became converts to conservatism; a few, like Franz Ziegler and Johann Jacoby, clung to their positions, isolated and impotent; most, like Benedikt Waldeck and Hermann Schulze-Delitzsch, capitulated to the spirit of compromise. When they reemerged in Prussian political life after 1859, few left-wing liberals still demanded a revolutionary transformation of the Prussian constitution. Although advocates of greater social and political equality, most had relinquished the goal of parliamentary government and had doubts about the advisability of universal suffrage. Thereafter they are best designated as "democratic" rather than "radical" liberals.[52]

Among moderates the reaction was more uniform. To be sure, two important figures, Robert von Mohl and Georg Gervinus, turned toward radicalism, the former to a belief in the necessity of popular sovereignty, the latter to the conviction that only a republic could guarantee human rights. But the bulk of the moderates adopted a "realistic" or "practical" position, abandoning what they now regarded as their "doctrinaire" politics in the pre-March period.

The first signs of this development came but a few weeks after the dissolution of the Frankfurt Parliament. In late June 1850 the moderates, summoned by Dahlmann and the Gagern brothers, assembled in Gotha to conclude that the aim they had sought in Frankfurt was more important than the "form" of its attainment.[53] They agreed to go to Erfurt and cooperate with the Prussian government in establishing the German union. Thereafter this group, in which "classical liberals" of the pre-March period predominated, were to be known as the *Gothaer* or "old-liberals." These "political professors" were repelled by the excesses of the radicals in Dresden and Baden, impressed by the durability of the old state structure, and discouraged by the impotence of the revolution. They set their hopes for the future upon the use of Prussian power to accomplish German unity under a constitution that, while preserving traditional authority, might at least leave open the way for the realization of a *Rechtsstaat*.

This increased respect for power found its philosopher in August Ludwig von Rochau. A journalist who had begun as a radical and gravitated before 1848 to the moderate position, Rochau distinguished sharply between philosophical speculation and practical politics (*Realpolitik*). The former dealt with what principles ought to rule, but the latter recognized that power alone rules. The subjection of power to law was "unreasonable," for the strong cannot let themselves be ruled by the weak. "Neither a principle, nor an idea, nor a treaty will unite the splintered German forces, but only a superior force that

---

[52] Krieger, *German Idea*, 341–397.

[53] Georg Witzmann, *Die Gothaer Nachversammlung zum Frankfurter Parlament im Jahre 1849* (Gotha, 1917), 71–73.

swallows up the rest." He concluded that the state could generate the power to unify Germany only with the help of the bourgeoisie.[54] In view of what had just occurred, however, the conclusion was non sequitur.

Although Rochau's position was perhaps more extreme than most, his work had considerable influence. Among right-wing liberals the conviction spread that even "despotism" was acceptable if it became an instrument for national unification. The youthful Heinrich von Treitschke declared, "I'll go with the party that shows the strongest national initiative"; methods were secondary; what mattered was the goal.[55] In many minds the romantic cult of genius and general discouragement over the efficacy of popular movements combined to produce a vague longing for a new Siegfried who would brave the flames to awaken the German nation from its sleep of centuries.[56]

[54] Ludwig von Rochau, *Grundsätze der Realpolitik, angewendet auf die staatlichen Zustände Deutschlands* (2d ed., 1859), 2–3, 224. In this work Rochau coined the word *Realpolitik*, soon to become common currency in German political discourse.

[55] Andreas Dorpalen, *Heinrich von Treitschke* (New Haven, 1957), 16, 31.

[56] Brandenburg, *Reichsgründung*, vol. 1, 342–343.

✠✠

The Internal Functions of Power

Bismarck's Childhood

ON APRIL 1, 1815, as the allied armies gathered for the final campaign against Napoleon, Otto von Bismarck was born on the estate of Schönhausen in Brandenburg. His heritage was both bourgeois and aristocratic. Through his father, Ferdinand, he belonged to a Junker family that had possessed estates in the Prussian Altmark for five centuries. His mother was Wilhelmine Mencken, descendant of a long line of German academicians and daughter of an able state official who had risen to the post of cabinet secretary to Frederick the Great and Friedrich Wilhelm II and III. Otto was the fourth of six children, only three of whom survived childhood (the others were Bernhard, born in 1810, and Malwine, born in 1827). His first five years were spent on the family estates at Schönhausen and Kniephof (Pomerania). In 1822 the family moved to Berlin. The boys boarded at the Plamann Anstalt, a private school, where Otto spent his sixth to twelfth years; thereafter, until age seventeen, he attended in succession the Friedrich Wilhelm and Graue Kloster *Gymnasien* in Berlin where he boarded with teachers.[1]

In later years Bismarck recalled his family and school life, except for two years at the Graue Kloster, with great distaste. "My mother," he wrote in 1847, "was a beautiful woman, who loved external elegance, who possessed a bright, lively intelligence, but little of what the Berliner calls *Gemüth*. She wished that I should learn much and become much, and it often appeared to me that she was hard, cold toward me. As a small child I hated her; later I successfully deceived her with falsehoods. One only learns the value of the mother for the child when it is too late, when she is dead. The most modest maternal love, even when mixed with much selfishness, is still enormous compared with the love of the child. Nowhere perhaps have I sinned more grievously than against my parents, above all against my mother. I really loved my father. When not with him I felt remorse concerning my conduct toward him and made resolutions that I was unable to keep for the most part. How often did I repay his truly boundless, unselfish, good-natured tenderness for

---

[1] On Bismarck's early years see the first volume of Erich Marcks's uncompleted biography, *Bismarcks Jugend, 1815–1848* (Stuttgart, 1909) and Ernst Engelberg, *Bismarck: Urpreusse und Reichsgründer* (Berlin, 1985), 1–362. For a perceptive interpretation see Wilhelm Lütgert, *Die Religion des deutschen Idealismus und ihr Ende* (Gütersloh, 1923–1930), vol. 4.

me with coldness and bad grace. Even more frequently I made a pretence of loving him, not wanting to violate my own code of propriety, when innerly I felt hard and unloving because of his apparent weaknesses. I was not in a position to pass judgment on those weaknesses, which actually annoyed me only when coupled with *gaucherie*. And yet I cannot deny that I really loved him in my heart. I wanted to show you how much it oppresses me when I think about it."[2]

At age thirty-two Bismarck looked back on his relationship to his father with deep disappointment. Although warm and good humored, Ferdinand was lethargic and ineffectual. He did not provide Otto with the strong, masculine image for which he longed. Bismarck's tribute to maternal love was a sop given to his fiancée, to whom the above letter was addressed. Never again, so far as the record shows, did he repeat even this feeble effort to understand his mother. For the rest of his life he spoke of her only with resentment. His complaints are not the only testimony we have concerning her. A childhood playmate, cousin Hedwig von Bismarck, remembered an uncle speaking of Wilhelmine's "fishlike nature." For all children, Hedwig recalled,

FERDINAND AND WILHELMINE VON BISMARCK AS BRIDE AND GROOM (FROM CONRAD MÜLLER,
BISMARCKS MUTTER UND IHRE AHNEN, VERLAG VON MARTIN WARNECK, BERLIN, 1909, P. 304).

[2] Bismarck to Johanna von Puttkamer, Feb. 23, 1847, in GW, XIV, 67. By comparing this letter with the original, an enterprising American historian discovered that some critical passages had been left out by the editors of Bismarck's collected works. See Charlotte Sempell, "Unbekannte Briefstellen Bismarcks," *Historische Zeitschrift*, 207 (1968), 609–616. For similar complaints by Bismarck about his mother see GW, VIII, 207, and Heinrich von Poschinger, *Bismarck-Portefeuille* (Stuttgart, 1899), vol. 4, 100.

she was unapproachable. "In my memory the prince's mother lives on as a cold woman relating little to the people about her. I cannot remember ever hearing from her a hearty utterance toward any of us. It was otherwise with Uncle Ferdinand! He always had a friendly word or an amusing joke for us, especially when Otto and I rode on his knees. She was often sick and then listless. The first time I heard the word nervous, so common today, was in connection with this woman. It was generally said that she made her life difficult and still more that of her husband and children by her nervousness."[3] Wilhelmine's involvement with her family satisfied her needs, not theirs. "She spoilt my character," Bismarck said.[4] He felt rejected and unloved; the severity of his adult censure measures the degree of his childhood frustration and disappointment.

In the dynamics of the parental household there are other clues to the formation of Bismarck's character. When she married in 1806, Wilhelmine Mencken, an orphan since 1801, was seventeen and her husband Ferdinand von Bismarck thirty-five. The disparity in age was not remarkable for that time, but, by all accounts, their relationship was. Contrary to the norm, she was the dominant partner in the marriage. Ferdinand was a country squire and former cavalry officer who retired from the Prussian army in 1795 after serving with distinction against France. In 1806, when Prussia again went to war, remained at home with his bride; in 1812–1815 he did not participate in the war against Napoleon, a dereliction held against his son four decades later by political opponents. During their years at Schönhausen and Kniephof, Wilhelmine is said to have intervened in the management of her husband's property, with unfortunate results. Reputedly the decision to lease the estates and move to Berlin in 1822 was dictated by her desire to return to Berlin society, to secure a better education for her two sons, and to provide them later with proper connections for successful careers in the state service.[5]

To the end of his life Bismarck never ceased to lament the change that occurred in his life when he was taken from the fields and stables of Kniephof and enrolled in the Plamann Anstalt. "At the age of six I entered a school whose teachers were demagogic *Turner* who hated the nobility and educated with blows and cuffs instead of words and reproofs. In the morning the children were awakened with rapier blows that left bruises, because it was too

[3] Hedwig von Bismarck, *Erinnerungen aus dem Leben einer 95 Jährigen* (5th ed., Halle, 1910), 28–31. Philipp zu Eulenburg talked to an elderly lady who had once known her, Frau Charlotte von Quast-Radensleben. "She was enthusiastic about Bismarck, but adopted a curiously serious expression when she once spoke of his mother. She shook her fine old head and said, 'Not a pleasant woman, very smart, but—very cold.' " *Aus 50 Jahren* (Berlin, 1923), 73.

[4] Quoted in Sir W. Richmond, "Bismarck at Home: Personal Impressions," *Daily News* (London), Aug. 2, 1898, 5.

[5] Gustav Wolf, *Bismarcks Lehrjahre* (Leipzig, 1907), 23–26; Marcks, *Bismarcks Jugend*, 40–53.

burdensome for the teachers to do it any other way. Gymnastics were supposed to be recreation, but during this too the teachers struck us with iron
rapiers! For my cultivated mother, child rearing was too inconvenient and she
freed herself of it very early, at least in her feelings."[6] Bismarck remembered
the Plamann school as a "prison" that ruined his childhood; the discipline
was harsh, the food poor and insufficient. Indeed the school routine was spar-
tan: twelve hours of instruction daily, including considerable training in gymnastics, fencing, and other sports. Its founder, Johann Ernst Plamann, was a
disciple of Pestalozzi, and one of its patrons was Wilhelm von Humboldt,
educational reformer of the Stein era. But the Plamann regimen had become
more Prussian than Pestalozzian.[7] Wilhelmine chose for her sons a school
whose tradition, if not its reality, reflected her own humanistic values: "the
views that I imbibed with my mother's milk," he wrote later, "were liberal
rather than reactionary."[8]

In his memoirs Bismarck related that he graduated from the *Gymnasium*
with the belief that a republic was "the most sensible form of the state." He
was, he observed with irony, a "normal product of our public instruction."
Having heard "so many bitter or denigrating criticisms of the ruler from
adults," he wondered what it was that "could cause millions of people continually to obey one individual." From his years in the Plamann school, where
the Jahn tradition predominated, he also "brought away German-national
impressions." But these "observations," he continued, were purely "theoretical" and "not strong enough to uproot inborn Prussian-monarchical feelings.
My historical sympathies remained on the side of authority." As a child he
regarded Harmodius, Aristogeton, and Brutus as "criminals" and grew indignant at every German prince who opposed the Holy Roman Emperor "before
the Thirty Years War." From the Great Elector onward, however, he sided
with the Hohenzollern against the Kaiser. On arriving at the university of
Göttingen in 1832, he considered joining the *Burschenschaft*, but was repelled
by their refusal to duel, their bad manners, and the "extravagance of their
political views." Thereafter he associated utopian theories with poor breeding.[9]

In these fluctuating and conflicting early views can be discerned the effect
of Bismarck's frustrating relationship with his parents. His hostility toward

[6] To Keudell while enroute to Leipzig, June 18, 1864. Robert von Keudell, *Fürst und Fürstin
Bismarck: Erinnerungen 1846–1872* (Berlin, 1901), to Robert Lucius and others at dinner, Mar.
30, 1878. Freiherr Lucius von Ballhausen, *Bismarck-Erinnerungen* (Stuttgart, 1920), 137–138.

[7] See Ernst Krigar, *Kleine Mittheilungen aus der Jugendzeit des Fürsten Bismarck in der Pla-
mannschen Pensions-Anstalt* (Berlin, 1873); Wolf, *Bismarcks Lehrjahre*, 26–51; Marcks, *Bismarcks
Jugend*, 53–65; Engelberg, *Bismarck*, 94–98.

[8] *GW*, XV, 14.

[9] *GW*, XV, 5–6.

FERDINAND VON BISMARCK (FROM ALFRED FUNKE, *DAS BISMARCK-BUCH DES DEUTSCHEN VOLKES*, TWO VOLS., W. BOBACH & CO., LEIPZIG, 1921, VOL. 1, P. 57).

the mother, who failed to provide the warmth and approval he required, and disappointment in the father, who failed to act out his role as the figure of authority in the household, were further complicated by displacement from a friendly environment (associated with the father, paternal ancestry and social milieu) to a hostile one (associated with the mother, maternal ancestry and

WILHELMINE VON BISMARCK (FROM ALFRED FUNKE, *DAS BISMARCK-BUCH DES DEUTSCHEN VOLKES*, TWO VOLS., W. BOBACH & CO., LEIPZIG, 1921, VOL. 1, P. 65).

social milieu). He never grew to like the urban world into which she sent him at such a tender age, determined that he should "learn much and become much." The fields and forests for which he longed as a child were indelibly associated with his Junker heritage. "As the pictures in house and church show," he once wrote of Schönhausen, "my fathers have been born and have lived and died in the same rooms for centuries."[10] The symbols of the Mencken line were academic books and documents of state; those of the Bismarcks were land, home, portraits, gravestones, and many other visible and tangible things. Through the Bismarck name he belonged to a privileged caste. Never did he display any sense of guilt at having been born a Junker. Rarely did he mention the Menckens and his maternal heritage.

Some of Bismarck's habits and attitudes in later years may have stemmed from these early experiences: his contempt for men dominated by wives; his dislike of intellectuals ("professor" was for him an epithet); his hostility toward bureaucratic government and suspicion of *Geheimräte* (his maternal grandfather's career); his late rising (pupils at the Plamann Anstalt were driven out of bed at 6:00 A.M.); his longing for the country and dislike of cities, especially Berlin; and his preference in agriculture for forestry (he never forgave his mother for ordering a stand of oak trees felled at Kniephof).[11]

The personal problem that began in the nursery became more complex in adolescence. As his social consciousness expanded, Bismarck became aware of the developing conflict in Germany between Junker and bourgeois, conservative and progressive, authority and freedom. A preliminary climax in that struggle came in the revolutions of 1830, the Hambach festival of 1832, and the Frankfurt Putsch of 1833—events that occurred between his fifteenth and eighteenth years. Bismarck's moment of decision came in 1832 when he turned his back on the *Burschenschaft* at Göttingen and joined a dueling corps. By that act he rejected his maternal for his paternal heritage, seeking in the traditional image of the Prussian aristocracy the strength and authority he missed in his father. Not every trans-Elbian Junker embraced conservatism in reaction to the growing attack on aristocratic values and interests. Given the circumstances of his childhood, Bismarck's choice was natural.[12]

Failure of a Formal Education

Although his marks were fair, Bismarck was little affected by his formal education. The classical ideal, which was its foundation, appears to have played no part in molding his intellect and character. As for so many, classical languages were formal intellectual exercises rather than avenues for the discovery

---

[10] GW, XIV, 74.

[11] For other views on Bismarck's childhood development see Charlotte Sempell, "Bismarck's Childhood: A Psychohistorical Study," *History of Childhood Quarterly*, 2 (1974), 107–124, and Judith M. Hughes, "Toward the Psychological Drama of High Politics: The Case of Bismarck," *Central European History*, 10 (1977), 271–285. Ernst Engelberg has aptly described the union of the Bismarck and Mencken families as a "social symbiosis" rather than a "mésalliance." Both families gained from it: for the bride, noble status; for the groom, access to the royal court at Potsdam, to which the Menckens had a relationship. Engelberg, *Bismarck*, 23–64.

[12] "Bismarcks Persönlichkeit," *Süddeutsche Monatshefte*, 19 (1922), 110.

of a philosophy of life. His later writings, speeches, and conversations show none of the classical interest in the fully developed man or the famous Greek "style." The unique clarity and force of his speech and writing did not derive from classical models. Always a person of manifold inner conflicts and tensions, Bismarck never understood the Greek admonition, "Be harmonious!" He retained some knowledge of Latin, the language of law and government, but forgot his Greek, the language of philosophy and aesthetics. His practical mind never acquired the habits of reflection and abstract speculation. He never felt the urge to penetrate to the essence of life or to acquire a metaphysical system capable of containing and explaining its phenomena. Nor did the classical tradition in its later forms appeal to him. He had no interest in the art and culture of the Renaissance or in the philosophy of German idealism.[13]

During his years in the *Gymnasium* (1827–1832) the productive period of German idealism was nearing its end. He was aware of the greatness of Goethe and Schiller and read their works with enjoyment. Although Goethe's realism was close to his own nature, the stirring drama and historical interest of Schiller attracted him more. But, again, the powerful humanistic impulse, which was the essence of idealism in its classical phase, left no impression upon him. What he read provided him with quotations, which later adorned his speech and writing, but did not change his way of looking at life. It did not mold his character or form his mind.

The foreign languages Bismarck learned best were French and English. Although fluent in French from childhood, he had little interest in French culture. Anti-French sentiment, dating from the war of liberation, was still alive in the schools he attended. Like many Germans of this epoch, he formed a lasting sympathy for things English.[14] Byron and Shakespeare were the authors he liked the best. In Byron he found a kindred spirit: bold, grandiose, and restless. Yet he quoted Shakespeare most often—not the deluded Othello, conscience-ridden Macbeth, or indecisive Hamlet, but the autocratic Coriolanus ("Go, get you home, you fragments!"). In music he preferred the exciting chords and crescendos of Beethoven to the classicism of Haydn and Mozart and, later, the somber romanticism of Wagner. Although these interests are perhaps symbolic of his nature, it is too much to say that

[13] Lütgert, *Idealismus*, vol. 4, 3ff.; Otto Graf zu Stolberg-Wernigerode, "Unbekannte Gespräche mit Bismarck," *Süddeutsche Monatshefte*, 27 (1929–1930), 312. Later he criticized his primary education as oriented more toward the head than the heart and condemned it as responsible for the moral and political degeneration of his time. Letter to Wilhelm Harnisch, Feb. 16, 1849. Hans Rothfels, ed., *Bismarck-Briefe* (Göttingen, 1955), 121.

[14] GW, XIV, 469. This had no influence upon his political outlook. Though he admired the English political system (as it was before the reform acts), he thought it impossible to duplicate in Germany because of the uniqueness of the German social order. BR, I, 125. See Eva Maria Baum, *Bismarcks Urteil über England und die Engländer: Münchener historische Abhandlugen*, 11 (Munich, 1936).

he "abandoned himself to the spirit of Lord Byron, Shakespeare, and Beetho-ven."[15] Music he liked for background, rather than serious listening; litera-ture, for diversion and usable quotations. Neither provided him with a vital, molding, inner experience.

Nor did the study of mathematics and natural science influence the forma-tion of his mind. His love of nature, both deep and abiding, was for the mead-ows, forests, and rolling hills of rural Pomerania, the land of his childhood. For nature as science he had little interest. Though skeptical of the results of scientific theory and experiment,[16] he was certainly affected by the growing scientific spirit of the age. He liked to describe himself as a natural scientist charged with the task of discerning the phenomena of politics as they are, not as they ought to be. Like Leopold Ranke, he knew little of the subject matter of science but was influenced by its spirit of objective inquiry. The practice of politics, however, he always regarded as an "art," not a science.

No more than the humanistic *Gymnasium* did the university influence the basic structure of his mind and thought. At Göttingen (1832–1833) he quickly took up the rowdy, dueling, beer-drinking life of a corps student, and in Berlin (1834–1835) he crammed for the law exam, his gateway to a career in the state service. At the time both universities were intellectual centers of importance. In Göttingen were Friedrich Dahlmann and Jakob Grimm; in Berlin, Friedrich Karl von Savigny and the scholars of the Hegelian school. During their student years many future leaders of Germany—for example, Rudolf Delbrück, Rudolf von Bennigsen, Gustav Mevissen, Gustav Freytag, Heinrich von Sybel, and Max Duncker—received in the university an intel-lectual stimulus that lasted a lifetime. But Bismarck's formal education had little apparent effect.[17]

During his three semesters at Göttingen, a university renowned as a train-ing ground for prospective statesmen and civil servants, Bismarck spent little time in the lecture halls of the law professors. What did appeal to him was history. Here his preference was the elderly Arnold Heeren, a scholar of ex-traordinary range (ancient to modern times), rather than the younger Dahl-mann, a man of strong liberal-national convictions deeply engaged in the political issues of the age. Under the influence of Montesquieu's *Spirit of Laws* and Adam Smith's *Wealth of Nations*, Heeren pioneered the study of material factors in the formation of the state systems in classical and modern times. Son of a Bremen merchant family, he focused on the concrete details of trade and politics and their interconnections in the formation of foreign policy, being much too sober of temperament to fantasize in the romantic-idealistic vein about the spiritual nature of states and nations. Apparently this is what attracted Bismarck, and it is possible that Heeren influenced Bismarck's con-

[15] Gustav A. Rein, *Die Revolution in der Politik Bismarcks* (Göttingen, 1957), 75; also 45ff.
[16] Lütgert, *Idealismus*, vol. 4, 5.
[17] Marcks, *Bismarcks Jugend*, 83ff.; Walter Nissen, *Otto von Bismarcks Göttinger Studentenjahre, 1832–1833* (Göttingen, 1982).

ception of the interest of state as the basis of foreign policy and of the European balance of power as the regulator of conflicts of interest between its member states.[18]

Otherwise Bismarck's peers, not his professors, seem to have contributed most to his education at Göttingen and Berlin. Among them were John Lothrop Motley, future American diplomat and historian, and Count Alexander von Keyserling, Baltic aristocrat and future scientist. Both were capable of serious intellectual discussion. Motley whetted Bismarck's appreciation of Shakespeare, Goethe, and Byron; Keyserling, a gifted pianist, his appreciation of Beethoven. The two essays Bismarck wrote in completing the formal requirements for a civil service career—one in philosophy, the other in political economy—were works of no originality. They were formal exercises on assigned topics, mere hurdles to be leaped on the way to a career.[19] Like many in his social class, Bismarck acquired in the university not an appreciation of intellectual disciplines but a general contempt for the academic mind. Ideas that he found unrealistic he dismissed as *"Doktorfragen"* or *"Professorenweisheit."*

During the years he spent in Kniephof and Schönhausen (1839–1847) Bismarck found the time and inclination to read. This was the period of frustration, of isolation and loneliness, after the failure of his attempt at a career and before his marriage and first appearance in public life. Here he cultivated his interest in history and stored up in a highly retentive memory the material with which he leavened many a speech and document in later years. What he acquired was largely factual knowledge; he had no interest in historical synthesis or in the philosophy of history. Although he read Hegel, he admitted not having understood him. He also read Spinoza and the young Hegelians, but it was their religious, not their philosophical, viewpoints that interested him. He was attracted by Spinoza's pantheism and by the biblical criticism of David Friedrich Strauss, Bruno Bauer, and Ludwig Feuerbach. But this also he soon rejected.[20]

The Will to Power

In a youthful novel, *Morton's Hope*, Motley painted a lively portrait of the young Bismarck he knew as a student in Göttingen.[21] Unlike its protagonist,

[18] Marcks, *Bismarcks Jugend*, 98ff.; Lothar Gall, *Bismarck: Der weisse Revolutionär* (Frankfurt a. M., 1980), 33–34.

[19] For the *Referendar* essays see Horst Kohl, ed., *Bismarck-Jahrbuch*, 2 (1895), 3–47. It is possible that Bismarck derived from his researches for the second of these essays the prejudice for indirect taxation to which he clung for the rest of his life. Georg Brodnitz, *Bismarcks nationalökonomische Anschauungen* (Jena, 1902), 78ff.

[20] Marcks, *Bismarcks Jugend*, 126–127, 246–247.

[21] *Morton's Hope, or the Memoirs of a Provincial* (2 vols., New York, 1839). Whether Bismarck ever read the novel is difficult to say. In 1850 he reported to their mutual friend Sharlach, "Motley writes very popular novels." GW, XIV, 162.

"Otto von Rabenmark," his Junker friend was not a skilled musician, "excellent classical scholar," or remarkable (though competent) linguist. Like Rabenmark, however, he was a roistering student and constant duelist. Beneath his "fool's-mask" Motley's hero was a man of serious purpose. "I have a certain quantity of time on my hands," he confessed. "I wish to take the university as a school for action. I intend to lead my companions here, as I intend to lead them in after life."[22] Like Bismarck, Rabenmark planned a career in diplomacy. But, unlike him, he got involved with a countess, slew two men, fled, was captured, stabbed his accuser in the courtroom, and ended it all by taking poison.

Motley's picture of Bismarck is that of a self-assured young man, conscious of unusual talents, of an aggressive and combative nature, driven by a dynamic urge to lead and dominate. According to another reminiscence, he was a natural leader in the play-battles of the children in the Plamann school. He advertised his arrival in Göttingen by challenging an entire student corps.[23] Bismarck was six feet four inches tall, powerfully built, and a terror on the dueling floor. During three semesters he fought no less than twenty-five *Mensuren* and lost only once—a slashed cheek that resulted, so he claimed, from a foul stroke.[24] In 1852 he exchanged shots in a duel with Georg von Vincke. Neither was struck and, while their seconds rejoiced, Bismarck lamented that dueling etiquette did not allow him, being the challenged, to demand another round. In 1866 an assassin fired five times at him on a Berlin street. As the pistol exploded, Bismarck turned upon his attacker and seized him by the throat. He had, he once remarked, a "natural lust for combat."[25]

The will to power was Bismarck's central characteristic. How he came to be this way no one can know with certainty. And yet some insight can be gained from a psychoanalytic model. Ideally the child gradually converts an empathic parental control over his behavior into an enduring psychic structure of self-control; egoistic drives and impulses are frustrated by parental authority until the standards imposed have become internalized to the point that the maturing child can accept them as his own. The child who makes this transition in an empathic environment provided by parents and parental surrogates (for example, nursemaids, schoolteachers) should develop a sense that the world is a secure and responsive place. Parental praise for and pride in the child gradually become internalized as a healthy sense of self-esteem.[26] Bismarck's early development deviated from this model. Whatever psychic

[22] *Morton's Hope*, vol. 1, 164.

[23] Marcks, *Bismarcks Jugend*, 55–56, 87.

[24] BP, I, 30.

[25] GW, XIV, 258; VII, 90, 116–117.

[26] Otto Pflanze, "Toward a Psychoanalytic Interpretation of Bismarck," *American Historical Review*, 77 (1972), 419–444. The author has benefited from the advice of Thomas Kohut in revising the views expressed in this article.

support Otto received from his parents—it may well have been more than he remembered in later years—did not suffice. "Fish-like" Wilhelmine could not give this precocious child what he needed. The personal warmth and contact he received from affable Ferdinand was squandered when the child, detecting a lack of finesse and authority, lost respect for the father.

It could be that the necessity of achieving self-reliance without the nurture of an empathic family life and early schooling produced in Bismarck a vital need to influence and control the world about him. For the gratification of such a need Bismarck's social environment (that of the Prussian gentry) offered two outlets: service to the monarchy either as an official or army officer. His parents wished their son to seek a military career, a profession that some paternal ancestors had pursued with distinction, including his Uncle Friedrich, a veteran of the Napoleonic wars who retired as a lieutenant general. But young Otto firmly resisted their entreaties.[27] He discharged his military obligation in short order—by a single year of officer training that led to a commission in the militia, not the regular army. And yet he liked to refer to himself in later years as a royal officer. After promotion to the rank of major general in 1866, he wore the uniform as normal dress.[28] In a Christmas letter to Wilhelm I in 1872 he regretted that it had been his lot to serve the royal house behind the writing desk rather than on the battlefront. He would much rather have won military than diplomatic campaigns.[29] Bismarck could conceive of himself as a commanding general but not as a junior-grade officer.

Bismarck's youthful aspiration was to enter the Prussian diplomatic service. Foreign Minister Johann Ancillon granted the applicant an interview but advised him to lower his sights by seeking entry into the Zollverein service by way of the Prussian provincial administration. The minister judged the Junker gentry too rustic and unsophisticated to master the fine art of European diplomacy, a conclusion to which Bismarck himself later came.[30] After passing the required preliminary examination, Otto entered Prussian service in May 1835 as a law clerk (Auskultator) at the superior court (Kammergericht) in Berlin. Within months he applied successfully for a transfer from the judiciary to the provincial administration at Aachen. On completing with praise the remaining requirements (two essays on assigned topics and an oral examination), he became in the early summer of 1836 an apprentice official (Referendar) at Aachen. His talents attracted the attention of the provincial governor, Count Adolf von Arnim-Boitzenburg, to whom he made known his ambition to

[27] GW, XIV, 5.

[28] One may doubt that the sole reason was the better protection the high collar provided against colds. Keudell, Fürst und Fürstin Bismarck, 386.

[29] Horst Kohl, ed., Anhang zu den Gedanken und Erinnerungen von Otto Fürst von Bismarck (Stuttgart, 1901), vol. 1, 232–233; see also GW, VII, 137.

[30] Marcks, Bismarcks Jugend, 83ff.

transfer as early as possible to the foreign service. But this was not to be. Although the governor provided him with a broad experience in provincial government by moving him about from department to department, the twenty-one-year-old *Referendar* was bored. He relieved the tedium by indulging in a series of love affairs that led to professional and financial disaster.[31]

Aachen was a spa with an international clientele and was far more diverting than the stiffly formal and unexciting court society Bismarck had known in Berlin. Soon after his arrival he wrote with obvious satisfaction to brother Bernhard that he was dining daily with English and French guests of high station at one of the spa hotels. Among them were the duke and duchess of Cleveland and their "enchantingly lovely" niece, Laura Russell. By September he claimed to be "as good as engaged" to her. But the diversion was expensive. His extravagantly circuitous journey from Berlin to Aachen (via Dresden, Frankfurt, Wiesbaden, Rüdesheim, Bingen, and Cologne) had already left him in debt and begging for help from his father. The relief he received "without reproach" (two hundred thalers) did not suffice to cover his needs. His attempt to recoup his fortunes at roulette in the spa casino merely deepened the problem.

In the autumn the ducal party returned to England, and Otto regretted that he had not formally proposed. He felt too young and too poor to start a family. In December came a revelation—actually a somewhat malicious rumor—that cooled his ardor. Laura, so it was said, was not the duke's niece but the illegitimate daughter of the duchess, a low-born courtesan whom the duke had married two years earlier. Bismarck believed he had narrowly escaped a union that would have produced ridicule and no dowry. He imagined himself being lorgnetted by high-born gossips: "Look there [at] that tall monster. That is the silly German baron, whom they have caught in the woods, with his pipe and his seal-ring."[32]

By January 1837 Otto had found solace in the arms of a *"femme de qualité* aged thirty-six, married, very well preserved, and a coquette with taste," whose company, he boasted, improved more than his French. In July the Cleveland party stopped off at Aachen for a day enroute to Wiesbaden, and Bismarck exploited their brief presence to meet Laura's good friend, Isabella Loraine-Smith, with whom he promptly fell in love. Isabella was seventeen, four years younger than Laura, and her antecedents were impeccable. Her family belonged to the gentry of Northamptonshire and Leicestershire; her father, the Reverend Loraine Loraine-Smith, was a graduate of Eton and

---

[31] Engelberg, *Bismarck*, 131–133, 140.

[32] *Ibid.*, 134–142. At the bottom of the rumor about Laura was the fact that the duchess had been in the regency era the companion (under a French alias) of the British banker Coutts. On the families of Laura and Isabella see Alan Palmer, *Bismarck* (London, 1976), 10–13, and "Bismarck, the Young Romantic," *The Times* (London), Apr. 17, 1976.

BISMARCK AT AGE TWENTY-ONE, 1836.

Cambridge, rector of Passenham, owner of a Leicestershire estate, and, with his daughter, a regular participant in the Grafton hunt. "The very archetype of an English beauty," Isabella was vivacious, self-assured, and captivating; her mere presence, Bismarck wrote (his metaphors out of control), "burns up my inflamed blood like steam." Bismarck joined the Loraine party (father, mother, and two English colonels) regularly at dinner and on excursions into the surrounding countryside. When they left for Frankfurt and Wiesbaden, the infatuated *Referendar* took leave from his job and hurried after them. He arrived at Wiesbaden to find the Lorraine-Smiths and Clevelands holding a happy reunion, a situation that must have taxed Bismarck's as yet undeveloped diplomatic talents. When the rector's party departed for the upper Rhine and Switzerland, Bismarck tagged along. On August 30 and September 13, 1837, he casually invited two old friends (Savigny and Scharlach) to attend his marriage, which was "apparently" to take place in late March at Scarsdale in Leicestershire.[33]

It may be that neither Laura nor Isabella took this tall, slender, reddish-blonde "baron" from Schönhausen very seriously, much as they enjoyed his company and attention. He was after all a rural Junker from an Altmark family without impressive connections in the German and European aristocracy. Both girls were constantly chaperoned, and their suitor was alone with neither for any length of time. Isabella's diary, which records in detail most of the events of that summer, is silent on the subject of her putative engagement. It could hardly have escaped the attention of the parents that neither the young *Referendar* nor his family was wealthy, despite Otto's madcap extravagances (champagne dinner by moonlight). When Scharlach asked in 1845 what had become of his English bride, he reported losing her to "a colonel of 50, with one arm, 4 horses and 15,000 in revenues." But this was patently fanciful. In 1840 Isabella married a Harrovian banker of twenty-nine years and became the mistress of Brixworth Hall, Northampton. In 1844 Laura—the legitimate and orphaned daughter of the duchess's brother, a naval officer—married the earl of Musgrave (later marquis of Normandy), who became successively the royal governor of Nova Scotia, Queensland, and New Zealand.[34]

His headlong pursuit of Isabella brought Bismarck close to bankruptcy and professional disgrace. Wiesbaden was notoriously expensive, and the rector patronized only the best hotels and restaurants. Again Bismarck sought to defray the cost of his follies at the casino, with the same misfortune as at Aachen. By September 1837 the Isabella affair had put him in arrears by seventeen hundred thalers, which took him years to repay. But that was not all.

[33] GW, XIV, 8–11; Engelberg, *Bismarck*, 143–145; Palmer, "Young Romantic."
[34] GW, XIV, 30; Palmer, "Young Romantic."

He had exceeded by many weeks the fourteen days' leave his superiors had granted. From Bern he wrote Governor von Arnim seeking two additional months, which were curtly refused. Bismarck decided not to return to Aachen, where creditors would have hounded him. (Articles of clothing he left behind were evidently impounded.) Instead he requested a transfer to Potsdam, far away from the temptations of the Rhineland spa. At the end of September he returned home to Kniephof, "poor in purse and sick at heart," traveling in a stranger's carriage. At Potsdam in 1838 he resumed his duties, sought diversion in gambling and drinking, ran up more debts, and resigned after five months.[35]

In a remarkable letter written in September 1838 to cousin Caroline ("Lienchen") von Malortie he explained to his family (Ferdinand and Bernhard received copies) why he had taken this step. The bureaucracy, he complained, had no place for an independent and critical spirit. The state official is like a musician in an orchestra, who must perform regardless of what he thinks of the melody or its interpretation. "But I want to play the tune the way it sounds good to me or not at all. . . . Pride bids me command rather than obey." In general, statesmen are motivated not by patriotism but by "pride, the desire to command, to become admired and renowned. I confess I am not free from these passions." Unsubmissive by nature, he could see only one way to scale the heights of his ambition: through a Prussian parliament. He envied states with "free constitutions," where individuals could make their influence felt and views effective. His imagination was fired by the examples of Peel, O'Connell, and Mirabeau.[36]

Like many documents from Bismarck's pen, this letter revealed some motives but concealed others less palatable to the recipient. The years in Berlin had left the Bismarck family as a whole in poor financial condition. Otto owed far more money than he dared admit. Before her death on January 1, 1839, Wilhelmine accepted the advice of her sons that the family return to the country to repair their fortunes.[37] His disappointing experiences at Aachen and Potsdam merely reinforced Otto's decision to exchange "the pen for the plow and the brief case for the hunter's bag." After completing a year of military training (1838–1839) in order to qualify for a commission in the militia, Bismarck became a rural squire at Kniephof and, after his father's death in 1845, at Schönhausen. In neither place could he resist the urge to play some role in public affairs, acting in Pomerania as assistant to his brother,

---

[35] GW, XIV, 10–11, 30–31; Engelberg, Bismarck, 145–148.

[36] GW, XIV, 13–17, 31. Years later Keyserling reminded him of a comment made in these years: "constitution unavoidable; this the path to outward fame; one must also be inwardly pious." Kohl, Anhang, vol. 2, 246ff.

[37] Sempell, "Unbekannte Briefstellen," 610–611.

the local *Landrat*, and in Brandenburg as dike reeve on the Elbe.[38] The life did not satisfy him for long.

From age twenty-three to thirty-two Bismarck underwent a period of gestation that corresponds closely to the "psychosocial moratorium" that Erik Erikson described in other personalities of like creativity.[39] During these years he was a restless, unhappy man. He drank, gambled, hunted, traveled to Switzerland, France, and Britain, and made vague plans for a trip to the Middle East and India. In the spring of 1844 he again attempted a bureaucratic career but quit after three months. He was contemptuous of the neighboring gentry, poked fun at their ignorance and piety, argued with them about politics and religion, and delighted in shocking them by boorish behavior—which earned him locally the sobriquet of the "wild" or "crazy" Bismarck. By his own admission he fell into "bad company" and "thought every sin permissible." During these years he also—typically according to Erikson—formed a deep attachment for a sibling, his younger sister Malwine, who kept house for him at Kniephof until her marriage in 1844.[40]

Bismarck's erratic conduct during his Aachen, Kniephof, and Schönhausen years reveals the disquiet within him. He had sought but could not find the balm with which to treat his injured narcissism. But in 1846–1848 his years of frustration were brought to an end by three events that promised better days: religious conversion, marriage, and the beginning of a political career. Conversion to pietistic Lutheranism ended his feeling that life was "shallow and fruitless" by providing him with a source of spiritual support. Marriage brought him a stable, dependable, and nurturing family life, in which he was unquestionably the dominant figure, free from contradiction and the threat of repudiation or rejection. In a parliamentary and diplomatic career he found the possibility of influencing the world about him. Above all, he moved closer to the valves and sluices of power with which he might one day fill the reservoir of his self-esteem.

Bismarck's Religion

In childhood Bismarck received no firm religious foundation. He could not remember a single discussion with his father on the subject of faith.[41] Not a

[38] Marcks, *Bismarcks Jugend*, 109, 149–150, 154.

[39] Erik H. Erikson, *Identity: Youth and Crisis* (New York, 1968), 142–161.

[40] Marcks, *Bismarcks Jugend*, 203–208; Werner Richter, *Bismarck* (Frankfurt, 1962), 29–39; GW, XIV, 46. After Ferdinand's death, Baron Senfft von Pilsach, governor general of Pomerania and favorite of Friedrich Wilhelm IV, sought to persuade Bismarck to enter government service. Bismarck was willing but refused to take the requisite examinations. Senfft to Moritz von Blanckenburg, Feb. 24, 1877. [Hans Goldschmidt, ed.], "Neue Briefe von und über Bismarck," *Deutsche Allgemeine Zeitung*, July 9, 1937, Nr. 304–305, 1. Beiblatt.

[41] GW, XIV, 67.

very religious man, the elder Bismarck was content with a simple, naive trust in God's love and mercy. His wife had been raised in the rationalist tradition and was not a churchgoer. Yet none of the watered-down religious formulas of the Enlightenment satisfied her. She took up the popular occultism of the time, interested herself in mesmerism and clairvoyance, and read the works of Swedenborg, Schubert, and Kerner.[42] Although confirmed by Schleiermacher in the *Dreifaltigkeitskirche* in Berlin, Bismarck maintained in later years that he had learned nothing from the great theologian.[43] Soon thereafter he decided to give up the nightly prayers he had offered since childhood. In later years he described the religious views with which he graduated from the *Gymnasium* variously as "deistic," "atheistic," and "pantheistic."[44] Although a skeptic, he arrived at no firm theoretical position with regard to his skepticism. Similarly, the religious faith that he finally acquired lacked theological content.

During his period of retirement at Kniephof, Bismarck debated religious questions with two devout Pomeranian neighbors, Moritz von Blanckenburg and Marie von Thadden, Blanckenburg's fiancée. Though he regarded most of the gentry with humor mixed with contempt, Moritz was a respected friend and Marie a person of wit and charm whom he came to love. Her father was Adolf von Thadden, an important rural leader of the Prussian religious revival and a close friend of Leopold and Ludwig von Gerlach. It was Marie who introduced Bismarck to Johanna von Puttkamer, his future wife. Both women worked diligently for his conversion. Marie's death in October 1846 was for Bismarck a shattering personal tragedy. The news of her approaching end wrenched from his tortured mind the first prayer he had uttered in sixteen years, and from that day onward prayer and devotion became an intimate part of his existence. In December he wrote the famous *Werbebrief* to Heinrich von Puttkamer in which he declared both his religious conversion and his love for Johanna.[45]

The revival movement to which Bismarck adhered began primarily as a lay movement within the Lutheran church. It was a resurgence of eighteenth-century pietism, which had declined among the educated classes during the high tide of German idealism. Although led by Junkers, many of whom were

---

[42] Marcks, *Bismarcks Jugend*, 72–73.

[43] GW, VII, 100. A similarity in their attitudes toward prayer leaves open the possibility that Schleiermacher actually influenced his pupil. Neither believed it possible to move God through prayer. See Friedrich Meinecke, *Preussen und Deutschland im 19. und 20. Jahrhundert* (Munich, 1918), 301–303, and Hajo Holborn, "Bismarcks Realpolitik," *Journal of the History of Ideas*, 21 (1960), 85.

[44] GW, VII, 11, 224; XIII, 463; XV, 5; Lucius von Ballhausen, *Bismarck-Erinnerungen* (Stuttgart, 1920), 492.

[45] Marcks, *Bismarcks Jugend*, 183ff., 251ff.; GW, XIV, 46–48.

OTTO AND JOHANNA VON BISMARCK IN 1849 (BILDARCHIV PREUSSISCHER KULTURBESITZ).

veterans of the war of liberation, the movement hoped to reach the lower classes. Like the mystics of the pre-Reformation epoch, the pietists sought a sense of union with God. Where the regular clergy was unsympathetic to their cause, their devotions were conducted by lay preachers in private dwellings. They rejected the rational, unemotional element that had penetrated the clergy during the Enlightenment. In place of reason they emphasized feeling; for theology they substituted divine and brotherly love.[46]

Pietism appealed to Bismarck because of its lack of dogmatism and its faith in the capacity of man to reach God without the mediation of priests and preachers. He had no interest in theology and, although daily prayer and Bible reading became a habit, he seldom attended church. In contrast to pietistic friends, he did not find in religion a doctrinal basis for his politics.[47] Scholars have differed concerning the nature of Bismarck's religious conversion.[48] Yet there can be little doubt of its sincerity, for it altered his personal conduct. In a letter of 1847 to his bride he confessed that he had acted "almost" like the fool in King Lear: "wine I love deeply, dice dearly, and in women outparamoured the Turk, false of heart, light of ear, bloody of hand."[49] Religion reinforced personal ambition in what must have been a titanic struggle for self-discipline. In July 1851, after weeks of unavoidable separation from his wife, he wrote to a friend, Hans von Kleist-Retzow, of the temptations that assailed him. "The chief weapon with which evil assaults me is not desire for external glory, but a brutal sensuality that leads me so close to the greatest sins that I doubt at times that I will gain access to God's mercy. At any rate I am certain that the seed of God's word has not found fertile ground in a heart laid waste as it was from youth. Otherwise I could not be so much the plaything of temptation, which even invades my moments of prayer. . . . I am often in hopeless anxiety over the fruitlessness of my prayer. Comfort me, Hans, but burn this without speaking of it to anyone."[50] Ultimately he concluded that the "usefulness of prayer" lay in its implied "submission to a stronger power," not in its efficacy for God's intercession. "I am conscious of that Power, which is neither arbitrary nor capricious."[51]

Political power was ultimately the means by which Bismarck fulfilled and realized himself. To assume that he wielded it only for self-aggrandizement

[46] Meinecke, *Preussen und Deutschland*, 296–337; Franz Schnabel, *Deutsche Geschichte im neunzehnten Jahrhundert* (3d ed., Freiburg i. Br., 1955), vol. 4, 383–399.

[47] Lütgert, *Idealismus*, vol. 4, 12.

[48] Friedrich Meinecke, "Bismarcks Eintritt in den christlich-germanischen Kreis," *Historische Zeitschrift*, 90 (1903), 56–92, reprinted in *Preussen und Deutschland*, 296–337; Marcks, *Bismarcks Jugend*, 244ff.; Otto Baumgarten, *Bismarcks Stellung zu Religion und Kirche* (Tübingen, 1900) and *Bismarcks Glaube* (Tübingen, 1915); Hans von Soden, *Bismarcks Glaube*, in Ernst Jackh, ed., *Der deutsche Krieg*, 40 (1915); Arnold Oskar Meyer, *Bismarcks Glaube im Spiegel der "Loosungen und Lehrtexte,"* in *Münchener historische Abhandlungen*, Erste Reihe, vol. 1 (Munich, 1933); Max Buchner, "Bismarck und die Religion," *Gelbe Hefte*, 11 (1935), 541–561. For later works on this subject see note 54.

[49] GW, XIV, 46.

[50] Bismarck to Hans von Kleist Retzow, July 4, 1851, in Joachim von Muralt, *Bismarcks Verantwortlichkeit* (Göttingen, 1955), 89–90. The passage was suppressed by the editors of Bismarck's collected works.

[51] Richmond, "Bismarck at Home," 5.

would be unfair. From the beginning to the end of his career he felt keenly the obligation he had undertaken. While granting freedom to act, power subjected him to its own necessity, imposing goals and purposes more important than the mere satisfaction of personal conceit. Such a sense of responsibility has led others into the morass of self-doubt and self-criticism. But upon Bismarck the effect was different. It made him hypersensitive to criticism and opposition, for his confidence in the superiority of his own judgment was absolute. The very qualities that prevented him from being a dutiful subordinate made him in later years an autocratic superior.

His highly developed sense of duty was reinforced by his religious faith. At the beginning of his diplomatic career in 1851 he wrote, "I am God's soldier and I must go where he sends me, and I believe that he sends me and fashions my life as he needs it."[52] Nevertheless, he did not conceive of himself as the mere passive tool of God's will. Unlike Friedrich Wilhelm IV, he did not feel compelled to wait upon divine inspiration. What he received from God, he believed, was the obligation to act according to the dictates of his reason and conscience. God was not the instigator of his actions but their judge. It was not impossible, however, for man to perceive God's will in the direction of human events. "I am happy," he remarked, "when I discern whither our lord God is going and can hobble after him."[53] Though he did not believe it possible to invoke divine intervention, he found sustenance in prayer and a feeling of subjection to a higher power. In times of great stress, like the war of 1870–1871, his faith fortified him in the titanic struggle to gain his will over great odds. In times of political frustration he found solace in the assumption that what he could not prevent or make otherwise was God's doing. His religion gave to his self-confidence a moral underpinning and added to the certitude with which he asserted his will over others.

It is highly doubtful, nevertheless, that Bismarck's religious conversion was a decisive turning point in the development of his character.[54] His need to dominate and direct did not spring from a sense of divine mission, but from an earlier, more elemental force in his personality. Conversion did not fundamentally alter his attitude toward his fellowman. His cynical view of minds and motives, his hatred and malevolence toward those who opposed him, his willingness to exploit and use others show that the Christian doctrine of love

[52] GW, XIV, 208, also 227.

[53] Meyer, Bismarcks Glaube, 9.

[54] The contrary viewpoint is held by S. A. Kaehler, "Zur Deutung von Bismarcks 'Bekehrung,' " in Heinrich Runte, ed., Glaube und Geschichte: Festschrift für Friedrich Gogarten (Giessen, 1948), 189–209; Wilhelm Schüssler, Um das Geschichtsbild (Gladbeck, 1953), 122–141; Otto Vossler, "Bismarcks Ethos," Historische Zeitschrift, 171 (1951), 263–292; Muralt, Verantwortlichkeit, 97. Though he accepted the general viewpoint of these authors, Pastor Franz Pahlmann was critical of their theology, "Der Stand des Gesprächs über Bismarcks Glauben," Geschichte in Wissenschaft und Unterricht, 7 (1956), 207–222.

and charity had little influence upon him. His faith provided the reinforcement, not the foundation, of his sense of responsibility. From feudal times the gentry had preserved the tradition of an aristocratic status group dedicated to the functions of government and defense in the interest of the whole. Through Frederick the Great the tradition was deliberately transformed into patriotic service to the Prussian nation-state. In relying solely upon the voice of conscience, Bismarck discarded the possibility of an objective moral code and was willing to disregard the limitations of law in his conduct of public affairs. Hence his religion was compatible with much of his earlier skepticism. It helped him put his personal life in order but produced no basic change in his social attitudes.[55]

On the contrary, the evidence suggests that the function of religion in Bismarck's psychology was to help him cope with the inner, purely personal problem created by the emotional starvation of his childhood. Religion gave him a sense of security, a feeling of belonging to a coherent, meaningful, and controlled world—the kind of environment that his parents did not provide. The God he worshipped was powerful (in contrast to his father) and loving, supportive, and omnipresent (in contrast to his mother). Unlike Wilhelmine, furthermore, Bismarck's God did not intervene and manipulate, yet provided the direction and leadership that the Junker from Schönhausen could never accept from mortals. God was the source of spiritual power that he tapped not only to shore up his moral defenses, but also to enable him through the confident use of innate political talent to satisfy his narcissistic needs.

Conception of the State

Bismarck was a royalist. Although both sides of his family had served the Hohenzollern, the Junker side was obviously the origin of his monarchist sympathy. Hence he preferred the vocabulary of feudalism to that of the modern state: "subject" instead of "citizen," "royal servant" instead of "state servant." In later years he often referred to himself as the "vassal" of his "liege lord," the king. Once he wrote, "He has the right to receive homage from every single subject and every corporation in the country when and where it pleases him."[56] Nevertheless, this attitude was directed more toward the person of Wilhelm I than toward the institution of kingship. Although he served no less than four successive rulers, his chosen epitaph ("A loyal German servant

---

[55] See Holborn, "Bismarcks Realpolitik," 87–90. Holborn revived the older viewpoint of Meinecke, Lenz, and Brandenburg. One of the descendents of the circle of Pomeranian pietists revived the doubts of nineteenth-century conservatives as to the genuineness of Bismarck's conversion. Reinold von Thadden-Trieglaff, *War Bismarck Christ?* (Hamburg, 1950).

[56] GW, XIV, 571; also III, 147, and Keudell, *Fürst und Fürstin Bismarck*, 110. See G. Adolf Rein, "Bismarcks Royalismus," *Geschichte in Wissenschaft und Unterricht*, 5 (1954), 330–349.

of Kaiser Wilhelm I")[57] gave homage to only one. Nor was his vassalage unconditional. Throughout their relationship he often used the threat of resignation to overcome the king's reluctance on critical policies.

With a frequency that carries conviction Bismarck maintained that the
Hohenzollern dynasty reigned by divine right ("by the grace of God"). From
this it cannot be assumed that he had any theoretical position with regard to
the institution of monarchy as such. Later we shall see from both his words
and actions that the argument of "legitimacy" had little meaning for him.
Once he wrote that the sovereignty claimed by the German small states was
an "unhistorical, Godless, unjust swindle."[58] Much has been made of his "organic" view of the state. But the proof consists of only a few brief quotations,
such as the phrase "permanent-identic personality," which he used only
once.[59] Certainly, the organic concept as understood by the romantic conservatives was alien to his thinking. He described his political attitude before
1847 as "*ständisch-liberal*." This meant that he sided with the aristocratic opposition to absolute monarchy.[60] His reasons, however, were practical rather
than doctrinaire.

In Friedrich Julius Stahl he found a viewpoint much closer to his own than
those of Karl Ludwig von Haller and the Gerlachs. Stahl and Bismarck began
their active political careers in the Prussian Landtag and Erfurt parliament.
They were associated in the founding of the Prussian Conservative party.
How much Bismarck was influenced by his learned colleague is difficult to
determine.[61] From Erfurt in 1850 he wrote of "our dear Stahl, who casts his
pearls here before the swine. He still has pearls for me, although with the
years the time will yet come . . . when our ways will separate."[62] Probably he
was attracted by Stahl's realism and his solution to the problem of combining
monarchical and representative institutions. It is safe to say, nevertheless,
that he passed over the theoretical structure by which the philosopher justified monarchical power. In one of his early speeches Bismarck announced his
adherence to the concept of the "Christian state" and remarked that the basic

[57] Inscription on Bismarck's sarcophagus at Friedrichsruh.

[58] GW, XIV, 578. On another occasion he spoke to Ludwig Gerlach of the "abstract sovereignty" of the lesser states. *Ibid.*, VII, 106.

[59] Hans Rothfels, *Otto von Bismarck: Deutscher Staat* (Munich, 1925), xxi, and Egmont Zechlin, "Bismarck und der ständische Gedanke," *Nationalsozialistische Monatshefte*, vol. 5, no. 1
(1934), 562.

[60] GW, XV, 16.

[61] See Erich Marcks, *Bismarck und die deutsche Revolution, 1848–1851* (Stuttgart, 1939), 154ff.,
and Bernhard Michniewicz, *Stahl und Bismarck* (Berlin, 1913), 108ff.

[62] GW, XIV, 157–158. Years later he remarked to Lothar Bucher, "Do you believe that Stahl
and company were sympathetic to me. Most certainly not! But at least they had a tangible goal,
and I could go a way with them; yet I knew very exactly where our ways separated." Quoted in
Michniewicz, *Stahl und Bismarck*, 162. The high point of the relationship was their joint author-
ship of an amendment to the Radowitz constitution in Erfurt. BR, I, 232ff.

purpose of political institutions was "the realization of Christian doctrine." But this appears to have been a convenient argument of the moment rather than a deep-seated conviction. He was debating against a measure to permit Jews to enter the state service.[63]

Bismarck believed that the state, like all else, was part of the divine world plan. His subordination of church to state and his belief in the duality of Christian morality and political necessity were characteristic of Lutheranism. Nevertheless, it cannot be proved that he actually shared with Luther and Stahl the conviction that the state had been instituted by God to protect the virtuous few from the sinful majority.[64] His attitude toward the state was pragmatic, not theological. What impressed him was not its divine, legal, idealistic, or cultural nature, but its power. In this he was by no means unique. We have seen that he appeared as an actor on the political scene at a time of transition toward political realism. And yet there was a vital difference between his view and that of most of his contemporaries. In contrast to Ranke and Treitschke, for example, he was incapable of thinking of the state as a "moral personality" or of its power as a "spiritual essence."[65] For him the state was primarily a device for governing and its power but a means to concrete, practical ends. What were those ends?

Historians have often asserted that Bismarck did not covet power for its own sake and did not use it irresponsibly, even though he did not employ it for ideal ends. His religion, aristocratic background, and traditional view of the art of statecraft imposed restraints. He belonged to the school of classical politics, which believed foreign and military policy must be dictated by the reasoned interest of state and pursued within the limits of the balance of power system. This "ethic" elevated him above the temptation of personal aggrandizement and shielded him from the passions of ideology and the irrational influence of popular movements.[66] Indeed, Bismarck never again spoke or wrote, so far as the record shows, of his "wish to command, to be admired, and to become famous" as frankly as he did in the letter of 1838. During his political career he saw himself as "the man of the state and the king," who stood above the chaos of social and political life, seeking without fear or favor,

[63] BR, I, 21–31. Stahl's Der Christliche Staat und sein Verhältnis zu Deismus und Judentum (Berlin, 1847) appeared after Bismarck's speech and shows some difference in viewpoint. Michniewicz, Stahl und Bismarck, 56ff. Others detected the influence of Ludwig von Gerlach. Ernst Ludwig von Gerlach, Aufzeichnungen aus seinem Leben und Wirken, 1795–1877 (Schwerin, 1903), vol. 1, 477.

[64] Muralt, who takes a contrary position, admits that there is no direct evidence to support it. Verantwortlichkeit, 106.

[65] Rothfels, Deutscher Staat, 71–72, 80, 84.

[66] See particularly Gerhard Ritter, Staatskunst und Kriegshandwerk: Das Problem des "Militarismus" in Deutschland (Munich, 1954), vol. 1; Hans Rothfels, Bismarck: Der Osten und das Reich (Stuttgart, 1960); Franz Schnabel, "Bismarck und die klassische Diplomatie," Aussenpolitik, 3 (1952), 635–642; and Muralt, Verantwortlichkeit.

prejudice or partisanship, the ideal line in foreign and domestic policy dictated by *raison d'état*.[67] "I am," he told the Prussian Chamber of Deputies in 1874, "a disciplined statesman who subordinates himself to the total needs and requirements of the state in the interest of peace and the welfare of my country."[68]

One need not question the sincerity of this statement in order to establish that the Bismarck of 1874 was still the Bismarck of 1838. What occurred may be understood in terms of a common psychic process that has been called the "evocation of a proxy." Instinctual impulses that the conscience cannot tolerate are either repressed or projected.[69] Bismarck projected his quest for power and renown onto the Prussian state. Goals that would have been intolerable if conceived as personal, could, when conceived as in the interest of state or public welfare, be sought without a sense of guilt and with all the formidable talents he possessed. Bismarck's religion may have had a similar function in his psychology. Being "God's soldier" and merely listening for "God's footsteps" relieved him of any sense of selfishness in his relentless pursuit of power and domination. By such projections Bismarck protected his ego from the sting of conscience.

It is doubtful, of course, whether the kind of objectivity Bismarck claimed for himself as a statesman is actually possible. Like the historian, the statesman is part of the historical process and not above it. His conception of what constitutes the public welfare is formed in the crucible of the mind, where it is inevitably alloyed with personal aims and social biases. Bismarck was no exception. His thought about the state was compounded of both subjective and objective elements. Internally its power was the means of his own self-fulfillment and of survival for the aristocratic order in a century of dynamic change; externally its power was the means of common protection against foreign aggression and of the expansion and aggrandizement of the Prussian nation-state.

Fortress of Aristocratic Interests

Bismarck began his political career in 1846–1847 as an effective and partisan champion of conservative interests. On taking possession of Schönhausen, he

---

[67] BR, VI, 129–131; VIII, 328–339; XI, 292; XII, 85; GW, VIc, 383.

[68] BR, VI, 131.

[69] Anna Freud, *The Ego and the Mechanisms of Defence*, tr. Cecil Baines (New York, 1946), 132–146. Though Anna Freud described the process, Martin Wangh provided the best descriptive term. The term "altruistic surrender" coined by Edward Bibring and used by Anna Freud has, as Wangh pointed out, a "passive renunciatory" quality that is not always appropriate. He preferred "evocation of a proxy" because of its "active quality, equally unconscious." See his "The 'Evocation of a Proxy': A Psychological Maneuver, Its Use as a Defense, Its Purposes and Genesis," *Psychoanalytic Study of the Child*, 17 (1962), 451–469.

assiduously cultivated the attention of the local gentry, sought and obtained the position of Elbe dike reeve, took a hand in the revival and reform of the manorial judicial powers of estate owners, gained election to the provincial Landtag, and became one of its six representatives in the United Diet of 1847. From the tribune of that body he opposed every reform that meant the least sacrifice to the aristocratic caste, whether proposed by the crown or liberal opposition. By late June when the assembly dissolved, he could boast to Johanna of having attained some influence within the "so-called court party and among other ultraconservatives."[70]

By his own account Bismarck heard of the Berlin uprising on March 18–19 from noblewomen fleeing the capital. At Schönhausen he organized and armed villagers willing to defy urban radicals from nearby Tangermünde and threatened to shoot a neighboring landlord of liberal persuasion if he should interfere. He hastened to the authorities in Potsdam with the extravagant claim that "the peasants are rising in our cause." But the army officers with whom he talked showed no enthusiasm for his proposal to raise a peasant militia to support the army in recapturing Berlin. They believed the troops under their command were adequate for such an effort but were indisposed to act without orders from Friedrich Wilhelm IV, then a virtual prisoner of the revolutionaries in Berlin. Yet they were interested in the possibility that one of the royal princes could be encouraged to assume leadership of such a coup, acting in behalf of the king, but without his express consent. Contrary to the impression created in his memoirs, Bismarck was only a peripheral participant in this plot, which was in any case soon overtaken by events. On March 25 the king arrived unexpectedly in Potsdam and told his assembled officers, "I have never been more free and secure than under the protection of my citizens." The reform program he had granted had been "long prepared" and accorded with his own convictions. Events had merely hastened the concessions and "no power can and will move me to take back what has been given."[71]

---

[70] GW, XIV, 89

[71] GW, XV, 18–23; Engelberg, Bismarck, 214–230, 243–251. The only consequence of Bismarck's peripheral participation in the officers' plot was the enduring enmity of the future Empress Augusta, then princess of Prussia and wife of Prince Wilhelm of Prussia, heir to the throne. In an audience Bismarck, acting on behalf of a Junker delegation, sought to entice from her a document in which the prince, before he had fled to England, was believed to have authorized an attack on Berlin in the event Friedrich Wilhelm IV should be deposed. Augusta refused with great indignation what she interpreted as a dishonorable attempt to compromise her husband. She extracted her visitor's "word of honor" never to involve either her husband or her son in a reactionary coup. Egmont Zechlin, Bismarck und die Grundlegung der deutschen Grossmacht (Stuttgart, 1930), 254; Engelberg, Bismarck, 271–276. For earlier accounts of the failed counterrevolution see G. Adolf Rein, "Bismarcks gegenrevolutionäre Aktion in den Märztagen 1848," Die Welt als Geschichte, 13 (1953), 246-262; Max Lenz, "Bismarcks Plan einer Gegenrevolution im

Like most who were present that afternoon in the palace at Potsdam, Bismarck was much grieved, even angered, by the monarch's words. But during the following days he began to reassess the situation, much to the distress of his pietistic associates. When the United Diet reassembled on April 2, he publicly accepted the revolution as an accomplished fact, saying that he had no other choice now that "the crown had buried its own coffin."[72] He had no wish to make trouble for the new government, he declared, and for some days his tone and manner were conciliatory. To Johanna he wrote with customary irony: "I am much calmer than earlier: [am] with Vincke heart and soul."[73] But this mood began to change when the new cabinet announced its fiscal program: to pacify the urban population by substituting for the grist tax a direct tax to be paid by the well-to-do; to revive the economy by extending credits to businesses suffering from the effects of the revolution. Bismarck denounced both measures as a "gift from the treasury to the cities," whose cost would ultimately be borne by the "country and the small towns." The minister of finance, he charged, saw the needs of the public "through the spectacles of industrialism."[74]

In May he decided not to become a candidate for the Prussian National Assembly, which replaced the United Diet, having concluded that he had no chance of election.[75] Impotently he watched while the new parliament drafted a constitution that would have abolished the formula of divine right and titles of nobility. Furthermore, the deputies ended the exclusive hunting rights of the Junkers; progress was made on a measure to eliminate their feudal judicial powers in the manorial courts; and bills were introduced providing for the abolition of the gentry's exemptions from the property tax and of certain payments and services still owed by the peasantry to Junker landlords. The tax reform, in particular, aroused Bismarck's ire. "A real estate tax," he wrote, "is not a tax, but a confiscation of capital." It was a conspiracy of the city against the country, of capitalists against Junkers. In the name of "order and justice" the liberals had begun to "plunder one class of citizens to reward an-

März 1848," *Sitzungsberichte der preussischen Akademie der Wissenschaften*, Jahrgang 1930, Philosophisch-Historische Klasse, 251–276; Marcks, *Bismarck und Revolution*, 19ff.

[72] BR, I, 45–46. At the end of March he amended the text of a proposed conservative proclamation submitted to him by Ludwig Gerlach by inserting the promise, "No reaction" and "readiness for personal sacrifice." Helmut Diwald, ed., *Von der Revolution zum Norddeutschen Bund: Politik und Ideengut der preussischen Hochkonservativen, 1848–1866; Aus dem Nachlass von Ernst Ludwig von Gerlach* (Göttingen, 1970), vol. 1, 89; Ludwig Gerlach, *Aufzeichnungen*, vol. I, 518–523; Hans J. Schoeps, "Unveröffentlichte Bismarckbriefe," *Zeitschrift für Religions- und Geistesgeschichte*, 2 (1949), 2–3. His moderation aroused bitter criticism from ultraconservative friends.

[73] GW, XIV, 103–104.

[74] BR, I, 51–56; Erich Jordan, *Die Entstehung der konservativen Partei und die preussischen Agrarverhältnisse vor 1848* (Munich, 1914), 128, 159.

[75] GW, XIV, 105.

other." The issue, he believed, was "literally one of the existence of a large part of the conservative party."[76]

In the program of the Frankfurt Parliament he found reason to fear for the "social and political existence of Prussia."[77] The program was, he later charged, more "social than national" in character. "If the revolution had been restricted to the national issue, the movement would have been limited to a few prominent people. Only by raising the social question were they able to cut the ground from under us. By misrepresentation they excited the greed of the unpropertied for the possessions of others, and the envy of the less well-to-do against the rich."[78] As revolutionary ardor cooled and news of the first victories of the counterrevolution in France (the "June days") and Italy (reconquest of Milan) arrived, conservatives who had been shaken by the events of March regained courage. Bismarck began to rebuild his relationship with those ultraconservatives offended by his speech of April 2. He helped finance and found a conservative journal, the Neue Preussische Zeitung (better known as the Kreuzzeitung) and assisted in the founding of a Prussian network of conservative sympathizers. These activities (aided by an apology for his apostasy of April) eased his acceptance by the Gerlachs into a secret camarilla of ultraconservatives, whose primary aim was to persuade the king to stage a coup d'état.[79]

What most excited his wrath now was the conviction that the king himself had been responsible for the defeat of the old regime. In March the army had never swerved in its loyalty to the crown. The troops would have crushed the revolution at the barricades, had Friedrich Wilhelm not ordered a premature withdrawal.[80] For the time being, however, Friedrich Wilhelm refused to act. In August Bismarck drafted a threatening petition for the signatures of conservative friends. The new financial legislation, it declared, was "a confiscation of private property" unequalled in history except by "conquerors and

[76] Kohl, Jahrbuch, vol. 1, 475–483; vol. 3, 399–400; vol. 6, 10–16; Ludwig Gerlach, Aufzeichnungen, vol. 2, 20; GW, XIV, 111–112; XV, 27–29; Hans-Joachim Schoeps, Bismarck über Zeitgenossen—Zeitgenossen über Bismarck (2d ed., Frankfurt a. M., 1981), 315–319.

[77] Letter to the Magdeburger Zeitung, Mar. 30, 1848. GW, XV, 26–27; XIV, 103. Apparently the final version of the letter was somewhat different. Marcks, Bismarck und Revolution, 26. On the social reforms to which he objected see Theodore S. Hamerow, Restoration, Revolution, Reaction: Economics and Politics in Germany, 1815–1871 (Princeton, 1958), 168ff.

[78] BR, I, 111.

[79] GW, XIV, 106–110; Hermann Witte, "Vom Nachlass Ludwig von Gerlachs, mit ungedruckten Briefen Bismarcks," Archiv für Kulturgeschichte, 31 (1943), 140–141. For the attitudes of other conservatives see Jordan, Entstehung der konservativen Partei, 130–132, 154ff. Until 1851 Bismarck was a constant contributor to the columns of the Kreuzzeitung. Few of his articles can be identified with certainty. The claim of Bernhard Studt to have identified 125 contributions is insecure. See his Bismarck als Mitarbeiter der Kreuzzeitung in den Jahren 1848 and 1849 (Bonn, 1903), and Hans J. Schoeps, "Der junge Bismarck als Journalist," Zeitschrift für Religions- und Geistesgeschichte; 3 (1951), 1–12.

[80] GW, XV, 47–48; also XIV, 160–162; X, 16.

dictators." For this neglect of their rights "the great majority of the Prussian people will hold your majesty responsible before God and the hereafter." Friedrich Wilhelm should understand, in other words, that where Junker rights and privileges were concerned there was a limit to royalism. On August 18–19, 1848, the squire from Schönhausen participated in a "Junker parliament" at Berlin, which organized the nobility for the defense of their interests.[81]

In Bismarck's eyes this was not mere self-seeking. As a candidate for parliament he was probably sincere in describing himself to voters as "independent and nonpartisan" in contrast to a merchant or industrialist. Without a sense of greed he could openly declare, "I am a Junker and want the advantage of being one."[82] The privileges of his caste, he believed, were justified by its unique contribution to the general welfare. In 1849 he devoted a speech to this subject. History proved that only those states with a hereditary aristocracy attained "lasting prosperity and power." The great victories of the Prussian army had been purchased with aristocratic blood. Opposed to both monarchical and democratic absolutism, they were the greatest bulwark of freedom in Prussian society. They were the keel and rudder that counterbalanced the raging winds of the *Zeitgeist*.[83]

In a letter of 1849 Bismarck argued that it was the patriotic duty of the Junkers to look after their own material interests. Without independent means this class could no longer continue to serve the state.[84] To the end of his days he held steadfastly to the view that the agricultural classes were the backbone of society. The endurance for victorious campaigns came from the cultivation of the land, rather than the tending of machines. The soil nourished the healthy instincts of patriotism and dynastic loyalty; the city bred the loathsome diseases of treason and revolution. The producing classes of German society were the farmers and rural nobility, not capitalists, factory workers, bureaucrats, court nobility, and *Geldadel*. They were the "worker bees" whose culture should be the main interest of political economy.[85] His defense of the nobility was not romantic, but realistic. He did not speak of the sacred trust of time, but of the utilitarian services of the nobility in the present.

By late summer 1848, Bismarck had become totally uncompromising in his defense of Junker interests and monarchical authority. He opposed and undermined the proposal of a Pomeranian neighbor, the Junker publicist Ernst

---

[81] GW, I, 1–2; Marcks, *Bismarck und Revolution*, 58–60. In June he had remonstrated personally to Friedrich Wilhelm, but was disarmed by the king's friendly candor. Herman von Petersdorff, *König Friedrich Wilhelm der Vierte* (Stuttgart, 1900), 13–14.

[82] GW, X, 22; VII, 15; XIV, 123–124.

[83] BR, I, 144–153.

[84] GW, XIV, 112.

[85] GW, IX, 90ff., 196ff.; XII, 611.

Der neue Peter von Amiens und die Kreuzfahrer.

LEOPOLD VON GERLACH AS "THE NEW ST. PETER OF AMIENS," HOLDING ALOFT THE PRUSSIAN IRON
CROSS (SYMBOL OF THE *KREUZZEITUNG*). ON HIS LEFT IS "ST. STAHL," GARBED AS A PRIEST; ON HIS
RIGHT, BISMARCK AS A "SWINDLER" KNIGHT IN COMICAL ARMOR, FAMILY TREE IN ONE HAND, SCOURGE
IN THE OTHER; BEHIND HIM, HERMANN WAGENER AS DON QUIXOTE. (WILHELM SCHOLZ,
KLADDERADATSCH, NOVEMBER 4, 1849).

von Bülow-Cummerow, for a "compact" alliance between the "propertied
classes, the *Mittelstand*, and the more intelligent circles of the nation" against
those whose aim was "not social reform but social revolution." Bismarck concluded that the monarchy was not in need of such support. When Friedrich
Wilhelm finally resolved to use force, the revolution proved to be a mere

"spook." Out of respect for public opinion the king had deceived himself about the "real relationships of power." In his memoirs Bismarck concluded that a *Realpolitiker* need concern himself with the clamor of press and parliament only insofar as it affected the loyalty of the troops.[86] This was also his view in 1849. In a speech of that year he declared that the struggle between popular sovereignty and divine right would never be settled by parliamentary debate. The final arbiter between bourgeois and Junker, liberal and conservative, was force, not oratory. Victory lay not with the parliamentary majority but with the mailed fist of the state.[87]

This must not be taken to mean that Bismarck regarded popular opinion as unimportant. No more than Machiavelli did he ignore moral forces in politics. Like the Florentine, however, he regarded them as objects of exploitation and manipulation, rather than as determinants of political action. They must be permitted neither to influence the conduct of policy nor to corrode the vital instruments of state power. Throughout the rest of his career Bismarck's first consideration in domestic politics was to preserve monarchical control over the means of force. We shall see, in fact, that this was precisely the issue that brought him to office in 1862. Behind his rigidity on this point lay the memory of events in 1848 and a recognition that the remaining autocratic powers of the monarchy were the fortress without which the nobility would lie exposed to the assaults of its enemies.

Rejection of Absolutism

Bismarck was never an absolutist. Like most conservatives, he regarded the state as a source of danger as well as safety. In the past the greatest threats to aristocratic interests had come from royal absolutism and bureaucratic liberalism. But in Bismarck's case the dislike of the bureaucratic machine was also personal. As we have seen, he was repelled by his brief experience as an official and frustrated by the lack of any other path to political power.

The United Diet of 1847 offered both a means of personal advancement and an opportunity to continue his old feud against the governmental apparatus. In that body he opposed reforms proposed by the bureaucracy as strongly as he did those stemming from the liberal opposition. With other conservatives he was angered by some liberal features of the constitution decreed on December 5, 1848.[88] Elected to the new Landtag, he argued vociferously against the efforts of the Manteuffel government to complete the liq-

---

[86] GW, XIV, 21; XV, 47–48; also XIV, 161; Engelberg, *Bismarck*, 311–312.

[87] BR, I, 77–78.

[88] GW, XIV, 120–121; Ludwig Gerlach, *Aufzeichnungen*, vol. 2, 36ff.; Leopold von Gerlach, *Denkwürdigkeiten* (Berlin, 1891), vol. 1, 259ff.; Hans Walter, *Die innere Politik des Ministers von Manteuffel und der Ursprung der Reaktion in Preussen* (Berlin, 1910), 44ff.

uidation of manorialism and put an end to peasant unrest.[89] So severe were his attacks that he was nearly expelled from the conservative faction.[90] When summer came, his rancorous pen scratched out a bitter denunciation. "The bureaucracy is cancerous from head to foot; only its mouth is healthy, and the excrement it issues in the form of laws is the most natural filth in the world." On other occasions he described state service as the embodiment of "Bonapartism" and "heathen-republicanism." The germ of this "disease" was a false education that inculcated habits of skepticism and criticism. Low salaries and slow promotions encouraged officials to promote innovations that might lead to their own advancement.[91]

There is no reason to doubt the sincerity of Bismarck's conviction that a parliament was required to counterbalance the "revolutionary" tendencies of bureaucratic liberalism. But what kind of parliament? How was it to be chosen and what were to be its powers?

Bismarck began as an advocate of the corporate state (Ständestaat). His ideal parliament was one chosen by estates and equipped only with the power of "public criticism." Under the influence of Stahl he saw in 1848 the wisdom of adding to the three traditional estates (nobility, peasantry, and burgher class) a fourth representing the urban proletariat.[92] His motive was practical, rather than romantic. What he wanted was not the resurrection of a medieval institution, but the creation of a representative body based upon occupational and interest groups in which landowners would have the dominant voice. Universal, direct, and equal suffrage he condemned because of its emphasis upon numbers, rather than intelligence and understanding. Their greater skill at party organization and political agitation would enable liberals to elect their candidates even though they represented a minority of the voters.[93]

Nor was he satisfied with the three-class system established by royal decree on May 30, 1849. It divided the electorate artificially according to wealth rather than interests and occupations. "We do not represent the people," he told the deputies. "Let's climb down from this pedestal upon which we have placed ourselves."[94] He denied that any system could accurately reflect the popular will. As this was the case, it was folly to speak of parliamentary rep-

---

[89] BR, I, 162ff.; GW, XIV, 144, 164; Kohl, Jahrbuch, vol. 3, 400–408. On the Manteuffel reforms see Hamerow, Restoration, Revolution, Reaction, 219ff., and Walter, Innere Politik Manteuffels, 73ff.; Georg Friedrich Knapp, Die Bauern-Befreiung und der Ursprung der Landarbeiter in den älteren Theilen Preussens (Leipzig, 1887), vol. 1, 217ff.; vol. 2, 411ff.

[90] Ludwig Gerlach, Aufzeichnungen, vol. 2, 93, 98.

[91] GW, I, 375; XIV, 159–160, 244, 328; BR, I, 303.

[92] Richard Augst, Bismarcks Stellung zum parlamentarischen Wahlrecht (Leipzig, 1917), 6ff.; Leopold Gerlach, Denkwürdigkeiten, vol. 1, 244. It is also possible that Bismarck's views on an assembly of estates were influenced by the writings of his Pomeranian neighbor, Ernst von Bülow-Cummerow. Marcks, Bismarcks Jugend, 222ff.

[93] BR, I, 88–89; GW, XIV, 124.

[94] BR, I, 302.

resentation as a natural right of the individual. The rest of this address was a spirited defense of the aristocratic order and of its right to govern in the public interest.[95]

During the first two years of its existence he hoped to see the Prussian lower chamber replaced by an assembly of estates.[96] In a letter of 1851 to Leopold Gerlach he argued that this could be done without violating the constitution. The crown should simply summon a new united diet, which would assume the legislative functions of the Landtag. The latter would wither on the vine.[97] Soon, however, he came to the conclusion that such a maneuver was unnecessary. Because liberals boycotted the election, the first chamber chosen under the three-class system was dominated by conservatives. In a memorial of 1853 to Prince Wilhelm of Prussia Bismarck asserted that "as long as times are peaceful the same persons reappear in the chamber whatever the election law." The best "guarantee" for the conduct of parliament was not a particular "recipe for its composition," but the limitation of its powers.[98]

Here he faced a crucial problem that bothered him for the rest of his career. If its powers were too feeble, parliament would be ineffective as a counterweight to the bureaucracy; if too strong, the chamber would become a threat to the crown. In either case the interests of the nobility were in danger. Where should the line be drawn?

The constitution decreed on December 5, 1848, and revised in the charter of January 31, 1850, gave the crown and both chambers an equal voice in the passage of legislation. Because the upper chamber was ultimately converted into a hereditary House of Lords, this meant that crown and nobility possessed an absolute veto. As a deputy in the lower chamber Bismarck vigorously opposed all attempts to increase its power. For the first time he expounded the famous "gap theory" (Lücketheorie), which was to be the crown's legal defense in the constitutional conflict of the 1860s. The constitution made no provision for settling serious disagreements between crown and parliament. In such cases, Bismarck argued, the will of the former must prevail.[99]

In the memorial of 1853 to Prince Wilhelm he amplified his views. "[Parliament] must be equipped with the means to ward off new laws and new taxes and to exercise a controlling criticism over the governmental system, namely over the financial housekeeping and the inner administration." But that was

---

[95] BR, I, 149–153.

[96] Augst, Bismarcks Stellung, 15; Ludwig Gerlach, Aufzeichnungen, vol. 2, 180–181; Schoeps, "Bismarckbriefe," 5–6. In 1851 Friedrich Wilhelm IV also wanted to reconstruct the lower chamber on a corporative basis, but Otto Manteuffel and others opposed the necessary coup d'état. Heinrich von Poschinger, ed., Unter Friedrich Wilhelm IV: Denkwürdigkeiten des Ministers Otto Freiherrn von Manteuffel 1848–1858 (Berlin, 1900–1901), vol. 2, 24, 47–51; vol. 3, 97ff.

[97] GW, XIV, 223–224. For Leopold Gerlach's view see Denkwürdigkeiten, vol. 1, 585ff.

[98] GW, I, 375–376.

[99] BR, I, 312–321. See also his article in the Kreuzzeitung, Jan. 23, 1850. Kohl, Jahrbuch, vol. 3, 411–413.

all. "It must never have the power to force the crown to act against the king's will or to coerce the king's ministers; otherwise, it will unfailingly misuse that power." To prevent this evil the crown must be able to prohibit any changes in the laws of the country undertaken without its consent. Parliament must be allowed no final control over the budget "or any part thereof." Pending approval of a new budget, the previous one must remain in effect. The crown must have the authority to continue levying taxes, once granted, without the further approval of parliament.[100]

From the beginning Bismarck believed in the importance of parliament as an institution. It was the means by which he had launched his own career. In 1858 he decried the "servility" and "inertia" that threatened the Landtag with "insignificance and oblivion" and encouraged "bureaucratic coups" by the cabinet. To remain healthy, the state required some "freedom of movement."[101] More than three decades later in retirement, he uttered similar complaints about the German Reichstag. But the impotence of the Prussian and German parliaments was the natural consequence of the largely negative functions he gave them. They were conceived for the "defensive" purpose of protecting the nobility from encroachments of the bureaucracy and the crown.[102] In any serious struggle for power he favored the monarchy over the legislature. Both royal absolutism and parliamentary government were hazards to the interests of the nobility, but the latter was decidedly the greater.

His utterances are notable in that age for their lack of philosophical reasoning. In sharp contrast to most of his contemporaries, whether liberal or conservative, his thinking about political questions was limited almost solely to practical considerations. What interested him in constitutional matters was not the validation of theoretical rights or of a historical theory, but the representation of concrete interests and the distribution of powers.

[100] GW, I, 375–376.
[101] To Leopold Gerlach, Mar. 2, 1858. GW, XIV, 485–486. The purpose of the letter was to oppose Ludwig's attempt to extend the parliamentary term to six years in the hope of warding off the reforms expected of the approaching "new-era" cabinet.
[102] GW, I, 375.

The External Functions of Power

A Prussian Nationalist

MONG German historians and political scientists the most common justification for authoritarian government has been geopolitical. Located on the open plains of northern Europe with no
adequate geographical barriers, the Prussians had to develop a
governmental system capable of reacting quickly and effectively against foreign attack. Ranke gave this view its classic statement in his *Dialogue on Politics*: "The position of a state in the world depends on the degree of independence it has attained. It is obliged, therefore, to organize all its internal
resources for the purpose of self-preservation. This is the supreme law of the
state."[1] In German political literature this principle became known as the
"primacy of foreign policy" (*Primat der Aussenpolitik*). Ranke was its philosopher, but Bismarck is generally considered to have been its greatest practi-
tioner.[2]

Although a secondary theme, the concept of the *Primat der Aussenpolitik*
does appear in Bismarck's recorded thoughts during the early period of his
career. In February 1851 he delivered a harsh speech opposing extension of
the financial powers of parliament on the grounds that the proper conduct of
foreign policy would be impossible in a government dominated by the second
chamber. In a body composed of five to six parties, majority decisions were
the "unsteady result of a very complicated diagonal of forces." The composition of the British House of Commons, on the other hand, was far different.
Here there were only two parties, one of which had a secure majority subject
to the "iron discipline" of leaders who were at the same time cabinet ministers.[3]

This praise of the British system cannot be taken at face value.[4] The House
of Commons was the great model of the Prussian liberals, and Bismarck liked
to irritate the deputies by pointing out the inadequacy of the parallel. A passage in his memorial of 1853 to Prince Wilhelm shows that he was opposed

---

[1] Theodore H. von Laue, *Leopold Ranke: The Formative Years* (Princeton, 1950), 167.

[2] See Max Lenz, "Ranke und Bismarck," *Kleine historische Schriften* (Munich, 1910), 383–408;
Otto Diether, *Leopold von Ranke als Politiker* (Leipzig, 1911), 518 ff.; Stephen Skalweit, "Ranke
und Bismarck," *Historische Zeitschrift*, 176 (1953), 277–290.

[3] *BR*, I, 300–301.

[4] On other occasions he wrote of the "incalculability" of England's foreign policy because of
its party system. *GW*, II, 143, 221; XIV, 429, 436, 440.

to parliamentary government whatever the composition of the chamber: "Prussia's greatness was by no means achieved through liberalism and free-thinking, but through a series of strong, resolute, and wise rulers who carefully nourished and saved the military and financial resources of the state. They held those resources, moreover, in their own unshackled hands until the favorable moment came to cast them with reckless courage into the scales of European politics. . . . The demand is undoubtedly justified that every Prussian should enjoy the degree of freedom that is consonant with the public welfare and with the course that Prussia has to take in European politics, but no more. One can have this freedom without parliamentary government."[5]

Bismarck's use of the *Primat der Aussenpolitik* at this time in his career differed from that of Ranke and other apologists for Prussian authoritarianism. Their argument was defensive; his, offensive. He maintained that monarchical control over the vital functions of government was necessary, not to defend Prussia from the threat of foreign aggression, but to take advantage of the opportunities that might arise for her expansion. His motive for expansion was not geopolitical, but nationalistic—for the greater glory and power of Prussia and the Hohenzollern dynasty.

Bismarck's nationalism was of the type formed by the state rather than by a common culture.[6] Only in his old age, and rarely even then, did he speak of the nation as a cultural phenomenon. To the end he regarded the "mediation" of dynastic loyalty as necessary for the creation of national sentiment. His family heritage made it natural for him to take this view. For centuries the Bismarcks had served in the armies of the Hohenzollern. Prussian patriotism was his birthright.[7]

This is not to say that the young Bismarck was devoid of German feeling. At school he was exposed to German national sentiment. In Göttingen he flirted briefly with the *Burschenschaft*, but was repelled by the "extravagance of their political views" and their unwillingness to "give satisfaction" by duelling.[8] His German patriotism was limited to the "spirit of 1812," as the conservative nobility had understood it. Most of the Junkers who went to war in 1812 did so to liberate German soil from the foreigner, not to unify Ger-

---

[5] GW, I, 375.

[6] See pp. 18–21.

[7] See Otto Pflanze, "Bismarck and German Nationalism," *American Historical Review*, 60 (1955), 559ff. Hans Rothfels's misinterpretation of this article was disingenuous. See his *Bismarck: Der Osten und das Reich* (Darmstadt, 1960), 64 (fn. 69). Otto Becker's view that Bismarck was always a German nationalist is based not on contemporary evidence, but upon the chancellor's words and writings after 1866. Otto Becker, *Bismarcks Ringen um Deutschlands Gestaltung* (Heidelberg, 1958), 33ff., 63. Becker denied the existence of a "Prussian nation" (47, 103), but this expression and its sentiment were common at the time. For a few examples of Bismarck's use of the term see GW, II, 383; IV, 31; X, 38, 43; XIV, 160, 666–667.

[8] GW, XV, 5ff.

many. What men of this conviction wished was the solidarity of Germany's princes, rather than the sovereign union of its peoples.[9]

Bismarck's opposition to the revolution of 1848 was, in part, owing to its threat to the integrity of the Prussian nation. He was outraged by the liberal plan for an autonomous Poland.[10] But an even greater danger came from the Frankfurt Parliament and the proposal to merge Prussia into Germany. In the Landtag debate on the Frankfurt constitution (April 1849), he declared it self-evident that "everyone . . . who speaks German wants German unity." But this remark was pure embellishment, for he continued in another vein. The proposed constitution "seeks to undermine and demolish that house of state constructed by centuries of glory and patriotism and cemented throughout by the blood of our ancestors." The Prussian government, he declared, should put forward its own plan for German unity.[11]

The German union plan, nevertheless, also excited his opposition. In September he denounced the intention to surrender Prussian independence to this "phantom." The powers given the Hohenzollern king in the small-German federation were not enough to compensate for the fact that Prussia could be outvoted in its governing body. The scheme meant the dissolution of Prussia, "the best pillar of German power." During the year of revolution she alone had saved Germany from foreign danger: "What preserved us was that which constitutes the real Prussia. It was what remains of that much stigmatized *Stockpreussentum*, which outlasted the revolution: that is, the Prussian army, the Prussian treasury, the fruits of an intelligent Prussian administration of many years' standing, and that vigorous spirit of cooperation between king and people that exists in Prussia. It was the loyalty of the Prussian people to their hereditary dynasty. It was the old Prussian virtues of honor, fidelity, obedience, and bravery, which permeate the army from its nucleus, the officer corps, outward to the youngest recruit. This army harbors no revolutionary enthusiasm. You will not find in the army, any more than in the rest of the Prussian people, any need for a national rebirth. They are satisfied with the name Prussia and proud of the name Prussia. . . . Prussian we are and Prussian we wish to remain."[12] In this passage appear all the elements that composed Bismarck's conception of the nation: dynastic loyalty, autocratic paternalism, military discipline, and patriotic sacrifice. During the following

[9] BR, I, 9–10; GW, XIV, 89; Friedrich Meinecke, *Weltbürgertum und Nationalstaat: Studien zur Genesis des deutschen Nationalstaates* (5th ed., Munich and Berlin, 1919), 298ff.

[10] BR, I, 49–51; GW, XIV, 104–106; Erich Marcks, *Bismarck und die deutsche Revolution, 1848–1851* (Stuttgart, 1939), 43–44.

[11] BR, I, 92–94. The occasional expressions of German national sentiment that Bismarck voiced in this period (another example: GW, XIV, 106) were obviously tactical, intended to dazzle the opposition and outdo them at their own game. References to Prussian patriotism are far more frequent and convincing.

[12] BR, I, 113, also 235–241; GW, XIV, 152ff.; Hans J. Schoeps, "Der junge Bismarck als Journalist," *Zeitschrift für Religions- und Geistesgeschichte*, 3 (1951), 2–12.

debate an opponent branded him "a lost son of the great German fatherland," to which Bismarck replied, "My country (*Vaterhaus*) is Prussia, and I have never left my country and I shall never leave it."[13]

Aggressive Nationalism

Both forms of the national idea are potentially aggressive. The cultural nationalist regards national unity, or national independence, as a moral right that transcends existing international law and the established distribution of power between states. The concept of national self-determination is easily transformed into a belief in national superiority and the right of dominion over alien cultural groups. Bismarck, on the other hand, was inclined to look upon Prussian expansion more as a matter of opportunity than of moral necessity. He found his model in the career of Frederick the Great rather than in the French Revolution and the wars of liberation. Personal ambition and Prussian pride, the need for self-fulfillment through political power and the desire for Prussia's aggrandizement in German and European politics, sprang from the same elemental force in his personality.

Bismarck's earliest recorded judgment on the subject of international politics indicates the direction of his thinking. During his Kniephof period he once remarked in a gathering of rural gentry that "the chief aim of the mighty upon earth is to widen their borders and extend the area of their dominion." "I am of the opinion that the time will again come when the kingdom of Prussia will undergo a significant expansion."[14] That this remark was remembered and later recorded suggests that it aroused antagonism at the time. Among pietistic Junkers the Frederician tradition was regarded with strong distaste. The conquest of Silesia had been a violation of the principle of legitimacy and of a solemn compact between princes.

During the spring and summer of 1849 Bismarck believed Prussia's great moment had arrived. At home the Hohenzollern monarchy was again firmly in the saddle; abroad there was no coalition capable of blocking her growth. England was apparently favorable to the idea of a small-German union under Friedrich Wilhelm IV. France was involved in internal difficulties. The state that had the most to lose, Austria, was still crippled by the revolt of Hungary. With the possible exception of Russia, no major power would have opposed Prussian hegemony in Germany. In his April speech against the Frankfurt constitution, Bismarck recommended that Prussia "give laws to Germany rather than receive them from others."[15]

The German union plan[16] excited his contempt not only because of its

[13] BR, I, 117.
[14] GW, VII, 4.
[15] BR, I, 93.
[16] See pp. 26–30.

content, but also because of the method chosen for its adoption. Friedrich Wilhelm eschewed violence and took the path of negotiation and parliamentary approval. In August Bismarck grasped immediately that the collapse of the Hungarian revolt had transformed the situation. The issue would be decided, he wrote, not by parliamentary procedure, but by diplomacy and war. "What we chatter and resolve about it has no more value than the moonlight reveries of a sentimental youth, who builds castles in the air and believes that some event for which he hopes will make him into a great man."[17]

In the Landtag on September 6, 1849 he subjected the king to a scathing comparison. What would Frederick the Great have done had he been alive and ruler at such a moment? There were two possibilities. He might have allied Prussia with Austria, "the old comrade-in-arms," and aided her in the destruction of the "common enemy"—liberal and national revolution. This would have given to the Prussian king the "brilliant role" played in Europe by Tsar Nicholas I; or at the risk of war he might have dictated a constitution to the German people "with the same right with which he conquered Silesia. . . . This would have been a truly national policy for Prussia." Either alone or in cooperation with Austria, Prussia would have gained for Germany "the power that is her due in Europe." "All of us want the Prussian eagle to spread its wings, to protect and rule from Memel to the Donnersberg." But these wings must remain free, unpinioned by a new Holy Roman Empire and unclipped by a liberal constitution of the Frankfurt type.[18]

This was no mere oratorical flourish. In his famous "blood and iron" speech of 1862 Bismarck reminisced about the "favorable moment" that had been allowed to "slip by." When he composed his memoirs in the 1890s the subject still teased him. Again he speculated over what a resolute monarch might have accomplished during that auspicious spring of 1849.[19] Even more striking is the fact that the two alternatives in the speech of September 6 were again uppermost in his mind during the years of crisis that ended in the civil war of 1866; should Prussia expand her power in Germany in agreement with Austria or alone and, if necessary, even against her?

A Conflict in Values

We have learned that the power of the state represented for Bismarck: first, the available means of self-expression and self-fulfillment; second, a fortress

---

[17] GW, XIV, 134–136; BR, I, 78.

[18] BR, I, 110–114. If he read this speech, Friedrich Wilhelm probably took no offense. When Hermann von Beckerath urged him to take the Frankfurt crown, the king replied, "If you could have directed your eloquent words to Frederick the Great, he would have been your man; I am no great ruler." Alexander Scharff, "König Friedrich Wilhelm IV: Deutschland und Europa im Frühjahr 1849," in Geschichtliche Kräfte und Entscheidungen: Festschrift zum fünfundsechsigsten Geburtstage von Otto Becker (Wiesbaden, 1954), 145.

[19] BR, II, 29–30; GW, VII, 422; XV, 46.

for the protection of the interests and values of his social class in a time of dynamic change; and, third, an instrument for advancing the Prussian national interest in foreign affairs. The last two functions were, however, not necessarily harmonious. Although he dismissed the ideological and religious objections of the romantic conservatives to an egoistic policy of state, Bismarck was well aware that such a policy might prove hazardous to aristocratic interests. The fate of the Junkers could not be completely separated from that of the European nobility as a whole; nor could the Hohenzollern dynasty hope to outlive for long the collapse of monarchical government in central and eastern Europe. Yet a policy of self-interest could also be severely handicapped by the necessity of upholding the Holy Alliance and observing the sovereign rights of the German princes. During the crisis that led to Olmütz, this conflict in values caused Bismarck to follow a zigzag course. When confronted by a choice between the interest of state and the conservative cause, he could not at this point make up his mind.

In November 1850 his initial reaction to the dismissal of Radowitz and the shift of Prussian policy from the German union to the issue of parity was exuberant and bellicose. "Now let war come, regardless where or with whom. Every Prussian saber will glisten high and joyfully in the sun."[20] But after his arrival in Berlin from Schönhausen, where he had heard the news, he joined the Manteuffel clique in the cabinet to rally the conservative party for peace. Certain practical considerations influenced this shift in attitude: from August von Stockhausen, the minister of war, he heard that the army had been so deployed to deal with the revolutionary uprisings of the preceding year that now it could not even defend Berlin; two of Radowitz's supporters were still in the cabinet, and it was possible that the German union might yet become the Prussian war aim.[21] Nevertheless, his about-face was also owing to a confusion in values. This is shown by his fluctuating attitudes over the occupation of Hesse-Kassel and the problem of parity between the dual powers in the confederation.[22]

As previously explained, the dual powers came close to war in November 1850 over whether Prussia, acting for the German union, or Austria and Bavaria, acting for the German Confederation, had the right to quell an internal disturbance in Hesse-Kassel. The issue was vital to Berlin, for across this principality ran the military roads connecting the eastern and western halves of

---

[20] GW, XIV, 179–180.

[21] GW, XV, 52–53; XIV, 181–182. Unknown to Bismarck, Stockhausen himself was chiefly responsible for Prussia's unpreparedness. The minister was opposed to the war, moreover, on political grounds. Friedrich Meinecke, *Radowitz und die deutsche Revolution* (Berlin, 1913), 513–515; Ludwig Dehio, "Zur November-Krise des Jahres 1859," *Forschungen zur brandenburgischen und preussischen Geschichte*, 35 (1923), 134–145. Apparently Bismarck was employed by Manteuffel as an agent in the diplomatic negotiations that led to Olmütz. GW, I, 2; XIV, 182–183, 185.

[22] Concerning these issues and the climax of Olmütz, see pp. 26–27.

the Prussian monarchy. One evening during the crisis, Bismarck had a heated argument with Leopold Gerlach. Though the general maintained that conservative monarchies must at all costs avoid conflict, Bismarck replied that Prussia could not tolerate "too much Austrian impertinence." "We cannot permit 100,000 Bavarians and Austrians to take up positions between our eastern and western provinces." Gerlach took the view, however, that the issue was "purely juridical." In occupying Hesse-Kassel, Austria was simply acting for the confederation, whose constitution was still valid law in Germany. According to Gerlach's daughter, Bismarck made a shocking rejoinder: "He recognizes no law in foreign affairs, only convenience. Friedrich II, 1740, is his example."[23]

Three days later, at the height of the crisis, however, he expressed views in a letter to his wife that were remarkably close to those of Gerlach. Radowitz, he declared, had sent Prussian troops into Hesse-Kassel "in violation of international and confederate law." Agreement had now almost been reached on the terms of a joint occupation. The question was "only a matter of military etiquette." How could anyone want to lay waste Europe over such a "petty issue?" "There is the greatest danger that for the sake of such bagatelles conservative armies, which love and respect each other, will slaughter one another and place the fate of Germany in the hands of foreigners." France lusted for the Rhineland. England would do nothing to aid Prussia. Her only allies would be the democrats of the national revolution. Should Prussia be victorious, they alone would profit. Had the understanding of Prussian honor sunk so low that it could be used for revolutionary purposes?[24]

But was the demand for parity worth a war? On November 19, 1850, Bismarck published an article in the *Kreuzzeitung* through which the public first learned of this demand. If Prussia were refused, it warned, "we also want war." The Junkers would raise the cry of their ancestors, "Dat walde Gott un kold Isen!"[25] Despite some suspicion, Bismarck seems to have been fairly confident that Austria would agree to "reconciliation . . . at the expense of the small states."[26] Yet he noted with approval his government's intention to continue military preparations until the negotiation was concluded. If war came, he wrote on the eighteenth, it would be fought "only against Austria and Bavaria and, God helping us, we are equal to the test."[27]

[23] GW, XIV, 182; Ernst Ludwig von Gerlach, *Aufzeichnungen aus seinem Leben und Wirken, 1795–1877* (Schwerin, 1903), vol. 2, 116. Leopold Gerlach's version of the debate is less revealing. Leopold von Gerlach, *Denkwürdigkeiten* (Berlin, 1891), vol. 1, 559; also 584. Years later a close friend remembered that in 1849 Bismarck had remarked, "What do I care about the [German] small states; my only concern is the security and increased power of Prussia." GW, VII, 18.

[24] GW, XIV, 182–183. The letter could scarcely have been more orthodox had it been written by Leopold Gerlach himself. See his *Denkwürdigkeiten*, vol. 1, 556ff.

[25] Horst Kohl, ed., *Bismarck-Jahrbuch*, vol. 3, 414–415.

[26] GW, XIV, 181, also 180, 183.

[27] GW, XIV, 181–182.

On December 3 Bismarck delivered a major speech in defense of the Olmütz agreement of November 29. By this time it was apparent that Russia too
had to be numbered among Prussia's potential foes. He began by pointing out
the futility of war against "two of the three greatest continental powers, while
the third mobilizes on our frontier, eager for conquest."[28] But then he admitted, "I would not shrink from such a war, nevertheless; in fact, I would advise
it, if someone could prove to me that it is necessary, or could show me a
worthy goal . . . that cannot be attained in any other way. Why do large
states go to war nowadays?" His reply to this rhetorical question has become
one of the most famous of Bismarck's quotations: "The only sound basis for a
large state is its egoism and not romanticism; this is what distinguishes a large
state necessarily from a small one. It is not worthy of a large state to fight for
a thing that is not in its own interest. Just show me an objective worth a war,
gentlemen, and I will agree with you."[29]

The German union, he continued, was not such an objective, for it meant
the mediatization of Prussia. A war to preserve the integrity of the Hessian
constitution would be just as quixotic. Furthermore, the passage of Austrian
troops across the military roads gave no cause for alarm. As long as Prussia
had the use of their length, Austria could be permitted to cross their width!
"Wars of principle" were to be decried; the only true criterion of foreign policy
was the interest of state. The Prussian interest, he insisted, lay in the "avoidance of every shameful alliance with democracy" and in the attainment of
parity with Austria. "We do not wish to make conquests. I do not want to
discuss here how much this fact is to be deplored, nor how willingly perhaps
one might conduct a war simply because his king and commander says, 'This
country strikes my fancy and I want to have it.' . . . At the moment this
question does not concern us." He admonished those eager for war to await
the outcome of the conferences to be held in Dresden. Until a "positive result" was achieved there, Prussia ought not to demobilize. "Then there will
still be time to go to war, if we actually cannot avoid it with honor, or do not
wish to avoid it."[30]

Apparently he had not been told that at Olmütz Friedrich Wilhelm had
already agreed to demobilize. We have no evidence of his immediate reaction
to this information, but later sources suggest further ambivalence. In a *Kreuzzeitung* article published on April 20, 1851, he described the Olmütz agreement and the prevention of war as "very fortunate."[31] Certainly the reasons

[28] This was a reference to France, which had mobilized an observation corps of forty thousand
men on the Rhine frontier.

[29] What Bismarck had in mind was not the romantic cosmopolitanism of the Gerlachs, but the
romantic sentimentalism that prompted Radowitz and Friedrich Wilhelm IV to embrace the national cause. This is shown by his letter to Sharlach, July 4, 1850. GW, XIV, 160–161. See also
his article of Nov. 19 in the *Kreuzzeitung*. Kohl, *Jahrbuch*, vol. 3, 414–415.

[30] BR, I, 261–279.

[31] Schoeps, "Bismarck als Journalist," 10. Luckily for Bismarck's future career the king, an-

he had advanced for avoiding war over Hesse-Kassel were equally valid for the issue of parity. In order to fight a war against Austria and her German allies, possibly supported by Russia, Prussia would have been forced to enter a "shameful alliance" with the popular forces of liberal nationalism. In his memoirs, nevertheless, Bismarck was still critical of the government's failure in the Dresden conferences of January–May 1851 either to obtain concessions from Austria or to find grounds for war.[32]

During his early years in politics Bismarck wavered between the seemingly opposite poles of the interest of state and the interest of conservative order. Faced by the necessity of choice, he was indecisive, but tended to give priority to the latter. During the next stage of his career the conflict was resolved and the priority reversed.

The Interest of State

The squire from Schönhausen was due a reward for his recent services to the monarchy. But what was suitable? Aside from his abortive service in Aachen and Potsdam, his experience in state administration was that of an assistant *Landrat* and dike captain on the Elbe. The tiny duchy of Anhalt-Bernburg needed a prime minister. Bismarck liked the idea: "the duke is a fool and the minister duke." But then it was proposed to make him a *Landrat*, which pleased him less. The final decision was startling. In April 1851 Friedrich Wilhelm, acting on Leopold Gerlach's advice, appointed him Prussian envoy to the diet of the German Confederation. His youthful dream had been fulfilled. Success as a deputy had vaulted him high over the laboring files of bureaucrats into the ranks of the powerful. At the moment Frankfurt was the most important post in the Prussian foreign service.[33]

Established in 1815 at the Congress of Vienna, the German Confederation was intended to provide security against the dangers of external attack and internal revolution. It was not a sovereign body, but a miniature United Nations composed of thirty-eight independent states of varying size and influence. Austria and Prussia, the "dual powers," were by far the largest and most powerful. By tradition Austria was the leading state and occupied the "presi-

---

gered by an accusation of treason against Radowitz in the article, never learned the author's name. *Ibid.*, 9.

[32] GW, XV, 57.

[33] GW, XIV, 190, 193, 202, 206–207; VII, 17, 31; Leopold Gerlach, *Denkwürdigkeiten*, vol. 1, 616, 618, 620, 637, 648; Hans J. Schoeps, "Neue Bismarckiana, 1851–1854," *Zeitschrift für Religions- und Geistesgeschichte*, 4 (1952), 167–168. Incredulously Prince Wilhelm asked, "And this militia lieutenant is supposed to be envoy to the confederation?" Heinrich von Poschinger, ed., *Preussens auswärtige Politik 1850 bis 1858: Unveröffentlichte Dokumente aus dem Nachlasse des Ministerpräsidenten Otto Freiherrn von Manteuffel* (Berlin, 1902), vol. 1, 208. Ludwig Gerlach, *Aufzeichnungen*, vol. 2, 124. Because of his inexperience he was apprenticed (counselor of legation) for three months to a career diplomat, Theodor von Rochow.

dency," a position of no executive authority other than that which her envoy was able to assume as presiding officer of the diet. After the dual powers came the "medium states": Bavaria, Saxony, Württemberg, Hanover, and Baden.[34] The "small states" ranged from the two Hesses, of moderate size, to the "free cities" and the Thuringian states, whose tiny dimensions were a cartographer's nightmare. Like the U.N. General Assembly, the diet was not a legislature, but a congress of diplomats whose votes were instructed by their respective governments. The most vital questions could be passed only by unanimous vote, matters of less moment by simple majority.

Until 1848 the confederation had been a relatively stable organization. In the interest of their entente with Russia in European affairs, the dual powers avoided friction in Germany. While protecting the prerogatives of the presidency, Metternich made no effort to increase its authority. Before Radowitz the Prussian government had shown no serious desire to alter the structure of the confederation or to challenge Austrian leadership in its affairs. The rare cases of positive action taken by the diet were the result of prior agreement between Vienna and Berlin.

After the revolution neither power was inclined to return completely to this state of affairs. Manteuffel hoped to attain parity between Austria and Prussia; Schwarzenberg, to enhance Austrian primacy in the diet by increasing the powers of the presidency and reducing the number of matters requiring unanimity in the actions of that body.[35] In the struggle that ensued, the lesser states played an important role. The dual powers had in the past combined to dominate them, but now each needed their support against the other. Until the climax of 1866, therefore, the contest between Austria and Prussia was essentially one for influence over the other members of the confederation. The lesser states tended to side with that power which, at the moment, was feared the least.[36] This was usually Austria. Because of the events of 1848–1850 the German princes were alarmed over the possibility of Prussian expansion in Germany. The parliaments of Frankfurt and Erfurt had shown, moreover, that the hopes and ambitions of the small-German nationalists were centered upon the Hohenzollern monarchy. The victory of this form of the national idea would mean mediatization and perhaps dispossession of the

[34] Denmark and the Netherlands were also members, the former for Holstein and Lauenburg, the latter for Limburg and Luxemburg. Neither exercised much influence upon confederate affairs.

[35] Arnold Oskar Meyer, *Bismarcks Kampf mit Österreich am Bundestag zu Frankfurt, 1851–1859* (Berlin, 1927), 19ff., 66ff.; Heinrich Ritter von Srbik, *Deutsche Einheit: Idee und Wirklichkeit vom Heiligen Reich bis Königgrätz* (Munich, 1935–1942), vol. 1, 385ff.; vol. 2, 92ff.

[36] On the policies of the medium states see Sigmund Meiboom, *Studien zur deutschen Politik Bayerns in den Jahren 1851–1859: Schriftenreihe zur bayrischen Landesgeschichte*, vol. 6 (Munich, 1931), and Walther P. Fuchs, *Die deutschen Mittelstaaten und die Bundesreform 1853–1860: Historische Studien*, vol. 256 (Berlin, 1934).

lesser dynasties. Hence they usually supported Austria on any issue of moment. Prussia found herself the minority party in the diet.

Under these circumstances any Prussian envoy would have faced an uphill struggle in Frankfurt. Bismarck's temperament, however, aggravated the quarrel. In later years he described himself as having been in a "state of political innocence" and a "rather good Austrian" when he entered the diet in May 1851.[37] But this was hardly the case. On informing his wife of the appointment on April 28, he wrote: "I cannot refuse to accept, although I foresee that it will be a fruitless and thorny office. In spite of my best efforts I shall lose the good opinion of many people. But it would be cowardice to decline."[38] Whose esteem did he fear to lose? Was it that of Gerlach, who expected him to support at all costs the cause of conservative solidarity with Austria? To others he is said to have remarked that the German small states were but a "hindrance" to Prussia; Austrian "arrogance" must be checked "at any price."[39]

His first letters and reports from Frankfurt show that even before the diet had undertaken any serious business Bismarck was sharply critical of his Austrian counterpart, Count Friedrich von Thun and Hohenstein, and of the confederation as such. One week after arriving he wrote, "No one, not even the most evil-intentioned skeptic of a democrat, would believe what charlatanry and pomposity lie hidden in this diplomacy." On the same day he wrote Hermann Wagener that he had "little hope for favorable results" from the diet. Once the two men had set up a channel of communication safe from espionage, he was more explicit. "The Austrians intrigue under the mask of jovial good fellowship; they lie, steal dispatches (even the most upright among them), gamble, whore, and seek to get the better of us in the small formalities that have thus far been the whole of our activity."[40]

[37] GW, II, 23; III, 239; VII, 113, 121–122; XIV, 441, 558; XV, 198. Historians once accepted these statements at face value. On Mar. 6 Bismarck defended the diet in the Chamber of Deputies as the most successful protector of Germany's unity and power since the Hohenstaufen. BR, I, 327–328; Meyer, Bismarcks Kampf, 22–25. Defense of the confederation was, however, his parliamentary duty as a party spokesman. Throughout the period leading to Olmütz his attitude toward Austria had been charged with hostility and suspicion, softened at times by concern over revolutionary subversion. In later years he exaggerated the change that occurred in his attitude at Frankfurt in order to heighten his case against Austria as the sole source of the friction that rent the confederation. More accurate is what he wrote to Otto Manteuffel at the end of his first month: "When I came here, my expectations of results from the diet's deliberations were not high, but since then they have decreased." GW, I, 17.

[38] GW, XIV, 206–207.

[39] Richard Schwemer, Geschichte der freien Stadt Frankfurt a. M., 1814–1866 (Frankfurt a. M., 1918), III/2, 61.

[40] GW, XIV, 213–214, 217, 228; I, 17, 22; XV, 198. See the letters of June 22 and July 4 to Leopold Gerlach and Kleist-Retzow. "The Austrians are and remain card sharpers." GW, XIV, 219–224, 230–231. Note also the sense of injury with which he reacted to his first interview with Thun. GW, VII, 23–24.

As the quarrel in the diet developed, he reached the conclusion that the primary motive in the conduct of foreign policy is self-interest. Like a "natural scientist," his sole aim was to see things as they actually are.[41] "In politics no one does anything for another, unless he also finds it in his own interest to do so."[42] This is, he concluded, the one fundamental rule of all political behavior. Such causes as the "principle of legitimacy" and the "interest of Germany" are moral camouflage with which statesmen conceal the egoistic aims of their countries.[43] "Alliances between large states," he wrote, "are of value only when they express the actual interests of both parties."[44] Conflicts, on the other hand, are the inevitable result of contradictory interests. The clash between Austria and Prussia was not arbitrary. History and geography were its source, not the whims of monarchs and ministers.[45] "In the middle of Europe it is impossible to wait passively upon the march of events or to try to stay removed from them." "If we do not prepare for ourselves the role of the hammer, there will be nothing left but that of the anvil."[46]

The quest for political advantage, he concluded, must be pursued with complete objectivity. For the statesman, as for the natural scientist, the only trustworthy guide is reason. Reward, revenge, and punishment have no place in politics. "Not even the king himself has the right to subordinate the interests of the fatherland to personal feelings of love or hatred toward foreigners."[47] Since the pursuit of rational self-interest seems natural to the conduct of states, he presumed that it is, like all things in nature, a part of the divine plan. The duty of the statesman is to discern that interest and dedicate himself to its fulfillment. This was for Bismarck, the devout Christian, a moral compulsion from which there could be no escape.[48]

The necessities of state, however, inevitably conflict with other values likewise sanctified by religious faith. In contrast to the Gerlachs, Bismarck held that the ordinary codes of human conduct are inapplicable to the statesman. He was highly critical of the "chivalric" attitude of King Friedrich Wilhelm, who disdained "to exploit the embarrassments of other states" for the benefit of his own.[49] In Bismarck's eyes this was a neglect of duty and of the responsibility imposed by the deity. His letters to Berlin complain bitterly of the lies

[41] GW, I, 40, 70, 104; III, 190; VII, 38; XIV, 441.

[42] GW, II, 231; XIV, 473. Although written in 1867, this judgment was already implicit in one of the first letters written from Frankfurt. GW, I, 17.

[43] GW, I, 401–402, 404, 456; III, 147–148; XIV, 327, 332, 335. See Rechberg's report of his talk with Bismarck on June 19, 1857. Meyer, Bismarcks Kampf, 551, 558.

[44] GW, I, 515; III, 382; XIV, 465.

[45] GW, I, 70, 119–120; II, 311; XIV, 441.

[46] GW, II, 231; XIV, 474, also 465, 467.

[47] GW, XIV, 465.

[48] GW, I, 238; II, 125–126; III, 148; XIV, 468–469, 549. Otto Vossler, "Bismarcks Ethos," Historische Zeitschrift, 171 (1951), 263ff.

[49] GW, I, 435.

told by the Austrian envoys; nevertheless, he was aware that truth could sometimes be dangerous to the interest of state.[50] One of his most striking talents was the capacity to mold an argument and create conviction by emphasizing the partial truth. But where an outright lie seemed essential he did not hesitate. What he detested was the unnecessary lie told out of habit, incaution, or personal malice. Looking backward at the end of his career, the sage of Friedrichsruh recognized the double standard of the statesman-cavalier and expressed the hope that in the hereafter his conduct as a Prussian officer would compensate for his sins as a diplomat.[51]

But what of the social and political viewpoint of conservatism? Must this value likewise be sacrificed on the altar of the interest of state? By no means did Bismarck abandon his belief that the protection of conservative institutions was a proper function of foreign policy. Where the Prussian interest did not interfere, he participated in the witch-hunts of the diet against liberal laws and constitutions in the lesser states.[52] In two letters, written to Gerlach and Manteuffel in 1857–1858 he made his viewpoint clear: "I also recognize as my own the principle of struggle against revolution, but . . . in politics I do not believe it possible to follow principle in such a way that its most extreme implications always take precedence over every other consideration." "In representing Prussia abroad one cannot be partisan to the same extreme degree as in domestic affairs."[53] Both motives remained, in other words, but priority now belonged to the interest of state.[54]

This change did not occur solely because Bismarck, in his new occupation as a diplomat, was in closer contact with the realities of foreign affairs and more aware of its problems. Even more important was the fact that he had a better perspective of the events of 1848. After Gotha it was apparent that moderate liberals had recoiled from their momentary alliance with the radical left. Shocked by the subterranean forces exposed in the revolution, they were forced into greater dependence than ever upon established authority. After the failure of the revolts in Saxony and Baden, the radicals were in a state of disintegration. By boycotting the first elections held under the three-class system in Prussia (1849), they delivered parliament into the hands of the conservatives.

Most striking of all, however, was the political apathy into which the mass

---

[50] GW, I, 389. "If I can't lie, I can't accomplish anything," he once remarked. Ludwig Gerlach, Aufzeichnungen, II, 273.

[51] GW, IX, 161; also VIII, 594.

[52] Richard Augst, Bismarcks Stellung zum parlamentarischen Wahlrecht, (Leipzig, 1917), 29ff.

[53] GW, XIV, 470; II, 323, also 227.

[54] It was once assumed that his experience in Frankfurt converted Bismarck from a "partisan politician" into a "statesman," that he lost his one-sided interest in the aristocratic-monarchical cause and thereafter devoted himself to the interest of state. What occurred, however, was an important shift in emphasis, not a fundamental conversion. See Hans Mombauer, Bismarcks Realpolitik als Ausdruck seiner Weltanschauung: Historische Studien, vol. 291 (Berlin, 1936), 37–38.

of the population had fallen. Scarcely a ripple remained of the tidal wave that swept Germany in March 1848. In the Prussian election of 1855 only one-sixth of the eligible voters went to the polls. By a program of agrarian reform and guild protectionism the regime of Otto Manteuffel did its best to appease the peasant and artisan classes. As the decade progressed, the tempo of industrialization and economic activity increased. Germany was caught in the grip of a material revolution that for a time absorbed the energies of the upper *Mittelstand*. Politics were left to the government and the conservative party.[55]

[55] See the excellent description of Prussia at mid-century by Ferdinand Fischer, *Preussen am Abschlusse der ersten Hälfte des neunzehnten Jahrhunderts* (Berlin, 1876); also Heinrich Heffter, *Die deutsche Selbstverwaltung im 19. Jahrhundert* (Stuttgart, 1950), 349ff.; Theodore Hamerow, *Restoration, Revolution, Reaction: Economics and Politics in Germany, 1815–1871* (Princeton, 1958), 219ff.; Hans Walter, *Die innere Politik des Ministers von Manteuffel und der Ursprung der Reaktion in Preussen* (Berlin, 1910), 62ff.; and Günter Grünthal, *Parlamentarismus in Preussen 1848/49–1857/58, Preussischer Konstitutionalismus—Parlament und Regierung in der Reaktionsära* (Düsseldorf, 1982).

✦✦✦

The Strategy of *Realpolitik*

The Art of the Possible

I N RETIREMENT after 1890 Bismarck had the leisure and occasion to express his views on the nature of political life and the strategies it imposes on statesmen. His reflections on this subject, recorded by listeners in interviews and informal speeches, were based on his political experience of nearly five decades. And yet they cannot be dismissed as merely the wisdom of hindsight. Instead, they reveal the instinctive perceptions that made him the most effective statesman of his century.[1]

His skepticism concerning the chances of the statesman in the stream of time was a recurrent theme. "By himself the individual can create nothing; he can only wait until he hears God's footsteps resounding through events and then spring forward to grasp the hem of his mantle—that is all."[2] In a person of other temperament this awareness of the smallness of man and the inadequacy of his best efforts would have ended in resignation and apathy. But, as we have seen, Bismarck was driven by a vital compulsion to seize the helm and steer. If man can do little, he has at least the moral duty to accomplish what he can.

The statesman's task is complicated not only by the overpowering flow of the time stream, but also by the unceasing clash of contradictory forces: "It is a principle of creation and of the whole of nature that life consists of strife. Among the plants—as a forester I experience this in my cultures—through the insects to the birds, from birds of prey up to man himself: strife is everywhere. Without struggle there can be no life and, if we wish to continue living, we must also be reconciled to further struggles."[3] He described the struggling forces as states, nations, social classes, political parties, economic and sectional interests, and even feuding individuals. The conflict of opposites he believed to be a condition of human progress and hence an intentional part of the divine plan.[4]

The unending clash of contradictory forces and the sweep of the time

---

[1] Otto Pflanze, "Bismarck's 'Realpolitik,' " *The Review of Politics*, 20 (October, 1958), 492–514.

[2] Arnold Oskar Meyer, *Bismarcks Glaube im Spiegel der "Loosungen und Lehrtexte,"* in *Münchener historische Abhandlungen*, Erste Reihe, vol. 1 (Munich, 1933), 9–10.

[3] GW, XIII, 555.

[4] GW, XIII, 559, 570; IX, 8ff. During the conflict of 1870, he described war as the "natural condition of mankind." GW, VII, 388.

stream make the tasks of the statesman forever inconclusive and beset his course with grave uncertainties: "My entire life was spent gambling for high stakes with other people's money. I could never foresee exactly whether my plans would succeed. . . . Politics is a thankless job, chiefly because everything depends on chance and conjecture. One has to reckon with a series of probabilities and improbabilities and base one's plans upon this reckoning. . . . As long as he lives the statesman is always unprepared. In the attainment of that for which he strives he is too dependent on the participation of others, a fluctuating and incalculable factor. . . . Even after the greatest success he cannot say with certainty, 'Now it is achieved; I am done with it,' and look back at what has been accomplished with complacency. . . . To be sure, one can bring individual matters to a conclusion, but even then there is no way of knowing what the consequences will be. . . . In politics there is no such thing as complete certainty and definitive results. . . . Everything goes continually uphill, downhill."[5]

Since this was the nature of political life, Bismarck concluded that its phenomena could not be systematized: "There is no exact science of politics, just as there is none for political economy. Only professors are able to package the sum of the changing needs of cultural man into scientific laws. . . . Already many have spoken of my political principles. The professors and their imitators in the newspapers constantly decry the fact that I have not revealed a set of principles by which I directed my policies. . . . Politics is neither arithmetic nor mathematics. To be sure, one has to reckon with given and unknown factors, but there are no rules and formulas with which to sum up the results in advance."[6]

"Professor" was not a complimentary word in Bismarck's vocabulary. Whom did he have in mind? Adam Smith, Thomas Malthus, David Ricardo, Jean de Sismondi, Jean-Baptiste Say, and Frédéric Bastiat were the names he mentioned. The "scientific laws" to which he referred, then, were such as laissez-faire, the "iron law of wages," and the Malthusian theory of population. The economic doctrines of liberalism, he argued, were formulated in the interest of industrial capitalism by "English clergymen," "Jewish bankers," and "French merchants and jurists." "The whole political economy given us by the academicians and the press is a political economy for commerce and not for agriculture as well." It ignores "the actual relationships and overriding circumstances," and "speaks only of one-sided, private interests where general interests are primarily at stake."[7]

What Bismarck objected to, however, was not merely the partiality of the economic doctrines of Manchesterism, but also the whole rationalistic belief

---

[5] GW, IX, 397ff.
[6] GW, IX, 90, 93, 420.
[7] GW, IX, 90.

in the existence of natural laws in society equivalent to those in the structure of the universe. The natural world he knew, as the owner of fields and forests, was the disorderly one of growing things and not that of algebraic equations and physical laws. In the popular biology of social Darwinism he found a better parallel between science and society. His views reflected the revolt of the nineteenth century against the seventeenth and eighteenth centuries, the period of biological discovery against that of astronomy and physics, the age of romanticism against that of rationalism, and, last but hardly least, the outlook of the conservative against that of the liberal.

If not a scientific discipline, what was politics in Bismarck's view? He gave his answer on several occasions:

"Politics is less a science than an art. It is not a subject that can be taught. One must have the talent for it. Even the best advice is of no avail if improperly carried out."

"Politics is not in itself an exact and logical science, but it is the capacity to choose in each fleeting moment of the situation that which is least harmful or most opportune."

"Because they have as yet scarcely outgrown the political nursery, the Germans cannot accustom themselves to regard political affairs as a study of the possible."[8]

The art of the possible—this was Bismarck's conception of statecraft. Every great artist, however, is a compound of genius and technical mastery. Hence we must ask whether a tactical pattern is identifiable in Bismarck's statesmanship, whether consciously or unconsciously he adopted a standard, though variable, tactic in coping with the successive situations he met in domestic and foreign affairs. On several occasions, particularly during his retirement years, Bismarck reflected aloud on the nature of politics and how the statesman can be effective in coping with its vagaries. If study of the past could yield no science of politics, Bismarck was far from thinking that it had no value for statesmen: "For me history existed primarily to be learned from. Even if events do not repeat themselves, at least circumstances and characters do. By observing and studying them one can stimulate and educate one's own mind. I have learned from the mistakes of my predecessors in the art of statesmanship and have built up my 'theory,' although one ought not to speak of such in the narrow sense of the word."[9] From the mistakes of Napoleon I he learned to exercise "wise moderation after the greatest successes," from those of Napoleon III not to "confuse slyness with falsehood." "I spoke the stark truth. That they often didn't believe me and then afterward felt very surprised and disillusioned is not my fault."[10]

[8] GW, IX, 399; XIII, 468; IX, 93; also XIII, 177. "Politics," he remarked on another occasion, "is a science of relatives." GW, III, 251.

[9] GW, IX, 90.

[10] GW, IX, 93–94.

Moderation in victory and deceptive frankness were important weapons in Bismarck's armory. It is doubtful, nevertheless, that he depended much on historical precedent as a guide to political action. Though he may indeed have learned from the fate of the first Bonaparte, Napoleon III was after all not a historical figure, but a contemporary opponent on the chessboard of European politics. Although well versed in recent European history, Bismarck drew upon its facts primarily to buttress arguments for decisions made on other grounds.[11] His knowledge of political tactics stemmed more from intuition and personal experience than from historical example.

"More than anything else politics demands the capacity to recognize intuitively in each new situation where the correct path lies. The statesman must see things coming ahead of time and be prepared for them. . . . An indispensable prerequisite is patience. He must be able to wait until the right moment has come and must precipitate nothing, no matter how great the temptation."

"From childhood I have been a hunter and fisher. In both cases waiting for the right moment has been the rule that I have applied to politics. I have often had to stand for long periods in the hunting blind and let myself be covered and stung by insects before the moment came to shoot."

"Correct evaluation of the opponent is also indispensable to success. This means the exercise of caution. In chess one should never base a move on the positive assumption that the other player will in turn make a certain move. For it may be that this won't happen, and then the game is easily lost. One must always reckon with the possibility that the opponent will at the last moment make a move other than that expected and act accordingly. In other words, one must always have two irons in the fire."

Patience and careful timing, the intuitive recognition of the correct path, and the accurate evaluation of his opponents were often characteristic of Bismarckian statecraft. And yet these characteristics are matters of judgment and temperament rather than a demonstrable technique of political action. The best clue to his method, both tactical and strategical, lies in the final words: "two irons in the fire." "Many paths led to my goal," he declared. "I had to try all of them one after the other, the most dangerous at the end. It was not my way to be single-handed in political action."[12] Here is the most significant explanation Bismarck ever gave of his effectiveness as a statesman. We shall see that he developed this method in the diplomatic quarrels of the 1850s and later applied it in many other situations in both domestic and foreign affairs.

"In major domestic and foreign affairs and questions," wrote a contemporary, "Prince Bismarck likes to provide himself with an alternative in order to

---

[11] Bismarck's use and conception of history were critically analyzed by Helmuth Wolff, *Geschichtsauffassung und Politik in Bismarcks Bewusstsein* (Munich, 1926). See also Maria Fehling, *Bismarcks Geschichtskenntnis* (Stuttgart, 1922).

[12] GW, IX, 400, 50; XIII, 468.

be able to decide the same in one of two opposed directions."[13] Frequently these alternatives were multiple solutions to a single political problem that could be simultaneously explored until the moment of final choice. Often they were multiple possibilities of alliance with opposed political forces between which a final choice had to be avoided as long as possible. In its many variations the strategy of alternatives provided Bismarck with a means of navigation amid the shifting currents and treacherous eddies of the time stream. It enabled him to gain and retain the initiative. The knowledge that his quiver held more than one arrow gave him the confidence and sureness that most of his opponents lacked. If one bolt fell short of the mark, another was ready to follow. By this means he minimized the risk, if at the last moment the most desirable objective appeared too costly. But the availability of another option could also be used to remove obstacles along the way. By candidly revealing the availability of a course more disadvantageous to his opponents than to himself, he might force them to yield. His options were seldom bluffs. No matter how drastic, they were usually practical threats that he was ready to carry out if so compelled. By monopolizing the alternative possibilities that the situation afforded, he often severely restricted his adversary's sphere of action.

His awareness of a world animated by the constant clash of competing forces made Bismarck sensitive to the possibility of exploiting their mutual antagonisms for the benefit of his own cause. Usually he sought the middle ground between conflicting interests, the point from which alliance with either was possible. By attaining and preserving freedom of choice between opposed interests he was often able to bring them into an equilibrium of mutual frustration. Through the static immobilization of hostile interests he gained the liberty to promote his own. The position for which he constantly strove was that of the fulcrum in a balance of power. By seizing the position of greatest mobility, he maneuvered others into those of least latitude. Sometimes Bismarck's alternatives were actually successive stages through which he hoped to pass toward the achievement of a desired objective.[14] His first move was often but a modest beginning from which he hoped to progress toward a hidden goal of more drastic character. What could not be achieved immediately might eventually be accomplished through organic growth. Today's acorn was tomorrow's oak.

These related patterns of strategy are evident in the recommendations of

[13] Max Freiherr Pergler von Perglas, Bavarian envoy in Berlin, quoted in Fritz von Rummel, *Das Ministerium Lutz und seine Gegner, 1871–1882* (Munich, 1935), 2; also Heinrich Ritter von Srbik, *Deutsche Einheit: Idee und Wirklichkeit vom Heiligen Reich bis Königgrätz* (Munich, 1935–1942), vol. 3, 70.

[14] This was the general theme advanced by Otto Becker, *Bismarcks Ringen um Deutschlands Gestaltung* (Heidelberg, 1958).

the 1850s and 1860s with which Bismarck urged his government into a more aggressive policy toward Austria.

The Fulcrum of Power

Like Bismarck, Otto von Manteuffel was a realistic, not a romantic, conservative. Yet the two men differed greatly in political temperament and technique. Although determined to surrender nothing to Austria, the foreign minister refused to take the initiative against her and strove to avoid a public quarrel. A pessimist, he feared the consequences of war for the conservative order. He favored reason and persuasion over threat and force. But Bismarck's "lust for combat," his personal ego, and his Prussian pride soon brought him into open conflict with Count Thun, the Austrian envoy, who presided over the diet.[15]

At stake were petty issues of protocol as well as matters of high policy. In the diet chamber, where previously only the presidential envoy had smoked, Bismarck drew out a cigar and asked Thun for a light. When the count received him in shirtsleeves on a hot day, the Prussian pulled off his own jacket. Forced to wait a few minutes in the presidential antechamber, he stalked out. Neither Thun nor his successor, Count Anton Prokesch von Osten, had the nerves to endure this kind of rancor. Count Johann von Rechberg, who arrived in 1855, had more staying power. But even he came close to a duel with the Prussian envoy.[16]

Back of this personal friction lay for Bismarck a serious political purpose: the determination to exact from Austria full recognition of Prussia's equality of status in the confederation. The Austrians had to realize that prior agreement with Berlin was necessary on any important business to be transacted by the diet. From another standpoint his aim was acceptance of the Prussian right of veto; votes had to be "weighed as well as counted."[17] He acted under orders from Berlin, but the character that the struggle assumed in Frankfurt was determined by the Prussian envoy. From his busy mind poured a steady stream of adroitly worded reports and letters designed to influence the decisions of Manteuffel and, through Leopold Gerlach, the king as well.

In Frankfurt his first tactic was obstruction. "When Austria hitches a horse in front, we hitch one behind."[18] With clever amendments he vitiated the

[15] Gunther von Richthofen, *Die Politik Bismarcks und Manteuffels in den Jahren 1851–1858* (Leipzig, 1915), 31ff.; Srbik, *Deutsche Einheit*, vol. 2, 174–175.

[16] Arnold Oskar Meyer, *Bismarcks Kampf mit Österreich am Bundestag zu Frankfurt, 1851–1859* (Berlin, 1927), 41ff.; Eduard von Wertheimer, *Bismarck im politischen Kampf* (Berlin, 1930), 9–10.

[17] GW, II, 259; also I, 114ff., 128ff., and Manteuffel's instruction in Heinrich von Poschinger, ed., *Preussen im Bundestag, 1851 bis 1859* (Leipzig, 1882–1884), vol. 1, 1–3.

[18] Quoted in Srbik, *Deutsche Einheit*, vol. 2, 175.

importance of measures backed by the Hofburg. In cases of the least doubt he denied the jurisdiction of the diet or insisted that voting be by unanimity rather than by majority. Traveling from court to court in southern Germany, he endeavored to win the confidence of rulers and statesmen in the hope of splitting apart the opposing coalition. Where persuasion failed, he incited the fear of retribution and sowed the seeds of mutual jealousy and discord. As a last resort he threatened Prussia's secession.

These tactics were entirely negative and not well suited to Bismarck's temperament. He wanted not only to halt the Austrian, but also to launch the Prussian offensive. In one of his first reports to Manteuffel he doubted that the confederation could ever meet the needs of the Prussian state. In the Zollverein he saw a useful precedent. Through similar treaties he proposed to expand Prussian influence "within the geographical area made dependent upon us by nature." By promoting the material interests of the population Prussia could make the confederation superfluous—a useless shell that would drop away from the growing kernel.[19] We shall see this possibility constantly recurring in his calculations down to the year 1870.

From the beginning, however, his main reliance was upon the coercive rather than the evolutionary approach. What Prussia required, he concluded, was a new source of power capable of forcing the opposition either to bend or buckle. Isolated in Germany, she must seek in Europe allies with which to threaten the security of Austria and the lesser states. "Fear and fear alone, that is the only thing which has any effect in the palaces from Munich to Bückeburg."[20]

This meant that the Prussian alliance with Austria must be abandoned in European as well as in German politics. In the past the eastern coalition between the dual powers and Russia had served two purposes: it had been the fortress of conservatism in Europe and had prevented the German medium states from seeking to escape the domination of Austria and Prussia by allying themselves with France. Bismarck maintained that the coalition no longer served either of these functions. Internally Germany now appeared fairly safe from a repetition of the events of March 1848, and abroad in Paris the Second Republic had yielded to the Second Empire, which he regarded as less menacing to the European order. Hence Prussia could afford to loosen her tie with Austria and create the specter of alliance with France.

During January 1853 Bismarck commenced to advocate such a policy in a series of letters to Gerlach and Manteuffel. It was wrong, he argued, for conservatives in Berlin to treat the imperial pretensions of Louis Napoleon with public contempt. The sneers of the *Kreuzzeitung* at the coming marriage of Louis to Eugénie de Montijo were needlessly provocative. "I am convinced

[19] GW, I, 17, 99, 140; II, 321; III, 268; VII, 24–25; XIV, 223.
[20] GW, XIV, 372.

that it could be a great misfortune for Prussia if her government should enter an alliance with France, but, even if we make no use of it, we ought never to remove from the consideration of our allies the possibility that under certain conditions we might choose this evil as the lesser of two." By wiping out the impression that Prussian antagonism toward France was irrevocable, it would be possible to regain the "freedom of position that our illustrious ruling house has in the past used so successfully for the expansion of its power."[21]

These documents are among the most significant of Bismarck's Frankfurt period. Here he revealed for the first time his conviction that Prussia must find outside Germany the sources of power with which to dominate the lesser states and force Austria into submission. "In the final analysis," he wrote a few years later, "the influence of a power in peace depends upon the strength that it can develop in war and on the alliances with which it can enter into the conflict. . . . The conquest of influence in Germany depends entirely upon the belief among the confederate states in the possibility, probability, or certainty that Prussia can count on foreign alliances in the event of war."[22] France appeared to be the only major power available for this purpose. Shunned because of his name and revolutionary origin, Napoleon III was a pariah in the society of European monarchs. He needed allies.

The policy that Bismarck now advocated for Prussia was precisely that for which he never tired of condemning Austria and the medium states. He often accused Austria of a willingness to come to terms with Napoleon III in order to exert pressure on Prussia in Germany. In tones bordering on righteous indignation he frequently warned that the medium states of the south would at the slightest opportunity return to the "politics of the Rhenish Confederation" (*Rheinbundpolitik*).[23] This was an accusation of potential treachery, for it harked back to the time when the southern dynasties sold out to Napoleon I in return for their own aggrandizement.

At this time, nevertheless, Bismarck was sincere in disclaiming any wish to see Prussia actually allied with France. His intention was not to substitute one coalition for another, but to adopt a strategy of alternative pressures. He de-

---

[21] GW, I, 285–287; XIV, 289–291; also I, 291. The view that Bismarck changed his attitude toward the eastern entente after the Crimean War is inaccurate. Thus Meyer, *Bismarcks Kampf*, 308–309; Hans Mombauer, *Bismarcks Realpolitik als Ausdruck seiner Weltanschauung: Historische Studien*, vol. 24, (Berlin, 1936), 49ff.; Egmont Zechlin, *Bismarck und die Grundlegung der deutschen Grossmacht* (Stuttgart, 1930), 102–103. The change began in the winter of 1852–1853 before the eastern crisis arose. The first sign was a letter of Nov. 24, 1852, to Manteuffel deploring the king's anti-Bonapartism. GW, I, 261. To Leopold Gerlach, on Dec. 4, he still maintained that friction with Austria must be restricted to Germany. But the letters of Jan. 27, 1853, criticizing the attitude of the *Kreuzzeitung* show a complete reversal in viewpoint. Later he used the consequences of the Crimean War to justify a policy actually arrived at on other grounds. GW, II, 141, 167, 217; III, 266; XIV, 352.

[22] GW, II, 221, also 231; XIV, 465.

[23] GW, XIV, 246, 284–286, 292, 295.

sired a mobile policy unencumbered by a firm commitment to any power, free to form a temporary intimacy when and where the situation demanded. Prussia should seek to hold a mediate position between Austria and France. Unbound to either, she could exploit the one against the other, making a definite choice only in the extremity of war.[24]

Here Bismarck hoped to find the coercive force that he had vainly sought within the confederation. Such a policy, he believed, would strike terror in the ranks of the lesser states, for a Franco-Prussian alliance might be the prelude to a series of annexations such as had so often changed the political geography of Germany. Fright would bring them under the influence of Prussia and reverse the relationships that had hitherto dominated the diet. Then Austria would find herself in the minority and be compelled to respond to Prussia's will.

At the time it was conceived this tactic had a major flaw. As long as the Austro-Russian segment of the eastern alliance remained intact, a Prussian flirtation with France might not have the effect Bismarck desired. With backing from Russia, Austria could still make a firm stand in Germany. Even while Bismarck wrote, however, a crisis was developing on the eastern horizon that soon dissolved the bond between Vienna and Petersburg.

The Crimean War

In May–July 1853 Turkish resistance to Russia's demand for a protectorate over the Christian population in the Ottoman Empire led to Russian occupation of the Danubian principalities. Encouraged by Britain and France, the sultan declared war in October. Six months later Europe stumbled into a major conflict that its statesmen neither wanted nor had the wisdom to avoid. Inevitably the conflict placed Austria and Prussia under severe pressure. To deploy troops against distant Russia, England and France needed their military support, and yet the Tsarist government confidently expected their assistance as conservative powers and members of the Holy Alliance.

In Vienna, Count Karl von Buol-Schauenstein, foreign minister since the death of Schwarzenberg in 1852, was alarmed by the appearance of Russian troops on the lower Danube. He also saw in the affair a golden chance to shut Russia permanently out of the Balkans and establish Austrian power in the area. But conservative ministers opposed him, and Franz Joseph was dubious. At first Buol steered down the middle, seeking both to avoid antagonizing Petersburg and to win friendship of the western powers. During 1854–1855

---

[24] In Berlin Legation Counselor Küpfer also advocated such a policy. Heinrich von Poschinger, ed., *Unter Friedrich Wilhelm IV: Denkwürdigkeiten des Ministers Otto Freiherrn von Manteuffel 1848–1858* (Berlin, 1900–1901), vol. 2, 268ff.

he moved dangerously close to war against Russia. For this he needed the backing of Prussia and the German Confederation.[25]

To Bismarck the proper course seemed obvious: Prussia should exploit the Austrian need to satisfy her own. Early in 1854 he advised Manteuffel to wait until Austria was thoroughly involved in the east. Once her troops were deployed on the Balkan front, Prussia should suddenly present the Hofburg with the alternatives of Prussian support or hostility. The price of the former ought to be a secret treaty establishing separate spheres of influence, "partly geographical, partly topical," between the dual powers in the German Confederation. In the diet the Austrians must respect the Prussian veto. If refused, Prussia could attack the exposed Bohemian frontier. "The great crises provide the weather for Prussia's growth." She was not a "satiated state."[26]

In Berlin there was no unanimity of opinion or purpose. The ultraconservatives were pro-Russian, Prince Wilhelm and his coterie prowestern. Buffeted by many counsels, the king steered an erratic course, alternately drawn by the desire for neutrality and driven by the fear of isolation. His conservative soul was tortured by the prospect that the eastern alliance might collapse; above all he wished to preserve Austro-Prussian solidarity in European politics. Hoping to control Austria, he granted a renewal (April 1854) of the defensive alliance that had bound the dual powers since 1851. In addition to a mutual territorial guarantee, it was established that Austria might act in the east only in agreement with Prussia. But if she should become involved with Russia, Berlin would mobilize one hundred thousand troops on the eastern frontier—two hundred thousand if the situation should worsen. Immediately the Hofburg took advantage of the compact. In June Buol delivered an ultimatum, forcing the tsar to withdraw his troops from the Danubian principalities, which Austria herself now proceeded to occupy.[27]

Bismarck's reaction to the April treaty illustrates his conception of political strategy. If Austria invoked the treaty, he advised Friedrich Wilhelm, Prussia ought to assemble her troops "not in the neighborhood of Lissa, but in Upper Silesia." Here they would be in a position "to cross either the Russian or the Austrian borders with equal facility." Because the forces of all other nations

---

[25] On Austrian policy see Heinrich Friedjung, *Der Krimkrieg und die österreichische Politik* (Stuttgart, 1907); Kurt Borries, "Zur Politik der deutschen Mächte in der Zeit des Krimkrieges und der italienischen Einigung," *Historische Zeitschrift*, 151 (1934–1935), 294ff.; S. A. Kaehler, "Realpolitik zur Zeit des Krimkrieges—Eine Säkularbetrachtung," *ibid.*, 174 (1952), 436ff.

[26] GW, I, 427–430; XIV, 347, 368ff.

[27] On the Prussian course see Kurt Borries, *Preussen im Krimkrieg, 1853–1856* (Stuttgart, 1930) and Reinhold Müller, *Die Partei Bethmann-Hollweg und die orientalische Krise, 1853–1856* (Halle, 1926). The source of the confusion lay in the inability of Friedrich Wilhelm to govern through his ministers and his willingness to permit the interference of his many camarilla and "kitchen cabinet" advisers. See Fritz Hartung, "Verantwortliche Regierung, Kabinette und Nebenregierungen im konstitutionellen Preussen, 1848–1918," *Forschungen zur brandenburgischen und preussischen Geschichte*, 44 (1932), 2–17.

were now deployed in the east, this was the true fulcrum of European power. "With 200,000 men your majesty would at this moment become the master of the entire European situation, would be able to dictate the peace and win for Prussia a worthy position in Germany." Although receptive, Friedrich Wilhelm was mostly just amused by this bold idea. "A man of Napoleon's sort," he replied, "can commit such acts of violence, but not I."[28]

Instead he proceeded to cooperate with Austria in a rather tentative fashion through most of 1854. To Bismarck this policy was "cowardly" and "shameful." Must Prussia, he asked, ever play Leporello to the Austrian Don Juan?[29] Fearing that Prussia might be dragged into a war against Russia for purely Habsburg interests, he worked desperately to keep her neutral. In this there was chance of assistance from the medium states, which, like Prussia, had nothing to gain from such a conflict. Meeting in Bamberg they formed a coalition to look after the interests of the "third Germany."[30] It now appeared possible for Prussia to split Austria from her German allies.

Again Bismarck came forward with a characteristic proposal. He urged that Prussia threaten to move in any one of three directions: first, alliance with Russia ("it is senseless to swear continually that we would never go with Russia"); second, alliance with France ("and indemnify ourselves at the cost of our perfidious comrades in the confederation"); or third, alliance with German liberalism ("a new cabinet oriented toward the left . . . so partial to the western powers that Austria would be outdistanced and forced to hold vainly to our coattails"). By these means he hoped to press the medium states into joining Prussia in a league of armed neutrality that would also include the Netherlands, Sweden, and Denmark.[31] But if the German states should "desert" her, neutrality would be impossible for Prussia. She must either go with Russia and execute a surprise attack upon the Bohemian frontier, or "with the west" and "divert the water of German public opinion into our own sluices" rather than let it flow to the "Austrian mill." "My policy," he declared, "would be the first named."[32]

Although Friedrich Wilhelm ignored this advice, he was finally compelled to change his attitude toward Austria. In December Franz Joseph overtaxed his friendship by signing a treaty with France and England that appeared to

[28] GW, XV, 72–73; VII, 221; XIII, 337.

[29] GW, I, 446–447; II, 143; XIV, 365–367, 375, 380, 514.

[30] Sigmund Meiboom, Studien zur deutschen Politik Bayerns in den Jahren 1851–1859: Schriftenreihe zur bayrischen Landesgeschichte, vol. 6 (Munich, 1931), 77ff.; Walther P. Fuchs, Die deutschen Mittelstaaten und die Bundesreform 1853–1860: Historische Studien, vol. 256 (Berlin, 1934), 36ff.

[31] GW, I, 503; II, 42; XIV, 334–335. Originally he included only the German middle states, Belgium, and Sardinia. GW, XIV, 310. Apparently the idea for such a league originated in Russia. Christian Friese, Russland und Preussen vom Krimkrieg bis zum polnischen Aufstand (Berlin, 1931), 75.

[32] GW, XIV, 370.

FRIEDRICH WILHELM IV IN 1855 (BILDARCHIV PREUSSISCHER KULTURBESITZ).

be the prelude to war. Next the Hofburg proposed mobilization of the confederate armies against Russia. But this move was frustrated in the diet by Prussia and the lesser states. Throughout 1855 Bismarck enjoyed the unaccustomed luxury of heading the majority. A brake was applied upon Austrian policy that prevented her from entering the conflict. When peace came, however, the coalition dissolved. Austria resumed her leadership of the lesser states, and Prussia returned to isolation. In Germany all was as before.[33]

The Chessboard of Politics

Europe, however, was not the same. The eastern alliance, which since 1815 had been the most important constellation in European politics, was now in a state of dissolution. By her *Realpolitik* in the Crimean War, Austria had severed the conservative bond that for decades had united her with Russia without gaining a substitute in France and Britain. In Petersburg her ultimatum was regarded as treachery and in the west her failure to join in the war was a disappointment. Prussia on the other hand had established a fund of goodwill in the Russian capital that in future years was to grow in value. But for the time being the greatest gainer was Napoleon, who emerged from the Congress of Paris as the dominating figure in European politics.[34]

The war had scarcely commenced before Bismarck began to calculate what new combinations might be erected over the wreckage of the old. In December 1853 his letters to Gerlach already speculated over the possibility of rapprochement between France and Russia. While arguing against Prussian support of Austria, he warned Manteuffel that cooperation between the dual powers in the east would force Russia to make peace and seek the alliance of Bonaparte. The tsar would find this "the most natural way out, if we make hell too hot for him." Such a combination would have irresistible attraction for the medium states. Austria too would seek to join it. In order to forestall her foes and avoid isolation, Prussia would be compelled to become the "third in this repugnant alliance."[35]

But he spoke differently to others. Marquis Lionel de Moustier, the French ambassador at Berlin, heard him say that a firm alliance with France and Russia was most in accord with Prussia's interests. In October 1854, Russian Attaché Glinka at Frankfurt reported that the Prussian envoy had described the alliance as his "political ideal," "the only combination that could satisfy the

[33] Borries, *Preussen im Krimkrieg*, 250ff.; Friedjung, *Krimkrieg*, 132ff.; Charles W. Hallberg, *Franz Joseph and Napoleon III, 1852–1864* (New York, 1955), 72ff.

[34] Kaehler, "Realpolitik," 443–444; Zechlin, *Grundlegung*, 453–454; Werner E. Mosse, *The European Powers and the German Question, 1848–1871* (Cambridge, Eng., 1958), 49ff.

[35] GW, XIV, 334, 346, 351–352, 405; I, 407, 426, 444, 490. Apparently Manteuffel was influenced by the argument. Borries, *Preussen im Krimkrieg*, 226.

political needs of the three countries."[36] At the court of the tsar this suggestion was taken seriously, and the attaché inquired whether King Friedrich
Wilhelm could be won for such a plan. With astounding self-assurance Bismarck replied that he could promise success, "if your government wishes to
intrust me with the task of convincing him." He left no doubt about the purpose he had in mind: "If we foresee the necessity for war against Austria, we
must be in a position to attack her while she is still unprepared and before she
can concentrate her troops on our frontiers."[37] At the moment French and
Russian troops were locked in fatal combat in the Crimea, and Berlin was
busy negotiating with Vienna over a fresh agreement to supplement the treaty
of April 1854!

And yet Bismarck's project was not lacking in realism. During the summer
and early fall French spokesmen had assured him that the war against Russia
was but an expedient for Napoleon; that there was no lasting source of conflict
between the two countries; that France intended to expand into Italy rather
than Germany; that Prussia could become the bridge for a tripartite alliance
against Austria.[38] In Russia Britain was regarded as the real enemy; toward
France there was little hostility and some speculation about the possibility of
future alliance.[39] But Tsar Nicholas shuddered at the idea of dealing with a
Bonaparte. On hearing of his refusal through Glinka, Bismarck sent the la-
conic reply: "Necessity will compel you to do it." The troubled Nicholas
wrote, "That is just as sad as it is possible." Within a few months he was dead.
His successor, Alexander II, was more accessible to the idea. In April 1856
he replaced Foreign Minister Count Karl Nesselrode, advocate of the eastern
alliance, with Prince Alexander Gorchakov, to whom the French coalition
was a near obsession.[40]

At this time Bismarck evidently regarded the Franco-Russian alliance as
not only probable but desirable. Though still careful to conceal his opinion
from Gerlach, he confessed to Manteuffel in February 1856, "I hope for more

---

[36] F. de Martens, *Recueil des traités et conventions conclus par la Russie avec les puissances étrangères* (St. Petersburg, 1874–1909), vol. 8, 444; Friedrich Frahm, *Bismarcks Stellung zu Frankreich
bis zum 4. Juli 1866* (Kiel, 1911), 32.

[37] Martens, *Recueil*, vol. 8, 453–454. On Friedrich Wilhelm's viewpoint see Borries, *Preussen
im Krimkrieg*, 227.

[38] GW, I, 465, 485–486, 494, 505.

[39] "Ein russisch-französisches Allianzprojekt von 1855," *Deutsche Revue*, vol. 21, no. 4 (1896),
292–300.

[40] Martens, *Recueil*, vol. 8, 454; Friese, *Russland und Preussen*, 8ff. Concerning rapprochement
between the two powers during and immediately after the war see V. Bourtenko, "Un projet
d'alliance franco-russe en 1856," *Revue historique*, 155 (1927), 277–325; W. E. Mosse, "The
Negotiations for a Franco-Russian Convention, November 1856," *Cambridge Historical Journal*,
vol. 10, no. 1 (1950), 59–74; François Charles-Roux, *Alexandre II, Gortchakoff, et Napoléon III*
(Paris, 1913), 112ff.; Ernst Schule, *Russland und Frankreich vom Ausgang des Krimkrieges bis zum
italienischen Krieg 1856–1859: Osteuropäische Forschungen*, Neue Folge, vol. 19 (Königsberg,
1935), 4ff.

than fear such an alliance, provided that we jump into it with both feet." For Bismarck this was a very unusual judgment; it meant that he no longer sought for Prussia the middle position in European politics. Apparently this decision arose from despair over the Prussian situation in the diet. From the outset he had been under no illusion concerning the permanence of the majority induced by the Crimean crisis. In view of its approaching dissolution, he believed Prussia must "accentuate [her] European more than [her] German relationships." A triple alliance was "the only means with which to escape the Austrian snare and domination by the medium states."[41]

When he discussed the problem again, however, Bismarck was more cautious. During 1856–1857 he addressed to both Gerlach and Manteuffel a long series of letters, among the most famous of his career, in which he analyzed thoroughly the Prussian position in German and European politics. In none of these documents did he again describe the alliance as one to be joined so impetuously. Perhaps he wished to sweeten a pill difficult for Gerlach and the king to swallow. But it is more probable that Bismarck himself had come to appreciate better the dangers that his policy involved. Although improving Prussia's position in Germany, it would have made her the least influential member of the most powerful coalition in European politics.

Hence Bismarck returned to the policy of the fulcrum. There was a strong possibility, he argued, that Europe would divide into two opposed power blocs, each desirous of Prussian support. A need for mutual support against common foes made a Franco-Russian alliance probable; this would summon into existence a countercoalition composed of Austria and England. As long as the cleavage between these blocs remained infirm, Prussia should ally with neither. She should "hold open every door and every turning." By exploiting this pivotal position she could extract favors from both sides.[42]

But if the Franco-Russian alliance should develop "warlike purposes," neutrality would become impossible for Prussia. Since the collapse of the eastern entente, the German Confederation was no longer a viable instrument for German security. In a war against France and Russia neither Austria nor the medium states would be trustworthy allies; England, moreover, could give Prussia little assistance on the continent. In this extremity Prussia would have to abandon her middle position in favor of alliance with the probable winners. It was wise to prepare this option in advance. The alliance would not be desirable for Prussia if she should become the "third member after its creation." Hence Prussia should hedge by keeping alive the French desire for a

    [41] GW, II, 120; also I, 456, 516; XIV, 425. This document was overlooked by Lenz in his controversy with Schiemann. Theodor Schiemann, "Bismarcks Audienz beim Prinzen von Preussen," Historische Zeitschrift, 83 (1899), 447–458, and Max Lenz, "Ein Apologet der Bismarck-Memoiren," ibid., 84 (1900), 39–71.

    [42] GW, XIV, 473; II, 150, 223.

"more intimate understanding." This appeared to be "the best means of hindering, delaying, or minimizing the harm" of a Franco-Russian alliance.[43]

This argument was, of course, but a facade. Bismarck sought to persuade his superiors in Berlin that rapprochement with France and Russia was a necessity of European politics, when in reality it was for him primarily a necessity of German politics.[44] As before, his aim was to coerce Austria into granting the expansion of Prussian influence. Only by tapping a new reservoir of power outside Germany could Prussia consolidate her position within. The first step must be to cultivate good relations with France. Merely by responding to the desire of Napoleon to make a state visit in Berlin, Prussia could create consternation in the rest of Germany. Even if an actual alliance were never signed, it was foolish to throw away the advantages that the dread of such an event would bring.

Though affected by the argument, Friedrich Wilhelm could not be brought to take any step that might lead to a breach with Austria.[45] The tradition of Austrian leadership and conservative solidarity were too deeply embedded in his thinking. Gerlach was highly shocked over the radical proposals of his "pupil." The two men argued the matter out in an exchange of letters famous for their illustration of the differences between the romantic and realistic views on foreign policy.[46] Basically the dispute was one of relatives, not of absolutes. The interest of state and the struggle against revolution were important to both, but Bismarck gave precedence to the former, Gerlach to the latter.[47]

As was his wont, Gerlach opposed rapprochement with Napoleon on the ground that the Napoleonic dynasty, having been founded on revolution, could have no place in the respectable family of European monarchs. Never-

---

[43] GW, II, 144, 222–223.

[44] In the views Bismarck expressed during the Crimean War Muralt saw the origins of his "policy of the European middle" in the 1870s and 1880s. Though accurate, this fails to consider the important distinction that Bismarck's purpose in the earlier period was offensive, in the latter period defensive. Muralt ignored the many documents of the 1850s in which the aggressive purpose of the policy is evident. Leonhard von Muralt, *Bismarcks Verantwortlichkeit* (Göttingen, 1955), 141–217.

[45] Friese, *Russland und Preussen*, 134ff.

[46] For the entire exchange see *Briefwechsel des Generals Leopold von Gerlach mit dem Bundestagsgesandten Otto von Bismarck* (Berlin, 1893). See also GW, XV, 110ff.; XIV, 46off.; Ernst Ludwig von Gerlach, *Aufzeichnungen aus seinem Leben und Wirken, 1795–1877* (Schwerin, 1903), vol. 2, 209; Manteuffel, *Denkwürdigkeiten*, vol. 3, 193–194; Richard Augst, *Bismarck und Leopold von Gerlach* (Leipzig, 1913).

[47] For discussions of this problem see Friedrich Meinecke, *Weltbürgertum und Nationalstaat: Studien zur Genesis des deutschen Nationalstaates* (5th ed., Munich and Berlin, 1919), 315, *Preussen und Deutschland im 19. und 20. Jahrhundert* (Munich, 1918), 279–295, and Otto Vossler, "Bismarcks Ethos," *Historische Zeitschrift*, 171 (1951), 271ff. Kurt Bigler, *Bismarck und das Legitimitätsprinzip bis 1862* (Winterthur, 1955), went too far in picturing Bismarck, in contrast to Gerlach, as a man of pure expediency.

theless, he buttressed this argument with another of different character. Because it was in the interest of France to do so, he believed, Napoleon would inevitably ally himself with the popular forces of liberal and national revolution. Using Bismarck's own words, he wrote that this was the "reality" that it was folly to "ignore."

Only the second of these arguments was capable of impressing Bismarck. Even so he thought it false. His interviews with Napoleon in 1855 and 1857 had convinced him that the emperor was of a far different calibre than his dreaded uncle. Where the latter had been bold, aggressive, and calculating, the former was sly, limited, and sentimental. There was no danger of a resurgence of French imperialism on a revolutionary scale; the founder of the Second Empire had neither the instincts of a conqueror nor the talents of a field commander. Nor was he impelled by the necessity of propagating revolution. On the contrary, liberalism was as great a threat to his own power as to that of any other European monarch. His imperialistic ambitions were centered on Italy, rather than on the Rhine, where French expansion would certainly recreate the coalition that had crushed the first Napoleon.[48]

Bismarck also refused to be impaled on the first prong of Gerlach's fork. The whole conception of "legitimacy" he dismissed as out of accord with his-

LEOPOLD VON GERLACH (BILDARCHIV PREUSSISCHER KULTURBESITZ).

[48] For Bismarck's view of Napoleon see Frahm, *Stellung zu Frankreich*, 37ff., and Herbert Geuss, *Bismarck und Napoleon III: Kölner historische Abhandlungen*, vol. I (Cologne, 1959), 23ff.

torical fact. Analyzing the origins of the so-called "legitimate" dynasties of Europe, he exposed the fact that the ultimate source of all authority, even that of the Prussian monarchy itself, was revolution. The Napoleonic regime had as good a claim to legitimacy as any other.[49] "As a romanticist I can shed a tear for his fate," he wrote of the deposed Louis Philippe. "As a diplomat I would be his servant, were I a Frenchman. Being what I am, however, I count France only as a piece and to be sure an unavoidable one in the chess game of politics, no matter who happens to be her ruler. In this game it is my business to serve only my king and my country."[50]

The Alternatives of Coercion

Since the beginning of the Crimean crisis Bismarck's attitude toward Austria had become increasingly belligerent. In January 1855 the Austrian ambassador in Berlin reported that on visits to the capital Bismarck had been heard to say that Austro-Prussian dualism could no longer be tolerated in Germany. Through the centuries it had always been productive of war. One more was needed to eject Austria from Germany. Three months later Rechberg reported from Frankfurt that Bismarck had been doing some loose talking "about the necessity for Prussia to expand not in Poland, but in Germany, namely in Saxony and Hanover." During a visit to Paris in August Bismarck told a Prussian diplomat, Prince Heinrich von Reuss, that war with Austria was unavoidable.[51]

In April 1856 he informed Gerlach and Manteuffel of his belief that "we shall have to fight for our existence against Austria in the not-too-distant future." Nevertheless, he disavowed any desire to precipitate such a conflict. It would come, he believed, in the natural course of events. "The Viennese policy being what it is, Germany is too small for the two of us." "We shall both plow the same disputed acre as long as no honorable arrangement has been made and executed concerning the influence belonging to each in Germany." Such an arrangement, he argued, should be a "political or geographical line of demarcation."[52]

More than a year later he spoke just as bluntly to his Austrian colleague in Frankfurt. Without any authorization from Berlin he told Rechberg, "The existing situation cannot continue and must lead either to an understanding or a decisive break." It was a delusion for Austria to assume that she could count on Prussian aid in the event of war. The imperial government must reckon with the "reality" that, if no settlement had been reached with Prus-

---

[49] GW, II, 226ff.; XIV, 470ff.

[50] GW, XIV, 465.

[51] Meyer, *Bismarcks Kampf*, 239–240, 261–262; Erich Marcks, *Otto von Bismarck: Ein Lebensbild* (Stuttgart, 1915), 40.

[52] GW, II, 142; XIV, 441.

sia, the latter would be found in the ranks of the enemy. Concerning the details of such a settlement he was again vague. The two powers, he said, must avoid holding any "point in common."[53] What he appears to have had in mind was the division of Germany into separate spheres along the Main.

Despite his bellicose utterances, it would be a mistake to assume that Bismarck believed war the only means of accomplishing this end.[54] What he had decided upon was the necessity, not of war, but of coercion. There were two possibilities: coercion by threat followed by a negotiated settlement or coercion by violence and a settlement dictated by the fortunes of war. The first course would result in the peaceful division of Germany into two spheres of influence, but the second meant that Prussia would seek to drive Austria out of Germany, expand her frontiers to link her eastern and western provinces, and reorganize the rest of Protestant Germany into a federation under her own domination. These were the alternative goals of the Prussian state, as Bismarck now conceived them. Both were to be considered and prepared. Being the less dangerous, the former was preferred, but in view of the nature of the conflict with Austria, the latter was more likely.

As has been shown, Bismarck sought the necessary means of coercion in the potential combinations of European politics. Through the separation of Austria and Russia, the Crimean War had given Berlin the possibility of seizing the fulcrum in the European balance of power. By placing herself in the pivotal position from which alliances in at least two directions were possible, Berlin could arouse fears in Vienna and the lesser capitals that might break their resistance to the expansion of Prussian power.

Brilliant though it was, this strategy had a serious shortcoming. If, as Bismarck anticipated, the mere threat of an alliance with France and Russia proved insufficient, Prussia might be compelled to promote such a combination in order to make war on Austria. Should she fight alone, Prussia would at least be compelled to stay close to these powers in order to prevent their coming to Austria's assistance. Or if they should conspire to make war on Vienna for their own ends, Prussia would have to join them as a secondary partner. In any event the abandonment of the favored position of the fulcrum was likely. Whatever gains she achieved in a successful war might be offset by restrictions imposed upon her in victory by her two mighty allies, both of whom had a traditional interest in a weak and divided Germany.

[53] Meyer, *Bismarcks Kampf*, 549–553. Naturally Bismarck made no mention of this unauthorized threat in his report of the interview. GW, II, 232ff.

[54] Those who recorded his remarks obviously remembered only their sensational import and forgot or ignored the qualifying phrases that appear everywhere in the documents that came from his pen during these years. His attitude is best expressed in a letter to Leopold Gerlach of June 1855. "We must hold open the bridge to Austria, but not cross it ourselves." GW, XIV, 406. During the Italian war of 1859 he told Gerlach, "We must go either with or against Austria." GW, VII, 39.

Toward the end of the 1850s, however, certain developments in German and European politics, when coupled with changes in Bismarck's own thinking, enabled him to readjust the pattern of strategy by which he hoped to promote the Prussian interest. By adding still other forces—national and material—to his system of pressures he increased its flexibility and reduced its hazards.

BOOK TWO

The Years of Decision,

1858–1863

Komm, Einzger, wenn du schon geboren,
  Tritt auf, wir folgen deiner Spur!
Du letzter aller Diktatoren,
  Komm mit der letzten Diktatur!

  —*Johann Georg Fischer in 1848*

✚

‡·‡

Materialism and Nationalism

Germany's Second Revolution

URING Bismarck's years in Frankfurt, Germany entered a new era of accelerated economic growth that exceeded by far any previous epoch in its history. Building on the accomplishments of the preceding fifteen years, the output of heavy industry and adjunct sectors of the economy mounted steadily from 1850 to 1873, despite brief setbacks in 1857–1859 and 1866–1867. In three decades Germany began to close the gap that for three centuries had separated its level of economic and social development from that of western Europe. The process of growth was an intertwining one in which demographic change, agrarian development, commercial expansion, and industrialization mutually reinforced each other.[1]

Between 1816 and 1864 the population living within the borders of the future German Reich rose from 23,522,000 to 37,819,000, despite massive emigration. When the growth in population temporarily exceeded employment opportunities in the 1820s and 1830s, the result was a fall in the birthrate. But a new wave of fecundity arrived in the wake of industrialization and continued into the late 1870s.[2] Europe's burgeoning population and urban development pushed food prices upward after 1830, a trend that continued into the 1860s. To meet the demand, German farmers plowed pasture, fallow, and waste land, steadily increasing the acreage under cultivation; in Prussia the area tilled mounted from 55.5 to 69.3 percent of the whole between 1800 and 1864 after which the percentage remained fairly constant. Crop rotation, improved implements, and (after 1850) increased use of artificial fertilizers improved yields. Between 1816 and 1865 the growth in agricultural production (135 percent) greatly exceeded the growth in population (59 percent). The surplus was exported to other European countries, particularly to Great Britain.[3]

---

[1] For the problems of economic growth in German economic history see Richard Tilly, "Soll und Haben: Recent German Economic History and the Problem of Economic Development," *The Journal of Economic History*, 29 (1969), 298–319. For the results of recent research see Reinhard Spree, *Wachstumstrends und Konjunkturzyklen in der deutschen Wirtschaft von 1820 bis 1913* (Göttingen, 1978); Hermann Aubin and Wolfgang Zorn, eds., *Handbuch der deutschen Wirtschafts- und Sozialgeschichte*, vol. 2 (Stuttgart, 1976), particularly Knut Borchardt, "Wirtschaftliches Wachstum und Wechsellagen, 1800–1914," 198–275; and Karl Erich Born, *Wirtschafts- und Sozialgeschichte des deutschen Kaiserreichs, 1867/71–1914* (Stuttgart, 1985).

[2] Walther Hoffmann, *Das Wachstum der deutschen Wirtschaft seit der Mitte des 19. Jahrhunderts* (Berlin, 1965), 172–173; Spree, *Wachstumstrends und Konjunkturzyklen*, 92–93.

[3] Wilhelm Abel, *Agrarkrisen und Agrarkonjunktur* (2d ed., Hamburg, 1966), 253–257; Walther

The most dramatic changes in the German economy in the third quarter of the century occurred in transport and industry. By 1835 German mercantile tonnage, after a slump of two decades, finally regained the level of 1816; between 1835 and 1870 it expanded from 293,000 to 1,008,000 tons, a growth indicative of the increasing exchange goods that followed the formation of the Zollverein and accompanied the acceleration of industrialization. After 1850 railway construction again became the chief engine of industrial growth, although the rate of expansion achieved in 1846 was not reached again until 1868. The network of 29,970 kilometers built between 1835 and 1875 produced a voracious demand for iron and coal, initially met by imports, ultimately by an expanded domestic production. Between 1840 and 1873 the output of pig iron rose from 172,982 to 2,240,575 tons, and that of hard coal from 3,188,169 to 36,392,000 tons; per capita consumption of pig iron spurted from 8.5 to 71.5 kilograms and of hard coal from 111 to 818 kilograms. The manufacture of locomotives gave "decisive impetus" to growth in the machine industry. Increases in per capita income were soon reflected in the growth of consumer industries, particularly textiles; in expanding cities the construction industry boomed to satisfy the demand for housing and work space.[4] Recent estimates of Germany's rate of economic growth (gross national product) show a healthy rise from 1.2 percent annually during 1830–1850 to 1.6 percent during 1850–1870, a surge that brought her abreast of the two leaders in European industrialization: Great Britain (1.4 and 1.6 percent) and Belgium (1.7 and 1.7 percent).[5]

Hoffmann, "The Take-Off in Germany," in W. W. Rostow, ed., *The Economics of Take-Off into Sustained Growth* (London, 1964), 101–103; Graf A. W. Finck von Finckenstein, *Die Entwicklung der Landwirtschaft in Preussen und Deutschland, 1800–1930* (Würzburg, 1960), 98ff., 326, 329.

[4] Hoffmann, "Take-Off," 104ff.; Arthur Spiethoff, *Die wirtschaftlichen Wechsellagen* (Tübingen, 1955), vol. 2, tab. 13 and 20. Economic historians have ceased to regard the advancing figures of production in heavy industry as proof of what happened in the rest of the economy. And yet studies have confirmed the view that in Germany railway construction was the "leading sector" that fueled a "take off into sustained growth." Carl-Ludwig Holtfrerich, *Quantitative Wirtschaftsgeschichte des Ruhrkohlenbergbaus im 19. Jahrhundert: Eine Führungssektoranalyse* (Dortmund, 1973); Reinhard Spree and Jürgen Bergmann, "Die konjunkturelle Entwicklung der deutschen Wirtschaft, 1840 bis 1864," in Hans-Ulrich Wehler, ed., *Sozialgeschichte Heute: Kritische Studien zur Geschichtswissenschaft* (Göttingen, 1974), vol. 11, 289–335; and Rainer Fremdling, *Eisenbahnen und deutsches Wirtschaftswachstum, 1840–1879: Ein Beitrag zur Entwicklungstheorie und zur Theorie der Infrastruktur* (Dortmund, 1975), 5–85.

[5] Paul Bairoch, "Europe's Gross National Product, 1800–1975," *Journal of European Economic History*, 5 (1976), 286; Carl-Ludwig Holtfrerich, "The Growth of Net Domestic Product in Germany, 1850–1913," in Rainer Fremdling and Patrick O'Brien, eds., *Productivity in the Economies of Europe* (Stuttgart, 1983), 124–132; Hartmut Kaelble, "Der Mythos von der rapiden Industrialisierung in Deutschland," in *Geschichte und Gesellschaft*, 9 (1983), 106–118. Kaelble challenged the assumption of some defenders of the *"Sonderweg* thesis" that Germany's industrialization was more rapid than that of other industrializing countries, which succeeded, where Germany failed, in developing political democracies. Yet he conceded that, in the period discussed here,

"The appearance of the country changed quickly," wrote Friedrich Engels. "Whoever last saw the Prussian Rhineland, Westphalia, the kingdom of Saxony, Upper Silesia, Berlin, and the seaports in 1849 found them unrecognizable in 1864. Everywhere machines and steam power had appeared. Steamships gradually replaced sailships, first in the coastal trade, then in maritime commerce. The railways multiplied in length many times. In the dockyards, collieries, and iron works there prevailed an activity of the kind that the ponderous German had previously thought himself utterly incapable."[6] The industrial revolution rescued Germany from the effects of overpopulation by providing employment for millions whom the land could not support. It set in motion an internal migration without parallel in German history until 1945, as the excess rural population drained into seven industrial regions: Rhineland-Westphalia, the Rhine-Main area, Saxony, Upper Silesia, Berlin, the northwestern seaports, and after 1871 the Saar and Lorraine.[7] Between 1852 and 1871 the number of cities in Germany with a population above 100,000 increased from twenty-six to forty-eight, those with 10,000 to 100,000 inhabitants from 108 to 126. Although 51 percent of Germany's work force was still engaged in agricultural pursuits in the 1860s (as against 28 percent in mining and manufacture), the figure was steadily declining.[8]

Among the Zollverein states Prussia was the chief beneficiary of these demographic changes. The areas of fastest population growth were on its soil in the northeast and in the Rhineland. By 1864 Prussia's population within the German Confederation outnumbered that of Austria by 2,700,000, and that of the larger middle states by 2,500,000; its total population was larger than all of the confederate small and middle states combined. In the 1860s Prussia accounted for nine-tenths of all coal and pig iron, two-thirds of the iron ore, and almost all steel and zinc produced in the German Zollverein. Two-thirds of the Zollverein's steam engines were located on its soil. In textiles its dominance was also evident, accounting for four-fifths of all flax spindles, over half of all worsted spindles, and three-fifths of all machines for weaving woolen goods. Only in the manufacture of cotton goods did Prussia take second place.[9] Since 1815 Prussia had controlled all of Germany's principal wa-

---

it was more rapid than before. On the problems encountered in assembling and using statistics measuring economic growth see especially Knut Borchardt, "Wirtschaftliches Wachstum und Wechsellagen, 1800–1914," in Aubin and Zorn, eds., *Handbuch*, vol. 2, 198–203.

[6] Quoted in Hans Mottek and others, *Studien zur Geschichte der industriellen Revolution in Deutschland* (Berlin, 1960), 165–166.

[7] Wolfgang Köllmann, *Bevölkerungsgeschichte Deutschlands: Studien zur Bevölkerungsgeschichte Deutschlands* (Göttingen, 1974), 37–38, and "Grundzüge der Bevölkerungsgeschichte Deutschlands im 19. und 20. Jahrhundert," *Studium Generale*, 7 (1959), 383–385. Only 43.6 percent of those residing in Berlin in 1871 had been born there; 20.2 percent came from Brandenburg, the rest from more distant provinces. Mottek, *Studien*, 230.

[8] Hoffmann, *Wachstum*, 131, 135.

[9] Wolfgang Köllmann, "Bevölkerungsgeschichte 1800–1970," in Aubin and Zorn, eds., *Hand-

terways, except the Danube; the Rhine, Weser, Elbe, and Oder crossed its soil. Earlier, to be sure, Prussia and Germany had lacked a natural center of transportation and commerce such as London provided for Britain and Paris for France. Railways made Berlin a center of communication between east and west; the growth of banking, bourse, and machine manufacture made it a nucleus for industry and finance as well. Between 1850 and 1870 Berlin's population nearly doubled from 400,000 to 763,000.[10] Long a nerve center of government, the Hohenzollern capital now became the principal ganglion of the Prussian and German economy.

During the two decades of Germany's leap into the industrial age there appear, in retrospect, to have been two great questions. The first was whether Prussia would convert its new economic sinew into political muscle. Continued leadership in the Zollverein, control over the lower reaches of Germany's waterways, the centralizing effect of the German railway system, and superior development in industry and finance—all of these factors pointed to the possibility of Prussia's future hegemony in Germany. Among the lesser states only Saxony experienced an industrial growth of significance in the same period, and Saxony had emerged from the Congress of Vienna greatly reduced in size and importance. In the Hapsburg Empire lower Austria and Bohemia made important progress in the middle decades. Yet the empire's national resources were scattered and less easily exploited than Prussia's. Its enterprises were weak in capital and unequal to foreign competition. Prussia, which since 1740 had gained, lost, and regained at least nominal equality with Austria in military and political affairs, was now rapidly drawing ahead in the spheres of industry and finance. During 1850–1853, Prussia's success in defeating Bruck's plan for a central European union and in renewing the Zollverein demonstrated the increasing orientation of material interests in Germany toward Berlin and away from Vienna.

The second question raised by Germany's rapid industrialization was whether the aristocratic-monarchical order in Prussia would succeed in containing the new social forces that industrialization produced. The old Prussian "establishment" (crown, cabinet, bureaucracy, Protestant church, officer corps, and gentry) was based economically on agriculture and socially on the big landowners east of the Elbe. But the growth of industrial capitalism and of the factory system of production was creating new forms of wealth and an altered social structure. In Max Weber's terms, status society began to yield to class society; traditional corporate groups and institutions, to the social classes and pressure groups typical of a modern pluralistic society.[11] At issue

---

buch, vol. 2, 15; Pierre Benaerts, Les origines de la grande industrie allemande (Paris, 1933), 647–648.

[10] Mottek, Studien, 230.

[11] Max Weber, Wirtschaft und Gesellschaft (4th ed., Cologne, 1958), 177–180, 285, 314. See also Jürgen Kocka, "Stand-Klasse-Organisation: Sozialer Ungleichheit in Deutschland vom

was whether the old order could and would satisfy the material interests and moral aspirations of part or all of these new economic and social forces. How fast and with what degree of thoroughness, in other words, would the shift proceed? Would the transformation occur at a revolutionary or evolutionary tempo?

At mid-century the answers to these two questions were by no means obvious. For their resolution both demanded leadership with comprehension and imagination, political nerve, and tactical skill. During the Napoleonic era the Prussian establishment had withstood the first great test of the modern age under the direction of able bureaucratic reformers. In 1848 it survived the second, this time largely because of the weakness, division, and limited aims of its foes. But thereafter the current of economic and social change accelerated. Whether the old order could produce a leadership capable of keeping it afloat upon the rushing stream of time remained to be seen.

Industrialism under the "Reaction"

The government that faced these challenges at mid-century was socially of mixed origin and in transition from bureaucratic absolutism to constitutional monarchy. Although still favored, the old landed nobility (*Landadel*) had not been able to monopolize Prussia's state service. Most officials were of bourgeois or humbler origin; some commoners had climbed the bureaucratic ladder to leading positions as diplomats, district presidents, privy counselors, and even ministers. Often they were rewarded with ennoblement, creating a service nobility (*Dienstadel*) without feudal roots.[12] Professionalization of the state service reshaped the old bureaucratic caste. The result was a relatively homogeneous official estate (*Beamtenstand*), proud of its status, conscious of its power, and still imbued with the tradition that the state it served was above the competing forces of civil society. The external distinction between official and nonofficial became sharper than the internal distinction between noble and nonnoble.[13]

At mid-century, however, there were tensions within the bureaucratic estate produced by a generational gap between senior officials, who were rela-

---

späten 18. bis zum frühen 20. Jahrhundert im Aufriss," in Hans-Ulrich Wehler, ed. *Klassen in der europäischen Sozialgeschichte* (Göttingen, 1979), 137–165.

[12] In 1847, 31 percent of the diplomats, 36 percent of the highest administrative officials, and 21 percent of the generals in the Prussian army were either bourgeois or recently ennobled. In 1862 the figures were 27 percent, 40 percent, and 31 percent, respectively. See Nikolaus von Preradovich, *Die Führungsschichten in Österreich und Preussen, 1804–1918* (Wiesbaden, 1955), 78ff.

[13] John R. Gillis, *The Prussian Bureaucracy in Crisis, 1840–1860* (Stanford, 1971), 29–30; Otto Hintze, *Der Beamtenstaat: Vorträge der Gehe-Stiftung zu Dresden*, vol. 3 (Leipzig, 1911). Jürgen Kocka doubted that Prussian-German officialdom could be classified as either class or estate, but surely its self-identification was *ständisch*. Kocka, "Stand-Klasse-Organisation," 156–157, 164.

tively well paid and for whom there was no set age of retirement, and junior officials, who were better educated but poorly paid. The ranks of the juniors were seriously overcrowded, and as a consequence they were compelled to wait longer than normal for tenure and promotion. During the unrest of 1847–1848 some of the dissatisfied emerged as participants in, and even leaders of, the liberal movement. The revolution of 1848 revealed a serious breach in both the corporate solidarity and the isolation of the official estate, a breach that constitutionalism tended to perpetuate. For more than two decades the Prussian Chamber of Deputies contained many officials who were elected either as supporters of the government (the predominant type during the 1850s) or as members of the liberal opposition (the predominant type during the 1860s).[14]

In economic policy, furthermore, the Prussian bureaucracy had inherited from earlier epochs two contradictory traditions: state paternalism and laissez-faire. The average German businessman in the early nineteenth century still resided in a small town and managed a small enterprise limited in capital; he was a "man of limited horizon, competent to do his daily business, but not to serve common interests or to develop new ways of life."[15] Government officials, trained in the Berlin Technical Institute, founded in 1821, and often sent abroad for study, had more technical expertise than the owners and employees of the mines and foundries of Rhineland-Westphalia. Hence the state continued the mercantilistic practice of controlling and regulating the successive phases of production and marketing in important industries. The state, furthermore, was an entrepreneur. The Ministry of Commerce owned, operated, and supervised many undertakings, including iron works and coal mines; in 1851 one-fifth of Prussia's coal was still produced in state-owned mines. Founded in 1772, the Prussian Overseas Trading Company (*Seehandlung*) evolved into a state bank heavily engaged in developmental activities. It raised funds to float private enterprises, sought new markets for Prussian products, constructed roads, owned and operated model factories, and acted as wholesaler for many manufactured products. The motives for this paternalistic activity were varied: to increase fiscal revenues, promote military potential, create employment in depressed regions, and provide a surrogate for the private capital and initiative that the country lacked. "Tradition died hard in Prussia, and the notion that the country was a vast estate to be managed by the king and his advisers survived into the modern age of steam engines and railways."[16]

[14] Gillis, *Prussian Bureaucracy*, 49ff.

[15] Wolfram Fischer, "Government Activity and Industrialization in Germany (1815–1870)," in Rostow, ed., *Economics of Take-Off*, 90, and *Wirtschaft und Staat im Zeitalter der Industrialisierung* (Göttingen, 1972). Joseph A. Schumpeter, *Business Cycles* (New York, 1939), vol. 1, 283–284.

[16] W. O. Henderson, *The State and the Industrial Revolution in Prussia, 1740–1870* (Liverpool,

Since the late eighteenth century, nevertheless, the doctrines of Adam Smith had penetrated the Prussian government. Reinforced by the humanistic impulse of German idealism, the concept of laissez-faire held that the common welfare and even the interest of state might best be served by freeing the moral energies of the individual from the bonds of corporatism. Beginning with Stein and Hardenberg, bureaucratic liberals had lifted many of those bonds by abolishing serfdom and by granting the free sale of noble estates, freedom of occupation (*Gewerbefreiheit*), and the free exchange of goods within the Zollverein. Although many restrictions remained, these new freedoms gave sufficient room for the growth of industrial capitalism.[17] By mid-century a new breed of entrepreneurs was emerging in Prussia. They were self-confident, market-oriented businessmen less needful of bureaucratic direction: foreigners (William Mulvaney, John and James Cockerill) with technical experience in mining and manufacture; Silesian magnates (prince of Pless, Count Henckel von Donnersmarck, Count von Schaafgotsch) who mined the coal underlying their properties; master mechanics and machine builders (Franz Egells, August Borsig) who expanded shops into factories; merchant-bankers (Gustav Mevissen, David Hansemann, Abraham and Simon Oppenheim) who invested in heavy industry; and many other individuals with personal or family backgrounds as merchants, small manufacturers, and state officials (Matthias Stinnes, Franz Haniel, Eberhard Hoesch, Alfred Krupp).[18]

Entrepreneurs of this stamp grew restive under bureaucratic paternalism. They resented the competition of state-owned enterprises, close supervision and control over mining operations, limitations imposed on the joint-stock form of business enterprise, inequitable and outmoded forms of taxation, and a monetary policy oriented more toward the fiscal needs of the state than the requirements of trade and industry. At the same time they demanded that the government raise and invest funds for improvements believed necessary for

---

1958), xix, 43ff., 96ff., 119ff., 150ff.; and Fischer, "Government Activity," 83ff.; Hans and Manfred Pohl, *Deutsche Bankengeschichte* (Frankfurt a. M., 1982), vol. 2, 43–52. The positive views of Henderson and Fischer on the contribution of the state to economic development in early industrialization have been challenged by Richard Tilly in "The Political Economy of Public Finance and the Industrialization of Prussia, 1815–1866," *Journal of Economic History*, 26 (1966), 484–497, and 27 (1967), 391, *Financial Institutions and Industrialization*, and "Soll und Haben," 298–319. For a review of the controversy see the essay by Friedrich Zunkel, which tends to support Tilly: "Die Rolle der Bergbaubürokratie beim industriellen Ausbau des Ruhrgebiets, 1815–1848," in Wehler, ed., *Sozialgeschichte Heute*, 130–147.

[17] On the laissez-faire policy of the restoration regime see Reinhart Kosselleck, *Preussen zwischen Reform und Revolution* (Stuttgart, 1967).

[18] Friedrich Zunkel, *Der rheinisch-westfälische Unternehmer, 1834–1870* (Cologne, 1962); Hartmut Kaelble, *Berliner Unternehmer während der frühen Industrialisierung* (Berlin, 1972); Jürgen Kocka, *Unternehmer in der deutschen Industrialisierung* (Göttingen, 1975); W. Stahl, *Der Elitekreislauf in der Unternehmerschaft* (Frankfurt a. M., 1973), 126–131.

industrial development but beyond the reach of private capital; namely, banking facilities, roads, canals, river channels, and especially railways. They wanted both greater freedom and greater assistance from the state. Liberal intellectuals of academic orientation thought of universal human rights and liberties and of their legal embodiment in bills of rights and constitutions, but the new businessmen concentrated on the concrete, practical needs of free enterprise and of the political influence and power needed to satisfy them.[19]

Internally divided between bureaucratic liberals and bureaucratic conservatives and their conflicting traditions in economic policy, the Prussian government was not able to arrive at a clear-cut policy either for or against the promotion of industrial capitalism. Faced with a series of decisions, it equivocated, responding alternately to the pressures of conflicting interests and to fears and anxieties that were natural in a society faced with change. Before and after the revolution of 1848 this ambivalence is evident in the government's attitude toward railway construction, the joint-stock form of business enterprise, and fiscal policy.

During the 1830s the Prussian cabinet refused to subsidize railways and was reluctant to authorize private railway construction. The reasons were many: the railway was a threat to feudal and agrarian society; joint-stock companies would draw capital away from trade and agriculture and depress the price of government bonds; landowners would have their property expropriated for the benefit of railway entrepreneurs; bureaucrats would lose control over the economy to large-scale private enterprises; the postal service would lose its monopoly over freight shipments and increased government debts would require higher taxes and constitutional concessions. After 1840 the policy was reversed. Generals came to appreciate the military advantages of mass transport; ministers and officials recognized that Prussia's great power status might be jeopardized by failure to keep abreast of technical progress; eastern landowners came to appreciate the profits to be made in domestic markets by the improved transport of grain. The railway boom of 1842–1846 was sparked by government subsidies and guarantees. By relaxing its restrictions on use of the joint-stock principle (first permitted under a statute of 1838), the government opened the sluices for a flood of private investment and speculation in railway shares. After 1843 restrictions were also eased in other industries, including mining and iron manufacture. Yet the entrepreneurial elite had obtained only part of what it wanted. In the United Diet of 1847 its representatives refused to cooperate with a government that denied them both more help and greater freedom.[20]

[19] Zunkel, Unternehmer, 133ff.

[20] Heinrich von Treitschke, Deutsche Geschichte im neunzehnten Jahrhundert (Leipzig, 1927), vol. 4, 577ff.; Tilly, "Political Economy of Public Finance," 489; and especially Dieter Eichholtz, Junker und Bourgeoisie vor 1848 in der preussischen Eisenbahngeschichte (Berlin, 1962). The king of

The revolution of 1848 gave Rhenish businessmen the chance to steer the government's economic policy into channels more in accord with their interests. Their moment of influence was brief. Shocked by the excesses of the revolution and fearful of social radicalism, they recoiled from politics under the "reaction." To assert, however, that German capitalists entered into an "alliance" with the aristocracy and bureaucracy during the 1850s is to distort a complex relationship.[21] Rhenish businessmen regarded the counterrevolution as a triumph of the gentry over the entrepreneurs, of eastern agrarianism over western industrialism, of the old over the new economic and social order. Gustav Mevissen sought to bridge the gap between eastern and western interests by proposing a bank based upon agrarian and industrial capital. He aimed to reconcile the Junkers to the transition from an agrarian to an industrial state, a transition that he realized was unavoidable if Prussia was to assert itself in the modern world. But the project was rejected by the government.[22]

Self-interest compelled bankers and industrialists, nevertheless, to maintain close relations with the bureaucracy. Governmental approval and assistance were required for numerous vital activities: charters for new joint-stock enterprises, authorization to issue new securities, and subsidies for new railway lines. Businessmen could benefit, furthermore, from inside information on policies and actions of the government that affected investments. If infrequent, corruption was not unknown.[23] Although staunchly conservative, the Manteuffel cabinet was not homogeneous. Under the collegial principle cabinet ministers were coequal and mutually responsible for ministerial decisions and actions. But equality tended to encourage independence rather than cooperation. Manteuffel succeed in gaining some precedence through the famous cabinet order of September 8, 1852. Only the minister-president and minister of war henceforth had the right of direct access to the ruler. Yet Manteuffel continued to complain about the lack of unity and mutual trust among his colleagues.[24]

Hanover was quoted as saying, "I don't want every shoemaker and tailor to travel as fast as I do." Mottek, *Studien*, 36.

[21] For examples of this commonly held thesis see Helmut Böhme, *Deutschlands Weg zur Grossmacht* (Cologne, 1966), 16; Walter Struve, *Elites against Democracy* (Princeton, 1973), 53; and especially Lothar Machtan and Dietrich Milles, *Die Klassensymbiose von Junkertum und Bourgeoisie: Zum Verhältnis von gesellschaftlicher und politischer Herrschaft in Preussen-Deutschland 1850–1878/79* (Frankfurt a. M., 1980), 15–33.

[22] Joseph Hansen, *Gustav von Mevissen: Ein Rheinsches Lebensbild, 1815–1899* (Berlin, 1906), vol. 1, 648, 659, 664–667, 722.

[23] On at least one occasion Minister-President Otto von Manteuffel is said to have sold his influence. Tilly, *Financial Institutions*, 96–100. Bismarck accused him of also using the foreign service for quick information on the movements of foreign stock markets. Moritz Busch, *Tagebuchblätter* (Leipzig, 1899), vol. 2, 484.

[24] Ernst Rudolf Huber, *Dokumente zur deutschen Verfassungsgeschichte* (2d ed., Stuttgart, 1964), vol. 2, 9.

The colleagues most responsible for economic policy were Minister of Finance Karl von Bodelschwingh, a Westphalian landowner, and especially Minister of Commerce August von der Heydt, a merchant-banker from industrial Elberfeld in the Rhineland. Before 1848 Heydt had been a prominent member of the liberal opposition, but civil disorder during the revolution had convinced him of the need for a strong monarchy. Conservatives regarded him as a spokesman for trade and industry, but his former associates saw him as a traitor to the liberal cause and to his own class. As minister he strove to protect the "interest of state" against the "one-sidedness and short-sighted egoism of private enterprise." His greatest achievement, the completion of the main lines of Prussia's railway network, did not win him the applause of the business community, for he regulated rates and services with a heavy hand and sought state ownership of the entire system. Opposition from railway entrepreneurs and advocates of free enterprise became increasingly vociferous and after 1859 Heydt's plan for public ownership was shelved.[25]

Other policies of Heydt were better received by the heavy industrialists. Between 1851 and 1860 the government gradually abolished the "direction principle" under which government officials had since 1766 closely controlled the management of private mining companies (including their technical operations, finances, and qualifications of their employees). In 1851 the tax on the gross income of mining companies was reduced from 10 to 5 percent.[26] Although the Prussian government eased still further its control over the general use of the joint-stock company in the 1850s, a royal charter was still required, the granting of which usually took more than a year; proof was demanded that the company had a "worthy" purpose consonant with the "general welfare" and that no other way could be found to raise the necessary capital; and the corporation's books were subject to examination by a royal official, who could summon meetings of stockholders and attend meetings of the board of directors.[27]

Heydt, Bodelschwingh, and other cabinet members remained opposed, moreover, to the use of the joint-stock principle in banking. They feared the financial power that could accumulate in corporate banks possessing the right to deal in securities. In this they were supported by many private bankers who did not want competition. For two decades the only such corporate bank chartered in Prussia was the *Schaaffhausen'scher Bankverein* founded in Cologne in 1848 while Rhenish businessmen held office in Berlin. Several private bank-

[25] Henderson, *State and Industrial Revolution*, 178ff.; Alexander Bergengrün, *Staatsminister August Freiherr von der Heydt* (Leipzig, 1908), 137ff., 173ff., 266ff.; Zunkel, *Unternehmer*, 182ff.

[26] Statutes of May 12, 1851, and May 21, 1860, in GSP (1851), 261–264 and GSP (1860), 201–206.

[27] Bergengrün, *Heydt*, 214–216; Mottek, *Studien*, 173ff.; Gerhard Gebhardt, *Ruhrbergbau, Geschichte, Aufbau und Verflechtung seiner Gesellschaften und Organisationen* (Essen, 1957), 5ff., 14ff., 23ff.

ers (for example, Simon and Abraham Oppenheim in Cologne and Gerson Bleichröder in Berlin) were prosperous enough to promote industrial enterprises. Yet these sources were inadequate to provide the capital needed for industrial expansion in the 1850s. Prussian financiers were compelled to exploit a loophole in the Prussian code permitting formation, without charter, of banking enterprises on the commandite principle (*Kommanditgesellschaft auf Aktien*), which combined active partners of unlimited liability with silent partners of limited liability. The two great Berlin banks established in this period—*Disconto-Gesellschaft* (founded in 1851, reorganized in 1856) and *Berliner Handelsgesellschaft* (founded in 1856)—were based on the commandite principle. Like the *Schaafhausen'scher*, both participated in company promotion through the floating of securities and granting of credits. Financiers were also able to evade the government's restrictions by founding joint-stock banks in neighboring states and free cities. Two Rhenish bankers (Abraham Oppenheim and Gustav Mevissen) participated, despite strong opposition from the Prussian government, in founding (1853) the *Bank für Handel und Industrie*, known as the *Darmstädter Bank*, on the pattern of the French *Crédit Mobilier*. Because of Prussia's dependence on foreign insurers, the government was more sympathetic to the founding of joint-stock insurance companies; the capital they accumulated was often invested in industrial development.[28]

Another obstacle to the growth of industrial capitalism was the restrictive monetary policy of the government; that is, its limitation of the supply of both coin and currency in the effort to control economic development. Yet financiers constantly found ways to evade the restrictions. Early in the century, when coin was the chief medium of exchange, they supplemented the Prussian silver Thaler with foreign coins. But this did not suffice to meet the needs of the economy for additional means of credit and exchange. Threatened by plans for the creation of a "German bank" in neighboring Anhalt-Dessau, the Prussian government relented by founding in 1847 the *Preussische Bank*, a joint-stock central bank of issue financed mostly by private capital but administered primarily by government officials. And yet its capitalization and note-issuing capacity were insufficient to feed the demand. While minister of fi-

[28] Alexander Bergengrün, *David Hansemann* (Berlin, 1901), 663ff.; Mottek, *Studien*, 169ff.; Pohl, *Deutsche Bankengeschichte*, vol. 2, 119–122, 171–186; Manfred Pohl, *Konzentration im deutschen Bankwesen, 1848–1980* (Frankfurt a. M., 1982), 44–96. The fate of two requests for joint-stock bank charters in 1856 is instructive. One consortium offered an initial capital of 30 million thalers, the other 24 million thalers. In the first group were the Duke of Ratibor, Prince of Hohenlohe-Öhringen, Count Reddern, Count Arnim-Boitzenburg, Count Solms-Baruth, Count Keyserling, Gustav Mevissen, Abraham Oppenheim, and the Mendelsohn Company. Members of the second were the Hereditary Prince of Bentheim, M. A. von Rothschild and sons, Louis Ravené, and Gerson Bleichröder. Naturally the bankers hoped that their aristocratic allies could influence the cabinet. But both projects were rejected by the ministers, who questioned the "economic and political" soundness of chartering financial undertakings of this magnitude. Bergengrün, *Heydt*, 232–233; Hansen, *Mevissen*, vol. 1, 664–667.

nance in the revolutionary government, David Hansemann secured passage of a statute authorizing private joint-stock banks of issue. Six were chartered by 1856, but the Manteuffel government kept their note issue capacity low. For a time Rhenish financiers solved the problem of monetary supply by founding joint-stock banks of issue in neighboring principalities. Their currency circulated within Prussia until finally prohibited in 1857. At the same time, however, the statutory limitation on the note-issuing capacity of the *Preussische Bank* was repealed, enabling it to take up the slack. Meanwhile, Prussian bankers had developed money surrogates in the form of bills of exchange, bank acceptances, and other means of payment. Government restrictions were not sufficient, in other words, to prevent financiers from accumulating the investment capital and creating the means of exchange needed to fuel the Prussian "take off" of the 1850s. With governmental cooperation their task would have been much easier, but even so it was not impossible.[29]

Although uneasy over its social consequences, Manteuffel and his colleagues did not deliberately obstruct the growth of industrial capitalism. The long mercantilistic tradition of stimulating economic growth and of equating business prosperity with state power, the penetration of liberal economics even into conservative circles, the increasing respect for private property and initiative, and the conflicting currents within the bureaucratic estate—all combined to dictate a governmental posture at least partially favorable to the businessman and his requirements.

Social Reform

The Manteuffel government of the 1850s has received poor marks from historians, who generally dismiss it as "reactionary." Certainly many of its actions merit the charge. Censorship, police espionage, and political repression were common. Not even Prince Wilhelm of Prussia, heir to the throne, and his circle were safe from police surveillance. Protestant church affairs were handed over to the extreme orthodox, and the administration and curricula of the schools were under their influence. Yet Catholics enjoyed, except for a brief interlude in 1852, greater religious freedom than elsewhere in Germany. Though the constitution was retained, the upper house was converted by royal decree into a largely hereditary "house of lords," which became the stronghold of the aristocratic gentry. The lower chamber was elected by universal, but indirect and unequal, suffrage. The three-class voting system based on income gave the louder voice to the wealthy. Bourgeois apathy and official pressure at election time enabled progovernment conservatives to control the chamber. Yet even this regime was capable of significant social reforms.

[29] Tilly, *Financial Institutions*, and "Finanzielle Aspekte der preussischen Industrialisierung, 1815–1870," in Wolfram Fischer, ed., *Wirtschafts- und sozialgeschichtliche Probleme der frühen Industrialiserung* (Berlin, 1968), 477–491; Pohl, *Deutsche Bankengeschichte*, vol. 2, 80–89, 154–158.

Since the 1840s a number of thoughtful observers, liberals as well as conservatives, had become concerned about "the social question," namely, the human consequences of industrialization and urbanization. Journalists, professors, officials, and entrepreneurs (Friedrich Harkort was a notable example) engaged in significant discussions about the fate of artisans in competition with the machine, working and living conditions of the urban poor, the spread and persistence of pauperism, and whether self-help or state intervention was desirable in alleviating social distress. The proposed remedies ranged widely: cooperatives, subsidized housing, savings banks, better education, tax reform, poor relief, trade unionism, arbitration courts, restrictions on child labor, minimum wages, maximum hours, and profit sharing.[30] Their commitment to laissez-faire and the brevity of their moment in power prevented moderate liberals from undertaking any significant social reform in 1848–1849. Instead the revolution revealed their vulnerability on this issue by exposing a cleavage between the middle and lower strata of Prussian society. Joseph Maria von Radowitz urged German rulers to find in the "lower and most numerous classes of the population" the "natural allies" of the monarchy in its struggle against bourgeois capitalism. "Any form of government," he advised Friedrich Wilhelm IV on March 28, 1848, "that defends its interests boldly and wisely, that advocates the progressive taxation, a system of poor relief, the regulation of conflicts between capital and labor, would win over the 'common man' and thus generate a mighty force. Certainly it is a dangerous course, but what other course is now without danger? Danger, in fact, without the prospect of victory."[31]

Following the coup of December 5, 1848, the counterrevolutionary government quickly exploited the opportunity Radowitz had discerned by demonstrating its solicitude for peasants, artisans, and other workers. During the first election campaign held under the new constitution the king himself spoke of his desire to improve the lot of the "poor and propertyless." On February 9, 1849, the cabinet issued under its "emergency" power a decree authorizing local authorities to establish industrial councils (Gewerberäte) empowered to found or reconstitute compulsory guilds in more than seventy crafts. The councils were elected by owners and workers (minority representation) engaged in handicraft production, factory production, and commerce. (By 1854, 4,650 craft guilds had been founded or reconstituted in Prussia.) The training of apprentices and administering of master's examinations were again recognized as guild functions. In the same statute steps were taken to appease proletarians by prohibiting both the truck system and involuntary Sunday labor, by authorizing arbitration courts (Gewerbegerichte) representing both la-

[30] See Donald Rohr, The Origins of Social Liberalism (Chicago, 1963); Nicholas Bullock and James Read, The Movement for Housing Reform in Germany and France, 1840–1914 (Cambridge, Eng., 1985), 17–35.

[31] Paul Hassel, Joseph Maria von Radowitz (Berlin, 1905), vol. 1, 577–578.

bor and management (one vote majority) to handle labor disputes, and by establishing through local legislation compulsory insurance funds (*Unterstützungskassen*) for sick and needy workers.

To become permanent, the emergency decree of February 9 required ratification by the Prussian Landtag. Hoping to make it palatable to businessmen, Heydt did not revive the economic-regulative functions of the old guilds and excluded from the list of affected crafts those significantly involved in large-scale mining or factory production. Nevertheless, the revival of corporatism was regarded as reactionary by the business community, for it reversed the trend toward free enterprise begun by Hardenberg in 1810 and completed in the industrial code of 1845. In the lower chamber the sharpest critics of compulsory guilds were bankers and manufacturers (Hermann von Beckerath, Ludolf Camphausen, and Friedrich Harkort), while the most vigorous defender was Bismarck. He praised the artisanry as the "nucleus of the burgher class"; their welfare was a prerequisite for the continued health of the "state organism." At the same time he denounced the factory system for enriching some individuals while breeding masses of undernourished workers, whose insecurity made them dangerous to the state. In conclusion, he dared to say what others had not: the statute was politically desirable.[32]

A statute of May 16, 1853, initiated by Heydt, prohibited child labor under the age of twelve and restricted the working hours of children aged twelve to fourteen to six hours daily. Other paragraphs prohibited night work (between 8:30 P.M. and 5:30 A.M.) and required schooling (three hours daily) for young workers under fifteen years. Enforcement was placed in the hands of government inspectors and the ordinary courts. Although enforcement was lax, the law itself was progressive at a time when the minimum age for child laborers was eight in England and France. Furthermore, the Manteuffel cabinet refused to follow other German governments in reintroducing restrictions on marriage and domicile.[33] Another positive step taken by the Prussian government was the reinforcement of workers' welfare associations. Communal governments were slow to found, and employers to contribute (one-half of the amount expected from workers) to, the new *Unterstützungsvereine* authorized by the statute of 1849. A statute of 1854 empowered the Ministry of Com-

[32] *Stenographische Berichte über die Verhandlungen der Zweiten Kammer* (1849), 697–790; BR, I, 134; GSP (1849), 93–124; Bergengrün, *Heydt*, 204–208; Theodore S. Hamerow, *Restoration, Revolution, Reaction: Economics and Politics in Germany, 1815–1871* (Princeton, 1958), 188–190. The arbitration courts (seen today as an ancestor of contemporary *Mitbestimmung* in West Germany) tended to polarize worker and employer representatives and soon dissolved. Heinrich Volkmann, *Die Arbeiterfrage im preussischen Abgeordnetenhaus, 1848–1869: Schriften zur Wirtschafts- und Sozialgeschichte* (Berlin, 1968), vol. 13, 39–46; Hans Jürgen Teuteberg, *Geschichte der industriellen Mitbestimmung in Deutschland: Ursprung und Entwicklung ihrer Vorläufer im Denken und in der Wirklichkeit des 19. Jahrhunderts* (Tübingen, 1961), 326ff.

[33] Statute of May 16, 1853. GSP (1853), 225–227; Bergengrün, *Heydt*, 208ff.; Hamerow, *Restoration, Revolution, Reaction*, 234–236; Volkmann, *Arbeiterfrage*, 47–59.

merce to order their establishment, one-half of the administrative cost to be borne by the local community. In the same year a similar statute reinforced the *Knappschaften*, long-established welfare associations (providing for sickness, disability, old age, burial, widows, and orphans) for mining and foundry workers. Humanitarianism was not the only purpose—such funds slowed the growth in public expenditure for poor relief.[34]

As the economy expanded in the 1850s and the memory of the "crazy year" (1848), faded, the fear of lower class violence declined and with it the impulse for reform. The Prussian establishment took comfort in the thought that increased employment and rising wages would of themselves solve the "social question." Although urban laborers benefited from the German "take off" of the 1850s and 1860s, it cannot be said that they received a just share of the new wealth their labors produced. Reliable statistics are scarce, but what we possess suggests that, while the nominal wages of industrial labor rose 16 percent in the 1850s, prices (particularly food) rose an astronomical 78 percent during 1850–1855 alone and were still 41 percent above the 1850 level in 1859. In the next decade labor enjoyed an additional 25 percent increase in wages, while prices fluctuated, showing a 12 percent gain by the end of the decade.[35] Although prohibited under the industrial code of 1845, strikes occurred, particularly during the depression of 1857–1859. Trade unions were outlawed under the same code; yet mutual aid associations often served as camouflaged trade unions. Not until repeal of anticombination laws in 1869 did nationwide trade unions become possible.[36]

The economic weapons at labor's disposal during the "reaction" were limited and largely impotent; so likewise were the political. The revolution of 1848 gave birth to local political clubs among artisans and workers, which, united by the *Allgemeine deutsche Arbeiterverbrüderung* (General Brotherhood

---

[34] Statutes of Apr. 3 and 10, 1854. GSP (1854), 138–142; Hans Mottek, *Wirtschaftsgeschichte Deutschlands* (Berlin, 1964), vol. 2, 232–233, 241–245; Elisabeth Todt, *Die gewerkschaftliche Betätigung in Deutschland von 1850 bis 1859* (Berlin, 1950), 71ff. Under the law of Apr. 3, the number of communities with statutes providing for *Unterstützungsvereine* expanded from 226 to 3,644 with 427,190 members, of whom 170,847 (40 percent) were factory workers. Prussia had 378,521 factory workers in 1861, which means that less than half were insured. Because the monthly contribution from employers was one-half of that from workers (sometimes even less), much depended upon the size of the membership, which averaged only 117 in 1860. Hence most associations were financially weak and the assistance they could provide was inadequate. Volkmann, *Arbeiterfrage*, 64, 76–77.

[35] Jürgen Kuczynski, *Die Geschichte der Lage der Arbeiter unter dem Kapitalismus* (Berlin, 1962), vol. 2, 146, 152, and Hoffmann, *Wachstum*, 492. Kuczynski's index of real wages (1900 = 100) sank from 88 to 55 between 1850 and 1855, recovering to 75 in 1858, a peak not reached again until the 76 of 1863; the highest level of the 1860s was 82 in 1864, followed by a downward slide to 67 in 1867. At the end of the decade the index was at 77, still appreciably lower than in 1850. For a critique of such price indices see W. G. Hoffmann and J. H. Müller, *Das deutsche Volkseinkommen, 1851–1957* (Tübingen, 1959), 14–15.

[36] Todt, *Die gewerkschaftliche Betätigung*, 51–70.

of German Workers) under the leadership of Stephan Born, survived into the
1850s. The brotherhood had a democratic, not a communistic program,
stressing the need for civil rights, universal suffrage, and social reform rather
than social revolution; yet it was regarded as communistic and revolutionary
by governments and police administrations throughout Germany. A Prussian
ordinance of March 11, 1850, required clubs organized for the purpose of
influencing public affairs to register with the police, authorized police to dissolve meetings on slight provocation, forbade participation by "women, students, and apprentices" (from whom presumably no rational discourse was
expected), and prohibited links between clubs that could lead to regional or
national federations. In the confederate diet, Austria, Prussia, and Baden
pressed for a common statute that would interdict working-class organizations
throughout the country. Bismarck, eager to protect Prussia's legislative autonomy, was a moderating influence. As finally approved in 1854, the confederate statute was generally consonant with Prussian law and obligated the states
to ban workers' clubs pursuing "political, socialistic, or communistic aims."
This was less than the outright prohibition of all political clubs proposed by
Austria. Yet the acts of the diet and the states sufficed during the 1850s to
dissolve the brotherhood and to interdict a budding, nonrevolutionary working-class movement that might have become a useful instrument for the assimilation of urban workingmen in German society. What survived and even
prospered, despite suppression in a few states, were nonpolitical cooperatives
and mutual aid associations. For politically motivated workers the 1850s were
years of police surveillance and espionage, arrest and imprisonment, flight
and exile. The result was a harvest of bitterness that fed the emerging socialist
movements of the 1860s.[37]

Agrarian Reform and Prosperity

The agrarian policy of the Manteuffel regime shows the same mixed pattern
of social reform for the lower and appeasement for the upper class. Under the
disadvantageous terms of Hardenberg's land settlements of 1811 and 1816,
360,233 former serfs had managed by 1848 to free themselves of all manorial
obligations associated with the land they tilled. Of these, 70,582 owned large
plots (six-sevenths of all former serfs possessing large plots); 289,651 owned
small plots (only one-quarter of all those owning small plots). The figures
show why servile dues were still a source of peasant unrest during the revolution. The Manteuffel cabinet addressed this problem in a statute of March 2,
1850, that created state land banks to issue mortgage bonds with which to

[37] GSP (1850), 277–283. On the workers' movement of the postrevolutionary years and its
suppression see Frolinde Balser, Sozial-Demokratie 1848/49–1863: Die erste deutsche Arbeiterorga-
nisation "Allgemeine Arbeiterverbrüderung" nach der Revolution (Stuttgart, 1962).

indemnify estate owners for all remaining dues and services. Through annual payments to the banks peasant proprietors could now amortize their mortgages, which were long term and at low interest. By 1865 most peasant homesteads, large and small, had been freed, effectively ending the financial side of manorialism. The rural nobility was appeased by the restoration of its right to establish entailed estates (1852), its powers in county and provincial government (1853), and its manorial police authority (1856). Except for former hunting rights and judicial powers, the Junkers had regained the prerogatives they possessed before the revolution.[38]

Agrarian reform from Stein to Manteuffel created a new class of independent farmers in the central and eastern regions of Prussia. Not all, however, were able to survive the transition to economic freedom. Many had too little land to become self-sufficient or were compelled by poor harvests, lack of bank credit, or poor management to sell their properties. They became day laborers bound to local landlords by yearly contracts, still subservient financially and morally, usually receiving their pay in kind until mid-century and thereafter in wages. Others became seasonal migrants who found employment where they could. Stripped of the protection of corporatism, these rural proletarians paid the cost of agrarian progress.[39]

The economy of rural Prussia was steadily changing and with it the character of the landowning class. Over the decades Junker landowners were gradually transformed from a closed hereditary caste into an open, professional, propertied, and acquisitive class. From a feudal estate subsisting on manorial dues and peasant services they evolved into agrarian entrepreneurs primarily concerned with the maximum return on invested capital. Even before abolition of the legal prohibition against the sale of noble estates to commoners in 1807, nearly 10 percent of those estates had gravitated in one way or another into the hands of owners who lacked the predicate von. During the agrarian depression of 1817–1830 debts and mortgages, bankruptcies, and foreclosures forced a startling number of gentry to sell their estates. By 1856 only 7,203 of 12,339 noble estates in Prussia (average size: 500 hectares, or 1,236 acres) were still in the hands of aristocratic families, including the newly ennobled.

Acquisition of a noble estate meant social ascent since feudal rights and privileges were an attribute of the estate rather than the owner. By this route bankers, merchants, industrialists, prosperous farmers, state officials, estate managers, and former leaseholders on royal domains promoted themselves to the status of Landjunker. In the beginning these parvenus were not socially accepted by haughty neighbors of aristocratic lineage, but after 1850 the so-

---

[38] GSP (1850), 77–138; A. Sartorius von Waltershausen, Deutsche Wirtschaftsgeschichte, 1815–1914 (2d ed., Jena, 1923), 140.

[39] Theodor Freiherr von der Goltz, Geschichte der deutschen Landwirtschaft (Stuttgart, 1903), vol. 2, 180ff., and Frieda Wunderlich, Farm Labor in Germany, 1810–1945 (Princeton, 1961), 8ff.

cial cleavage closed as commoners became more feudal in outlook and aristocrats less so. With thousands of commoners who owned latifundia not classified as noble estates—in 1866 numbering 7,047 of the 18,197 Prussian farms of more than 133 hectares (329 acres)—they formed a relatively homogeneous class of agrarian landowners similar in outlook and interests.[40]

The period of Germany's industrialization and of her unification were the most prosperous that German landowners experienced during the nineteenth century. Urban growth in central and western Europe and rising average incomes created a strong demand for food; Zollverein and railway opened up distant markets and fresh prospects for profit through exports. By plowing new land, adopting crop rotation as developed by Albert Thaer, and eventually using farm machinery, Prussian farmers and estate owners increased grain production from 5,164,000 tons in 1822 to a peak of 9,389,000 tons in 1864. Higher food prices, expanding production, and mounting land prices fostered an agrarian boom, which, since it lasted more than four decades, appeared to be unending. Optimism encouraged speculation in farm land and expedited the transition from manorial to capitalistic agriculture. The trans-Elbian region profited in particular from the export trade to Great Britain after repeal of British Corn Laws in 1846. In contrast to their British counterparts, the Prussian gentry became enthusiastic advocates of free trade. They did not fear foreign competition for their own produce, and they benefited from low prices on imported manufactures.[41]

The new technology of agriculture (that is, machinery and crop rotation) favored large over small proprietors. Those with capital or credit enlarged their holdings at the cost of the small farmer and impoverished nobility. Many landowners (including Bismarck) became petty industrialists through the construction of breweries, distilleries, saw mills, paper mills, and sugar refineries—operations requiring capital investment, business accounting, and professional management. During the 1850s grain exports, rural industries, and the land settlement of 1850 gave eastern landowners (again Bismarck was an example) capital to invest in government bonds, railway shares, and industrial corporations. A gulf remained between the agrarian east and industrial west—with the bureaucracy suspended somewhere between. And yet bridges had begun to appear.[42]

[40] Hans Rosenberg, "Die Demokratisierung der Rittergutsbesitzerklasse," in Zur Geschichte und Problematik der Demokratie: Festgabe für Hans Herzfeld (Berlin, 1958), 463–466. See also Goltz, Geschichte der deutschen Landwirtschaft, vol. 2, 165ff., Finckenstein, Entwicklung der Landwirtschaft, 109ff.; Ernst Klein, Geschichte der deutschen Landwirtschaft im Industriezeitalter (Wiesbaden, 1973), 69–91.

[41] Abel, Agrarkrisen und Agrarkonjunktur, 244–257. On crop yields see Finckenstein, Entwicklung der Landwirtschaft, 99, 326, 329; on prices see Hoffmann, Wachstum, 552, and Alfred Jacobs and Hans Richter, Die Grosshandelspreise in Deutschland von 1792 bis 1934: Sonderhefte des Instituts für Konjunkturforschung, vol. 37 (1935), 52–53.

[42] Goltz, Geschichte der deutschen Landwirtschaft, vol. 2, 171–177; Wolfgang Zorn, "Wirtschafts-

Economics and Politics

Although the changes that occurred in the economic and social life of Prussia during 1850–1873 were highly significant, their political effect was not immediately apparent. The wealthy merchant or industrialist who purchased a Pomeranian estate, the bourgeois university graduate who rose to ministerial rank, and the bourgeois officer who attained the rank of general usually adopted the social and political attitudes of the aristocracy. Although lacking, until ennobled, the final symbol of status, they were largely assimilated into the Prussian establishment. Nor did the Silesian prince who became an industrialist by exploiting the coal lying beneath his land fundamentally change his political and social convictions any more than did the Pomeranian Junker who expanded his acreage, shipped his grain to urban centers in the west, and erected a distillery to consume his potato crop. Undoubtedly these men did become more aware of the world at large, more conscious of the economic transformation under way, and more open to suggestions for modernization and change—as long as the fundamental distribution of power and privilege remained unaltered. Despite grumbling, no Fronde appeared to combat Manteuffel's agrarian reforms of the kind that led Hardenberg in his time to incarcerate Counts Marwitz and Finckenstein. Prussia still had its ultras like the Gerlach brothers; but a new social environment was evolving that ultimately had an effect upon Prussian conservatism. During the 1850s there were already signs that an agrarian conservatism based upon the self-interest of landed capital was beginning to take precedence over an ideological conservatism based upon Protestant theology and general theories of history and society.[43]

Naturally the acceleration of German industrialization in the 1850s began to enlarge the size and wealth of the upper *Mittelstand*. Had this expansion occurred in the prerevolutionary period, group egoism, material interests, and liberalism might have combined to change the course of German politics. But the chronology was otherwise, and, when an entrepreneurial elite finally appeared in strength, the revolutionary impulse within German liberalism was already spent. Such zeal for political change as the business class had possessed was dulled in 1848–1849 by fears of social disorder. They had witnessed mobs

---

und Sozialgeschichtliche Zusammenhänge der deutschen Reichsgründungszeit (1850–1879)," *Historische Zeitschrift,* 179 (1963), 327ff. Of the 480 original investors in 61 joint-stock companies founded in the 1850s, 31.7 percent were merchants, 14.8 percent were manufacturers, 12.9 percent were civil servants, 10.8 percent were bankers, 6.9 percent were big landowners, 1.3 percent were army officers. Horst Blumberg, "Die Finanzierung der Neugründungen und Erweiterungen von Industriebetrieben in Form der Aktiengesellschaften während der fünfziger Jahre des neunzehnten Jahrhunderts, am Beispiel der preussischen Verhältnisse erläutert," in Mottek, *Studien,* 196.

[43] William O. Shanahan, *German Protestants Face the Social Question* (Notre Dame, 1954), vol. 1, 278, 321–322.

in the streets, artisans and proletarians at the barricades, and assaults on private as well as public property. Paris had had its "June uprising," Vienna its "September revolution." The specter of class warfare haunted the memory of the "crazy year."[44] The hectic pace of business life in the 1850s, furthermore, left little time for political activity. If the state had completely ignored their needs or grievously harmed their interests, the new bourgeois might have drifted into political radicalism, but this was not the case. The regime left them enough room to satisfy their ambitions in the collieries, factories, banks, and stock exchanges.

What the new business interests objected to was not the governmental system as such, but some of its features and many of its practices. The preference given to Junkers at court and in the civil service, officer corps, and rural government was galling. The most successful entrepreneurs found that wealth alone could not always win entry into the social elite. They resented the exclusiveness of the Prussian nobility, its arrogant assumption of superiority by dint of birth, its military code of honor, and its contempt for Mittelstand values. What the new entrepreneur had to achieve through personal accomplishment came to the Junker through status, family, and official connections. In addition, the extensive regulatory power of the "police state" over affairs affecting the daily lives and activities of most citizens was considered burdensome and unnecessary. The individual was believed to have inadequate protection against the abuse of those powers by officials. Financiers wanted the abolition of usury laws (limiting interest to 6 percent); employers, the liquidation of many restrictions on free enterprise and mobility of labor. Owners of heavy industry deplored the lack of tariff protection against foreign imports; merchants, importers of raw materials and foreign manufactures, and owners of light industry with foreign markets joined big landowners in support of free trade.

Perhaps the greatest annoyance of all was the handicap placed upon the expansion of trade and growth of industry by German disunity. Although the Zollverein and railway had created a single market for small-Germany and the adoption in 1861 of a common code had produced order in the field of commercial law, German businessmen were still plagued by the confusion in currencies, weights, measures, and freight rates, discrepancies in business laws and regulations, restrictions on domicile and residence, and lack of support and protection in world trade.[45]

Apparently these grievances were not serious enough to lead the business

---

[44] Hans Rosenberg, *Rudolf Haym und die Anfänge des klassischen Liberalismus* (Munich, 1933), 143ff.

[45] On the social and political attitudes of the new business class see particularly Friedrich Zunkel, *Unternehmer*; Eugene Anderson, *The Social and Political Conflict in Prussia, 1858–1864* (Lincoln, 1954), 18ff., 148ff.; and Theodore Hamerow, *The Social Foundations of German Unification, 1858–1871: Ideas and Institutions* (Princeton, 1969), 97ff.

class to take a very active role in political life. The typical businessman of the postrevolutionary period expended his energies in the pursuit of profits, leaving the great issues of freedom and constitutionalism to a discouraged liberal intelligentsia. Political freedom was not a necessity as long as he enjoyed a sufficient measure of economic freedom to attain his material goals. Some may have followed Gustav Mevissen in assuming that the shift from an agrarian to an industrial economy would of itself transform society and government and realize liberty.[46] Their concern over political issues tended to be limited to economic and social legislation affecting their immediate interests. No general consensus existed concerning the virtues of economic liberalism. Even capitalists were capable of fearing the consequence of unrestrained acquisitive instincts for humanistic values. Those who gained their understanding of society from Hegel, furthermore, believed that the regulatory powers of the state over civil society, and of the corporative bodies located within it, were necessary to curb the excesses on unrestrained capitalism.

On the local level, to be sure, businessmen participated in the political process, often dominating city governments and liberal party caucuses, where candidates were selected for the Chamber of Deputies and later the Reichstag. But most declined to become candidates themselves, in contrast to their counterparts in Great Britain, where businessmen stood for Parliament in increasing numbers after the Reform Act of 1832. Despite changes in Prussia's social structure in the 1850s, the same social groups continued to supply political leadership in the lower chamber of the Landtag. In the chamber of 1848, 7.5 percent of the seats were held by businessmen; in 1862 the figure was 7.2 percent. Within the Chamber of Deputies the leadership of the liberal party was largely in the hands of landowners and state officials. The "young Lithuanians" who founded the Progressive party in 1861 were country squires from East Prussia who had found their way to liberalism via the doctrine of free trade and Kantian ethics. They were joined by bourgeois officials from the lower ranks of the bureaucracy (particularly the judiciary) who had been nurtured politically by the same sources. They came, in other words, from within the establishment rather than from outside it.[47]

What occurred after 1859 was not the entry of new groups into the political process but the election of liberal rather than conservative deputies from the same social groups that had traditionally provided political leadership. Before

[46] To Mevissen, the disciple of Hegel and St. Simon, it appeared "that the material interests are the one point from which we may shape a better future." Hansen, Mevissen, vol. 1, 616, 694–695, 708, 738.

[47] James Sheehan, German Liberalism in the Nineteenth Century (Chicago, 1978), 82–88; Anderson, Social and Political Conflict, 445. See also Preradovich, Führungsschichten, 154ff., and Reinhard Adam, "Der Liberalismus in der Provinz Preussen zur Zeit der Neuen Ära und sein Anteil an der Entstehung der deutschen Fortschrittspartei," in Verein für die Geschichte von Ost- und Westpreussen, Altpreussische Beiträge (Königsberg, 1933), 145–181.

and after that date more than 60 percent of the lower chamber was composed of that academically trained elite (*Bildungsbürgertum*) that by virtue of education, office, or occupation was regarded by the electorate as best suited for political leadership. They were notables (*Honoratioren*), men of social and professional prestige, but mostly without independent status, more inclined toward political discussion than political conquest. The voters who elected the electoral college that chose such deputies in 1863 were spread evenly across the income and occupational strata of the *Mittelstand*; the percentage of votes cast for liberal candidates was approximately the same in all three categories of the Prussian three-class electoral system: 65.17 percent of class I, 67 percent of class II, and 67.67 percent of class III in urban districts; 43.89, 41.13, and 35.6 percent, respectively, in rural districts.[48]

Party politics was not, however, the only channel through which the new social groups and material interests could vent their aspirations. During the middle decades of the nineteenth century technical improvements (rotary press, dandy rolls, wood pulp paper, and, eventually, Linotype) in combination with increasing literacy and urban concentration revolutionized the publishing trade. Here businessmen could reconcile the pursuit of both politics and profit. Between 1824 and 1869 the number of newspapers published in Prussia rose from 845 to 2,127. Of the larger newspapers about half were located in Berlin, accounting for one-third of the total German press run of about 300,000 daily in the early 1860s. Most of the dailies were liberal in editorial policy, for example: in Berlin, the *Volkszeitung, Spenersche Zeitung, Vossische Zeitung, National-Zeitung*; in the provinces, the *Kölnische Zeitung, Magdeburgische Zeitung, Schlesische Zeitung, Königsberger Hartungsche Zeitung*. Only about forty newspapers in Prussia supported conservative causes (most notably, the *Kreuzzeitung* and *Norddeutsche Allgemeine Zeitung*). The newspaper press was supplemented by political journals such as the liberal *Preussiche Jahrbücher*, conservative *Berliner Revue*, and satirical *Kladderadatsch*. Of the dailies the *Volkszeitung* had the greatest circulation at 36,000; *Kladderadatsch* reached 40,000. Some non-Prussian newspapers attained national circulation: the *Augsburger Allgemeine Zeitung, Grenzboten* (Leipzig), *Hamburger Nachrichten*, and *Neue Frankfurter Zeitung*. Although no German newspapers had yet achieved mass circulation, the press as a whole had become a significant force among businessmen and professional people both for the molding and expression of public opinion.[49]

[48] Zunkel, *Unternehmer*, 182ff.; Hangeorg Schroth, *Welt- und Staatsideen des deutschen Liberalismus in der Zeit der Einheits- und Freiheitskämpfe, 1859–1866: Historiche Studien*, vol. 201 (Berlin, 1931), 59–74; and Adalbert Hess, *Das Parlament dass Bismarck widerstrebte* (Cologne, 1964); Sheehan, *German Liberalism*, 81–83.

[49] Werner Sombart, *Die deutsche Volkswirtschaft im neunzehnten Jahrhundert* (2d ed., Berlin, 1909), 466; Otto Bandmann, *Die deutsche Presse und die Entwicklung der deutschen Frage, 1864–1866* (Leipzig, 1910), 182–191.

Another development of significance in German public life was the proliferation of "voluntary associations," chiefly under the auspices of the *Mittelstand*. Such organizations first appeared in the late eighteenth century, evidently to satisfy general social purposes not met by the guilds and corporations of earlier times. After 1840 the voluntary associations began to assume, under the impact of economic and social change, a more specialized and differentiated character. They were formed to promote specific economic, social, cultural, religious, recreational, and altruistic interests. Many also became forums for political discussion and agitation. The depression that struck in 1857 accelerated this conversion by impelling businessmen to unite for common action. In 1858 mining concerns in the Ruhr area created the Association for Mining Interests under the leadership of Friedrich Hammacher, a successful industrialist and parliamentary deputy. The Congress of German Economists was established in 1858 to agitate for free enterprise and free trade. Its founders and leaders were liberal politicians and journalists (including Hermann Schulze-Delitzsch, Otto Michaelis, Julius Faucher, and John Prince-Smith) who espoused Manchesterism out of conviction. Though few businessmen participated in the congress, its views were popular with important interests (merchants, landowners, and small manufacturers).

In 1858 local chambers of commerce (*Handelskammer*) formed the Prussian Commercial Association (*Handelstag*), which in 1861 joined with similar bodies from other states, including Austria, to establish the German Commercial Association. David Hansemann, director of the *Disconto-Gesellschaft*, became the first chairman of the association, which was composed of businessmen (primarily merchants, but also bankers and industrialists). In economic matters the congress and association paralleled two other political organizations, to be discussed later: the small-Germanist Nationalverein (founded in 1859) and great-Germanist Reformverein (founded in 1862). The connections between the congress, Nationalverein, and German Progressive party (founded in 1861) were particularly close, many individuals belonging to all three. National organizations of workingmen reappeared in 1863 with the founding of the General German Workers Association by Ferdinand Lassalle and of the Convention of German Workers Clubs (*Vereinstag deutscher Arbeitervereine*), led after 1867 by August Bebel.[50]

[50] Thomas Nipperdey, "Verein als soziale Struktur in Deutschland im späten 18. und frühen 19. Jahrhundert," in Hartmut Boockmann, Arnold Esch, Hermann Heimpel, Thomas Nipperdey, and Heinrich Schmidt, eds., *Geschichtswissenschaft und Vereinswesen im 19. Jahrhundert* (Göttingen, 1972), 1–44; Gebhardt, *Ruhrbergbau*, 20–21; Helmut Böhme, *Deutschlands Weg zur Grossmacht: Studien zum Verhältnis von Wirtschaft und Staat während der Reichsgründungszeit, 1848–1881* (Cologne, 1966), 87–90, 104–105; Zorn, "Zusammenhänge," 236; Hamerow, *Social Foundations*, vol. 1, 340–348. The Nationalverein evaded the legal prohibition against political clubs by founding a national organization without local branches, a possibility unforeseen by the lawmakers of the early 1850s. This served as a model for the Reformverein, the German Progressive party, and Lassalle's General German Workers Association. The Convention of German Work-

The upsurge of voluntary associations during the 1850s, particularly of the kind just described, shows that Germany was evolving into a pluralistic society under the impact of economic change and improved communications. Often these associations represented pressure groups whose objective was not to change the fundamental structure of society and government but to influence public policy. Behind them stood material forces and moral aspirations that no government, not even an autocratic one, could safely ignore. But the new interest groups and popular causes also offered opportunities to a statesman capable of exploiting their inner contradictions of idealism and self-interest.

New Weapons in Foreign Policy

Bismarck's early views on economics and society were those to be expected of a person of his paternal background and financial interests. As shown earlier, he saw the revolution of 1848 as a conflict between industrial capitalists and landed gentry, between the large cities and the small towns and countryside.[51] As a journalist and parliamentary deputy during 1848–1851 he was a staunch defender of the interests of the gentry against the reforms of both the revolutionary and counterrevolutionary governments. His views on taxation were predictable: property taxes were confiscatory; income derived from work should be taxed less heavily than that derived from invested capital; indirect taxes, such as the urban milling and slaughter taxes, were "easiest and best" and did not burden the poor more than the rich; and protective tariffs deprived the citizen of the freedom to purchase goods where they were cheapest. Compulsory guilds ought to be restored, he believed, to protect artisans from "the pressure of capital" and from overproduction resulting from free enterprise. Artisans, peasantry, and gentry were the social foundation of the state; hence their welfare ought to be the first concern of economic policy. Factory owners and capitalists merely enriched themselves at the cost of others and produced "a mass of proletarians" so badly nourished and precarious in their existence that they endangered the state.[52] We shall see that Bismarck retained some of these views for the rest of his life—his preference for agriculture and for indirect taxes, his opposition on principle to the property tax, and his concern over the social and political effects of industrialization.

During the 1850s Bismarck's economic and social attitudes began to change. Even while defending restoration of the guilds in 1849, he had admitted that industrial freedom did offer the public certain advantages. "It produces inexpensive goods." But he insisted that the citizen who wore cheap,

---

ers followed a different route, founding local clubs that officially had no common organization, only an annual meeting. Balser, *Sozial-Demokratie*, vol. 1, 483–489.

[51] See pp. 58–62.

[52] GW, X, 18–20, 47–86, 110–129; XIV, 160–161.

machine-made garments ought to be uneasy, knowing that he had robbed some artisan of his daily bread. By 1853, he had concluded that the Frankfurt guilds, which were more intact than any he had previously known, were but a device "to exploit the public and exclude competition."[53] Other experiences in Frankfurt also enlarged his economic and social perspective. The free city on the Main was the banking capital of middle and southern Germany and an important commercial center. In its society noblemen and patricians (diplomats, bankers, and merchants) associated on an equal footing. Meyer Carl Rothschild became a social as well as business acquaintance. Bismarck shared the general prejudice of Frankfurt bankers and his own government against joint-stock banks that sprang up in the lesser states to promote industrial undertakings; the *Darmstädter Bank* he described as merely "the most prosperous of the new swindling businesses."[54]

In his earliest reports from Frankfurt, Bismarck pointed out the value of mobilizing German public opinion as a Prussian weapon against the diet majority. The dynasties of the lesser states were compelled to keep company with Austria because the interests of their subjects ran parallel to those of Prussia. The experiences of 1848–1850 had revealed the potential affinity between German nationalism and Prussian imperialism. Should these two forces ever combine, crowns would topple and sovereignties be destroyed. Bismarck urged his government to exploit the fear of such an alliance by actively promoting the material interests of the German commercial and industrial classes.[55] "I would consider it very useful if we concerned ourselves in time with questions of German material welfare," he wrote to Leopold Gerlach in June 1851. "Whoever seizes the initiative, whether it be the diet, the Zollverein, or Prussia alone will gain a great advantage in winning the sympathy of those affected, for these matters *quae numero et ponder dicunter* are more important to the majority of Germans than to you and me. Although I don't value uniformity in weights, measures, bills of exchange, and other gimcracks of that sort very highly and regard them as difficult to put into effect, we must still show goodwill and make some noise about it, but more through Prussia than the confederate diet."[56]

As Prussian envoy to the Bundestag Bismarck became deeply involved in the struggle over the renewal of the Zollverein and many other economic issues, such as the enactment of a German code of commercial law, railway construction, monetary policy, and postal affairs. Although he judged these issues primarily from the political standpoint, his involvement dictated a broader view of German capitalism than he had earlier displayed. In the diet he engaged Count Thun in a hot contest for public favor. Both posed as

[53] *GW*, X, 49; XIV, 302.
[54] *GW*, II, 137.
[55] *GW*, I, 17, 114; II, 321; VII, 24–25.
[56] *GW*, XIV, 223.

champions of the national welfare. By means of front organizations and a heavily subsidized press Bismarck's legation became an effective center for the dissemination of Prussian propaganda in central and southern Germany.[57] His experiences confirmed Bismarck's conviction that Prussia could easily outdistance Austria and the medium states in any conclusive struggle for popular opinion.[58]

For the time being, nevertheless, he sought the coercive power with which to break apart the opposing coalition in the combinations of European politics rather than in the movement for German national unity. But he continued to speculate on the potential utility of the latter for Prussia. During the Crimean crisis, as we have seen, he listed "a new cabinet oriented toward the left" as one of three alternative courses open to Prussia. In Frankfurt he experimented with the possible effect of such a change: "With the tone of one who has had nothing to do with it and is not pleased by the prospect I have described this to several of my colleagues as the probable development of Prussian policy. In every case my hearers became very agitated and upset about it. They fear such a possibility more than cholera and concede that Austria would be immediately outdistanced and forced into the defensive on the question of hegemony in Germany."[59] In his memorial of 1853 to Prince Wilhelm of Prussia, he stated his belief that "parliamentary liberalism" might be exploited as a "temporary means" with which to gain for the Hohenzollern monarchy a satisfactory solution of the German question.[60]

This shows how far the fear of revolution had receded in Bismarck's mind. He judged it possible for the king to appoint a liberal cabinet, use it to carry out a stroke in foreign affairs, and then dismiss it without jeopardizing his own authority. The "liberals" whom he had in mind, of course, were the moderates. From their actions in the revolution and their conduct at Gotha and Erfurt it was evident that they were not fundamentally antipathetic to authority and that their interest in national unity far outweighted their dedication to liberal principle. In November 1853 Bismarck wrote to Gerlach: "We are in the same position with regard to the Gothaer as were Louis XIII and XIV to the German Protestants; at home we have no use for them, but in the

---

[57] GW, I, 52ff., 63, 121, 246ff. Also Friedrich W. Lange, *Bismarck und die öffentliche Meinung Süddeutschlands während der Zollvereinskrise, 1850 bis 1853* (Giessen, 1922), and Arnold Oskar Meyer, *Bismarcks Kampf mit Österreich am Bundestag zu Frankfurt, 1851–1859* (Berlin, 1927), 355–356.

[58] GW, II, 239. Bismarck's appreciation of the value of popular support for foreign policy is also shown by his desire to encourage the Landtag to take a stand on the issues dividing Austria and Prussia. GW, I, 116; II, 299, 320–324; III, 70–71; XIV, 487, 544. He believed the overzealous harrying of democrats by Berlin police to be harmful to Prussia's foreign relations, but he advocated the suppression of journals that opposed or failed to support government policy. GW, I, 317, 515–516; XIV, 390.

[59] GW, I, 505–506.

[60] GW, I, 375.

small states they are the only elements that want anything to do with us."[61]
At the dawn of the age of classical diplomacy, Cardinal Richelieu had exploited the ideological force of Lutheran Protestantism in the interest of state against the Hapsburg monarchy. In its twilight Bismarck, the Prussian conservative, proposed to exploit the ideological force of German nationalism to a similar end.

During the 1850s Louis Napoleon provided a persuasive example. This latter-day Bonaparte possessed the qualities of both Machiavelli and Mazzini, a blend of realistic self-interest and crusading idealism. By promoting the cause of national self-determination in Europe he hoped to overturn the settlement of 1815 and open the way for French expansion. Through the elevation of France's power in Europe he expected to identify his regime with the French nation and win the favor of French nationalists. But he also curried favor with French Catholics by appeasing the Papacy and with French businessmen, laborers, and farmers by promoting their material interests. By gaining the support of all important interest groups in French society he hoped to perpetuate his dynasty.

While in Frankfurt Bismarck followed with keen interest what transpired beyond the Vosges. As always it is difficult to say how much he acquired from others. In later years he spoke of having learned from Napoleon's mistakes, but he said nothing about having profited from his successes.[62] It is more probable that what happened in France merely reinforced his own observations about the tactical possibilities inherent in the German political situation. Events had shown that nationalism was not necessarily hostile to authoritarian institutions. Far from being the inseparable companion of liberalism, it might easily be converted into an antiliberal force. The foreign policy of Napoleon demonstrated that the ideal of ethnic self-determination, when applied to the divided and submerged cultural nations of central and eastern Europe, was capable of supplying a vital élan and moral approbation to an aggressive foreign policy executed in the interest of state.[63]

---

[61] GW, XIV, 329.

[62] GW, IX, 90–94.

[63] Bismarck's "Bonapartism," much discussed by his contemporaries, has also been discussed in numerous essays and books in recent historical literature. If Napoleon III's policies and actions in the 1850s taught Bismarck something about the nature of politics, especially political tactics, he could hardly have been impressed by the emperor's course in the 1860s in either domestic (the liberal empire) or foreign affairs (the Mexican debacle, Austro-Prussian war, and Luxemburg crisis). The residual resemblances in their policies—those of Napoleon in the 1850s and Bismarck in the 1860s—are probably more attributable to similarities in their situations and possibilities than to any conscious emulation by Bismarck of a man whom he held in general contempt. Out of these perceived similarities Wehler, Stürmer, and others devised a model, which has not gained universal acceptance. See Hans-Ulrich Wehler, Das deutsche Kaiserreich, 1871–1918 (4th ed., Göttingen, 1980); Michael Stürmer, Regierung und Reichstag im Bismarckstaat: Cäsarismus oder Parlamentarismus (Düsseldorf, 1974); Lothar Gall, "Bismarck und der Bonapartismus,"

During the 1850s Bismarck came to appreciate the potential value of German nationalism for Prussian foreign policy because of its capacity to stir moral fervor and promote material progress. Not until later, after the Prussian constitutional conflict began, did he come to appreciate its potential value for the Hohenzollern monarchy in domestic affairs. In the beginning his purpose was not to weaken a domestic opposition by the theft of the national cause, but to find in the ideal of national unity a point of contact, as in 1848–1850, between the monarchy and the German liberal movement. Years later he reflected on what he had learned in his Frankfurt years: "In Europe's present situation, in the present state of civilization, it is impossible to undertake great political and perhaps warlike actions for secret reasons of cabinet diplomacy that may be unraveled later by historians. Now one can only conduct war out of national motives, from motives that are national to the degree that their compelling nature is recognized by the great majority of the population."[64]

Historische Zeitschrift, 223 (1976), 618–624; Elisabeth Fehrenbach, "Bonapartismus und Konservatismus in Bismarcks Politik," *Francia*, Sonderheft (1977); and Allan Mitchell, "Bonapartism as a Model for Bismarckian Politics," comments by Otto Pflanze, Claude Fohlen, and Michael Stürmer, *Journal of Modern History*, 49 (1977), 181–209; Otto Pflanze, "Bismarcks Herrschaftstechnik als Problem der gegenwärtigen Historiographie," *Historische Zeitschrift*, 234 (1982), 562–599.

[64] To the Reichstag, Apr. 22, 1869. GW, XI, 50.

❖❖❖❖❖❖❖❖❖❖❖❖❖❖❖❖❖❖❖❖❖❖❖❖❖❖❖❖❖❖❖❖❖❖❖❖❖❖❖

Petersburg and Paris

The New Era

N OCTOBER 1857, King Friedrich Wilhelm IV was incapacitated by a stroke. For a year Prince Wilhelm of Prussia, his brother and heir, acted as his deputy. When it became apparent that the king would not recover, the prince established a regency. In 1861 the ailing monarch died, and Wilhelm succeeded to the throne. In many respects the brothers contrasted sharply. Friedrich Wilhelm was a man of sensitivity and imagination, of keen artistic interest and understanding, prone in governmental affairs to impractical dreaming, sudden enthusiasms, and easy disillusionments. Until it became apparent that the king would be childless, Wilhelm had not expected to rule. Like most younger sons of the royal family, he received an entirely military education. In bearing and outlook he remained to the end a soldier—sober, realistic, and accustomed to command.[1]

On matters of principle the brothers were in basic agreement. Both were divine-right monarchists, firmly convinced that to rule was both a right and duty imposed by God. Friedrich Wilhelm had vague ideas about restoring the feudal *Ständestaat*, but Wilhelm adhered firmly to the absolutist tradition of his house. Friedrich Wilhelm often wanted to tear up the constitution, that "scrap of paper" he had granted in 1850. In a political testament he advised his heir to refuse the oath to uphold it on ascending the throne—the first step toward its revision. Although opposed in principle to a constitution of mixed powers, in which the monarch shared legislative power with an elected parliament, Wilhelm refused to cultivate unpopularity by beginning his reign with a coup against the constitution.[2]

During the 1850s the Prince Wilhelm had disapproved of the repressive chicanery of the Manteuffel regime. In this he was reinforced by his wife, Augusta, a Weimar princess with liberal views. From their residence in the Rhineland city of Koblenz the royal pair maintained contact with leaders of the "liberal-conservative" opposition in the Landtag's Chamber of Deputies. That opposition was composed of moderates of both liberal and conservative persuasion, popularly called the *Wochenblattspartei*, from the journal that expressed their views. Led by Moritz von Bethmann-Hollweg, their main objec-

---

[1] For a comparison of the two personalities see Herman von Petersdorff, *König Friedrich Wilhelm der Vierte* (Stuttgart, 1900), 1ff., and Erich Marcks, *Kaiser Wilhelm I* (9th ed., Berlin, 1943), 65ff.

[2] Petersdorff, *Friedrich Wilhelm IV*, 165ff.; Marcks, *Wilhelm I*, 127ff.; GW, XV, 132–133.

tive was to preserve the constitution of 1850 against reactionary attacks by ultraconservatives of the *Kreuzzeitungspartei*, who dominated court and cabinet in Berlin.[3]

The royal brothers were also in disagreement on foreign policy. Although critical of its constitution, Wilhelm had supported the Radowitz plan in 1850. Unlike the romantic conservatives, he considered the Olmütz capitulation a shameful defeat. He found it hard to forgive the tsar for siding with Austria in the crisis. During the Crimean War he favored cautious cooperation with Austria in order to avoid isolation; Bismarck's advice he dismissed as that of a "schoolboy." His interest in German unity was more positive and lasting than that of his brother. In May 1849 he wrote: "Whoever wishes to rule Germany, must conquer it. . . . Our whole history shows that Prussia is destined to lead Germany, but the question is when and how." During the 1850s he regarded "moral" rather than "physical" conquest as the "how" of Prussian policy. "Wise legislation" and "elements of unification like the Zollverein," rather than violence, were the proper course. He was firmly convinced of Prussia's right to parity in the confederation and fundamentally suspicious of Austria. As a soldier he deplored the inadequacy of Germany's military defenses. He came to power with the determination to reorganize both the Prussian and confederate armies. His aim was the division of confederate forces during wartime into two commands, Prussian and Austrian, operating on a common plan of campaign.[4]

His program for Germany required a fresh beginning in Prussia, a new regime with greater popular support. Hence one of Wilhelm's first acts on becoming regent was to dismiss Manteuffel. The new cabinet was drawn from the "liberal-conservative" opposition of the 1850s. Three of its members— Rudolf von Auerswald, Baron Erasmus Robert von Patow, and Count Maximilian von Schwerin—had served in the liberal government of 1848. The minister-president was Prince Karl Anton of Hohenzollern-Sigmaringen, Wilhelm's distant relative. At the Foreign Ministry was Alexander von Schleinitz, like Karl Anton and Auerswald a close friend of the regent and Augusta; at the Ministry of War Eduard von Bonin, who had been dismissed

---

[3] Siegfried Bahne, "Vor dem Konflikt: Die Altliberalen in der Regentschaftsperiode der 'Neuen Ära'," in Ulrich Engelhardt et al., ed., *Soziale Bewegung und politische Verfassung* (Stuttgart, 1976), 154–161; Walter Schmidt, *Die Partei Bethmann-Hollweg und die Reaktion in Preussen, 1850–58* (Berlin, 1910); Justus von Gruner, "Rückblick auf mein Leben," *Deutsche Revue*, vol. 26, no. 2 (1901), 180–193; Reinhard Müller, *Die Partei Bethmann-Hollweg und die orientalische Krise, 1853–1856* (Halle, 1926).

[4] Ernst Berner, ed., *Kaiser Wilhelms des Grossen Briefe, Reden, und Schriften* (Berlin, 1906), vol. 1, 203, 230–234, 269–275, 449, 479–482; Heinrich von Poschinger, ed., *Preussens auswärtige Politik 1850 bis 1858: Unveröffentlichte Dokumente aus dem Nachlasse des Ministerpräsidenten Otto Freiherrn von Manteuffel* (Berlin, 1902), vol. 1, 44–45, 72–73, 107–111; vol. 2, 349; Horst Kohl, ed., *Anhang zu den Gedanken und Erinnerungen von Otto Fürst von Bismarck* (Stuttgart, 1901), vol. 1, 47; APP, II/1, 266; Marcks, *Wilhelm I*, 98ff.

as "too constitutional" from the same post in 1854. From these ministers Wilhelm expected a new moral tone, obedience to the constitution, reforms of a moderate nature, but no fundamental changes and no sacrifice of royal authority. With brutal frankness Bismarck warned him that the new cabinet did not contain "a single individual of statesmanlike calibre."[5]

To shrewd observers the change did not appear very drastic. Instead of feudal conservatives, aristocratic whigs were now in power.[6] To the general public, however, any change from the previous regime was progress. Many believed that a fresh page had turned in Prussian and German history, and they dubbed it "the new era." Within months the cabinet received a resounding endorsement from the electorate. The chamber chosen in 1855 had contained 218 supporters of the government, opposed by 116 moderates or "conservative liberals" (as some dubbed themselves). In November 1858 the Manteuffel conservatives withered to 57, facing 263 backers of the new era. Members of the new majority were all too conscious that no act of theirs had brought about this change. Their watchword was: "Just don't press!" Whether of conservative or liberal inclination (the shadings of opinion were so spectral that such distinctions are dubious at best), they supported the constitutional system of mixed powers, and their main objective was parliamentary government but a harmonious and productive relationship with the ruler and his cabinet. Former radicals of 1848—Franz Benedikt Waldeck, Johann Jacoby, Hermann Schulze-Delitzsch, Hans Viktor von Unruh, and Johann von Rodbertus—took no active part in the election and even instructed their followers to vote for moderates. Although a few aspired to form an independent party of the extreme left, Waldeck refused to cooperate, and without him there was no chance. The radical tradition was nearly extinct.[7]

For the first time in Prussian constitutional history, monarch, cabinet, chamber, and people appeared united. From the unhorsed ultraconservatives

---

[5] GW, V, 141. Budberg, the Russian envoy, was of like opinion. APP I/1, 55. On the political complexion of the cabinet see Alexander Bergengrün, *Staatsminister August Freiherr von der Heydt* (Leipzig, 1908), 247ff.; Gruner, "Rückblick," 333ff.; Heinrich von Poschinger, ed., *Erinnerungen aus dem Leben von Hans Viktor von Unruh* (Stuttgart, 1895), 198–199; and Karl Heinz Börner, *Die Krise der preussischen Monarchie von 1858–1862* (Berlin, 1976), 39–54.

[6] See Sigmund Neumann, *Die Stufen des preussischen Konservatismus: Historische Studien*, vol. 190 (Berlin, 1930), 130ff.

[7] Bahne, "Vor dem Konflikt," 162–164; Börner, *Krise der preussischen Monarchie*, 49–50; Friedrich Thorwart, ed., *Hermann Schulze-Delitzschs Schriften und Reden* (Berlin, 1909–1913), vol. 4, 18–19; vol. 5, 133–134; Gerhard Eisfeld, *Die Entstehung der liberalen Parteien in Deutschland* (Hanover, 1969); Schmidt, *Partei Bethmann-Hollweg*, 219–245; Wilhelm Biermann, *Franz Leo Benedikt Waldeck: Ein Streiter für Freiheit und Recht* (Paderborn, 1928), 253–255, 290. On Waldeck see particularly Ludwig Dehio, "Benedict Waldeck," *Historische Zeitschrift*, 136 (1927), 25–57. The desire for parliamentary government on the English model appears so seldom in the literature of German liberalism as to be anomalous. For one such instance (qualified by "under certain circumstances") see the letter by Georg Vincke to Justus Gruner, Nov. 26, 1856, quoted by Bahne in "Vor dem Konflikt," 162.

of the *Kreuzzeitungspartei* came the only dissent. Without support from the crown they were powerless. And yet even before the election Wilhelm was already suspicious of the popular response his actions had aroused. "What have I done," he asked querulously, "to merit praise from that crowd?"[8]

The Booklet

In March 1858 Bismarck made an effort to influence the foreign policy of the coming regime in a memorial known as the *Booklet* because of its length.[9] He predicted that in the near future Austria would seek a decision in the struggle against Prussia. She would maneuver Berlin into the position of having to choose between violation of the confederate constitution and surrender of Prussian independence. Because Prussia must choose the former, this would expose her to a war of "execution" intended to end her resistance for all time. It is highly doubtful that Bismarck actually believed this an imminent possibility. But his exaggeration of Austria's intentions enabled him to give a sense of urgency to the question that followed: with what means could Prussia defend herself against such a development? The medium states, he believed, were the key to the situation. The effectiveness of Austrian policy in Germany depended upon their support; only by gaining control over them could Prussia recover the initiative. It was futile to try to win them by acts of friendship. They must be coerced.

In the *Booklet* there is no mention of the combinations of European politics that for five years had played the primary role in Bismarck's calculations on this point. He now took the view that the only suitable source of power with which to buttress Prussian foreign policy was the moral pressure of German public opinion. In contrast to their governments, the interests of most Germans outside Austria coincided with those of the Prussian state. In order to make this fact apparent, Berlin need only encourage the Prussian press and parliament to take a more active interest in questions of foreign policy. Bismarck had no doubt that the general symphony of public opinion would follow the score composed by the government. Outside Prussia the theme would be taken up by the press and legislatures of the lesser states. Before such a demonstration the other German governments must inevitably give way.

Whatever promoted the interest of Prussia, he declared, added to the welfare of the German nation. For Bismarck this was a new and significant argument. The first hint of it had appeared in a memorial to Manteuffel of May 1857. Here he accused the princes of the lesser states of being aware that their "exaggerated sovereignty" was an "evil for Germany." "They know very well

---

[8] Friedrich von Bernhardi, ed., *Aus dem Leben Theodor von Bernhardis* (Leipzig, 1893–1905), vol. 3, 156–157; Ernst II., Herzog von Sachsen-Coburg-Gotha, *Aus meinem Leben und aus meiner Zeit* (Berlin, 1887–1889), vol. 2, 393–394.

[9] GW, II, 302–322.

that Prussia's disunited situation is difficult enough in itself to bear and that the unnatural compulsion of the small intervening states to assert their independence has become a severe handicap for us and for German life and development." Arguing for rapprochement with France, he wrote, "Only outside Germany are the means available to consolidate our position in the interest of Germany itself."[10]

In the *Booklet*, however, Bismarck found these means *within* Germany, and hence his contention was all the more persuasive. The true promoter of the national welfare, he declared, was Prussia, not the confederation, whose majorities were "dependent upon non-German interests." As a "pure German state" Prussia's "needs and course of development" were "homogeneous with those of the rest of the German population." Prussia was the "natural crystallization point" for associations among German states to attain common objectives on customs regulations, commercial and exchange law, cartel conventions, railways, postal systems, banking, currency, and other similar matters. Whereas Austria and her German allies wished to make these affairs subject to confederate legislation, Prussia could outtrump them by attaining the same objectives outside the diet through agreements with neighboring states on the pattern of the Zollverein. "There is nothing more German than precisely the development of the particularistic interests of Prussia rightly interpreted."[11]

This argument had a discordant sound coming from the archreactionary of 1848 and even from the diplomatic realist of the 1850s. Since 1851 he had consistently derided those of his colleagues who appealed to the "German" interest. He had scornfully rejected the criticism that his filibustering in the diet had harmed Germany by preventing any united action on the part of the confederation. In Frankfurt and Vienna he had challenged his opponents to abandon the hypocritical phrases of German patriotism and negotiate realistically on the basis of self-interest. However inconsistent his arguments, Bismarck's purpose was undeviating. His aim was to expand the power of the Prussian state and he was willing to consider all possible means to that end. This was the narrow bridge leading across the chasm that had previously separated him from the German national cause.

By March 1858 Bismarck had conceived a revolutionary plan for Prussian expansion, the execution of which would one day startle Europe. He proposed that Prussia exploit the moral and material power of German nationalism in the interest of state, that a conservative monarchy deliberately employ the sentiment for national unity to reinforce its foreign policy at the cost of a conservative foe. For the time being, however, he had little success with his proposals. During the summer he conferred with Wilhelm in Baden-Baden,

---

[10] GW, II 217–223.
[11] GW, II, 317–322, also 370–371.

but apparently got nowhere. When the new cabinet took office in the fall, Wilhelm and Schleinitz decided on rapprochement with Austria and Britain. It was a popular decision in Prussia. Friendship with Britain was a basic tenet of liberal politics. But even conservatives (including Gerlach) approved because of their alarm over French and Russian "Caesarism."[12] Naturally this choice meant that the bellicose Junker from Schönhausen had to be recalled from Frankfurt. In March 1859 he traveled for seven days across drifted plains and frozen streams to his new post in St. Petersburg. With bitter irony he wrote of having been "put in cold storage on the Neva."[13]

Revival of the National Cause

Even as Bismarck's sleigh hissed across the hard-packed snow toward the Petersburg railhead, the course of European politics changed in his favor. At Plombières in July 1858 Napoleon had met with Count Cavour, the Sardinian prime minister, to plot the unification of Italy. At a reception on New Year's Day 1859, the emperor surprised the Austrian ambassador by saying, "I regret that our relations are not as good as I wished, but please report to Vienna that my personal feelings toward the Kaiser are unchanged."[14] On March 3 he prepared the way for war by securing the benevolent neutrality of Russia. But Buol precipitated the conflict by sending an ultimatum to Sardinia on April 23. Once more the forces of national revolution, quiescent since 1849, were set in motion. Like the sorcerer's apprentice, Napoleon summoned the spirits that ultimately overwhelmed him.

With remarkable prescience Bismarck had anticipated the new epoch and its potentialities for Prussia. From Petersburg he urged his government to seize the opportunity. "Ours will be the winning card in the present situation," he wrote to Gustav von Alvensleben, the regent's adjutant, "if we let Austria become deeply involved in the war with France and then burst out with our entire army to the southward, taking our boundary stakes in our knapsacks and planting them again on the Bodensee or where the Protestant faith ceases to predominate." The divided segments of the Prussian state must be united. Within twenty-four hours the incorporated peoples would fight for their new master, "especially if the prince regent will do them the favor of rebaptizing the kingdom of Prussia as the kingdom of Germany." This was the "safest

---

[12] APP, I/1, 52–54, 60–62, 67; Boris Nolde, *Die Petersburger Mission Bismarcks, 1859–1862: Russland und Europa zu Beginn der Regierung Alexander II* (Leipzig, 1936), 1–2; Christian Friese, *Russland und Preussen vom Krimkrieg bis zum polnischen Aufstand* (Berlin, 1931), 152ff.

[13] GW, XIV, 495. As usual, he blamed his political misfortune upon feminine intrigue, maintaining that his replacement's wife, Countess Usedom, hankered for the society and climate of Frankfurt. GW, XV, 135ff.

[14] Joseph A. von Hübner, *Neun Jahre der Erinnerungen eines österreichischen Botschafter in Paris unter dem zweiten Kaiserreich, 1851–1859* (Berlin, 1904), vol. 2, 150–151.

play" Prussia could make. If "too adventurous," Berlin should at least exploit the situation "either to change our relationship to the confederation or to release ourselves from it."[15] To Schleinitz he wrote that "Prussia would soon be able to construct better and more natural relations with her German neighbors," once the confederation were dissolved. "I would like to see the word 'German' instead of 'Prussian' inscribed on our banners only when we are more closely and more suitably united with our countrymen than previously; it loses some of its charm when used as it is now in connection with the confederate diet."[16]

But again Bismarck's counsel was ignored in Berlin. Like his brother in the Crimean War, Wilhelm was unable to arrive at a clear and decisive policy. Although sympathetic toward Austria, he deplored Buol's ultimatum, which cut short his own efforts to preserve peace. The revolutionary implications of Napoleon's attack alarmed him, but so did the national indignation in Germany against France. He wished neither to ally with Austria nor to exploit her distress for the expansion of Prussian power in Germany. After the Habsburg defeat at Magenta on June 4 he mobilized six army corps and proposed in London and Petersburg "armed mediation" to halt the struggle. In Vienna he demanded the right of command over the confederate contingents.[17]

Bismarck was outraged at the prospect that his government would "draw the Habsburg chestnuts out of the fire." Zealously he reported the threats of Alexander and Gorchakov that Russia would never permit France to go down to defeat under the weight of Austrian and Prussian arms; from the moment of Prussian entry into the conflict, Germany, rather than Italy, would be the main theater of war.[18] In the Russian capital he made no secret of his disagreement with the policy of Wilhelm and Schleinitz. Word of his disloyalty filtered back to Berlin. For a time Wilhelm considered either a reprimand or recall.[19]

But suddenly the fighting stopped. Shocked by the bloodshed, alarmed over the pace of Italian unification and uncertain of Prussian policy, Napoleon negotiated the peace of Villafranca. None of the major powers was satisfied

[15] Bismarck to Alvensleben, May 5, 1859. [Hans Goldschmidt, ed.], "Neue Briefe von und über Bismarck," Deutsche Allgemeine Zeitung, Mar. 14, 1937, Nr. 121–122, p. 1, 1. Beiblatt. Fragments of this letter were published in GW, XIV, 517, and Arnold Oskar Meyer, Bismarcks Kampf mit Österreich am Bundestag zu Frankfurt, 1851–1859 (Berlin, 1927), 480–481.

[16] GW, III, 38. See also III, 33–34, and Leopold von Gerlach, Denkwürdigkeiten (Berlin, 1891), vol. 2, 652.

[17] APP, I/1, 172–176, 274–284, 421–424, 467–468, 546–555, 646–647, 654–657, 749–756; Berner, Kaiser Wilhelm, vol. 1, 453–461, 497–501; Hans Kentmann, "Preussen und die Bundeshilfe an Österreich im Jahre 1859," Mitteilungen des Österreichischen Instituts für Geschichtsforschung, Ergänzungsband 12 (1933), 297–415.

[18] GW, III, 22–23, 33, 58, 61; VII, 40–41; XIV, 516, 519; Nolde, Petersburger Mission, 62ff.

[19] Johannes Schultze, ed., Kaiser Wilhelms I. Weimarer Briefe (Berlin, 1924), vol. 2, 15–16; Gruner, "Rückblick," 78; Nolde, Petersburger Mission, 67.

with the results: Austria lost a province; Prussia had antagonized all and gained nothing; Russia and France had some grounds for satisfaction, but both were soon alarmed at the speed with which Italian unification proceeded and the form it assumed. Sardinia devoured the chestnuts, while the rest came away with scorched fingers.

The appointment of the new-era cabinet and the French attack upon Austria produced startling changes in the whole political climate of Germany. Throughout the country the fall of the feudal party in Berlin was greeted with enthusiasm. Because Wilhelm and several of his ministers had supported Radowitz in 1850, those German nationalists who looked to Prussia for leadership were filled with fresh hope. It was chiefly the war of 1859, however, that aroused the question of German unity from a decade of uneasy slumber. Romantic conservatives and liberal nationalists alike were disturbed by the French attack upon a member of the confederation. In Italy the first Napoleon had begun the career of conquest that brought the borders of France to the Rhine. The crisis refreshed the memory of 1812–1813 and produced a demand for war. Over the course of the conflict there was general disappointment. The failure of Austria and Prussia to come to terms demonstrated again the incapacity of the German Confederation. Fresh rumors of an entente between France and Russia kindled the fear of a hostile coalition against which Germany had no adequate defense.[20]

These anxieties produced the demand for a German state capable of defending the nation against foreign attack. In turn this brought up the further question of the inclusion or exclusion of Austria. Once again the politically conscious public began to divide upon the issue of great- or small-German unification. The strength of the great-Germanists lay mostly in the south among farmers and rural noblemen, small town burghers, and politically active Catholics; the small-Germanists were strongest in Protestant Germany among members of the upper strata of the *Mittelstand*, especially businessmen in industry, commerce, and finance, professional people, and intellectuals (most notably, the popular historians). From the beginning the small-German movement attained the greater momentum. Its leaders dominated the Nationalverein founded in September 1859 to agitate for German unity. For the first time German liberals of many political viewpoints coalesced in a common organization that transcended their differences. Although many southern liberals remained aloof, the Nationalverein succeeded by virtue of the vagueness of its first platform in uniting moderates and democrats who

[20] On the development of German national sentiment see Heinrich Ritter von Srbik, *Deutsche Einheit: Idee und Wirklichkeit vom Heiligen Reich bis Königgrätz* (Munich, 1935–1942), vol. 2, 297ff., 377ff.; also Kurt von Raumer, "Das Jahr 1859 und die deutsche Einheitsbewegung in Bayern," in Herman Haupt, ed., *Quellen und Darstellungen zur Geschichte der Burschenschaft und der deutschen Einheitsbewegung* (Heidelberg, 1925), vol. 8, 273–327; and Annie Mittelstaedt, *Der Krieg von 1859: Bismarck und die öffentliche Meinung in Deutschland* (Stuttgart, 1904).

had split in 1848–1849 over the decision to invite Friedrich Wilhelm IV to become the constitutional monarch of a united Germany. The inclusion of former radicals produced internal tensions that lasted throughout the organization's history, but leadership remained in the hands of moderates and "realistic" democrats willing to accept the unification of Germany under a constitution preserving the autocratic authority of the Hohenzollern monarchy. At a second congress in 1860 they succeeded in establishing this as the association's program.[21]

The Nationalverein was not a mass movement, but an elite body of a few thousand members led by a Hanoverian nobleman, Rudolf von Bennigsen. To be sure, the journalists, deputies, professors, and other notables who belonged had a public influence greater than their actual number. Nevertheless, the membership was largely of the upper *Mittelstand* and intentionally so. Repeatedly the association refused to lower its dues to encourage workingmen to join.[22] The primary purpose of its founders was to put governments, not the masses, in motion. They did not intend to attack the ruling system, but to gain its cooperation for national ends. Their immediate hopes were placed on the new-era cabinet.

Bismarck, Schleinitz, and the Nationalverein

In July 1859 Bismarck returned to Germany in wretched health. A quack doctor in Petersburg had treated his rheumatic knee with a mustard plaster that ate into the flesh and destroyed a vein. An eminent Russian surgeon advised amputation. In Berlin he lay for two weeks in a hotel consulting other doctors and considering other cures. But even in this condition his mind was politically active. From the press he learned of the intent to form the Nationalverein and grasped immediately its significance for his plans. A chance contact gave him the opportunity to establish liaison between its leaders and the Prussian cabinet. One day Viktor von Unruh called upon him at the Hotel Royal.[23] An industrialist and leading liberal, Unruh had first met Bismarck in the United Diet. Although politically in strong disagreement, the two men

[21] See Srbik, *Deutsche Einheit*, vol. 3, 3ff., and Adolf Rapp, *Grossdeutsch-Kleindeutsch*, in *Der deutsche Staatsgedanke* (Munich, 1922); Hermann Oncken, *Rudolf von Bennigsen* (Stuttgart, 1910), vol. 1, 346ff., 435ff.; Paul Herrmann, *Die Entstehung des deutschen Nationalvereins und die Gründung seiner Wochenschrift* (Leipzig, 1932); Walter Grube, *Die Neue Ära und der Nationalverein: Ein Beitrag zur Geschichte Preussens und der Einheitsbewegung* (Marburg, 1933); Kurt Bachteler, *Die öffentliche Meinung in der italienischen Krise und die Anfänge des Nationalvereins in Württemberg 1859* (Tübingen, 1934).

[22] Hermann Oncken, "Der Nationalverein und die Anfänge der deutschen Arbeiterbewegung 1862–1863," *Archiv für die Geschichte des Sozialismus und der Arbeiterbewegung*, 2 (1912), 120–127.

[23] GW, XV, 158–159; Robert von Keudell, *Fürst und Fürstin Bismarck: Erinnerungen 1846–1872* (Berlin, 1901), 72.

held each other in high personal regard.[24] Unruh was completely unprepared for what he now heard. "Prussia is completely isolated," Bismarck told him. "There is but one ally for Prussia, if she knows how to win and handle them . . . the German people!" Laughing at Unruh's astonishment, he hastened to reassure him. "I am the same Junker of ten years ago, . . . but I would have no perception and no understanding if I could not recognize clearly the realities of the situation."[25]

The response to this parley was agreeable. On September 12, 1859, three days before the meeting in Frankfurt that created the Nationalverein, Unruh composed a letter to Bismarck. The leaders of the national revival, he declared, were waiting "with great suspense" to see how Prussia would react to their movement. Austria had already announced its vigorous opposition. By "energetic action in the national question" Prussia could win many hearts in Germany. But if Prussia failed to give forthright support, "we will not be able to do anything in Prussia's interest." Zeal for the national cause was their only motive. "We, including Herr von Bennigsen, would be sincerely pleased if you should be named minister of foreign affairs."[26] Bismarck received this note in Baden-Baden, whence he had been called to consult with the regent. While there, he discussed the liberal overture freely with Schleinitz. Returning to Berlin in late September, he again met with Unruh, who reported that the general mood of the Frankfurt meeting had been highly favorable to Prussia. "Rather the most severe Prussian military government than the misery of petty disunion," the democrat August Metz had cried out to great applause. Years later Unruh admitted that on this occasion he had discussed with Bismarck the possibility of a "temporary military despotism," insisting he had meant the dictatorship of a revolutionary government, not that of a legitimate monarchy.[27] But at the time Bismarck understood otherwise.

Schleinitz found Unruh's information "noteworthy—gratifying." Nevertheless, he was suspicious of popular forces and sought to steer a middle course, neither hostile toward nor allied with the national movement. Although sympathetic to the cause of national unity, he had too great a respect

[24] Unruh had been the last speaker of the Prussian national assembly before its dissolution in December 1848. During 1856 Bismarck had tried to protect him from persecution by the Manteuffel regime. GW, XIV, 560; Unruh, Erinnerungen, 194ff.

[25] GW, VII, 37–39. The date of this interview is uncertain. Unruh's account was written sometime after the event and the circumstances he describes do not fully correspond with any of Bismarck's visits in Berlin during this period. Willy Andreas dated it "mid-March." Ibid. Erich Eyck accepted this view. Bismarck: Leben und Werk (Zurich, 1941–1944), vol. 1, 296. But Egmont Zechlin chose Sept. 24. Bismarck und die Grundlegung der deutschen Grossmacht (Stuttgart, 1930), 155. Boris Nolde appears to have picked the more likely time, the latter half of July. Petersburger Mission, 204.

[26] Horst Kohl, ed., Bismarck-Jahrbuch, 4 (1897), 154–157.

[27] Unruh, Erinnerungen, 209ff.; GW, III, 64; VII, 129; XIII, 155.

for law and legitimacy to follow a revolutionary policy.[28] He was a man of suavity and charm, but lacking in energy and decision. Even the supporters of the new-era cabinet complained of his "vacillating weakness, his way of saying nothing in his dispatches that he does not retract in the next sentence, this constant 'to be sure—but—yet—indeed—nevertheless.' "[29] So great was his fear of France that he wished to accept an Austrian offer of alliance. But his colleagues in the cabinet were inclined toward a national policy in opposition to Vienna.[30] In March 1860 Karl Anton and Auerswald persuaded the regent to look for another foreign minister. Bismarck was an obvious candidate.[31]

By chance he was still in Germany. During the winter he had lain desperately ill of pneumonia and rheumatic fever on a friend's estate in Pomerania— by his diagnosis "an explosion of all the anger I accumulated during eight years in Frankfurt." Indeed his host at the time, Alexander von Below-Hohendorf, concluded that Bismarck's problem was more psychological than physical. The best medicine, Below thought, was biblical: "Love thine enemies!" But that was advice the patient showed no disposition to follow.[32] By March Bismarck had recovered sufficiently to return to Berlin at the height of the crisis over Schleinitz. The ubiquitous Theodor von Bernhardi wrote in his diary on the twenty-ninth that Bismarck was "seeking contact with the liberals and telling everyone willing to listen that he has been misunderstood, even slandered, and that he is actually a man of liberal outlook."[33]

Early in April 1860 the regent summoned Bismarck and Schleinitz to present their opposing views. As usual the former argued for the revision of Prussian policy toward Austria and for rapprochement with Russia. Apparently he made no mention of his desire for close relations with France. But he did present his case for drastic revision of the confederation and creation of a German parliament. Schleinitz, on the other hand, maintained that France, rather than Austria, was Prussia's foremost foe. Solidarity with Austria against this hazard was the traditional policy of the Hohenzollern monarchy. In view

[28] L. Raschdau, ed., *Bismarcks Briefwechsel mit dem Minister von Schleinitz, 1858–1861* (Stuttgart, 1905), 47; Kohl, ed., *Anhang*, vol. 2, 304; Grube, *Neue Ära und Nationalverein*, 36ff. Certainly he was not encouraged by Bismarck's disclosure of Unruh's desire to see Bismarck as foreign minister. Unruh, *Erinnerungen*, 209.

[29] Heinrich von Sybel quoted in Bernhardi, *Aus den Leben*, vol. 3, 313. See also APP, II/1, xi.

[30] APP, II/1, 63–64, 80–83, 259–266; Rudolf Haym, *Das Leben Max Dunckers* (Berlin, 1891), 211ff.; GW, XIV, 545.

[31] GW, XV, 161ff.

[32] GW, III, 67; Alexander von Below-Hohendorf to Moritz von Blanckenburg, Dec. 7, 1859. "Neue Briefe von und über Bismarck," *Deutsche Allgemeine Zeitung*, July 9, 1937, Nr. 312–313, Beiblatt.

[33] Bernhardi, *Aus dem Leben*, vol. 3, 305, also 309. In the Landtag Bismarck heard an old enemy, Georg von Vincke, praise him for opposing Austrian hegemony in Germany. There were even rumors of a coming Vincke–Bismarck cabinet. Eyck, *Bismarck*, vol. 1, 350.

of a possible Franco-Russian combination, the danger from across the Rhine was more acute than ever. Popular opinion was opposed to alliance with Russia.[34]

Immediately after Schleinitz ended his presentation the regent declared that he would make no change in the Foreign Ministry. Bismarck concluded that Wilhelm had staged the conference merely to appease Karl Anton and Auerswald. Yet for many weeks the regent refused Bismarck's request for permission to return to Petersburg. Apparently he was still uncertain what use to make of this talented, volatile man. In June the order finally came; Bismarck returned to the Neva for another winter. The Hohenzoller, said Karl Anton, had declined to "give billy goat the job of gardener."[35]

Bismarck in Isolation

Wilhelm's decision had indeed already been made. In a crown council on March 26 he had listened to the conflicting views within the cabinet and afterward composed for Schleinitz a directive dictating a policy of rapprochement, though not alliance, with Austria against France.[36] Despite his weakening confidence in Schleinitz, there appeared to be no other choice. Recent events had made Bismarck a highly dubious choice as foreign minister. At the moment Europe appeared on the verge of a fundamental readjustment in power relationships that would end the chaos produced by the Crimean War. This readjustment threatened Bismarck's plans and, even worse, his career.

In May 1859 the rash Buol, architect of disaster, had been replaced at Vienna by Count Johann von Rechberg, Bismarck's old opponent at Frankfurt, a disciple of Metternich and advocate of the Holy Alliance. At the Quai d'Orsay Count Alexandre Walewski, conservative and Russophile, lost his position as foreign minister in January 1860 to Édouard Thouvenel, radical and Russophobe. During the same month came the first reports of Napoleon's intention to annex Nice and Savoy; in March he claimed them as his reward for permitting the unification of central Italy under Sardinia. In the tense atmosphere created by the recent war this event was interpreted as the beginning of a new era of Bonapartist expansion. His next target was expected to

---

[34] GW, XV, 161–162; VII, 113. The date of this conference is uncertain. On Mar. 26 the ministers debated the issue in a crown council, and Wilhelm made his decision for a middle course. On Apr. 5 Schleinitz presented his resignation, which was refused. APP, II/1, 282–285. On Apr. 10 Bismarck wrote that, if there actually had been a crisis over the position of foreign minister "ten days ago," it was "now" over, although the question of policy was still unsettled. Eight days earlier the regent had granted him permission to return to Petersburg, but his pass had not arrived. GW, XIV, 545. The press reported Bismarck's presence in the palace on Apr. 3 and 11. Horst Kohl, ed., Fürst Bismarck: Regesten zu einer wissenschaftlichen Biographie des ersten Reichskanzlers (Stuttgart, 1891–1892), vol. 1, 166.

[35] Haym, Duncker, 213.

[36] APP, II/1, 259–266, 282–285.

be the "natural frontier" of the Rhine. From the Thames to the Neva a wave of anxiety swept Europe. Lord Palmerston and the British cabinet lost what remained of their faith in Napoleon. Tsar Alexander and his advisers were shocked by the consequences of their bargain in the preceding year. The cost of revenge against Austrian perfidy was high. In Rumania, Hungary, and Poland the cause of national self-determination made new progress. During May came the dramatic landing of Garibaldi in Sicily followed by the collapse of the Neapolitan kingdom. The specter of revolution hovered over Europe. In July Wilhelm and Franz Joseph met at Teplitz and in October they assembled at Warsaw with Alexander. The Holy Alliance appeared close to its day of resurrection.[37]

These developments placed Bismarck in a difficult situation. In recent years he had made no secret of his disagreement with the anti-French policy of his government. Naturally his views were distorted. Among liberals and conservatives alike he was reputed to be a "Bonapartist," the unprincipled advocate of alliance with Napoleon whatever the cost. As he neared the vortex of power these rumors circulated with increased velocity.[38]

In May 1860 he sought to counteract this "nonsense" among ultraconservatives by explaining his point once more to Leopold Gerlach. Formerly the two men had differed on both policy and principle, but now they disagreed on principle alone. "Fundamentally," wrote Bismarck, "you want nothing to do with Bonaparte and Cavour; I do not want to go with France and Sardinia—not because I hold it to be morally wrong, but because I consider it harmful to the interest of our security." It was a matter of "complete indifference" who ruled France. Considerations of law, justice, and legitimacy could never be used as criteria for foreign relations; the one and only consideration was "political utility." "I am a child of other times than yours, but just as true to mine as you to yours." "To me France would be the most dubious of all allies, although I must hold open the possibility of such an alliance, because one cannot play chess if 16 out of 64 squares are excluded from the game."[39]

[37] Werner E. Mosse, *The European Powers and the German Question, 1848–1871* (Cambridge, Eng., 1958), 87ff.; Nolde, *Petersburger Mission*, 135ff.

[38] Leopold Gerlach, *Denkwürdigkeiten*, vol. 2, 718–719; Haym, *Duncker*, 213; Bernhardi, *Aus dem Leben*, vol. 3, 328–329, 337–339; vol. 4, 14, 32, 294, 306.

[39] GW, XIV, 548–549; also VII, 39. To his old friend Moritz Blanckenburg he was blunter. "Russia concedes little to us, England nothing, but Austria and the ultramontanes are worse for us than the French. France will often be our enemy out of insolence and lack of restraint but it can at least live without fighting us. But Austria and her allies (*Reichensperger*) can only flourish on a field where Prussia has been plowed under as fertilizer. To cling to the slavic-romanic mixed state on the Danube and to whore with Pope and Kaiser is just as treasonable against Prussia and the Lutheran faith, indeed against Germany, as the most vile and bald Rhenish confederation. The most we can lose to France is provinces and that only temporarily; to Austria, the whole of Prussia and for all time." Bismarck to Moritz von Blanckenburg, Feb. 12, 1860. "Neue Briefe von und über Bismarck," *Deutsche Allgemeine Zeitung*, July 9, 1937, Nr. 312–313, Beiblatt.

After returning to Petersburg, Bismarck came under sharp attack in the nationalist press. Since September 1859, the leaders of the Nationalverein had given up the idea of cooperating with the Hohenzollern monarchy. They were disappointed by the flabby policy of Schleinitz and had lost confidence in Bismarck, the agent through whom they had hoped to consummate the union. His reputed willingness to sacrifice German soil to Napoleon made the latter a convenient target.[40] In the conservative press no voice was raised in his defense. Bismarck felt betrayed by these men with whom he had so often "eaten from the same bowl." "One ought not to rely upon people," he commented bitterly. "I am thankful for every impulse that draws me within myself."[41]

The man from Schönhausen was isolated. His views on foreign policy had alienated his old friends among the Prussian conservatives, but had failed as yet to gain him the support of German liberals. He fought back by directing an old associate in Frankfurt, Carl Zitelmann, to show trusted journalists certain documents that would refute the accusations made against him. Furthermore, he asked Zitelmann to seek out Unruh. "Perhaps he can explain to you why the Nationalverein attacks me despite the fact that for nine years I have steered against wind and weather a course that, although for conservative aims and purposes, was nevertheless parallel to theirs."[42] But still the attacks continued.

The greatest hazard to Bismarck's future, however, was that the charges might be believed by those close to the regent. In desperation he requested of Gorchakov an official Russian denial that the Prussian envoy had ever proposed a three-power alliance against Austria involving the cession of German soil. But the vice-chancellor refused: *Qui s'excuse, s'accuse.*[43] Next Bismarck wrote to Auerswald: "Since 1856, I have characterized the alliance of France and Russia in my official reports to his majesty, the king, as an eventuality whose realization we must hinder with all our resources, because our position, as a member of such an alliance, will be a subordinate one and, as an opponent, a weak one." Because of the friction between Austria and Prussia, nevertheless, the German Confederation was not a viable institution for the defense of Germany in a dangerous war: "If, in spite of all our efforts, a Franco-Russian alliance cannot be prevented, we must in good time either

[40] Oncken, *Bennigsen*, vol. 1, 341ff., 364ff., 377–378, 521–522; Otto Westphal, *Welt- und Staatsauffassung des deutschen Liberalismus: Historische Bibliothek*, vol. 41 (Munich, 1919), 141ff. Typical was a pamphlet by Karl Twesten which asserted, as though it were a matter of general knowledge, that the Junker envoy had sought during his stay in Germany in 1860 to bring about an alliance with France and Russia at the cost of German soil. *Was uns noch retten kann: Ein Wort ohne Umschweife* (Berlin, 1861), 47.

[41] GW, XIV, 561–562.

[42] GW, XIV, 560.

[43] GW, III, 100–101.

ally ourselves closer with Russia than with France or come to such a fundamental understanding with Austria that we can count on an honorable collaboration between the two powers and thereby upon an inner strengthening
of the Austrian monarchy. I have always had the courage of my convictions,
and, if I considered advantageous the furtherance of the Franco-Russian alliance and our union with the same, I would openly say so." In the existing
situation the promotion of such an idea would be "proof of inconsequence
and lack of judgment." He feared that such rumors would reflect upon the
"soundness of my political understanding." "If I have desired an alliance in
recent years, it has been one with England and Russia, but this is easier to
talk about than bring about."

Auerswald should know, he maintained, from their conversations of the
previous spring "that I am neither Austrian, nor French, nor Russian, but
Prussian, and that I see our welfare only in trust in our own strength and that
of the German national movement."[44] In a letter to Below-Hohendorf he
reiterated this point. "During the entire period of my visit in Germany," he
wrote, "I never advised anything else but reliance upon our own strength and,
in event of war, upon that evoked by us from the German nation."[45]

A Revision in Strategy

From his defense of 1860 against the attacks of the Nationalverein and ultraconservatives it is evident that Bismarck's views had undergone a considerable change since 1857. The shift was one of strategy rather than conviction.
As before, his basic aim was to further the interests of Prussia. He was not a
convert to the cause of German nationalism, but he had come to appreciate
its potential utility for the expansion of Prussian power. This was now, in fact,
the primary force with which he hoped to coerce Austria and the lesser states
into granting the Prussian demands. No longer did he count upon a Franco-
Russian alliance to achieve this end. He conveniently forgot that in 1856 he
had wanted to jump "with both feet" into such an alliance. Now he even
maintained that this coalition must be prevented if at all possible. What were
the reasons for this revision?

Since the Crimean War, events had shown that, despite its apparent logic,
grave obstacles stood in the path of a Franco-Russian alliance. To be sure,
neither of the powers could succeed in its major objectives without support

[44] GW, XIV, 558–560. In November he again wrote Auerswald, "In the long run we have
actually but one reliable support, the national strength of the German people (if we do not
intentionally reject it). This will be true as long as they see the Prussian army as their defender
and their hope for the future and do not see us conducting wars for the benefit of other dynasties
than the Hohenzollern." GW, XIV, 564–565.

[45] GW, XIV, 561–562. Concerning Bismarck's influence on Below see Ernst Ludwig von Gerlach, Aufzeichnungen aus seinem Leben und Wirken, 1795–1877 (Schwerin, 1903), vol. 2, 233.

from the other: France in the revision of the settlement of 1815 and Russia in the revision of that of 1856. Without Russia's benevolent neutrality Napoleon would have hesitated to move against Austria in 1859 and without French assistance Russia had little chance of liquidating the restrictions placed on her sovereignty in the Black Sea. Yet Napoleon was reluctant to part company with London; he feared British sea power, for which Russia could supply no substitute. Furthermore, Tsar Alexander was much too conservative to relish entering into a genuinely revolutionary compact with Napoleon. After the annexation of Nice and Savoy he became increasingly cool to the idea.[46] But Gorchakov was incorrigible. Even in the midst of the conservative rapprochement of 1860 he continued to hold out an arm to Paris, eager for the most feeble handshake.[47]

In Petersburg, Bismarck had the chance to study at close hand the mind and character of the Russian vice-chancellor. Superficially brilliant, fluent of thought and adept at phrases, he was more political technician than statesman. Bismarck recognized that France offered the only possible "maneuver terrain" for Russian policy. Nevertheless, after observing for some time the prince's "repetitive game of advance and withdrawal" he began to doubt its seriousness. Russia was absorbed in internal problems and could give little time or energy to foreign affairs. For reasons of prestige Gorchakov maintained the appearance of an active policy, but it was "basically just a sham fight having neither aim nor result, a gymnastic performance executed with elegance and distinction by this brilliantly capable artist and then repeated."[48]

It was never Bismarck's way to cling to outworn possibilities. When the alliance failed to develop, he ceased to base his plans upon it. But he was probably honest in disclaiming any desire for such a coalition. As his letter to Auerswald shows, he now fully appreciated its dangers for Prussia. During recent years Napoleon's policies had shown a general shiftiness that inspired caution. "It is Napoleon's great talent," Bismarck wrote Schleinitz, "to conceal himself in a cloud of vapor in such a way that no one knows where or whether he will emerge. Perhaps he will remain within and steam leisurely

---

[46] The desire for alliance with France and Prussia, which Alexander expressed to Bismarck in June 1860, was based on the belief that the two conservative powers might in this way keep a close rein on Napoleon. A few days later Bismarck reported evidence of Alexander's growing antipathy against France. Ludwig Raschdau, ed., *Die politischen Berichte des Fürsten Bismarck aus Petersburg und Paris, 1859–1862* (Berlin, 1920), vol. 1, 115–116, 128–129.

[47] On the general problem of rapprochement between Paris and Petersburg see Ernst Schüle, *Russland und Frankreich vom Ausgang des Krimkrieges bis zum italienischen Krieg 1856–1859: Osteuropäische Forschungen*, Neue Folge, vol. 19 (Königsberg, 1935), 141–149; Friese, *Russland und Preussen*, 13ff., 88ff., 124ff.; Mosse, *European Powers*, 87–93; also Alfred Stern, "Ein russischfranzösischer Bündnisplan 1858," *Europäische Gespräche*, 9 (1931), 30–39.

[48] GW, III, 305; also 390; Friedrich Frahm, *Bismarcks Stellung zu Frankreich bis zum 4. Juli 1866* (Kiel, 1911), 50ff. On Gorchakov see Nolde, *Petersburger Mission*, 25ff., and François CharlesRoux, *Alexandre II, Gortchakoff, et Napoléon III* (Paris, 1913), 115–116.

away ad infinitum." His hidden ambitions and slippery character made the gray-eyed man in the Tuileries indeed a "dubious" ally.[49]

Nevertheless, it would be false to assume that France and Russia had ceased to play important roles in the system of pressures by which Bismarck hoped to gain his ends in Germany. On the contrary, he continued to argue that Prussia must constantly dangle the possibility of alliance with France before the eyes of Austria and the medium states. In 1860–1861 he did his best to soften the suspicions of Schleinitz and Wilhelm that Napoleon would attempt to annex the Rhineland as he had Nice and Savoy. The emperor was well aware, Bismarck maintained, that such a move would seriously upset the European balance and bring into existence a countercoalition similar to that which had defeated his uncle. Furthermore, he would be inclined to attempt it only if assured of the active cooperation of the German medium states. In order to prevent this, Prussia need only preserve a more intimate relationship than the medium states with France. The function of a Franco-Prussian rapprochement in Bismarck's altered strategy was to isolate Austria and the medium states, not to prepare a military alliance against them.[50]

His purpose in promoting good relations with Russia was similar. In Petersburg he worked constantly and with success to ingratiate himself with Gorchakov and the royal family.[51] His reports to Berlin left out what might harm and emphasized what might improve relations between the two powers. Nevertheless, it is grotesque to maintain that the contact with Russia, which proved so useful in future years, was entirely of his manufacture.[52] Its foundation had been laid in the Crimean War and in the close family tie between the Romanovs and Hohenzollerns (Alexander's mother was Wilhelm's sister). The failure of Gorchakov's French policy and of the attempt to renew the Holy Alliance left Russia no other potential ally than Prussia. After the Warsaw conference in October 1860 the fear of revolution receded and Austro-Russian rivalry in the Balkans increased. It was apparent, nevertheless, that Russian policy had entered a dormant stage. By 1861 Bismarck had little to report from Petersburg other than domestic conditions.[53] The most that could

[49] GW, III, 207; XIV, 549; VII, 39. To Bernstorff in Jan. 1862 he wrote, "France and Austria are, each in their own way, destined as a rule to be opponents of Prussia, not through the arbitrary will of their momentary rulers, but by the weight of enduring historical circumstances." GW, III, 315.

[50] GW, III, 69–70, 220, 251, 289–290; also I, 505.

[51] GW, III, 291; Friese, Russland und Preussen, 238–239; Gerhard Heinze, Bismarck und Russland bis zur Reichsgründung (Würzburg, 1939), 25–26. Long before arriving in Petersburg he was known to the tsar as a "useful and very devoted friend." F. de Martens, Recueil des traités et conventions conclus par la Russie avec les puissances étrangères (St. Petersburg, 1874–1909), vol. 8, 453.

[52] Mosse, European Powers, 93–101.

[53] GW, III, 174, 305, 327; Friese, Russland und Preussen, 247–248.

be expected of Russia in any future clash with Austria was benevolent neutrality.

Great Britain had also been drawn into his scheme. Previously he had discounted altogether the importance of London for Prussian policy. In 1857 he had told Leopold Gerlach that Britain could never be regarded as a reliable ally. The Reform Act had placed her foreign policy at the mercy of shifting majorities in parliament. His purpose at the time, however, was to dissuade Manteuffel and the king from ever joining Britain and Austria to counteract a Franco-Russian alliance. Even then he recognized that Britain was Prussia's "unnatural enemy." Their interests were not in conflict; only the momentary combinations of European politics threatened to force the two countries into opposed camps. When the danger of an Austro-British coalition passed, the "unnatural enemy" became a "natural ally."[54]

Nevertheless, Bismarck's statement to Auerswald concerning his desire for alliance with Britain and Russia must be treated with caution. The government of the new era was partial toward London. Britain had long been the mecca of German liberal opinion. During and after the Crimean War, Wilhelm had favored a pro-British policy. Albert, the prince consort, had been his friend and adviser. By adding Britain to his list of Prussia's potential allies, Bismarck brought his own policy, with no sacrifice to its essential purpose, a little nearer to the dominant current in the Prussian court.[55] As he indicated to Auerswald, however, a union between Britain and Russia was most improbable. Throughout the nineteenth century the interests of these two powers were in conflict from the Balkans to India; no other cleavage among European powers was more difficult to bridge.[56]

Even if attainable, an alliance with Britain and Russia could never have performed the function that Bismarck had originally expected of a coalition with France and Russia. Russia had to be discounted for reasons already analyzed, and Britain was not a land power capable of effective military assistance against Austria. Throughout the century London had steadily avoided entanglement in continental struggles in which she had no direct, tangible interest; only a French attack upon the Rhineland or a renewal of the Russian drive toward the Mediterranean would have created such a situation. Bismarck's purpose in promoting an understanding with Britain and Russia was, there-

[54] GW, XIV, 436, 440, 468.

[55] Lord Bloomfield, British ambassador in Berlin, believed Bismarck's motive was to ingratiate himself with Prince Wilhelm. Veit Valentin, "Bismarck and England in the Earlier Period of His Career," *Transactions of the Royal Historical Society*, 4th series, 20 (London, 1937), 28.

[56] He recognized that Gorchakov's interest in such a combination was insincere. Its purpose was to disrupt the Anglo-French entente and force France to seek an understanding with Russia. GW, III, 158; Friese, *Russland und Preussen*, 240. For Bismarck's efforts to improve relations with Russia and Britain see GW, III, 30–33, 156–158, 247, 264, 315; Raschdau, *Berichte aus Petersburg und Paris*, vol. 1, 74, also 96–97.

fore, to isolate Austria rather than create a dynamic alliance for her military coercion.[57]

In 1860 yet another piece was added to Bismarck's diplomatic chessboard. To Schleinitz he described the enlarged Sardinia as "our natural ally against France, if the occasion should arise, as well as against Austria. The French alliance would cease to be dangerous and dictatorial for Turin if she could gain support from Prussia."[58] After Napoleon's incorporation of Nice and Savoy he shifted his policy, though not his principle. In the letter of May 1860 to Leopold Gerlach, already quoted, he wrote, "In my opinion this is not the time to stiffen Sardinia's back against France; the moment is either behind or ahead of us. I believe the prospect remote in view of the personal situation at home, but I do not consider it impermissible."[59] The "personal situation" was the attitude of the regent, who was shocked by the overturning of so many thrones and sovereignties in Italy and alarmed at the apparent inclination of Napoleon to round out France's frontiers to their "natural boundaries."

European legitimists were angered even more when the house of Savoy continued to spread its rule over the rest of Italy (except for Rome and Venice). Tsar Alexander was especially outraged by the conquest of Naples in which his dynasty had a long-standing interest. Through Bismarck, Gorchakov sought to persuade the regent, who was both indignant and undecided, to join Russia in severing relations with Turin.[60] In Berlin the *Kreuzzeitung* faction agitated for the same cause. On this subject Bismarck was a poor intermediary. He used the opportunity to explain to Schleinitz how greatly his own views now differed from those of the *Kreuzzeitung*.[61] "Our sword of justice cannot reach over the whole world." The only objective of Prussian policy must be the "consolidation" of Prussia's interests. "Although I can be wrong, I am convinced that the creation of a strong Italian state in the south between France and Austria is beneficial to Prussia"—beneficial abroad, because the creation of a potential ally would add to Prussian security, and beneficial at home, because a friendly policy toward Italian national unity would make a favorable impression upon German liberal nationalists. During 1861 Bismarck urged his government to recognize the new state. "In my opinion we would have had to invent the kingdom of Italy, had it not come into existence on its own."[62]

Italy was a useful pawn. As long as Venice lay in Austrian hands, the new

[57] Heinze, *Bismarck und Russland*, 16.

[58] GW, III, 70.

[59] GW, XIV, 549.

[60] GW, III, 115, 118; APP, III/1, 653–655, 663–669. Cavour countered conservative protests with the argument that in supporting Garibaldi he had saved the monarchical principle in Italy by stealing the national cause from the republicans! APP, III/1, 683–685.

[61] Nolde, *Petersburger Mission*, 127–128, 135ff., 148ff.

[62] GW, III, 147–148, 179, 314, 319.

state would inevitably be found in the ranks of Habsburg foes. In peace or war, Italy could be used to exert pressure on Austria's southern flank, weakening her resistance to Prussia in the north. Nevertheless, this "natural ally" had only limited value for Prussia. Italy's diplomatic and military strength was not great, and geography decreed that she would be of little use in the diplomatic struggle for hegemony over the German medium states.

A German Parliament

It is now apparent that in Bismarck's strategic plan the Franco-Russian coalition had been replaced by the movement for German national unity.[63] The function expected of the latter was that previously assigned the former: to supply a means of pressure with which to gain the initiative in the struggle against Austria and the medium states. This vital substitution was made possible and in some degree dictated by the changing conditions of Prussian and European politics. But Bismarck also saw that an alliance with German nationalism had none of the drawbacks of a coalition with France and Russia. Having lost their revolution, the German liberals were a controllable ally. In this combination the Hohenzollern monarchy had the best chance of remaining the dominant partner.

But how was the national movement to be mobilized against Austria and her German allies? As early as 1858, at the time of the composition of the *Booklet*, Bismarck believed that this could best be done by raising the demand for a German parliament. The proposal appears for the first time in a letter of that year to Below-Hohendorf. In it Bismarck foresaw that in 1865, when the customs treaties were to expire, Prussia might be forced to dissolve the Zollverein and begin anew. It would then be necessary "to adopt one of the features of the union project of 1849 by establishing a kind of customs parliament with provision for *itio in partes*, if the others demand it." Such an institution would give to the German taxpayer a way in which to counteract the particularistic economic policies of the lesser states. Through this channel the most important economic interests of the nation could be brought to the support of Prussian policy in Germany. Congruent interests made them obvious allies.[64]

Two years later he raised this proposal again in a memorial addressed to Schleinitz. The chief issue of the moment was again that of Hesse-Kassel. Backed by Austria and the majority in the confederate diet, the elector had once more attempted to subvert the liberal constitution of his principality. Although Schleinitz was inclined to give way, Bismarck argued that Prussia

---

[63] Zechlin took a similar view, but saw the accompanying motives in a somewhat different light. *Grundlegung*, 157–158.

[64] GW, XIV, 486–487. For Below's letter see Kohl, ed., *Jahrbuch*, vol. 3, 127–129.

should seize the opportunity to subvert the German Confederation. At the minister's request he drafted a Prussian declaration that roundly condemned the diet for interfering in the domestic affairs of its members. The confederation was incapable, it declared, of realizing the national aspirations of the German people. The common feeling of national unity was the "only cement that can make the confederate contract into something more than an ordinary treaty of state between neighboring sovereigns." In an accompanying note to Schleinitz he proposed that the declaration also include the call for a "representative assembly in the confederation."[65] It was the most radical statement yet to come from Bismarck's pen. As he anticipated, Schleinitz made no use of it.

In the summer of 1861 the opportunity came to advance his plan once again under more favorable circumstances. A year had passed since Wilhelm had made his choice between Bismarck and Schleinitz. The latter had been generally unsuccessful in his attempt at alliance with Britain and Austria. Lord Russell, the British foreign secretary, had shied away from any policy that might force France to combine with Russia. In the autumn, the British press raised a clamor over the alleged mistreatment of a traveler named Mac-Donald arrested by the Prussian police. During the winter the British public reacted critically to news of the growing conflict in Berlin between king and parliament. The climate of opinion, once seemingly favorable to such an alliance, appeared to be growing cold.[66]

Schleinitz's policy toward Austria had been equally calamitous. The rapprochement begun so hopefully at Teplitz in July 1860 collapsed when the attempt was made to negotiate concrete terms. No more than in 1859 were the Austrians willing to concede either the dual division of command over confederate forces during wartime or the Prussianization of the lesser contingents through their adoption of the Prussian military system. Wilhelm was gravely disappointed. In this mood he was open to suggestions for a Prussian diplomatic offensive in the German question.[67]

Since 1859 it had become more and more difficult for German rulers to ignore the issue of German national unity. Among professional groups (lawyers, historians, physicians, theologians, schoolteachers, and book dealers) it had become common to hold national conventions with political overtones. Even more significant were the ever-larger national festivals of choral, hunting, and gymnastic societies. Their meetings sparkled with nationalistic oratory, their banquets with patriotic toasts. On Bastille Day 1861, a fanatic named Becker fired several shots at Wilhelm in Baden-Baden because he had not "done enough for German unity." All that the Hohenzoller suffered was

[65] GW, III, 71–76.

[66] Friese, Russland und Preussen, 243ff.

[67] Paul Bailleu, "Der Prinzregent und die Reform der deutschen Kriegsverfassung," Historische Zeitschrift, 78 (1897), 385–402.

a contusion and stiff neck. When the reactionary Hessian minister, Baron Reinhard von Dalwigk zu Lichtenfels, tried to exploit the incident by urging suppression of the Nationalverein, Wilhelm replied sharply that the wiser course was to satisfy the just demands of the German people.[68]

In Baden Wilhelm was surrounded by liberal-national influences. His son-in-law, Grand Duke Friedrich I, and the latter's foreign minister, Baron Franz von Roggenbach, had been warned by old-liberal correspondents in Berlin that the ailing new-era cabinet could be rescued only by a strong initiative in foreign affairs.[69] To Wilhelm they presented a plan for the federal union of small-Germany with a national parliament and Prussian executive, to be made acceptable to Austria by a constitutional guarantee of the entire Habsburg Empire. But conservatives were also active. Summoned from Petersburg by Minister of War Albrecht von Roon,[70] Bismarck was asked for his views on the matter. The result was his famous "Baden-Baden memorial."[71]

In it he argued once more that Prussia's role in the existing confederation was not adequate in view of the burden she bore for the defense of Germany. The confederation was incapable of satisfying the popular aspiration for national unity. Hence Prussia should publicly announce her support of "a national assembly of the German people." By insisting that its members be chosen by the state legislatures Prussia could make certain of their "intelligence and conservative outlook." In such an organ Bismarck saw "the only unifying force that can supply an adequate counterweight to the tendency of the dynasties to adopt separate and divergent policies."[72]

Austria and the lesser states would certainly never voluntarily consent to

[68] Grube, Neue Ära und Nationalverein, 119–120; Friedrich Curtius, ed., Denkwürdigkeiten des Fürsten Chlodwig zu Hohenlohe-Schillingsfürst (Stuttgart, 1907), vol. 1, 111; Wilhelm Schüssler, ed., Die Tagebücher des Freiherrn Reinhard von Dalwigk zu Lichtenfels aus den Jahren 1860–1871 (Stuttgart, 1920), 39ff.

[69] Hermann Oncken, ed., Grossherzog Friedrich I. von Baden und die deutsche Politik von 1854–1871 (Stuttgart, 1927), vol. 1, 115–153, 251ff.

[70] The cabinet crisis that occasioned Roon's message was over domestic rather than foreign policy. The new-era ministers had opposed Wilhelm's ambition to receive from the "estates" of the realm an oath of fealty at his coronation in Königsberg as out of place in a constitutional monarchy. Roon and Edwin Manteuffel saw in the crisis the possibility of splitting the cabinet and driving out the remaining liberal ministers. By the time Bismarck arrived in Germany, however, Wilhelm had given in and the crisis had passed. Zechlin, Grundlegung, 194–195.

[71] There are two versions of this document: one drafted in July for the king and another in September for leaders of the Conservative party. The earlier draft has the more radical phrasing, for it had to compete with a similar plan by Roggenbach, whereas the later version was intended to convert the conservatives to a new policy in the German question. Hermann Oncken, "Die Baden-Badener Denkschrift Bismarcks über die deutsche Bundesreform (Juli, 1861)," Historische Zeitschrift, 145 (1931), 106–130. Oncken printed the July version; the September version is in GW, III, 266–270.

[72] In the July version the wording is a little different: "the most effective, perhaps the only and the necessary unifying force."

BISMARCK IN MARCH 1860 (FROM FÜRST HERBERT VON BISMARCK, ED., *FÜRST BISMARCKS BRIEFE AN SEINE BRAUT UND GATTIN*, J. G. COTTA'SCHE BUCHHANDLUNG NACHFOLGER G.M.B.H., STUTTGART, 1900, P. 449).

such a program,[73] so Prussia ought to strive for the same objective by an alternate route. Following the plan he had once outlined to Below, Bismarck advocated that Prussia work for the erection of a Zollverein parliament. By "skillful leadership" of such an organ she could force the lesser states into agreements similar to the Zollverein treaties but dealing with military affairs. The ultimate goals were a common military organization supported by income derived from tariffs and related taxes, and a representative assembly made up of the combined legislatures of the member states and equipped with the power to legislate in matters dealing with trade and commerce.

While the king pondered this proposal, Bismarck urged it upon leaders of the Conservative party as a party platform. In a letter to Below-Hohendorf he deplored the purely "negative" and "defensive" attitude of Prussian conservatives. Such an attitude could never conquer "terrain and adherents" and even jeopardized the party's existence. The idea of conservative solidarity in foreign affairs was a "dangerous fiction." Such "quixotry" was incompatible with the primary task of the Hohenzollern monarchy: "the protection of Prussia against injustice." The "sovereignty" of the lesser states was an "unhistorical, Godless, and unjust swindle" dangerous to the future of Prussia and Germany. The conservatives should declare for a confederate or Zollverein parliament. "Until now very modest concessions to the national cause have always been considered worthwhile. One could create a very conservative national assembly and still reap the thanks of the liberals."[74] In other words, the conservatives should capture the national cause from their foes. Far from harmful to the interests of the conservative aristocracy, it might well be the means of survival in this dynamic century, a life preserver on the raging flood of the "time stream."

In German nationalism Bismarck had found a new "moral basis" for the expansion of Prussian power. Even though the plan for a confederate parliament would certainly be rejected in the Frankfurt Diet, he believed its announcement alone would bring Prussia a resounding victory in the fight for public opinion. As his memorial in the Hesse-Kassel affair shows, Bismarck conceived such a declaration as a tactical gambit that would give Prussia the initiative in the struggle against the diet majority. It might shock the opposition into concessions. Even if it did not, Prussian manipulation of the Zollverein would soon convince them that the threat was no bluff. Should pres-

---

[73] The July draft argued that acceptance of the proposal in non-Austrian Germany was "not outside the realm of the politically possible," but that Austria was the stumbling block to its universal acceptance. In both versions he recognized that acceptance by Austria would be possible only if she divided her German and non-German provinces so drastically that the only remaining link would be "personal union" under the emperor.

[74] GW, XIV, 578–579. The letter was a criticism of the platform of the conservative Volksverein being founded by Hermann Wagener. See Felix Salomon, *Die deutschen Parteiprogramme* (3d ed., Leipzig, 1924), 104–105.

sure in this direction lead to conflict, Berlin would have the best possible moral ground upon which to go to war.[75]

If successful either by peaceful or warlike means, Prussia would have laid the cornerstone of a new structure in Germany favorable to her interests. In the national parliament she would find an instrument with which to counteract the pressures of particularism. But the parliament too had to be held in check. According to Roggenbach, Bismarck also planned an upper chamber composed, like the confederate diet, of state representatives that would debate and vote in secret. In short, centripetal and centrifugal forces would counterbalance each other, leaving the decisive power in the hands of the "holder of the balance." Like Europe, Germany was to have its balance of power with the Hohenzollern monarchy in the pivotal position of greatest control.[76]

By no means did Bismarck regard an alliance with German nationalism as the only possible course. In accordance with his general views on political strategy he considered it but one of the alternative combinations available to Berlin. As before, Prussia must hold open every door and every turning. In applying pressure against Austria and the medium states she must preserve the choice of rapprochement with either German national opinion or France and Russia. As the situation permitted, either weight (or both) might be used to depress the scales. Should war against Austria be necessary, Prussia must rely primarily upon her own strength and that of the German national movement. The former would supply the punching power for victory and the latter the moral cause for which to fight. If France should threaten to intervene, the pact with German nationalism would also be a useful means of pressure against the Tuileries.[77] Against Austria, Italy alone among the European powers was a prospective ally. She could be rewarded with Italian rather than German soil, and there was little prospect that in victory she would ever become an uncomfortable rival for Prussia. The friendship of the other European powers was to be cultivated, not as a source of military assistance, but as a means of isolating Austria and her German allies.

The Conflict Joined

The revolution in Prussian foreign policy, however, was not to commence with Bismarck. Wilhelm was afraid of this "red reactionary" with his formidable talents and daring plans. Instead he chose to replace Schleinitz as for-

---

[75] Since the 1850s the idea of a Zollverein parliament had been under public discussion. In 1861 it was approved by the first German *Handelstag*, a convention of businessmen under the chairmanship of David Hansemann. W. O. Henderson, *The Zollverein* (Cambridge, Eng., 1939), 285ff.; Oncken, *Bennigsen*, vol. 1, 499; HW, I, 113.

[76] Zechlin, *Grundlegung*, 164–165.

[77] GW, XIV, 555.

eign minister with Count Albrecht von Bernstorff, Prussian ambassador at London. Although conservative, the count was acceptable to the remaining new-era ministers. He favored rapprochement with France and a strong Prussian initiative in the German question. At Ostende on September 7, 1861, Wilhelm and Bernstorff conferred with Roggenbach and accepted in general the Baden program for confederate reform.[78]

Those German nationalists who learned of these negotiations were hardly satisfied with the results. When Roggenbach submitted the details of his program, the Prussians objected to liberal features, such as ministerial responsibility and a parliament chosen by direct election. Grand Duke Friedrich and his minister readily consented to drop these points. Nevertheless, they grew timid about submitting the plan to the other German states.[79] When finally advanced by Bernstorff on December 20, it came not as a demand, but as a rebuttal to another proposal by Baron Friedrich von Beust of Saxony. In rejecting Beust's plan for a tripartite reorganization of the confederation under Austria, Prussia, and the lesser states, Bernstorff declared that only a small-German federation within the existing great-German confederation could satisfy the German need for national unity. Although the language was mild, the Austrians were shocked. Prussia had revived the Radowitz plan.[80]

In 1862 the tempo of popular agitation quickened again. Leading members of the ailing Nationalverein gathered at Easter and agreed to promote periodic congresses of nationalist deputies from German diets and parliaments. The event was reminiscent of the Offenburg assembly of 1847 and the preparliament of 1848. But the most dramatic occurrence of the year was a gigantic hunting festival held in Frankfurt. In July ten thousand men armed with hunting rifles paraded through the Eschenheimergasse before the confederate diet. The hunters had nothing but pasteboard targets in mind, but even the Prussian and Austrian legations thought it best to display that day the black-red-gold tricolor of 1848.[81]

Although small-German sentiment predominated at such affairs, the great-Germanists were by no means inactive. They gained encouragement and added strength from contrasting political developments in Berlin and Vienna. While the Hohenzollern monarchy fell ever deeper into the pit of reaction, the Habsburg Empire seemed on the ascent toward constitutional govern-

[78] Kurt Promnitz, *Bismarcks Eintritt in das Ministerium: Historische Studien*, vol. 60 (Berlin, 1908), 19–32.

[79] Oncken, ed., *Grossherzog Friedrich I*, vol. 1, 278–312; Karl Ringhoffer, *The Bernstorff Papers* (London, 1908), vol. 2, 90ff.; Gruner, "Rückblick," 159. During his year in office Bernstorff made no real attempt to establish liaison with the Nationalverein. Grube, *Neue Ära und Nationalverein*, 128ff.

[80] Ludwig Aegidi and Alfred Klauhold, eds., *Das Staatsarchiv: Sammlung der officiellen Aktenstücke zur Geschichte der Gegenwart*, vol. 2, (1862), 1–21; DPO, II, 53–55; Srbik, *Deutsche Einheit*, vol. 3, 375–376.

[81] Oncken, *Bennigsen*, vol. 1, 566–567; Zechlin, *Grundlegung*, 263–265.

ment. The defeat of 1859 had revealed the bankruptcy of the old policy of centralized absolutism inaugurated by Schwarzenberg. In the "October diploma" of 1860 provincial diets were restored and in the "February patent" of 1861 a central parliament was created for the whole empire. The reform was nothing but a "constitutional overcoat" beneath which lay intact the absolute powers of the crown. For the time being, nevertheless, German liberals were impressed.[82]

These basic laws also made it easier for Vienna to approach the problem of reform in Germany. Through the device of a "narrow" parliament, which excluded Hungary, reform minister Anton von Schmerling created the possibility of dissociating for some purposes the Austrian half of the empire, which belonged to the German Confederation, from the eastern half, which did not. This opened the possibility of consolidating the confederation on a great-German basis. There were good reasons for such a policy. The Schmerling system was based on the German population of the empire. To be successful it required the backing of 40 million confederate Germans against ambitious Czechs and troublesome Magyars. In the Foreign Ministry he found a willing ally in Baron Ludwig von Biegeleben, the influential secretary for German affairs and advocate of an aggressive German policy. Together they pressured the reluctant Rechberg into a policy of confederate reform.[83]

The Austrians based their plan on that of Beust as modified by Dalwigk. To the existing structure of the confederation was to be added a chamber of delegates drawn from the parliaments of the member states, an executive committee representing their governments, and a high court with the power to interpret confederate law. In such a system Prussia could be permanently outvoted by Austria and her middle state allies. The method of adoption was clever—overly so. Rather than propose an organic change in the confederate constitution, which Prussia would certainly veto, Vienna intended to present a bill that would have called upon state parliaments to create a chamber of delegates to advise the diet on pending legislation for confederate law codes. The Austrian coalition would then have seen to it that the chamber, once in existence, remained in session to become an organic part of the confederate government. By the same route the proposed high court and executive committee would also appear.[84]

In January 1862 a secret envoy from Vienna went from capital to capital in Germany seeking support for the plan. With some reservations the middle states agreed to assist in the Austrian power play. They even agreed to form a new organization without Prussia, if the confederation should fall apart during

[82] On the Austrian reforms see Josef Redlich, *Das österreichische Staats- und Reichsproblem* (Leipzig, 1920–1926), also A.J.P. Taylor, *The Hapsburg Monarchy* (London, 1941), 112ff.

[83] Enno Kraehe, "Austria and the Problem of Reform in the German Confederation, 1851–1863," *American Historical Review*, 56 (1951), 274–294.

[84] DPO, II, 67ff.; Srbik, *Deutsche Einheit*, vol. 3, 376ff.

the ensuing struggle. But when it came to action the lesser states dragged their heels. Not until July did the ministers assemble to draft the details. As always they were reluctant to take a decisive step, fearing to cut their ties with Berlin and yet prodded by their greater fear of Prussian imperialism and the swelling agitation for national unity. Finally the wavering ended. Bavaria, Württemberg, Hesse-Darmstadt, Saxony, and Hanover joined Austria in presenting the bill to the diet.

On August 14, 1862 the diet assembled at Frankfurt to deliberate on a motion to refer the Austrian proposal to committee. No one was sure how Count Guido von Usedom, the Prussian envoy, would vote. Would Prussia, racked by internal conflict and desperately in need of popular favor, actually vote against a measure that promised greater national unity? Usedom "surprised even the least hopeful with the vehemence of his denunciation." Not only did he reject the idea of confederate reform by majority vote; he loudly challenged the assembled envoys to join Prussia in undertaking a real constitutional reform, including a strong executive and a national parliament. Only in this way, he declared, could the German longing for greater power and respect abroad be satisfied. By overwhelming majority, nevertheless, the chamber voted for committee consideration. Austria had crossed the first hurdle.[85]

The German Confederation was not the only arena in which the two German great powers contended during 1860–1861. In gaining renewal of the Zollverein for twelve years in 1853, Prussia had agreed to reconsider after 1860 Austria's bid for an economic union. This gave Austrian Minister of Commerce Ludwig Bruck the opportunity to try again to establish the great central European common market that had been his goal since 1848. Bruck had expected that by 1860 Austrian industry would be ready for the lower tariffs that Prussia had fostered in the Zollverein. Yet the course of economic development was the reverse of what he hoped. The industrial boom of the mid-1850s and the depression of 1857–1860 widened the gap between the German and Austrian economies. In Prussia the depression struck trading interests more severely than it did heavy industry. The affected agrarians, merchants, and light industrialists reacted by calling for still lower tariffs in order to widen their markets in western Europe. But in Austria coal, iron, and textile producers were the most injured interests, and their demands for protective tariffs increased. The Crimean and Italian wars, furthermore, left Habsburg finances in disorder and discouraged any tariff experiments that might lower public revenues.[86]

---

[85] Kraehe, "Problem of Reform," 287; DPO, II, 444ff.; Staatsarchiv, vol. 3, (1862), 154–159.

[86] Helmut Böhme, Deutschlands Weg zur Grossmacht: Studien zum Verhältnis von Wirtschaft und Staat während der Reichsgründungszeit 1848–1881 (Cologne, 1966), 81ff. See also Eugen Franz, Der Entscheidungs-Kampf um die wirtschaftspolitische Führung Deutschlands (1856–1867): Schriften-

Nevertheless, it was recognized in Vienna that Prussia's dominance over the Zollverein in the industrial age could have serious political consequences. Until his death in 1861 Bruck and, after him, Rechberg determined to push the negotiations provided for in the treaty of 1853. Again the Austrians were badly outflanked. In March 1862 Bernstorff and Rudolf Delbrück hurriedly negotiated a free-trade treaty with France. Since 1860 the French Empire had concluded a series of such treaties with England, Belgium, and Switzerland. If ratified, the new treaty would give Berlin access to a steadily widening European free market in accordance with the wishes of Prussia's predominant agrarian and commercial interests. For Austria the prospects were disastrous. If she should try to follow suit, her struggling industries would be suffocated by foreign competition. Hence the move threatened to frustrate again Austria's ambition to join the Zollverein. By granting France "most favored nation" status, furthermore, the treaty would destroy Austria's special relationship to the Zollverein, which was all that Vienna had been able to salvage from the debacle of 1853.[87]

Even so, it appeared for a time that Austria might actually benefit from the Prussian démarche. Under the rules of the Zollverein any change in the tariff laws of a participating state had to be approved by all members. The governments of most of the medium states were incensed by the far-reaching character of the French-Prussian agreement and its consequences for their Austrian ally. Southern landowners and textile manufacturers (particularly in Württemberg) were protectionist and hence pro-Austrian. But even southern governments hesitated to abandon the Zollverein. Economic union with Prussia offered material advantages that Austria could not match. The surge in industrialization and railway construction in the 1850s had heightened the economic interdependence of the Zollverein states. The flow of goods and produce from one region to another had increased greatly and with it the regional division of labor. But capital too had begun to migrate across political frontiers, as bankers and entrepreneurs availed themselves of new opportunities for investment. The dominant trend in the economic thought of the day was toward laissez-faire. Under the agitation of John Prince-Smith and the Congress of German Economists, Manchesterism had made further converts in Germany. In economic policy Prussia appeared progressive, Austria reactionary.[88]

Desperately Austria maneuvered to meet the Prussian challenge. Even

reihe zur bayerischen Landesgeschichte, vol. 12 (Munich, 1933), 34ff., 145ff.; Henderson, Zollverein, 273ff.; Ringhoffer, Bernstorff Papers, vol. 2, 143ff.

[87] Böhme, Deutschlands Weg, 99, 103; Franz, Entscheidungskampf, 3ff., 169ff.

[88] Franz, Entscheidungskampf, 159ff.; Julius Becker, Das deutsche Manchestertum: Eine Studie zur Geschichte des wirtschaftspolitischen Individualismus (Karlsruhe, 1907), 26ff. Born in London, Prince-Smith spent his career in Germany as a publicist and agitator for the doctrines of Adam Smith, Malthus, Ricardo, and Bentham.

Austrian industrialists realized that drastic steps were necessary if the Habsburg monarchy was to avoid isolation in Europe and if its internal social and political structure were to be preserved. With their support Rechberg officially revived in July 1862 Bruck's old plan by proposing that the Zollverein and Habsburg Empire unite into a common market beginning in 1865, the equalization of tariffs to be accomplished by 1877. Together the dual powers would negotiate new commercial treaties with France and England. Austria was ready, he declared, "to make exertions and sacrifices" in order to prevent a "wall" from being erected between itself and its German allies. The offer was the most far-reaching Vienna had made. On July 21, Bernstorff counterattacked by recognizing the Kingdom of Italy and, on August 2, by signing the March agreement with France. All that remained to put the latter into effect was an exchange of ratifications, which was delayed while Prussia rounded up the votes of the Zollverein states. At stake, Austrian Ambassador Count Alois von Károlyi told Bernstorff, was Austria's very existence. "Likewise for Prussia," was the reply. Should Austria persist, the result would be a "struggle of life and death."[89]

Paris Interlude

With Bernstorff's appointment the curtain went up on a drama whose dénouement was to be reached on the battlefields of Bohemia in 1866. Months before Bismarck came to power in September 1862, the Prussian government began to shape the foreign policy that he was to pursue with resounding success. In the German Confederation and in the Zollverein Bernstorff reacted to the Austrian assault with a counteroffensive that mobilized the basic ideas and forces that Bismarck was to manipulate to great effect: German nationalism, laissez-faire, and the special interests they served. While locked in bitter conflict with parliament over the most basic issues of military and constitutional policy, the Prussian government began to put together in foreign affairs the combination of idealism and materialism that ultimately provided the weapons for victory both at home and abroad.

Nevertheless, Bernstorff was a minor character who prepared the scene and set the mood while the leading actor waited impatiently in the wings for his cue. In ill health, the count had accepted the Foreign Ministry with great reluctance. During his year in the Wilhelmstrasse he repeatedly asked to be allowed to return to London. For Bismarck it was a time of uncertainty and depression. After attending Wilhelm's coronation in Königsberg (October 18, 1861), he wearily took the road back to Petersburg for another winter in

[89] Böhme, *Deutschlands Weg*, 114–115, and *Vor 1866: Aktenstücke zur Wirtschaftspolitik der deutschen Mittelstaaten: Hamburger Studien zur neueren Geschichte*, vol. 7 (Frankfurt a. M., 1966), 101–111; Franz, *Entscheidungskampf*, 220; Kohl, ed., *Jahrbuch*, vol. 6, 155–156; *Staatsarchiv*, vol. 3, (1862), 228ff.

the frozen north. "Three years ago," he complained, "I would still have made a useful minister, but now, when I think about it, I feel like a sick equestrian facing a series of jumps."[90]

In March 1862 a sudden crisis in the developing struggle with parliament prompted his recall to Berlin. Still Wilhelm could not bring himself to accept the ministerial candidate urged upon him by Roon. The post of minister without portfolio was discussed. But Bismarck had no wish to mount the horse without the reins. To end the quandary he demanded either dismissal or appointment to a new diplomatic post. In late May he was posted to Paris, his chest newly decorated with the Order of the Red Eagle, first class. It was recognized, however, that his services would soon be needed in Berlin. In their parting audience Wilhelm told him to remain *au qui vive*. Bismarck was deeply vexed by this indecision.[91] Nevertheless, Paris offered him the opportunity to probe once more the mind of the man who was so vital to the success of his whole strategy of foreign policy.

During Bismarck's last visit in 1857 Napoleon had made proposals of alliance so far-reaching that Bismarck was reluctant to report them to Berlin, knowing how they would shock Gerlach, Manteuffel, and Friedrich Wilhelm IV. On that occasion the emperor had denied any ambition to expand toward the Rhine (except for a "small rectification" of the frontier). Such a move would arouse the whole of Europe against France. Instead he confessed his intention to promote the cause of Italian unification and obtain for France territory on the Mediterranean. In return for Prussia's benevolent neutrality in a war with Austria, France would favor her acquisition of Hanover and Schleswig-Holstein. This would enable her to develop a navy. Europe was lacking in sea powers of second rank capable, in combination with France, of opposing the oppressive naval supremacy of Great Britain.[92]

Relations between Prussia and France had improved since their nadir in 1860. As his attitude toward Austria stiffened, Wilhelm was not averse to some degree of rapprochement. In October 1861 he made a state visit to Compiègne. A few months later the commercial treaty followed. Hence it was natural that Napoleon should again speak frankly to the Prussian diplomat who for years had been the reputed advocate of a French alliance. On June 5, 1862, Bismarck dined in the Tuileries and afterward listened to Napoleon advise that a German national policy was the best solution to Prussia's internal difficulties.[93] Three weeks later envoy and emperor conferred again at Fontainebleau. Suddenly Louis posed the crucial question: "Do you believe

[90] Ringhoffer, *Bernstorff Papers*, vol. 2, 83ff.; GW, XIV, 581.

[91] Promnitz, *Bismarcks Eintritt*, 33–36; Kohl, ed., *Bismarck-Regesten*, vol. 1, 175–176; GW, XV, 163ff.

[92] See Frahm, *Stellung zu Frankreich*, 53–74; Richard Fester, "Bismarcks Gespräche mit Napoleon III. im April 1857," *Historische Zeitschrift*, 84 (1900), 460–465.

[93] GW, III, 366–368.

that the king would be disposed to conclude an alliance with me?" Bismarck parried: "For an alliance there must be an aim or a motive." What he intended, Bonaparte replied, was not an "adventurous project," but an "intimate and durable entente" based on common interests. "You could never imagine what singular overtures were made to me by Austria a few days ago."[94]

In reporting this episode Bismarck was careful to stress that he did not advise a formal treaty with France. His major emphasis was upon the fresh evidence of Austrian perfidy. Nevertheless, his dispatch touched Wilhelm in a sensitive spot. In the press, rumors of a French-Russian-Prussian alliance mingled with those of Bismarck's coming appointment to the Foreign Ministry. "Tell him," the king instructed Bernstorff, "that I shall never consent to an alliance with France."[95]

Except for these interviews there was little to report from Paris. This was the dead season in European politics when rulers and ministers took time out to nurse their ailments at the baths. On an excursion to London Bismarck conferred at length with Lords Palmerston and Russell, listened to their advice on the introduction of a parliamentary system in Prussia, and replied that liberal opposition to military appropriations would vanish, should the government adopt the aims of the Nationalverein.[96] At a formal dinner he had the chance to speak to Disraeli. Revealing his coming appointment, he frankly told the conservative leader of his intent to find a pretext for war against Austria and to suppress the lesser states in the name of German unity. "Take care of that man!" the shrewd Englishman warned. "He means what he says."[97]

Daily Bismarck expected word from Berlin, and daily he was disappointed. His nerves were on edge. His letters home complained of Wilhelm's indecision, the ambiguity of Bernstorff's position, and the unsettled nature of his own existence. "My things are still in Petersburg and will be frozen in there; my carriages are in Stettin, my horses in the country near Berlin, my family in Pomerania, and I on the highway."[98] In disgust he departed southward on an extended leave. From late July to early September 1862 he bathed at Trouville and Biarritz, climbed in the Pyrenees, sampled the local wines, and fell in love with a Russian princess, vivacious Katharina Orlov. Katharina evoked

[94] GW, III, 381–383; XV, 173–174.

[95] Promnitz, Bismarcks Eintritt, 44–49; Kohl, ed., Jahrbuch, vol. 6, 155; Otto Nirrnheim, Das erste Jahr des Ministeriums Bismarck und die öffentliche Meinung: Heidelberger Abhandlungen zur mittleren und neueren Geschichte, vol. 20 (Heidelberg, 1908), 38ff., 57ff., 281ff. This episode probably heightened Wilhelm's distrust of Bismarck. On Sept. 12 he dismissed the suggestion of his appointment to the cabinet with the remark, "Bismarck is pressing for an alliance with France, which I will never accept." Promnitz, Bismarcks Eintritt, 103.

[96] GW, III, 384–386.

[97] Carl Friedrich Vitzthum von Eckstadt, St. Petersburg und London in den Jahren 1852–1864 (Stuttgart, 1886), vol. 2, 158–159.

[98] GW, XIV, 619.

in him memories of Marie von Thadden, but she too was attended by a husband. Evidently the relationship remained platonic.[99]

As the vacation idyll neared its end, Bismarck's mind turned again to politics. In Toulouse on September 12 he resolved to force the issue, even if it meant being minister without portfolio. Returning to Paris, he received coded telegrams of reply from Bernstorff and Roon. Roon's message was emphatic: "*Periculum in mora. Dépêchez-vous.*" Early on the morning of September 19, Bismarck boarded the train for Berlin. Twenty-four hours later he arrived to confront the greatest domestic crisis of the Hohenzollern monarchy since that fateful day in March 1848 when the revolutionists manned the barricades.[100]

[99] See Nikolai Orloff, *Bismarck und Katharina Orloff: Ein Idyll in der hohen Politik* (Munich, 1936).

[100] GW, XIV, 619; XV, 177; Zechlin, *Grundlegung*, 287–291; Promnitz, *Bismarcks Eintritt*, 105–116, 155–198.

‡•‡

CHAPTER SEVEN

Germany at the Crossroads

Failure of the New Era

ISMARCK first conceived his plan for the exploitation of German nationalism in 1858–1859, when conditions for its execution appeared particularly ripe. The prince regent was intent on reconciling the crown with its subjects; most politically conscious Germans were enthusiastic about the new-era cabinet; the Nationalverein appeared willing to act as a bridge between the Hohenzollern monarchy and the German nation. When Bismarck came to power, however, these conditions had disappeared. In Prussia the period of harmony had passed; by 1861 crown and parliament were bitterly at odds over the issue of military reform. Repulsed by Schleinitz and virtually ignored by Bernstorff, the Nationalverein had turned away from the Prussian state to seek its ends through the liberal movement. At Coburg in October 1862 the association raised a demand for the Frankfurt constitution of 1849.[1]

From the outset the new era was an illusion. Not for a moment did Wilhelm waver from his belief in divine-right absolutism. The moderate liberals he chose as ministers were never in full control of the governmental apparatus. Occupying the important posts of justice and commerce were two ministers, Ludwig Simons and August von der Heydt, held over from the previous regime. The three closest advisers of the regent—Gustav von Alvensleben, Edwin von Manteuffel, and Albrecht von Roon—were generals of absolutistic and antiliberal conviction. Beneath the cabinet the key administrative officials responsible for carrying out ministerial decisions were mostly ultraconservatives appointed during the period of reaction. The House of Lords remained a stronghold of reactionary power possessing the veto with which to kill any legislation of which the conservatives disapproved.[2]

When the first reform bills stumbled against these obstacles, the broad "liberal-conservative" coalition that composed the majority in the Chamber of

---

[1] Walter Grube, *Die Neue Ära und der Nationalverein: Ein Beitrag zur Geschichte Preussens und der Einheitsbewegung* (Marburg, 1933), 128–143; Hermann Oncken, *Rudolf von Bennigsen* (Stuttgart, 1910), vol. 1, 580ff. On the development of the conflict see Fritz Löwenthal, *Der preussische Verfassungsstreit, 1862–1866* (Munich, 1914), 1–108.

[2] On the complexion of the cabinet see Alexander Bergengrün, *Staatsminister August Freiherr von der Heydt* (Leipzig, 1908), 247ff. As a matter of "principle" the new-era ministers refused to remove lesser officials for political reasons. Friedrich von Bernhardi, ed., *Aus dem Leben Theodor von Bernhardis* (Leipzig, 1893–1906), vol. 3, 271, 275.

Deputies began to dissolve. A few members (henceforth dubbed "old-liberals") remained loyal to the new-era cabinet, but most joined "committed liberals" (*entschiedene Liberalen*) in founding the German Progressive party in 1861. As the title indicates, the party program was both liberal and national.[3] Like the Nationalverein, in which many of its leaders were active, the new party embraced both moderate and democratic liberals, the former predominating. Brought together by mutual distrust of the new-era cabinet, the two factions differed in the constituencies for which they spoke and aspects of the liberal philosophy and program they emphasized. The democrats aspired to represent the "little people," that is, artisans, shopkeepers, and others of modest means in the lower *Mittelstand*; moderate liberals, the elite of *Bildung und Besitz*, that is, the merchants, industrialists, and educated elite of the upper *Mittelstand*. The emphasis of the democrats was on egalitarianism; that of moderate liberals, on national unity and laissez-faire economics. Symptomatic of this cleavage was the conflict over suffrage during the discussions that led to formation of the party: democrats wanted universal and equal male suffrage; moderates preferred a limited suffrage based on wealth. In the interest of unity the subject was sidestepped in the founding program. In December 1861, the progressives scored a surprising victory at the polls, capturing 109 seats. With other oppositional groups they controlled 161 votes in the chamber, opposed by 164 conservatives and old-liberals.[4]

By now it was evident that Prince Wilhelm and the progressive deputies had completely different conceptions of the role that the new-era cabinet was to perform. Liberals looked upon the cabinet as an instrument of reform; the regent considered it a means for reconciling parliament and popular opinion to the royal will. The consequence was that by the end of 1861 the cabinet lay spread-eagled between monarchy and parliament, able neither to progress, nor retreat, nor stand upright. The liberal ministers could make no firm decision for either monarchy or parliament. To bend to the will of the regent meant the betrayal of political convictions and sacrifice of popular support. But to follow the dictates of parliament meant dismissal, loss of power and position, and the triumph of ultraconservatives. Like the liberal ministers of 1848, they were embarrassed by the drift to the left in the chamber. If they

---

[3] Oncken, *Bennigsen*, vol. 1, 564–565; Martin Philippson, *Max von Forckenbeck: Ein Lebensbild* (Dresden, 1898), 61ff.; Siegfried Bahne, "Vor dem Konflikt: Die Altliberalen in der Regentschaftsperiode der 'Neuen Ära'," in Ulrich Engelhardt et al., eds., *Soziale Bewegung und politische Verfassung* (Stuttgart, 1976), 154–196; Heinrich August Winkler, *Preussischer Liberalismus und deutscher Nationalstaat: Studien zur Geschichte der Deutschen Fortschrittspartei 1861–1866. Tübinger Studien zur Geschichte und Politik*, vol. 17 (Tübingen, 1964), 1–15.

[4] Ludwig Bergsträsser, "Kritische Studien zur Konfliktszeit," *Historische Vierteljahrschrift*, 19 (1919), 353–354; Gerhard Eisfeld, *Die Entstehung der liberalen Parteien in Deutschland 1858–1870* (Hanover, 1969), 71–116.

broke with the king, they would have no choice other than to join forces with democratic liberals, to whom they were fundamentally opposed.[5]

For that matter Prince Wilhelm and the new parliamentary opposition were faced with a like dilemma. Divided by factions, wavering in determination, uncertain of popular support, and lacking experienced leadership, the liberals hesitated to open an irreparable breach between themselves and the crown. Even left liberals were reluctant to bring about the fall of a cabinet that had begun its labors with so much hope and promise and with which they had earlier identified themselves. Despite growing mistrust, Wilhelm also found it difficult to dispense with his liberal ministers. He did not want to return to the Gerlach–Manteuffel school of politics and could see no alternative source from which to draw a new government.[6]

The consequence of these antagonistic motives and vacillating attitudes was a series of crises and compromises in the years 1860–1861, the most important of which concerned the bill for reorganization of the Prussian army.

The Military Conflict

Under the great military reform of 1814–1815, Prussian citizens were obliged to serve three years in the regular army (called the "line"), followed by two years in its reserve and thereafter fourteen years in the militia (*Landwehr*). The latter was divided into two levies of seven years each. In war the fighting army consisted of the line, reserve, and first levy of the militia. Because of economies in the military budget the size of the army had not kept pace with the rapid expansion of the population. Of those youths who were eligible, only one-half could actually be drafted. For the same reason the usual term of service in the line had come to be two years; increased to three years in 1856, it had been reduced again to two-and-one-half in practice. The ranks of the reserve and militia were filled out by recruits who received but a few weeks of training. Instead of being an extension of the regular army, as originally intended, the militia had practically become a separate organization. Most of its officers had received only one year of formal military training.

On coming to power in 1859, Wilhelm was fully determined to change this system, which he had long considered defective. Three years of training for infantry and four years for other branches, he insisted, were necessary to inculcate the habits of discipline and obedience essential to an effective fighting force. By raising the number of draftees, lengthening by six months their period of service, and increasing service in the reserve to five years (later re-

[5] Bernhardi, *Aus dem Leben*, vol. 3, 272–273, 285–286; vol. 4, 159–160.

[6] *Ibid.*, vol. 4, 107, 160; Philippson, *Forckenbeck*, 56; Ludwig Dehio, "Die Taktik der Opposition während des Konflikts," *Historische Zeitschrift*, 140 (1929), 287ff.; Hermann Oncken, ed., *Grossherzog Friedrich I. von Baden und die deutsche Politik von 1854–1871* (Stuttgart, 1927), vol. 1, 323.

KING WILHELM I IN 1863 (FROM HORST KOHL, ED., ANHANG ZU DEN GEDANKEN UND ERINNER-UNGEN VON OTTO FÜRST VON BISMARCK, TWO VOLS., STUTTGART, 1901, VOL. 1).

QUEEN AUGUSTA IN 1862 (FROM ALFRED FUNKE, DAS BISMARCK-BUCH DES DEUTSCHEN VOLKES, TWO VOLS., W. BOBACH & CO., LEIPZIG, 1921, VOL. 1, P. 585).

duced to four), he proposed to double the size of the army. But he also wished to introduce radical changes in the militia. Most of his life he had been distressed by the sight of those "dirty militia men" who marched past at military reviews in ragged ranks and moth-eaten uniforms. He doubted that even a reformed *Landwehr* could be expected to fight side by side with, and as competently as, the line. Hence he proposed that during wartime the fighting army consist only of the strengthened line and its reserve. The militia, in other words, was to be separated altogether from the regular army and relegated to the rear.[7]

The regent and his generals were not alone in the belief that serious reforms were necessary. After the Italian war all political factions in Prussia recognized that the army was inadequate in size and organization. Flushed with renewed enthusiasm for the national cause, the liberals expected Prussia, headed by a liberal cabinet, to become the nucleus of a small-German unification for whose achievement the use of force, or at least its threatened use, would be necessary. In their minds national unity was inextricably linked to

---

[7] Gerhard Ritter, *Staatskunst und Kriegshandwerk: Das Problem des "Militarismus" in Deutschland* (Munich, 1954), vol. 1, 144ff.; Gordon A. Craig, *The Politics of the Prussian Army, 1640–1945* (Oxford, 1955), 188ff. See particularly Wilhelm's remarks to the cabinet on Dec. 3, 1859. Ernst Berner, ed., *Kaiser Wilhelms des Grossen Briefe, Reden, und Schriften* (Berlin, 1906), vol. 1, 461–478.

the cause of political freedom. The obligation to defend Germany from foreign attack compelled Prussia to bear a much greater military and financial burden than its population could shoulder. In a united Germany the burden would be spread over a much larger population, enabling Prussia to reduce its tax burden proportionately. But other significant benefits might also be expected. The significance of the army in Prussian public life would be diminished, the geopolitical argument for an authoritarian government weakened, and a better climate provided for the growth of a parliamentary democracy and a more egalitarian society. Under these circumstances liberal suspicion of the army as the traditional instrument of autocratic power diminished.[8]

But the old fears returned as soon as the regent's plan became known. The enlarged army meant an increase in taxation of 25 percent, which alarmed the commercial interests, just recovering from the depression of 1857. The primary objection, however, was not financial, but social and political. Behind the changes planned for the militia and the lengthened period of military service, the liberals detected a plan by the Junker military caste to strengthen the authority of the monarchy and buttress its own position in Prussian society at the cost of commoners.[9] This was, in fact, the case.

Like local self-government and universal military service, the militia system had originally been intended by the reformers of 1807–1815 to give the general public a vested interest in the Prussian state and the success of its army in wartime. This had been lacking in the largely mercenary army of the eighteenth century, which was the personal instrument of the monarch. Through the militia and general conscription, Scharnhorst and Hermann von Boyen wished to put forces in the field animated more by patriotism and willingness to sacrifice for the commonweal than by professional efficiency, loyalty to the king, and the "cadaver obedience" that was the pride of Prussian militarism. Although the reform was incomplete, their conception of the army as a partly civilized force became as important to the liberals as the *Rechtsstaat*, constitutionalism, and the rights of man.[10]

Wilhelm and his military advisers were hostile toward the militia system for the very reasons that liberals were attracted to it. In a famous memorial of 1858, through which he won the confidence of the regent, Roon condemned it as a "politically false institution." The militiaman, he declared, was not a soldier, but a civilian in thought and attitude. There was no proof that in war patriotic enthusiasm was an adequate substitute for the iron discipline and esprit de corps imparted by years of formal military training. In domestic politics, moreover, the militia was a positive hazard to royal authority. As long

[8] Winkler, *Preussischer Liberalismus*, 28–33; Egmont Zechlin, *Bismarck und die Grundlegung der deutschen Grossmacht* (Stuttgart, 1930), 173ff.

[9] Eugene N. Anderson, *The Social and Political Conflict in Prussia, 1858–1864* (Lincoln, 1954), 109ff.; Bernhardi, *Aus dem Leben*, vol. 3, 284–285; Craig, *Prussian Army*, 145–146.

[10] Ritter, *Staatskunst*, vol. 1, 125ff.

as a vital part of the army consisted of "civilians in uniform" whose wishes had to be considered, the king would never be master of his own house. One purpose of Wilhelm's reform, therefore, was to get rid of Boyen's compromise between a royal and popular army. The army was to become again what it had been in Frederician times: the personal and "nonpolitical" instrument of royal will.[11]

Unlike some reactionary absolutists of the two previous reigns, Wilhelm and Roon had no intention of abolishing universal conscription in favor of a purely mercenary army. Quite the contrary. It was their deliberate purpose to employ the three years of military training as a means of implanting habits of loyalty and obedience to the monarchy that would make the conscript a staunch supporter of the crown and its political authority for the rest of his days. The army was to become the "school of the nation." Whereas Scharnhorst and Boyen had wished to revive the Prussian army with an injection of civic patriotism, Wilhelm and Roon desired to use the draft to inject military attitudes into civil life.[12]

From the purely military-technical side there was no real need for a three-year training period. In April 1862 a board of fifteen generals (including Helmuth von Moltke), appointed by Wilhelm to study the problem, agreed on the adequacy of two-and-one-half years with furlough during the winter months. Under certain conditions they granted that two years would not impair military efficiency. Three decades later during the reign of Wilhelm II the term of service was actually reduced to two years with the approval of the army command, despite the more complicated weapons and tactics that had to be taught. In 1914 the shortened term stood the test of war.[13]

Liberals sensed the ulterior political aim of the military reorganization. In reacting against it, the democratic progressives themselves developed an offensive purpose. Speaking to the hunters' festival in Frankfurt (July 1862), Hermann Schulze-Delitzsch openly declared that constitutional development would never be assured until "parliament is backed by a people's army standing amid an armed people." Later he maintained he had meant a future German parliament, not the Prussian Landtag. But his speech confirmed Wilhelm's belief that the progressives aimed at parliamentary control over the armed forces. Though this was not the case, the deputies ultimately did open an attack upon important aspects of the Prussian military state. In April 1863 the military committee of the Chamber of Deputies recommended limitation of the jurisdiction of military courts to military offenses, liquidation of cadet schools and military courts of honor, selection and promotion of officers ac-

[11] Waldemar von Roon, *Denkwürdigkeiten aus dem Leben des General-Feldmarschalls Kriegsministers Grafen von Roon* (4th ed., Breslau, 1897), vol. 2, 521–572; also vol. 1, 345ff.

[12] Ritter, *Staatskunst*, vol. 1, 154ff.

[13] Bergsträsser, "Kritische Studien," 349–350.

cording to ability rather than social caste, and equality of pay between the elite *Gardekorps* and regular troops.[14]

Another vital issue was the relationship between political and military authority. In 1852 Otto Manteuffel had modified the collegial structure of the Prussian cabinet by obtaining from Friedrich Wilhelm IV an order limiting the right of access to the king by his fellow ministers.[15] An exception was made in the case of the minister of war. Invariably a general and a career officer, he had the privilege of taking matters to the king without prior approval of the minister-president. This meant that no intermediate civil authority stood between himself and the monarch. Although officially responsible only to the king, the minister of war was required by the constitution to appear in parliament to explain and defend government bills dealing with military affairs. This necessity did at least subject his actions to a degree of popular review.[16]

This was not true, however, of the chief of the military cabinet. Under the Prussian system the king was technically the acting commander of the armed forces, a duty and prerogative that could not be delegated to a minister. To assist them in this function the Hohenzollern had turned to the personnel division in the war ministry, which thereby acquired a dual character. As a division of the war ministry, its members were concerned with such matters as the selection and promotion of officers, but, as aides and advisers to the commander-in-chief, they formed an unofficial "military cabinet." Their chief had direct access to the king and hence the opportunity to bypass the minister of war and the whole civil cabinet. Through this channel men of purely military training and outlook could influence the entire course of the government. "To ambitious and power-hungry personalities it presented an opportunity for uncontrollable political influence 'behind the scenes.' "[17]

In 1848 an attempt was made to abolish this position, which menaced any kind of democratic government. Although the military cabinet was reintegrated into the Ministry of War, an informal "camarilla" of military advisers took its place. During the rest of the reign of Friedrich Wilhelm IV this shadow cabinet, headed by Leopold Gerlach, directed the reactionary mea-

[14] Friedrich Thorwart, ed., *Hermann Schulze-Delitzschs Schriften und Reden* (Berlin, 1909–1913), vol. 4, 106–107, 128–131; vol. 5, 224–225; SBHA (1863), IV, 656–658.

[15] For the cabinet order see Otto Küsel-Glogau, *Bismarck: Beiträge zur inneren Politik* (Berlin, 1934), 70; Ernst Rudolf Huber, *Dokumente zur deutschen Verfassungsgeschichte* (Stuttgart, 1964), vol. 2, 9. To reach the king the other ministers had to go through the minister-president, who had the privilege of being present during the audience.

[16] Ritter, *Staatskunst*, vol. 1, 207ff.; Rudolf Schmidt-Bückeburg, *Das Militärkabinett der preussischen Könige und deutschen Kaiser* (Berlin, 1935), 46ff.

[17] Ritter, *Staatskunst*, vol. 1, 223. On the development of the military cabinet see Heinrich O. Meisner, *Der Kriegsminister, 1815–1914* (Berlin, 1940), 7ff., and Schmidt-Bückeburg, *Militärkabinett*, 57ff.

sures that emasculated the work of the revolution and sealed the daily conduct of the government against the infection of liberal ideas.[18]

One of its members, Edwin Manteuffel, remained behind to serve the regent in the dual role of chief of military cabinet and head of the personnel division. A man of uncompromising absolutistic views, the general was determined to reconstruct the power of the military cabinet at the cost of the Ministry of War and hence of constitutional government. Although this ultimately brought him into conflict with Roon, who replaced Eduard von Bonin as minister of war in late 1859, both men shared the objective of securing the army from every constitutional restriction. In January 1861 Manteuffel succeeded in getting Wilhelm's approval of a cabinet order that removed from the signature of the minister of war all military orders except those dealing with purely administrative matters and those requiring legislation or dealing with the budget.[19]

In a pamphlet published in 1861 Karl Twesten, a prominent progressive, painted Manteuffel as a highly sinister figure. The general, he charged, was primarily a courtier, long out of contact with the army, where he was little liked. His power to dispose over military personnel was conducive to whim and nepotism; his usurpation of functions of the Ministry of War complicated military administration. What crisis would be required to "remove this unwholesome man from an unwholesome position?"[20] Manteuffel demanded that the deputy retract not only the personal attack, which was indeed slanderous, but also his entire criticism of the military cabinet, much of which was accurate. When Twesten refused, the general sent a challenge and shot him through the arm. Manteuffel's purpose, Twesten believed, was to silence all public criticism of the army.[21]

The Prussian army was often called a "state within a state." Through Roon and Manteuffel most of its vital affairs were removed from any kind of political control, whether by cabinet or parliament. Of its higher officers 90 percent were carefully chosen from the Junker caste. After the purges conducted by

---

[18] Meisner, *Kriegsminister*, 16ff.; Fritz Hartung, "Verantwortliche Regierung, Kabinette, und Nebenregierungen im konstitutionellen Preussen, 1848–1918," *Forschungen zur brandenburgischen und preussischen Geschichte*, 44 (1932), 2ff.

[19] On Manteuffel see Gordon Craig, "Portrait of a Political General: Edwin von Manteuffel and the Constitutional Conflict in Prussia," *Political Science Quarterly*, 66 (1951), 1–36; Ludwig Dehio, "Manteuffels politische Ideen," *Historische Zeitschrift*, 126 (1926), 41–71, and "Edwin von Manteuffel und der Kaiser," *Deutsche Rundschau*, 206 (1926), 40–48, 149–157; a more favorable view is given by Wilhelm Gradmann, *Die politischen Ideen Edwin von Manteuffels und ihre Auswirkungen in seiner Laufbahn* (Düsseldorf, 1932).

[20] Karl Twesten, *Was uns noch retten kann: Ein Wort ohne Umschweife* (Berlin, 1861), 81–82.

[21] HW, I, 62–65. On Twesten see Dehio, "Taktik der Opposition," 294ff. Regretfully Wilhelm had to go through the formality of confining Manteuffel, deploring the temporary loss of his services as a "triumph of democracy." Berner, ed., *Kaiser Wilhelm*, vol. 2, 15; also Roon, *Denkwürdigkeiten*, vol. 2, 21.

EDWIN VON MANTEUFFEL (BILDARCHIV
PREUSSISCHER KULTURBESITZ).

KARL TWESTEN IN THE 1860S (BILDARCHIV
PREUSSISCHER KULTURBESITZ).

Manteuffel, they were mostly of conservative and absolutistic views. The oath they swore was to the person of the king, not to the constitution or civil government. They were a pressure group that the king himself could not ignore, even if he desired. They were the one fully dependable support for his own authority.[22]

Lord and Vassal

In the beginning both cabinet and parliament sought to avoid a head-on collision over the military bill. Many old-liberals who had served in the chamber of 1860 believed, in fact, that the measure should be accepted, distasteful though it was, in order to avoid embarrassing the new-era ministers. But the liberal press was critical and the deputies responded to its pressure. While approving the proposed expansion, the committee on military affairs insisted on certain economies and rejected the regent's plans for the militia and the three-year period.

To the relief of the deputies the government then withdrew the bill and asked for a "provisional appropriation" to enable it to proceed with the expansion alone. This was granted, but only after the minister of finance, Baron von Patow, had given verbal assurances that those parts of the general plan

[22] "I know," remarked Friedrich Wilhelm IV, "that my army is the condition for the existence of my throne." Quoted in Meisner, *Kriegsminister*, 18. See also Johannes Schultze, ed., *Kaiser Wilhelms I. Weimarer Briefe* (Berlin, 1924), 64.

to which parliament objected would not be put into effect. On Edwin Man-teuffel's urging Wilhelm chose to ignore this promise, which apparently he had not authorized. By royal command thirty-six infantry regiments of the militia were separated from the army and replaced by a like number of new regiments of the line. On January 18, 1861, their standards were ceremoniously dedicated over the tomb of Frederick the Great.[23]

This high-handed action outraged liberal opinion, but still the moderates who controlled parliament hesitated to precipitate an open break. When the matter came up again in 1861, they granted a second provisional appropriation. In December came the rousing electoral victory of the progressives, already mentioned, which greatly strengthened the opposition in the Chamber of Deputies. During March 1862 the deputies forced the issue by passing the "Hagen bill." By requiring the itemization of the military budget for 1862, the bill would have made it impossible for the government to continue shifting funds to purposes not authorized by parliament. Wilhelm reacted by dissolving the chamber and replacing the remaining new-era ministers with conservatives. Despite severe bureaucratic pressure on the voters, the election in May was catastrophic for government candidates. Conservative strength shrank to ten seats; the old-liberals were severely reduced. But the opposition grew to 223, of whom 135 were progressives. The government's critics were now clearly in control of the chamber.[24]

These developments created a sense of emergency in the royal palace. For more than a year Edwin Manteuffel had predicted revolution. With his associates he drafted a detailed plan for the remorseless conquest of the city, street by street, should the opposition take to the barricades. There was to be no repetition of the capitulation of March 1848. From his ready talk of "bloody heads" it seems certain that Manteuffel not only expected but also desired an uprising. Its ruthless suppression would permit the crown to abolish parliament and the constitution. He pictured himself as the Strafford who would purge the political opposition and rescue the monarchy from its enemies.[25] Roon too was thinking of Strafford, but more of his fate than his achievement. Someone had once prophesied that the general would die "by the neck."[26]

Manteuffel's chance never came. Not even the democratic liberals had any serious thought of revolution.[27] In the summer and early fall came a final

[23] Craig, *Prussian Army*, 146ff.; Eugen Frauenholz, *Das Heerwesen des XIX. Jahrhunderts*, in *Entwicklungsgeschichte des deutschen Heerwesens* (Munich, 1941), vol. 5, 250–254.

[24] Bergsträsser, "Kritische Studien," 353–368; Karl Ringhoffer, *The Bernstorff Papers* (London, 1908), vol. 2, 180ff.; Philippson, *Forckenbeck*, 82.

[25] Ludwig Dehio, "Die Pläne der Militärpartei und der Konflikt," *Deutsche Rundschau*, 213 (1927), 91–100.

[26] Roon, *Denkwürdigkeiten*, vol. 2, 107.

[27] Outside Prussia a few radicals—Wilhelm Rüstow, a renegade Prussian officer, Ludwig

attempt at compromise. Since 1860 the moderates had abandoned their opposition to the militia part of the government's program; hence the one demand upon which the liberal factions were still united was the reduction of the service period from three to two years. Rather than risk open conflict with parliament, the cabinet advised Wilhelm to concede the shorter term. Even Roon was unnerved by the determined attitude of the chamber. With Heydt, the minister of finance, he was in contact with the moderates in search of a compromise. Before parliament on September 17, 1862, he openly spoke of his willingness to come to terms. But two days later he was compelled to reverse himself, for Wilhelm had flatly refused to budge. On the evening of Roon's first speech the king bluffed his ministers by dramatically summoning Crown Prince Friedrich Wilhelm. This was a threat of abdication, a prospect that conservatives had every reason to dread.[28]

Those who are teased by what "might-have-been" in history have always found the character of Friedrich Wilhelm a fascinating study. In 1862 he was strongly opposed to the course that his father was taking. Through his mother, a Weimar princess, and his wife, a daughter of Queen Victoria and an earnest advocate of the English system, he had been exposed to liberal influences. Among his friends and associates were men close to the old-liberals and progressives. Though believing in the necessity of military reform, he was willing to compromise on the length of service. Had he ascended the throne, the issue would have been settled.

But would German history have taken a radically different course? As with most "ifs" in history the answer is not wholly clear. Friedrich Wilhelm was not a resolute personality with a clearly reasoned political philosophy. His liberalism was of the compromising sort common to the old-liberals, who were his chief political advisers. By rebuilding the government of the new era he wished to steer a mediate course between absolutism and parliamentary democracy. Basically the prince was "more Hohenzollern than Coburg." There was an "authoritarian tendency" in him that leaves open to doubt whether, had he become king in 1862, he could have maintained the delicate balance of liberal and conservative forces that was his political ideal.[29]

Schweigert, a former captain in the Austrian army, and Fedor Streit, prominent on the extreme left of the Nationalverein—seriously speculated on the possibility of organizing rebellion. But their illusions were not shared by most radical refugees, including Marx. Gustav Mayer, *Ferdinand Lassalle: Nachgelassene Briefe und Schriften* (Stuttgart, 1921–1925), vol. 5, 15ff.

[28] On the September crisis see particularly Wilhelm Treue, "Wollte König Wilhelm I. 1862 zurücktreten?" *Forschungen zur brandenburgischen und preussischen Geschichte*, 51 (1939), 275–310; also Kurt Promnitz, *Bismarcks Eintritt in das Ministerium: Historische Studien*, vol. 60 (Berlin, 1908), 67–99, 117–154; Zechlin, *Grundlegung*, 291ff.; Ringhoffer, *Bernstorff Papers*, vol. 2, 193ff.; Bergengrün, *Heydt*, 301–306; Johannes Schultze, ed., *Max Duncker: Politischer Briefwechsel aus seinem Nachlass* (Stuttgart, 1923), 334.

[29] Heinrich O. Meisner, ed., *Der preussische Kronprinz im Verfassungskampf 1863* (Berlin, 1931), 47–62; Heinrich O. Meisner, ed., *Kaiser Friedrich III.: Tagebücher von 1848–1866* (Leip-

Nevertheless, the possibility existed that without a political talent such as Bismarck to help him (and there was none in the old-liberal camp) Friedrich Wilhelm might have been swept along by the liberal tide from one compromise to another. But there was yet another possibility. The army too was a political force. After openly clashing with the Bismarck government in 1863 the crown prince suspected that the generals were conspiring to replace him as heir to the throne with his reactionary uncle, Prince Friedrich Karl, or the latter's son.[30] Had he become king during these vital years of decision, the Prussian conservatives would hardly have let their royalism stand in the way of their interests. Who can say what might have come out of the collision of popular and reactionary forces that would then have ensued? In any case Wilhelm certainly had no intention of giving way to Friedrich Wilhelm, unless ministers could not be found who were willing to carry out his military policy and rule the country without a legal budget. On the evening of September 17, the threat of abdication was sufficient to drive the shocked cabinet into line, but two days later Heydt and Bernstorff handed in their resignations. After a futile attempt to mediate between the king and his defecting ministers Friedrich Wilhelm hurried off on the twentieth to rejoin his family in Thuringia. From his father's final remarks he assumed that Bismarck's appointment was not imminent. Three days later he was shocked to learn from a telegram that he had been misled.[31]

Since May Wilhelm had held Bismarck in reserve for just such a crisis. Yet he was still apprehensive of this man who wanted to "turn everything upside down." Queen Augusta and Friedrich Wilhelm vigorously protested his qualifications. In desperation, the queen sought to prejudice her husband by describing how Bismarck had tried in March 1848 to involve him without his knowledge (Wilhelm had fled to England) in a military coup against the revolution. But the king was apparently more interested in current than past politics. As late as September 7, he remarked to Roon that Bismarck was impossible, for he favored alliance with France. On the sixteenth, nevertheless, Wilhelm allowed Bernstorff to summon Bismarck to Berlin. Three days later the dissolution of the cabinet left the king with no other choice. But still he could not fully make up his mind. Would even this daring and resolute man accept the conditions refused by the retiring ministers?[32] Wilhelm's un-

zig, 1929), xiv ff., xliv ff.; Martin Philippson, *Friedrich III., als Kronprinz und Kaiser* (Berlin, 1893), 77–78.

[30] Friedrich III, *Tagebücher 1848–1866*, pp. xxvii–xxviii; Meisner, ed., *Kronprinz im Verfassungskampf*, 161–162; Bernhardi, *Aus dem Leben*, vol. 5, 339.

[31] Treue, "König Wilhelm I," 291ff.; Friedrich III, *Tagebücher 1848–1866*, 160–161; Bernhardi, *Aus dem Leben*, vol. 4, 334; Philippson, *Friedrich III.*, 97.

[32] Ernst II., Herzog von Sachsen-Coburg-Gotha, *Aus meinem Leben und aus meiner Zeit* (Berlin, 1887–1889), vol. 2, 497; Promnitz, *Bismarcks Eintritt*, 27; Zechlin, *Grundlegung*, 252–256, 279–280; Ernst Ludwig von Gerlach, *Aufzeichnungen aus seinem Leben und Wirken, 1795–1877*

certainty grew when he learned that Bismarck had conferred with the crown prince immediately on arriving from Paris. Had Bismarck come only to serve his son?

On September 22, 1862, Bismarck drove to the Gothic summer palace at Babelsberg for the fateful interview that was to decide his and Germany's future. Pointing to the draft of his abdication proclamation, Wilhelm explained the situation. In good conscience he could no longer reign unless ministers could be found who would "conduct my government without subjecting me to the will of the parliamentary majority." When he paused, Bismarck asserted his willingness to serve with Roon in a new cabinet and his confidence that other ministers could be found to replace any who might resign. But the king was still uncertain and pressed him with specific questions. Would Bismarck carry through the military reorganization? The answer was "Yes." Against the will of the majority in parliament? Once more came an emphatic affirmative. Wilhelm was impressed. He had expected reservations, conditions, arguments. But Bismarck judged man and mood with complete accuracy. Despite his doubts about the wisdom of the course Wilhelm was following, he assumed the role of a feudal vassal come to learn his lord's will. The king made up his mind, "Then it is my duty to try to continue the struggle, and I will not abdicate."[33]

Bismarck's appointment is the best possible demonstration of the authoritarian power of the Hohenzollern monarchy. He gained his position by the personal decision of the king, and he was to retain it through varying vicissitudes for more than a quarter of a century for the same reason. In 1862 he did not have the full support of a single faction in the Prussian Landtag. Even the conservatives were dubious of this "democrat in disguise."[34] The king himself was tortured by doubt. Only Roon resolutely desired his appointment. To the general he was the final hope of rescue. Wilhelm's abdication appeared to mean surrender of the army to parliamentary control and the end of the Prussian military state.[35]

Bismarck judged the situation in similar terms. The central issue, he told the king in Babelsberg, was not one of "liberalism or conservatism of one

---

(Schwerin, 1903), vol. 2, 248; Roon, *Denkwürdigkeiten*, vol. 2, 120–121. On Bismarck's relationship to Augusta see pp. 57n, 131–132.

[33] *GW*, XV, 177–180. For Wilhelm's brief account of the interview and the draft of his abdication proclamation see Friedrich III, *Tagebücher 1848–1866*, 497–500.

[34] *GW*, VII, 140; Herman von Petersdorff, *Kleist-Retzow* (Stuttgart, 1907), 366ff.; Promnitz, *Bismarcks Eintritt*, 99–101. On Sept. 24 Wilhelm Dilthey wrote to Hermann Baumgarten, "Not a single party is for Bismarck; all of the vague hopes that have been placed on him vanish with his entry into the present cabinet." Not even the most "fantastic" politician could attempt a stroke in foreign policy without a solution of the military question. *HW*, I, 117.

[35] On Sept. 21 the cabinet warned Wilhelm that abdication would mean "self-destruction" for the crown. Friedrich III, *Tagebücher 1848–1866*, 494–497. On the long personal relationship between Roon and Bismarck see Roon, *Denkwürdigkeiten*, vol. 2, 19–20, 27–28; *GW*, XV, 206.

shading or another," but of monarchical or parliamentary government. The latter had to be avoided at all costs—even if it meant a "period of dictatorship." "In this situation I shall be quite open in giving you my opinion, if your majesty should request of me things that I do not consider right, but if you insist on your own judgment I would rather go down with the king than desert your majesty in the contest against parliamentary government." Undoubtedly this argument was ad hominem, designed to inspire confidence and whip up the fighting mood of his soldier-monarch. Nevertheless, Bismarck often repeated it under other circumstances during the years that followed.[36]

Although many thought so, it is not certain that in 1862 Prussia (ultimately Germany) actually stood on the dividing line between monarchical and parliamentary government. It will be shown that none of the liberal parties or factions openly aimed at parliamentary control over the executive power. And yet the clash of ideals and interests may well have led in the end to changes in constitutional relationships more radical than any of the participants initially intended. It is safe to say at least that, if Wilhelm had abdicated, the Prussian Chamber of Deputies would have attained a greater degree of influence over state policy and German parliamentary life a greater vitality. Originally the system of mixed powers was the common form of constitutional government in Europe, but elsewhere legislatures ultimately came to dominate the executive branch, creating parliamentary government. This was the direction of constitutional development in England, France, Italy, the Netherlands, and Scandinavian countries. Under Friedrich Wilhelm such a development might have occurred in Prussia, but the longevity of Wilhelm I and the political talent of Bismarck assured that Germany was to be different. Here the system of mixed powers endured, to become by the end of the century the uniquely "German form" of constitutional monarchy.

[36] For example, BR, II, 78, 285.

❖❖

CHAPTER EIGHT

Thrust, Parry, Riposte

An Attempt at Compromise

O N THE DAY after Bismarck's first visit to Babelsberg the parliament, with but eleven dissenting votes, struck out of the budget for 1862 the funds already expended by the government for military reorganization.[1] By this act the deputies finally ended the temporizing with which, since 1860, they had sought to avoid an open breach with the crown. It was expected that the government would now be compelled either to concede to their wishes with regard to the two-year service period or restore the army to its status as of 1859. With this ultimatum the question of military reform retreated into the background and the more fundamental issue of the constitutional powers of king and parliament came to the fore. The "army conflict" was transformed into a "constitutional conflict."[2]

Despite his fighting words in Babelsberg, Bismarck was neither pleased by the prospect of a final test of strength between crown and parliament nor reconciled to its necessity. Although he had come to power because of the internal crisis, his primary interest was still foreign affairs. In the "Baden-Baden memorial" of 1861 he had advised Wilhelm to avoid conflicts with parliament because of their damaging effect upon external policy. To achieve its ends in Germany, Prussia must give the impression abroad that "all organs and forces of the country" were united behind the government.[3] But now the situation was worse than ever. With his usual flexibility Bismarck determined upon a final attempt to reconcile the conflicting parties.

The maneuver was hazardous. If awkwardly carried out, it could have destroyed the impression he had made in Babelsberg, but also given weight to

[1] Indicative of the immaturity of parliamentary practice in Prussia was the absence of any deadline for the passage of budget bills. Even as the deputies debated the budget for 1862, the funds it was to grant were being expended. Because the government had presented the budget for 1863 in May, the chamber had before it simultaneously two budget bills. Waldeck had to convince the deputies that the two measures should be considered individually rather than lumped together in a single debate. H. B. Oppenheim, *Benedikt Franz Leo Waldeck: Der Führer der preussischen Demokratie, 1848–1870* (Berlin, 1880), 163.

[2] On the parliamentary situation leading to the September crisis see Kurt Promnitz, *Bismarcks Eintritt in das Ministerium: Historische Studien*, vol. 60 (Berlin, 1908), 25–38, 50ff., 117ff.; Fritz Löwenthal, *Der preussische Verfassungsstreit, 1862–1866* (Munich, 1914), 75–108; Gerhard Ritter, *Staatskunst und Kriegshandwerk: Das Problem des "Militarismus" in Deutschland* (Munich, 1954), vol. 188.

[3] GW, II, 320–321.

demands of extremists for a reactionary cabinet under Edwin Manteuffel. On the night of October 3, 1862, Bismarck dined with an old associate of Petersburg days, Kurd von Schlözer, and told how he intended to get away with it: "We drank a lot of champagne, which loosened even more his naturally loose tongue. He exulted about pulling the wool over everybody's eyes. Partly by himself and partly through others, he is seeking to get the king to concede the two-year service period. In the House of Lords he paints the reaction he plans in colors so black that, as he puts it, the lords themselves are becoming anxious about the conditions he says he will bring about if need be. Before the gentlemen of the second chamber he appears at one moment very unbending, but in the next hints at his desire to mediate. Finally, he intends to make the German cabinets believe that the king is hard put to restrain the Cavourism of his new minister. There is no denying that until now people are impressed by his spirit and brilliance. *C'est un homme!*"[4]

Where parliament was concerned, there was some reason to believe that these tactics would be successful. Far from being firmly united against the government, the deputies were divided into parties, caucuses, and factions with differing aims. On the right was a caucus known as the "constitutionalists," the remaining core of the "liberal-conservative" coalition that had recently dominated the chamber. Although dissatisfied with the course chosen by the king and unhappy about the fate of their colleagues in the cabinet, they were deeply suspicious of those further to the left who had taken control of the chamber. One wing under Georg von Vincke wished to come to terms with the government at whatever cost; the other under Wilhelm Grabow was reluctant to break the bonds of liberal solidarity by such a surrender.[5]

The bulk of the opposition came from the Left Center and Progressive parties, which together controlled two-thirds of the chamber. Sometimes called the "Bockum-Dolffs caucus" from the name of its leader, the Left Center was composed of moderate liberals largely from the Rhineland. Most hoped for a government surrender on the term-of-service issue; otherwise they were willing to cooperate with progressives to force the Junker cabinet out of office. From its inception the Progressive party was plagued by internal tensions that forecast its ultimate division in 1866. Many moderates, like Karl Twesten and Viktor von Unruh, dreaded the prospect of fruitless conflict with the government. Fearing that either the crown or liberal majority might be driven to extremes, they sought an acceptable basis for compromise. But the democratic wing, led by Baron Leopold von Hoverbeck, Rudolf Virchow, and Hermann Schulze-Delitzsch, was inclined to hold its ground. On the extreme left a democratic faction of about forty deputies led by Benedikt Waldeck was

---

[4] Kurd von Schlözer, *Petersburger Briefe, 1857–1862* (Stuttgart, 1921), 261.

[5] For the general viewpoint of this party, see Otto Westphal, *Welt- und Staatsauffassung des deutschen Liberalismus: Historische Bibliothek*, vol. 41 (Munich, 1919).

determined to force the issue. Waldeck's influence was on the rise. His was the measure passed on September 23, 1862, to compel the government to restore the army to its condition as of 1859. The coalition of left centrists and progressives was a marriage of convenience rather than love. Once the common objective was achieved, the followers of Bockum-Dolffs hoped to split apart the progressives, of whose democratic wing they strongly disapproved. The Left Center would then become the nucleus of a party of moderates that would supply the ministers for a new cabinet.[6]

By finding the right formula Bismarck hoped to precipitate this cleavage. First he withdrew the budget bill for 1863 and called for an "armistice." Next he sought out influential liberals of all parties to point out why every effort should be made to come to terms. The internal conflict was a "serious handicap to our prestige and actions abroad." In German politics his aims were those of the opposition; the army reform was "indispensable" for their achievement. Liberals ought to cooperate with the new cabinet, for its appearance had saved the country from complete reaction. The two-year term was "harmless" and might even be "advantageous." But time was required. Like a horse, he told Twesten, Wilhelm balked at anything new; force made him all the more stubborn. Through persuasion and the influence of the generals, he could ultimately be brought around. Meanwhile, the liberals must not complicate the task.[7]

On September 30 he presented his case to the budget committee of the lower chamber. It was his first crucial test as minister-president. Some found him "pleasant" and "conciliatory"; others, nervous and uncertain. His hands shook, and his speech, always uneven in tempo, was very abrupt. But for a "Mark Junker" he had considerable wit. Ideas and suggestions cascaded from his lips. A witness described the swift pace of Bismarck's mind as "kaleidoscopic"; the colors changed almost too quickly for the eye to follow. The effect was dazzling. Only later did the listener conclude that he had tasted "not wine, at the most soda."[8]

---

[6] On the tensions within and between the liberal parties see Promnitz, *Bismarcks Eintritt*, 64ff. Ludwig Dehio, "Die Taktik der Opposition während des Konflikts," *Historische Zeitschrift*, 140 (1929), 288ff.; *HW*, I, 75ff.; Herman von Petersdorff, *Kleist-Retzow* (Stuttgart, 1907), 341–342; Martin Philippson, *Max von Forckenbeck: Ein Lebensbild* (Dresden, 1898), 77ff.

[7] *GW*, VII, 55–62; Heinrich O. Meisner, ed., *Kaiser Friedrich III.: Tagebücher von 1848–1866* (Leipzig, 1929), 500–503; Eduard von Simson, *Erinnerungen aus seinem Leben* (Leipzig, 1900), 354–355; Heinrich von Poschinger, ed., *Erinnerungen aus dem Leben von Hans Viktor von Unruh* (Stuttgart, 1895), 214–215; Robert von Keudell, *Fürst und Fürstin Bismarck: Erinnerungen 1846– 1872* (Berlin, 1901), 112. According to some reports, he even offered cabinet posts to certain old-liberals. Heinrich von Sybel, *The Founding of the German Empire by William I* (New York, 1891), vol. 2, 511–512; Ludolf Parisius, *Leopold Freiherr von Hoverbeck* (Berlin, 1897–1900), II/ 1, 87–88. The ultras were shocked. Petersdorff, *Kleist-Retzow*, 341–342.

[8] Otto Nirrnheim, *Das erste Jahr des Ministeriums Bismarck und die öffentliche Meinung: Heidel-

BUDGET COMMITTEE OF THE PRUSSIAN CHAMBER OF DEPUTIES IN 1862. FIRST ROW, CENTER: HEINRICH
VON BOCHUM-DOLFFS (PRESIDING). SECOND ROW, FROM LEFT: SECOND PERSON IS RUDOLF VIRCHOW;
FOURTH, MAX VON FORCKENBECK; SIXTH, KARL TWESTEN. THIRD ROW, FROM LEFT: FIFTH PERSON IS
LEOPOLD VON HOVERBECK (FROM EGMONT ZECHLIN, *BISMARCK UND DIE GRUNDLEGUNG DER
DEUTSCHEN GROSSMACHT*, J. G. COTTA'SCHE BUCHHANDLUNG NACHFOLGER,
STUTTGART AND BERLIN, 1930, P. 274).

Bismarck fed the committee a sharp blend of threat, blandishment, and appeasement. His was a difficult task. Unable to promise publicly the two-year period, he had to hint that it was in prospect. Speaking of reconciliation, he had to leave the impression that he had no urgent need of concession or compromise. For dramatic effect he drew from his cigar case an olive branch, a precious souvenir of Avignon and Katharina Orlov. But the deputies were not cowed, diverted, or mollified. After two years of waiting and compromising they had lost all confidence in the commitments of the government.[9]

Luckily for Bismarck, Wilhelm apparently did not hear of his secret promises to liberal leaders. Nevertheless, his candid remarks to the budget committee produced the first crisis in his relationship with the king. In the opposition press his veiled threats aroused a sharp reaction; even Roon disapproved of the "witty digressions" with which his cabinet colleague had entertained the deputies. At Baden-Baden, whence he had gone after appointing the new minister-president, Wilhelm was surrounded by those who disagreed with his choice—Augusta, Friedrich Wilhelm, and Grand Duke

berger Abhandlungen zur mittleren und neueren Geschichte, vol. 20 (Heidelberg, 1908), 89, 91; BR,
II, 37–38.
    [9] BR, II, 16–36.

Friedrich of Baden. Bismarck surmised that there was talk of Louis XVI, Strafford, and Polignac.

Anxiously he hurried out to meet the royal train returning from the south
on October 4. Boarding at Jüterbog, he found Wilhelm alone and morose in
an ordinary first-class compartment. "I foresee exactly how all this is going to
end," the Hohenzoller declared. "Out there in the Opernplatz under my windows they will cut off your head and a little later mine." Carefully Bismarck
chose his ground. What better fate than to die for such a cause?—"I in the
struggle for the cause of my king and your majesty for the rights that are yours
by the grace of God." Wilhelm should think of the noble death of Charles I,
not the ignominious end of Louis XVI. "Your majesty is faced with the necessity of fighting. You cannot capitulate. You must oppose tyranny, even if you
incur bodily danger."[10]

As Bismarck saw him, Wilhelm had most of the virtues and failings of a
Prussian officer: indifferent to danger, unquestioningly obedient to command,
driven by an exalted sense of duty, but uncertain when acting on his own
responsibility, oversensitive to criticism, and fearful of the judgment of history. With words of duty and courage Bismarck pumped confidence into Wilhelm's veins. When the train pulled into the Berlin station the Hohenzoller
was again in a fighting mood.[11] But this tactic rendered even more difficult
the task of gaining Wilhelm's consent to the plan recommended by Roon and
his associates on October 10.

Modeled after the system of Napoleon III, the plan would have permitted
conscripts to purchase release from military service after two years. Those
unable or unwilling to pay were to serve a third year. The money raised would
be used to attract volunteers. In this way the king would have been provided
with a skeleton of professional soldiers within the body of a conscript army;
the well-to-do were to be allowed to buy their way into the reserve. Left out
of the bargain were those who lacked the means to buy their releases. In addition, the plan would have established the size of the army at 1 percent of
the population and its support at a fixed sum per soldier. Henceforth these
matters were to be beyond the challenge of the Chamber of Deputies. Roon
wished to seduce the *Mittelstand* and its parliamentary spokesmen into compromising the basic principle of the *Volksheer*, that of equal and universal
service, and the most fundamental power of any parliament, that of annual
control over military appropriations.

---

[10] GW, XV, 194–195; also XIV, 622–623. Bismarck's surmise concerning what had taken
place in Baden-Baden was incorrect. The subject of the Prussian crisis was avoided. When the
nationalist demand for the constitution of 1849 was mentioned, Wilhelm exploded with anger,
yelling at his son-in-law so loudly that he could be heard in the street. Hermann Oncken, ed.,
Grossherzog Friedrich I. von Baden und die deutsche Politik von 1854–1871 (Stuttgart 1927), vol. 1,
337.
[11] GW, XV, 195.

But Wilhelm disapproved. He studded the margins of the document with such comments as "ruin of the troops," "death warrant of the army." He was encouraged in his refusal by Edwin Manteuffel, to whom any law delimiting the powers of the monarchy in military matters was anathema. One after another, the offending clauses were struck out of the draft. When finally presented to parliament in 1863, the bill had no chance of accomplishing Bismarck's purpose of splitting the opposition.[12]

Throughout these negotiations Bismarck apparently remained on the sidelines. But Roon certainly acted with his approval, and some ideas in the draft may have come from him. Five years later he incorporated its method of setting the size and financial support of the army in the German constitution. For the present, however, he was in no position to insist. To Bernstorff, now Prussian envoy in London, he explained: "For the infantry two years, with volunteers, would be satisfactory. But if the king insisted on ten years, I would not refuse obedience in such matters. In my opinion there are more important questions than that of purchasing momentary peace with the present Chamber of Deputies by this concession. Peace with such people would not be lasting. As far as I'm concerned, therefore, no surrender."[13]

Motives and Tactics

Reconciliation had failed and capitulation was unthinkable, so ways had to be found to overcome the chambor's opposition. More than a year before his appointment as minister-president Bismarck had outlined to Roon what his tactic would be in this situation. The crown, he wrote, could disengage itself at home only by a successful diversion abroad. "For fourteen years we have cultivated the taste of the nation for politics without satisfying its appetite, and hence it seeks nourishment in the gutter. We are almost as vain as the French. If we can persuade ourselves of our importance abroad, we are willing to let many things at home go by the board."[14]

In his appearance before the budget committee he tried to dazzle the deputies with the prospect of a revolutionary use of Prussian power. The Nationalverein, he declared, had no true appreciation of the importance of the Prussian army for the attainment of its ends. The Prussian people had always had a liking for more armor than the slim body of the state could bear. Now the time had come to use it. Prussia's leadership in Germany did not depend upon the degree of her liberalism, but upon the extent of her might: "Prussia must build up and preserve her strength for the advantageous moment, which has

[12] Ludwig Dehio, "Bismarck und die Heeresvorlagen der Konfliktszeit," *Historische Zeitschrift*, 144 (1931), 31–47; Kriegsministerium, *Militärische Schriften weiland Kaiser Wilhelms des Grossen Majestät* (Berlin, 1897), vol. 2, 479–488.

[13] GW, XIV, 628.

[14] GW, XIV, 571; see also III, 367, 381, 385–386.

already come and gone many times. Her borders under the treaties of Vienna are not favorable for the healthy existence of the state. The great questions of the day will not be settled by speeches and majority decisions—that was the great mistake of 1848 and 1849—but by blood and iron."[15] Seen in context, this famous quotation, so often misinterpreted, was a crude attempt to distract the deputies from the domestic quarrel by dangling before them the prospect of foreign conquest. But the overly dramatic phrase he chose was immediately singled out for attack by the liberal press and gave him the reputation of an unprincipled man of violence that haunted him and his memory ever after.

Although he overdid it, there were good reasons for believing in the persuasive appeal of national power and prestige for the liberal mind. Since 1859 the Nationalverein had tended to languish. Disappointed by the Prussian government, its leaders had turned to popular agitation. But the movement lagged, despite the surface activity of sporting and professional groups, the many rallies, conventions, and floods of oratory. With the exception of Baden, voters everywhere failed to elect deputies devoted to the cause. Liberals were despondent. How could the governments and people of Germany, they repeatedly asked themselves, again be set in motion toward national unity?[16]

Some old-liberals hoped for another national crisis like those of 1812, 1840, and 1859—for a "national war" that would dissolve the hard crust of German particularism and close the fissures of Prussia's internal conflict.[17] A generation steeped in Hegelian thought longed for the "world-historical personality" who would unleash the latent power of the Prussian state. "The German question," wrote Max Duncker, historian and adviser to the crown prince, "is a question of power and will never be solved without the deployment of Prussian power, without proofs of the national use of power and success of power." For the sake of a German national policy he was willing to accept a "military dictatorship" in Prussia. The Karlsruhe historian Hermann Baumgarten yearned for the appearance in Berlin of "a great and firm man," "a great genius or mighty tyrant" capable of "quick and decisive action."[18] Soon after Bismarck's appointment, the journalist Constantin Rössler wrote that "a bold, lasting, irrevocable deed in the German question" would make

[15] BR, II, 29–30.

[16] Hermann Oncken, Rudolf von Bennigsen (Stuttgart, 1910), vol. 1, 477ff.; Johannes Schultze, ed., Max Duncker: Politischer Briefwechsel aus seinem Nachlass (Stuttgart, 1923), 315–321; HW, I.

[17] Ludwig Dehio, "Die Pläne der Militärpartei und der Konflikt," Deutsche Rundschau, 213 (1927), 99; Rudolf Haym, Das Leben Max Dunckers (Berlin, 1891), 261–262; Friedrich III, Tagebücher 1848–1866, xxvi–xxvii; Friedrich von Bernhardi, ed., Aus dem Leben Theodor von Bernhardis (Leipzig, 1893–1906), vol 4, 314, 325–326; Duncker, Briefwechsel, 301, 304; HW, I, 160–163; Hans Rosenberg, ed., Ausgewählter Briefwechsel Rudolf Hayms (Stuttgart, 1930), 193–194, 199, 208, 211.

[18] HW, I, 39, 59, 61, 71; Duncker, Briefwechsel, 317.

liberals forget "within days" what Bismarck had previously said and done. "Then the reaction would be at an end, but likewise the opposition." A jubilant nation would shout, *"Eine Diktatur für einen Mann!"*[19]

The opposition movement in the Prussian Chamber of Deputies was aware of Bismarck's Bonapartism, but doubted that he would succeed. Although discouraged about the strength of the popular movement, most were inclined to believe that unity could never be achieved under other than liberal auspices. The first step toward this end, they reasoned, must be the liberalization of Germany's most powerful state. A liberal government in Berlin, achieved by peaceful means, would launch a national revolution that would end the German Confederation, liquidate Austro-Prussian dualism, and unify small-Germany under Prussian leadership. In the thinking of democratic liberals, at least, the necessity and inevitability of this scenario was axiomatic. The axiom had its corollary: any attempt on the part of a conservative Prussian government to undertake a warlike venture in foreign policy was foredoomed to failure. How could this Junker of reactionary reputation, who had been summoned by the king as a last resort in the quarrel with parliament, possibly tap the reservoir of German national patriotism for his ends? By standing firm on the issues of military reorganization and constitutional rights, left liberals hoped to find the leverage to influence foreign policy. For a time the government might be able to defy the powers claimed by parliament in budgetary matters and finance the state from sources of income previously authorized. But the outcome would be different when Bismarck attempted his "grand action." At the crucial moment the population would refuse its moral support, and parliament would reject the extraordinary credits necessary for war.[20]

Whether the liberal opposition in the constitutional conflict deliberately sought to inaugurate parliamentary government in Prussia on the British model is still a subject of debate.[21] At no time, not even at the height of the

---

[19] Constantin Rössler, *Ausgewählte Aufsätze* (Berlin, 1902), xviii.

[20] See Dehio, "Taktik der Opposition," 28off.; Friedrich Thorwart, ed., *Hermann Schulze-Delitzschs Schriften und Reden* (Berlin, 1909–1913), vol. 3, 192, 207.

[21] At one time historians generally assumed that parliamentary government was the actual, although discrete, goal of the parliamentary opposition. See, for example, Adalbert Wahl, "Beiträge zur Konfliktszeit," *Tübinger Universitätsprogramm von 1914*, 52ff.; Egmont Zechlin, *Bismarck und die Grundlegung der deutschen Grossmacht* (Stuttgart, 1930), 203–204; Arnold Oskar Meyer, *Bismarck: Der Mensch und der Staatsmann* (Stuttgart, 1949), 201–202; Johannes Ziekursch, *Politische Geschichte des neuen deutschen Kaiserreiches* (Frankfurt a. M., 1925–1930), vol. 1, 52; Ernst Rudolf Huber, *Deutsche Verfassungsgeschichte seit 1789* (Stuttgart, 1956–1963), vol. 3, 293. Representatives of the opposing point of view are Hans Boldt, "Deutscher Konstitutionalismus und Bismarckreich," in Michael Stürmer, ed., *Das kaiserliche Deutschland 1870–1918* (Düsseldorf, 1970), 123–124; James Sheehan, *German Liberalism in the Nineteenth Century* (Chicago, 1978), 115–116; Michael Gugel, *Industrieller Aufstieg und bürgerliche Herrschaft: Sozioökonomische Interessen und politische Ziele des liberalen Bürgertums in Preussen zur Zeit des Verfassungskonflikts 1857–1867* (Köln, 1975), 11–20, 63–66, 72–74; and Lothar Machtan and Dietrich Milles, *Die Klassensymbiose von Junkertum und Bourgeoisie: Zum Verhältnis von gesellschaftlicher und politischer Herr-*

constitutional conflict, did any party or faction raise the cry for a politically
responsible cabinet, although this may have been the goal of a few individuals.[22] When Bismarck accused the opposition in parliament of having such an
aim, the reply was an indignant chorus of denial. Heinrich von Sybel suggested that, without "an understanding royal leadership," parliament was
"not yet equal to the task" of governing; the monarchy and parliament were
still necessary to each other. "The issue between the liberal and feudal parties," Franz Duncker explained, "is essentially this: Which can win the monarchy? Which can move the monarchy over to its side?"[23]

Both sides of the chamber were influenced by the enduring tradition that
in Prussia crown, cabinet, and bureaucracy represented the whole against all
special interests, including political parties—a view that persisted despite the
accumulating evidence to the contrary. This perception had found its most
persuasive philosophical expression in Hegel, for whom the state, as the "vessel of the *Weltgeist*," exercised a controlling and mediating influence over civil
society, a conception that dominated the lecture halls and seminars of German universities, where politically active members of Germany's upper *Mittelstand* (including liberal officials in the ranks of the Progressive party) received their education. Popular sovereignty, a concept already firmly
grounded in French and Anglo-Saxon political life, never had wide currency
among educated Germans. The radical fringe of the liberal movement, which
had advanced that concept in the 1840s, faded after 1848. After that year
German liberals, whether of moderate or democratic persuasion, mounted no
serious challenge to the basic division of powers under the Prussian constitution. What they fought against in 1862–1866 was the upset of that division
in favor of the government.

Looking backward to the seventeenth century, members of the parliamentary opposition of the 1860s could cite many instances in which the Prussian
crown, under both monarchical and bureaucratic absolutism, had deprived
the Junker nobility of powers and privileges in the interest of state. What
most expected of the new-era government and subsequently from Bismarck's

---

schaft in Preussen-Deutschland 1850–1878/79 (Frankfurt a. M., 1980), 36–46, 59–60. Heinrich
August Winkler took a mediate position, concluding that the great majority of liberals strove to
gain the power of political decision—"not formally, to be sure, but in fact." *Preussicher Liberalismus und deutscher Nationalstaat: Studien zur Geschichte der Deutschen Fortschrittspartei, 1861–1866.
Tübinger Studien zur Geschichte und Politik*, vol. 17 (Tübingen, 1964), 21–22. For a critique of
these works see Friedhelm Grützner, *Die Politik Bismarcks 1862 bis 1871 in der deutschen Geschichtsschreibung: Eine kritische historiographische Betrachtung* (Frankfurt a. M., 1986), 15–52.

[22] Winkler cites private letters by Twesten, Virchow, and Bamberger espousing parliamentary
government. See his *Liberalismus und Antiliberalismus: Kritische Studien zur Geschichtswissenschaft*,
vol. 38 (Göttingen, 1979), 294–295.

[23] BR, II, 365; HW, I, 105 (Sybel); Duncker, *Briefwechsel*, 284; Ludwig Bergsträsser, "Kritische
Studien zur Konfliktszeit," *Historische Vierteljahrschrift*, 19 (1919), 370–372; Hansgeorg Schroth,
Welt- und Staatsideen des deutschen Liberalismus: Historische Studien, vol. 201 (Berlin, 1931).

fall was not a change of system but yet another act of political realism by the crown (not unlike the suppression of the Brandenburg and Prussian diets under the Great Elector, the reforms of Stein and Hardenberg under Friedrich Wilhelm III, and the embrace of constitutionalism under Friedrich Wilhelm IV) that would bring representatives of the *Mittelstand*, which they sometimes dubbed "the general estate," into the government and thereby accelerate the progress of national unity, economic growth, and general modernization.

Seen from this perspective, the struggle was between two status groups (estates), each of which claimed for itself the right to advise and influence the crown on state policy—the *Adelsstand*, whose claim rested on its centuries-old status as the fighting and governing arm of Prussian society, and the *Mittelstand*, whose claim rested on its status as the repository of enlightened thought and "modern" values. The two estates represented different economic orders: the rural gentry, seeking to hold on to its traditional dominance in the Prussian establishment, and the urban elite of "culture and property" (*Bildung und Besitz*), seeking political influence with which to expedite the interests of mercantile, industrial, and finance capitalism. Each of these interest groups saw itself as the best representative of Prussian society as a whole, the gentry because of its traditional role as the governing estate under feudal corporatism, the urban elite because it was the cutting edge of economic, social, and cultural progress. Neither attributed to the rural and urban understratum either the right or capacity to play an independent role in political life. Without its support, liberals of the constitutional conflict had little chance of forcing through a fundamental change in constitutional relationships. They would have had to appeal for support to an understratum composed of journeymen, wage earners, day laborers, and unemployed—a social category that German burghers regarded as unripe for politics. By arousing the political participation of the masses, liberals feared to unleash social forces that might eventually escape their control. European history since 1789 was replete with examples.

The constitutional conflict cannot be explained as a clash over material issues between urban and rural elites based on rival systems of production. We shall see that throughout the constitutional conflict crown and parliament cooperated on economic issues of significance such as the renewal of the Zollverein on a free-trade basis in 1865, the year in which the parliamentary struggle reached a new high. On the liberal benches in parliament, furthermore, sat many aristocratic landowners and civil servants, who were moved more by idealism than class interests. The causes for which they and their bourgeois colleagues fought had a genuine liberal, emancipatory character: for constitutionalism—the *Rechtsstaat*, juridical responsibility of ministers, preservation of the lower chamber's budgetary powers, freedom of press and speech, and preservation of civil values in the armed forces—and against arbitrary government by a monarch and ministers who still clung to the Prussian traditions of monarchical absolutism and the military state. By persistent defense of the *Rechtsstaat*, liberals hoped to frustrate the Bismarck government, ultimately make it untenable, and induce the crown to turn it out. Naturally this was an attractive strategy for the many lawyers, jurists, academicians, and state officials in the liberal ranks. Good strategy seemed to coincide with good law.[24]

At bottom the constitutional conflict of 1862–1866 has to be seen as an effort by the opposition to replace Prussia's political leadership, not to effect a structural change in its dualistic constitution. By making it impossible for Bismarck to govern, liberals expected to force his resignation and the appointment by the crown (whether under Wilhelm I or his successor) of a new cabinet willing to respect the rights of parliament under the constitution.

And yet the opposition deputies were no less conscious than were Wilhelm I, Bismarck, and the conservatives at court and in the cabinet that the progressives, if they succeeded in this effort, would set a precedent. If the crown should yield on the constitutional issue of parliament's budget rights, other objectives might also be attainable. Perhaps the first would be a statute establishing the juridical responsibility of ministers, for which liberals had striven in vain for more than a decade.[25] If that were achieved, could political responsibility be far behind? The erosion of the monarch's authority over the executive branch of the government might one day lead to the supremacy of parliament—if not under the present ruler (now over sixty years of age), then under his successor who was known to be sympathetic toward liberal causes. The alternative to this development was even clearer: the acceptance of Bismarck's interpretation of the constitution, the reduction of parliament's voice in public finance, the execution of Roon's plan to eradicate civil influences in the army, and the ideological sterilization of the state bureaucracy through the disciplining of its officials.

The division of governmental authority under the Prussian constitution of 1850 was no longer stable. The aggression of the crown and the parliament's reaction to it had left little or no middle ground. At the time the only possible outcome appeared to be the heightened authority of either the crown or the parliament. Confronted with these alternatives, liberal deputies were compelled to back the cause of parliament. And yet the experience of the constitutional conflict did not radicalize the liberal movement. Their reluctance to

---

[24] The best analysis of liberal aims and motives in the middle decades is by Sheehan, *German Liberalism*, 79–140. But see also Dehio, "Taktik der Opposition," and "Benedict Waldeck," *Historische Zeitschrift*, 136 (1927), 50–57; and Gerhard A. Ritter, *Arbeiterbewegung, Parteien, und Parlamentarismus: Kritische Studien zur Geschichtswissenschaft*, vol. 23 (Göttingen, 1976), 10–20, 102–115, 158–186.

[25] Otto Pflanze, "Juridical and Political Responsibility in Nineteenth-Century Germany," in *The Responsibility of Power: Historical Essays in Honor of Hajo Holborn* (New York, 1967), 162–182.

demand parliamentary government shows how ambivalent they were, even under these circumstances, toward the Hohenzollern monarchy. They were attracted by the potential utility of its power for national purposes, but repelled by its autocratic form, militaristic tradition, and reactionary policies. Moderates stressed the attraction; democrats, the repulsion. The attitudes of Prussian and non-Prussian liberals also diverged. The former, now embittered by the constitutional conflict, were inclined to fight it through; the latter tended to deplore the whole affair and hope for its settlement. Removed from the immediate scene, uninvolved in its personal feuds and passions, non-Prussians were far more concerned with what to them was the greater issue of national unity.

The liberal coalition to which fell the task of conducting the struggle against the crown in Prussia was an uneasy coalition of factions whose mutual distrust had been bridged only by the necessity of forming a common front. None of the liberal groups that composed the alliance was sure of its own internal cohesion. Prussian parliamentary life was still in its infancy. Even the progressives had no adequate party organization. Hence the primary concern of the deputy was the electorate that sent him to Berlin, meaning the small group of local magnates who had the important votes. In parliament he tended to assert his independence of party ties and decisions. Any attempt by the members to bind the party to a positive program was likely to endanger its existence. For this reason the reshuffling of party groupings was a constant phenomenon.[26] But the greatest weakness of the liberal opposition was the persistent suspicion of its leaders that they had no firm popular following. As the conflict reached an early climax in the summer of 1862, Max von Forckenbeck, a spokesman for the moderate progressives, expressed his fear that, if the deputies should force a fresh dissolution, it would "drive the undecided people—and that is the great majority—to the other side and thus make victory doubtful for the near future."[27] Parliamentary liberals had the uncertainty

[26] Dehio, "Taktik der Opposition," 287–288; Eugene N. Anderson, *The Social and Political Conflict in Prussia, 1858–1864* (Lincoln, 1954), 243ff.; Unruh, *Erinnerungen*, 231–232.

[27] Philippson, *Forckenbeck*, 84–85; Ernst Schraepler, "Linksliberalismus und Arbeiterschaft in der preussischen Konfliktszeit," in Richard Dietrich and Gerhard Oestreich, eds., *Forschungen zu Staat und Verfassung: Festgabe für Fritz Hartung* (Berlin, 1958), 385–401; Winkler, *Preussischer Liberalismus*, 92 (fn) and *Liberalismus und Antiliberalismus*, 25. At the height of the enthusiasm over the regency and new-era government, Minister of Interior Eduard Heinrich von Flottwell concluded, on the basis of routine reports received from regional and local state officials, that most of the population was unmoved. "Least excited by the governmental changes are the farmers, the class of small burghers and workers in the cities, because these strata of the people are not accustomed to being noticeably affected by the daily press. For a long time they have been used to following the impulses coming from above, from state agencies and great landowners." They had cast their ballots in the recent election but remained "for the most part true to the monarchy." Flottwell to prince of Prussia, Mar. 5, 1859. Siegfried Bahne, "Vor dem Konflikt: Die Altliberalen in der Regentschaftsperiode der 'Neuen Ära'," in Ulrich Engelhardt, ed., *Soziale Bewegung und politische Verfassung* (Stuttgart, 1976), 168–169.

of frontline troops thinly deployed before a determined foe and backed by no reserves.

Advance and Retreat in Germany

Recent biographers of Bismarck have concluded that he was driven into a ("white") revolutionary foreign policy by internal "forces" that compelled him to exceed his actual intentions. This argument for the "primacy of internal policy" during the era of national unification is based on the assumption that the parliamentary opposition in the constitutional conflict was backed by a large majority of the Prussian people. It is presumed that Bismarck, in order to cope with this putatively overwhelming opposition, had to yield to its foreign policy program.[28] But neither Forckenbeck nor other leading deputies of the Progressive party believed that they had a secure popular following. It will be shown that, as the years advanced, so also did their uncertainty of public support.

Bismarck's quarrel with Austria and the formulation of his strategy for its resolution predated the constitutional conflict and the founding of the Progressive party by years. In the months following his appointment as minister-president he repeatedly denounced as "frivolous" the accusation that he sought in foreign affairs "a means of settling our internal differences." "The means would be worse than the evil itself."[29] Certainly Bismarck would have sneered at the historian's proposition that the strength of the parliamentary opposition in 1862–1866 forced him to adopt the foreign policy of the Progressive party. The most that can be said is that the domestic quarrel added to the urgency of executing a stroke in the German question originally conceived on other grounds. A single blow might bring a double victory. But his first year in office was one of frustration and near disaster.

At the moment of his appointment the struggle between the dual powers neared a climax in both the confederation and Zollverein. During the fall of 1862 the Austrian drive for a favorable reform of the confederation gained momentum.[30] On October 28 a convention of great-Germanists created a German Reformverein to combat the Nationalverein. Although in dissension about the details of the reforms proposed in August, Austria and her allies

---

[28] Lothar Gall, *Bismarck: Der weisse Revolutionär* (Frankfurt a. M., 1980), 248–292; Ernst Engelberg, *Bismarck: Urpreusse und Reichsgründer* (Berlin, 1985), 438–454, 568–588, 619–621, 694–700. In the absence of public opinion surveys, election results are our only statistical source, but they are inconclusive because of the Prussian system of open, indirect, and unequal (three-tiered) balloting and the low voter turnout on election day. Eugene N. Anderson, who located and analyzed the only known election statistics, concluded that Prussia was "overwhelmingly" liberal in 1862—or "potentially" so! The weakness of this conclusion reflects the uncertainty of his evidence for it. See his *Social and Political Conflict in Prussia*, 440.

[29] BR, II, 31, 98. Cited by Gall, *Bismarck*, 258, 282.

[30] HW, I, 135.

agreed in November to press for their adoption "in principle" by the confederate diet. Except for Saxony, the medium states continued to oppose the
Prussian free-trade treaty with France. Among businessmen, however, the
treaty gained in favor. In September–October both the Congress of German
Economists and, by a narrow margin, the German Commercial Association
endorsed it.[31]

Following the strategy he had planned for nearly a decade, Bismarck moved
first to seize the pivotal position of alternative choice. At the end of October
he journeyed to Paris, ostensibly to take leave of Napoleon as Prussian ambassador. Apparently he received assurances from Napoleon and the new foreign minister, Édouard Drouyn de Lhuys, that France would maintain "unconditional neutrality" in the event of war between Austria and Prussia.[32]
Before leaving Paris, he delivered his first stroke. Calling on Austria's ambas-

BISMARCK, IN AMBASSADORIAL DRESS, TAKES FORMAL LEAVE OF NAPOLEON III, WHO ADMONISHES THE
DEPARTING ENVOY TO DEMONSTRATE AS PRUSSIA'S NEW MINISTER-PRESIDENT THAT HE LEARNED
SOMETHING USEFUL AT THE EMPEROR'S "INSTITUTE OF DECEMBER 2" (DATE OF THE COUP D'ÉTAT IN 1851
THAT LIQUIDATED THE REPUBLICAN ASSEMBLY AND PREPARED THE WAY FOR THE SECOND EMPIRE);
(WILHELM SCHOLZ, KLADDERADATSCH, OCTOBER 18, 1862).

[31] Eugen Franz, *Der Entscheidungskampf um die wirtschaftspolitische Führung Deutschlands (1856–
1867): Schriftenreihe zur bayerischen Landesgeschichte*, vol. 12 (Munich, 1933), 241ff.; W. O. Henderson, *The Zollverein* (Cambridge, Eng., 1939), 294ff.; Heinrich Ritter von Srbik, *Deutsche
Einheit: Idee und Wirklichkeit vom Heiligen Reich bis Königgrätz* (Munich, 1935–1942), vol. 3, 399,
428ff.; Erich Zimmermann, *Der deutsche Reformverein* (Pforzheim, 1929).

[32] GW, IV, 10–11; XIV, 627; VII, 65–67. The replacement of Thouvenel by Drouyn de Lhuys
as foreign minister had aroused apprehension that Napoleon was bent on rapprochement with
Austria. APP, III, 41–43.

sador, Prince Richard Metternich, he candidly declared that his aim was to establish Prussia's leadership in the economic, political, and military affairs of northern Germany. He preferred to attain it "through understanding and close union with Austria," but, if opposed, he would use "every means . . . without special scruple" to gain his ends.[33] In early December he repeated this grim warning to Count Alois von Károlyi, the Austrian ambassador in Berlin. He advised the Habsburg monarchy to locate its sphere outside Germany in the east, ruling Hungary not as an appendix but as a vital part of the empire. As inducement he offered a "firm alliance" in European politics and a promise of "unconditional" support for Austrian interests in Italy and eastern Europe. If spurned, Prussia would "go with" Paris in any future crisis.[34]

Nevertheless, his first aggressive move in Germany came to naught and then the whole offensive miscarried. In November he dispatched an ultimatum to the Elector Friedrich Wilhelm of Hesse-Kassel, ordering him to end his quarrel with the Hessian parliament or risk the consequences. By marching troops into Kassel, Bismarck expected to alter the balance of forces among the lesser states in favor of the French customs treaty and renewal of the Zollverein. But the unpopular prince evaded him by responding to the ultimatum, and the Hessian pawn remained in play.[35] In December the Frankfurt Diet neared a vote on the Austrian reform plan, and Bismarck began to prepare for war. "What would France do if things got hot in Germany?" he asked French Ambassador Charles de Talleyrand. The reply was not what he expected. If the struggle remained local, France would be a spectator, but, if the destruction of the confederation and a shift in the European balance were threatened, "the emperor would then seek the combination offering the greatest guarantees for the security of his state and the peace of Europe."[36] A few days later this straw in the wind from Paris was followed by another.

As was his custom, Bismarck was moving forward simultaneously on a second front. In the course of negotiations with Paris on the implementation of the free-trade treaty, he had asked the French for a guarantee that they would not make similar agreements with other Zollverein states. His aim was to make Berlin's Brandenburger Tor the "only door" through which the latter could enter the European system of free trade. Thus armed, he hoped that in 1866, after the expiration of the Zollverein treaties, Prussia could force the

[33] GW, XIV, 628; Freiherr von Hengelmüller, "Graf Alois Károlyi: Ein Beitrag zur Geschichte der österreichisch-ungarischen Diplomatie," *Deutsche Revue*, 38/4 (1913), 35–36. Rechberg was not impressed by the threat. Hengelmüller, "Karolyi," *Deutsche Revue*, 38/3 (1913), 304.

[34] GW, VII, 69–72; IV, 14–16, 22–25; APP, III, 145–146; DPO, II, 635–637. Again Rechberg's reply to Károlyi was uncompromising. DPO, II, 623–626, 649–653.

[35] GW, VII, 62–65; IV, 13–14; XIV, 630–631.

[36] APP, III, 131–132, 143. The Italian ambassador was asked bluntly whether Prussia could depend upon military assistance in a conflict with Austria. Although mistrustful, the Italians were interested. APP, III, 129–130, 134.

lesser states to accept procedure by majority vote and a parliament capable of counterbalancing the "political divergencies of the governments." In place of a reformed diet, equipped with a great-German assembly under Austrian control, he intended a reformed customs union, equipped with a small-German parliament under Prussian hegemony. But on December 30, 1862, Drouyn refused the Prussian stipulation.[37]

Although the French shift was a severe disappointment to Bismarck, his system of strategy allowed for such situations. From the pivotal position it was now necessary to draw away from Paris and closer to Vienna. The French had to be shown that the Wilhelmstrasse could be reconnected with the Ballhausplatz.[38] But this posed a difficult task. Even while seeking rapprochement with Vienna, he had to defeat the Austrian reform plan and convince the Austrians of the futility of attempting another. But Bismarck was adept at squaring the circle. In his interviews with Thun and Károlyi in early 1863 the themes of appeasement, threat, enticement, and diversion appear in rapid succession. One minute he talked of the desirability of an "offensive-defensive alliance" and in the next stressed Prussia's self-sufficiency; he spoke of the dangers of the European revolution and then disclosed plans to exploit revolutionary forces for Prussia's advantage; denying any intention of dividing Germany into two spheres, he proposed plans that would ultimately have that effect. Finally, he suggested that the dual powers "abstract" their European from their German relationships, cooperating in the one area while disagreeing in the other. Károlyi found it "truly astonishing with what rapidity Herr von Bismarck goes from one extreme to another diametrically opposed."[39]

As the vote in the diet neared, he employed the tactic of "fear and fear again" toward the lesser states, warning them that, if voted down, Prussia would immediately declare herself no longer bound by the confederate constitution. Until the last minute some of the smaller states wavered, torn between fright and hatred of Prussia. But when the votes were counted on January 22, 1863, the Austrian plan had lost, nine to seven. The sensation of the day, however, was the message that accompanied the Prussian vote. "The German nation," it declared, "can find a competent organ through which to influence the course of common affairs only in a representative body chosen directly by the people of each confederate state according to its population." To be workable such a "German parliament" would have to be equipped with a "legislative power" sufficient to make it an effective "counterweight" to the

[37] GW, IV, 16–19, 28–33; APP, III, 140–142; Franz, *Entscheidungskampf,* 259ff.

[38] The danger was made acute by the fact that Gorchakov was again considering an alliance with France. APP, III, 108–109, 120, 128; GW, XIV, 633–634.

[39] DPO, II, 719–721, 738–746, 750–758, 791–797, 809–814; APP, III, 186–187, 194, 198–199, 203–204. Thun was convinced of Bismarck's change of heart, but not Károlyi. DPO, II, 762.

diet.[40] What the shocked envoys heard was a powerful warning that, if the Austrian coalition continued on the path of great-German reform, Prussia would ally herself with the forces of small-German nationalism. In such a competition Berlin could offer far more than Vienna.

While the Prussian envoy spoke, events were taking place in the east that again badly disrupted Bismarck's scheme and soon even brought him close to disaster. On the night of January 21 the Poles arose once more in revolt against Russian domination. Although Prussian Poland was not affected, Berlin immediately ordered four army corps into the area, and their commander issued a proclamation tantamount to martial law. In February 1863 General von Alvensleben was sent to Petersburg to consult on "common measures." It may be that he exceeded his instructions by wiring back to Berlin the draft of a convention providing for the possibility of military cooperation in pursuit of rebels across the Prussian frontier. But Bismarck quickly accepted it, for the convention appeared to signify the end of Russian attempts to appease the Poles.[41]

Bismarck's opposition to the Polish cause was more political than racial or cultural. An independent Poland, he feared, would inevitably strive for the frontiers of 1772, including Posen and West Prussia. Because of these ambitions a Polish state would be a "natural ally of France." Within the Russian government, moreover, those who favored Polish autonomy were also supporters of the French alignment.[42] But his view of the Polish question was also charged with emotion. Toward no other people did he express himself with such violent antagonism. "Harry the Poles so that they despair of their lives," he wrote to his sister in 1861. "I have every sympathy for their plight, but if we are to exist we can do nothing other than exterminate them." Undoubtedly this was written in an exuberant moment. At no time did Bismarck ever officially advocate or follow a policy of extermination against a national minority. But a letter to Bernstorff of the same year was nearly as savage. "Every success of the Polish national movement is a defeat for Prussia; we cannot carry on the struggle against this element according to the rules of civil justice, but only according to those of war."[43]

[40] GW, IV, 38–40; Enno Kraehe, "Austria and the Problem of Reform in the German Confederation, 1851–1863," American Historical Review, 56 (1951), 291–294.

[41] APP, II, 222–224, 231ff. On the problem of the origins of the convention see Zechlin, Grundlegung, 430ff.; Gerhard Heinze, Bismarck und Russland bis zur Reichsgründung (Würzburg, 1939), 29–37; Robert H. Lord, "Bismarck and Russia in 1863," American Historical Review, 29 (1923), 24–48; Hellmuth Scheidt, Konvention Alvensleben und Interventionspolitik der Mächte in der polnischen Frage 1863 (Würzburg, 1937).

[42] GW, IV, 59–61; XV, 210ff.; APP, III, 400; Zechlin, Grundlegung, 421ff.; Srbik, Deutsche Einheit, vol. 3, 470ff.; Christian Friese, Russland und Preussen vom Krimkrieg bis zum polnischen Aufstand (Berlin, 1931), 269ff., 295ff.

[43] GW, XIV, 568; III, 298–299. For Bismarck's general attitude toward the Polish question see Joseph Feldman, "Bismarck et la question polonaise," Revue Historique, 173 (1934), 540–588,

Since 1861 he had advised the Russians against all concessions to the Poles. Now he became obsessed by the fear that the reform party in Petersburg, led by Gorchakov, might actually withdraw Russian troops and abandon the Poles to themselves. He determined to occupy the vacated region and attach it to Prussia. In a rare lapse of judgment he sounded out the governments in London and Paris on the matter.[44] One evening at a court ball he spoke to Heinrich Behrend, vice-president of the Chamber of Deputies, about the possibility of "Germanizing" Russian Poland.[45]

Whatever the future value, there can be little doubt that the Alvensleben convention, judged by its immediate consequences, was a bad mistake. Both London and Vienna protested Prussia's intervention. But the most dangerous reaction came from Paris. The convention rescued Napoleon from a dilemma. He had need of rapprochement with Russia to relieve his dependence upon Britain, but the doctrine of national self-determination dictated support of the rebels, and the French public was intensely interested in their fate. Now he was able to train his diplomatic artillery on Berlin rather than Petersburg. On February 21, 1863, he proposed identic notes from Paris, London, and Vienna censuring Prussian intervention.[46]

When London and Vienna refused, Napoleon turned to another scheme even more dangerous for Prussia. In early March he asked Vienna for an alliance. If events should require the surrender of Galicia to an independent Poland, Austria would receive "material compensations" and "exclusive preponderance" in the Balkans. If she would surrender Venetia to Italy, the two powers could join in dismembering the Italian kingdom into three segments (Piedmont, Papal States, Naples); Austria would receive "material compensation" in Germany, where her "preponderance" would be assured.[47] Earlier Empress Eugénie, gesticulating at a map, had revealed to Metternich the full scope of the fantasy that hovered over the Tuileries. In a general exchange of territories France was to gain the Rhine; Austria to gain Silesia, Bosnia, and Herzegovina, and "all that she wished south of the Main"; Prussia to gain Saxony, Hanover, and the duchies north of the Main; Russia to gain Asiatic Turkey, Poland to gain Posen and part of Galicia; the dispossessed princes would be used to "civilize and monarchize" the American republics on the

summarized in "Bismarck und die polnische Frage," *Ostland-Berichte*, 5 (1931), 222–230; Heinze, *Bismarck und Russland*, 21–25, 27–46; Hans Wendt, *Bismarck und die polnische Frage: Historische Studien*, vol. 9 (Halle, 1922).

[44] APP, III, 237–238, 256–259. Bernstorff's reply was discouraging. *Ibid.*, 280–282.

[45] Zechlin, *Grundlegung*, 470–472; APP, III, 354; BP, I, 24–25. In his account of this conversation Bismarck did not mention "Germanization." GW, IV, 70–71. The reports of the Saxon and British ambassadors likewise fail to mention it. APP, III, 271–272, 278. Two years later, however, Bismarck wrote to Bodelschwingh about the "political" wisdom of gradually "Germanizing" Posen. GW, V, 69–70.

[46] Zechlin, *Grundlegung*, 450ff.; Lord, "Bismarck and Russia," 31ff.; APP, III, 286–287.

[47] RKN, I, 10–16.

pattern of Mexico. Metternich concluded that Louis shared the "phantasma-goria" of his impetuous wife. "His language recalls the great epochs of his reign, those that preceded the Crimean and Italian wars."[48] Nevertheless, much of his army was committed in Mexico, where the decisive battle was yet to be fought; France was in no condition to fight a major continental war. Hence everything depended upon the success of the insurrection on the Vis-tula, which was to inaugurate the long chain of sacrifice and compensation. But the rebel cause faltered, and the Austrians declined. The mirage evapo-rated.[49]

Napoleon's actions, however, forced Bismarck into hasty retreat. In Lon-don, Vienna, and Paris he maintained that the convention was of "no prac-tical importance"; having never been ratified, it did not "formally" exist; Rus-sia's success in Poland had made it a "dead letter." Toward Austria and Russia he spoke the language of the Holy Alliance, pleading for a common front against revolution and vigorously denying any thought of alliance with small-German nationalism or of "any kind" of German parliament. "Given a choice between two evils, the lesser is preferable; concern for the security of a coun-try takes precedence over plans for its growth."[50]

It was Britain that finally routed the French offensive. In rejecting the French proposal of February 21, Lord Russell proposed that the powers send identic notes to Petersburg rather than Berlin, recommending a more liberal treatment of Poland. This transformed the issue. Russia and her Polish policy came to the center of the stage, while Prussia and the Alvensleben conven-tion retreated to the wings. During the months that followed, French policy gyrated desperately from one plan to another. Finally Napoleon joined Britain and Austria in a series of démarches to Petersburg in the vain hope of coercing Alexander into liberating Poland. Twist and turn though he might, Gorcha-kov was compelled to reject the notes with increasing sharpness. Because Vi-enna and London now let the matter rest, Napoleon was impotent. His Polish intervention had failed and with it, as time was to prove, his last chance for alliance with Russia. In the future Alexander and his government leaned in-creasingly on Prussia in European politics.[51]

Point and Counterpoint

No sooner had one threat subsided than Bismarck was faced by another. Through the Polish affair Austria had acquired the pivotal position in Euro-

[48] RKN, I, 3–10.

[49] See Gustav Roloff, "Napoleon und der polnische Aufstand im Jahre 1863," Historische Zeit-schrift, 164 (1941), 49–65, and Charles W. Hallberg, Franz Joseph and Napoleon III, 1852–1864 (New York, 1955), 314ff.

[50] APP, III, 299–304, 316ff.; Zechlin, Grundlegung, 487ff.

[51] Srbik, Deutsche Einheit, vol. 3, 480ff.; Friese, Russland und Preussen, 309ff.

pean politics. Schmerling and Biegeleben now insisted that Vienna exploit this situation by renewing the struggle for a confederate reform consonant with her own interests. Although their plan was an improvement in most respects over the previous one, it provided for a collective executive body in which Prussia would have been permanently "majoritized." Naturally Bismarck found that unacceptable. The method of adoption was again guileful. Instead of trying to pass over the Prussian veto, the Austrians stoked the fires of a steamroller with which to flatten every obstacle. While Wilhelm was taking his yearly cure in Bad Gastein in early August, Franz Joseph suddenly presented the plan and invited him to a "congress of princes" to consider the matter. The date was August 3, 1863, and the congress was to meet in Frankfurt on the sixteenth.[52]

Only with the greatest effort was Bismarck able to persuade his king not to attend. The idea of such a conclave of reigning monarchs appealed to the

THE CONGRESS OF PRINCES AT FRANKFURT AM MAIN IN 1863. EMPEROR FRANZ JOSEPH STANDS ON THE FIRST STEP IN WHITE COAT; TO HIS RIGHT, KING GEORG OF HANOVER; TO HIS LEFT, KINGS JOHANN OF SAXONY AND MAXIMILIAN II OF BAVARIA (BILDARCHIV PREUSSISCHER KULTURBESITZ).

[52] APP, III, 683–684, 688–701; DPO, III, 229–234; Zechlin, *Grundlegung*, 566ff.; Srbik, *Deutsche Einheit*, vol. 4, 39ff.; Max Lenz, "König Wilhelm und Bismarck in Gastein, 1863," *Kleine Historische Schriften* (Munich, 1910), 429–474, and "Die Begegnung König Wilhelms I. mit dem Kaiser Franz Joseph in Gastein am 3. August 1863," in Alfred Doren et al., *Staat und Persönlichkeit: Festschrift für Erich Brandenburg* (Leipzig, 1928), 169–213.

Hohenzoller. All other princes accepted, so he feared the discourtesy of a refusal. In his memoirs Bismarck describes that dramatic midnight argument in Baden-Baden that ended with Wilhelm in tears; the minister relieved his feelings by smashing a washbasin on the floor. With it shattered the last real attempt at a great-German solution to the German question. Ridden by fears and jealousies, the lesser princes agreed at Frankfurt to the Austrian reform proposal, but only on condition that Prussia again be invited to give her consent.[53]

For weeks Bismarck delayed his reply to this invitation. Finally on September 22, 1863, he delivered a slashing counterattack. Only a central parliament elected directly by "the entire nation" and sharing legislative power, he declared, could adequately counteract dynastic particularism; in contrast to Austria the interests of Prussia were identical with those of the German people.[54] Such a parliament would have split the German from the non-German parts of the Habsburg Empire—precisely what Schmerling wished to avoid. For the second time within a year Bismarck halted the Austrian diplomatic offensive by revealing that Prussia had within reach an option compatible with her own interests but poisonous to Austria's. It was a threat to ally the Prussian state with German national sentiment.

Originally the Prussian note had an even more radical clause, providing for "eventual" agreement with the "popular assembly" on a constitution. Perhaps on Wilhelm's objection this was left out of the final draft.[55] Outwardly the Prussian note looked like an offer of universal and equal suffrage. When the British objected to a German national parliament as conducive to revolution, Bismarck replied that the "smallest property qualification" would offer a "better guarantee against revolutionary excesses" than most German electoral laws, including the Prussian. For that matter even a "high property qualification" could be satisfactory. Wilhelm, furthermore, was thinking in terms of a "conservative franchise."[56] But these reservations were hidden from the public.

Standing amid the ruins of their attempt at great-German reform, Rechberg and his colleagues suddenly found themselves under attack from Paris. On November 5 Napoleon declared that the treaties of 1815 had "ceased to exist." Only a European congress could preserve the peace by drafting a fresh settlement. More than any other country in Europe, Austria had reason to

[53] GW, XV, 227–241; Horst Kohl, ed., *Anhang zu den Gedanken und Erinnerungen von Otto Fürst von Bismarck* (Stuttgart, 1901), vol. 1, 74; Johannes Schultze, ed., *Kaiser Wilhelms I. Weimarer Briefe* (Berlin, 1924), vol. 2, 38–51. For a detailed study of the *Fürstentag* affair see Hans Scheller, *Der Frankfurter Fürstentag 1863* (Leipzig, 1929).

[54] Ludwig Aegidi and Alfred Klauhold, eds., *Das Staatsarchiv: Sammlung der officiellen Aktenstücke zur Geschichte der Gegenwart*, vol. 8 (1865), 206–213; GW, IV, 174–176.

[55] APP, III, 764–765, 779–786.

[56] Ibid., 813–814; IV, 53–54; DPO, III, 239–240.

fear such a congress, for it would certainly raise the question of national self-determination. Austria, rather than Prussia, now seemed to be the target of French imperialism. Vainly Rechberg pleaded for a concerted answer of the four great powers. On Bismarck's advice Wilhelm's reply to Napoleon was "friendly in tone," but "held open every path." As he undoubtedly anticipated, the British cabinet torpedoed the congress plan with a brusque rejection. Queen Victoria thought it an "impertinence."[57]

After a year of crisis and disappointment Bismarck now had reason for satisfaction. Once more Prussia had the middle position in European politics. Napoleon's fumbling had poisoned his relationships with St. Petersburg and London. His policy on Poland and his talk of revising the settlement of 1815 had ended the threat of a Franco-Russian alliance and had destroyed the working entente with Britain established in the Crimean War. Rebuffed by Austria, the emperor had no choice other than to resume his courtship of Berlin.[58] But in Vienna as well there was a change in attitude. Very discouraged by the negative results of their attempt at confederate reform and frightened by the dangerous turn in Napoleonic policy, the Austrians were now ready to cooperate with Prussia. Within a few months Bismarck led them deep into the morass of the Schleswig-Holstein question.

[57] George E. Buckle, ed., *The Letters of Queen Victoria*, 2d ser., vol. 1, 114; APP, IV, 119–120, 135–137, 148–150, 170–172.

[58] As early as June, reports from Paris had shown that the weathercock on the Tuileries was again shifting toward Berlin. APP, III, 633–635, 647–648. In September Napoleon and Drouyn hinted broadly at their desire for an alliance. APP, III, 751–755, 757–758; IV, 40. But Bismarck was wary. APP, III, 633–634, 765–766; IV, 109. At the moment he was probing Petersburg over the prospect of an alliance against Austria. Should France interfere, "the line of the Weser is more important to us than that of the Rhine." APP, III, 758–762, 786–793. But the Russian reply was negative. APP, III, 802, 804, 807–809.

A Period of Dictatorship

Prussian Constitutionalism

THE COLLAPSE of his attempt at reconciliation at home and his failure to achieve a coup abroad left Bismarck with no popular foundation for his policies either in foreign or domestic affairs. Since 1858 the Conservative party had suffered a series of catastrophic defeats. Not even vigorous bureaucratic interference in the election of March 1862 had been able to halt the decline. Part of the fault lay in an inadequate party organization and press. Among the rural gentry the tasks of practical politics were considered denigrating and distasteful. Proud of their traditional function as the ruling estate, they saw no need to legitimate it now by appealing to the popular will.[1]

A conservative who did understand this necessity was Bismarck's old friend and associate of the revolutionary period, Hermann Wagener. In September 1861 he had helped found the Prussian Volksverein, the conservative answer to the Nationalverein and Progressive party. Socially the organization was an alliance of landowners and artisans to protect what remained of manorialism and the guild system against liberalism, laissez-faire capitalism, and the factory system. With official patronage it achieved minor success, reaching a membership of twenty-six thousand in 1862 and fifty thousand in 1865. During Bismarck's first months in office the Volksverein promoted a flood of "loyalty declarations," which arrived at the royal palace from the provinces almost daily. Many were borne by delegations that included peasants and artisans. In October 1862 a companion organization, *Die Patriotische Vereinigung*, was formed under the leadership of Moritz von Blanckenburg. A monster petition was launched denouncing the "unpatriotic" and "revolutionary" attitude of the opposition. By January 1863 it had accumulated a half-million signatures.[2]

Still it was obvious that the cabinet had no significant popular support. Where the masses stood was uncertain, but the organs of public opinion, both

[1] Eugene N. Anderson, *The Social and Political Conflict in Prussia, 1858–1864* (Lincoln, 1954), 352ff.

[2] See Hugo Müller, *Der preussische Volks-Verein* (Berlin, 1914); [Ludwig Hahn, ed.], *Die innere Politik der preussischen Regierung von 1862 bis 1866* (Berlin, 1866), 128–131. Liberals spoke of the "petition swindle" because of the way in which many signatures were obtained. Otto Nirrnheim, *Das erste Jahr des Ministeriums Bismarck und die öffentliche Meinung: Heidelberger Abhandlungen zur mittleren und neueren Geschichte*, vol. 20 (Heidelberg, 1908), 100ff.

press and parliament, were overwhelmingly on the side of the liberal opposition. Hence Bismarck had no better choice than to introduce that "period of dictatorship" whose possibility he had foreseen in Babelsberg.

For this purpose the Prussian constitution was an effective instrument. Edwin Manteuffel's assertion that in Prussia the old monarchy was the reality and the constitution "as yet mere theory" contained more than a little truth.[3] The vital clauses were phrased with a careful ambiguity that left open the possibility of authoritarian interpretation. "When crown and ministers are in agreement," Bismarck had declared in 1851, "governmental authority is stronger and firmer in Prussia than in any country in the world. There will always be an inclination to obey, as long as his majesty does not lose the will to command. . . . Through the manner in which it has been reshaped and interpreted during the last two years the constitution has ceased to restrict the process of governing and is becoming more and more just the receptacle whose content is determined by those who rule."[4] In withdrawing the budget bill for 1863 on September 28, 1862, Bismarck promised to reintroduce it, along with a new bill on compulsory military service, in the chamber's next session. But the king was obligated under the constitution to summon parliament between early November 1862 and mid-January 1863, which meant that the deputies might not receive the bill in time to take action before January 1 of the year to which it applied. Hence Forckenbeck introduced a resolution calling on the government to conform to the law by summoning parliament early enough to discharge its duty.[5]

In his appearance before the budget committee on September 30, Bismarck responded by citing article 99 of the constitution: "All revenues and expenditures of the state must be estimated in advance for each year and must be entered in the state budget. The latter is to be established each year by law." Because the phrase "in advance" was in the first, not the second sentence, he maintained that the budget need not be established by law before the beginning of the budget year. For twelve years this had, in fact, been parliamentary practice. The budget for 1862, from which the chamber had just stricken the funds for military reorganization, was a case in point. Bismarck then turned to Forckenbeck's demand that the government cease making expenditures of public funds for purposes not authorized by the chamber. Under the constitution, he said, the crown, House of Lords, and Chamber of Deputies had equal voices in the passage of legislation. To the crown, however, were reserved all rights not expressly granted by the constitution to the two chambers. If the three organs could not agree on a budget, the monarchy must

[3] Heinrich O. Meisner, ed., *Der preussische Kronprinz im Verfassungskampf 1863* (Berlin, 1931), 106.

[4] *GW*, I, 62.

[5] Martin Philippson, *Max von Forckenbeck: Ein Lebensbild* (Dresden, 1898), 104ff. On Oct. 7 the resolution passed, 251 to 36.

follow the "law of necessity" and allocate expenditures as it saw fit. "The question of law easily becomes a question of power."[6]

In a later speech Bismarck elucidated the point. Compromise, it had been asserted, was the essence of constitutional government. But if one side insisted dogmatically upon its point of view the series of compromises was broken. "In their place conflicts appear, and, since the life of the state cannot stand still, conflicts become a question of power. Whoever holds the power then proceeds according to his own will, for the life of the state cannot remain still even for a second." This was the famous *Lücketheorie*, the theory of a constitutional hiatus.[7] Against the legal side of the argument the liberals had no good defense, for it was indisputable that the constitution did not provide for the settlement of differences between crown and parliament. The deputies were compelled to take their stand less on the constitution itself, which was purposefully inadequate, than upon the constitutional practices of other countries, which were irrelevant. Nevertheless, Bismarck's use of the theory was not legalistic, but realistic. He argued the case less from the standpoint of law than of power. At one point he even maintained that it was an open question whether in cases of irreconcilable conflict the constitution itself did not become inoperable and the right of absolute government return to the crown.[8]

With this statement of the crown's position there began a duel of endurance between cabinet and parliament that lasted four years to the climax of 1866. From France in June 1862 Bismarck had outlined to Roon the tactics to be used. "The longer the affair is drawn out the more the chamber will sink in public esteem, for they have committed the mistake, and will commit it again, of involving themselves in petty details and have no speakers who do not increase the boredom of the public." While the cabinet continued to rule the country, the deputies must be engaged in "trifling" disputes over the con-

---

[6] BR, II, 19–38. Bismarck's exegesis of the budget clauses in the constitution was no improvisation but merely a restatement of the crown's long-prepared position. See Günter Grünthal, "Grundlagen konstitutionellen Regiments in Preussen 1848–1867," in Gerhard A. Ritter, ed., *Regierung, Bürokratie, und Parlament in Preussen und Deutschland von 1848 bis zur Gegenwart*, 41–55, and *Parlamentarismus in Preussen 1848/49–1857/58, Preussischer Konstitutionalismus—Parlament und Regierung in der Reaktionsära* (Düsseldorf, 1982), 52–65, 129–150.

[7] BR, II, 76–87. As Bismarck confessed, the theory was not his invention, but a loophole deliberately intended by those who drafted the constitution. *Ibid.*, 83–84. It had been defended in the *Sternzeitung* on Aug. 14 and 19 and advanced by the king in his debate with the cabinet. [Hahn, ed.], *Innere Politik*, 26–32; Kurt Promnitz, *Bismarcks Eintritt in das Ministerium: Historische Studien*, 60 (Berlin, 1908), 67–99; Alexander Bergengrün, *Staatsminister August Freiherr von der Heydt* (Leipzig, 1908), 301–304.

[8] BR, II, 84. See Rudolf von Gneist, *Die Militärvorlage von 1892 und der preussische Verfassungskonflikt von 1862 bis 1866* (Berlin, 1893), 19–32. After Bismarck's victory students of constitutional law conceded the validity of his legal position on all points except that of expenditures for military reorganization unauthorized by legislation. Nirrnheim, *Bismarck und die öffentliche Meinung*, 82.

stitution. Ultimately they would tire, hope vainly that the government would "lose its wind," and long for a settlement.[9]

Early in October the House of Lords rejected the amended budget bill for 1862 and exceeded its authority by accepting the original bill proposed by the government. As intended, this embroiled the two chambers in controversy over the powers of the upper house. Amid the uproar Bismarck strode to the rostrum and prorogued the Landtag.[10] For three months the hall was vacant and the liberals deprived of a forum to propagate their views. Meanwhile, Bismarck strove to put pressure on the deputies from other directions. He appealed to the provincial diets to take a stand in favor of the government's position and endeavored to split the small Catholic faction from the opposition by alternately supporting the Papacy against the Italian state and threatening Rome with reprisals against the Catholic church in Prussia.[11] On January 14, 1863, the deputies reassembled as determined as ever. First, they tried the tactic of appealing to the king about the misconduct of his ministers. But Bismarck refused to transmit their petition. "There is a limit to what a king of Prussia can hear." Reached through another channel, Wilhelm replied sharply that the liberal deputies, not his ministers, were violating the constitution.[12]

Soon the Polish insurrection presented the chamber with yet another issue. Although the threat of war hung over the land, the only source of public information was the foreign press. Bismarck refused to answer interpellations concerning the Alvensleben convention, denying the right of parliament to inquire into diplomatic negotiations. Unruh, Waldeck, Sybel, and others fiercely attacked his competence. The convention, they charged, had gratuitously elevated the Polish rebellion from a local to a European crisis and shifted the odium of the "man hunt" in Poland from Petersburg to Berlin. In reply Bismarck accused the deputies of siding with the Poles and inviting foreign attack. Called to order by the speaker, he contemptuously denied that ministers were subject to parliamentary discipline. During April the chamber was further agitated by the Schleswig-Holstein issue. In the event of war against Denmark, Twesten warned, the chamber would not support the government. "I can assure you and I can assure the world," Bismarck lashed out,

[9] GW, XIV, 601. See also Friedrich von Bernhardi, ed., Aus dem Leben Theodor von Bernhardis (Leipzig, 1893–1906), vol. 5, 12; DPO, III, 193.

[10] BR, II, 50ff.; Fritz Löwenthal, Der preussische Verfassungsstreit, 1862–1866 (Munich, 1914), 131–134.

[11] Ludolf Parisius, Leopold Freiherr von Hoverbeck (Berlin, 1897–1900), II/1, 107; Herman von Petersdorff, Kleist-Retzow, (Stuttgart, 1907), 349; HW, I, 120; GW, IV, 4–5; APP, III, 50–51. On the conduct of the Catholic faction see Egmont Zechlin, Bismarck und die Grundlegung der deutschen Grossmacht (Stuttgart, 1930), 345ff.

[12] BR, II, 63–69, 99–103; GW, IV, 48; Horst Kohl, ed., Anhang zu den Gedanken und Erinnerungen von Otto Fürst von Bismarck (Stuttgart, 1901), vol. 1, 47–48.

"that, if we find it necessary to carry on a war, we shall do so with or without your consent." The deputies roared with anger.[13]

While Ludwig Loewe replied for the progressives, Bismarck ostentatiously got up and left the chamber. The deputies protested, and he returned amid a gale of laughter, which changed to fury after he spoke. The speaker, he declared, could be heard well enough behind closed doors; the minister-president had more important matters to attend to. Actually he was writing a letter to his old friend Motley. The pen scratched across the paper, vibrating with rancor and contempt: "I hate politics. . . . At this moment my ears are full of it. I'm compelled to listen to unusually silly speeches from the mouths of unusually childish and excited politicians . . . *querelle d'allemand.* You anglo-saxon yankees have something of that too . . . but your battles are bloody, ours verbose; the babblers cannot rule Prussia. . . . They have too little wit and too much self-satisfaction, are stupid and impudent."[14]

To the spice of anger was added the oil of patriotism. On March 17, 1863, occurred the fiftieth anniversary of the founding of the Prussian militia. Bismarck and Wilhelm saw the chance to remind the public of a time when all had "rallied enthusiastically to the king" and sacrificed "for throne and country." Veterans were invited to garrison banquets, bearers of the Iron Cross to dine with the king and witness a great parade down Unter den Linden.[15] But the effect was cold. In parliament a Polish deputy made everyone uncomfortable by referring to the Polish revolt as a "war of national liberation." Berliners could find no space in their homes for the two thousand knights of the Iron Cross. Workers refused to parade, because they were asked to march behind the troops. A sparse crowd cheered the crown prince and let the king ride by in "icy silence."[16]

At the end of February the deputies had passed a resolution condemning the Alvensleben convention. Bismarck wished to reply by proroguing parliament. But only Roon came to his support in the cabinet. To Ludwig Gerlach, Bismarck vented his anger. He could neither educate his colleagues nor get rid of them; invariably they rejected his proposals; never did they have any of their own. In May the matter was decided by a turbulent scene in the chamber. Like Bismarck, Roon refused to recognize the right of the presiding officer to call him to order. The authority of the speaker, the cabinet insisted, extended "up to the ministers' bench and no further." When the king backed

[13] SBHA (1863), I, 255–265, 327–353, 358–389, 397–419; II, 898–906. On the Polish debates see Irmgard Goldschmidt, *Der polnische Aufstand von 1863 in den Verhandlungen des preussischen Abgeordnetenhauses* (Cologne, 1937).

[14] SBHA (1863), II, 907–910; GW, XIV, 639.

[15] GW, IV, 19–20; XIV, 631–632; Kohl, ed., *Anhang,* vol. 1, 43–44, 49; BR, II, 69–73.

[16] Goldschmidt, *Polnischer Aufstand,* 22; Bernhardi *Aus dem Leben,* vol. 5, 41–42; HW, I, 138; Martin Philippson, *Friedrich III. als Kronprinz und Kaiser* (Berlin, 1893), 72–73; Nirrnheim, *Bismarck und die öffentliche Meinung,* 195–196.

his ministers, the chamber resolved that the matter could be settled only by a "change of persons and, even more important, a change of system." On May 26 parliament was prorogued. No action had been taken on either the military or budget bills.[17]

Throughout the session Bismarck had been deliberately provocative, his manner haughty, his words scornful and derisive. He had a tactical purpose. Some of his colleagues disapproved of the Alvensleben convention; ultraconservatives were still dubious about his appointment; foreign governments plotted his downfall. On February 25 Theodor Bernhardi reported, "Everyone thinks Bismarck's government finished and is convinced that he can't hold out any longer."[18] By irritating the deputies into taking sides with the Polish rebels, however, the man from Schönhausen convinced Wilhelm afresh that he was struggling against the forces of revolution in Europe. Years later Bismarck confessed having deliberately played the "Junker reactionary." "In the palace the king heard from every side insinuations to the effect that I was a democrat in disguise. I could gain his complete trust only by showing him that I was not afraid of the chamber."[19]

His tactic aroused among the opposition deputies a burning resentment. In the press doubts were raised as to his sanity. To Karl Samwer he seemed "always in half-drunken condition." "He is a gambler," observed Max Duncker, "who doesn't hesitate to risk the existence of Prussia and the dynasty." "Bismarck's end," predicted Prince Karl Anton, "will probably be frightful."[20]

"Disciplining" the Bureaucracy

While the quarrel with parliament intensified, Bismarck and his fellow ministers launched a series of repressive measures against the opposition. The first were aimed at liberal state officials. Both the state administration and judiciary contained many officials who identified themselves with the liberal movement. Having survived the Manteuffel regime, they had enthusiastically served the new-era government and now deplored its passing. Many had seats in the Chamber of Deputies. Since 1847 dual careers in bureaucracy and parliament had been common in Prussia. The principle of separation of powers and functions was weakly developed in a system so recently evolved from

---

[17] GW, VII, 73; SBHA (1863), II, 1189–1190, 1207, 1247–1248, 1262, 1306. Three ministers, among them Eulenburg, were still in doubt about the wisdom of prorogation. Kohl, ed., Anhang, vol. 1, 67–71.

[18] Zechlin, Grundlegung, 526ff.; Bernhardi, Aus dem Leben, vol. 5, 37; Fritz Hartung, "Verantwortliche Regierung, Kabinette und Nebenregierungen im konstitutionellen Preussen, 1848–1918," Forschungen zur brandenburgischen und preussischen Geschichte, 44 (1932), 29–30.

[19] GW, VII, 140; Heinrich von Poschinger, ed., Erinnerungen aus dem Leben von Hans Viktor von Unruh (Stuttgart, 1895), 220–223.

[20] Nirrnheim, Bismarck und die öffentliche Meinung, 142ff.; HW, I, 134; Bernhardi, Aus dem Leben, vol. 5, 107.

absolutism. Of 352 deputies in the Chamber of Deputies, 215 (61 percent) elected in 1855 were officials on active service; in 1862, 142 (40 percent). (In 1862 landowners with 24 percent were the next largest group in the chamber.) During the reaction the cabinet had encouraged *Landräte* to stand for election, and no less than 72 sat in the chamber of 1855. They were the royal officials most often in contact with the voting public, and they had been handpicked for loyalty and subservience. Under the new era an increasing number of judicial officials entered the chamber. Their occupation, security of tenure, and largely bourgeois origin inclined them toward liberalism. In 1862, 111 were elected, constituting 33 percent of the chamber.[21]

Liberals in the state service had always been an anathema to Bismarck; liberal officials actively engaged in politics, doubly so. They were both a source of dissension within the government and the core of the opposition in parliament. To a person of his autocratic temperament this was intolerable. The bureaucracy, he argued, had once acted as a counterweight to the crown, but parliament had assumed this function after 1847. Consequently the bureaucracy must now support the crown against parliament.[22] "Political officials," however, represented opportunity as well as danger. By turning the screws of bureaucratic pressure, the government might coerce them into silence or even into reversing their stand in parliament. Prussian law permitted the removal by administrative action of a number of key officials—from cabinet ministers down to *Landräte*, state's attorneys, and diplomats—"in the interest of the service." Other administrative officials could be dismissed on proof of "hostile partisanship against the government." Judicial officials, on the other hand, could be removed only through a disciplinary procedure designed to protect them against arbitrary punishment. Bismarck would gladly have done away with these legal restrictions by royal fiat, but other ministers objected. Short of this extreme, however, there were many other opportunities for reprisal.[23]

On the suggestion of Hermann Wagener, he proposed in mid-October 1862 measures too punitive for even his reactionary colleagues. Officials serving in the chamber were to be billed for the cost of substitutes whether needed or not. Per diem payments were to be stopped, except for those paying for substitutes. The ministers of commerce and interior, Heinrich von Itzenplitz and Gustav von Jagow, opposed these steps and were supported by most col-

---

[21] Grünthal, "Grundlagen," 50–53; Anderson, *Social and Political Conflict*, 25–26, 445; see also Fritz Hartung, "Zur Geschichte des Beamtentums im 19. und 20. Jahrhundert," *Abhandlungen der deutschen Akademie der Wissenschaften zu Berlin*, Jahrgang 1945/46, Philosophisch-historische Klasse, Nr. 8 (Berlin, 1948), 21ff.

[22] Horst Kohl, ed., *Bismarck-Jahrbuch*, 1 (1894), 16ff.

[23] Zechlin, *Grundlegung*, 348–349: Harro-Jürgen Rejewski, *Die Pflicht zur politischen Treue im preussischen Beamtenrecht (1850–1918): Schriften zur Rechtsgeschichte*, vol. 4 (Berlin, 1973), 68–69.

leagues. All that Bismarck obtained at this time was the dismissal of one *Landrat* and two state's attorneys; six tenured officials were transferred to less desirable posts. The most prominent victim of the transfers was Bockum-Dolffs, the leader of the Left Center and chairman of the house budget committee, who was moved from Koblenz on the Rhine to East Prussian Gumbinnen (Prussia's equivalent of Siberia). These measures were taken despite a constitutional guarantee (article 84) against reprisals for attitudes expressed in parliament. It was a reversion to the practices of the Manteuffel era, to which Wilhelm himself had once strongly objected. The king was troubled but found a way to ease his conscience. Officials who acted out of conviction, he declared, should not be punished "in any way" for opposing the government in parliament; the affected officials had been motivated by "personal considerations." Bismarck justified the action on the grounds that the positions taken by liberal officials in parliament misled the voters concerning the real desires of the king.[24]

The deputies were not alone in feeling the heavy hand of official displeasure. Bismarck was determined to "restore discipline at any cost" throughout the state service. His aim was to convert the bureaucracy into an effective instrument for influencing the electorate. To this end the difficult Jagow was replaced in December 1862 by Count Friedrich zu Eulenburg in the vital Ministry of Interior, which controlled most state officials. Simultaneously Bismarck brought yet another supporter into the cabinet by securing the appointment of Werner von Selchow as minister of agriculture.[25] Eulenburg's first act was to instruct his subordinates that their primary duty was to support the crown "unconditionally." Royal officials must act in all matters with "unity of spirit and will, decisiveness and energy." Differences of opinion within the bureaucracy must not be allowed "to weaken or shake" the crown's authority in public opinion. In April 1863 the cabinet ordered provincial governors to report on the political conduct and sympathies of their subordinates as the first step toward disciplinary action. The responses were thorough, extending even to the conduct of officials in communal governments, state-owned enterprises (railways, mines, foundries, salt works), and state-employed physicians and surgeons.[26]

The most difficult problem was the Ministry of Justice. Since Frederick the

[24] Zechlin, *Grundlegung*, 349–351; Wolfgang Saile, *Hermann Wagener und sein Verhältnis zu Bismarck: Tübinger Studien zur Geschichte und Politik*, vol. 9 (Tübingen, 1958), 67; Kohl, ed., *Anhang*, vol. 1, 31–33; Rejewski, *Pflicht zur Treue*, 65–66; Bernard Steinbach, *Die politische Freiheit der Beamten unter der konstitutionellen Monarchie in Preussen und im Deutschen Reich* (dissertation, Bonn, 1962), 51–52.

[25] GW, XIV, 627, 629; [Hahn, ed.], *Innere Politik*, 132. It was not easy to find a candidate willing to take the resolute action desired. Heinrich O. Meisner, ed., *Kaiser Friedrich III.: Tagebücher von 1848–1866* (Leipzig, 1929), 506–507.

[26] Rejewski, *Pflicht zur Treue*, 63–66.

Great the independence of the judiciary had been a cherished principle in Prussian law. In December 1862 the minister of justice, Count Leopold zur Lippe, directed presiding judges to report on the political activities of subordinate justices and state's attorneys. Although he refused Bismarck's demand that political orientation, rather than seniority, be made the basis of promotion, Lippe did establish this as the criterion for elevating state's attorneys to judgeships. Use was made, furthermore, of the regulation that for unbecoming conduct judges might be transferred or dismissed by a special disciplinary court.[27]

How many officials were affected by Bismarck's "sharp Razzia" is difficult to determine. A liberal deputy, himself a victim, estimated that during the entire period of the conflict at least one thousand suffered reprisals for their political opinions and activities. Twenty were deputies, including nine judges. A "national fund" was established to assist those in need and was deposited in Britain beyond the reach of the Prussian police. Collectors were prosecuted; officers of the militia who signed the appeal were dismissed.[28] Apparently steps were also taken to eradicate liberal influence in the armed forces. Although never as divided as the bureaucracy, the army had some officers of liberal viewpoint. From a correspondent Bernhardi heard of a resurgence of "spying and terrorizing" within the ranks. "They have fear of the people and are afraid they can't be certain of the army any more." "It is generally accepted," he wrote, "that in a certain quarter they want to arouse a spirit of animosity between military and civilians." An "older and wiser group of officers" disapproved, but they hesitated to speak out against what obviously had the support of Edwin Manteuffel and the military cabinet. In the election of September 1863 the troops were forbidden to vote. Roon and Wilhelm regarded the election campaign as hazardous to military discipline.[29]

The Press Edict

Another object of concern during Bismarck's first months in office was the newspaper press. Long ago during the revolution he had learned its political value as a collaborator of the *Kreuzzeitung*. In 1862 the conservative press was hopelessly outclassed. By one estimate it had a daily printing run of about 40,000 copies and a reading public of 200,000; liberal journals published

[27] Bernhardi, *Aus dem Leben*, vol. 5, 160–161; Parisius, *Hoverbeck*, II/1, 171–172; Ludwig von Roenne, *Das Staatsrecht der preussischen Monarchie* (2d ed., Leipzig, 1864), I/1, 247ff. On the political attitudes of the county judges see Anderson, *Social and Political Conflict*, 289–291.

[28] Ludolf Parisius, *Deutschlands politische Parteien und das Ministerium Bismarcks* (Berlin, 1878), 68; Walter Reichle, *Zwischen Staat und Kirche: Das Leben und Wirken des preussischen Kultusministers Heinrich von Mühler* (Berlin, 1938), 129; Zechlin, *Grundlegung*, 350–351.

[29] Anderson, *Social and Political Conflict*, 438; Berhardi, *Aus dem Leben*, vol. 4, 329–330, 338–339; vol. 5, 30–31, 98; Philippson, *Friedrich III.*, 106; Waldemar von Roon, *Denkwürdigkeiten aus dem Leben des General-Feldmarschalls Kriegsministers Grafen von Roon* (4th ed., Breslau, 1897), vol. 2, 166–167.

250,000 copies seen by perhaps 1,250,000 readers. In conference with Wagener, the most important conservative journalist of the day, Bismarck considered ways to dam this liberal stream and expand the conservative trickle into a torrent.[30]

One of his first acts was to end government support of the *Sternzeitung*, a journal of poor circulation long compromised by official connections. Secretly he bought the services of the *Norddeutsche Allgemeine Zeitung*, whose editor was August Brass, a revolutionary of 1848 and former exile. One of his colleagues was the Marxian socialist, Wilhelm Liebknecht, who indignantly resigned when he learned the source of Brass's new income. Camouflaged by its left-wing editor, the *Allgemeine* became the government's consistent defender. The minister-president himself often dictated or corrected articles for its columns. Nourished by this kind of patronage, its circulation steadily increased.[31]

The *Allgemeine* was but one of many newspapers that began to benefit from the public treasury. The financial records of the Ministry of State list an impressive number of journalists and publications in the secret pay of the government.[32] Another form of subsidy was news itself. Beginning in November 1862, all public information was channeled into the columns of the official *Staatsanzeiger* and friendly publications. Under Bismarck's leadership the government began a thorough reorganization and expansion of the official press. For this purpose an embryonic newspaper chain was already in existence. In years past the state administration had established relations with private local newspapers, especially in rural areas, for the purpose of transmitting official information to the public. Where such journals were lacking they had been founded and edited by the county governments. Under orders from Berlin these *Kreisblätter* were now enlarged, given a political character, and made nominally independent. Later they carried the "provincial correspondence," a feature edited by the press bureau of the Ministry of Interior. On occasion Bismarck himself directed what they were to print. The entire system was supported by the state and the taxpayer, but it propagated the partisan views of the Bismarck cabinet and the Conservative party.[33]

---

[30] Anderson, *Social and Political Conflict*, 343; Saile, *Wagener und Bismarck*, 73–78. On the earlier efforts of Wagener and the Volksverein to build up the conservative press see Müller, *Volks-Verein*, 58ff.

[31] GW, XIV, 628; Franz Mehring, *Karl Marx: The Story of His Life* (London, 1936), 331–332; Irmgard Loeber, *Bismarcks Pressepolitik in den Jahren des Verfassungskonfliktes, 1862–1866*, in *Zeitung und Leben*, 24 (Munich, 1935), 16–17; Parisius, *Hoverbeck*, II/1, 125–126, 144–145. For Bismarck's later relationship to the *Allgemeine* see Kurt Forstreuter, "Zu Bismarcks Journalistik: Bismarck und die Norddeutsche Allgemeine Zeitung," *Jahrbuch für die Geschichte Mittel- und Ostdeutschlands*, 2 (1953), 191–210.

[32] Loeber, *Bismarcks Pressepolitik*, 18ff., 64ff. Subsidies were passed to south German newspapers and French journalists through the legations in Frankfurt and Paris.

[33] *Ibid.*, 23ff.; Anderson, *Social and Political Conflict*, 36off. In Jan. 1864 Bismarck told the

Meanwhile, various measures were considered for checking the opposition press. Bismarck proposed a "correction system," which would have compelled editors to print rectifications of purportedly inaccurate statements. But he was persuaded that such "chicanery" was unworthy of the Prussian government. Then he considered either prohibiting or hindering the distribution of liberal journals through the mails. But Eulenburg objected that this was of doubtful legality and too underhanded for the Hohenzollern monarchy. Instead the minister favored use of the press law of 1851.[34]

Although article 27 of the constitution forbade censorship and guaranteed freedom of expression, the framers had been careful to add an escape clause: "Every other restriction upon freedom of the press shall be made only by way of legislation." The press law of 1851 gave the government the power to license and control all media of printed expression. Issues might be confiscated and editors fined or imprisoned for propagating falsehoods, slander, distortions of fact, and incitement to hate or contempt. Under this statute the Manteuffel cabinet had introduced a rigid censorship. Even Wagener's *Kreuzzeitung* was repeatedly confiscated. Because the new-era cabinet had failed to repeal the law, Bismarck and his colleagues were able to put this weapon once more to use. In late 1862 confiscations and prosecutions were stepped up, particularly in Berlin.[35]

But the ministers were dissatisfied with the results. Liberal judges persisted in viewing truth as a factual, not a political matter. Furthermore, the cabinet became impatient with the judicial process itself. Before the bench the state's attorney had to prove his case with specific quotations from the publication in question. The liberal press, it was complained, had long since learned how to make the "most hateful attacks and insinuations against the government, even against the crown itself," without providing evidence usable in court. Even when the government obtained a favorable decision, it affected the individuals accused but not the newspaper itself, which might continue publication in other hands.[36]

On June 1, 1863, five days after parliament had been prorogued, the king signed an edict silencing the opposition press. It provided that a newspaper or periodical could be banned after two warnings because of a "general attitude" considered "dangerous to the public welfare." To the bureaucracy, rather than the courts, was given the power to decide what constituted "public welfare." Appeals could be heard only by the cabinet, not by any judicial

---

Chamber of Deputies, "There is no official press; my first task on becoming a minister was to abolish it." *BR*, II, 300.

[34] Loeber, *Bismarcks Pressepolitik*, 14–17.

[35] *GSP* (1851), 273–287, also 121–122; Anderson, *Social and Political Conflict*, 64–65; Zechlin, *Grundlegung*, 351–353.

[36] Loeber, *Bismarcks Pressepolitik*, 32–33; [Hahn, ed.], *Innere Politik*, 196–197; Anderson, *Social and Political Conflict*, 205–208.

body. Political agitation, it was asserted, had created an "impassioned and unnatural excitement." Journalists misused their freedom to "undermine every foundation of orderly government and of religion and morality as well."[37]

Bernhardi recognized that the edict had been modeled after the press laws of Napoleon III. But Bismarck had gone even further than the dictator across the Rhine. In France a newspaper could be suppressed only for a "specific, judicially provable reason"; in Prussia, for its "general attitude." The diarist felt that the minister-president had crossed the critical dividing line between legitimate rule and arbitrary government. He had arrogated to the crown the right to legislate, interpret, and enforce the law.[38]

The edict was issued under article 63 of the constitution, which granted the king the right to issue decrees while parliament was not in session, but only when "urgently" required to do so "for the preservation of public safety or the settlement of an unusual emergency." Furthermore, such edicts could not conflict with any other provision of the constitution. These conditions had not been met. Nothing had happened that could be construed as a state of emergency; the public safety was in no apparent danger; the decree had obviously been prepared before the Landtag adjourned; the constitution guaranteed freedom of speech. Unanimously the law faculties of Kiel, Göttingen, and Heidelberg declared it unconstitutional.[39]

The king himself was uneasy about the matter. In the crown council of June 1 Bismarck, backed by the other ministers, assured him that there was "no reasonable doubt" about constitutionality. Although not immediately apparent, a threat to public safety would most certainly arise once a "bad press" had corrupted those "classes of the population incapable of independent political judgment." The loyalty of the army might be affected. Finally the prickling of Wilhelm's conscience was soothed by the desire to be convinced. On the protocol he wrote that he had signed the decree "under the assumption" that it did not violate his oath or the constitution and only after being assured that measures would be taken "now or later" to soften its effect upon public opinion.[40] Bismarck could be content. The protocol went into the files for the benefit of historians, the edict into the statute books for immediate use.

The conscience of the crown prince was less easily appeased. For months he had been deeply troubled by the course of the new government. During cabinet meetings he maintained an icy silence. Bismarck's efforts to win him had been in vain. His back was stiffened by his strong-willed English wife and their relatives in the distant palaces of Coburg, Brussels, and London. As the breach between crown and parliament widened, he began to fear for the Hohenzollern the fate of the Stuarts and Bourbons. Before leaving Berlin for

---

[37] GSP (1863), 349–351; [Hahn, ed.], *Innere Politik*, 195–198.
[38] Berhardi, *Aus dem Leben*, vol. 5, 110–111.
[39] Roenne, *Staatsrecht*, I/2, 167.
[40] Meisner, ed., *Kronprinz im Verfassungskampf*, 66–67.

East Prussia on May 31, 1863, he advised his father against "violation or circumvention of the constitution." Now he learned of the press edict in the cold type of a provincial newspaper. Deeply offended, he publicly stated in Danzig that he had had "no part" in the matter.[41]

Wilhelm was shocked and wrathful. He forgot that once during the Crimean War he had contemplated a similar step against his brother, Friedrich Wilhelm IV. For a time he considered court-martial and confinement, the punishments meted out to Frederick the Great as crown prince.[42] But Bismarck persuaded him that the "reason of state" must take precedence over "paternal anger." The affair should be "blunted, ignored, and hushed up."[43] So it would have been had not copies of the letters that passed between father and son leaked into the foreign press. Once again tempers flared. Yet Friedrich Wilhelm lacked the nerves, resolute will, and filial impiety to conduct an open struggle against the king. They reached an uneasy reconciliation. But the relationship between crown prince and minister-president was worse than ever. Like Queen Augusta, Friedrich Wilhelm hated and feared the "Catiline" in the Wilhelmstrasse who seemed to be leading the monarchy into the abyss.[44]

Energetic use was made of the powers granted by the press edict. On June 5 the first warnings were issued in Berlin against six leading newspapers that had published a joint protest. By August 19, according to one estimate, eighty-one warnings had been delivered throughout the country, of which fourteen were in Berlin. Attempts at subterfuge were fruitless. The *Berliner Reform* received its second warning for reprinting passages from Lamartine on the press laws of Charles X. Most editors and publishers bowed to the inevitable. Rather than risk suppression and financial loss they outwardly conformed to the law. A "graveyard stillness" spread through the liberal press, over which could still be heard the strident voices of the conservative newspapers and the bought journals of the government.[45]

    [41] *Ibid.*, 10–22, 65–73; Frederick Ponsonby, ed., *Letters of the Empress Frederick* (New York, 1930), 40–48; Philippson, *Friedrich III.*, 73ff. In a letter to Itzenplitz on June 14 Count Dönhoff reported that Friedrich Wilhelm, to whom he had recently talked, was chiefly resentful about not having been told of the impending decree. BFA, Itzenplitz file. But in his diary the crown prince wrote that his intent was to make himself "publicly known as an opponent of Bismarck and his evil theories." Friedrich III, *Tagebücher, 1848–1866*, 198.

    [42] Heinrich von Poschinger, ed., *Unter Friedrich Wilhelm IV: Denkwürdigkeiten des Ministers Otto Freiherrn von Manteuffel 1848–1858* (Berlin, 1900–1901), vol. 2, 419, also 443. Field Marshal Wrangel favored court-martial, and Edwin Manteuffel advised that such was the king's prerogative. The prince offered to resign his military command and accept any place of exile "where I can remain entirely away from politics." Meisner, ed., *Kronprinz im Verfassungskampf*, 19–29, 74–75, 107.

    [43] GW, XV, 218; Meisner, ed., *Kronprinz im Verfassungskampf*, 77–82.

    [44] Meisner, ed., *Kronprinz im Verfassungskampf*, 23ff., 75–77; Kohl, ed., *Anhang*, vol. 2, 349–352.

    [45] Loeber, *Bismarcks Pressepolitik*, 34ff.

Power or Law?

In the great debate of January 1863 on the *Lücketheorie* Bismarck had vigorously defended himself against the charge of having asserted that "power takes precedence over law."[46] There can be no doubt, however, that this was his actual position. His willingness to go beyond the law is evident in the measures he proposed against liberal officials and newspapers. The press edict stretched even the rubbery Prussian constitution beyond the breaking point. But the most conclusive proof is to be seen in his thoughts about the possibility of a coup d'état during 1863.

On November 11, 1862, Ludwig Gerlach spent an hour in the Wilhelmstrasse and came away deeply disturbed by Bismarck's "absolutism." "One can accomplish a great deal even under a constitution by such ordinary means as fear, enticement, and the like," Bismarck had told him. "If nothing avails, one can still resort to a coup d'état." A few months later, after the deputies had dared to attack the Alvensleben convention, Bismarck remarked that such "injuries" could not be suffered indefinitely or "all authority would be undermined." Decrees against the press and for the suspension of officials might be necessary "and as a last resort abolition of the election law." To the crown prince he confessed that the greatest obstacle to "changes in the constitution" was the king, who took his oath seriously. The ministers too had sworn to uphold it "conscientiously." "What if conscience bids me not to respect it?"[47]

In a crown council on June 16, 1863, the minister-president clashed with colleagues who wished to dissolve parliament and appeal to the electorate afresh. He preferred to rule the country as long as possible without parliament and an opposition press. To hold an election would be a confession of weakness, an admission that in order to govern, the crown needed a majority in parliament. To dissolve parliament would inaugurate a "chain of dissolutions" that could be broken only by a *Staatsstreich*. The crown, he maintained, was not obligated to summon the Landtag before mid-January 1864. In view of the "state of war" existing in Prussia, it was vital that the monarchy use "all means within its power that do not run counter to the constitution."

But other ministers disagreed. Karl von Bodelschwingh, the minister of finance, pointed out that under article 99 the budget was "to be established each year by law." The Landtag must be given a chance to finish the deliber-

---

[46] *BR*, II, 86–88.

[47] Ernst Ludwig von Gerlach, *Aufzeichnungen aus seinem Leben und Wirken, 1795–1877* (Schwerin, 1903), vol. 2, 249–250; Friedrich III, *Tagebücher, 1848–1866*, 510–511. This long-established evidence contradicts the view of Leonhard von Muralt that Bismarck "loyally subjected" himself to the constitution. *Bismarcks Verantwortlichkeit* (Göttingen, 1955), 197, 228. The same is true of Gerhard Ritter's statement that "he actually had nothing in common with the *Staatsstreich* plans of the military cabinet and reactionary hotspurs." *Staatskunst und Kriegshandwerk: Das Problem des "Militarismus" in Deutschland* (Munich, 1954), vol. 1, 203.

ations interrupted in May, if the crown was to show its loyalty to the constitution. Wilhelm found the argument unconvincing. To deal further with a chamber that had openly refused its cooperation was beneath the government's dignity.[48]

In August at Bad Gastein Wilhelm confessed to the crown prince (their first meeting since the Danzig episode) that he too foresaw the likelihood of a series of dissolutions and elections. "Above all obedience must be reestablished in the country." Bismarck painted a similar picture. A "constitutional regime" was "untenable" in Prussia; under parliamentary government the monarchy would inevitably fall apart. Friedrich Wilhelm replied that this was "peculiar talk" coming from a Prussian minister-president. If that was the minister's attitude, why did he continue to govern under the constitution at all? Bismarck replied that he would observe existing laws as long as he could, but the time would yet come when it would be "otherwise"![49]

Because of these remarks Friedrich Wilhelm understood the true meaning of the royal rescript of September 2, 1863, which dissolved parliament. He kept silent during the crown council in which the formal decision was reached. But next day he had it out with his father. A cryptic entry in his diary records the conversation:

C.P.: I didn't want to express my doubts yesterday in front of the ministers. But what about the future?

King: Repeated dissolutions, one after the other.

C.P.: But to what end shall these measures finally lead?

King: Obedience in the country, scaffold, possibly a rupture of the constitution by barricades in the streets and then naturally suspension of the same.

C.P.: In Gastein Bismarck spoke of the untenability of the constitution and of the coming necessity of its abandonment.

King: The Kaiser of Austria and I are both convinced that in twenty years there will be no more constitutions.

C.P.: What then?

King: I don't know. I won't be alive then. But this abominable constitutional system can't continue; it will only bring about the destruction of royal authority and the introduction of a republic with a president as in England [sic]. Scoundrels of the opposition, like Schulze-Delitzsch, have to be shown who is king of Prussia.

This angry exchange produced a new crisis in the royal family. Encouraged by wife and mother, Friedrich Wilhelm refused to attend further sessions of

[48] Meisner, ed., *Kronprinz im Verfassungskampf*, 86–87, 150. Roon and Itzenplitz sided with Bismarck, Eulenburg with Bodelschwingh. Itzenplitz to Bismarck, Aug. 28, 1863. BFA, Itzenplitz file.

[49] Friedrich III, *Tagebücher, 1848–1866*, 209; Meisner, ed., *Kronprinz im Verfassungskampf*, 135, 171–172.

the cabinet. But the Danzig episode was not repeated; the crown prince chose "passive resistance."[50]

In his personal dealings with cabinet members, however, he was far from passive. "When I see him," Roon reported, "he looks like a thundercloud." For a few days after September 2, Bismarck was absent from Berlin, and Roon had the feeling that this alone prevented a "catastrophe." Finally the crown prince and Bismarck met. In his memoirs Bismarck wrote that he would never forget that "hostile expression and olympian dignity" with which the crown prince, his face red and head thrown back, rejected the idea that Bismarck could ever expect to enter his own service. Bismarck spurned the suggestion just as sharply: "That I shall never do!"[51] For many reasons, personal and political, he dreaded the day when this young Hohenzoller would ascend the throne. The possibility was not remote. Wilhelm was sixty-six.

"Now begins the election swindle," Bismarck commented on September 4. During the campaign he attempted to influence voters by an appeal to both Prussian patriotism and German nationalism. The congress of princes and the Austrian reform plan were treated as an attack upon Prussia's existence; their failure, as a triumph of Prussian policy. The call for a popularly elected national parliament was an appeal to small-German sentiment. Silenced on the domestic crisis, liberal journals were compelled to concentrate on foreign news. The Austrian plan was severely criticized and its rejection by Prussia acclaimed. Nevertheless, liberals were not impressed by Bismarck's reply. Although the moderate right ignored it, progressive journals indignantly refused an offer of national unity from such a source. They took solace in the assumption that it was a purely tactical move of no consequence. They were determined to fight the election on domestic issues.[52]

During the campaign the government relied heavily upon the system of bureaucratic intervention that Wilhelm had decried during the 1850s.[53] Efforts were made to discourage liberal officials from standing for election. By cabinet decision (*Staatsministerialbeschluss*) of September 22, 1863, officials serving as deputies were assessed the cost of substitutes appointed by the government. A directive of September 24 from Eulenburg informed them that, if elected, they were bound by oath to follow, both as voters and deputies, the "constitutional way" as determined by the crown. Government employees

---

[50] Friedrich III, *Tagebücher, 1848–1866*, 213; Meisner, ed., *Kronprinz im Verfassungskampf*, 44–47, 160–161. The prince continued to attend crown councils. For a time Wilhelm feared he intended to force the issue by publicly breaking with the regime. From Windsor Castle Queen Victoria wrote her "dear brother" Wilhelm, trying to mediate between father and son. Meisner, ed., *Kronprinz im Verfassungskampf*, 150–153, 161–162.

[51] *GW*, XV, 222.

[52] *GW*, XIV, 652–653; [Hahn, ed.], *Innere Politik*, 221–234; Nirrnheim, *Bismarck und die öffentliche Meinung*, 568ff.

[53] On the character of the campaign see the report of the special investigating committee of the Chamber of Deputies. *SBHA* (1863–1864), IV (Anlagen), nos. 90 and 95.

were ordered to give energetic support to conservative candidates.[54] Wilhelm informed the voters that "an inimical attitude toward my government is incompatible with loyalty to my person." Liberals were thereby branded as unpatriotic and even treasonable.[55]

Otto Manteuffel's rubber-stamp parliament had been elected largely through the efforts of the *Landräte*. Thirteen out of 19 million Prussians lived in rural areas governed by these royal officials. They possessed extensive powers under the Prussian "police state" to regulate local affairs; hence many citizens were dependent upon their favor. They drew up voting lists, delineated precinct boundaries, and supervised the election. Most functioned as election commissioners (*Wahlkommissare*) and, under Prussia's open voting procedure, they actually recorded the votes on election day—even when they were themselves candidates. With assistants they could travel about the country and electioneer at government expense. In the election of 1863 tavern keepers were threatened with loss of license for permitting the opposition to assemble or distribute political literature on the premises. Taverns were the usual places for political assembly, so this was an attempt to interdict the liberal campaign.[56]

Village mayors were threatened with fines and loss of position for voting against government candidates. In some cases they were ordered to stand for the electoral college, there to cast votes for the conservative candidate, perhaps the *Landrat* himself. University professors who criticized were censured. Teachers were admonished to show "piety toward the king and authority" by voting conservative. Pastors preached the Christian virtue of voting as the king desired. Junker landlords put pressure on their tenants and other dependents. Renters of public property were instructed to support the government or suffer consequences. Employees of government-owned railways were likewise coerced. Bismarck was responsible for the suspension of a group of railway workers who failed to prevent a hostile demonstration against himself at the Pomeranian station of Belgard.[57]

This remorseless use of the governmental apparatus for partisan purposes was not without effect on October 20. When the votes were in, the conservatives could count thirty-six deputies in the chamber as against their previ-

---

[54] Bernhard Mann, "Zwischen Hegemonie und Partikularismus," in Gerhard A. Ritter, ed., *Regierung, Bürokratie, und Parlament in Preussen und Deutschland von 1848 bis zur Gegenwart* (Düsseldorf, 1983), 85; Steinbach, *Politische Freiheit*, 46–50. Anderson, *Social and Political Conflict*, 386–387. Apparently other cabinet members (except the minister of justice) issued similar rescripts. Beneath the cabinet level the heads of bureaus and governors of provinces and districts followed suit. *SBHA* (1863–1864), IV (Anlagen), 604ff. See also Bismarck's directive to Ernst von Senfft-Pilsach, *GW*, XIV, 653–654. According to one authority, twenty officials were punished under these directives. Parisius, *Hoverbeck*, II/1, 176, 183.

[55] [Hahn, ed.], *Innere Politik*, 241; Löwenthal, *Verfassungsstreit*, 203–204.

[56] Anderson, *Social and Political Conflict*, 386ff.; Steinbach, *Politische Freiheit*, 48–49.

[57] Anderson, *Social and Political Conflict*, 395; Steinbach, *Politische Freiheit*, 52; *GW*, XIV, 656.

ous ten. In many cases liberal deputies were reelected by greatly reduced majorities. With 258 out of 350 seats, however, they still dominated the chamber. Once again a migration toward the left was apparent. Although progressives and left centrists gained a few seats, the old-liberal constitutionalists were seriously reduced; even Georg von Vincke went down to defeat. The number of officials in the house was reduced to 126, of whom 90 were judges—none of them conservative.[58]

The result was about what Bismarck had expected. The only cause for gratification was that the elected conservatives included some "greater capacities" than before, notably Wagener and Blanckenburg. But the great issue between crown and parliament remained undecided and Bismarck's doubts about the viability of the Prussian system unchanged. "The Prussian monarchy and our present constitution," he told Schleinitz on October 26, "are irreconcilable." Many obstacles, he confessed, stood in the way of the "complete and unconditional elimination" of the latter. The chief of these was the king.[59] But experience had shown that Wilhelm's conscience was malleable.

[58] Anderson, *Social and Political Conflict,* 412; Parisius, *Hoverbeck,* II/1, 180–181; Steinbach, *Politische Freiheit,* 49.
[59] Meisner, ed., *Kronprinz im Verfassungskampf,* 171–172.

Speculation about the Masses

A Test of German Liberalism

URING Bismarck's first year in office German liberalism underwent its greatest test between the revolutions of 1848 and 1918. Since September 1862 the Prussian opposition had been subjected to a steady crescendo of dictatorial measures. The press law, an obvious breach of the constitution, was the climax. How did liberals react?

Twenty-three liberal newspapers published a common protest, branding the edict as unconstitutional. First warnings were immediately issued by the Ministry of Interior, and the journals lapsed into silence on the domestic crisis rather than incur financial ruin. On June 4, 1863, the Berlin city council voted to send a delegation to the king protesting arbitrary actions by the government. Other city councils followed suit. But the cabinet reacted swiftly. On June 6 Interior Minister Eulenburg issued an order forbidding city governments to take any notice of national politics and threatening mayors and other municipal officials with disciplinary action in the event of disobedience. The movement subsided. On the proposal of Hermann Schulze-Delitzsch a "society for the preservation of the constitutional freedom of the press in Prussia" was founded. It solicited legal opinions from the law faculties in Kiel, Göttingen, and Heidelberg (all of them critical) and published warnings issued by the government to the press in order to demonstrate their tyrannical character. But, otherwise, the society appears to have accomplished little.[1]

Reports of the crown prince's Danzig speech appeared in most German newspapers and aroused considerable comment. But the effect was dulled, as Bismarck hoped, by the absence of outward consequences. Friedrich Wilhelm was not summoned back to Berlin and summarily stripped of his rank and command. Instead he continued his inspection tour, while the king departed for Karlsbad and his annual cure. The "indiscretion" of the letters was the sensation of the European press in July, but no Prussian newspaper dared print the story. Those who heard about the matter got their information through

---

[1] [Ludwig Hahn, ed.], *Die innere Politik der preussischen Regierung von 1862 bis 1866* (Berlin, 1866), 199–200; Ludolf Parisius, *Leopold Freiherr von Hoverbeck* (Berlin, 1897–1900), II/1, 170–171; Otto Nirrnheim, *Das erste Jahr des Ministeriums Bismarck und die öffentliche Meinung: Heidelberger Abhandlungen zur mittleren und neueren Geschichte*, vol. 20 (Heidelberg, 1908), 204–205, 216ff.

the uncertain media of leaflets and rumor. Because of the source there was general skepticism.[2]

"The spirit here on the Rhine is excellent," Sybel reported on June 17. In Bonn "liberals and clericals" combined to hold a "great celebration" for the returning deputies. Forbidden by the police to demonstrate, the students drafted a declaration of support. In Krefeld, Sybel's constituency, "the entire town was in motion." A series of petitions and delegations were to be dispatched to king and cabinet.[3] But Prince Karl Anton judged the mood "antiministerial," rather than "antiroyal." The least act of reconciliation by the king would reverse the situation. In Prussia "it is never too late." In July Karl Friedenthal informed Max Duncker that farmers had lost interest in the quarrel. The urban agitation, which had aroused them, was exhausted; the promise of a reduced military service remained unfulfilled. There was a general feeling that in military and political questions the king's judgment was authoritative. From Silesia the deputy Baron Karl von Vincke reported (June 9) that there was almost no talk of politics in the country. The general attitude was: "Nothing comes of it; better let the king rule by himself once more."[4]

Originally the deputies planned to distribute from Berlin a flood of leaflets to substitute for the suppressed journals. But in mid-July Schulze-Delitzsch complained of a dearth of manuscripts. "The best talents are away traveling; the whole press is on vacation."[5] But so were the deputies. Baron Leopold von Hoverbeck, a leader of the democratic progressives, returned home so weary of politics that he could hardly bring himself to visit his constituents. He was overcome by a sense of futility, inclined to believe that the ministers whom the deputies fought were mere "tools" of "unresponsible" personalities beyond their reach.[6] On July 14, 1863, Rudolf Haym, editor of the *Preussische Jahrbücher*, wrote to Eduard Simson: "The conduct of the lot is as miserable as was to be expected. Whoever can seeks a pretext to withdraw, saying, " 'After all, we can't push our way through, we must let the storm blow over,' and the like. He who is involved, fancies himself uninvolved, spares his strength, relaxes from the strain, and leaves the struggle to others. Later he will reappear and be all the louder when the friends of the constitution have been victorious or when some favorable event in foreign affairs has turned the page." But Haym's bravery was confined to letters. Wishing to avoid even a

[2] Heinrich O. Meisner, ed., *Der preussische Kronprinz im Verfassungskampf 1863* (Berlin, 1931), 38–39.

[3] *HW*, II, 155–156.

[4] Johannes Schultze, ed., *Max Duncker: Politischer Briefwechsel aus seinem Nachlass* (Stuttgart, 1923), 347, 356, 365.

[5] *HW*, I, 161; also Ludwig Dehio, "Die Taktik der Opposition während des Konflikts," *Historische Zeitschrift*, 140 (1929), 322, and Friedrich Thorwart, ed., *Hermann Schulze-Delitzschs Schriften und Reden* (Berlin, 1909–1913), vol. 3, 198–200.

[6] Parisius, *Hoverbeck*, II/1, 169.

first warning from the government, he published in the June issue of the *Jahrbücher* two editorials so conciliatory to the Bismarck cabinet that they provoked a furious denunciation from his former collaborator, Heinrich von Treitschke.[7]

Outside Prussia leaders of the Nationalverein were highly disturbed by the feeble reaction to the edict. From Heidelberg the journalist August Ludwig von Rochau complained bitterly to Rudolf von Bennigsen about "the pflegm, the indolence, the indecision" of the Progressive party. But Schulze-Delitzsch calmly replied that outsiders could hardly realize the difficulties of transacting business in a country as large and dispersed as Prussia. He went on to insist that "at this moment" there be "no hurrying, no excessive haste that could rob us of the fruits gained in the struggle."[8] To Gustav Freytag, who was also impatient, he wrote: "The present pause is both natural and necessary. . . . It is a pause not of indolence or exhaustion, but for gathering strength." For one-and-a-half years the deputies had engaged in unrelenting struggle. On vacation they were now "repairing the damage, reprovisioning themselves, in order to be able to renew the contest in the autumn with new strength." Attempts under these circumstances "to force any kind of real agitation" would most certainly fail and in the process do considerable damage to the liberal cause. If the masses were to be brought into motion, it could only be through some "internal calamity" or "great event abroad."[9]

His letter to Bennigsen, however, contained a challenge. It did little good to insist that *something* be done, "when one does not know one's self what."[10] Indeed this was the crux of the matter. In his attack on Haym, published in Freytag's *Grenzboten*, the vitriolic Treitschke wrote darkly of the possibility of revolution in Prussia. "It must be dared," he wrote privately, "as soon as there is prospect of success." But even he complained of the "cowardice" and the "unwillingness to sacrifice" of the "great mass of the liberals."[11] "In the whole of Prussia," Sybel informed Hermann Baumgarten, "you will not find a single person who does not hold open violence to be an act of folly and a crime."[12]

[7] HW, I, 162–163; *Preussische Jahrbücher*, 11 (1863), 627–653; Karl M. Schiller, ed., *Heinrich von Treitschke: Aufsätze, Reden, und Briefe* (Meersburg, 1929), vol. 3, 182–189; Hans Rosenberg, ed., *Ausgewählter Briefwechsel Rudolf Hayms* (Stuttgart, 1930), 313ff.

[8] Hermann Oncken, *Rudolf von Bennigsen* (Stuttgart, 1910), vol. 1, 595–597. See also Nirrnheim, *Bismarck und die öffentliche Meinung*, 182–186, 219–222.

[9] HW, I, 160–161.

[10] Oncken, *Bennigsen*, vol. 1, 595.

[11] Treitschke, *Aufsätze, Reden, Briefe*, vol. 3, 185; vol. 5, 546–548. In the letter in which he broke with Haym, Treitschke asserted that the editor's attitude could only weaken still further "the unfortunately all too feeble indignation of the country." *Ibid.*, vol. 5, 552. Treitschke's call for revolution was more an expression of personal temperament than a judgment of the actual state of affairs in Prussia. See Hildegard Katsch, *Heinrich von Treitschke und die preussisch-deutsche Frage von 1860–1866: Historische Bibliothek*, vol. 40 (Munich, 1919), 27ff.

[12] HW, I, 156.

Riots occurred in the streets of Berlin in early July, but the eviction of a saloonkeeper was the cause, not the prorogued parliament or muzzled press.[13] On September 11 Sybel reported again from Berlin, "No one here wants to precipitate revolution."[14]

Even if the Prussian liberals had been inclined toward violence, there were good reasons for doubting its success. The secret plans of the army for dealing with a popular uprising were still in readiness. In February 1863 Field Marshal Baron Friedrich von Wrangel had increased the number of battalions to be used from fifty to eighty. When the Prussian army of thirty-seven thousand men marched against Denmark a year later, one of nearly equal size (thirty-five thousand) remained behind in the neighborhood of Berlin.[15] At no time during the constitutional conflict did the liberals question that the army, both officers and men, would stand behind the crown against an uprising. In a letter of May 26 historian Sybel wrote that he knew of no occasion in history when "a people had ever been able to accomplish anything by force" when opposed by a trained and disciplined army of two hundred thousand men loyal to the regime.[16]

Since revolution was out of the question, what possibilities remained? The best weapon of any parliament against the executive is financial. By finally denying the funds needed to carry out the military reorganization, the deputies had taken the first step. Under the *Lücketheorie*, nevertheless, the crown continued to expend funds as it saw fit. The constitution provided that taxes, once authorized, might be levied indefinitely without further parliamentary approval. It was the misfortune of the deputies that the period of the constitutional conflict was one of steadily rising national income and increasing tax yields. While the deputies struggled against the crown, their political supporters were piling up the profits and paying the taxes that were to bring about parliament's defeat.

The only possibility of robbing the state of this income was to organize a taxpayers' strike. There was precedent for such an action. Before their dispersal in November 1848 liberals of the Prussian national assembly had vainly called upon the public to refuse taxes for the reactionary government. According to Sybel and Twesten, there was much talk in June 1863 of a similar step. "Nevertheless," the former added, "this, clearly, must begin with the upper bourgeois, if it is to be effective, and among them the matter must ripen

[13] Parisius, *Hoverbeck*, II/1, 171; *HW*, I, 162. Bismarck saw in the affair a possible pretext to banish political agitators, especially writers and journalists, from the city. *GW*, XIV, 644–645; Horst Kohl, ed., *Anhang zu den Gedanken und Erinnerungen von Otto Fürst von Bismarck* (Stuttgart, 1901), vol. 2, 352–353.

[14] *HW*, I, 171, also 98, 102.

[15] Ludwig Dehio, "Die Pläne der Militärpartei und der Konflikt," *Deutsche Rundschau*, 213 (1927), 95–96.

[16] *HW*, I, 153.

somewhat." "Everyone agreed," Twesten wrote, that to call suddenly for a widespread strike was impossible. Ludolf Parisius judged that in any case it would be unconstitutional! In and around Essen a few such acts of defiance by taxpayers did occur, but the government reacted vigorously and the movement collapsed.[17]

Having rejected revolution and discarded a taxpayers' strike, Prussian liberals were bankrupt of ideas. Their ears were closed to the strategy proposed by Ferdinand Lassalle. A radical revolutionary in 1848, the gifted Lassalle now belonged to the left wing of the Progressive party. In speeches of 1862 he had proposed a kind of parliamentary strike. Undisguised absolutism, he argued, was no longer possible in an increasingly industrialized society with an expanding burgher class. Consequently, authoritarian monarchies had been forced to resort to sham constitutionalism. To be victorious, the deputies need only rip away this veil of deception by adjourning the lower chamber until the government yielded. Under modern conditions, he asserted, no monarchy could rule indefinitely without parliament. "A government that has its hands continually in everyone's pocket must assume at least the appearance of having everyone's consent."[18]

By this proposal Lassalle, who had already taken the first step toward founding a socialist movement, probably intended to challenge the liberals and expose their unwillingness to undertake decisive action that might have a revolutionary outcome. If so, he was soon proved right. His suggestion was immediately attacked by the entire liberal press. The one deputy who endorsed it was so isolated that he resigned his seat in parliament.[19]

Even after the election of October 1863 the deputies were disinclined to force the issue by taking any positive step. To be sure, they reelected the presiding officers (Grabow and Bockum-Dolffs) who had clashed so bitterly with Roon and Bismarck in the preceding session. They exercised their right under the constitution to vote down the press edict, which thereby became inoperative. A committee investigated and recorded the abuses of the government in the election.[20] The army bill was again rejected, and the funds for military reorganization were struck out of the budget for 1864. Nevertheless, the deputies turned down once more the motion that the budget bill be rejected outright without debate or amendment.[21] Nothing came of the pro-

[17] HW, I, 156, 159, 175–176; Parisius, Hoverbeck, II/2, 1–2.

[18] Ludwig Maenner, ed., Ferdinand Lassalle: Reden und Schriften in Friedrich Meinecke and Hermann Oncken, eds., Klassiker der Politik (Berlin, 1926), vol. 15, 177–207.

[19] Hermann Oncken, Lassalle: Eine politische Biographie (4th ed., Stuttgart, 1923), 280–282; Schlomo Na'aman, Lassalle (Hanover, 1970), 569ff.; Martin Philippson, Max von Forckenbeck: Ein Lebensbild (Dresden, 1898), 109–110; Fritz Löwenthal, Der preussische Verfassungsstreit, 1862–1866 (Munich, 1914), 197–198.

[20] SBHA (1863–1864), I, 75–111.

[21] Ibid., II, 713ff. The debate on this subject is most illuminating for the conflicting views on tactics within the liberal movement.

posal that the chamber pass a series of "striking resolutions," culminating in a demand for resignation of the cabinet and a call for a taxpayers' strike.[22]

The inactivity of Prussian liberals in 1863 was not merely a fault of inadequate leadership. Behind their unwillingness to engage in decisive action—whether revolution, taxpayers' strike, or parliamentary strike—was the crippling uncertainty of popular support. In the midst of the election campaign Bernhardi noted signs that the public was "completely fed up with politics."[23] Even the slender gains made by conservatives on election day had a depressing effect. The journalist Wilhelm Wehrenpfennig estimated that another election might increase by threefold the number of conservative deputies; Haym judged that repeated dissolutions would produce a ministerial majority. Twesten, who favored outright rejection of the budget bill, reported that most believed such an act "would ruin us with the voters, particularly the rural ones." From Berlin Karl Mathy, a prominent Baden liberal, wrote to Freytag on November 13, "The longing for compromise hovers in the air. . . . The progressives are tame; they no longer feel so certain in their trust that the voters will persevere."[24]

Uncertainty about the constancy of the voters is not the only explanation for the opposition's indecision in 1863. Since 1848 no significant leader and no faction—wherever situated in the spectrum of liberal politics—had openly and consistently striven for the conquest of state power. To engage in decisive action against the Bismarck government and the crown required not only an appeal to the bottom strata of German society, the uneducated and unperfumed masses whom they regarded as unready for politics, but also a readiness on their own part to assume full responsibility for governing. At most what "committed liberals" had striven for was the opportunity to replace the Junker cabinet by demonstrating to king and country that Prussia could only move forward in domestic and foreign politics under a liberal cabinet drawn from the *Mittelstand* and representing its values.[25] But Bismarck's performance belied the assumption of inevitability that underlay that claim. The liberal fort was built on sand, and, while the deputies anxiously watched for the first cracks, Bismarck considered ways and means to rip away the whole foundation.

Search for a Popular Foundation

Contrary to what the crown prince assumed, Bismarck had not made up his mind to abandon the Prussian constitution. Undoubtedly the king was nearer the truth when he wrote to his son in October. "You always come back to

[22] Meisner, ed., *Kronprinz im Verfassungskampf*, 171–172.
[23] Friedrich von Bernhardi, ed., *Aus dem Leben Theodor von Bernhardis* (Leipzig, 1893–1906).
[24] HW, I, 177–178, 181, 185–186; Rosenberg, ed., *Haym: Briefwechsel*, 225.
[25] See pp. 165, 186–189.

Minister von Bismarck's utterance that we could reach the point of dispensing with the constitution. In his conversation with you at Gastein he presented this as one . . . possibility, while you make it out to be the goal of his efforts."[26] As in the struggle against Austria, many paths had to be explored, of which the most dangerous was the last. But none of the routes tried during Bismarck's first year in office had led anywhere. Hence the possibility of a coup d'état became increasingly real.

What form ought it to take? Here apparently Bismarck was not in agreement with the king. Wilhelm was still troubled by his oath to uphold the constitution. Rather than openly violate it, he preferred to wait until the opposition's hatred boiled over into rebellion. By resorting to the barricades, the liberals would themselves break the law and thereby release the monarch from the obligation to obey it. While his generals crushed the revolt, following the plan long prepared, Wilhelm would scrap the constitution and return to the type of personal rule that existed before 1848.

For Bismarck this was not a pleasing prospect. Although willing to accept it as a last resort, he had never been sympathetic to the idea of absolutism. Such a move would be tantamount to an admission that the monarchy's only secure foundation was the army. Bismarck wished to enlarge rather than restrict the base of the government's support. By returning to absolutism Prussia would further isolate itself in Germany; German nationalists would regard as an utter farce the Hohenzollern proposal for a national parliament. Furthermore, Bismarck saw no reason for discarding the whole constitution. On the contrary, the document designed by Manteuffel and his reactionary colleagues had proved sufficiently elastic to meet the needs of the monarchy in the constitutional conflict. The only gap of embarrassing size had been covered by the *Lücketheorie*. The fault lay not with the constitution itself, but with one of its details—the electoral law.[27]

In Bismarck's opinion the political complexion of the Chamber of Deputies was the artificial consequence of the three-class voting system, not the actual state of Prussian opinion. The law of May 30, 1849, divided voters into three categories according to the amount of taxes paid. In the beginning this enabled aristocratic owners of eastern latifundia to concentrate their strength in classes I and II, which paid two-thirds of the taxes and chose two-thirds of the electors. By the late 1850s, the increased tempo of industrialization had created a new plutocracy with incomes greater than the gentry. Many who had previously voted in the first division were forced into the second, others from the second into the third. By 1861 class I contained 159,000 voters; class II, 454,000; class III, 2,750,000. Although they achieved majorities in all three

[26] Meisner, ed., *Kronprinz im Verfassungskampf*, 176–177.

[27] Revision of the electoral law was the last resort mentioned to Gerlach in their talk of Mar. 4. GW, VII, 73. See Richard Augst, *Bismarcks Stellung zum parlamentarischen Wahlrecht* (Leipzig, 1917), 42ff.

divisions in the elections of 1861–1863, liberals were strongest among the men of new wealth who now dominated the first two.[28]

Theoretically universal (that is, for males), Prussia's suffrage was actually very limited because of its inequality. Despite the great agitation in chamber and press, 65 percent of those eligible did not vote in the election of 1862, nearly 70 percent in 1863. The number of delinquents was highest in the two western provinces, the traditional strongholds of liberal influence; in Westphalia 80 percent and in the Rhineland 82 percent of the electorate failed to vote in 1863. Most significant of all is the fact that throughout Prussia the greatest proportion of absentees belonged to class III. In 1863, 43 percent of class I, 56 percent of class II, and 73 percent of class III did not go to the polls. In the new industrial towns of western Germany the percentage of lower class delinquents was often above 90.[29]

What were the reasons for this failure? The poor man knew that his vote was worth only one-seventeenth that of a wealthy person. Voting was indirect and by voice rather than ballot. The procedure of open voting was time-consuming and potentially hazardous for those financially dependent upon others of contrary political views. For urban workers, moreover, the problem of daily bread was more immediate and pressing than what went on in the Landtag. On the land the peasantry had been accustomed for centuries to the idea that political questions were the proper concern of someone higher up. The Stein reforms and the revolution of 1848 had made some inroads upon this lethargy, but both had been followed by long periods of political stagnation. One suspects that the constitutional conflict had the appearance of a quarrel between the upper classes, between those who had the power and those who had the votes. Those who had neither busied themselves with other matters.

In this untapped reservoir Bismarck hoped to find new sources of support for the monarchy. His strategy was the same as on previous occasions. In 1853 he had sought outside Germany a political force capable of exerting pressure on the Austrian coalition in the Bundestag; after 1858 he saw in German nationalism a potential ally of similar utility; now he sought in the lowest social strata a new reserve that could be set in motion against the liberal views of the middle and upper *Mittelstand*. Unlike Wilhelm, he was not content

[28] Johannes Ziekursch, *Politische Geschichte des neuen deutschen Kaiserreiches* (Frankfurt a. M., 1925–1930), vol. 1, 59–61. On the Prussian electoral system in general see Eugene Anderson, *The Social and Political Conflict in Prussia 1858–1864* (Lincoln, 1954), 255ff. For Bismarck's view of it see Hans J. Schoeps, "Unveröffenlichte Bismarckbriefe," *Zeitschrift für Religions- und Geistesgeschichte*, 2 (1949), 15; *BR*, II, 94–95; Ernst Ludwig von Gerlach, *Aufzeichnungen aus seinem Leben und Wirken, 1795–1877* (Schwerin, 1903), vol. 2, 255.

[29] Ziekursch, *Politische Geschichte*, vol. 1, 61–62; Anderson, *Social and Political Conflict*, 413ff.; Löwenthal, *Verfassungsstreit*, 147. Bismarck estimated that only one-seventeenth of those eligible voted, with the consequence that those who reached the chamber were "the distilled bourgeoisie . . . the organized revolution." Gustav Mayer, *Bismarck und Lassalle: Ihr Briefwechsel und ihre Gespräche* (Berlin, 1928), 34, 36.

merely to retreat behind the moated and bristling battlements of the Prussian military state. He much preferred to maneuver in open country, mobilizing new forces with which to turn the flanks of the foe and, if possible, strike him in the rear.

The idea of exploiting workers and artisans against the new elite of "culture and property" was not a sudden one for Bismarck. Never had he doubted the loyalty of the peasantry to the monarchy; liberalism and rebellion were in his view the natural products of cities. In 1848 he first became aware of a "bitter tension" between burghers and workers in Berlin and of its potential value for the nobility. Although the former supported the revolution, the latter were partial to "king and military" and wanted the crown to regain its authority.[30] The democratic radicals of the extreme left, moreover, had a certain fascination for him. During the years of reaction he often sought their company and conversation, finding them more congenial than the moderates. In 1851, he reported receiving "the most respectful greetings" from the "reddest of the red here and abroad." Their press was "flattering." "They love us of the extreme right in contrast to the way they feel about the Gothaer."[31]

After 1849 he watched the government of Otto Manteuffel seek through social reform to win the support of peasants and artisans. Originally he shared the conservative prejudice favoring artisans ("the backbone of the burgher class") and the guild system that protected their interests. During his years in the great commercial city of Frankfurt, however, he became convinced of the inefficiency of the guilds and of the virtues of mass production; he became a convert to the cause of industrial freedom. His conversion removed a major obstacle to his future collaboration with Germany's capitalists.[32] But it also marked his realization that the spread of the factory system was inevitable and that the factory proletariat was destined to replace handicraftsmen as the working class of the future. This was the first step toward the recognition of its social interests—and its political potential.

The Social Problem

Once the depression of 1857 had been overcome, Germany entered another decade of rapid industrial progress. New clusters of smokestacks belched their soot into the air; humming machines demanded the presence of more and more workers; the social cleavage between owner and worker deepened. Once

[30] GW, XIV, 114. Josef Maria von Radowitz told Friedrich Wilhelm IV that workingmen were the logical allies of conservatives against bourgeois liberals. Friedrich Meinecke, *Radowitz und die deutsche Revolution* (Berlin, 1913), 77–78, 531–532; Theodore S. Hamerow, *Restoration, Revolution, Reaction: Economics and Politics in Germany, 1815–1871* (Princeton, 1958), 72ff., 174ff. There is some evidence of a deliberate effort by conservatives to arouse Berlin workers against the revolutionary government in 1848. Erich Jordan, *Die Entstehung der konservativen Partei und die preussischen Agrarverhältnisse vor 1848* (Munich, 1914), 285–296.

[31] GW, VII, 15–16, 24; XIV, 150, 189, 192.

[32] BR, I, 130ff.; GW, XIV, 302; Hamerow, *Restoration, Revolution, Reaction*, 248–251.

more the artisans were in retreat before the inexorable advance of factory production. Their proletarian rivals, on the other hand, suffered many of the typical evils of early industrialism: long hours, rising prices, uneven employment, poor housing, and penury in sickness and old age. Except for some efforts to provide decent lodging, most entrepreneurs were smugly content not to worry about the social consequences of their business activities. Liberal economics required them to believe that any artificial interference with "natural laws" of supply and demand in the labor market would spell disaster for employer and employee alike. Under the influence of Manchesterism, the new-era government began to strip away guild protectionism, but did nothing to repeal the law prohibiting trade unions.[33]

Liberals were little conscious of the wisdom of binding urban workingmen to the *Mittelstand* in a common struggle against the monarchy. At most they desired only their moral and passive support. In the absence of an independent proletarian movement in Germany, it was assumed that this could be had without any effort to satisfy the social needs of labor. Liberal interest in the lower classes was limited to the founding of educational societies for workers (*Arbeiterbildungsvereine*). Workers should not be encouraged to become politically active until they reached an educational level sufficient to enable them to appreciate liberal ideas. The attitude of the Nationalverein is instructive—though willing to finance a workers' delegation to the industrial fair in London in 1861, the association repeatedly refused to lower its dues to encourage proletarian membership. Though critical of the three-class system, most liberals favored suffrage restrictions of some kind. As long as they prospered under the three-class system, they could see no reason to agitate against it. The issue was unmentioned in the progressive platform of 1861. Even Waldeck, leader of the extreme democratic faction, believed that the time had not yet come to strive for equal suffrage. Liberals were repelled by the very example that inspired Bismarck: Napoleon's exploitation of universal suffrage for autocratic purposes. Only a few individuals on the outer fringe of the movement, like Franz Ziegler and Lassalle, favored an equal franchise for the masses.[34]

[33] Hamerow, *Restoration, Revolution, Reaction*, 238ff.; Julius Becker, *Das deutsche Manchestertum: Eine Studie zur Geschichte des wirtschaftspolitischen Individualismus* (Karlsruhe, 1907), 79ff.; Pierre Benaerts, *Les origines de la grande industrie allemande* (Paris, 1933), 573ff.

[34] Ernst Schraepler, "Linksliberalismus und Arbeiterschaft in der preussischen Konfliktszeit," in Richard Dietrich and Gerhard Oestreich, eds., *Forschungen zu Staat und Verfassung: Festgabe für Fritz Hartung* (Berlin, 1958), 385–401; Hermann Oncken, "Der Nationalverein und die Anfänge der deutschen Arbeiterbewegung 1862–1863," *Archiv für die Geschichte des Sozialismus und der Arbeiterbewegung* (1912), vol. 2, 120–127; Paul Herrmann, *Die Entstehung des deutschen Nationalvereins und die Gründung seiner Wochenschrift* (Leipzig, 1932), 113; Walter Gagel, *Die Wahlrechtsfrage in der Geschichte der deutschen liberalen Parteien 1848–1918* (Düsseldorf, 1958), 22ff.; Hans Neumann, "Franz Ziegler und die Politik der liberalen Oppositionsparteien von 1845–1866," *Forschungen zur brandenburgischen und preussischen Geschichte*, 37 (1925), 280–281; Wil-

A major exception was Schulze-Delitzsch. With some success he sought to bind workers to the liberal cause by promoting its economic interests within the limits of liberal economic doctrine. His program was one of "self-help" through the founding of workers' cooperatives with the aid of private capital. But the chief beneficiaries were members of the lower *Mittelstand*, especially artisans, not industrial workers. Credit, raw material, storage, and consumer cooperatives strengthened their ability to survive the calamities of an increasingly big business economy. For indigent proletarians he had only the limp advice that by saving they might accumulate enough capital to join the cooperative system. Nor did he succeed in winning the Progressive party to the principle of equal suffrage.[35]

This was the heart of Lassalle's program. Disgusted by the impotence of progressives in the constitutional conflict, the fiery agitator turned to industrial workers for realization of his ideal of a democratic Germany. In April 1862, he called upon proletarians to recognize themselves as the "fourth estate" to whom the future belonged. Attacking Schulze-Delitzsch's "self-help" cooperatives as futile, he demanded factory cooperatives based on "state-help." To obtain this assistance, labor must first gain political power through the grant of universal, direct, and equal suffrage. On March 1, 1863, Lassalle issued the manifesto that led to the creation of a General German Workers Association to agitate for this end. By their obtuseness on the social and political needs of the emerging stratum of factory workers, German liberals opened the way for its estrangement.[36]

In this they were not entirely alone. Prussian conservatives were almost equally blind to the potentialities of the social question. Their rural background was no preparation for an understanding of the social upheaval produced by the industrial revolution. The social relationship to which they were accustomed was that between noble landowner and submissive peasant. Their blindness was also owing to the character of their religious belief. The propagation of faith, not social welfare, was regarded as the proper concern of the Lutheran church. Christian morality was primarily a matter of inner piety rather than social service. In conservative thought the idea persisted that proletarians should regard themselves as a new estate (*Arbeiterstand*), functioning like *Adelsstand* and *Mittelstand* within the organic body of society. That many refused to conform to this romantic pattern and aspired to equality was regarded with irritation and impatience.[37]

---

helm Biermann, *Franz Leo Benedikt Waldeck: Ein Streiter für Freiheit und Recht* (Paderborn, 1928), 296.

[35] Schulze-Delitzsch, *Schriften und Reden*, V, 186–187, 201.

[36] Oncken, *Lassalle*, 293ff.; *Lassalle: Reden und Schriften*, 209–245; Schraepler, "Linksliberalismus und Arbeiterschaft," 393–401; Gustav Mayer, "Die Trennung der proletarischen von der bürgerlichen Demokratie in Deutschland, 1863–1870," *Archiv für die Geschichte des Sozialismus und der Arbeiterbewegung* (1912), vol. 2, 1–67.

[37] See William O. Shanahan, *German Protestants Face the Social Question* (Notre Dame, 1954),

Although they shared these prejudices, Victor Aimé Huber and Hermann Wagener had a better understanding of the social developments in their time than did most conservatives. A teacher and publicist, Huber was troubled by the deterioration of religious faith in working class families. The reason lay, he believed, in their social circumstances. Through cooperatives of various kinds, particularly housing, he hoped to raise living standards and integrate the proletarian estate into a stable Christian society. Like Schulze-Delitzsch, he believed in "self-help" rather than state assistance. An independent and disputatious soul, Huber had no talent for practical politics and never sought to found a movement.[38]

For Wagener, the political aspect of the social problem was all important. Failure to grasp the social issue, he predicted, would lead to the ruin of the monarchy and aristocratic order. With others of similar opinion he published the Berliner Revue, whose columns favored agrarianism, anti-Semitism, and "social realism." To the state, Wagener argued, belonged the primary responsibility for social welfare. He rejected the plans of Huber, Lassalle, and Schulze-Delitzsch, yet proposed that the government foster model productive associations as yardsticks for determining wages, hours, and working conditions in different industries. This would be a guide to future legislative action and government control.[39]

Wagener's social view had some of the characteristic limitations of the conservatives. Although interested in promoting the interests of factory workingmen, he understood best the artisan class. His Volksverein was an alliance of landowners and handicraftsmen. He favored the right to organize, but opposed strikes and believed that trade unions should take their place, like the guilds, in the corporative structure of society. He rejected the three-class voting system and wanted to reorganize the electorate into occupational estates of traditional character.[40] He believed that such a program would be popular among workers and that through it the monarchy could easily win any serious contest for the allegiance of workers. "This is the sore spot that the Progressive party carries around on its body." The monarchy must establish itself as the protector of the masses. "This is the secret of the popularity of Bonapartism."[41]

Throughout Europe conservative politicians found the political system of Napoleon III an enlightening phenomenon. Nationalism, democracy, and

---

and Fritz Fischer, "Der deutsche Protestantismus und die Politik im 19. Jahrhundert," Historische Zeitschrift, 171 (1951), 473–518.

[38] Shanahan, German Protestants, 382ff.

[39] Ibid., 362ff. See also Adalbert Hahn, Die Berliner Revue: Ein Beitrag zur Geschichte der konservativen Partei zwischen 1855 und 1875. Historische Studien, vol. 241 (Berlin, 1934).

[40] Hugo Müller, Der preussische Volks-Verein (Berlin, 1914), 22ff., 114, 117–120; A. Hahn, Berliner Revue, 96ff.

[41] Adolf Richter, Bismarck und die Arbeiterfrage im preussischen Verfassungskonflikt (Stuttgart, 1935), 26.

socialism were the three principal ingredients in his political recipe. Universal suffrage preserved the fiction of popular participation; the Bonapartist tradition stimulated national pride; state socialism eased the material wants of the lower classes. Through public works, particularly the reconstruction of Paris, Napoleon temporarily reduced unemployment and improved wages. Some progress was made in public housing for workers. Government support was provided for private cooperatives and health insurance undertakings. By selling government bonds in small denominations to people of moderate means he sought to build a sense of identification with the state.[42]

These ideas and experiments were grist for Bismarck's mill. During the 1850s he had studied the structure of the Napoleonic system and had already borrowed parts of it. Wagener was an old friend and collaborator. After a period of eclipse he had reemerged under the new era as the organizer and leader of the Conservative party apparatus. It was only natural that Bismarck should consult him soon after coming to power.[43]

At the minister-president's request the publicist wrote three memorials outlining ways and means of "destroying" the Progressive party. His advice concerning the disciplining of officials, organization of an official press, and suppression and subornation of opposition journals may well have influenced the first actions of the cabinet. His chief recommendation, however, was to base the monarchy upon the masses by promoting their material interests against the "domination of finance capital." Implicit in his argument was the assumption that divine right and aristocratic support were no longer an adequate foundation for monarchical authority. To command the future, the crown must "place itself at the head of the movement" by promoting the "moral and material interests of the masses." In the new age there were only two possibilities: parliamentary government or the imperial system of Napoleon III.[44]

Bismarck underlined the more significant passages in Wagener's memorials. But during the winter of 1862–1863 he was apparently much too busy to launch such a program. In March 1863 he asked Eulenburg to look into the possibility of private old-age pension funds under state supervision. A month later he prodded Itzenplitz to consult Huber for suggestions on social reform. "For political reasons" the government must "act with vigor." But nothing came of these forays. Both ministers were too much under the influence of liberal economic doctrine to believe in the wisdom of state action in such matters.[45]

[42] H. Gollwitzer, "Der Cäsarismus Napoleons III. im Widerhall der öffentlichen Meinung Deutschlands," *Historische Zeitschrift*, 173 (1952), 23–75; Walter Vogel, *Bismarcks Arbeiterversicherung* (Braunschweig, 1951), 16–19.

[43] Wolfgang Saile, *Hermann Wagener und sein Verhältnis zu Bismarck: Tübinger Studien zur Geschichte und Politik*, vol. 9 (Tübingen, 1958), 65ff.; Hermann Wagener, *Erlebtes* (2d ed., Berlin, 1884), vol. 2, 17.

[44] Saile, *Wagener und Bismarck*, 133–144.

[45] GW, IV, 84–85, 94–95; Richter, *Arbeiterfrage*, 87–90.

The Talks with Lassalle

Perhaps through Wagener Bismarck became aware of the split among the progressives signified by the founding of the General German Workers Association. In May 1863 he took the extraordinary step of summoning Lassalle for a secret talk. Over the next ten months the radical agitator and minister-president conferred repeatedly. Years later Bismarck testified that Lassalle was "one of the most clever and attractive men with whom I have ever talked. . . . Our conversations went on for hours, and I was always sorry when they ended." For all that divided them, they had much in common. Both were bold, outspoken, pragmatic, and brilliant. And they shared the same foe.[46]

While frankly admitting the "revolutionary" nature of his movement, Lassalle maintained that he had no dogmatic ideas about governmental forms. "The working class," he declared, "is instinctively inclined toward dictatorship," but it must first be convinced that "this power will be exercised in its own interest." Proletarians would shed their republicanism and willingly accept a "social dictatorship" by the crown, if the latter would only "strike out in a truly revolutionary and national direction and transform itself from a monarchy of the privileged classes into a social and revolutionary people's monarchy."[47]

HERMANN WAGENER IN 1871 (BILDARCHIV PREUSSISCHER KULTURBESITZ).

FERDINAND LASSALLE, ABOUT 1860 (BILDARCHIV PREUSSISCHER KULTURBESITZ).

[46] GW, XI, 606.

[47] Mayer, *Bismarck und Lassalle*, 60–61; Schlomo Na'aman, "Lassalles Beziehungen zu Bismarck—Ihr Sinn und Zweck," *Archiv für Sozialgeschichte*, vol. 2 (1962), 55–85, and Lassalle. *Reden und Schriften*, 622–625.

In the end the discussion centered upon the crucial subject of the election law. According to Lassalle, Bismarck declared his intention "some day" to ally the monarchy with the people through the proclamation of equal suffrage. But how was it to be introduced? The majority in the Chamber of Deputies would vote against it, and the king was against a coup d'état. Lassalle had the answer. Having been established by decree, the three-class system could be repealed the same way. This would automatically resuscitate the law of 1848, which had provided for universal, direct, and equal male suffrage.[48]

The king's unwillingness openly to break the law was not the only reason for Bismarck's reluctance. He was unconvinced that universal suffrage would in itself produce a governmental majority. What if the lower classes continued to stay away from the polls even if given the equal vote? Once more the facile Lassalle found a "magic formula." Able-bodied citizens who failed to vote in two successive elections should lose their civil rights for ten years. But still Bismarck was not impressed. He wanted assurance that the voters would not only go to the polls, but also vote conservative when they got there.[49] For all his talk about the "instinctive" royalism of the masses, he was not fully certain of their support. Later he described what he had in mind to his colleagues in the cabinet. One way to assure the "influence of the government on the spot" would be to send election commissioners to poll the population, house by house. Or the existing election law might be changed so that government candidates would automatically receive the ballots of those who failed to vote.[50] Such were the terms in which Bismarck thought of universal suffrage at the time of his talks with Lassalle.

The drift of events discouraged Lassalle. Within weeks after their first meeting came the press edict. Such measures, the radical warned, would make the proposed alliance impossible.[51] During the fall of 1863 his speeches and writings brought him into conflict with the police and bureaucracy. His appeals to Bismarck had no effect. Apparently Bismarck preferred to keep him under restraint. Early in 1864 a note of desperation appeared in Lassalle's messages. The imminence of war with Denmark caused him to fear that the minister-president had chosen the path of foreign adventure over internal reform. When the conflict came, Bismarck did sever their relationship.[52] In August Lassalle fell in a duel over a love affair.

The reasons for Bismarck's decision against an alliance with the proletarian left in 1863 are not difficult to discern. Despite the exertions of its dynamic

---

[48] Mayer, *Bismarck und Lassalle*, 28–29, 41, 61.

[49] *Ibid.*, 42–43, 81–84.

[50] *Ibid.*, 35–36.

[51] *Ibid.*, 61.

[52] *Ibid.*, 80, 87–88; GW, VII, 94–95; Hermann Oncken, "Bismarck, Lassalle und die Oktroyierung des gleichen und direkten Wahlrechts in Preussen," *Historisch-politische Aufsätze und Reden* (Munich, 1914), vol. 2, 195–196.

leader, the workers' association enjoyed only limited success. When he died, there were forty-six hundred members, of whom three thousand were Prussian. In Berlin, where Schulze-Delitzsch reigned supreme, the followers of Lassalle were just thirty-five. "What could Lassalle offer and give me?" Bismarck asked in 1878. The "poor devil" had "nothing behind him."[53]

[53] Oncken, *Lassalle*, 440; *GW*, XI, 606.

BOOK THREE

The Years of Triumph,

1864–1867

Exalt his self-esteem toward foreigners and
the Prussian forgets whatever bothers him
about conditions at home.

—*Bismarck in 1858*

Woe to the unfortunate devotee of principle who thinks of the past,
who is so naive and so unrealistic to assert that right
is still right and wrong still wrong, that
success can create power, but never right!

—*Wilhelm Liebknecht in 1866*

✠

CHAPTER ELEVEN

The Conquest of Schleswig-Holstein

The Problem of the Duchies

O
N THE SURFACE the Schleswig-Holstein question appeared to present Bismarck with a fine chance to strike at the domestic opposition through an impressive coup in foreign affairs. Since 1848 the "North Mark" had been a cause célèbre of German nationalism. In that year the government in Copenhagen had first attempted to incorporate Schleswig into Denmark. With Holstein and tiny Lauenburg, Schleswig was a possession of the Danish crown, but, unlike them, it did not belong to the German Confederation. By tradition, nevertheless, the two larger duchies were inseparable, and the Danish action threatened to split them apart. The Germans in the duchies rose in revolt, and the Frankfurt Parliament commissioned Prussia to intervene in their behalf. But after a short campaign Berlin withdrew under pressure from the European powers, and the parliament was impotent to succor the rebels. More than any other event of 1848, this episode revealed the powerlessness of the assembly in the Paulskirche. The failure in Schleswig-Holstein presaged the failure of the German revolution itself.[1]

The Danes also suffered frustration. Although Austria and Prussia agreed with the other great powers in the treaty of London (May 1852) to respect the integrity of the Danish monarchy, Denmark was compelled to promise the dual powers (treaty of December 1851) never to incorporate Schleswig or take any steps toward that end; in addition, the king promised to consult the ducal estates concerning any future constitutional union with Denmark. This left the ambitions of Danish nationalists unsatiated and the practical problem of ruling the duchies unsolved. During the 1850s the issue remained alive, and in 1863 King Frederick VII issued his "March Patent," which established a new constitutional arrangement without the required consultation and augured a fresh attempt to incorporate Schleswig. During the next six months the Frankfurt Diet ponderously ground out an order of execution against Denmark. But the Danes were not discouraged. Europe was preoccupied with the Polish question; the diet was quarreling over confederate reform; Prussia was troubled by an internal conflict; England and France seemed friendly to Denmark; and from Sweden came vague promises of military assistance.[2]

---

[1] On the problem of the duchies see the classic study by Lawrence D. Steefel, *The Schleswig-Holstein Question* (Cambridge, Mass., 1932).

[2] *Ibid.*, 55ff.

Suddenly, on November 15, 1863, the Danish case was thrown into confusion by the unexpected death of King Frederick. He had no direct heir. In the treaty of London the powers had sought to take care of this problem by recognizing in advance the claims of Prince Christian of Glücksburg to both the Danish kingdom and the duchies. Nevertheless, the German Prince Friedrich of Augustenburg, on hearing the news from Copenhagen, immediately proclaimed himself "Friedrich VIII, Duke of Schleswig-Holstein." At Gotha, under the protection of Duke Ernst of Coburg, he immediately began to assemble a government. Within a short time his sovereignty, although of doubtful legality, had been recognized by most of the German lesser states.

The Augustenburg cause was also quickly taken up by liberal nationalists throughout Germany. The fate of the duchies was regarded as a critical test of the vitality of German nationalism. If unable to meet the challenge of tiny Denmark, Germany could hardly expect to generate the power necessary to create a nation-state. For many the issue was also a test of the German will to political freedom. On hearing the news from Copenhagen, Gottfried Planck, professor of law at Kiel, wrote to his old friend Rudolf von Bennigsen, "Upon the outcome depends not only the rescue of the duchies for Germany and the entire position of Germany abroad, but also the course of our inner development for many years to come." Failure would result in either revolution or,

PRINCE FRIEDRICH VON AUGUSTENBURG AS "DUKE FRIEDRICH OF SCHLESWIG-HOLSTEIN" (BILDARCHIV PREUSSISCHER KULTURBESITZ).

more likely, a general relapse into the crudest kind of reaction.[3] To men of his conviction unity and freedom were still synonymous; progress toward one meant progress toward the other.

The Augustenburg cause appeared to embody both. Prince Friedrich was known to be of liberal and nationalistic conviction. His good friend, Duke Ernst, was the patron of the Nationalverein. In 1848–1850 the prince had served with his father in the revolutionary army of Schleswig-Holstein.[4] Nevertheless, support of his claims placed the German liberals in the anomalous position of upholding the principle of legitimacy and seeking to increase the number of lesser states. On both points they had reversed themselves.

Immediately after the death of the Danish king, the leaders of the Nationalverein hastened to exploit the new situation. On November 18 Bennigsen summoned the executive committee to meet in Berlin. There it was quickly decided to give Prince Friedrich every possible assistance. A highly inflammatory appeal was released to the public. Schleswig-Holstein, it asserted, must not be allowed to suffer the fate of Alsace-Lorraine. The Germans must reclaim the northern duchies from Denmark, just as their ancestors had reconquered East Prussia from Poland, Pomerania from Sweden, and the Rhineland from France. As "sons of the common fatherland," the German princes must take note of their responsibilities. Although willing to "pardon and forget many wrongs," the people would never forgive "betrayal of their honor and freedom to foreigners." Patriotic associations were called upon to hold in readiness men, money, weapons, and matériel. A coordinating committee was set up in Göttingen under the Hanoverian politician Johannes Miquel.[5]

But soon the Nationalverein reduced its activity in favor of a new organization with a broader base. On the subject of Schleswig-Holstein and the claims of Augustenburg the association found itself in agreement with its rival, the Reformverein. Combining their efforts, the small-German and great-German organizations summoned the deputies of all German parliaments to rally in Frankfurt on December 21. Nearly five hundred came and voted unanimously to make the cause of Augustenburg that of Germany itself. Although the great-Germanists objected, a permanent "committee of thirty-six" was created to act as a "center of legal activity" in marshaling support for the duchies. Intoxicated by their new-found unity of purpose, the nationalists proposed to exploit popular indignation to sweep the German governments into action. Here was their opportunity to demonstrate the existence of a

[3] Hermann Oncken, ed., *Grossherzog Friedrich I. von Baden und die deutsche Politik von 1854–1871* (Stuttgart, 1927), vol. 1, 621; Johannes Ziekursch, *Politische Geschichte des neuen deutschen Kaiserreiches* (Frankfurt a. M., 1925–1930), vol. 1, 129–130.

[4] On the Augustenburgs, father and son, see Johann H. Gebauer, *Christian August, Herzog von Schleswig-Holstein* (Stuttgart, 1910), and Karl Jansen and Karl Samwer, *Schleswig-Holsteins Befreiung* (Wiesbaden, 1897), 103ff.

[5] Hermann Oncken, *Rudolf von Bennigsen* (Stuttgart, 1910), vol. 1, 621ff.

national movement of overwhelming power, which in the future no German statesman dare ignore.[6]

Hatred of the foreigner is the best possible cement for a divided nation. Even the Prussian conservatives joined the swelling chorus of moral outrage. Where the rights of German principalities against outsiders were concerned they were not immune to national sentiment. Many were impressed by the argument of legitimacy. Since 1848 the Danish experiments with liberal constitutions had been a thorn in the flesh of conservative Europe. Impressed by these arguments, King Wilhelm himself favored recognition of Augustenburg. The crown prince, who had known Prince Friedrich as a student in Bonn, was his warm supporter.[7]

Amid the general enthusiasm a ripple of uneasiness spread through the minds of Prussian liberals. What if the sinister man at Wilhelmstrasse 76 should turn the situation to his own advantage? Would he seek to head a great national crusade against Denmark? Dared they carry out their threat to refuse credits for such a war? If so, what would be the consequence for their own prestige in Germany? Would they be tortured by the necessity of choosing between national unity and political freedom?[8]

Their equanimity was soon restored. On November 28, 1863, Prussia and Austria publicly based their case against Denmark on the treaties of 1851–1852, rather than on the claims of Augustenburg. A month later they branded the committee of thirty-six as "revolutionary" and called upon the states of the confederation to suppress it.[9] Throughout Germany these actions were regarded by liberals as a "betrayal" of the national cause. In Prussia the leaders of the opposition returned to the attack. Apparently they had been absolutely right in believing that a Junker reactionary could never act for the good of the nation.[10] Denmark and Bismarck could now be condemned in the same breath.

Bismarck had good reasons for passing up such a favorable opportunity.

[6] Erich Zimmermann, *Der deutsche Reformverein* (Pforzheim, 1929), 75–88; Theodor Schieder, *Die kleindeutsche Partei in Bayern: Münchener historische Abhandlungen*, vol. 12 (Munich, 1936), 41ff.; Adolf Rapp, *Die Württemberger und die nationale Frage, 1863–1871: Darstellungen aus der württembergischen Geschichte*, vol. 4 (Stuttgart, 1910), 59ff.; Liselotte Konrad, *Baden und die schleswig-holsteinische Frage, 1863–1866: Historische Studien*, vol. 265 (Berlin, 1935), 44ff.

[7] Gerhard Ritter, *Die preussischen Konservativen und Bismarcks deutsche Politik, 1858–1875* (Heidelberg, 1913), 89ff.

[8] Ludwig Dehio, "Die Taktik der Opposition während des Konflikts," *Historische Zeitschrift*, 140 (1929), 325–327; Ludolf Parisius, *Leopold Freiherr von Hoverbeck* (Berlin, 1897–1900), II/1, 195; Oncken, *Bennigsen*, vol. 1, 630–631; HW, I, 183, 187. Bernhardi and Max Duncker hoped Bismarck would exploit the Schleswig-Holstein affair in order to end the domestic crisis. Friedrich von Bernhardi, ed., *Aus dem Leben Theodor von Bernhardis* (Leipzig, 1893–1906), vol. 5, 146, 154–155.

[9] APP, IV, 148.

[10] Dehio, "Taktik der Opposition," 327ff.

Despite outward appearances, the Augustenburg cause did not fit his purposes. To have backed it would have ruined his own secret plans for the duchies and aroused diplomatic complications of a dangerous kind.

The Strategy of Alternatives

Bismarck had long been familiar with the Schleswig-Holstein problem and alive to its possibilities for Prussia. In 1856 he confessed to Bernhard von Bülow, the Danish minister in Frankfurt, that "he was no friend of a sentimental or national policy and much too Prussian to make any distinctions in his feelings between Spaniards, Bavarians, or Danes. His only concern was whether Prussia had an interest in quarreling with Denmark or disrupting the Danish monarchy. For the time being this was not the case."[11] Hence he advised his government to pose before the public as the defender of German national honor in the duchies, but to make no earnest attempt to solve the problem. Instead Prussia should delay a settlement until such time as she might extract some "practical gain" from it.[12]

By "gain," of course, he meant an increase in power. In his opinion, the solution desired by German nationalists would not add to Prussia's might. Quite the contrary, it would create another medium state that, like Hanover and Hesse, would inevitably fear Prussia and flirt with Austria. What Bismarck wished, long before he could openly say so, was incorporation of the duchies into Prussia. His mind brimmed with thoughts of expansion. "Prussia's mission," he declared, "is to extend itself."[13]

The odds against success were enormous. In Europe, Germany, and Prussia itself there was scarcely an important person or interest sympathetic to Bismarck's purpose. Among the great powers England and Austria were completely opposed to Prussian annexation, Russia mildly so. Although Napoleon encouraged it, his support was costly and possibly treacherous. All of the German lesser states backed Augustenburg. The Prussian king and crown prince had no thought of seizing the opportunity to expand their kingdom. Bismarck's own subordinates in the foreign service, some of whom had direct access to the royal ear, were against his policy. In the Chamber of Deputies all parties were inclined toward or committed to Augustenburg. Only the left-liberal Benedikt Waldeck, completely unaware of Bismarck's intention, came

---

[11] Arnold Oskor Meyer, "Die Zielsetzung in Bismarcks schleswig-holsteinischer Politik von 1855 bis 1864," *Zeitschrift der Gesellschaft für Schleswig-Holsteinische Geschichte*, 53 (1923), 112–113. In mid-February 1864 he told Ludwig Gerlach, "I am a Prussian, not a German." What he ought to say, Gerlach replied, was, "I am a Prussian and therefore a German—or vice versa." Ernst Ludwig von Gerlach, *Aufzeichnungen aus seinem Leben und Wirken, 1795–1877* (Schwerin, 1903), vol. 2, 262.

[12] GW, II, 240.

[13] OD, IV, 118.

out immediately for annexation. With him, no more than with Napoleon, could there be any thought of compact.

After three difficult years, nevertheless, Bismarck got what he wanted. That he was able to maneuver his way through and over these many obstacles is one of the amazing feats in the history of politics. In later years he spoke of it as his "proudest" achievement.[14] His approach to the problem was characteristic. In the beginning he was only sure of what he wanted. He knew neither how, when, nor whether it could be attained. At the close of the war in 1864 he wrote, "This trade teaches that one can be as shrewd as the shrewdest in this world and still at any moment go like a child into the dark." That Prussia had been successful he attributed to divine aid, for God had not left him alone in his blindness.[15] Bismarck's faith, however, was not one of resignation. God helps those, he firmly believed, who know how to help themselves.

In typical fashion he analyzed the situation in terms of alternative possibilities. They were three: annexation to Prussia, continued "personal union" of the duchies with Denmark under the Danish crown, or their independence under the house of Augustenburg and inclusion in the German Confederation. If the first alternative were unattainable, which of the other two was to be preferred? German scholars have long disputed this point. His partisans have been quick to deny, his critics to affirm, that Bismarck was willing to leave Germans under alien rule rather than accept a solution disadvantageous to Prussia.[16] What he himself said about the matter varied according to his purpose of the moment. While seeking to coerce Augustenburg into concessions in return for Prussian aid (early 1864), he gave the second option as his preference. After concluding his alliance with German nationalism (late 1866), he maintained that the Augustenburg option had been his second choice. This was also the order listed in his memoirs.[17]

To insist that Bismarck made a choice in 1863–1864 is to misunderstand his whole approach to politics. Everything depended upon the circumstances of final decision. If England and France had intervened and Austrian support failed, he would have had no alternative but to leave the duchies under Danish sovereignty. Certainly a limited Danish sovereignty was preferable to a fully independent Schleswig-Holstein under Augustenburg. The latter solution would probably have been permanent; the former, temporary. The issue could have been reopened at some future date under circumstances more favorable for Prussian conquest. If compelled to accept Augustenburg, on the

---

[14] Moritz Busch, *Bismarck: Some Secret Pages of His History* (London, 1898), vol. 1, 130.

[15] GW, IX, 49; XIV, 672.

[16] Meyer, "Zielsetzung," 103–104; Erich Eyck, *Bismarck: Leben und Werk* (Zurich, 1941–1944), vol. 1, 550.

[17] Meyer, "Zielsetzung," 105–106, 128–130; GW, XV, 254.

other hand, Bismarck intended to exact a heavy price that would have been tantamount to Prussian annexation.

Bismarck's great opportunity lay in the fact that the forces that opposed his primary aim were disunited. Their conflicting interests and ambitions enabled him to occupy his favorite position of the pivot. Again and again he used the availability of choice to frustrate the maneuvers of his opponents. Pressure was met by counterpressure in a precarious balance that for months oscillated back and forth in imminent threat of upset. That it did not was owing to Bismarck's extraordinary skill.

In the beginning this strategy was possible only because his opponents were ignorant of his intention to annex. Otherwise they might have united long enough to wreck his chance of success. Like a hunter crossing a marsh, he remarked to Wagener, "I never advance a foot until certain that the ground to be trod is firm and safe." First, he clung to the treaties of 1851–1852; then, he raised the idea of personal union; finally, he appeared to accept Augustenburg. Each project was dropped or permitted to collapse once its usefulness was over, until eventually the only practical alternative remaining was that of annexation. His conduct of the war shows the same step-by-step progression: first, the confederate execution in Holstein; then, Austro-Prussian occupation of Schleswig; finally, the invasion of Jutland. Either excessive delay or precipitate haste could have brought disaster. Years later he explained to Lothar Bucher, "The individual actions were trifles in themselves; to see that they dovetailed was the difficulty."[18]

Bismarck's Masterpiece

The twists and turns of Bismarckian diplomacy in the Schleswig-Holstein affair are much too intricate to be related here in full. For that matter, no one will ever fully comprehend the dexterity of his performance without reading through the several documentary collections that record, as well as any written record can, his daily decisions and actions. Here it will suffice to trace the broad outline of the story.

Long ago Bismarck had concluded that the duchies could not be acquired without war.[19] Militarily Denmark and Prussia were no match. Prussia's population was 16,000,000; Denmark's was 2,500,000, of whom 30 percent were Germans of doubtful loyalty. Bismarck's task was to see to it that the Danes fought alone. From Great Britain came the greatest threat of intervention. Any weakening of the Danish monarchy was regarded as dangerous to British interests in the Baltic. Without another great power as an ally, however, Brit-

---

[18] BP, II, 24; Steefel, *Schleswig-Holstein*, 95. His success, he remarked to Ludwig Gerlach, was a "matter of luck and circumstances." Gerlach, *Aufzeichnungen*, vol. 2, 267.

[19] APP, III, 133; see also 90–91.

ain could not easily engage in a continental war. Russia was almost out of the question, so Austria and France were the likely candidates. It was necessary then to bind Austria securely to Prussia and keep France and Britain apart.[20]

To this end Bismarck first adopted a policy of outward moderation and strict legality. All that Prussia asked, he declared, was that Denmark live up to her obligations to the German powers under the agreements of 1851–1852. For its part Berlin would hold to the treaty of London and had no intention of threatening the integrity of the Danish monarchy. Within the Prussian government the obstacles to such a policy were considerable. Although disturbed by the liberal character of the Augustenburg movement, Wilhelm was partial to the prince's cause and anxious to be rid of the treaty of London. From every quarter he was bombarded with advice by people of similar views: fellow princes, the queen and crown prince, friends in the old *Wochenblatt* party, and some of Bismarck's own subordinates in the foreign office. At crucial moments the minister-president was able to hold the king in line only by marshaling the support of his cabinet colleagues and threatening to resign.[21]

The London treaty was the rope with which Bismarck took the Austrian government in tow. Because of popular clamor over the duchies Franz Joseph and Rechberg could scarcely pursue a purely negative, "do nothing" policy in the Danish affair, and yet any "national solution" to the problem would have been a dangerous precedent for Vienna. The Habsburg monarchy could not easily support the cause of national self-determination abroad and continue indefinitely to deny it at home. Hence the Austrians were relieved to learn that Bismarck was willing to turn his back upon Augustenburg and the German national movement.[22] After November 1863 the men in the Ballhaus and Hofburg were afflicted by a curious apathy. It was as though, exhausted by the futile struggle of recent years, they had lost the will and energy to protect Austria's interests.[23]

Certainly they realized that there was only one way to avoid the perils of liaison with Bismarck: by binding Prussia firmly to the principle that under no circumstances would Christian's succession to the duchies be open to question. This alone would have made it impossible for Berlin to acquire the duchies or create a small state under Prussian influence. At each successive step of

---

[20] On British and Russian policy see Werner E. Mosse, *European Powers and the German Question, 1848–1871* (Cambridge, Eng., 1958), 146ff.

[21] APP, IV, 188–190, 242–245, 259–262, 264–265, 291–292; Horst Kohl, ed., *Anhang zu den Gedanken und Erinnerungen von Otto Fürst von Bismarck* (Stuttgart, 1901), vol. 1, 86–87; Alfred Stern, *Geschichte Europas seit den Verträgen von 1815 bis zum Frankfurter Frieden von 1871* (Stuttgart, 1899–1924), vol. 9, 582–584; GW, XV, 250ff.

[22] DPO, III, 443–444; APP, IV, 163–164, 186.

[23] "One can say," wrote Moritz Blanckenburg to Ludwig Gerlach on Dec. 4, 1863, "that the Vienna cabinet is now located in the Wilhelmstrasse in Berlin." Gerlach, *Aufzeichnungen*, vol. 2, 259. In April 1864 Bismarck remarked to Keudell that it was "incomprehensible" why the Austrians had followed Prussia into Schleswig. GW, VII, 85.

FRANZ JOSEPH I, KAISER OF AUSTRIA, IN 1861 (BILDARCHIV PREUSSISCHER KULTURBESITZ).

COUNT JOHANN VON RECHBERG (BILDARCHIV PREUSSISCHER KULTURBESITZ).

the dual powers in the Danish affair Rechberg and his colleagues sought to put the Prussians into this restraining harness: before the confederate execution in Holstein, before the Austro-Prussian invasions of Schleswig and Jutland, and finally during the London conference in May 1864.

On each occasion, Bismarck evaded them by use of his balancing technique. As far as he was concerned, so he said, the Austrians could have their guarantee, but, alas, Wilhelm would never accept it. Week after week, he tortured the nerves of Károlyi and Rechberg with the details of his struggles against the Augustenburg faction at the Hohenzollern court. By pressing their demands too far, he warned, the Austrians would push Wilhelm in a radical direction. It was a convincing performance. Even Károlyi, usually less than gullible, concluded that Bismarck had undergone a genuine conversion. All that the Austrians succeeded in extracting was a vague commitment, made before the invasion of Schleswig, that, if Danish resistance should lead to war and abandonment of the treaty of London, the question of the succession would be decided "in no way other than through mutual agreement."[24]

In Frankfurt the dual powers joined forces to insist that the treaties of 1851–1852, not the claims of Augustenburg, must be the basis for action against Denmark. If voted down, they warned, Berlin and Vienna would pro-

---

[24] DPO, III, 436–438, 454–458, 598–606, 616ff., 629–634, 666ff.; IV, 36–37, 47–48, 79ff.; APP, IV, 439ff., 477, 491, 501–502, 737–741.

ceed on their own in defiance of the diet.[25] For years Austria had led the confederate majority against Prussia; now she accepted de facto Bismarck's old position that the diet could not outvote the two great powers. The effect was electrifying. "So they put a knife to our throats!" shouted the Bavarian minister-president. From Frankfurt the Austrian envoy reported that the loss in Austrian prestige among the lesser states was catastrophic.[26]

But again, the lesser states showed themselves incapable of maintaining a solid front against the dual powers. In December 1863 they accepted, by a majority of one, the treaties of 1851–1852 as the basis for intervention in Holstein and Lauenburg. Once Saxon and Hanoverian troops had occupied the southern duchies in the name of the confederation, however, they rejected a proposal of the dual powers that the same motivation be used to justify an invasion of Schleswig. As a consequence, Austria and Prussia made good their threat. In late January 1864 their forces began to cross Holstein in the direction of Schleswig, ready to fight either the Danes or the Saxons and Hanoverians. Sullenly the confederate troops gave way. The high-handed manner in which the Prussians took over the strategic towns and military quarters in Holstein excited fresh indignation. Meeting in Würzburg, ministers of the lesser states resolved to press again for confederate recognition of Augustenburg. Bismarck's reaction was severe. He let the "sheen of the blade show above the scabbard" by mobilizing an army corps on the Saxon frontier. In Vienna Edwin Manteuffel obtained a commitment from Rechberg to join Prussia, if necessary, in an "armed action against Germany." The revolt subsided.[27]

His profession of loyalty to the London treaty was also useful to Bismarck in the British capital. For a time it helped him lull the suspicion of the British cabinet concerning his intentions.[28] The controversy over Schleswig-Holstein was very embarrassing to Russell and his colleagues. Their interests and sympathies, as well as those of the British public, lay with Denmark, and yet the government in Copenhagen appeared to be in the wrong. Repeated attempts at mediation by the British shattered against the persistence of the Danes in clinging to the March Patent. Only the adoption by Germany of the Augustenburg cause would have provided Britain with a satisfactory case for intervention.

Repeated warnings from London on this score provided Bismarck with another weapon. They helped him dampen Wilhelm's enthusiasm for the prince and gave weight to his insistence that the course advocated by the lesser states could result in a major war. On the other hand, his difficulties with the Au-

[25] APP, IV, 255–257.

[26] DPO, III, 476–479, also 449–451.

[27] DPO, III, 720–722. Heinrich Ritter von Srbik, *Deutsche Einheit: Idee und Wirklichkeit vom Heiligen Reich bis Königgrätz* (Munich, 1935–1942), vol. 4, 104ff.

[28] APP, IV, 327–328. See also Steefel, *Schleswig-Holstein*, 132.

gustenburg movement were also useful in London. Pressure from this direction, he argued, compelled Prussia to make her adherence to the London treaty dependent upon Danish fulfillment of her agreements of 1851–1852 with the dual powers. Whenever Russell tried to pin him down as to what constituted fulfillment, Bismarck grew vague.[29]

The crucial moment in British policy came when the dual powers announced their intention to invade Schleswig. Palmerston and Russell were not convinced by Bismarck's argument that a choice had to be made between "invasion of Schleswig and revolution in Germany." But the queen and most of the cabinet were unwilling to go to war over the issue. In any case Britain could not act without the support of France, and in Paris Foreign Minister Drouyn de Lhuys told the British envoy with apparent satisfaction that "the question of Poland had shown that Great Britain could not be relied upon when war was in the distance." The Anglo-French entente was finished.[30]

Had they known what was transpiring between Berlin and Paris, Palmerston and Russell would have been even more perturbed. Since November 1863 Napoleon had been trying to entice Prussia into a policy of annexation. He held out the possibility of her acquiring both the German population of Schleswig-Holstein and the "crowd of small states" hampering Prussian power. "If you now have something to whisper into our ears," Drouyn told Prussian Ambassador Count Robert von der Goltz, "we shall listen attentively."[31] By encouraging Prussia to destroy the German Confederation, the French apparently hoped to give the coup de grâce to the settlement of 1815. Without making any commitments Bismarck kept the suitor hopeful. The "favorable disposition" of the emperor, he explained to Goltz, was necessary as "a means of pressure on England."[32] To keep him in the proper mood, Bismarck stressed repeatedly his willingness to sacrifice the Rhine frontier.[33]

As the invasion neared, he resorted to a typical maneuver. Prussia had a choice, he warned Britain and Russia, "between two alternatives": she could

---

[29] APP, IV, 188–190, 194–197, 213, 219–221, 252–255, 268–270, 286–287, 292–293, 300ff., 357–359, 369–372.

[30] APP, IV, 361; Steefel, *Schleswig-Holstein*, 166–167; Mosse, *European Powers*, 159ff.

[31] APP, IV, 197–201, 207–209, 223–224, 344–346.

[32] APP, IV, 334–337.

[33] To Talleyrand and Károlyi (Dec. 16) and Fleury (Dec. 24) he declared that, if faced with a choice between Prussia's Polish possessions and the left bank of the Rhine, he would advise surrendering the latter. APP, IV, 324; DPO, III, 505. Fleury reported, "As for the Rhine frontier, the word has been spoken; should it be stressed?" "Don't speak of the Rhine," Napoleon replied, "and play down Poland." OD, I, 4. On the significance of these remarks see Herbert Geuss, *Bismarck und Napoleon III.: Kölner Historische Abhandlungen*, vol. 1 (Cologne, 1959), 97–98, and Gerhard Ritter, "Bismarck und die Rheinpolitik Napoleons III.," *Rheinische Vierteljahrsblätter*, 15–16 (1950–1951), 353–354. Geuss and Ritter were probably correct in considering the enticement a mere "maneuver" intended to keep Napoleon's favor. But this should not be dogmatized into the assertion that the sacrifice of German soil was unthinkable to Bismarck.

maintain the London treaty and preserve the recent entente between the four great powers against France, or she could abandon the treaty and "make common cause with the rest of the confederation and perhaps with the French cabinet." Although the second course "would facilitate our position considerably," Berlin preferred to continue upon the first. To Sir Andrew Buchanan, the British ambassador, he expressed the hope that Great Britain "would not give a signal for the commencement of a steeplechase to Paris."[34]

This strategy sufficed to isolate the battlefield in Schleswig, but soon the problem arose again in connection with the projected invasion of Jutland. Retreating from the fortified line of the Dannevirke, made vulnerable by thick ice over the Schlei, the Danes had withdrawn northward into Jutland and behind the trenches of Düppel in eastern Schleswig. While Bismarck was secretly negotiating with the Austrians to extend the war beyond the Schleswig frontier, a detachment of Prussian troops unexpectedly crossed into Jutland and occupied the town of Kolding. Once more the British contemplated intervention. On the Seine there were ominous signs that Napoleon might reverse his policy and join them.[35] But the majority in the London cabinet voted against the venture, and the emperor appears to have reconsidered. Bismarck reinforced the French decision in characteristic fashion. Opposition from Paris, he warned French Ambassador Charles de Talleyrand, would force Prussia to halt the Jutland operation. London, Vienna, and Petersburg were already making difficulties. Berlin could not afford to alienate all of these powers. "From the moment that you show us *faccia feroce*, we must put ourselves on good terms with Austria."[36]

The diplomatic struggle of the Danish War reached a climax at the international conference that began to assemble in London on April 20, 1864, two days after German troops had stormed and taken the trenches at Düppel, the last Danish foothold on the mainland. In summoning the conference, Russell had hoped to find a way to end the conflict with as little change as possible in the status quo ante bellum. Bismarck saw in it a chance to get rid of the London treaty, which, after screening the German advance up the Danish peninsula, had now outlived its usefulness. After informing the conference on May 12 that they no longer regarded the treaties of 1851–1852 as binding, the dual powers left open the possibility of "personal union" between the duchies and Denmark under King Christian. To the great distress of the Austrians the Danes obstinately refused to consider such a proposal. Even if they had, no agreement would have been likely. Bismarck had already suc-

---

[34] APP, IV, 466, 482–483; also 438, 458–465, 651–652.

[35] Steefel, *Schleswig-Holstein*, 186ff.; Mosse, *European Powers*, 179ff. The Austrians were shocked by Bismarck's suggestion that rapprochement with France would provide a means of pressure on Great Britain. DPO, 716–720, 772; APP, 592–597.

[36] OD, II, 15, 49. Later he claimed to Gorchakov that the threat had been effective: APP, IV, 622.

BASTION OF DANISH FORTIFICATIONS AT DÜPPEL DESTROYED BY THE PRUSSIAN ASSAULT, APRIL 18, 1864
(BILDARCHIV PREUSSISCHER KULTURBESITZ).

ceeded in getting Austrian consent to a number of "essential conditions" too
onerous for the Danes to accept.[37]

The failure of "personal union" exposed the bankruptcy of Austrian policy.
The London treaty and the principle of the integrity of the Danish monarchy
were dead. With them had expired the only possibility of a satisfactory outcome of the war for Vienna. There remained only a choice between Augustenburg and Hohenzollern rule, between a "national solution" to the German
question and a significant expansion of Prussia power in Germany.

The Danish Capitulation

On February 3, 1864, only two days after the invasion of Schleswig, Bismarck
began to shove forward the alternative of annexation. In a crown council he
openly confessed that this was his ultimate goal. "I reminded the king that
each of his immediate forebears, except his brother, had won for the state an
increase in territory . . . and encouraged him to do the same." But the Hohenzoller was troubled. To the protocol that recorded the discussion he added
that annexation was not the objective of Prussian policy, but merely a possible

[37] APP, IV, 755–756; DPO, IV, 8off.

outcome of the affair. Honest Wilhelm needed time to get accustomed to the idea and more arguments to square it with his conscience.[38]

During the following months Bismarck carefully prepared the ground. Under Baron Constantin von Zedlitz, the Prussian commissioner, the civil administration of occupied Schleswig began to assume a Prussian character. In the duchies a petition was circulated demanding close union with Prussia. In Prussia conservative leader Adolf von Arnim-Boitzenburg launched with Bismarck's connivance a petition bidding the king to seek either a Prussian protectorate or annexation. Conservative members of the Schleswig-Holstein estates appealed to Wilhelm against Augustenburg.[39]

The wind from Paris was fair. In March Napoleon proposed that the London conference consult the "wishes of the population" concerning their future. The other great powers abruptly refused. Bismarck was more subtle. He agreed to the division of Schleswig on national lines, but asserted that the will of the German population could best be ascertained by consulting the ducal estates rather than by popular referendum. Rechberg was shocked by Bismarck's agreement to such a revolutionary proposition.[40] The Austrian's agitation would have been even greater had he known what else had been agreed upon in Berlin and Paris. On April 9 Drouyn consented to Bismarck's view, adding that France would "deplore" a vote for Augustenburg, but support a decision for Prussia. In return she wanted no territory, just a "frank and vigorous entente in other areas." Bismarck's reply was favorable, but cautious. Even so, it cost Wilhelm a sleepless night. Annexation, the king feared, would leave Prussia alone in Europe with her "arch enemy and its inscrutable leader." Would Bonaparte demand "rectification" of the Rhine frontier?[41]

His chief minister was fully aware of the hazard of falling into dependence upon France. Once the threat of British intervention had passed, the main concern of Bismarck's diplomacy—one which was to last until the climax of 1866—was to maintain the delicate balance in Prussia's relations with France and Austria. Napoleon's objective, he well knew, was to sever the line between Berlin and Vienna and fashion the one from Paris to Berlin into a leash.

The easiest way out was to get the Austrians to agree voluntarily to Prussian annexation. In January 1864 he began to plant the idea in the minds of Rechberg and his colleagues that this, after all, might be the best solution to the problem. On the fourteenth he casually told Károlyi that annexation was being discussed in Berlin, adding that he had "firmly" rejected the idea. If the

---

[38] Stern, *Geschichte Europas*, vol. 9, 584–586; GW, XV, 254. On the problem of dating the council see Steefel, *Schleswig-Holstein*, 108–109, and R. Sternfeld, "Der preussische Kronrat von 2./3. Jan. 1864," *Historische Zeitschrift*, 131 (1925), 72–80.

[39] Srbik, *Deutsche Einheit*, vol. 4, 149–150.

[40] OD, II, 144–145; APP, IV, 667, 688, 700–701, 716–717.

[41] APP, IV, 709, 730–735.

course of events should make it a serious possibility, Austria would be compensated in Italy. When Biegeleben visited Berlin in April, the minister-president told him that by giving Prussia a "glorious peace" Vienna would win for herself "not a province, to be sure, but the Prussian army." To Count Bohuslav Chotek, the Austrian chargé, he spoke of the "inauguration of a policy of mutual compensation." In view of Rechberg's distaste for Augustenburg, he seems to have thought that the Austrians might actually accept.[42]

But in this he erred. His own policy ruined by the obstinacy of the Danes, Rechberg was compelled to choose the least harmful of two undesirable options. He chose Augustenburg. Although probably caught by surprise, Bismarck was quick to squeeze advantage out of necessity. With Austrian help it was now possible at least to wrench the duchies conclusively away from Denmark. On May 28 the dual powers astonished Europe by announcing to the London conference their support of the "complete separation" of the duchies from Denmark "and their union in a single state" under the prince of Augustenburg, who "in the eyes of Germany" had "the greatest right to the succession."[43]

Austria's decision drove Bismarck into a corner, but as usual he had a door of escape. Previously he had gotten Austrian agreement to an impressive list of conditions that were to be forced upon the Danes if they agreed to "personal union." Now these conditions were applied to Augustenburg—only the list was longer.

Rebuffed in Berlin, Prince Friedrich had hoped to ride to power on the ground swell of popular sentiment in Germany. No sooner had confederate troops entered Holstein than he established his headquarters in Kiel, which became a center of agitation for the Augustenburg cause in the duchies. To prove his liberalism he proclaimed his support of the revolutionary constitution of 1848, which provided for parliamentary government. Nevertheless, he grasped that Prussian support was indispensable and that it would have to be bought, if it was to be had at all. In April he assured Wilhelm of his willingness to accept inclusion of the duchies in the Zollverein, construction of a peninsular canal and a Prussian naval base at Kiel, erection of a confederate fortress in Rendsburg garrisoned by Prussia, and organization and training of the ducal armed forces on Prussian lines.[44] Three days after the joint declaration in London in his favor he arrived in Berlin for the interview with Bismarck that proved decisive for his cause.

Even before they met, the minister had made known to the prince that

[42] DPO, III, 621; IV, 80, 120; APP, IV, 734, 742–743.

[43] Ludwig Aegidi and Alfred Klauhold, eds., Das Staatsarchiv: Sammlung der officiellen Aktenstücke zur Geschichte der Gegenwart vol. 7 (1865), 23–24.

[44] Jansen and Samwer, Schleswig-Holsteins Befreiung, 116, 163ff., 200ff., 320ff., 717–719; C. Boysen, "Ein Brief Bismarcks an Herzog Friedrich," Zeitschrift der Gesellschaft für Schleswig-Holsteinische Geschichte, 62 (1934), 349–351.

Prussia would require "guarantees of a conservative system of government" in the duchies. In effect, this meant repudiation of the 1848 constitution. During their three-hour interview he also brought up the subject of territorial compensation for Prussia. But the prince refused to bargain away land and peoples without consent of the ducal estates, or for that matter to enter into any written agreement with Prussia. By doing so he would have damaged his own position in the duchies. In his report to the king, Bismarck made the prince out to be an ingrate who, far from being thankful for Prussia's aid, thought to reduce her just demands by appealing to Austria and the ducal estates. So black did he paint him that Wilhelm, who before the interview had thought the issue settled, now began to turn against the Augustenburg cause.[45] Later Bismarck boasted that at London he had "hitched" the Augustenburg "ox" to the plough. "As soon as the plough was in motion he unhitched the ox."[46]

The Austrian-Prussian declaration for Augustenburg left the London conference with nothing to discuss but the partition of Schleswig. In accord with Napoleon, Bismarck was willing to accept a division based on nationality, but the British proposed the line of the Dannevirke far to the south of the language frontier between Danish and German. Still hopeful of British aid, the Danes held to this line, and on June 25 the conference broke up without decision. Although Palmerston and Russell were belligerent, Queen Victoria was horrified at the thought of war against Germany, and the cabinet voted it down. After months of bluster and threat the British abandoned the Danes to their fate. They "recoiled with vigor," sneered Drouyn.[47]

On June 26, 1864, the armistice, which had halted the fighting during the conference, expired. Three days later Prussian forces crossed the narrow channel from the mainland to the island of Alsen, which the Danes were compelled to evacuate. This defeat shattered Danish confidence in the inaccessibility of Zealand. On July 8 a new cabinet took office in Copenhagen, which immediately offered to treat. In the preliminary peace of August 1 and in the final one signed on October 30, King Christian of Denmark ceded forever his rights in the duchies to Austria and Prussia. The Danish phase of the Schleswig-Holstein problem was over, but the question of who would ultimately possess the duchies remained.

Schönbrunn and Rechberg's Fall

With the successful detachment of Schleswig-Holstein from Denmark, the purpose of Bismarck's alliance with Austria would seem to have been fulfilled.

---

[45] Boysen, "Ein Brief Bismarcks," 33off., 730–736; GW, IV, 448–450.
[46] Steefel, Schleswig-Holstein, 256.
[47] Ibid., 240ff., 253.

In fact, Vienna was now the one major obstacle in the way of his next objectives: annexation and the expansion of Prussian power in Germany. Recent
experiences had shown that neither Britain nor Russia would intervene, and
from France came positive encouragement. For eighteen months, nevertheless, Bismarck clung to the Austrian alliance, and even after the final separation began in January 1866 he left open the possibility of return. "Many
paths" had to be explored, "the most dangerous at the end."[48]

Bismarck's aim was to extract from the Hofburg an ever higher price for the
continuation of an alliance that the Austrians were reluctant to sever. Without it they would be isolated and exposed in Europe. To Rechberg and Franz
Joseph it was also the necessary bulwark against France and the forces of revolution in Europe. By careful exploitation of frictions arising from condominium over the duchies, Prussia could make the Austrians, plagued by internal
difficulties and worried about their Italian frontier, long for a settlement—any
settlement to get rid of the affair. A prolonged occupation would enable Berlin to suppress the Augustenburg movement and foster annexation sentiment
in the duchies. Obligated by the peace treaty to pay the cost of the war and
assume their share of the Danish national debt, the ducal taxpayers would
soon see the wisdom of shifting the burden to Prussia. From the nearly bankrupt Austrian treasury there was no prospect of succor.[49]

In late August 1864, soon after the fighting ended in Denmark, Bismarck
had an opportunity to probe once more the minds and intentions of Franz
Joseph and his ministers. On the twenty-first he accompanied Wilhelm to
Vienna on a state visit. Precisely what transpired at the famous Schönbrunn
conference has long been the subject of dispute.[50] Did Bismarck actually offer
Rechberg an alliance against France and Italy for the defense of Venetia and
the recovery of Lombardy, in return for Prussia's annexation of Schleswig-
Holstein and dual solidarity against the middle states? Such an offer would
have been most unlike him, for his system of strategy depended upon the
avoidance of such a choice. Apparently what he did was to dangle once more,
as so often in the past, the enticing possibility of such a bargain. What he
wanted was to acquire the duchies in return for a vague, verbal promise that
at some future date, which might never arrive, Prussia would not object to
Austrian reconquest of Milan, a war she could scarcely undertake without
active Prussian support, which need never be forthcoming.

But Rechberg took him literally. On the morning of the twenty-fourth he

---

[48] GW, IX, 50.

[49] GW, V, 95; OD, VI, 214–215.

[50] See Walter Lipgens, "Bismarcks Österreich-Politik vor 1866," Die Welt als Geschichte, 10
(1950), 240–262; Heinrich Ritter von Srbik, "Die Schönbrunner Konferenzen vom August
1864," Historische Zeitschrift, 153 (1935–1936), 43–88; Rudolf Stadelmann, Das Jahr 1865 und
das Problem von Bismarcks Deutscher Politik: Beihefte der Historischen Zeitschrift, vol. 29 (Munich,
1933).

suddenly presented to the assembled monarchs and ministers the draft of an agreement that stated with uncomfortable exactness that Prussia would receive the duchies if Lombardy were reconquered. Bismarck got rid of the document in typical fashion. Without opposing the proposition himself, he let it trip and fall over the obstacle of Wilhelm's conscience. The critical moment came when Franz Joseph bluntly asked Wilhelm whether he really desired to annex the duchies or whether he was satisfied merely to acquire certain rights in them. There was a tense pause. While Wilhelm groped for a reply, Bismarck had a chance to ward off the question. But instead he encouraged it by declaring that he too wished to learn the king's will. Slowly and in some embarrassment Wilhelm replied that "he had no right to the duchies and hence could lay no claim to them." In his memoirs Bismarck maintained that this avowal put himself "out of action." But in reality it was Rechberg's draft that fell by the wayside. All that the Schönbrunn conferences produced was a meaningless promise of mutual cooperation in the affairs of the confederation.[51]

Rechberg and Franz Joseph continued their erratic course. They wanted to preserve the alliance with Prussia as well as that with the medium states. Suspicious of Prussian ambition, they were still hopeful of keeping Berlin upon the narrow path of conservative virtue. Schmerling, Biegeleben, and their followers were sharply critical of the fluctuations that rose from the incompatibility of these objectives. In October 1864 Biegeleben presented to Franz Joseph a memorandum that bluntly asserted the necessity of either a definite alliance with Prussia or an agreement with France. There being no acceptable ground for the former, Austria must choose the latter. But the Kaiser was unconvinced. He accepted Rechberg's counterplan: no firm alliance with any power, but rapprochement with Britain and Russia and improved relations with France. By this policy of the "middle line" he hoped to halt Prussian aggression in Germany.[52]

Rechberg's days, however, were already numbered owing to the failure of his economic policy. By cooperating with Prussia in the Danish affair, he had hoped to wrest concessions on the issue of the Zollverein. In February 1864 he had renewed his pressure upon Berlin to accept his proposal of 1862 for a central European customs union between the Habsburg Empire and the Zollverein.[53] But Bismarck dragged out the negotiations and blithely continued to force the lesser states to accept renewal of the Zollverein on the basis of the free-trade treaty with France, which Austria could not accept. In December 1863 the Prussian government, backed on this issue by the Landtag, had officially declared that, unless the lesser states agreed to the French treaty,

[51] Lipgens, "Bismarcks Österreich-Politik," 244ff.
[52] DPO, IV, 330–340; Srbik, Deutsche Einheit, vol. 4, 193, 211.
[53] See pp. 158–160.

AT THE RAILROAD CROSSING. RECHBERG TO BISMARCK, "TAKE CARE, COLLEAGUE, THAT WE DON'T
COME APART! WE ARE APPROACHING A DANGEROUS SPOT." (WILHELM SCHOLZ,
KLADDERADATSCH, MARCH 27, 1864.)

the Zollverein would come to an end in 1865 with the expiration of the treaties signed in 1853. No difficulties were encountered with Saxony, Baden, Brunswick, Oldenburg, the free cities, and Thuringian states. After Prussia, Saxony was the most industrialized German state, and its economy was much too closely linked to that of Prussia to contemplate the end of the Zollverein. Major opposition came from Bavaria, Württemberg, Hanover, Hesse-Darmstadt, Hesse-Kassel, and Nassau. Yet their efforts at the Zollverein conferences of 1863–1864 to establish a "third force" (*Trias*) foundered, as so often in the past, upon their conflicting fears and interests. The key state in this combination was Hesse-Kassel because of its central location between the Prussian frontiers and between Hanover and the south. Under heavy pressure from Berlin, the Hessians capitulated at the end of June 1864. In the weeks that followed the "third Germany" dissolved and by mid-October even the southern states had accepted renewal of the Zollverein on the basis of the French treaty.[54]

The blow to Rechberg's prestige was severe. In August his critics in the Austrian government had challenged him to prove the worth of his policy toward Prussia by just one success, if only in the field of economic affairs. Now he tried to bolster his position by demanding that Prussia at least leave open, as in 1853, the possibility of future negotiations for a central European customs union. Bismarck was amenable to this concession—he feared that Rechberg might be replaced by someone more formidable. Yet even this sop to Austrian sensibilities was resolutely opposed by the Prussian ministers of trade and finance and by the economic counselor Rudolf Delbrück, who was the driving force in Prussian economic policy. When the issue came to a head, Bismarck was on vacation in southern France, and his written protests were disregarded. By the time he succeeded in getting his way it was too late. Rechberg, undermined within the government and severely attacked in the press (partly directed by Schmerling), had no choice other than to resign (October 27, 1864).[55]

The reestablishment of the Zollverein and the final defeat of the Bruck–Rechberg plan for a central European customs union were events of major importance in German history. The entry of the Zollverein through the

[54] Helmut Böhme, *Deutschlands Weg zur Grossmacht* (Cologne, 1966), 140ff.; Wolfgang Zorn, "Wirtschafts- und sozialgeschichtliche Zusammenhänge der deutschen Reichsgründungszeit (1850–1879)," *Historische Zeitschrift*, 197 (1963), 329–330; Chester W. Clark, *Franz Joseph and Bismarck: The Diplomacy of Austria before the War of 1866* (Cambridge, Mass., 1934), 91; Eugen Franz, *Der Entscheidungskampf um die wirtschaftspolitische Führung Deutschlands (1856–1867): Schriftenreihe zur bayerischen Landesgeschichte*, vol. 12 (Munich, 1933), 341ff.

[55] *GW*, IV, 544–575; V, 1–3; XIV, 678, 683–684; Waldemar von Roon, *Denkwürdigkeiten aus dem Leben des General-Feldmarschalls Kriegministers Grafen von Roon* (4th ed., Breslau, 1897), vol. 2, 290–291. The figure behind Rechberg's fall may have been Count Moritz Esterhazy, rather than Biegeleben or Schmerling; the real issue, one of domestic rather than Zollverein politics. See Clark, *Franz Joseph and Bismarck*, 146ff., 240–241.

French treaty into the western European trading system demonstrated that Germany had overcome the economic and social aspects of the cleavage that had previously separated it from the west. The fault line in the economic and social geography of Europe had moved eastward from the Rhine to the Austrian frontier. But Prussia's victory also demonstrated how much the economies of the southern states had come under the dominance of the emerging industrial and financial colossus of the north. The common market, railways, banks, joint-stock companies, and bourse had begun to produce an interlocking, interdependent economic order throughout the small-German region. The Zollverein had become indispensable for the material prosperity of the entire area. Twist and turn through they did, the governments of the lesser states were unable to free themselves from the web of material interests that the Zollverein had helped to create.

Yet it is too much to say that with the renewal of the Zollverein the struggle for hegemony in central Europe was decided in favor of Prussia. Economic preponderance did not lead necessarily to political domination.[56] On the contrary, Prussia's success in the economic sphere made the lesser states, their people as well as their governments, all the more determined to defend their political independence. Its own plans shattered, the government in Vienna was now resolved to preserve its traditional political influence in German affairs against further encroachment by Prussia. Without Bismarck's narcissistic determination, his diplomatic skill, and Prussia's military might this resistance could not have been overcome. Here is one of those moments in the processes of history where a single personality, by his capacity to manipulate the forces within his grasp, influenced the course of history and the lives of millions.

The Gastein Convention

The immediate consequence of Rechberg's fall was not as severe as Bismarck feared. The actual author of Austrian foreign policy was not the foreign minister, but the Kaiser, to whom the Biegeleben policy of rapprochement with France and resumption of the offensive against Prussia in the confederation was as uncongenial as ever. As Rechberg's successor he chose Count Alexander von Mensdorff, likewise dedicated to a policy of the "middle line." Nevertheless, Mensdorff was a general with no experience in diplomacy and more dependent upon Biegeleben's counsel than his predecessor. Gradually Austria drifted back toward cooperation with the medium states, and the alliance with Prussia began to loosen. Within weeks after assuming office,

---

[56] Thus Pierre Benaerts, *Les origines de la grande industrie allemande* (Paris, 1933), 646ff., and Böhme, *Deutschlands Weg zur Grossmacht*, 15–17, 182. For the author's view of Böhme's interpretation see "Another Crisis among German Historians? Helmut Böhme's *Deutschlands Weg zur Grossmacht*," *Journal of Modern History*, 40 (1968), 118–129.

Mensdorff found himself deeply involved in the first of a series of sharp crises that were to trouble the German Confederation with increasing intensity until the climax of 1866.

Once the fighting was over, Bismarck resolved to liquidate the confederation's share in the occupation of Schleswig-Holstein. In July 1864 Rechberg had given him a start by agreeing—once more without gaining any real equivalent for Austria—to exclude the diet from the peace negotiations and to provide in the treaty for the cession of sovereignty over the duchies to the dual powers alone. During the same month Prussian troops rudely expelled the Hanoverian forces from the fortress of Rendsburg and Bismarck harshly protested agreements between the confederate commissioners and the Hanseatic cities on the use of telegraph lines in Holstein. On November 14 he followed this up by pressing Vienna for a joint demand that Hanover and Saxony withdraw their troops and officials. Confederate law, he pointed out, did not permit continued occupation after the successful completion of an execution. Because Austria and Prussia were now sovereign in the duchies, their troops alone might legally remain.[57]

As the atmosphere grew cloudy, Prussia and the medium states began to deploy troops in the expectation of violence. From Vienna came the counterdemand that Berlin join in presenting the peace treaty to the diet along with the proposal that confederate troops be withdrawn after sovereignty had been granted to Augustenburg. In late November the affair was settled by a "compromise," which gave Bismarck the essence of what he wanted. He dropped the demand that the dual powers disregard the diet; Mensdorff gave up the demand for Augustenburg, and both powers joined in getting the diet to vote, nine to six, for the withdrawal of confederate troops and commissioners.[58]

Now the question of disposition became more acute than ever. None of the Austrian statesmen was interested in the duchies for their own sake. By his Schönbrunn proposal Rechberg had shown that he was not opposed in principle even to Prussian annexation. What he, Mensdorff, and the Schmerling–Biegeleben faction desired was a settlement that would not disturb the power balance in the confederation to Prussia's advantage. Shortly after assuming office, Mensdorff had asked Prussia to choose between two alternatives: creation of a new principality under Augustenburg rule, or Prussian annexation accompanied by compensation to Austria (the Hohenzollern enclaves in Württemberg and certain border districts in Silesia). Although the message was heavily lathered with conservative principle, Austria had now made clear that, however reluctantly, she was willing to settle the fate of the duchies on the basis of mutual gain.[59]

[57] *GW*, V, 4ff.
[58] *GW*, V, 18–19, 29ff.; XIV, 689–690; *DPO*, IV, 429ff.
[59] *DPO*, IV, 371ff.

While Mensdorff pressed for quick decision, Bismarck answered with a mixture of double-talk and delay. Wilhelm would never agree to the cession of Hohenzollern soil, but Prussia might offer financial rather than territorial compensation. A possible solution was temporary partition of the duchies between the dual powers; someday Austria might grant Holstein to Prussia in return for her assistance in Italy. As for Augustenburg, the legal claims of the grand duke of Oldenburg also had to be considered, and likewise those of the Prussian king as ruler of Brandenburg! Prussia would have to wait upon the opinion of a crown tribunal summoned to judge the legal aspects of the case. In any event, Prussia's willingness to give up annexation would depend upon the extent of the special rights granted her in the duchies.[60]

Previously Bismarck had always avoided being very precise about the nature of these special rights, but now the Austrians pressed for the bill. Week after week Bismarck dallied with his reply, to the increasing irritation of the men in the Ballplatz. When it finally arrived, the content was startling. For all practical purposes the army and navy of Schleswig-Holstein were to be absorbed by Prussia; servicemen were even to swear allegiance to the king of Prussia. Other demands were the cession to Prussia of certain key coastal positions, Prussian construction and control over an isthmian canal, a Prussian garrison in a confederate fortress, and entry of the duchies into the Zollverein.[61] Mensdorff found these "February conditions," as they came to be called, "without precedent in all history." To the astonished Franz Joseph they were "quite unacceptable."[62]

The Austrians had no other choice than to continue the existing condominium in Schleswig-Holstein. Under cover of this policy, however, they strove to construct a firmer defense against the annexation movement. The matter was urgent. By buying up the press and appealing to material interests, Bismarck was making a vigorous effort to win the inhabitants; Baron Zedlitz, the Prussian commissioner, ruled Schleswig as though it were already a Prussian province. In Baron Anton von Halbhuber Vienna finally found a commissioner tough enough to block Zedlitz's encroachment and protect the Augustenburg movement, which now began to bloom. Turning again to the middle states, Mensdorff encouraged Bavaria to submit a resolution to the diet recommending that the dual powers hand over the administration of Holstein to Augustenburg. After a sharp contest for votes it passed, nine to six (April 6, 1865). On the previous day Roon had announced in the Prussian Landtag the government's intent to establish a naval base at Kiel. The Austrians protested sharply. Ominously Bismarck wrote, "We are reaching a bifurcation. . . . Unfortunately our tickets are on diverging lines."[63]

[60] DPO, IV, 387ff.; GW, V, 43–47, 59–66, 77–81.
[61] GW, V, 96–103.
[62] Clark, Franz Joseph and Bismarck, 197.
[63] Ibid., 198ff.; GW, V, 136ff., 158ff.; DPO, IV, 641ff.

The denouement appeared close. In the duchies Bismarck redoubled his efforts to cripple the Augustenburg movement. By March 1865 Wilhelm had been fully won to the idea of annexation. The army, he was assured, demanded it. In fact, the pressure for annexation at the cost of war waxed even stronger than Bismarck desired. On May 29 a crown council was summoned to consider the matter. "Sooner or later," the minister-president admitted, the war would come; at the moment the international situation was favorable. Nevertheless, the wisest course was to eliminate from the February conditions the two points that had met the greatest objection: the oath of allegiance and the "amalgamation" of the Prussian and ducal armed forces.[64]

Why this moderation? Those who believe in the "blood and iron" Bismarck, whether as critics or admirers, have long stumbled over this question. Was it because Prussia could not finance a war?[65] Rising prosperity and tax income had bolstered the government's position in the constitutional conflict, but additional millions were needed for mobilization and military operations. In the months before Gastein Bismarck had hounded the ministers of finance and commerce for fiscal initiatives that would strengthen his hand against Vienna. By manipulating the money market (for example, driving up interest rates), he hoped to make Vienna, whose treasury was in disarray, wary about the possibility of financing a war. But he also urged the reluctant ministers to take bold steps to fill the Prussian war chest.[66] In contrast to Minister of Finance Karl von Bodelschwingh, who had scruples about breaking the constitution, Bismarck was willing to raise a loan without parliament's consent, although only as a last resort.[67] Nine million thalers in state bonds, authorized in 1859 but never issued, were withdrawn from the vaults of the *Seehandlung* and placed on the market.[68] Whether the crown had the right to dispose of state-owned mines and railways without parliament's approval was questionable. But this did not bother Bismarck, any more than it did financiers eager to profit from the liquidation. On July 18, 1865, the Prussian government contracted to sell its options for Cologne-Minden railway shares, acquiring 5,705,000 thalers in cash (3,000,000 payable by October 1, 1865,

[64] Clark, *Franz Joseph and Bismarck*, 542–547; GW, V, 189–190.

[65] The question has been raised by John C. G. Röhl, "Kriegsgefahr und Gasteiner Konvention" in Immanuel Geiss and Berndt Jürgen, eds., *Deutschland in der Weltpolitik des 19. und 20. Jahrhunderts* (Düsseldorf, 1973), 89–103, and by Fritz Stern, *Gold and Iron: Bismarck, Bleichröder, and the Building of the German Empire* (New York, 1977), 62–65.

[66] Röhl, "Kriegsgefahr," 95–99; GW, XIV, 697–699.

[67] Bismarck to Roon, July 3, 1865. GW, XIV, 697–698.

[68] Bleichröder and Bismarck preferred to sell these bonds to the Frankfurt house of Rothschild, soaking up investment capital that might otherwise go to Vienna, but Otto von Camphausen, head of the *Seehandlung*, stubbornly insisted on par, refusing the final Rothschild offer of 99½. Ultimately the bonds were sold at par on the Berlin market in small quantities. As late as Aug. 8, Bismarck telegraphed nervously to Berlin to inquire when the money would be available. Stern, *Gold and Iron*, 64; APP, VI, 318.

the remainder by January 2, 1866); in addition, Prussia received negotiable railway shares worth 7,295,000 thalers and, evidently, the disposal over 17,000,000 thalers previously held in escrow for interest payments. On July 23 Bismarck telegraphed to the crown prince, "The decisions made by his majesty, the king, in the cabinet meeting at Regensburg [held on July 21] have made available about 60,000,000 thalers in funds for a complete mobilization and a military campaign lasting a year."[69] Not all of these funds were immediately accessible, and yet Prussia evidently had the means either in hand or in prospect with which to launch a war in late August 1865. By contrast, Austria was nearly bankrupt.[70]

During June and July the tension rose. Despite Bismarck's recommendations, Wilhelm refused to surrender any of the February conditions. Austrian counterproposals were judged insufficient. Bismarck pressed for the "restoration of order" in the duchies, meaning the suppression of Augustenburg agitation and public criticism of the Prussian occupation. Both sides began to calculate the ponderabilities of war. Bismarck hurried his diplomatic preparations in Turin and Paris. Whether he was satisfied with the results is unclear.[71] In dispatches to Goltz and Usedom on August 16, he stressed that Prussia must either arrive at an understanding with Austria consonant with Prussia's honor and interests or take steps to reinforce its position in the duchies in a way that would render a peaceful solution impossible. Before those steps could be taken, the king must have time to return home (he was at Bad Gastein for his annual cure) and the "financial operations with the Cologne-Minden railway" had to be "sufficiently advanced."[72]

In the summer of 1865 Bismarck continued on his double course because

---

[69] GW, V, 240. For the details of the Cologne-Minden railway transaction see Stern, Gold and Iron, 62–64, 67–68.

[70] On Aug. 1, 1865, Roon wrote to Moritz von Blanckenburg, "There is money, enough to give us a free hand in foreign policy and, if necessary, to mobilize the entire army and pay for an entire campaign. That gives our conduct toward Austria the necessary aplomb, so that we may hope that the Austrians will yield to our justified demands even without a war, which none of us wishes." Denkwürdigkeiten vol. 2, 354–355. From the available evidence it appears that Prussia's financial position was actually better in 1865 than in 1866, when a slump in business activity depressed the stock market, impeded the marketing of Cologne-Minden shares, and made bankers generally wary. By contrast, Austria's position improved in late 1865, owing to the successful negotiation of a loan from French banks for 90 million Gulden. Stern, Gold and Iron, 71–80.

[71] GW, V, 223ff., 242ff., 282ff. Srbik followed the older view that Bismarck had no certainty of the intentions of Italy and France; Stadelmann argued forcefully that he had no reason to doubt Italian aid and French neutrality. Röhl believed that lack of funds forced Bismarck to preserve peace in the summer of 1865. Srbik, Deutsche Einheit, vol. 4, 280ff.; Stadelmann, Das Jahr 1865, 57ff.; Röhl, "Kriegsgefahr," 103.

[72] GW, V, 271, 275. As these dispatches show, the problem of finance was for Bismarck at this point a deterrent of no greater magnitude than the task of getting Wilhelm to break off his cure and return home before hostilities broke out. What saved the peace that summer was not lack of money but Austrian concessions. If Vienna continued to yield, war was unnecessary. With more time, furthermore, the sale of securities could be completed on the best possible terms—before "the ball begins to roll and the bourse to sink." Röhl, "Kriegsgefahr," 98–99.

he was not yet convinced that Austria had reached the end of the long road of concession and compromise. From his remarks in the crown council on May 29 it is clear he regarded the February conditions, even without incorporation of the ducal forces into the Prussian army, as tantamount to annexation. The difference between open and camouflaged incorporation was not great enough to fight about, especially because in time the latter was likely to lead to the former. If war came, he wanted to fight for a "higher aim"—the "creation of a constitutional relationship between Prussia and the German medium and small states."[73] He needed time to prepare Germany for this fate (in 1866 more than two months ensued between Prussia's manifesto for reform and the outbreak of war). Yet he would have gone to war in 1865 if the Austrians had held their ground. Again they retreated.

In a last attempt for a settlement Franz Joseph sent Count Gustav von Blome to confer with Bismarck and Wilhelm at Bad Gastein. In outlook Blome stood much closer to Rechberg than to Mensdorff and Biegeleben. He feared that a second Olmütz would bring another new-era cabinet to power in Berlin with a foreign policy still more hazardous for Vienna than Bismarck's. On August 1 he returned with a proposal that stemmed from Bismarck, although he represented it as his own: the dual powers would divide the duchies, Austria assuming sovereignty in Holstein, Prussia in Schleswig. But the cabinet in Vienna restricted the agreement to the "administration" of the duchies, leaving joint sovereignty nominally intact. Lauenburg was to be sold to Prussia outright. On August 20 the agreement was signed in the episcopal palace at Salzburg.[74]

Blome miscalculated badly. He judged Bismarck to be more "party man" than statesman, interested primarily in the suppression of "democracy" at home rather than in warring against Austria. He expected Berlin to find in Schleswig her Venetia, a constant source of discontent that would lame her foreign policy. Although Mensdorff was inclined toward war, Franz Joseph thought he saw in the draft a way to save the peace and conservative front by avoiding a final choice between the German Confederation and Prussian alliance. Nevertheless, it meant the division of the "indivisible duchies," the abandonment of Augustenburg, and a sharp loss of Austrian prestige among the medium states.[75]

For Bismarck the treaty was one more step along the rocky road of expan-

---

[73] Clark, *Franz Joseph and Bismarck*, 545, 547; OD, VI, 213; Arnold Oskar Meyer, "Der preussische Kronrat vom 29. Mai 1865," in *Festgabe für Heinrich Ritter von Srbik* (Munich, 1938), 308–318. Although aware of the anti-Prussian views of Schmerling and Biegeleben, he banked on the conservatism and "goodwill" of Mensdorff and Franz Joseph, GW, V, 75. He may have been influenced by the fact that on May 23 Werther had reported Mensdorff's willingness to allow Prussian annexation of Lauenburg in return for a reduction in Austria's war costs. Stadelmann, *Das Jahr 1865*, 39.

[74] Stadelmann, *Das Jahr 1865*, 43ff.; DPO, IV, 811ff.; V/1, 1–5.

[75] DPO, V/1, 5ff.

sion. The question of Prussian annexation was only "adjourned."[76] Again the Austrians had failed to obtain any commitment closing the door to such an outcome. By preserving the principle of joint sovereignty, they foolishly handed Prussia a pretext for future intervention in Holstein. The special rights Prussia obtained in that duchy (naval base in Kiel, garrison in Rendsburg, construction of a canal, and rights of access to Schleswig) presented ample opportunity to infiltrate the southern duchy and plenty of combustible material with which to ignite future difficulties.

The Parting of Ways

Throughout the period of fluctuating crisis that followed the end of the Danish War Bismarck continued to observe his fundamental rule that Prussia must hold the pivotal position between France and Austria, using the threat of a firm settlement with Vienna to moderate Napoleon's demands on Berlin and a close relationship with France to weaken Austria's resistance to Prussian importunity in the duchies.[77] Continually he held out to the French the prospect that both their selfish and idealistic motives might be realized. In Schleswig, he stressed, Prussia was favorable to a new frontier that would separate the Danish- and German-speaking populations, and in Italy Prussia had no thought of guaranteeing Austrian possession of Venetia. While seeking to divert Napoleon's imperial ambition toward Belgium and Luxemburg, he carefully left open the possibility of his acquiring German soil as well. It would be folly for Paris to launch an aggressive war for the Rhineland. "The one who can give the Rhenish provinces to France is the one who possesses them."[78]

The most critical moments in this policy came at the time of Schönbrunn and Gastein. Immediately after both conferences Bismarck hastened to calm French suspicion. During Rechberg's formal dinner at the conclusion of Schönbrunn, he drew Gramont, the French ambassador, aside and assured him that no final settlement had been reached and that for the time being "plenty of ink" would be spilled, but no blood.[79] A year later the Gastein treaty produced a serious reaction in Paris. But again Bismarck warned that French hostility could only compel Prussia to reconstruct the eastern alliance of conservative monarchies, while French encouragement could only strengthen the anti-Habsburg front. The division of the duchies was "provisional and to be regarded as but the first step" toward Prussian annexation of both and the "triumph" of Prussian "hegemony" in the regions north of the

[76] GW, V, 276.
[77] See his instructions to Goltz. GW, V, 72–76, 92–95, 266–273.
[78] OD, IV, 62.
[79] OD, IV, 58ff.

Main. In return for her support France might expand "everywhere in the world where French is spoken."[80]

Early in October 1865 Bismarck went to Biarritz, ostensibly on vacation, but actually to confer with Napoleon and his chief advisers. Exactly what was said on the terrace of Eugénie's oceanside villa and later in Paris and St. Cloud is still in doubt. Some believe that Bismarck actually sought agreement on the cost of France's benevolent neutrality in the event of war.[81] That he did not report it later to Wilhelm is, of course, no proof to the contrary.[82] But the conjecture is improbable. Bismarck was not yet ready to part with Austria, and it was unlike him to make commitments so far in advance of their necessity. In all probability he wished to allay French anxiety over Gastein and reassure Wilhelm concerning Napoleon's intentions in Germany. It may also be that he used the occasion to suggest again that France seek her compensation in French-speaking Europe, rather than on the Rhine.[83] In his major purpose at least he was successful. Napoleon was ready to forget Gastein, he reported, and "dance the cotillion with us, without knowing in advance when it will begin or what figures it will include."[84]

The French did not have long to wait for proof that Gastein did not mean peace between the dual powers. While still in Biarritz Bismarck began yet another test of Austria's will to continue the alliance with Prussia at any cost. On October 1 deputies of the German parliaments had convened in Frankfurt to challenge the legality of the Gastein treaty, and on October 29 a congress of the Nationalverein was expected to take a similar stand. At Bismarck's urging the dual powers delivered sharp protests to the senate of the free city for permitting such demonstrations. But the burghers firmly rejected this interference in their sovereign rights.[85]

Bismarck forced the issue. In Vienna he proposed that the dual powers proceed against the senate through the confederate diet and, if voted down, act on their own authority. He recognized that the convention of deputies had been a failure and admitted that the gathering of the Nationalverein was not in itself a "misfortune" for Prussia. Nevertheless, he harbored an intense

---

[80] RKN, I, 67; OD, VI, 267, 453–454; VII, 64, 91; GW, V, 285ff., 300–302.

[81] In general, this view has been taken by Fester, Frahm, and Eyck. Richard Fester, "Biarritz: Eine Bismarck-Studie," Deutsche Rundschau, 113 (1902), 212–236; Friedrich Frahm, "Biarritz," Historische Vierteljahrschrift, 15 (1912), 337–361; Erich Eyck, Bismarck: Leben und Werk (Zurich, 1941–1944), vol. 2, 98–99.

[82] GW, V, 307–311. See also his relation to Goltz in Otto Graf zu Stolberg-Wernigerode, Robert Heinrich Graf von der Goltz (Oldenburg, 1941), 403–408.

[83] Erich Brandenburg, Untersuchungen und Aktenstücke zur Geschichte der Reichsgründung (Leipzig, 1916), 451–453. Geuss's view that the purpose of the journey lay in Bismarck's relationship to Wilhelm rather than to Napoleon appears distorted. Geuss, Bismarck und Napoleon, 145.

[84] GW, XIV, 707.

[85] GW, V, 312–315; Staatsarchiv, vol. 9 (1865), 312ff.; Richard Schwemer, Geschichte der freien Stadt Frankfurt a. M., 1814–1866 (Frankfurt, 1918), III/2, 221ff.

antipathy toward the liberal city on the Main. By resolute action against it he hoped to intimidate the Prussian liberals at home.[86] Yet his major purpose was to force Vienna to choose once more between the Prussian alliance and the lesser states and to undermine the confederation further by demonstrating the joint dictatorship of the dual powers in Germany.

But Mensdorff had finally resolved that the concessions must end. He parried with the proposition that the two powers be content to push through the diet a motion calling for stricter observance of confederate rules for the suppression of "revolutionary" associations and assemblies. Bismarck's reaction was severe. In the Prussian press and in talks with Chotek he declared that there could be no "half-relationship" between the dual powers. The Hofburg must choose between an "upright alliance" and war "to the knife."[87]

The refusal of Mensdorff and colleagues to join in chastising Frankfurt seems to have convinced Bismarck that the usefulness of the Austrian alliance was about over. The course of events in the duchies offered further proof. At Gastein he had calculated that within months Vienna would agree to some kind of monetary compensation for Holstein.[88] But French assistance eased the Habsburg financial crisis, and Franz Joseph was against further concessions to Prussia. Edwin Manteuffel, newly installed as Prussian governor of Schleswig, systematically exploited the principle of joint sovereignty to interfere in the Austrian administration of Holstein. Much to Bismarck's irritation he also contributed, by his authoritarian acts, to the growing popularity of the Augustenburg movement.[89] When Ludwig von Gablenz, the Austrian governor, unwisely permitted a demonstration for the prince in Altona on January 23, 1866, a harsh note left the Wilhelmstrasse for Vienna. It had the sound of an ultimatum.

Complaining of Austrian "aggression," the note demanded that Vienna suppress "democratic" and "revolutionary" agitation in the duchies. "A negative or devious answer" would compel Prussia to consider the alliance at an end and to assume "complete freedom for our entire policy." Although apologetic over the Altona incident, the Austrian reply (February 7) was indeed negative. A few days later Károlyi reported an "ominous stillness" in the Wilhelmstrasse. After weeks of voluble irritation Bismarck was suddenly silent. "The polemic between Vienna and Berlin," he was reported as saying, "is now at an end."[90]

For more than two years Bismarck had exploited the Austrian desire for cooperation with Prussia, repeatedly tricking and forcing Vienna into aban-

[86] GW, V, 301, 312–313, 315. See also Johannes Schultze, ed., Kaiser Wilhelms I. Weimarer Briefe (Berlin, 1924), vol. 2, 62–68.

[87] DPO, V/1, 59ff., 90–93, 97ff., 118; GW, V, 332–333, 338–345.

[88] GW, V, 309. Bleichröder urged this solution. Stern, Gold and Iron, 67–68.

[89] Clark, Franz Joseph and Bismarck, 317ff.; GW, V, 342ff., 346–349; DPO, V/1, 164ff.

[90] GW, V, 365–368; DPO, V/1, 181–182, 196.

doning its vital interests, while he steadily advanced, step by measured step, those of Berlin. Constantly aggressive, he invariably depicted himself as on the defensive; always injuring, he continually assumed the role of the injured; ever working for the upset of the status quo, he steadily posed as a genuine conservative. For Austria it was a long story of futility and frustration. Her protests were met by declarations of innocence and indignation, her attempts to temporize and delay by the threat that Prussia would act alone, her efforts to halt Prussian encroachments by the charge that they endangered the monarchical cause. But at last in the winter of 1865–1866 Bismarck reached the line of hard resistance. What he could not achieve through popular will in the duchies and further capitulation in Vienna he now resolved to acquire by force.

The Magnetism of Power

Unity or Freedom?

ISMARCK'S successes in foreign policy during the years 1863–1865 created new problems for the Prussian opposition. In November–December 1863 the Landtag parties were thrown into confusion by the deepening crisis over the duchies. Acting for the moderate liberals, the deputies Friedrich Stavenhagen and Rudolf Virchow moved a resolution urging the king to recognize Augustenburg and give "effective support" to his cause. They were emphatically opposed by Benedikt Waldeck and his democratic faction of thirty-five deputies. Completely ignorant of Bismarck's secret intention, Waldeck favored annexation to Prussia as a step toward the development of German naval power. But he was against backing the government in any aggressive action against Denmark, for it would morally commit the chamber to grant the hated Bismarck cabinet the means with which to fight a war. Patriotic excitement, it was feared, would drain off energies needed in the constitutional conflict.[1]

Here again was the basic dilemma of German liberalism. For Waldeck and his followers freedom took precedence over unity; the victory of parliament over the crown was more important than a German triumph over Denmark. The moderates were of the opposite opinion. "We value freedom at home very highly," declared Ludwig Loewe, "but independence abroad above all." What mattered was the "glory and greatness of Germany." Many deputies were torn between these extremes. "It was pitiful," wrote Karl Twesten, "to see how most sought to weasel through: don't spoil matters with the Nationalverein and the rest of Germany, therefore forward despite the cabinet; don't spoil matters with the radicals and abstainers, hence no cooperation with the cabinet. No one could bring himself to be quiet."[2]

Both factions agreed that the reactionary cabinet would never follow the recommendations of the lower house. By clinging to the London protocol, Bismarck appeared to prove once more the liberal axiom that a conservative government could do nothing for the national cause. Waldeck feared that war would merely fortify the cabinet's position, but his opponents confidently asserted that it would never survive such a crisis. "With the first blow of a real

---

[1] *SBHA* (1863–1864), I, 114–115, 209–214; III, 37–38; *HW*, I, 182–183; Friedrich von Bernhardi, ed., *Aus dem Leben Theodor von Bernhardis* (Leipzig, 1893–1906), vol. 5, 156–157, 159, 161–162; Ludolf Parisius, *Leopold Freiherr von Hoverbeck* (Berlin, 1897–1900), II/2, 19–21.

[2] *SBHA* (1863–1864), I, 232; *HW*, I, 195–196.

storm we will be free of this bad government," orated Loewe, while Bismarck listened from the ministers' bench. War was to be the midwife of freedom. When the debate ended, the petition passed by a large majority.[3]

Now the situation foreseen by Waldeck actually arose. On December 9 Bodelschwingh presented a bill authorizing a credit of 12 million thalers to finance Prussian support of the confederate execution against Denmark. Because the treasury had no need of the money, the government's purpose was to heighten the confusion among the deputies and alienate their public support in the event of refusal. For days they could not make up their minds. Waldeck made progress with his plea for outright rejection. Outside Prussia leading German nationalists pressed for acceptance, even at the cost of the liberal position in the constitutional conflict. In the end the moderates moved a resolution stating the readiness of the chamber to adjourn the internal conflict, if only the cabinet would adopt a "national policy" against Denmark.[4]

Bitterly Virchow reproached Bismarck for giving precedence to the "European" over the "German" aspect of the Schleswig-Holstein question. The Junker had shifted from one standpoint to another so often that "no one can define his actual position." He had no program or "guiding principle," was "antinational" and devoid of any understanding of the national interest. Bismarck's reply was equally sharp. "As long as we live in Europe we must place ourselves on the European standpoint." Being a scientist, Virchow (an eminent pathologist) should understand that some things were difficult for the expert to explain to laymen. "Politics is not an exact science"; as the situation changes, so must the method of its exploitation. "I really believe, gentlemen, that without exaggeration I understand these matters better." The resolution passed, 207 to 107, the Waldeck faction voting with the conservatives in the negative.[5]

During January 1864 Bismarck continued his patronizing pedagogy in the debate on the authorization bill. Foreign policies, he explained, were based on the interest of state. Without a German state there could be no German interest. Prussia's departure from the London treaty was a matter of "opportunity rather than law." To be effective legal opinions must be backed by power. Should the lower house refuse the requested funds, "we must take them where we find them." Ultimately the government would "conquer." "I believe that you too are no longer stranger to the feeling that it will turn out this way." The deputies laughed. On January 22 they rejected, 275 to 50, the requested authorization.[6]

[3] SBHA (1863–1864), I, 232, 242, 248, 258; HW, I, 204–205. Members of the old-liberal faction were busy drawing up a list of ministers for the next cabinet. Johannes Schultze, ed., Max Duncker: Politischer Briefwechsel aus seinem Nachlass (Stuttgart, 1923), 369–371.

[4] SBHA (1863–1864), I, 508–509; HW, I, 203–204; Parisius, Hoverbeck, II/2, 195–197.

[5] SBHA (1863–1864),I, 481–492, 504–507.

[6] BR, II, 247ff.

Only Waldeck seems to have believed that rejection would seriously hamper the government. What the rest apparently hoped to accomplish was Bismarck's dismissal. Wilhelm was known to be sympathetic to Augustenburg, and Berlin was rife with rumors of a cabinet crisis. Through indirect channels Twesten "stormed" the king with promises that the chamber would support "any other minister," even a conservative, if only his policy were national.[7] As the session neared its end and Bismarck was still in the saddle, the liberals became desperate. Because the ministers had violated the constitution for two years, Twesten declared, the deputies were no longer bound to observe it. "In this case every means is justified that can lead to the fall of such a government." The choice of means was no longer a question of law, but policy. Parliament, asserted Rudolf Gneist, had reached the end of the path of legal resistance.[8]

On January 25, 1864, the chamber resolved to condemn the expenditure of public funds without parliamentary approval as a breach of the constitution; on the same day a royal decree prorogued the Landtag. Once more the Prussian liberals had the chance to determine whether there was indeed any other "means" at their disposal than parliamentary protest. Was the German national cause any more capable of arousing a genuine popular movement than the constitutional conflict?

Even in January leaders of the Nationalverein were complaining, "Nowhere is the movement and agitation for Schleswig-Holstein further behind (Austria naturally excepted) than in Prussia. They do not assemble, do not press, do not contribute." Heinrich von Sybel too found the public mood "lamentable." Two centuries of absolutism had lamed the capacity for popular initiative. No one was willing to sacrifice for the cause, not even financially. On January 29 Theodor Mommsen wrote to Gustav Freytag, "I have completely given up the idea that the nation will interfere with real energy." A few days later he commented, "What calls itself the German Progressive party is on the whole but a negative mass."[9] Although there was again talk of a taxpayers' strike, those who may have taken it seriously were soon disabused. On returning to his East Prussian estate, Kurt von Saucken-Tarputschen, a Waldeck supporter, wrote, "The feudal party is fast gaining ground among all those who are in any way dependent, and a large part of the farmers are like soft wax, to be molded by anyone who knows how to approach them. The Berliners have no conception how things actually are in the country."[10]

[7] H. B. Oppenheim, *Benedikt Franz Leo Waldeck* (Berlin, 1880), 186; Berhardi, *Aus dem Leben*, vol. 5, 224–225; *HW*, I, 203–204.

[8] *SBHA* (1863–1864), II, 715–717, 924. The context shows that what Twesten had in mind was not revolution, but a flat rejection of the budget bill without amendment, to be followed by a tax boycott. Although he thought it justified, he opposed such a drastic step because he doubted its success. See also *HW*, II, 215.

[9] *HW*, I, 210–216.

[10] Parisius, *Hoverbeck*, II/2, 1–2, 19.

Into this political vacuum now rushed the first great achievement of the Bismarck cabinet and the reorganized army. On January 30 Johann Gustav Droysen reported that the army was jubilant over the prospect of war. After the opening battle he expected a similar mood among the public. "Bets are being made that with the first successes Herr von Bismarck will become popular." Indeed the dramatic victory at Düppel filled army and nation with pride. For the first time in half a century Prussian troops had tasted victory. In April and May, Theodor von Bernhardi, a supporter of Augustenburg, detected a "very perceptible reversal of public opinion" in Bismarck's favor. "If he should now dissolve the chamber, he would gain 100 seats."[11] The magnetism of national power had begun to exert its attraction.

Power or Right?

During January, Bismarck had commenced to stir up Prussian national sentiment in preparation for annexation. Accused of "wanting to ignore Germany," he charged in turn that the deputies "wanted to ignore Prussia." They wished Prussia to exist "as the domain of the Nationalverein or not at all. To gain their confidence the cabinet would have to "depart from the Prussian constitution . . . from Prussia's traditions, from Prussia's history, from Prussian popular feeling." Repeatedly he harped upon this theme. "An open profession of the Prussian interest, of Prussian nationalism is not to be found on your side. . . . You reject the Prussian *Volksgeist*. . . . You reject the glorious traditions of our past, for you disavow the position, the great power position, of Prussia acquired through heavy sacrifice in the people's blood and property."[12]

In May 1864 came the petition of Arnim-Boitzenburg for annexation. Within weeks it had accumulated seventy thousand signatures, chiefly from conservatives and right-wing liberals. Though leaving open the possibility of either Prussian annexation or a protectorate, the document leaned toward the former. Many conservatives who in the beginning had favored Augustenburg and been repelled by his alliance with the liberals found in annexation a welcome alternative. Although a few of the romantic school, like Ludwig Gerlach, were morally outraged by the idea, most found the renewal of Prussian

[11] R. Hübner, ed., *Johann Gustav Droysen: Briefwechsel* (Stuttgart, 1928), vol. 2, 830; Bernhardi, *Aus dem Leben*, vol. 6, 89, 102, 110–111, 116. Some cabinet members wished to exploit the victory by dissolving parliament, but Bismarck and Roon decided otherwise. Nearly a year passed between the end of the 1863–1864 session and the beginning of that of 1865. GW, XIV, 670; Waldemar von Roon, *Denkwürdigkeiten aus dem Leben des General-Feldmarschalls Kriegministers Grafen von Roon* (4th ed., Breslau, 1897), vol. 2, 257–258. Horst Kohl, "Aus der Korrespondenz des Grafen Friedrich Eulenburg mit dem Fürsten Bismarck," *Deutsche Revue*, vol. 25, no. 1 (1900), 43–44.

[12] BR, II, 264–283. "I wouldn't mind," he lamented to Below-Hohendorf in May 1864, "if our nation were so strongly inflated by Prussian pride that the government would have to moderate, rather than vivify it." GW, XIV, 667.

Machtpolitik "irresistibly attractive."[13] But liberals too were affected by the prospect of territorial gain.

Before Düppel and the London conference, to be sure, the Augustenburg phalanx remained fairly intact. In April 1864 the "thirty-six committee" drafted a declaration affirming that the duchies belonged to the prince both by inheritance and popular will and denying the right of an international conference to decide otherwise. Ultimately the document was signed by 1,362 deputies from various parliaments, of whom 186 were members of the Prussian Left Center and Progressive parties. Scornfully Waldeck denied their right to speak for the German nation or to dispose of what had been gained through Prussia's "independent military and diplomatic action." Nevertheless, eighteen of his thirty-five supporters, made uncertain by the conservative campaign for annexation, now switched to Augustenburg.[14]

As the news of victory sped over the telegraph wires, the liberal front began to dissolve. The *Preussische Jahrbücher*, which in November 1863 had come out for Augustenburg, concluded in May 1864 that annexation would be a "more national goal than the creation of a small state" and in September that Prussian self-interest alone was adequate reason for demanding the duchies.[15] In December Wilhelm Wehrenpfennig, editor of the *Preussische Jahrbücher* since Rudolf Haym's retirement in June, accepted an article by Ludwig Häusser opposing annexation, but immediately engaged Treitschke to write a reply. Earlier an ardent supporter of Augustenburg, the volatile historian had completely reversed himself. He reveled in the display of military power at Düppel and returned to his earlier conviction that only Prussian expansion could create the unity capable of ending German particularism and the political impotence that was its consequence. According to Wehrenpfennig, the Treitschke article, a good example of his fiery eloquence, had considerable impact upon the deputies in Berlin.[16]

On November 9, 1864, Rudolf von Bennigsen reported, "The Bismarck course (that is, the worship of military power and diplomatic success) is growing in a shocking way." Soon afterward Wehrenpfennig wrote that the question of annexation had "wrought havoc among all political parties." Although most old-liberals had been won over, the Left Center and Progressive

---

[13] Gerhard Ritter, *Die preussischen Konservativen und Bismarcks deutsche Politik, 1858–1875* (Heidelberg, 1913), 100ff.

[14] Parisius, *Hoverbeck*, II/2, 4–7, 21–22.

[15] Friedrich C. Sell, *Die Tragödie des deutschen Liberalismus* (Stuttgart, 1953), 211ff.; *Preussische Jahrbücher*, 12 (1863), 540ff.; 12 (1864), 661ff.; 14 (1864), 456ff.

[16] HW, I, 223–234, 237, 243; *Preussische Jahrbücher*, 15 (1865), 84ff., 169ff. Bennigsen's friend, Victor Böhmert, thought the article had "an enormous effect." Hermann Oncken, *Rudolf von Bennigsen* (Stuttgart 1910), vol. 2, 655. On Treitschke's shift in viewpoint see Andreas Dorpalen, *Heinrich von Treitschke* (New Haven, 1957), 88–89, 98–99, and Hildegard Katsch, *Heinrich von Treitschke und die preussisch-deutsche Frage von 1860–1866: Historische Bibliothek*, vol. 40 (Munich, 1919), 64ff.

parties were deeply split. Of the progressive leaders only Virchow, Ludwig von Rönne, Franz Duncker, and Hermann Schulze-Delitzsch held to their original position; Mommsen and Twesten (both natives of Schleswig-Holstein) led the fight for annexation. An eminent historian and liberal of unquestioned integrity, Mommsen's views carried considerable weight. Like Treitschke, he believed that Germany's primary problem was unity and that it could be achieved only through the expansion of Prussian power and creation of a strong executive. Despite all his difficulties with the existing government, Twesten again followed the course dictated by conscience. He deplored the attitude of unconditional opposition that gripped many of the deputies and was willing to support the cause of a greater Prussia even if it strengthened the Bismarck cabinet.[17]

Nevertheless, the annexationists were troubled by a basic dilemma. Their case against Denmark had always been based upon the liberal principle of national self-determination. Yet it was evident that most inhabitants of the duchies favored Augustenburg. Wehrenpfennig got over the difficulty by believing that pride in the power and prestige of the state—"the most valuable possession of the citizen"—would surely win them to Prussian rule. In his article Treitschke argued that the Schleswig-Holsteiners could not be permitted to decide an issue affecting the whole of Germany. A small independent principality would have much less prospect of Germanizing the Danes in northern Schleswig. Even Mommsen, a man of firmer liberal conviction than Treitschke, maintained that the right of self-determination, although basic to the liberal creed, must be limited where the general interest of the German nation was concerned.[18]

But many found these arguments unconvincing. So deep was the division of opinion that the Chamber of Deputies was unable to adopt anything more than a "passive" attitude during the session of 1865. It was an "evil situation."[19] To go on record for annexation meant capitulation to the principle of "power over right," violation of the principle of self-determination, and surrender to the Bismarck cabinet on a vital issue. To reject annexation was to deny Prussia her reward for military success, increase the number of small states, sacrifice the prospect of Prussian naval power, and lose the chance for progress toward German unity through the expansion of Prussia. The liberals divided according to which of these considerations they gave the greater value.

[17] Oncken, *Bennigsen*, vol. 1, 647; *Duncker: Briefwechsel*, 380–381; *HW*, I, 234, 246–249, 251. Concerning Mommsen's views on the Schleswig-Holstein question see Alfred Heuss, *Theodor Mommsen und das 19. Jahrhundert* (Kiel, 1956), 172ff., and Albert Wucher, *Theodor Mommsen: Geschichtsschreibung und Politik* (Göttingen, 1956), 151ff.

[18] *HW*, I, 236, 253–255; *Preussische Jahrbücher*, 15 (1865), 179ff.; Wucher, *Mommsen*, 181–182.

[19] *HW*, I, 186, 243.

Upon one point, nevertheless, there was little disagreement: if Augustenburg were to rule the duchies, their sovereignty must be sharply limited in favor of Prussia. Journals of all political viewpoints adopted Bismarck's February conditions as the minimum program acceptable to Prussia. Remembering the humiliating fate of the navy of 1848, the liberals were enticed by the prospect of Prussian naval power.[20] With the approval of Augustenburg lead-

DIFFERING PERSPECTIVES. "WHERE SHADOWS ARE, THERE CAN ALSO BE LIGHT"—OR "WHERE LIGHT IS, MUST THERE ALSO BE SHADOWS?" (WILHELM SCHOLZ, *KLADDERADATSCH*, SEPTEMBER 14, 1865).

[20] Oncken, *Bennigsen*, vol. 1, 657, 672–674; Otto Bandmann, *Die deutsche Presse und die nationale Frage, 1864–1866* (Leipzig, 1909), 22ff. The navy had been sold at auction during the reaction.

ing members of the thirty-six committee and Nationalverein assembled in Berlin in March 1865 to accept most of the conditions.[21]

Yet the Augustenburg cause continued to wither. At Bismarck's request, the Prussian "crown syndicate" (a tribunal composed of members of the House of Lords) had been asked for a judgment on the prince's claims. After solemn deliberation the lords ruled that the lawful heir to the duchies was the king of Denmark! Wilhelm, at least, found the ruling convincing. Bismarck's next gambit was to publish his one-sided account of the talk with Friedrich in June 1864. Fearing to be "trapped" by a lawsuit, the prince issued no public denial. The consequence was that many deputies came to believe the charge of his ingratitude and deserted his cause.[22]

The drift in Prussia toward annexation created new tensions within the German liberal-national movement. There had long been a precarious balance between advocates of a federal and a centralistic German union, but also between the moderates, who were willing to compromise with an authoritarian Prussia, and the democrats (particularly in south Germany), who wished a more decisive stand against the regime in Berlin. Bismarck's policy of self-interest, the support it attracted in Prussia, and the revulsion it aroused among southerners threatened to split the national movement along the axis of the Main.[23]

In September 1865 the cleavage became glaringly evident in the response to the call of the thirty-six committee for another congress of German deputies to be held in Frankfurt. The purpose was to condemn the Gastein treaty. At a caucus in Berlin most Prussian deputies voted not to attend. In public letters Mommsen and Twesten explained that the majority regarded the rally as an attack upon the Prussian state itself, not merely upon its existing government. Only the Prussian state was capable of unifying Germany. From the south came public replies from Wilhelm Schaffrath and Julius Frese. "No German," warned the former, "wants a Germany without Prussia, but neither does any German want the absorption of Germany into Prussia." If the Prussian deputies must as a matter of duty support Bismarck's foreign policy, Frese continued, this meant the end of the constitutional conflict. They must choose between "the politics of power and the politics of right."[24]

[21] This was the so-called "Berlin compromise." Not accepted were the oath to the Prussian flag, Prussian control of conscription, and Prussian administration of customs, post, and telegraph. Oncken, Bennigsen, vol. 1, 661.

[22] Erich Eyck, Bismarck: Leben und Werk (Zurich, 1941–1944), vol. 2, 45–47; Parisius, Hoverbeck, II/2, 58.

[23] Oncken, Bennigsen, vol. 1, 644ff.; Friedrich Thorwart, ed., Hermann Schulze-Delitzschs Schriften und Reden (Berlin, 1909–1913), vol. 3, 221ff. Bandmann, Deutsche Presse, 33ff.; Theodor Schieder, Die kleindeutsche Partei in Bayern: Münchener historische Abhandlungen, vol. 12 (Munich, 1936), 41–92.

[24] HW, I, 253–262. Bennigsen, who did his best to bridge the fissures, felt that the summons

But even the Augustenburg faction in Berlin felt compelled to stay away from Frankfurt. Schulze-Delitzsch explained that by attending they would "compromise" their position at home. They would "discredit" themselves with the electorate and drive annexationist liberals into the arms of Bismarck. Viktor von Unruh put it more bluntly: "We are ready to let ourselves be locked up, but not on account of a spectacle doomed in advance to failure." Eduard Lasker, newly elected to parliament in a Berlin by-election, felt that the convention would only serve to reveal cleavages within the national movement. "Schleswig-Holstein has taught me," he confessed, "that the feeling of unity is not yet sufficiently developed for an instinctive solution of the German question. For the present, German unity still cannot expect any adequate help from the masses."[25]

Months before its final trial German liberal nationalism had been split apart by the Schleswig-Holstein question. But even now the first doubt had been raised whether it was supported any more in its nationalism than in its liberalism by the German people as a whole.

Parliament in 1865

The victory over Denmark also embarrassed the liberals on the issue of military reform. In January 1864 Sybel wrote that in the Rhineland many were saying, "Apparently the reorganization has proved itself militarily after all." Following Düppel, Hermann Baumgarten reported that in Karlsruhe the military reform was considered a fait accompli, and Karl Mathy, a Baden minister, advised the progressives to surrender on this point, lest "the idea of the state" be lost. Both proposed compromise: the military bill for recognition of parliament's budget rights. But Mathy's soundings showed that the mood of the progressives was unchanged. Sybel reported that not even twenty votes were to be had for such a bargain; the king, moreover, would just "laugh" at the idea. On December 16, 1864, twenty-five leading deputies caucused to consider their strategy in the coming session. They resolved to stand fast on the military issue and be "as passive as possible" on foreign policy.[26]

When the term commenced in January 1865, nevertheless, many deputies yearned for a settlement. According to Georg von Seydlitz, the conviction was growing that "the general public is weary of this dispute." Should it last much longer, the country would learn to accept the policies of the government and bask in the reflection of its military achievements. A few months

---

to Frankfurt, being the work of south German radicals, was "folly." Oncken, *Bennigsen*, vol. 1, 671.

[25] Oncken, *Bennigsen*, vol. 1, 672–674; Schulze-Delitzsch, *Schriften und Reden*, vol. 3, 240–254; HW, I, 263.

[26] HW, I, 217, 223–224, 229–230.

before, Twesten had observed with bitterness that "from day to day" both officials and common citizens were becoming "more servile."[27]

Because of the imminence of war with Austria, Bismarck and Roon were also inclined toward compromise. The speech from the throne that opened parliament on January 14 expressed an "urgent wish" for the adjustment of differences. The military bill that the government presented soon afterward was the same as that previously rejected by the chamber, but the two ministers were willing to consider amendments. In the palace they broached once more the scheme Wilhelm had rejected in October 1862. The three-year service period was to be reduced and the size and financial support of the army geared to the increase in population. But again Wilhelm was negative. Next they turned to an amendment introduced by Gustav von Bonin, an old-liberal deputy, who proposed that the three-year period be kept and the standing army limited to 160,000 men. Such a limitation, Wilhelm replied, was "nothing less than an expression of mistrust against me personally."[28] Nor was the chamber sympathetic to the idea. After a debate marked by an acrimonious exchange between Gneist and Roon the entire bill was rejected.[29]

Despite the doubts it raised in the minds of many deputies, the Schleswig-Holstein affair had by no means stilled the spirit of opposition in the chamber. The few conciliatory words in the throne speech were lost in a vigorous reassertion of the crown's position. After reelection as speaker, Wilhelm Grabow delivered his usual scathing indictment of the government; "no power on earth" could budge the deputies in their "reverence for constitutional right." Against the arguments of Wehrenpfennig, Heinrich von Bockum-Dolffs maintained that even at the cost of abandoning Schleswig-Holstein the deputies must continue to uphold the constitution. The leader of the Left Center was supported in this view by many progressives. Despite some desertions, Schulze-Delitzsch declared, the "entire liberal party" was ready to continue the struggle against the "Bismarck system without regard for the victory swindle."[30]

The debate on the budget bill for 1865 took the usual course. Once more the motion of Virchow, Leopold von Hoverbeck, and others for outright rejection without amendment was turned down. Max von Forckenbeck voted against it because such a "dangerous demonstration" ought logically to be

[27] Martin Philippson, *Max von Forckenbeck: Ein Lebensbild* (Dresden, 1898), 124–125; HW, I, 228, 231, 240–241.

[28] SBHA (1865), I, 1–4; Bernhardi, *Aus dem Leben*, vol. 6, 169–170, 177–178, 200, 209; Roon, *Denkwürdigkeiten*, vol. 2, 325–326, 331–334. There is evidence that as early as the summer of 1864 Roon had negotiated with the moderates on the terms of the Bonin amendment. HW, I, 238–239.

[29] SBHA (1865), vol. 2, 1196–1355; vol. 6, 878–893.

[30] HW, I, 238–239, 242–243; Bernhardi, *Aus dem Leben*, vol. 6, 180; Oncken, *Bennigsen*, vol. 1, 657.

followed by a taxpayers' strike, for which there was no public support. Once again the deputies struck from the budget, along with other items, the funds requested for military reorganization. But this year they were faced with a new problem. Collection of the real estate tax passed in 1861 was to begin in 1865. Its yield would reinforce the financial independence of the crown. Waldeck's proposal that the chamber simply strike the tax out of the budget on the grounds that the Landtag of 1861 had no power to legislate for 1865 was rejected. Instead the deputies futilely insisted that the yield from the tax be limited to the sum originally estimated.[31]

Aware of their weakened position, the deputies tried to advance a program of greater popular appeal. The "naked legal question" of constitutional rights, they realized, had little interest for the lower classes; it was necessary to state their case in terms of the "material" welfare of the public. The budget committee prepared a "general report" surveying the entire financial structure of the state and ending with the recommendation that sums clipped from the military budget be used for "productive purposes" such as river improvement, road construction, land reclamation, science and education, with salary increases to teachers, lesser officials, soldiers, and noncommissioned officers.[32] Against power and patriotism the deputies raised the standard of financial self-interest.

But not even in this field were they able to assert themselves. The government presented a series of bills dealing with economic matters whose obvious purpose was to divide the chamber and, in the event of rejection, to discredit it. To be sure, the Zollverein treaties were readily accepted; economic unity and free trade were important chapters in the liberal textbook. Nevertheless, they were an uncomfortable reminder of a signal success in Bismarck's diplomacy. Other bills on state aid for railway construction threw the deputies into confusion. No issue, Hoverbeck observed, was more suited to split the majority into warring factions. Principle conflicted with local self-interest, and the latter conquered. The proposal of Otto Michaelis, a progressive, that the chamber refuse even to consider the bills until a legal budget was in existence was voted down 178 to 108. Over the protests of the laissez-faire faction and democratic liberals, all but one of the measures were then accepted.[33] A government bill to extend the operations of the Bank of Prussia throughout Ger-

[31] Philippson, Forckenbeck, 132; Parisius, Hoverbeck, II/2, 47–48; Oppenheim, Waldeck, 199; SBHA (1865), vol. 1, 471ff.; vol. 5, 466–467.

[32] Parisius, Hoverbeck, II/2, 28–29; SBHA (1865), vol. 5, 433–469; Philippson, Forckenbeck, 122–129; Fritz Löwenthal, Der preussische Verfassungsstreit, 1862–1866 (Munich, 1914), 236–237.

[33] Parisius, Hoverbeck, II/2, 30–33; SBHA (1865), vol. 2, 779–796, 813–853, 1117–1133, 2141–2151. See also Werner Schunke, Die preussischen Freihändler und die Entstehung der nationalliberalen Partei (Leipzig, 1916), 23ff.

many, on the other hand, was rejected, despite the support of important commercial interests.[34]

The tactical purpose of two other bills was equally evident. Tongue in cheek, the minister of finance asked the chamber to approve the government's financing of the recent war: the expenditure of 1,300,000 thalers withdrawn from the treasury and 12,000,000 thalers in surplus revenues piled up by a booming economy in 1863–1864. Despite Twesten's admission that Bismarck's diplomacy had been "bold, clever, successful," the deputies felt compelled to reject the request and with it an amendment from Hermann Wagener calling for annexation of the duchies. On that very day they had resolved to hold cabinet members liable for funds taken from the public treasury without parliamentary approval.[35] The naval construction bill was equally harassing. To build two armed frigates and a naval base at Kiel 19,600,000 thalers were requested, of which 10,000,000 thalers were to be borrowed. Since 1848 naval power had been a favorite cause of German liberal nationalism. The suitability of Kiel as a naval base was one of the motives behind the swing toward annexation in Prussia. In the budget bill of 1865 the finance committee had voluntarily increased by more than a million thalers the amount of the naval appropriation. But now the deputies, laden with embarrassment, had to reject the naval bill on the ground that without a legal budget no new funds could be granted the government.[36]

His enemies were exposed, and Bismarck struck with malicious skill. Like the false mother in the judgment of Solomon, the liberals would rather condemn the child than lose it. For twenty years Germany had dreamed of a fleet. Now that it was within reach the chamber was "impotently negative." The deputies accused him of incompetence; yet he had achieved over their obstruction what they themselves had demanded: the reconstruction of the Zollverein and the separation of Schleswig-Holstein from Denmark. All that stood in the way of a settlement with Augustenburg was the validation of his claims and acceptance of the February conditions. To fight the policy of the government was to fight one's own country in league with its enemies.[37] On June 17, 1865, the Landtag was prorogued.

The parliamentary term of 1865, longest of the constitutional conflict, marked yet another stage in the deterioration of the Prussian opposition. Cloven in one direction by the issue of annexation, they were riven in another by that of the priority between external power and internal right. Still other fissures were opened up by the bank and railway bills. In mid-March a liberal

---

[34] SBHA (1865), II, 856–909.

[35] Ibid., VII, 1549–1593; also III, 2087–2139.

[36] SBHA (1865), III, 1833–1903; VIII, 1601–1615; Löwenthal, Verfassungsstreit, 242–243. In April 1864 Gustav Droysen, previously a supporter of Augustenburg, wrote that Prussia's next task was dominium maris baltici. Droysen, Briefwechsel, vol. 2, 836.

[37] BR, II, 353ff., 378ff. See also GW, V, 161.

editor, August Lammers, wrote of an "unbelievable disorganization" in the liberal majority. "Instead of a single united party, we have ten to twenty little factions." Although some, like Twesten and Mommsen, were impressed by Bismarck's parliamentary performance in June, the effect was marred by an unfortunate incident. For questioning Bismarck's veracity Virchow received a challenge. The affair was settled without bullets, but the deputies regarded it as another assault upon parliamentary freedom. Mommsen reported, "The Bismarck-madness is spreading here with every passing day." Among the deputies there was now only a single issue: "for or against Bismarck."[38]

The strategy Bismarck had planned in 1862 was proving successful. Many deputies were weary of the struggle, worn out by endless friction and frustration. As the years passed, parliamentary life seemed less and less realistic. While the cabinet submitted bills that had no chance of becoming law, the opposition deliberated endlessly upon amendments that had no chance of acceptance by the crown. While the deputies resolved and petitioned, the ministers governed the country independent of every parliamentary influence. Most discouraging of all was the revelation that Bismarck had been right in declaring that the government could carry on war with or without parliament's consent. What did it achieve to declare ministers liable for the unconstitutional disposal of public funds when the lower house possessed no means with which to bring them to account?

By two further acts, committed soon after parliament adjourned, the ministers showed how little impressed they were by the threat. On July 5, 1865, the cabinet published in the official *Staatsanzeiger* the budget approved by the king, including provisions for the construction and arming of the fleet. It had the appearance of a royal decree. A month later, the cabinet approved, without consulting parliament, a contract by which the government sold its right to purchase the stock of the Cologne-Minden railway. In securing the measure Bismarck overrode the legal scruples of Karl Bodelschwingh and Heinrich Itzenplitz. By this fresh breach of the constitution the crown acquired nearly 30 million thalers with which either to purchase Austrian rights in Schleswig-Holstein or finance a future mobilization against her.[39]

Some deputies took comfort in the belief that the chamber had at least scored a great "moral success" with the public by its unyielding stand. But Hoverbeck feared this an "illusion." On returning home in June he wrote, "Those circles of the population that read newspapers at all or concern themselves in some degree with politics have long ago taken their position on these questions." Many had been driven by official pressure either into silence or

[38] HW, I, 244–245, 250–251; SBHA (1865), VII, 1886, 1897–1903, 1956–1964; GW, XIV, 695.

[39] Ludwig Aegidi and Alfred Klauhold, eds., *Das Staatsarchiv: Sammlung der officiellen Aktenstücke zur Geschichte der Gegenwart*, vol. 10 (1866), 74ff.; Löwenthal, *Verfassungsstreit*, 268–271; Schunke, *Freihändler*, 26–27; GW, XIV, 697–698.

into changing their views. "All our deliberations," he confessed, "have had no influence upon the great masses of the people, that is, upon the voters of the third and, in part, the second classes, for they never hear anything about them." Those who work for popular freedom, he concluded, "do not stand on solid ground." A fresh election might easily bring Prussia back to "naked absolutism."[40]

Preparations for a Coup d'État

Hoverbeck was not alone in this thought. Many ultraconservatives longed for an "inner Düppel" that would destroy the constitution and restore absolutism. After a talk with Alvensleben, Bernhardi concluded that the "camarilla" reactionaries wished to make Edwin Manteuffel minister-president to carry out the coup. Within the cabinet Bismarck's colleagues pressed for action, and Wilhelm was similarly inclined. But Bismarck believed the time was not yet ripe.[41] In a crown council on June 19, 1865, he confessed that for a long time it had been his conviction that Prussia could not be ruled under the existing constitution. The "blow" must come either during the coming winter or the following one. It must be prepared by more vigorous steps against liberal deputies and state officials.[42]

Since 1863 the pressure upon opposition deputies and officials had been unrelenting. After the election of that year severe reprisals were carried out against liberal voters, electors, and candidates.[43] Johann Jacoby, one of the few surviving radicals, was sentenced to six months in prison for lese majesty. Seventeen East Prussian deputies were prosecuted and fined because of an election broadside mildly critical of the cabinet. Similar cases were initiated against Deputies Eduard von Möller, Karl von der Leeden, Otto Lüning, Julius Frese, and Franz Duncker. Conscience itself, declared Waldeck, was on trial. In May 1865 many citizens of Cologne refused to join in the celebration commemorating the fiftieth anniversary of Rhineland's union with Prussia, and the local branch of the Progressive party organized a countercelebration honoring the opposition deputies following prorogation of the Landtag in June. On Bismarck's initiative the festival was forbidden. Eighty deputies appeared, but they were repeatedly blocked by policemen and soldiers from con-

[40] Parisius, Hoverbeck, II/2, 53–56.

[41] Ritter, Konservativen, 116–118; Bernhardi, Aus dem Leben, vol. 6, 171–172; Duncker, Briefwechsel, 392; Heinrich O. Meisner, ed., Kaiser Friedrich III.: Tagebücher von 1848–1866 (Leipzig, 1929), 530–533.

[42] Alfred Stern, Geschichte Europas seit den Verträgen von 1815 bis zum Frankfurter Frieden von 1871 (Stuttgart, 1899–1924), vol. 9, 587. See also Ernst Ludwig von Gerlach, Aufzeichnungen aus seinem Leben und Wirken, 1795–1877 (Schwerin, 1903), vol. 2, 273.

[43] See particularly the report of the investigating committee of the chamber of deputies. SBHA (1863–1864), IV, 624ff.

vening. Arrests were frequent, and newspapers critical of this interference with the right of free assembly were confiscated.[44]

Firms connected in some way with the opposition were passed over in the purchase of military supplies. Liberal physicians were ignored for positions in public health. Lottery collectors and bank agents lost their franchises. Masonic lodges were admonished to support the crown. Liberal mayors chosen by municipal parliaments were not confirmed by the government. After the same candidate had been repeatedly reelected in Königsberg and rejected by Berlin, the government arbitrarily appointed a "commissar" to administer the city. Eight of nine members elected to the Berlin city council in 1865 were not confirmed, and one was arbitrarily replaced by a government agent. In May 1864 Bismarck succeeded in getting Wilhelm to approve salary increases for judges on the basis of political conformity rather than seniority. Count Leopold zur Lippe, the minister of justice, objected that "rule and right" ought to prevail, but Bismarck replied, "The government must reward its friends and punish its enemies."[45]

Within the judiciary there was constant conflict between liberal and conservative judges. Although most lower courts were presided over by liberals, the higher tribunals were nearly monopolized by conservatives. The fate of cases brought against the treasury by officials who had been assessed the cost of substitutes while serving in parliament was typical. Most plaintiffs won in the courts of first instance, although only a few survived the second, and the rest lost in the supreme court. The liberal judges on the latter tribunal, of whom Waldeck was one, were outnumbered by a reactionary majority. Sitting as the "disciplinary senate" of the state service, the supreme court issued two decisions in September 1863 and October 1864 that read political meaning into the law of 1851, under which judges might be punished for unbecoming conduct.[46] The courts were no longer inviolable. "For those in disfavor," lamented Hoverbeck, "there is no justice any more in Prussia!" He feared that this "very systematic" attack would silence the bureaucratic opposition in the next election with disastrous consequences for the liberal cause. "Are our people independent and perspicacious enough to find out by themselves what is right, especially in the face of such pressure? One could doubt it. It is very possible that through intimidation the reaction will conquer." Weary of "ineffectual opposition," the progressive leader was even inclined to hope for a

---

[44] Thomas Parent, "Passiver Widerstand" im preussischen Verfassungskonflikt: Die Kölner Abgeordnetenfeste. Kölner Schriften zu Geschichte und Kultur, vol. 1 (Cologne, 1982), 261–383, 415–418; SBHA (1865), I, 374–381; (1866), I, 13–14, 34–35, 185–186; Parisius, Hoverbeck, II/2, 56–61. Of 253 deputies invited, only 160 accepted, of whom only half appeared. The east Prussian deputies declined on the grounds that there was nothing to celebrate.

[45] Parisius, Hoverbeck, II/2, 15; SEG (1865), 170, 174, 176, 180; Bernhardi, Aus dem Leben, vol. 5, 160–161; vol. 6, 118; HW, I, 231.

[46] Parisius, Hoverbeck, II/2, 23–24.

government coup that would end the struggle. Open absolutism was better than the existing state of affairs. At the end he foresaw the dread possibility—after a "terrible deterioration in the entire character of the people"—of popular revolution.[47]

Not all officials were easy to silence. On May 20, 1865, Twesten delivered in the Chamber of Deputies a blistering indictment of Lippe and the government for converting the courts into instruments of political oppression. The treasured Prussian tradition of an independent judiciary was now only an "illusion." Decisions of the supreme court were no longer based upon law, but upon the "interests and prejudices of the ruling party." As a county judge Twesten was well acquainted with conditions in the judiciary and had himself been repeatedly "disciplined" for political activities. On June 2 Deputy Johann Frentzel, previously the victim of two months' imprisonment for lese majesty, also attacked the government for destroying the Prussian tradition of the *Rechtsstaat*. Two weeks later the House of Lords called upon the government to prosecute "defamatory and other criminal utterances" in the lower chamber. In the crown council of the nineteenth Bismarck advocated the prosecution of Twesten and Frentzel. Now he was ready to pursue the opposition into the sanctuary of parliament itself.[48]

But still he had no intention of resorting to open absolutism. As before he was well aware that repression must be accompanied by positive efforts to attract the support of the masses. Roon hinted to Bernhardi that "appropriate liberal arrangements" were being considered, not a relapse into "Caesarism."[49] On June 17 Bismarck had informed Max Duncker that, should the next session of the Landtag turn out like the last, there were but two choices: either a convention to revise the constitution or "simply the reestablishment of direct and equal suffrage."[50]

Nevertheless, the old difficulties remained. Equal suffrage could not in itself supply the answer to the government's need. There had to be some assurance that, when given the vote, the masses would actually use it to elect deputies favorable to the government. Although aware that the lower classes were not behind the liberals, Bismarck could not be sure that they were behind the government. What seemed more likely was that, at least where artisan and factory workers were concerned, there existed a political void that

[47] *Ibid.;* 15–16.

[48] SBHA (1865), I, 284–299; SBHH (1865), I, 299.

[49] Bernhardi, *Aus dem Leben*, vol. 6, 209; see also Roon, *Denkwürdigkeiten*, vol. 2, 337, 346, 348–350.

[50] Friedrich III, *Tagebücher 1848–1866*, 532–533. In the crown council on June 19 Eulenburg stated that the electoral law could only be changed in the direction of equal male suffrage, but he expressed serious doubts about the wisdom of such a step; once taken, it could never be rescinded. Stern, *Geschichte Europas*, vol. 9, 587.

could be filled by the crown only through concrete steps to care for their material wants.

Experiment in Social Reform

Despite his absorption in foreign affairs, Bismarck did not lose sight of the problem of social reform during 1864–1866. Again his colleagues were hostile to his ideas and probably resentful of his interference. In May 1863 he pressed Itzenplitz to draft a bill legalizing trade unions. But the minister was doubtful and dilatory; not until December 1864 did the matter reach the cabinet. Before the ministers could act, such a bill was introduced in the lower chamber by a group of deputies headed by Schulze-Delitzsch. Speaking for the cabinet, Itzenplitz favored legalization, but only in combination with "positive measures," such as workers' cooperatives, for the amelioration of social distress. Wagener taunted the liberal deputies with the specter of equal suffrage, state-supported cooperatives, and a proletariat hostile to the bourgeoisie. Nevertheless, the bill presented to parliament in February 1866 and finally passed in 1869 granted the right to unionize, but made no mention of cooperatives. Bismarck's retreat on this point was partly owing to the failure of his model cooperative in Silesia.[51]

By halting the flow of raw cotton, the American Civil War had plunged the Silesian textile industry into depression. In October 1862 the factory owners of Reichenbach county, including Leonor Reichenheim, a liberal member of parliament, had proposed construction of a workhouse. They were infuriated by the way in which the local *Landrat*, Olearius, rejected the idea in a report that came to Bismarck's attention. "It is purely a question of saving from hunger a large number of people," Olearius declared, "who have fallen into need through no fault of their own, who have scarcely ever had the chance to save a penny for such a situation, and through whose effort others have become rich. For them a workhouse?"[52]

In May 1864 a delegation of three weavers, sent by two hundred workers of the Reichenheim works in Wüstegiersdorf, appeared in Berlin. Through Olearius and Wagener they reached Bismarck who, over the opposition of Eulenburg and the provincial governor, saw to it that they were sympathetically received by the king. But a committee of inquiry, appointed to investigate the matter, delivered a report favorable to the owners. Adopted without essential change by the ministries of interior and commerce, it reached Bis-

---

[51] Adolf Richter, *Bismarck und die Arbeiterfrage im preussischen Verfassungskonflikt* (Stuttgart, 1935), 252–257; SBHA (1865), I, 119–202; IV, 208, 312–316. The motives of the liberals were mixed. Freedom to organize was regarded as a fundamental right like industrial freedom. Being the weaker party, labor had greater need of that right than capital. As long as the prohibition was in effect, the workers would suffer from the delusion that what held down their wages was the law of the state, not the "natural law" of supply and demand in the labor market.

[52] Richter, *Arbeiterfrage*, 37–47; SBHA (1863), I, 23–28; III, 1–2.

marck in the summer of 1865.[53] A few days after Gastein, he took time out from diplomacy to write a devastating, fifty-seven page critique of its contents. The bias of the committee, he charged, was evident from its procedure. Although it justified successive reductions in wages, the committee had made no investigation of business profits. The problem was one of actual conditions, not doctrines. He rejected the argument that, because the state could not make a general practice of alleviating social distress, it could not help the Silesian weavers. "Ought it therefore to help no one? The state can."[54]

Meanwhile, Bismarck had directed Olearius to found and subsidize a model producers' cooperative in Wüstegiersdorf, employing the workers discharged by Reichenheim for petitioning the king. From the outset the experiment was plagued with difficulties. Eleven weavers joined the project, but the *Landrat* had trouble locating materials and quarters. The men were accustomed to cotton yarn, but all Olearius could supply was linen. The quality of the product was poor, and no regular market could be found. An attempt to get soldiers to buy it failed. Itzenplitz bought a few bolts, and Eulenburg tried vainly to get his friends to buy. Two weavers were sent with merchandise to the Frankfurt fair, but sold below cost. When the American conflict ended, the value of the yarn in stock fell precipitously. The weavers quarreled and intrigued against each other; Olearius concluded that they had always regarded the project as a "milk cow." Finally he was compelled to liquidate the venture.[55]

Bismarck was disappointed. In February 1865 he had defended the experiment in the Landtag against the attacks of Reichenheim and others with the ringing words, "The kings of Prussia have never been exclusively kings of the rich." He had hoped Wüstegiersdorf would serve as the model for a large-scale program for the founding of artisan cooperatives. After its failure he limited state aid to existing organizations. During 1865–1866 he repeatedly intervened on behalf of cooperative banks and producers' associations threatened with bankruptcy. His aim was admittedly to demonstrate to the workers the inadequacy of the private support advocated by Schulze-Delitzsch and other liberals. To the same end he backed a plan to found a home for invalided workers and a proposal to shift the tax burden imposed on the lower classes during the new era to the merchants and manufacturers.[56]

In the 1880s these experiments in social reform were accompanied by acts

[53] AWB, I, 20–25, 30–33, 49; GW, IV, 442; Richter, Arbeiterfrage, 53ff.

[54] Richter, Arbeiterfrage, 92–117, 235ff. Unfortunately this document was never published in full. See the excerpts in Hans Rothfels, ed., Otto von Bismarck: Deutscher Staat (Munich, 1925), 353–360, and AWB, I, 62–65. The ministers accepted many changes proposed by Bismarck, but the final report was not completed until July 1867. At that time its publication was decided against on the grounds that the issue was no longer so important "since the events of last summer." Richter, Arbeiterfrage, 247–248.

[55] Richter, Arbeiterfrage, 63–91.

[56] BR, III, 317; AWB, I, 32–33, 54, 68–70, 76, 78–83; GW, V, 335, 384–385; XIV, 691; Karl Thieme, "Bismarcks Sozialpolitik," Archiv für Politik und Geschichte, 9 (1927), 386.

of repression against the proletarian movement. After his death Lassalle's workers association had continued to grow despite squabbling among its leaders. In January 1865 the first party journal, *Der Sozialdemokrat* edited by Johann Baptist von Schweitzer, began publication in Berlin. The early issues carried an evaluation of Bismarck's Caesarism in foreign and social policy so favorable that Karl Marx, Friedrich Engels, and Wilhelm Liebknecht severed relations with the journal. Through Countess Sophie von Hatzfeldt, Marx had learned of Lassalle's talks with Bismarck. Rumor had it that Schweitzer was in the pay of the government. In July, however, the *Sozialdemokrat* attacked the government for suppressing the Cologne festival and called for mass meetings of protest. The government's reaction was severe. Issues of the journal were repeatedly confiscated; the Berlin branch of the workers' association was dissolved by police order; Liebknecht and Bernhard Becker, Lassalle's successor, were given twenty-four hours to leave the country; Schweitzer, a naturalized citizen, was sentenced to sixteen months and the loss of his civic rights for a year.[57]

Workers and Businessmen

In the 1860s Bismarck probably had a better chance to win German workers for the monarchy than two decades later when he finally made the attempt. As yet the party founded by Lassalle was not pledged to the revolutionary doctrine of the *Communist Manifesto*. Nor could it truthfully claim to represent proletarians as a whole, for they were largely uncommitted politically. Although the time was ripe, the palliatives Bismarck had in mind would hardly have gained the political loyalty of Germany's laborers. He did not contemplate large factory or mining cooperatives; an establishment the size of the Krupp works, he remarked to the Reichstag in 1878, could operate only under a monarchical, not a republican constitution. His purpose was to found small cooperatives in industries, such as textile manufacture, that had not yet completed the transition to large-scale production. Those whom he wanted to assist were primarily distressed artisans. Although they still outnumbered mine and factory workers, the artisans were the working class of the past, not the future.[58]

---

[57] Gustav Mayer, *Johann Baptist von Schweitzer und die Sozialdemokratie* (Jena, 1909), 110–142; Franz Mehring, *Geschichte der deutschen Sozialdemokratie* (Stuttgart, 1903), vol. 3, 195ff.; SEG (1865), 175. That there was a connection early in 1865 between the government and the *Sozialdemokrat* is confirmed by the fact that Eugen Dühring was commissioned by Bismarck to write articles for the publication. Richter, *Arbeiterfrage*, 57, 259. In October Lothar Bucher, now Bismarck's aide, offered employment to Karl Marx as a columnist on financial subjects for the official Prussian *Staatsanzeiger*. Marx refused. Franz Mehring, *Karl Marx: The Story of His Life* (London, 1936), 342–344.

[58] GW, XI, 609.

At any rate Bismarck was too busy with foreign affairs to give more than offhand attention to the problem. Not until the late 1870s, when his triumphs in foreign affairs had been achieved and partially consolidated, did he become as involved in domestic as in foreign policy. Not until then, furthermore, did he possess the personal ascendancy over the Prussian cabinet that enabled him to effect fundamental changes in Prussian economic and social policy. The ministers and counselors in charge of these affairs in the 1860s were too committed to laissez-faire and industrial capitalism to undertake a program of state socialism, either as a means of achieving social justice or of mobilizing wage earners against the upper *Mittelstand* in order to undermine liberal opposition in the Chamber of Deputies.

Earlier it was shown that laissez-faire was the one reform of the Stein–Hardenberg era whose progress was not choked off by reaction after 1820.[59] Laissez-faire had made inroads on mercantilistic practices under every successive Prussian regime after 1807. The liquidation of serfdom, free sale of noble estates, industrial freedom, abolition of internal tariffs, creation of the Zollverein, lifting of many restrictions on the joint-stock company—all of these decisions by successive governments in Berlin had reduced the role of government in economic affairs, promoting economic freedom and the growth of industrial capitalism. Despite many second thoughts, resulting in delays and temporary reversals, the course of Prussian economic policy for more than half a century had been primarily in the direction of free enterprise. Even political conservatives and bureaucratic absolutists within the government had come to accept that this was the best path to economic growth. About the wisdom and necessity of economic growth itself they were equally certain.

During the years 1862–1865—while Bismarck conferred with Wagener and Lassalle, conducted the experiment at Wüstegiersdorf, and attempted to initiate other measures of social reform—the Prussian bureaucracy continued on its earlier course by coercing the Zollverein to accept free trade during 1862–1865 and by completing deregulation of the mining industry in 1863. Although primarily a stroke of power politics in the continuing struggle with Austria, the free-trade treaty with France would have been impossible had it not corresponded to the interests of important segments of the German economy. As grain exporters and consumers of manufactured products, eastern landowners favored free trade. They were reinforced by merchants, who favored low tariffs in order to expedite the exchange of goods, and by many light industrialists, who did not need to fear foreign competition. Political economists lauded free trade as the key to economic growth. Whatever their thoughts about the political course of the Prussian government in the 1860s, agrarians, merchants, light industrialists, and academicians were in agreement with its economic policy. In 1862 the free-trade treaty with France was

[59] See pp. 108ff.

approved overwhelmingly by the Congress of German Economists and narrowly by the German Commercial Association. When polled by the government, most regional chambers of commerce in Prussia likewise endorsed the
French treaty. The chief opposition came from Prussian iron and steel industrialists, who suffered from British competition but were not yet weighty
enough to dictate tariff policy.[60]

On tariff matters the laissez-faire majority in the Prussian Chamber of Deputies was in full agreement with the government and the predominant agrarian and business interests. In September 1862 the deputies accepted the
French treaty and approved, with only twenty-six dissenting votes, the government's warning to the lesser states that rejection of the French treaty
would be regarded as rejection of the Zollverein itself. Three years later, the
new Zollverein treaties based on the agreement with France were approved
by the chamber without a single dissent. Liberal deputies rejoiced that Germany had joined hands with the "progressive peoples" of western Europe at
least in the field of economic policy.[61]

Although frustrated on the issue of tariffs, heavy industrialists found the
Bismarck government no different than its predecessors in responding to their
other needs. Since 1851 successive statutes had freed the mining companies
from governmental control and given them tax advantages.[62] The government transition from government "direction to inspection" over the mining
industry was finally completed in the statute of June 10, 1861, which abolished all local regulatory agencies (Bergämter) and limited provincial agencies
(Oberbergämter) chiefly to the regulation of mine safety. In the same year
(1861) in which the land tax reform ended the tax exemption of noble estates
the tax on the gross income of mining companies was reduced from 5 to 2
percent.[63] In 1865, while the constitutional conflict still raged, the Landtag
accepted a government bill establishing a mining code that incorporated in a
single statute all remaining regulatory acts.[64]

The laws that culminated in the code of 1865 ended governmental paternalism for the owners, but also for mine workers. Wages, hours, and working
conditions previously subject to state control were now established by work
contracts between workers and employers, an unequal partnership. Welfare

---

[60] Helmut Böhme, Deutschlands Weg zur Grossmacht: Studien zum Verhältnis von Wirtschaft und
Staat während der Reichsgründungszeit, 1848–1881 (Cologne, 1966), 116–117, 120–121; Wolfgang
Zorn, "Wirtschafts- und sozialgeschichtliche Zusammenhänge der deutschen Reichsgründungs-
zeit (1850–1879)," Historische Zeitschrift, 179 (1963), 325.

[61] SBHA (1862), 1549–1551, and (1865), 2228–2229; Heinrich Winkler, Preussicher Liberalismus und deutscher Nationalstaat: Studien zur Geschichte der Deutschen Fortschrittspartei, 1861–1866
(Tübingen, 1964), 71.

[62] For the history of this legislation see Wolfram Fischer, Wirtschaft und Gesellschaft im Zeitalter
der Industrialisierung (Göttingen, 1972), 139–178, 497–500.

[63] GSP (1861), 225–226, 425–430.

[64] GSP (1865), 705–760.

organizations (*Knappschaften*) that had previously provided a channel for the relief of worker grievances were reduced to the function of providing social insurance, sickness and disability compensation, and support of widows and orphans. The code marked the final triumph of the free-enterprise system in the mining industry and was also a milestone in the development of class consciousness among Ruhr miners. Unprotected by the state in the struggle against employers over wage contracts, the miners turned in the late 1850s to mass protests and work stoppages and in the following decades to unionization and socialism.[65]

Studies of the attitudes of businessmen toward the Prussian government during the 1860s show that the conflicts over the military bill and the constitution left them somewhat embarrassed. Traditionally Prussian businessmen were pacifistic and antimilitary. They had never been completely reconciled to the loss of exemptions enjoyed by the burghers before introduction of universal military conscription; they resented the arrogance and exclusiveness of the aristocratic officer corps and they preferred a larger fleet to a larger army for the better protection it would give to overseas trade. In 1848–1849, nevertheless, they had come to appreciate the utility of a loyal army for the preservation of social stability and private property in time of social unrest, and they accepted the judgment of Wilhelm and the generals that the mobilization of 1849 had shown grave deficiencies in the size and organization of the army. Nor was there strong objection to the separation of the *Landwehr* from the line army in wartime, for this reduced the military burden of bourgeois officers.[66]

The business community could scarcely have objected to the government's decision to pay for the enlarged army by abolishing (with compensation) the exemption from the land tax enjoyed by eastern estate owners. But the Junker estates had to be assessed before the tax could be levied, and the assessment was not completed until 1865; meanwhile, the needed funds for the army were acquired through surtaxes of 25 percent on income and on meal and slaughter taxes.[67] These taxes fell most heavily on urban dwellers, who resented the added burden. Nevertheless, the three-year service period for draftees was the only "reform" upon which the Chamber of Deputies refused

[65] Klaus Tenfelde, *Sozialgeschichte der Bergarbeiterschaft an der Ruhr im 19. Jahrhundert* (Bonn–Bad Godesberg, 1977), 163–191, 397–422; Gerhard Gebhardt, *Ruhrbergbau: Geschichte, Aufbau, und Verflechtung seiner Gesellschaften und Organisationen* (Essen, 1957), 22–25; Wilhelm Brepohl, *Der Aufbau des Ruhrvolkes im Zuge der Ost-West-Wanderung* (Recklinghausen, 1948), 181–184, 202–207.

[66] Friedrich Zunkel, *Der rheinisch-westfälische Unternehmer 1834–1879* (Cologne, 1962), 205–217; Eugene Anderson, *The Social and Political Conflict in Prussia, 1858–1864* (Lincoln, 1954), 18–22; Theodore Hamerow, *Social Foundations of German Unification, 1858–1871: Struggles and Accomplishments* (Princeton, 1972), 192–237.

[67] GSP (1859), 244; (1860), 278; (1861), 341.

in the end to yield, and this issue did not vitally engage the self-interest of German businessmen.

The constitutional issues that arose during 1862–1863, especially the government's violation of the constitution through the press ordinance of 1863, did radicalize some liberal businessmen. A return to arbitrary rule, they reasoned, might affect the government's economic policy to their disadvantage. Hence Rhenish electoral districts that had hitherto sent conservative or old-liberal deputies to Berlin now elected progressives. Yet there was no prospect of revolutionary action or even of participation in a taxpayers' strike. Had there been a depression, a failure of the government to extend assistance to business, or legislation hostile to entrepreneurial interests, Prussian businessmen might have taken a more determined stand with the Chamber of Deputies against the government. But this was not the case. The period 1861–1865 was one of steadily growing prosperity and industrial expansion.

In a letter of March 1865 to Karl Friedrich von Savigny, Bismarck exulted over the effect of renewed prosperity on the royal treasury. "Our financial balance for the last year (1864) shows that we need only 2 (two) million from the state treasury for the Danish War. Everything else is covered by the surpluses for 1863–1864. This information, although very gratifying, is to be kept secret because of the legislature. The financiers are pressing loans on us without parliament's approval but we could wage the Danish War twice over without needing one."[68] In 1863 Rhenish bankers had offered to convert government-owned mines of the Ruhr into joint-stock companies. In March–June 1866 the Cologne banker Abraham Oppenheim made a similar offer with regard to government mines, railways, and forests in the Saar basin. In December 1862 the Berlin banker Gerson Bleichröder proposed that the government replenish its coffers by selling its options on shares of the Cologne-Minden railway, one of the lines earmarked by Heydt for state ownership. In July 1865 Oppenheim and Bleichröder executed the sale for the government without parliamentary approval. Bleichröder, Bismarck's private banker since 1858, not only joined in these and other financial operations beneficial to the government but also carried out unofficial diplomatic missions for the minister-president.[69] Doing business with the government was a major source of profit for German financiers. For them the constitutional conflict was not a deterrent but an opportunity.

Businessmen in general appear to have lost interest in the struggle by 1864–1865. As practical men engaged in practical tasks, they deplored the tendency of professors, lawyers, and officials in the chamber to talk so much about the inviolability of principle. For the same reason they were impressed by Bis-

[68] GW, XIV, 693; translation from Theodore Hamerow, *Social Foundations of German Unification, 1858–1871: Ideas and Institutions* (Princeton, 1969), 14.

[69] Fritz Stern, *Gold and Iron: Bismarck, Bleichröder, and the Building of the German Empire* (New York, 1977), 38, 62–64; Zunkel, *Unternehmer*, 221; Böhme, *Deutschlands Weg*, 192–307.

marck's political realism and its success in the Schleswig-Holstein affair. A classic conversion was that of David Hansemann, minister of finance in the revolutionary government of 1848 and founder and head of the *Disconto-Gesellschaft*. In 1862 Hansemann denounced Bismarck as "frivolous"; before his death in late 1864, he concluded that Bismarck was "smarter and more foresighted than I have been." Gustav Mevissen rejoiced that at last a man of will and action was at the helm, and Ludolf Camphausen, leading minister of the 1848 government, conceded that Bismarck was the first statesman capable of bold action in Prussia since 1815. Viktor von Unruh, one of the few industrialists in parliament, complained to Schulze-Delitzsch, "The well-to-do bourgeois are politically stunted." They lacked "political nerve" and "energy" when faced by a man like Bismarck.[70]

During Bismarck's early years in office the Prussian government was at odds with parliament on political but not on basic economic issues. Acceptance of government policy on the economic front tended to weaken and undermine liberal opposition on the political one. To have launched a large-scale program of social reform would have destroyed this advantage. In the spring of 1866 Bismarck chose German nationalism rather than state socialism as his ultimate weapon in the struggle with parliament. Like the free-trade policy in the Zollverein, it carried a multiple warhead, capable of striking simultaneously at both domestic and foreign opposition.

[70] Zunkel, *Untermehmer*, 217–218; Alexander Bergengrün, *David Hansemann* (Berlin, 1901), 740–744; Joseph Hansen, *Gustav von Mevissen: Ein rheinisches Lebensbild, 1815–1899* (Berlin, 1906), vol. 1, 742; Schulze-Delitzsch, *Schriften und Reden*, vol. 4, 18–19, 256–257, and vol. 5, 133–134.

CHAPTER THIRTEEN

The Conquest of Northern Germany

On the Razor's Edge

ARRIVING in Berlin on February 15, 1866, Lord Augustus Loftus, the British ambassador, found the political atmosphere "loaded." "It smelled of powder."[1] On the twenty-eighth a crown council assembled in the Wilhelmstrasse. The diplomatic corps noted uneasily that the list of participants was unusual. In addition to the king, crown prince, and cabinet ministers, Generals Moltke and Alvensleben were present, as were Ambassador Goltz, who had been summoned from Paris, and Edwin Manteuffel, who came from Schleswig. The diplomats had reason to be nervous. Behind the closed doors of the foreign office the subject of discussion was war.

Wilhelm's opening remarks show how well he had learned the lessons Bismarck drilled into him. Since August 1865, he charged, Austria had steadily sabotaged the Gastein agreement. She was playing the old game: "*Il faut avilir la Prusse, pour la détruire.*" Prussia's mission, Bismarck added, was to lead Germany. An envious Austria had consistently blocked this "natural and very justified" ambition. A decisive struggle was only a matter of time. At the moment conditions in Germany and Europe were favorable for Prussia. Out of the conflict would come the solution of the German question. Another result, Eulenburg pointed out, would be the conquest of the Prussian opposition. This could not be the motive for war, Bismarck replied, but only its byproduct. Of those present only the crown prince spoke for the avoidance of hostilities.[2]

---

[1] Lord Augustus Loftus, *Diplomatic Reminiscences*, 2d ser. (London, 1894), vol. 1, 39.

[2] We possess three protocols of this critical meeting, two of which show that Eulenburg's comment was the only one to which Bismarck took exception during the council meeting. APP, VI, 611–619; Heinrich O. Meisner, ed., *Kaiser Friedrich III.: Tagebücher von 1848–1866* (Leipzig, 1929), 541–544; Walter Reichle, *Zwischen Staat und Kirche: Das Leben und Wirken des preussischen Kultusministers Heinrich von Mühler* (Berlin, 1938), 170–171. Yet historians have tended to attribute Eulenburg's remark to Bismarck himself, ignoring the two accounts by Konrad von Moltke and Heinrich von Mühler, which prove the contrary. See Michael Stürmer, *Regierung und Reichstag im Bismarckstaat 1871–1880* (Düsseldorf, 1974), 34; Fritz Stern, *Gold and Iron: Bismarck, Bleichröder, and the Building of the German Empire* (New York, 1977), 70; Immanuel Geiss, "Sozialstruktur und imperialistische Disposition im Zweiten Kaiserreich," in K. Holl and G. List, *Liberalismus und imperialistischer Staat* (Göttingen, 1975), 53; Hans-Ulrich Wehler, *Das deutsche Kaiserreich, 1871–1914* (2d ed., Göttingen, 1980), 35–36. Lothar Gall attributed the remark to no one in particular and ignored Bismarck's objection to it: *Bismarck: Der weisse Revolutionär*

What Wilhelm desired was not an immediate decision for military action, but preparation for its eventual necessity. Nor had Bismarck abandoned his double course. He was never one to confuse probability with inevitability. During the months ahead many things could happen. French policy might shift; the Italian alliance might not develop; Wilhelm's final scruples might not be overcome; the Austrians, isolated in Europe and nearly bankrupt at home, might compromise once more.

Like two boxers, Bismarck and Mensdorff circled warily, the one aggressive, the other defensive. The Junker's task was to find, the general's to avoid, a casus belli that would place Austria in the wrong. In the age of the newspaper press and popular interest in public affairs it had become important to unload the burden of blame on someone else's back. Bismarck had yet another motive. Under the Prussian constitution the king alone tipped the scales for peace or war, and Wilhelm was a man of stubborn conscience. He judged political questions more in terms of right and wrong than of power and possibility. If persuaded that his rights were being violated or his authority disputed (so Bismarck told French Ambassador Count Vincent Benedetti), Wilhelm could be brought to take the most "energetic measures" and even to think of them as stemming from his own initiative. For months Bismarck flooded the Ballplatz with recriminatory messages whose actual purpose was to convince Wilhelm of the righteousness of his cause. Like a clock, it was said in Berlin, the king had to be wound up each morning by his minister-president.[3]

Mensdorff's problem was different. In the Austrian government his voice, reinforced by that of Moritz Esterhazy, was that of moderation. He favored gradual concessions to Prussia in northern Germany, but was determined not to yield to the threat of force. Although he had advocated military resistance during the Gastein crisis, he now realized that Austria's position had deteriorated. Isolated and internally weak, she was unequal to a two-front war. Consequently Mensdorff wished to avoid any overt act that would furnish Bismarck with the pretext he sought. But Franz Joseph and his generals feared that this policy would place the Austrian army at a disadvantage. The Austrian mobilization system was an ox compared to the Prussian racehorse. Given an equal start, the Habsburg army would be left at the post. A prema-

---

(Frankfurt a. M., 1980), 346–347. Ernst Engelberg selected for quotation the Moltke version of Bismarck's objection: "the domestic situation does not require a foreign war, although it is an additional reason that makes war appear advantagous," passing up Mühler's account, which has a more negative shading: "Bismarck took exception to the assumption [by Eulenburg] that domestic questions can be the motive for war, [though] their solution may be a fruit of it." *Bismarck: Urpreusse und Reichsgründer* (Berlin, 1985), 570. The "coercive situation" (Engelberg's phrase) that Bismarck depicted that day was entirely one of foreign affairs.

[3] GW, V, 396, 399; VII, 123; OD, VII, 214, 222–223, 257–258.

ture mobilization would destroy the delicate web of Mensdorff's peace efforts, but a delayed one might mean loss of the war itself.[4]

On March 14, 1866, the generals persuaded Franz Joseph, over the protests of Mensdorff and Esterhazy, to assemble a few regiments to strengthen the Bohemian defenses.[5] Reports of the Austrian movement soon reached Berlin and, properly exaggerated, gave Bismarck the weapon he sought. Now he could play before Germany and Europe his favorite role of the injured party. In dispatch after dispatch he accused the Austrians of warlike intentions. The Austrian measure also enabled him to wind up the royal clock once more. On March 29 the king signed an order to strengthen the frontier regiments and fortresses. Up to the last minute Bismarck feared he might back down. It was Maundy Thursday and Wilhelm's mood was pious![6]

In desperation Mensdorff strove to counter the Prussian offensive. Bluntly he asked whether it was Berlin's intention to tear up the Gastein treaty. But it did little good to try to embarrass Bismarck with such a question. "No," he replied, and added sardonically that up to the eve of an attack no other answer could be expected from any power. Mensdorff's next démarche was more effective. On March 31 he informed Europe that Austria's intentions were peaceful, and he challenged Prussia to say the same.[7] Behind the scenes he helped to mobilize a formidable array of forces to weaken Wilhelm's will to war: Duke Ernst of Coburg, Queen Victoria, Queen Augusta, the crown prince and princess, the dowager queen, and the king's sister, Alexandrine. All were convinced of Bismarck's folly and the necessity of his fall. Others who wished him ill were Counts Goltz and Bernstorff (his two most influential subordinates), Baron Schleinitz, now Hohenzollern "house minister," and Justus Gruner, former state secretary in the foreign office.[8]

The "Coburg intrigue," as it was called, had some effect. Wilhelm found Bismarck's reply to Mensdorff's challenge "very cold and abrupt" and insisted on moderating the tone. Nevertheless, the note of April 6 was still barbed

---

[4] DPO, V/1, 202, 427; Heinrich Ritter von Srbik, *Deutsche Einheit: Idee und Wirklichkeit vom Heiligen Reich bis Königgrätz* (Munich, 1935–1942), vol. 4, 327–328; Chester W. Clark, *Franz Joseph and Bismarck: The Diplomacy of Austria before the War of 1866* (Cambridge, Mass., 1934), 239ff.

[5] The Austrian step was prompted by the warlike temper of the Prussian official press, an unusual practice mobilization in Berlin, and rumors of the Prussian intent to occupy Saxony immediately on the outbreak of war. Clark, *Franz Joseph and Bismarck*, 363ff.; 562–563. Since November the French military attaché had been reporting abnormal military preparations in Prussia. OD, VII, 171ff.

[6] APP, VI, 707ff.; GW, V, 416ff.; XIV, 710.

[7] DPO, V/1, 298–299, 302–323, 306–309; GW, V, 410–411; Ludwig Aegidi and Alfred Klauhold, eds., *Das Staatsarchiv: Sammlung der officiellen Aktenstücke zur Geschichte der Gegenwart*, vol. 10 (1866), 352–353.

[8] DPO, V/1, 240, 292ff., 312, 380–395; GW, XIV, 710–711; Srbik, *Deutsche Einheit*, vol. 4, 335ff.; Clark, *Franz Joseph and Bismarck*, 374ff.; Otto Graf zu Stolberg-Wernigerode, *Robert Heinrich Graf von der Goltz* (Oldenburg, 1941), 146ff.

enough to arouse Vienna. Within twenty-four hours a hasty and ill-considered rebuttal, drafted by the acid pen of Biegeleben, was dispatched to Berlin. Instantly Bismarck recognized it as a "crude and clumsy error."[9] Its caustic phrases provided a fresh irritant to rub into Wilhelm's wounded feelings. Now the Prussian moves came in quick succession. On April 8 a military alliance was concluded with Italy; next day Berlin called for a confederate reform, including a German parliament based on universal suffrage.

In the crown council of February 28 Moltke had given his professional opinion that Italian participation in a war against Austria was indispensable. Only if Austria were squeezed in the vise of a two-front war was Prussian superiority certain. In 1865 the Gastein agreement had disappointed the government in Florence. Consequently Alfonso La Marmora, the premier, was now determined to bind Prussia to a definite timetable for war on Austria. But this was impossible for Bismarck. Wilhelm was not yet ready for the final step, and Napoleon's position was still uncertain. Hence Bismarck had to leave open the alternative of a settlement with Austria. On March 14 an Italian general, Giuseppe Govone, arrived in Berlin to reconcile these differences. While Károlyi watched suspiciously from his window across the street, the Italians came and went at Wilhelmstrasse 76, until finally, with customary skill, Bismarck got his way. He achieved a secret treaty that left the exact timing of the war up to Prussia. But the Italians were committed to join only if the attack were begun within three months.[10]

The crisis of 1866 sharply revealed for the last time the fundamental dilemma of Austrian foreign policy. The Habsburg monarchy was faced with the necessity of choosing between its positions in Germany and Italy. Lacking the power for both, the empire had either to come to terms with Prussia in order to concentrate on Italy, or voluntarily cede Venetia in order to assert itself in Germany. After Gastein, La Marmora made a last attempt to obtain the province by purchase and the promise of an alliance. Told that the Italians had offered 500 million francs, Bismarck exclaimed, "Oh what folly! A war would cost only 300 million!"[11] In January he had hinted again that Austria, by surrendering her primacy in Germany, might receive Prussian aid in the reconquest of Lombardy.[12] For Franz Joseph, however, it was an abiding principle, ultimately fatal for the empire, not to surrender except under duress any fragment of his inherited power either at home or abroad. He deluded

---

[9] *Staatsarchiv*, vol. 9 (1866), 356–357, 362–364; Horst Kohl, ed., *Anhang zu den Gedanken und Erinnerungen von Otto Fürst von Bismarck* (Stuttgart, 1901), vol. 1, 127ff.; GW, V, 452.

[10] APP, VI, 599–604, 626–627, 653ff., 709–711; GW, V, 395ff., 412–413; DPO, V/1, 337. See also Friedrich Beiche, *Bismarck und Italien: Ein Beitrag zur Vorgeschichte des Krieges 1866: Historische Studien*, vol. 208 (Berlin, 1931).

[11] Srbik, *Deutsche Einheit*, vol. 4, 296–297. DPO, V/1, 209, also 201; OD, VII, 299.

[12] DPO, V/1, 153.

himself that Austria was equal to a two-front war as long as France or Russia did not intervene on the opposing side.

During the latter part of April, Mensdorff made yet another valiant attempt to influence Wilhelm and undercut Bismarck. For the moment the voices of the war party in Vienna were muffled by the desperate financial condition of the monarchy. It was estimated that the enormous expense of arming could be met only by manipulating the currency.[13] Mensdorff found his opportunity in the Prussian note of April 15, which, while rejecting Biegeleben's demand for Prussian disarmament, offered to follow suit if Austria herself disarmed. In a conciliatory reply Mensdorff now declared that the Habsburg troops in Bohemia would be ordered back to their original stations on April 25, if the Prussians would do likewise "on the same or even the following day."[14]

Disarmament proposals have little realism unless coupled with the easing of political tensions. Nevertheless, the note had a strong effect upon Wilhelm. The prospect of war was not popular in Prussia, and the influence of the "Coburg intrigue" lingered in his mind. On his insistence the Prussian reply of April 21 was also moderate. Vienna must take the initiative in ordering a return to the status quo ante, but Prussia would "keep in step."[15] The gap between the Prussian and Austrian views was narrowing, and the possibility loomed that it might actually close. Only a matter of etiquette seemed to stand in the way.

Desperately Bismarck struggled to control the king's mind. As often happened when he met such opposition, he fell ill with a "nervous rheumatic" disorder. To Roon he complained that he could "no longer bear this awful friction." Like a wounded boar, wrote Károlyi, he lay on a divan nursing his lame leg and looking more like a conspirator than a triumphator. Edwin Manteuffel came to his aid with a letter warning Wilhelm against a "second Olmütz." The old man reacted with a "magnificent display of anger" at Austria. Roon followed up with a "most sharp and cutting discourse on what we want and what we decidedly do not want." Bismarck's health began to improve. But it was the Austrians who made him well.[16]

On April 20 alarming reports reached Vienna from the south. Along the Venetian frontier, it was said, the Italians were busily assembling men and supplies. On the advice of his generals, and with Mensdorff's reluctant approval, the Kaiser hastily ordered, only a day later, the mobilization of the southern army. The reports were exaggerated. Károlyi suspected Bismarck was

[13] DPO, V/1, 443; Srbik, Deutsche Einheit, vol. 4, 354.

[14] GW, V, 452–454; Staatsarchiv, vol. 10 (1866), 366. See also the protocol of the ministerial council in which the Austrian reply was discussed. DPO, V/1, 498ff.

[15] GW, V, 460; VII, 109–110.

[16] DPO, V/1, 486; GW, V, 461; XIV, 712; Waldemar von Roon, Denkwürdigkeiten aus dem Leben des General-Feldmarschalls Kriegsministers Grafen von Roon (4th ed., Breslau, 1897), vol. 2, 400ff., 421.

the source. At any rate Victor Emmanuel II now made them a reality by openly mobilizing the entire Italian army. On May 1 Franz Joseph concluded that war was "unavoidable." Orders went out to strengthen further the northern army, and the treasury resorted to a dubious currency conversion to raise the necessary funds. News of the Austrian decision reached Berlin on the evening of May 3, and Wilhelm, swollen with indignation, ordered mobilization.[17]

The natural fruit of mobilization is war. So great are the expenses and dislocations that both sides feel the pressure to act lest the sacrifice appear in vain. And yet even now, while troops and cannon rumbled toward their stations, Bismarck found a way to continue his double course. The opportunity came in the plan of the brothers Ludwig and Anton von Gablenz for a compromise peace.

By heritage and interests the Gablenz brothers had a better chance than most to view the German quarrel objectively. They belonged to a family of imperial knights: Ludwig was Austrian proconsul in Holstein; Anton was a Prussian landowner and Landtag deputy (old-liberal). On April 20 Anton departed from Kiel for Vienna with the draft of an agreement that the brothers hoped would avert the threatening conflict. Under their plan an independent Schleswig-Holstein would be ruled by a Hohenzollern prince; the duchies would reimburse Austria for her costs in the war of 1864; Prussia would gain the most important special rights she had demanded; Germany would be divided into two military units along the river Main, Berlin commanding the north, Vienna the south. Backed by Germany, Austria would be able to protect her trans-Alpine possessions against Italy and France.

In Vienna and Berlin, Anton succeeded in gaining direct and secret access to the foreign ministers. For more than a month he shuttled back and forth between the Spree and the Danube bearing proposals and counterproposals. From the start he received only encouragement from Bismarck, who accepted the plan, with a few minor changes, as a "basis for negotiation." Bismarck's subordinate, Rudolf Hepke, worked out a more detailed plan, combining a dual reorganization of Germany with the national parliament Prussia had proposed on April 9. At the end of May, however, Anton heard from Mensdorff that Franz Joseph would consent to the Gablenz plan only if it were backed by one or more medium states. This ended the matter, for such consent was not to be had.[18]

There were several possible motives for Bismarck's encouragement of Ga-

---

[17] DPO, V/1, 523ff., 553; Srbik, *Deutsche Einheit*, vol. 4, 363–364; Ernst Berner, ed., *Kaiser Wilhelms des Grossen Briefe, Reden, und Schriften* (Berlin, 1906), vol. 2, 124.

[18] DPO, V/1, 521–523, 560; GW, V, 479; Otto Becker, *Bismarcks Ringen um Deutschlands Gestaltung* (Heidelberg, 1958), 121ff.

blenz.[19] As at Gastein, Prussia stood to gain the most from the agreement: Austria would have to concede Prussia's equal status in Germany; the lesser states would again feel betrayed by Vienna; even with the provision for *itio in partes* a confederate parliament based on universal suffrage would be more likely to support Hohenzollern than Habsburg interests. An Austrian rejection, on the other hand, would help convince Wilhelm of her perfidy. Most important of all, backdoor negotiation through Gablenz enabled Bismarck to leave open a line of retreat. In it he saw the means of continuing, up to the threshold of war, the basic strategy of alternatives that was his best security in the treacherous game of politics. During the weeks that remained before the shooting began, it was his only insurance against outside intervention.

The possibility that London or Petersburg would intervene was slight. The Russian government was still largely absorbed with internal problems. After her failure in Schleswig-Holstein and the death of Palmerston in 1865 Britain had reduced her involvement in continental politics. Bismarck's main concern was France.

Caesar on the Seine

Bismarck had no difficulty in recognizing Napoleon's basic strategy. It was the same as his own: a "double policy," seeking "to preserve the possibility of stepping at the right moment to one side or the other."[20] But Napoleon lacked Bismarck's acute sense of timing, certainty of purpose, and suppleness in maneuver. Although reasonably successful in foreign affairs until 1859, he had fumbled consistently thereafter. His loss of control over Italian unification, his equivocations in the Polish affair, the folly of the Mexican adventure, and the collapse of the British entente showed increasing ineptitude. In the German question he steered a zigzag course that has left his intentions open to dispute.

The developing crisis of 1864–1866 seemed to offer France a golden opportunity to refurbish the prestige of the Second Empire. Because both sides needed either France's support or, at least, its benevolent neutrality, Napoleon and his ministers had the possibility of extracting advantageous agreements from both Berlin and Vienna. Their primary aim was to detach Venetia from Austria and fulfill Napoleon's long-standing promise to the Italians. The grant of Venetia might also be a useful lever with which to limit the Italian union in a way favorable to France. Similarly he wished to restrict Prussian expansion to the region north of the Main and to replace Austrian with French influence among the south German states. Out of the coming cata-

---

[19] For a review of the widely diverging judgments on the significance of Bismarck's handling of the Gablenz plan see Otto Becker, "Der Sinn der dualistischen Verständigungsversuche Bismarcks," *Historische Zeitschrift*, 169 (1949), 264ff.

[20] GW, V, 95.

clysm, moreover, would emerge the chance, probably even the necessity, of further territorial gains for France. He wavered between many temptations: the frontier of 1814, Bavarian Palatinate, Belgium, Luxemburg, French Switzerland, and a buffer state on the Rhine. But France was not to be the only beneficiary. For a time Napoleon envisioned a European congress that would recarve European frontiers for the reciprocal benefit of the participating great powers. For surrendering Venetia to France, which would hand it on to Italy, Austria would receive the Danubian principalities (Moldavia and Walachia) or parts of Bosnia and Herzegovina or Silesia. Prussia would receive Schleswig-Holstein (minus northern Schleswig, which would go to Denmark), other small principalities in northern Germany, and the right to reorganize the German Confederation. France alone would gain without sacrifice, a feat that would win the hearts of Napoleon's subjects. If the congress failed, the fortunes of war would determine the outcome of this agenda.[21]

In the crown council of February 28, 1866, Bismarck had explained the necessity of obtaining "more definite guarantees" from France. Returning to Paris in early March, Goltz carried to Napoleon a personal letter from Wilhelm requesting a "more intimate entente." But the emperor evaded Bismarck's effort to "fix" the French position in advance of the war. Although he alluded to several possibilities for compensation ranging from the Alps to the channel, Napoleon declared that France would remain neutral and seek an agreement with Prussia to secure French interests only if the European balance were jeopardized.[22] For four years he had refused to snatch at the bait Bismarck dangled with his talk of the Rhine and French-speaking Europe. He was, however, surrounded by chauvinists—Eugénie, Drouyn, Persigny, and Prince Napoleon—who favored a ruthless exploitation by France of the German crisis. Less rash than they, he feared to arouse the whole of Europe by a policy of expansion toward the Rhine.[23]

Fluctuating between the poles of caution and ambition, Napoleon was unable to follow a resolute policy. Repeatedly he sought to entice from Bismarck a concrete offer without raising a concrete demand. In March he responded to soundings from Goltz by referring vaguely to Luxemburg and the Bavarian Rhineland. In mid-April he proposed a European congress to preserve the peace, by which he expected to put both Austria and Prussia under pressure to come to terms with France. One evening at a court ball, which fairly vibrated with politics, he drew Goltz aside to say that France was tempted by

[21] E. Ann Pottinger, *Napoleon III and the German Crisis, 1865–1866* (Cambridge, Mass., 1966), 24–150.

[22] APP, VI, 615; GW, V, 286–287; OD, VII, 293; RKN, I, 89–90, 98–99, 108.

[23] Gerhard Ritter saw Napoleon as more "shoved than shover." See his "Bismarck und die Rheinpolitik Napoleons III.," *Rheinische Vierteljahrsblätter*, 15–16 (1950–1951), 339–370; also "Die Politik Napoleons III. und das System der Mainlinie," *Korrespondenzblatt des Gesamtvereins der deutschen Geschichts- und Altertumsvereine*, 80 (1932), 178–182.

THE HERO OF NIAGARA. BISMARCK SEEKS TO OUTDO THE WIRE WALKER CHARLES BLONDIN—WHO
CROSSED NIAGARA ON THE "LONGEST CABLE YET KNOWN"—BY CARRYING A WEIGHT "MUCH HEAVIER
THAN HIMSELF" FROM 1865 TO 1866 (WILHELM SCHOLZ, *KLADDERADATSCH*, JULY 9, 1865).

far-reaching offers from Vienna. Lacking counteroffers from Berlin, he might
have to accept. France could not stand idly by while other powers aggrandized
themselves. "The eyes of the entire country are on the Rhine." On May 7 in
the published version of a speech delivered at Auxerre he said that, like most
Frenchmen, he "detested" the treaties of 1815.[24]

[24] *RKN*, I, 140ff., 165ff., 180ff.

The Auxerre speech was interpreted in France as favoring Prussia and Italy and inferring the possibility that France might join in the war on Austria. That thought elicited a sharply adverse reaction in French public opinion and a steep decline on the Paris bourse. Evidently the speech was yet another attempt on Napoleon's part, like the call for an international congress, to coerce Austria into surrendering Venetia. But the reaction revealed the depth of anti-Prussian and pacifistic sentiment in France.[25] In May, nevertheless, he made one more démarche in Berlin through an informal, and deniable, channel—an Hungarian expatriate, Nikolaus Kiss de Nemeskér, who had personal contacts with Bismarck and Prince Napoleon. Kiss brought to the German capital a draft treaty providing that, if Austria should decline to participate in the proposed congress and refuse to surrender Venetia and her rights in Schleswig-Holstein, France would join Prussia and Italy in a war whose aim would be a number of annexations. Italy would obtain Venetia; Prussia would acquire territories (evidently in northern Germany—the list has been lost) inhabited by seven to eight million people and the freedom to reorganize the German Confederation; France's portion would be the triangle of German territory lying between the Rhine and Mosel rivers and belonging to Prussia, Bavaria, and Hesse.[26] Bismarck refused to consider this last clause, but he is said to have sent back a counterproposal through another Hungarian emigré offering Belgium, Luxemburg, and a border region in the Rhineland.[27]

As war neared, Napoleon gave up the effort to reach agreement with Prussia and concentrated on the negotiation with Austria. His military advisers were nearly unanimous in the conviction that the Austrian army was superior to the combined forces of Prussia and Italy. In Vienna Mensdorff and Franz Joseph were finally convinced of the necessity of coming to terms with France. But their procrastination had a price. In March they might still have bought peace with Italy by ceding Venetia; in June they agreed to surrender it, not to avoid a two-front war, but to secure France's neutrality and approval of Austria's war aims in Germany. They were willing to grant Belgium to France and to create a buffer state in the Rhineland.[28] But Napoleon drove a hard bargain. He would not commit France to support Austria's acquisition of Silesia and agreed to Habsburg expansion in Germany only if it did not upset the

[25] Lynn M. Case, "French Opinion and Napoleon III's Decision after Sadowa," *Public Opinion Quarterly*, 13 (1949–1950), 441–461, and *French Opinion during the Second Empire* (Philadelphia, 1954), 196ff.; Pottinger, *Napoleon III*, 117–127.

[26] *RKN*, I, 241–246; Pottinger, *Napoleon III*, 136–141.

[27] John W. Bush, *Venetia Redeemed: Franco-Italian Relations 1864–66* (Syracuse, 1967), 73; Pottinger, *Napoleon III*, 141.

[28] *DPO*, V/1, 61, 185–186, 527ff., 549; *RKN*, I, 144, 160, 164–165, 180, 202ff., 227ff. Though the buffer state was not mentioned in the treaty, it was verbally agreed that this was to be France's compensation. *RKN*, I, 268; *OD*, X, 145; *GW*, VIb, 108 (n. 3). See also Heinrich Ritter von Srbik, "Der Geheimvertrag Österreichs und Frankreichs vom 12. Juni 1866," *Historisches Jahrbuch*, 57 (1937), 454–507, and Pottinger, *Napoleon III*, 82–105, 142–150.

European equilibrium. The contract was a poor one, but on June 12 the Austrians signed in the belief that it was the only way to assure French neutrality. Napoleon's knife, said Richard Metternich, was at Austria's throat.[29]

Bismarck was surprised by the extent and timing of Napoleon's demands in late April. They compelled him to leave open through the Gablenz plan the last door to a compromise settlement with Austria.[30] And yet the day was fast approaching when Prussia must make the final option for peace or war. If the choice was war, Napoleon's neutrality would have to be bought. What did Bismarck expect to pay? Some German historians found comfort in the fact that Bismarck, in contrast to the Austrians, made it clear from the outset that Wilhelm would never tolerate the cession of German soil.[31] His critics, on the other hand, can point to two highly suspicious documents, recording audiences with General Govone, the Italian agent, on June 2 and Count Benedetti, the French ambassador, on June 4.[32] According to the former, Bismarck confessed that, being "much less German than Prussian," he was willing to cede the region between the Rhine and Moselle, but the king would never agree to it.[33] The latter quoted him as saying that Wilhelm preferred to see Napoleon find his compensation in French-speaking areas. Nevertheless, the Hohenzoller might possibly be persuaded to grant the region of the upper Moselle, which, with Luxemburg, would nicely round out the French frontiers. As for the lower Rhine (Mainz, Bonn, Cologne), Bismarck asserted that he would sooner quit politics than consent to its surrender.[34]

Years later, after the publication of the first document, Bismarck angrily denied its accuracy. His ablest defenders explained away the second as an offer he knew Napoleon could not accept, extended in order to smoke out the terms being offered Paris by Austria. Can there be any doubt, asked Gerhard Ritter, of Bismarck's determination not to sacrifice one single inch of German soil to France?[35] Again the facts are obdurate. On April 30, the minister-president proposed to the Prussian cabinet that the state-owned mines of the Saar be sold to private investors in order to prevent financial loss to the government should the exigencies of war require ceding the region to France.[36]

---

[29] *RKN*, I, 247ff., 264ff., 290; *OD*, X, 114ff., 147ff., 164ff.

[30] *GW*, V, 482ff.

[31] *GW*, V, 389, 394. See Ritter, "Rheinpolitik Napoleons III.," 366; Erich Brandenburg, *Untersuchungen und Aktenstücke zur Geschichte der Reichsgründung* (Leipzig, 1916), 409, and the editorial comments of Oncken and Thimme, *RKN*, I, 245, and *GW*, V, 518.

[32] See Erich Eyck, *Bismarck: Leben und Werk* (Zurich, 1941–1944), vol. 2, 218ff.

[33] U. Govone, ed., *General Govone: Mémoires (1848–1870)* (Paris, 1905), vii–viii, 206–207.

[34] *RKN*, X, 31.

[35] Ritter, "Rheinpolitik Napoleons III.," 367.

[36] *GW*, V, 474ff. Fritz Hellwig, an Oncken student, asserted that Bismarck's aim in the memorial of Apr. 30 was financial rather than diplomatic, but he ignored the vital passage that refutes his thesis. See his *Der Kampf um die Saar 1860–1870: Beiträge zur Rheinpolitik Napoleons III.*, in Hermann Oncken, ed., *Forschungen zur neueren und neuesten Geschichte*, pt. 3 (Leipzig,

He foresaw, in other words, the likelihood of having to sacrifice at least the frontier of 1814. In an extremity it is probable that he would have surrendered even more. Unlike his historians, Bismarck was never inclined to dogmatize political possibilities.

As usual, Bismarck saw the problem of dealing with France as one of alternatives. The "easier way," he wrote on May 7, was to show Napoleon that "what Austria can offer him at our expense is more readily obtainable from us." The harder way was to threaten Napoleon with the anger of the German nation. As early as March 24 he had written Goltz that French ambitions made it all the more imperative to establish for Prussia "a firm and national foundation" by opening the "German question."[37] Before Europe the great advocate of national self-determination would be forced to choose between his principles and his interests. If he should choose the latter, Prussia would fall back, as in 1812, upon the volcanic passions of national hatred.

The War Begins

Meanwhile, the dual powers were engaged in a hard contest for the loyalty of the medium states. "We appeal to the noble sentiments: patriotism, honor, principles of law, energy, courage, decision, sense of independence, etc.," complained an Austrian diplomat. "He reckons on the lower motivations of human nature: avarice, cowardice, confusion, indolence, indecision, and narrow-mindedness."[38] In Hanover, Kassel, and Dresden, Bismarck promised territorial expansion; in Munich, hegemony over southern Germany. Those who opposed Prussia, he warned, might expect the lash of revenge. The result was failure. From the outset King Johann and Baron Beust placed Saxony securely in the Austrian camp. After months of wavering the rulers of Hanover and Hesse-Kassel staked their future at the last minute upon confederate law and Austrian power.[39]

In the south everything depended upon Bavaria. Barons Dalwigk, Varnbüler, and Edelsheim, the leading ministers, respectively, of Hesse-Darm-

---

1934), 172–173. As Ritter himself pointed out, the project was dropped because of the opposition it aroused in the Saar and not, as he argued in another place, because of a sudden surge of confidence on Bismarck's part in the success of Prussian arms. Had Napoleon responded to Wilhelm's March request for a "more intimate entente," the promise of the 1814 frontier would have been unavoidable, not as the result of a "catastrophic war development," as Ritter asserted, but in advance of actual hostilities. "Rheinpolitik Napoleons III.," 360, 367. According to Johannes Haller, Bismarck ordered a map showing the frontier brought to Nikolsburg during the intervention crisis of late July. Otto Scheel, *Bismarcks Wille zu Deutschland in den Friedensschlüssen 1866: Veröffentlichungen der Schleswig-Holsteinischen Universitätsgesellschaft*, vol. 44 (Breslau, 1934), 90 (n. 2).

[37] GW, V, 357–358, 414–415, 488–489.

[38] DPO, V/1, 270.

[39] GW, V, 390ff., 419ff., 430ff., 443ff., 466–467, 489ff., 547ff.

stadt, Württemberg, and Baden, were pro-Austrian, but without Bavaria their support was strategically ineffective. In Munich Baron von der Pfordten first declared Bavaria neutral and sought to mediate between the dual powers. Vain and self-important, he enjoyed being courted by both, but he was also fearful of French intervention in a German civil war. Ludwig II, a romantic dreamer absorbed in Wagnerian fantasies, was stubbornly insistent on peace whatever the issue, and the officer corps had serious doubts about Austria's military strength. Despite Bismarck's flattery and promises, Pfordten drifted steadily, almost unconsciously, into the harbor of the Austrian alliance. Although Austria too appealed to their cupidity, the motive that dominated the thoughts of the rulers and statesmen of the lesser states was dread of Prussian hegemony.[40]

On May 9 the Frankfurt Diet voted, ten to five, for a Saxon resolution calling upon Berlin to explain her mobilization. Three weeks later Austria forced the issue by formally placing the future of the duchies in the hands of the confederation. The aim was to compel Berlin to defy the diet and furnish the pretext for confederate mobilization. By formally breaking the Gastein treaty, however, the Austrian action enabled Bismarck to bring Wilhelm into the home stretch.[41] On June 7 Edwin Manteuffel, following orders from Berlin, sent his forces over the Eider into Holstein. Tensely the men in the Ballplatz and Wilhelmstrasse waited for news of the first skirmish. To their mutual distress Gablenz withdrew over the Elbe into Hanover without being attacked. The casus belli was lacking![42]

The scene shifted back to Frankfurt and the German question. On June 10 a dispatch from Berlin presented an "outline" of Prussia's plan for a German union excluding Austria. Even now Bismarck lacked Wilhelm's final consent for war. "I've led the horse to the ditch," he remarked. "*Il faut, qu'il saute.*"[43] The final prod came from Vienna. On June 11 Baron Aloys von Kübeck, the Austrian envoy, began to push through the diet, in defiance of its rules, a motion for immediate mobilization of all confederate forces (except for Prussia). It passed on the fourteenth, nine to five. Karl von Savigny answered for Prussia by declaring the confederation dissolved. Next day Berlin sent ultimatums to Dresden, Hanover, and Kassel. They were rejected. At midnight the Prussian columns began to move.

Bismarck had entered upon the greatest gamble of his life. Ludwig Gerlach noted something "restless, desperate in his attitude." On May 7 he had faced an assassin, Ferdinand Cohen-Blind, on the avenue Unter den Linden. Five

[40] Srbik, *Deutsche Einheit*, vol. 4, 337ff., 367ff.; Eugen Franz, *Ludwig Freiherr von der Pfordten: Schriftenreihe zur bayerischen Landesgeschichte*, vol. 29 (Munich, 1938), 353ff.

[41] DPO, V/2, 800ff.; GW, V, 519ff.

[42] GW, V, 526ff.; XIV, 714.

[43] GW, V, 534–536; Eduard von Wertheimer, *Bismarck im politischen Kampf* (Berlin, 1930), 250.

COHEN-BLIND FIRES AT BISMARCK, WHO COUNTERATTACKS, AS, FIRST, THE MASTER BOOKBINDER
GUSTAV BANNEWITZ AND, THEN, A PASSING MILITARY DETAIL COME TO HIS AID. BANNEWITZ WAS
WOUNDED BY ONE OF THE FIVE SHOTS AND BY THE BAYONET OF A SOLDIER, WHO MISTOOK HIM FOR
THE ASSASSIN. THE ARTIST: CARL RÖHLING (BILDARCHIV PREUSSISCHER KULTURBESITZ).

bullets were fired at him from a revolver, two while his back was turned, one
as he advanced on his attacker, two more as they grappled. Initially Bismarck
thought he had been badly, perhaps mortally, wounded by the final shots.
They were fired point-blank, the pistol pressed against his body. But low muz-
zle velocity, a thick overcoat, and three other layers of clothing saved him
from harm except for painful contusions. Afterward he ascribed his survival
to God's intervention. "I consider it good fortune to give one's life for our
king and country, and I pray to God to grant me such a death. This time God
has decided otherwise. He wants me to remain alive and do my duty." To
Gerlach he spoke of his escape as a matter of indifference; he had made his
peace with God. Indeed, those who witnessed the assault and its aftermath
on that busy street described his composure as remarkable. On the night of
June 15 he strolled with Lord Loftus in the garden behind the foreign office.
As the clock tolled twelve he informed the ambassador of the Prussian attack.
"If we are beaten, I shall not return here. I shall fall in the last charge. One
can but die once; and if beaten, it is better to die."[44]

[44] Ernst Ludwig von Gerlach, *Aufzeichnungen aus seinem Leben und Wirken, 1795–1877*
(Schwerin, 1903), vol. 2, 292; Helmut Diwald, ed., *Von der Revolution zum Norddeutschen Bund:*

Revolution from Above

With the assault on Austria Bismarck commenced to reconstruct the foundations of the Hohenzollern monarchy. Previously its supporting pillars had been dynastic loyalty, Prussian patriotism, Protestantism, Junker nobility, and the Prussian army and bureaucracy. To these were now added a new and eventually massive column: German nationalism.

In a public message on March 24 he wrote that Prussia must seek "in Germany the security once provided by the Austrian alliance." This was her natural course because of "her position, her German character, and the German outlook of her princes." The interests of Prussia and Germany were identical. Experience had shown, Savigny told the Frankfurt Diet on April 9, that neither the debates of an elected parliament (1848–1849) nor negotiations between governments (1863) were capable of overcoming the evil of German disunion. Only the two combined could give new institutions to Germany. Hence the diet should "summon an assembly chosen by direct election and universal suffrage from the entire nation" to deliberate upon a new constitution to be presented by the German governments. In May and early June Bismarck kept the opposition under pressure by gradually releasing details of the constitution Prussia intended to propose. Included were a parliament equipped with extensive legislative authority, the electoral law of the Frankfurt constitution of 1849, a dual army under Prussia and Bavaria, and the exclusion of Austria.[45]

On June 16 Wilhelm issued a manifesto, "To the German People," composed by Bismarck. The German Confederation, it declared, had lost the trust of the nation in a half-century of impotent existence. By mobilizing illegally against Prussia, the German states had destroyed it. Only the "living unity of the German nation" remained. Governments and peoples must "find for this unity a new, vital expression." Prussia's struggle was for the unrestricted "national development of Germany."[46]

In accord with the strategy planned since 1857, Bismarck set out to exploit the idea of nationalism and the yearning for national unity in the interest of

---

Politik und Ideengut der preussischen Hochkonservativen, 1848–1866; Aus dem Nachlass von Ernst Ludwig von Gerlach (Göttingen, 1970), vol. 1, 479–480; Robert von Keudell, *Fürst und Fürstin Bismarck: Erinnerungen 1846–1872* (Berlin, 1901), 263; Loftus, *Reminiscences*, vol. 1, 60. Although Bismarck strove to prove the contrary, Cohen-Blind appears to have acted alone. A reputedly gifted student at the Hohenheim agricultural academy in Württemberg, he was the twenty-two-year-old stepson of Karl Blind, a prominent radical of 1848 then in exile in London. By killing Bismarck, he hoped to avert the approaching civil war. While under police interrogation, Cohen-Blind committed suicide by slashing his throat. Julius H. Schoeps, *Bismarck und sein Attentäter: Der Revolveranschlag, Unter den Linden am 7. Mai 1866* (Berlin, 1984), particularly 38–41.

[45] GW, V, 418–419, 432–434, 447–449, 491, 514–515, 534–536.

[46] GW, V, 550–551.

Prussia. Hopefully it would provide the moral basis for the war and the means with which to arouse popular enthusiasm for the conflict. It was a terrain upon which Austria could not travel because of the multinational character of the empire. But it also provided a means with which to ward off French intervention. South of the Alps it helped to convince suspicious Italians that Prussia was serious about undertaking the war of "major dimensions" they demanded. In Germany it might sow confusion among the medium states and weaken their war efforts. Within a new, federal union it would supply the centripetal pressure with which to counteract the habits of particularism. Finally it was a way to end the internal conflict in Prussia by reconciling liberal nationalists to authoritarian rule and by providing an electoral system that might produce majorities favorable to the government.

Although an early proponent, Bismarck was not the first to forge the idea of a national parliament for the arsenal of Prussian foreign policy. We have seen Bernstorff bare the weapon before Austria and the medium states in December 1861 and again in August of the following year to meet the first of Schmerling's plans for great-German reform. Bismarck's contribution was the addition of universal, direct, and equal male suffrage. Originally he had advocated a parliament chosen by the legislatures of the states. But the Austrians incorporated this idea in their reform plan of 1862. Consequently Bismarck was compelled to go a step further. In January and September 1863 his counterattacks against Rechberg and Schmerling advocated "direct election" and hinted at universal suffrage. Early in 1866 Mensdorff, backed by Biegeleben, futilely urged Franz Joseph to regain the initiative by calling for a "German parliament."[47] But Bismarck outtrumped him in April with the electoral law of the Frankfurt Parliament. This had been the most radical product of the Paulskirche. By resurrecting it, Bismarck aligned the Prussian monarchy with the revolutionary tradition.

At the time of his talks with Lassalle, Bismarck had doubts that universal suffrage would produce, unless modified by some conservative device, a chamber sympathetic to the government. Nor was the promise of April 1866 unhedged by conservative features. As yet the word "equal" was avoided, and there was no promise of secret suffrage. Privately Bismarck spoke of prohibiting both the remuneration of deputies and the election of state officials.[48] Whatever his inner doubts and reservations, Bismarck defended the enfranchisement of the masses in Munich, Petersburg, and London as a "conservative principle," offering "greater guarantees for the conservative conduct of parliament than any of the artificial electoral laws that are calculated to achieve manufactured majorities." The masses were more interested in polit-

[47] Otto von Völderndorff, "Deutsche Verfassungen und Verfassungsentwürfe," *Annalen des deutschen Reichs* (1890), 402 (n. 2); Clark, *Franz Joseph and Bismarck*, 350ff.

[48] Becker, *Bismarcks Ringen*, 172.

ical order than were the leaders of the bourgeoisie. Through universal suffrage the monarchy could be brought into contact with the "healthy elements" in society. In Prussia nine-tenths of the population were loyal to the crown. [49]

German political leaders of most factions, from ultraconservatives deep into the ranks of the Progressive party, were dismayed over this "plunge into the dark," this "crude and frivolous experiment." Only the democratic liberals and Lassallean socialists rejoiced. [50] In Paris the reaction was divided. Drouyn was upset, while Napoleon remarked that "henceforth the two countries would pay homage to the same political system." In London, according to Bernstorff, the move was regarded as "completely revolutionary"; politicians were "alarmed" over the influence it might have upon the debate over the moderate reform bill of Gladstone. Gorchakov and Tsar Alexander considered it a grave attack upon the monarchical principle. Mensdorff protested it as "either revolutionary or an unworthy toying with the German reform question." From Frankfurt Kübeck denounced it to Mensdorff as both "perfidious" and "dangerous"; the envoys were unanimous in expressing "their abhorrence for the criminal gamble of the Prussian government with revolutionary elements." But neither Austria nor the medium states dared publicly oppose the measure, fearing the subterranean forces their satanic opponent wished to invoke. They chose the tactic of delay. Before a national parliament could assemble, they insisted, the German states must reach agreement on the proposals it might entertain. There the matter stood at the outbreak of war. [51]

For months Bismarck had talked and written the language of monarchical conservatism. In Berlin, Vienna, and Petersburg he had constantly accused Austria of damaging the monarchical cause and promoting "democratic revolution" by backing Augustenburg. We have seen him pushing for reactionary measures against the Nationalverein and Frankfurt senate. But all the while he was anticipating with sardonic satisfaction the turn of events that might require a sudden about-face. After Gastein he was reported as saying, "They accuse me of being reactionary . . . but I would march if need be even with revolution." In Dresden he treated Beust to one of those frank talks that often produced "astonishment bordering on stupefaction" in his hearers. "For all your courage and spirit," he is said to have remarked, "you would not know

[49] GW, V, 393, 421–422, 456–458; VI, 13; Keudell, Fürst und Fürstin Bismarck, 351–352; BP, I, 60–61.

[50] Martin Philippson, Max von Forckenbeck: Ein Lebensbild (Dresden, 1898), 158–159; Johannes Schultze, ed., Max Duncker: Politischer Briefwechsel aus seinem Nachlass (Stuttgart, 1923), 437; Ludwig Dehio, "Die preussische Demokratie und der Krieg von 1866," Forschungen zur brandenburgischen und preussischen Geschichte, 39 (1927), 258–259; Andreas Dorpalen, Heinrich von Treitschke (New Haven, 1957), 124ff.; Franz Mehring, Geschichte der deutschen Sozialdemokratie (Stuttgart, 1903), vol. 3, 239ff.

[51] RKN, I, 125–127, 130; Richard Augst, Bismarcks Stellung zum parlamentarischen Wahlrecht (Leipzig, 1917), 78; GW, V, 455–456; DPO, V/1, 444, 446; Srbik, Deutsche Einheit, vol. 4, 347ff., 372–373.

how to place yourself at the head of the revolutionary party in Germany. As for me, I could at any time become its chief."[52]

Judging from what Bismarck told Govone, it was not an easy task to get Wilhelm's approval for such a radical step as universal suffrage. "Why, that is revolution you're proposing to me," the king protested. "But there is no harm in that," Bismarck replied. "Your majesty will be seated on a rock above the flood. All who don't wish to perish will have to seek safety there."[53] In all probability, however, his most telling argument was that of its conservative purpose. His skill in managing Wilhelm during these months was everywhere the subject of wonder. In Berlin the wits were saying that Bismarck was "his last mistress, for only such a creature can wield so magic a power over an old man."[54]

Bismarck's exploitation of revolutionary forces in 1866 went far beyond his proposals for a national parliament and universal suffrage. Seven years before, Napoleon had started Italy on the way to national unity; except for Rome, Bismarck now brought her to the journey's end. To conservatives Victor Emmanuel was a "robber king," sitting on a revolutionary throne.[55] The Prussian alliance, while an act of expediency, gave a powerful boost to the radical principle of self-determination in Europe.

Even more startling were Bismarck's plans for the incitement of national uprisings within the Habsburg Empire. Of all its peoples the Hungarians had proved the most difficult to rule. The crushing of Louis Kossuth's republic in 1849 and the years of repression that followed left undiminished the Magyar will to national autonomy. In 1862 Bismarck had already made contact with the Hungarian underground through an émigré, Count Arthur Seherr-Thoss. In March 1866 Count Usedom, now Prussian minister at Florence, began to report the possibility of a "Hungarian–south Slav diversion" in the event of war. He was directed to keep in touch with the émigré colony in Italy without committing Prussia. For the present Wilhelm had to be "spared" involvement with revolutionaries. In late May Bismarck conferred in Berlin with Kiss de Nemeskér, an agent of Kossuth. On June 3 Count Theodor Czaky and Generals Stefan Türr and Georg Klapka, veterans of 1848, were hurriedly summoned to Berlin. Preparations began for the recruitment in Prussia of a Magyar legion under Klapka. From Italy a second "free corps" under Giuseppe Garibaldi was to assault the Dalmatian coast.[56]

---

[52] GW, V, 42, 57–58, 68–69, 156–158, 296ff., 301, 320, 363, 365, 369; OD, VII, 12–13, 72–73.

[53] Govone, Mémoires, 186.

[54] DPO, V/1, 313. Bismarck himself was not above such jokes. See Govone, Mémoires, 211.

[55] Gerlach, Aufzeichnungen, 279, also 247, 282ff.

[56] GW, VII, 65–67, 125–127; APP, VI, 719; GW, V, 423, 505–506, 536ff., 549; Johann Reiswitz, Belgrad-Berlin, Berlin-Belgrad, 1866–1871 (Munich, 1936), 58ff.; Wertheimer, Bismarck

The operation became doubly urgent when it was learned that the Italians planned to limit their attack to the quadrilateral fortresses south of the Alps. Bernhardi, who had been sent to Florence for military liaison, reported that the Hungarian diversion appeared to be the "only means" by which La Marmora could be induced to undertake an invasion of Austria.[57] Certainly Usedom acted in accord with the spirit of his instructions in drafting the famous "stab-in-the-heart dispatch" of June 17, in which he urged the Italians to march on Vienna in support of the Hungarian and Slavic insurgents.[58]

In every quarter of the empire Bismarck sought to uncoil the springs of nationalistic discontent. The success of Garibaldi's legion was believed to depend on a rising of the southern Slavs. In Belgrade Captain Anton Oreskovich, a former Austrian officer, had long been conspiring, with the approval of Prince Michael Obrenovich, to effect an insurrection among the troops of the Habsburg military frontier. On June 1 Bismarck telegraphed his approval of the recruitment of a "Slavic corps" in Serbia. Nine days later a Prussian envoy, Counselor of Legation Pfuel, was dispatched to Belgrade and Bucharest, followed by General Türr. On arriving in the Rumanian capital, Türr conferred in secret with Prince Karl, ruler of the Danubian principalities, about the possibility of support for a Hungarian-Rumanian uprising. A Hohenzollern prince and Prussian officer, Karl had accepted the throne in April on Bismarck's secret urging. Though sympathetic to the Prussian cause, he was far too insecure to engage in such a quixotic enterprise. Nor were the Prussians any more successful with the Czechs and Slovaks. On entering Bohemia the advancing troops distributed a proclamation: "If our cause is victorious, the moment may come when Bohemia and Moravia can, like Hungary, realize their national ambitions." But the response was limp.[59]

Before the Hungarian and south-Slav expeditions could get under way, the Prussian army struck a sledgehammer blow, which for the time being rendered

---

im politischen Kampf, 235ff. According to Arthur Brauer, Prussians were also recruited into the Klapka legion. Im Dienste Bismarcks: Persönliche Erinnerungen (Berlin, 1936), 7–8.

[57] Reiswitz, Belgrad-Berlin, 59–60.

[58] "Austria will lose in the same measure in which we win; the thrusts to be directed at Austria should strike at its heart, not its members." Max Straganz, Zur Geschichte der "Stoss ins Herz-Depesche" des Grafen Usedom (Innsbruck, 1922), 25. In 1868, when his policy toward Austria had radically changed, Bismarck repudiated the "linguistic crudity" of the dispatch (published by La Marmora), but not its basic purpose. Ibid., 42–43; GW, VIa, 401–409.

[59] Hermann Wendel, Bismarck und Serbien im Jahre 1866 (Berlin, 1937), 19ff., 45–56; Stefan Türr, "Fürst Bismarck und die Ungarn: Reminiscenzen aus dem Jahre 1866," Deutsche Revue, vol. 25, no. 1 (1900), 313ff.; GW, V, 431, 446–447, 516–518; VII, 107ff., 111; XIV, 711; Karl I, Aus dem Leben König Karls von Rumänien (Stuttgart, 1894–1900), vol. 1, 69–70, 89; T. W. Riker, The Making of Roumania (Oxford, 1931), 557–558; Hans Raupach, Bismarck und die Tschechen im Jahre 1866 (Berlin, 1936), 7. The incitement of the Czechs aroused protests in both Berlin and Petersburg. To the tsar Bismarck excused it as a mere gesture to keep the population friendly during the Prussian occupation. Had the war continued, however, he was prepared to grant Bohemia an "independent constitution." GW, VI, 58–60.

them unnecessary. On July 3 Moltke's converging columns attacked the Austrian position at Königgrätz. That evening Benedek's shattered troops streamed back in disorder along the road to Vienna. Despite an earlier victory over Italy at Custozza, Franz Joseph was compelled to treat. Anticipating the disaster, Mensdorff had already telegraphed on July 2 a request for French mediation.

Intervention and Revolution

Throughout Europe the swiftness and finality of the Prussian victory caused consternation. This was particularly true in Paris. Napoleon had allowed for an Austrian victory or for a long war exhausting both sides, but not for what came. For the first time he became fully aware of the implications of the Prussian reform plan of June 10 and feared that the proposed national parliament meant that Berlin was bent on hegemony over the whole of Germany. Drouyn, seconded by Eugénie, urged him (July 5) to take command of the situation by mobilizing eighty thousand men on the exposed Rhine frontier.

THE PRUSSIAN HIGH COMMAND ON A HILL OVERLOOKING THE DEPLOYING TROOPS ON THE MORNING OF THE BATTLE AT KÖNIGGRÄTZ. FROM LEFT TO RIGHT IN FRONT: PRINCE KARL OF PRUSSIA, THE GRAND DUKE OF MECKLENBURG-SCHWERIN, BISMARCK, ROON, MOLTKE, AND KING WILHELM I. RETOUCHED PHOTOGRAPH BY H. SCHNAEBELI (BILDARCHIV PREUSSISCHER KULTURBESITZ).

Napoleon agreed, then quickly reversed himself, settling on a policy of "friendly mediation." It may be that he was influenced by reports that French public opinion was pacifistic. But he was also confronted by the arguments of advisers Eugène Rouher and Felix La Valette that he dare not repudiate the doctrine of national self-determination and face the terrors of an aroused German nation.[60]

At any rate, Bismarck preyed upon the latter possibility. French threats, he instructed Goltz, were to be countered by the menace of "a national uprising in Germany" on the basis of the Frankfurt constitution of 1849. Prussia would use "every means, regardless of party standpoint," to excite national resistance. "Progressives and democrats" were ready "for every sacrifice in a war against France." Prussia would bring about "the complete ignition of the national spirit."[61]

Simultaneously he again held out the tantalizing possibility of compensation. On July 26 he was quoted as saying that the 1814 frontier offered "no difficulty"—except for getting the approval by Wilhelm and the Landtag! On August 4 Drouyn finally demanded outright the frontier of 1814, the left bank of the Rhine as far as Mainz (that is, the Bavarian and Hessian Palatinates), and the severance of all connections between Prussia, Limburg, and Luxemburg.[62] But the French were too late, for the treaty of Nikolsburg had already been signed. With Austria at his feet, Bismarck refused all German soil. "If you want war, you shall have it. We shall arouse the entire German nation against you." Even the rehabilitation of the confederate diet and a military alliance with Austria were conceivable. In such a war, he declared, "revolu-

[60] RKN, I, 38, 213, 285 (n. 4), 328ff.; Case, "French Opinion," 458ff.; Pierre Renouvin, Le XIXe Siècle (Paris, 1953–1955), vol. 1, 370–371. On the French efforts at mediation and compensation see Willard Allen Fletcher, The Mission of Vincent Benedetti to Berlin, 1864–1870 (The Hague, 1965), 80–140.

[61] GW, VI, 45, 55.

[62] RKN, II, 21–22; OD, XI, 394ff.; GW, VI, 101. On July 26, 1866, Benedetti, acting on instructions from Drouyn, sounded out Bismarck on the possibility of a secret treaty granting the frontier of 1814 and Luxemburg. Bismarck's immediate reaction was bellicose, but then he quickly calmed down and gave the response recorded above. By his own account he refused Benedetti's suggestion that the king of the Netherlands be compensated in East Friesland for the loss of Luxemburg. Benedetti's version was that Bismarck mentioned the possibility of ceding the Bavarian Palatinate either to France or to the Dutch king. RKN, II, 4–7; OD, XI, 219–225. Oncken believed that the most he could have offered was the surrender to the latter of the crown lands in the Palatinate. RKN, II, 5–6. Otto Scheel indignantly rejected as "fantastic" the possibility that Bismarck could have considered cession of the Palatinate. Bismarcks Wille, 258. But on July 8 Bismarck mentioned such a possibility to the crown prince. Friedrich III, Tagebücher, 1848–1866, 458. What he had been willing to grant under the duress of war, however, he certainly had no intention of conceding in the moment of victory. In this he was aided by Benedetti's admission that a refusal would result, not in war, but only in diplomatic hostility. RKN, II, 36. According to one report, the "characterless people" of the Palatinate might easily have accepted French rule. Friedrich Curtius, ed., Denkwürdigkeiten des Fürsten Chlodwig zu Hohenlohe-Schillingsfürst (Stuttgart, 1907), vol. 1, 161.

tionary strokes" might occur, against which the German thrones were more secure than that of a Bonaparte. Wilhelm himself now talked of "proclaiming a national war in all Germany" and of stopping at nothing in a conflict with France.[63]

Napoleon was not the only recipient of these warnings. In July and August the Russian government sought to organize a tripartite (Russia, England, France) intervention in Germany and advocated a European congress to review and moderate Prussia's war aims. Bismarck's reply was sharp. Outside interference would force Prussia "to unleash the full national strength of Germany and the bordering countries." This was a threat to exploit even the national ambitions of the Poles. When Tsar Alexander complained of Prussia's revolutionary policy, Bismarck became even more explicit. "Pressure from abroad will compel us to proclaim the German constitution of 1849 and to adopt truly revolutionary measures. If there is to be revolution, we would rather make it, than suffer it." If Napoleon came to terms with Austria or Russia, he told Govone on August 10, "we would conduct a war of revolution; we would incite rebellion in Hungary and organize provisional governments in Prague and Brünn."[64]

If we are to judge accurately this amazing man, it is imperative to determine to what lengths he would actually have gone in July and August 1866, the most critical moment of his career. No statesman was ever more conscious than he of the hazards of bluff. On this, as on most occasions, his words were not idle. On July 8 he pressed Eulenburg to organize a "preparliament," using the title of the revolutionary body that preceded the Frankfurt Parliament in 1848. "The proclamation of the Reich constitution [of 1849] can be useful to us as a final means in an extremity against France." He admitted, nevertheless, that "really it is serviceable to us only after a fundamental revision." As a war measure he was prepared to resurrect the document that embodied the highest hopes of German liberal nationalism. The struggle won, he would have broken the compact by "purifying" the document of its most liberal features.[65]

The threat to disintegrate the Habsburg Empire poses an even greater problem. In 1859 Napoleon had also conspired with Kossuth and Klapka to produce an uprising in Hungary. What came naturally for Bonaparte, however, seems grotesque in the mind of a Prussian Junker. Would Bismarck knowingly have touched off mines of nationalistic discontent that might have destroyed one of the bulwarks of the conservative order in Europe? Had the interest of

[63] GW, V, 106–111; VII, 148–149; RKN, II, 45; OD, XII, 22–25.

[64] GW, VI, 93, 120; VII, 156; Werner E. Mosse, The European Powers and the German Question, 1848–1871 (Cambridge, Eng., 1958), 243–247; and Eberhard Kolb, "Russland und die Gründung des Norddeutschen Bundes," in Richard Dietrich, ed., Europa und der Norddeutsche Bund (Berlin, 1968), 191–214.

[65] GW, VI, 59; XV, 285ff.; V, 397–398. See also Becker, Bismarcks Ringen, 189–191.

state triumphed so completely over conservative principle? Or did he have in reserve, as in the case of the Frankfurt constitution, some means by which the revolutionary character of the step could be blunted in the conservative interest?

As the intervention crisis reached its zenith at the end of July, Bismarck called for an Italian plenipotentiary empowered to negotiate "new agreements with further concealed aims." The preparations for Magyar and Serbian insurrections, relaxed after Königgrätz, were renewed. The recruitment and arming of the Hungarian legion was resumed. Another Hungarian émigré officer, General Eber, was dispatched to Bucharest to confer with Prince Karl. In Belgrade Stephen Türr was ordered to keep his "organization" intact.[66] Eighteen months later Bismarck told Carl Schurz that, if France and Austria had joined hands, "we would have been forced to explode every mine" in Germany, Serbia, and Hungary. "If this primer had been ignited, of course, retreat would no longer have been possible. To treat with Austria would have been out of the question. Her destruction would have been unavoidable. A great empty space would have been opened between Germany and Turkey. It would have been necessary to create something to fill this vacuum. We could not have left our Hungarian friends in the lurch." In an extremity Bismarck was prepared in 1866 to unleash forces that he recognized were beyond his power to control. He stood poised, match in hand, over the powder keg of national revolution.

Nevertheless, he did everything possible to avoid having to set it off. "Such eccentric means," he told Schurz, were to be used only as a last resort. He preferred to avoid war with France at such a cost. The existence of Austria was "necessary for Europe." "New creations in this area," he wrote in his memoirs, "could only be of a continually revolutionary character."[67] If possible, he was prepared to buy Austrian neutrality and even her alliance. But the threat of French intervention was not the only reason for his desire to give Austria an easy peace. By inflicting unnecessary wounds, he feared to incur her enduring hostility. He remembered Frederick the Great's long feud with Maria Theresa. The relationship with Vienna must not be permitted to become an organic fault in Prussian foreign policy.[68]

Wilhelm, whom he had dragged into the conflict, became most immoderate in his rage against Austria and in the demands to be made on her. His generals regarded with contempt the efforts of a civilian diplomat like Bismarck to limit the war and were outraged by his interference in military op-

[66] GW, VI, 93, 103, 114; Reiswitz, Belgrad-Berlin, 7off.; Karl I, Aus dem Leben, vol. 1, 94–95. Disappointed by the armistice of July 26, Klapka and his fifteen hundred men invaded Hungary after Aug. 1 on their own. But the public received them coldly, and they were forced to retreat. A. Kienast, Die Legion Klapka (Vienna, 1900), 199ff.

[67] GW, VII, 234–235, 242; XV, 278. See also The Reminiscences of Carl Schurz (New York, 1907–1908), vol. 3, 272.

[68] GW, XV, 272–273.

erations. They wished to march on Vienna and dictate a conqueror's peace. At Nikolsburg on July 24–25 Bismarck's insistence on a preliminary peace treaty without loss of territory by Austria led to one of the worst personal conflicts monarch and minister experienced in their long relationship. At one point Bismarck fled the room, burst into tears, thought of leaping to his death through an open window, and, in a calmer moment, of resignation. He was saved only by the intervention of the crown prince, whom he had recently striven to conciliate and who was convinced by his arguments. After listening to his son, the old man still complained about having to "bite into this sour apple." But bite he did.[69]

Bismarck's most revolutionary act in 1866, however, was not the plan for the disintegration of the Habsburg monarchy, which proved unnecessary, or his attempt to arouse the sleepy giant of German nationalism, which failed, but the destruction of thrones and sovereignties, which came with the expansion of Prussia's frontiers and the establishment of her hegemony over northern Germany.

Immediately after Königgrätz king and minister were apparently in agreement that the northern enemy states were to be greatly reduced in size, but not liquidated. Soon Wilhelm was busy with fantastic plans for recarving German frontiers without butchering the principle of legitimacy. One called for a Prussian gerrymander reaching into the south to reclaim the traditional Hohenzollern lands of Ansbach-Bayreuth. Back home there was some public pressure for the complete annexation of Saxony, Hanover, and Hesse-Kassel. To his wife Bismarck wrote on July 9 that he had the "thankless task of pouring water into the bubbling wine and making clear that we do not live alone in Europe." On the same day he wrote to Goltz that the annexations were not worth "gambling anew with the fate of the monarchy." Nevertheless, he instructed the ambassador to sound out the French on the possibility of Prussia's acquiring most of the northern states in toto. Within hours it became apparent that Napoleon would object only to the inclusion of Saxony. Instantly Bismarck shifted to the principle of complete incorporation: "every full annexation attainable without the cession of Prussian territory is better than the half by way of reform."[70]

He convinced Wilhelm that, rather than create irredenta, it was better either to take entire states or leave them intact. By the former policy he hoped to speed assimilation of conquered peoples, by the latter the reconciliation of

[69] GW, VI, 78–81; Friedrich III, *Tagebücher 1848–1866*, 470–473.

[70] GW, VI, 40–47. Thimme's editorial note to these documents superseded the earlier accounts of Brandenburg, *Untersuchungen*, 558–569, and G. Roloff, "Brünn und Nikolsburg: nicht Bismarck, sondern der König isoliert," *Historische Zeitschrift*, 136 (1927), 457–501. Nevertheless, it is unlikely that Bismarck's shift to full annexation was owing, as Thimme asserted, to the pressure of public opinion. As usual, he judged the matter in terms of options, with the final decision dependent upon the danger of provoking foreign intervention. See Johannes Petrich, *Bismarck und die Annexionen 1866* (Hamburg, 1933), 9ff.

defeated rulers. What he sacrificed was the principle of legitimacy. Only under Napoleon I had Europe experienced such a ruthless destruction of sovereignties. To genuine conservatives Prussia appeared to have taken the perilous path of Caesarism. "The monarchical principle," Tsar Alexander indignantly complained to Wilhelm, "has suffered a rude shock," not at all mitigated by the fact that it came from royal rather than revolutionary hands.[71]

On July 26 at Nikolsburg and on August 23 at Prague the treaties were signed that ended the "seven weeks' war." While granted a peace without annexation, Franz Joseph was compelled to concede the dissolution of the German Confederation and the reorganization of Germany into two new federations north and south of the Main. Except for Saxony, Prussia might make such territorial changes as she wished in Germany. In separate treaties Bismarck left Baden, Württemberg, and Bavaria intact; Hesse-Darmstadt lost some segments of territory. Indemnities were imposed on all the defeated states. On September 20, 1866, Prussia annexed Hanover, Hesse-Kassel, Nassau, and the city of Frankfurt. Toward the old confederate capital on the Main, isolated and helpless, Bismarck could vent all the vindictive hatred that he denied himself in *die grosse Politik*. Under the threat of plunder and hunger 25 million gulden were demanded of the hapless burghers, whose sole offense was their liberal reputation and dislike of Prussia.[72]

Napoleon too was among the losers. Had he insisted, he might have prevented Prussia's territorial expansion. What he did receive was the limitation of Prussian hegemony to the region north of the Main and the possibility of French influence in the south. By claiming his reward much earlier, he might have attained the border of 1814, perhaps even the Bavarian Palatinate. But during these vital weeks he was physically ill and mentally indecisive. Later he claimed that Drouyn, not he, was the author of the formal demands presented at Nikolsburg. When Bismarck refused, he repudiated the foreign minister, who resigned. With much of her army committed in Algeria and Mexico, France was in no condition to fight a European war.[73]

Pounding his fist on the table, Bismarck exulted: "I have beaten them all! All!"[74] Not the least of the defeated were the Prussian liberals.

[71] GW, XV, 278–279; VII, 147; APP, VIII, 42–43.

[72] The city had never declared war on Prussia and had already paid a levy of 6 million gulden. Despite Edwin Manteuffel's brutal twenty-four-hour ultimatum, the senate successfully delayed paying the ruinous sum. After the city had been officially annexed, its collection was more difficult. Owing to the intervention of Queen Augusta, the indemnity demand was dropped. But this was too late to save the life of the mayor, who in despair hanged himself. Eyck, *Bismarck*, vol. 2, 268ff.; Richard Schwemer, *Geschichte der freien Stadt Frankfurt a. M., 1814–1866* (Frankfurt, 1918), III/2, 317ff.

[73] RKN, II, 125ff.; Henry Salomon, "Napoléon III à la veille et au lendemain de Sadowa," *Le Monde Slave*, Nouvelle Série, 2 (1925), 168–212.

[74] GW, VII, 140.

Rügen

Königsberg

Lübeck

Varzin

Hamburg
Mecklenburg

Oldenburg
Bremen

Berlin

Elbe

Oder

Vistula

Langensalza

Dresden

Ems
Hesse
Thuringian
States
Saxony

Frankfurt
Prague
Königgrätz
Galicia

Sedan

Mainz
Darmstadt

Moselle

Palatinate

Bavaria

Karlsruhe
Rastatt
Stuttgart
Nikolsburg

Strassburg
Württemberg

Ulm
Rhine
Baden
Sigmaringen
Munich
Vienna
Danube

Belfort
Buda Pest

Austria-Hungary

GERMANY
1866-1870

———— North German Confederation

Custozza

Sedan
Luxemburg
Trier

Lor
Prussia

Moselle
Saar

Verdun
Spichern

Mars la Tour
Metz
Gravelotte
Weissenburg
Wörth

2nd Army

3rd Army

Nancy
Strassburg

France

Boundary of
1871

Alsace

Rhine

Belfort

War of 1870-1871

❖❖

CHAPTER FOURTEEN

The Conquest of Prussia

Absolutism Restored

ON JANUARY 15, 1866, the Prussian Landtag met for the last time before the Austrian War. Before convening, the liberals desperately tried to close ranks. "We are able to unite only in negation or on phrases!" lamented Unruh. "If that were only the case!" Hoverbeck replied. "But we can't even do that!"[1] Although the Schleswig-Holstein controversy had receded, the deputies divided again on the question of tactics in the coming session. Once more the issue was whether to go through the long process of amending the government's budget or to reject it outright without debate. By a bold action many hoped to force a denouement in the long drama of the constitutional conflict.

Without being aware of it, the more decisive party leaders neared the position of Lassalle, so contemptuously rejected three years before. Twesten asserted, "We ought not to maintain any longer the appearance that the constitution is still in effect." Lasker wished to show that "in almost every respect the country is being governed absolutely in the true sense of the word." Hoverbeck concluded that despotism was better than "sham constitutionalism." The world must know that "force has destroyed law." For once the opposition must "speak the full truth and then be silent until called upon to act." Nevertheless, he was not at all certain that the summons would actually come. In the event of a dissolution he foresaw that "by an energetic application of all bureaucratic screws" the government might very well bring about the defeat of the liberals. Many battles, he concluded, would have to be fought before the ultimate triumph of liberty. Freedom would always be in danger until "an absurd loyalty" had been erased from "the feelings of the people."[2]

At the beginning of the session the issue of tactics was raised in a caucus of the Progressive and Left Center (Bockum-Dolffs) parties. As expected, the extremist faction was in the minority. Included in it, however, were most of the prominent names among the progressives: Twesten, Hoverbeck, Lasker, Schulze-Delitzsch, Forckenbeck, Virchow, and Loewe. Supported by Rudolf Gneist, Waldeck stubbornly took his customary stand on the necessity of fulfilling the parliamentary function, come what might. His group was joined by moderates of the Left Center, who deplored the constitutional conflict and would do nothing to intensify it. To the delight of conservatives the dispute

---

[1] Ludolf Parisius, *Leopold Freiherr von Hoverbeck* (Berlin, 1897–1900), II/2, 64–65; HW, I, 267.

[2] Parisius, *Hoverbeck*, II/2, 55–56, 64ff.; HW, I, 265–269.

erupted in the liberal press and on the floor of the chamber when the budget bill was introduced. With the support of conservatives, left centrists, and Waldeck progressives, the extremists were voted down. The bill was referred to committee.[3]

But here the defeated faction had the upper hand. On February 21, 1866, the committee completed a "preliminary report" composed by Virchow. After recapitulating the history of the constitutional conflict and listing the abuses of the government, the report concluded: "It is clear as day that absolutism has been restored in Prussia and indeed absolutism without the self-imposed limitations of the pre-March period. There is no longer any control over finances or any legal budget; the *Staatsanzeiger* has replaced the statute books; the superior accounting office no longer has any function; the treasury and property of the state are at the free disposal of the government. One point alone has not been attacked. It is the one upon which the old absolutism failed and constitutionalism was won in Prussia. Still in effect is the clause in article 103 of the constitution reading: 'treasury loans may be raised only through legislation.' " On June 2, 1865, the Chamber of Deputies had resolved, "The house is not in position to grant loans to the present cabinet."[4]

The point was futile. Bismarck was quite willing if necessary to violate article 103.[5] But the need did not arise. Later, when war came, August von der Heydt, who replaced Bodelschwingh at the Ministry of Finance, raised the necessary funds from the treasury reserve and the sale of state-owned railway shares through a state bank (*Seehandlung*). The deputies hotly protested the constitutionality of these actions,[6] but they were helpless to stop them. No more than in 1864 had they the power to cripple Bismarck's foreign policy.

The debates of January and February 1866 bristled with constitutional issues. The deputies voted to condemn the government's violation of the right of free assembly through the suppression of the Cologne festival. They took note of the prosecution of Leeden, Frese, Lüning, Jacoby, and Franz Duncker for utterances critical of the cabinet. By acquiring Lauenburg without consent of parliament, they charged, the government had violated no less than three articles in the basic law. In a clever speech, sparkling with irony, Bismarck demonstrated once more the rubbery character of Friedrich Wilhelm IV's constitution.[7]

It was the judicial persecution of Twesten and Frentzel, however, that produced the greatest outburst of indignation in the chamber and provided a climax for the constitutional conflict itself. The prosecution of deputies for

[3] Parisius, *Hoverbeck*, II/2, 67ff.; *HW*, I, 269; Wilhelm Biermann, *Franz Leo Benedikt Waldeck: Ein Streiter für Freiheit und Recht* (Paderborn, 1928), 299; *SBHA* (1866), I, 19–29.

[4] Parisius, *Hoverbeck*, II/2, 68–70.

[5] *GW*, XIV, 697–698.

[6] Fritz Löwenthal, *Der preussische Verfassungsstreit, 1862–1866* (Munich, 1914), 278ff.; *SBHA* (1866), II, 162–177.

[7] *SBHA* (1866), I, 58–83, 222–250.

speeches delivered on the floor of the chamber was not only a breach of the constitution (article 84), but also an assault upon the parliamentary process itself. The courts of first and second instance had declared the charge inadmissible, but the judges of the supreme court ruled (January 29) the contrary by a majority of one. In doing so, the court reversed decisions of 1853 and 1865. The desired result was achieved only by packing the court with two "relief judges" of conservative views.[8] Three days after the verdict Hoverbeck introduced a motion that the chamber declare the action of the court, both in its procedure and decision, to be illegal and invalid. In succession the best speakers of the opposition blasted the perversion of the courts by the government. Lippe and Bismarck replied lamely that the chamber itself was guilty of illegal action in attempting to interfere with the courts. The minister-president flatly denied that the deputies had any greater freedom inside than outside of parliament. Hoverbeck's resolution passed, 263 to 35. In the major cities protest meetings were held, two of which (in Berlin and Königsberg) were dispersed by the police.[9]

On February 22 the chamber received the refusal of the cabinet to accept the censures on Lauenburg, the Cologne festival, and the Twesten–Frentzel case. The charges of unconstitutionality were themselves rejected as unconstitutional. In the tangle of legal claims and counterclaims Bismarck could hope to blunt the public effect of parliamentary criticism. On the same day he climbed the rostrum to read, before the surprised and angered deputies, a royal decree proroguing the Landtag. The session had lasted but forty days and eleven sittings, the shortest in the history of the Prussian parliament. Immediately afterward, agents of the government seized the papers and documents of the house. When the Rheinische Zeitung published Virchow's critical report, the edition was confiscated by the police.[10]

The liberal deputies had assembled quarreling, but departed in harmony, welded once more into a solid front by the tyranny of the government. On February 23 none attended the closing ceremony in the palace, where Bismarck read the royal message. The days of their new-found unanimity, however, were numbered.

Balky Liberals and Obedient Masses

By seizing the initiative in the national cause, Bismarck hoped in April 1866 "to put the German people in motion."[11] His aim was to convert the conflict

---

[8] HW, I, 270–275; Parisius, Hoverbeck, II/2, 70–72.

[9] SBHA (1866), I, 110–181. Over two hundred deputies signed Hoverbeck's motion in order, by virtue of their number, to escape prosecution. Parisius, Hoverbeck, II/2, 70–71.

[10] SBHA (1866), Anlagen II, 1–3, 30–33, 54, 137, 141, 184–185; SEG (1866), 164. The abrupt adjournment prevented presentation of Virchow's report, which did not become part of the formal record of the session.

[11] GW, VII, 110.

with Austria from a civil into a national war, to mobilize the peoples of Germany against pro-Austrian rulers and governments, and to add the élan of national sentiment to the striking power of the Prussian army. This he believed attainable within weeks after the Twesten–Frentzel case, the abrupt closing of the Landtag, and the seizure of its papers had brought the liberals to a new height of indignation. To one who had witnessed the migration of the moderates from Frankfurt via Gotha to Erfurt in 1849–1850 the possibility seemed far from absurd. But his cynicism was not entirely justified. When it came, the great reversal in German liberal opinion was produced less by the appeal to German nationalism than by the demonstration of Prussian military power.

As the conflict neared, the mood of vocal public opinion was nearly the opposite of what Bismarck hoped. In Austria there was considerable support and even enthusiasm for the conflict. In the southern states the small-German nationalists voted apathetically for the necessary war credits on the grounds that Prussia was the aggressor.[12] In Prussia itself popular agitation against war reached a dimension that Wilhelm termed "very unpleasant." From Solingen, where an antiwar rally was held on March 25, a wave of protest meetings spread through the monarchy. A torrent of resolutions and addresses descended on Berlin. Nor did the critical attitude change generally after Prussia came out for national reform on April 9. Within a few days the liberal press ran the gamut of "excitement, clamor, astonishment, laughter." *Kladderadatsch*, the famed humor magazine, announced it would cease publication: "We have been dealt a hard blow. . . . The Bismarck cabinet appeals to the German nation and supports itself upon the people! Hahahaha! Who's laughing? All Europe and adjacent parts of the world! We aren't up to such competition." The sudden switch from Hyde to Jekyll was far too swift to carry conviction. That no details of the plan were given until June 10 prevented many from taking it seriously. It had the appearance of a mere gambit on the chessboard of German politics, a momentary tactical stroke destined for oblivion once the game was won.[13]

During the first months of 1866 the Prussian opposition actually seemed to be leading a genuine mass movement. Indignation over arbitrary actions of the government in January and February, followed by general antagonism toward war in March and April, gave the opposition for a time the popular

[12] Otto Bandmann, *Die deutsche Presse und die nationale Frage, 1864–1866* (Leipzig, 1909), 106ff.; Chester W. Clark, *Franz Joseph and Bismarck: The Diplomacy of Austria before the War of 1866* (Cambridge, Mass., 1934), 381, 470; Theodor Schieder, *Die kleindeutsche Partei in Bayern: Münchener Historische Abhandlungen*, vol. 12 (Munich, 1936), 95ff.; Hans Ruider, *Bismarck und die öffentliche Meinung in Bayern, 1862–1866: Deutsche Geschichtsbücherei*, vol. 1 (Munich, 1924), 128ff.

[13] Horst Kohl, ed., *Anhang zu den Gedanken und Erinnerungen von Otto Fürst von Bismarck* (Stuttgart, 1901), vol. 1, 135; SEG (1866), 51; DPO, V/1, 511–512; Bandmann, *Deutsche Presse*, 126, 142–143; Ursula Schultz, *Die Politik Bismarcks in den Jahren 1862–1866 im Spiegel der rheinischen Presse* (Zella-Mehlis, Thür., 1933), 120ff.

foundation it had previously lacked. But the voices of protest were not in unison. In the Rhineland the influence of non-Prussian Germany was greater; Catholics feared the growth of Protestant power; businessmen dreaded the disruption of commerce. In the east, stronghold of Prussianism, many were less opposed to war than to the regime that presumed to conduct it. "For this cabinet not a penny!" was the battle cry.[14]

The liberal leadership was similarly divided. In a manifesto the Progressive party pledged itself anew to the twin ideals of unity and freedom and blamed the war on the lack of parliamentary influence in Prussia. Once more Schulze-Delitzsch and others were buoyed by the thought that a reactionary government could not possibly survive the stresses and strains of a major conflict. But Waldeck and his clique refused to take part in the protest movement. Every Prussian conquest was a step toward their ideal of a German unitary state. Among the moderates, voices were already heard demanding that the issues of liberty be postponed for the duration. Twesten and Lasker were by no means convinced that the party could make good its position of unconditional opposition. Differences of opinion were also evident among the old-liberals. A few—Schwerin, Patow, Gruner, and Bethmann—regarded the war as "frivolous." But most supported it. Max Duncker and Bernhardi had for years wanted war as the best way out of the internal conflict. Others—Sybel, Haym, Treitschke, and Wehrenpfennig—rated a Prussian victory over Austria as more important than the internal conflict. Although granting the indispensability of Bismarck and Roon, they wished to replace the most reactionary ministers: Eulenburg, Bodelschwingh, and Lippe.[15]

Nor were opinions about the Prussian reform plan harmonious. The progressives were not opposed to the reform itself, but to the unclean hands that offered it. Summoned by Loewe, Schulze-Delitzsch, and Franz Duncker, members of the Nationalverein in Berlin crowded the Tonhalle on April 11 to approve unanimously a resolution refusing support for the reform until constitutional government was restored in Prussia. Only a liberal government, it was confidently believed, could marshal popular support in a war for such an objective.[16] But others were not so sure that the reform should be rejected

[14] Clark, Franz Joseph and Bismarck, 512; Martin Spahn, "Zur Entstehung der nationalliberalen Partei," Zeitschrift für Politik, 1 (1907–1908), 365ff. On Catholic opposition to the war in the Rhineland and Westphalia see Jonathan Sperber, Popular Catholicism in Nineteenth-Century Germany (Princeton, 1984), 156–159.

[15] Felix Salomon, Die deutschen Parteiprogramme (3d ed., Berlin, 1920–1924), vol. 1, 127–129; Ludwig Dehio, "Die Taktik der Opposition während des Konflikts," Historische Zeitschrift, 140 (1929), 335ff.; Bandmann, Deutsche Presse, 92–94; Rudolf Haym, Das Leben Max Dunckers (Berlin, 1891), 380; HW, I, 280, 284–287, 292–293, 299, 305.

[16] Bandmann, Deutsche Presse, 101–102, 135ff.; Spahn, "Entstehung," 383ff.; Hermann Oncken, Rudolf von Bennigsen (Stuttgart, 1910), vol. 1, 693; Friedrich Thorwart, ed., Hermann Schulze-Delitzschs Schriften und Reden (Berlin, 1909–1913), vol. 3, 254–262; V, 255–256, 281–282, 295–298.

because of its origin. Impressed by the endurance of the Bismarck cabinet, Twesten, Lasker, and associates longed for a reversal of its internal policies that would enable them to support it on the national issue. In Halle a group of old-liberals led by Rudolf Haym resolved that the question of power should take precedence over that of freedom. Although it condemned the war, a "democratic" branch of the Nationalverein in the same city resolved to agitate for the government's proposal for a national parliament. In Bremen a right-wing branch of the Nationalverein also announced its support, although "without enthusiasm." If forced to wait on a more acceptable minister-president in Berlin, the liberals might never attain their goal. They trusted in the "overwhelming power" of the parliamentary idea to secure the ultimate aims of liberty.[17]

In January 1866 Bismarck had boasted to Benedetti that Prussia could with equal ease "fight the Nationalverein or make a compact with it." Undoubtedly the general reaction to the Prussian reform plan was a keen disappointment. Nevertheless, he perceived and sought to exploit the cleavages of opinion in the liberal camp. From mid-April until late June he conferred successively with Max Duncker, Bernhardi, Roggenbach, Bennigsen, Miquel, and Duke Ernst of Coburg. On Bismarck's request the latter reconnoitered the liberal parties and factions in southern Germany. Through these leaders and the popular forces they represented, Bismarck hoped to undermine the wavering governments of the medium states. He also sought to infiltrate the Prussian opposition by talking with Twesten, Unruh, and others of like opinion. Should battles be lost, the support of these moderates might become indispensable to the regime. It was necessary to learn their terms.[18]

The available records of these conferences show a consistent line of attack. Bismarck usually began by "confessing" that he might have to resign. Smiling ironically, he asked, "Is a liberal cabinet possible at this moment? Who would be foreign minister?" Progressives and old-liberals alike admitted the poverty of their talent. Since 1849 the reaction had been so successful, Unruh wearily conceded, that there were no longer "in high official circles" any liberal who possessed "the necessary energy, endurance, and general trust."[19] Only trained officials seem to have come into question. Having never experienced power, the Progressive party had no other reservoir of trained talent upon which to draw for the state's most sensitive position. The system did not provide for it.

In these talks Bismarck began to construct his own myth, one that patriotic Germans (historians included) were subsequently only too glad to believe.

[17] Spahn, "Entstehung," 370ff.; Oncken, *Bennigsen*, vol. 1, 696–697; Hans Rosenberg, ed., *Ausgewählter Briefwechsel Rudolf Hayms* (Stuttgart, 1930), 244–246.

[18] OD, VII, 243; GW, VII, 110, 130; Otto Becker, *Bismarcks Ringen um Deutschlands Gestaltung* (Heidelberg, 1958), 159ff.

[19] GW, VII, 109–110, 112–113, 131.

Since Frankfurt days, he told Bernhardi and Bennigsen, his "program" had been confederate reform and a German parliament. To Unruh he spoke of national unity as "the great goal of my efforts for sixteen years."[20] Having chosen the option of national reform, he now described it as his sole objective from the start. The mold of his personal history had to be reshaped, the statue recast, the popular image reformed. To contemporaries and to posterity he must appear in the pose of a German nationalist.

But leaders of the Nationalverein were cautious and mistrustful. Bennigsen refused to commit himself to the Prussian plan without knowledge of its details and assurances that Bismarck would make concessions in the constitutional conflict. Roggenbach concluded that the parliament plan had to be supported, for a defeated Prussia could never "fulfill its future mission." But then the Badenser, frightened by premature publicity, abruptly left Berlin. He feared to jeopardize his political future by dealing with the hated minister. Nor was Miquel impressed by the argument that to support Prussia was his "national duty." Like Bennigsen, he found the constitutional conflict an insurmountable obstacle. Bismarck also failed in his effort to recruit Treitschke to draft nationalistic manifestos for the Prussian government. Although sympathetic to the Prussian cause, the Freiburg professor feared to compromise himself.[21]

As the resolutions in Bremen and Halle show, the views of Bennigsen were not those of the entire Nationalverein. Anxiously the Hanoverian queried his agents throughout Germany. Should the organization support the Prussian plan or sit on the fence for the time being? The answers were inconclusive. Only one-eighth replied, of whom thirty-one advocated immediate agitation for the plan and eight a reserved attitude. Meeting in Berlin on May 13–14, the central committee condemned the prospect of civil war and avoided commitment to the parliament proposal. Six days later a congress of German deputies, with Bennigsen serving as vice-president, met in Frankfurt and "damned the threatening conflict as a cabinet war serving only dynastic interests." The rulers and ministers responsible for such an "unnatural war" would be guilty of a "terrible crime against the nation."[22]

The conferences with Twesten and Unruh were also unsatisfactory. Already burdened by a sense of defeat, the former restricted his price to the confirmation of the chamber's budget rights. This, he insisted, was the only way the crown could make it "legally and morally possible" for the deputies to cooperate in the war. At the minister's request he drafted a passage on this

[20] GW, VII, 113, 130.

[21] Oncken, Bennigsen, vol. 1, 702ff.; Friedrich von Bernhardi, ed., Aus dem Leben Theodor von Bernhardis (Leipzig, 1893–1906), VI, 298ff., 306ff.; GW, V, 463, 481–482; VII, 118–119: HW, I, 278ff.; Andreas Dorpalen, Heinrich von Treitschke (New Haven, 1957), 105–107.

[22] Oncken, Bennigsen, vol. 1, 708–709; Schulze-Delitzsch, Schriften und Reden, vol. 3, 282–295.

point for the next "throne speech."[23] It is questionable whether, as Bismarck asserted to Unruh, the Twesten draft actually reached the king after being accepted by the cabinet. At any rate Unruh refused to weaken the passage in order to meet Wilhelm's reputed objections. Nor did Bismarck get anywhere by reminding the deputy of his willingness in 1859 to accept a "temporary military despotism" for the sake of national unity. Internal peace, Unruh insisted, was to be had only by a return to the constitution.[24]

As yet Bismarck had little to offer for what he asked. He had no real intention of taking any liberal into the cabinet, unless compelled to do so by the fortunes of war. Contrary to what Bernhardi thought, he carefully avoided the subject in talking to Roggenbach. When Twesten's name was mentioned as a possible candidate, he merely laughed. Nor was he ready to fulfill Bennigsen's two requirements. The liberals should have no cares, they were told, "about the little bit of liberalism" they might sacrifice by supporting his government. "You will later be able to recoup that within six weeks under the first good liberal cabinet, and in any case a new government will take office under the crown prince." If the delegates to the coming parliament would "take the initiative and begin with a revision of the constitution of 1849, I'll accept that with a kiss." "Don't bother yourselves about the constitution now; later, when we have conquered, you should have constitution enough." But his hearers resisted these blandishments. They wanted proof of his sincerity in the form of a detailed program and concrete actions.[25]

On the extreme left he had better luck. Through an assistant, Lothar Bucher, the turncoat revolutionary of 1848, he was in touch with what remained of the old radical liberal movement. There is reason to believe that Bismarck instigated the impassioned war speech that Franz Ziegler, friend and adviser of Waldeck, delivered in Breslau. The result was a widely publicized resolution of the Breslau city council favoring the war. Karl Rodbertus—radical politician, social theorist, and admirer of Bismarck's "Caesarism"—also became a propagandist for the government. Count Oskar von Reichenbach, proscribed radical of 1848, ended his long exile in England. Acting on secret instructions from Robert von Keudell, another trusted Bismarck assistant, he traveled through southern Germany encouraging resistance to war. Two other veteran radicals, Arnold Ruge and Gottfried Kinkel, were also enlisted in the Prussian cause.[26] With the socialists too Bismarck had some success. Three

[23] HW, I, 307, 312–313, 497–499; Heinrich von Poschinger, ed., Erinnerungen aus dem Leben von Hans Viktor von Unruh (Stuttgart) 1895), 251. What Twesten understood by "budget rights," however, was rather far-reaching. See Spahn, "Entstehung," 393–394.

[24] GW, VII, 128–130. Gerhard Ritter, "Die Entstehung der Indemnitätsvorlage von 1866," Historische Zeitschrift, 114 (1915), 24.

[25] Bernhardi, Aus dem Leben, vol. 5, 303; Oncken, Bennigsen, vol. 1, 705 (n. 3); Ludwig Dehio, "Die preussische Demokratie und der Krieg von 1866," Forschungen zur brandenburgischen und preussischen Geschichte, 39 (1927), 254; GW, VII, 112, 115, 119.

[26] Dehio, "Preussische Demokratie," 230ff.; Ludwig Dehio, "Beiträge zu Bismarcks Politik im

days after the Prussian commitment on German reform he lent 2,500 thalers without interest to keep Schweitzer's *Sozialdemokrat* from bankruptcy. On May 9 the editor was prematurely released from prison. Immediately he set out to reinvigorate the faltering workers' association. At a convention held in Leipzig on June 17 the party, on his urging, resolved to commence general agitation for universal suffrage and a national parliament.[27]

But these results were meager. The predominant "movement" among the German people in April–June 1866 was antiwar and anti-Bismarck. The Junker would have been amused, however, by Károlyi's judgment that popular opinion would prevent him from going to war. "One doesn't shoot at the enemy with public opinion," he told Bernhardi, "but with powder and lead." "We don't need you at all," were his parting words to Miquel. The agitation against war, he wrote Goltz, was the "superficial" creation of the bourgeoisie, unsupported by the masses. "At the moment of decision the masses will stand by the monarchy, whether it follows the liberal or conservative stream." The king had but to command; they would obey.[28]

The mobilization in May was not unaffected by the public mood. Militiamen resented the rude interruption of their private lives for purposes not wholly clear. "Scandals" occurred at some assembly points. Nevertheless, the traditional Prussian discipline prevailed. As the troops massed on the Austrian frontier, the war-spirit rose. To one observer the militia now appeared even more bellicose than the line. In the minor battles of the west and south and in the decisive clash at Königgrätz Prussian troops struck down their fellow Germans with the same efficiency, if without the same degree of enthusiasm, shown earlier against the Danes and later against the French. Back home, Schulze-Delitzsch noted, the public followed the news reports with an increasing sense of involvement. Because of military conscription almost every family had a member under arms. Prussia's isolation and the proximity of her foes heightened the feeling of common danger. The good citizens shuddered at the reputed savagery of the "Austrian hordes." The necessity of winning the war became more important than the issue of its origin.[29] Bismarck's confidence was thoroughly vindicated.

Sommer 1866 unter Benutzung der Papiere Robert von Keudells," *Forschungen zur brandenburgischen und preussischen Geschichte*, 46 (1934), 155ff.; Hans Neumann, "Franz Ziegler und die Politik der liberalen Oppositionsparteien von 1848 bis 1866," *ibid.*, 37 (1925), 286–288; Becker, *Bismarcks Ringen*, 162.

[27] Gustav Mayer, "Der allgemeine deutsche Arbeiterverein und die Krisis 1866," *Archiv für Sozialwissenschaft und Sozialpolitik*, 57 (1927), 170–171; *Johann Baptist von Schweitzer und die Sozialdemokratie* (Jena, 1909), 161ff.; "Die Lösung der deutschen Frage im Jahre 1866 und die Arbeiterbewegung," in *Festgaben für Wilhelm Lexis* (Jena, 1907), 221–268; Franz Mehring, *Geschichte der deutschen Sozialdemokratie* (Stuttgart, 1903), vol. 3, 250–251.

[28] *DPO*, V/1, 243, 269; *GW*, V, 429–430; VII, 119, 121.

[29] *SEG* (1866), 506; Johannes Schultze, ed., *Max Duncker: Politischer Briefwechsel aus seinem Nachlass* (Stuttgart, 1923), 413; Schulze-Delitzsch, *Schriften und Reden*, vol. 3, 299ff.

Intoxication of Conquest

"Every Prussian," wrote Benedetti in March 1866, "has something of Frederick the Great in him, whatever his views on the issues of liberty." Bismarck would readily have agreed. In recommending draconian measures against the Frankfurt senate in October 1865, he wrote, "In my opinion every development of willpower and might that we accomplish in Germany will be of substantial help in overcoming our inner conflict." If carried out in defiance of the views of the liberals, this would be all the more true, provided that the action were taken "decisively" and not as a "half-measure."[30] The ruthless use of power, he judged, commands respect regardless of its purpose.

Certainly this was true of Germany in 1866. The remarkable display of will and energy with which Bismarck carried Prussia into war against great popular opposition and the crushing power with which Prussia, supported by no other German state and opposed by most, swept all before her soon had their effect. What ceaseless propaganda from the government press and the bold exploitation of liberal and national ideals had been unable to accomplish in the preceding months was achieved within days by powder, smoke, and the intoxication of conquest.

On May 9 the Landtag had been dissolved, and, as the war neared, the voting dates were set for June 25 and July 3. It was what the British call a "khaki election." "For or against the soldiers" was the official slogan. On June 17, 18, and 19, Prussian troops occupied successively Hanover, Dresden, and Kassel. "Already," reported *Das Deutsche Museum* on June 20, "[Bismarck] is followed by rejoicing crowds whenever he appears in the street."[31] On June 22–23 the invasion of Bohemia was begun without resistance. Two days later a shift to the conservatives commenced in voting for the electoral college. Hoverbeck, Forckenbeck, Grabow, and Waldeck were defeated and forced to seek safer districts for the final election. On June 26–29 came the first victories of the invading Prussian armies in Bohemia and on the twenty-eighth the capitulation of the Hanoverian army at Langensalza. While Prussian troops were storming the heights of Chlum on July 3, the electors cast their ballots at home. The conservatives captured 142 seats in contrast to their previous 28; the left centrists sank from 110 to 65, and the progressives from 143 to 83.[32] Had the election been held a few days later, after arrival of the news from Bohemia, the conservative victory would undoubtedly have been still greater. Even so, by allying with the old-liberal faction of nine members, the conservatives could now control the chamber.

[30] *OD*, VII, 392; GW, V, 315.

[31] Quoted in Spahn, "Entstehung," 388.

[32] Johannes Ziekursch, *Politische Geschichte des neuen deutschen Kaiserreiches* (Frankfurt a. M., 1925–1930), vol. 1, 192. Defeated in East Prussia, the liberals did best in the Catholic Rhineland, where some aversion for the war remained. Parisius, *Hoverbeck*, II/2, 93–95.

But the conservative victory and the liberal defeat were not as clear-cut as first appeared, for the dramatic events of July 1866 had produced an incredible confusion in all parties. No longer were conservatives unanimous in support of the Bismarck cabinet. Nor were liberals still united against it. Out of the chaos emerged an astonishing realignment of political forces. The catalyst that dissolved the old compounds and combined the new was the indemnity bill.

The "Golden Bridge"

In the exultation of victory ultraconservatives naturally expected the government to make the liberal defeat conclusive by suspending or revising the constitution. Yet on July 4 Bismarck agreed with the crown prince on the necessity of settling the internal conflict. Having chosen the path of national reform, he recognized the impossibility of basing his government on "anti-German particularists" of the *Kreuzzeitung* party. "The power of the monarchy in Prussia must be supported by a powerful army," he was even reported as saying. "But it must go with the opinion of the nation. It is the duty of every Prussian minister to regard the will of the king as authoritative, but at the same time to let the will of the king be saturated with the opinion of the nation."[33]

Although the war had been fought without public support, the peace Bismarck planned could not be made secure without it. Inside Prussia the incorporated masses had to be reconciled to their new situation, their loyalties to the deposed dynasties erased. A creation of Prussian *Machtpolitik*, the North German Confederation could not survive in the mass age without popular legitimation. These needs were to be met by German nationalism. It had the centripetal force to overcome the centrifugal habits of particularism. A continuation of the constitutional conflict would have driven German patriots, north and south, into the opposing camp. By identifying its cause with that of the nation, Prussia could cut off all hope of revenge on the part of the defeated states and undermine their resistance to a future completion of German unification under Prussian hegemony. As early as July 4, Bismarck spoke of the coming North German Confederation as but a "stage" toward German unity.[34] Such an undertaking required that Prussia have the support of an aroused nation, for it would involve, in all probability, war with France.

To break off the internal struggle was also for Bismarck a matter of personal insurance. Given Wilhelm's advanced age, he had to reckon that Friedrich Wilhelm might soon ascend the throne. Under him the quarrel, if still in

[33] GW, VII, 137, 141, 147; XV, 282ff.; Friedrich III, *Tagebücher 1848–1866*, 454.
[34] GW, VII, 137; XV, 293.

progress, would most certainly be ended—but by another cabinet.[35] In any case Bismarck had never believed in the viability of an extended period of naked absolutism in Prussia. Since parliament was a necessity, he had to find within it a majority willing to support his policies. Despite the conservative victory at the polls, the liberals were still a political force. They would be reinforced by voters in the annexed lands. The populations of Hanover, Hesse-Kassel, Nassau, and Frankfurt could be expected to vote more like the liberal Rhineland, with which they were socially akin, than the conservative east. Only in Mecklenburg could the conservatives expect political reinforcement. But in the other federal states of northern Germany—not to speak of those to be added in the south—Prussian conservatism would stand little chance at the polls.

To form a government majority, therefore, it was essential to attract the moderate liberals. Certainly Bismarck was aware that, despite all the clamor of the constitutional conflict, they were not fundamentally hostile to monarchical institutions or to the type of "mixed constitution" that he intended for Germany. He knew that their alliance with democratic liberals was an uneasy one, the unnatural child of a common cause in the constitutional conflict. In 1862 he had sought to split it apart as his first maneuver in domestic politics. In succeeding years he had witnessed the inner cleavages of the liberal movement and observed their weariness and insecurity, their longing for a settlement. By giving in on the budget issue, he could meet their conception of the *Rechtsstaat*. By taking up the cause of German unity, he could bring them to support an essentially conservative order. This was the "golden bridge" over which he hoped to lead the moderates.[36]

His interviews with Twesten and Lasker apparently convinced him that the opposition could be reconciled only by a sweeping concession. Further evidence was the unwillingness of Bennigsen, Miquel, and others in mid-July 1866 to cooperate in summoning a "preparliament," despite the pressure of French intervention.[37] After Königgrätz, moreover, Bismarck could afford to grant what he had previously withheld. No longer could the liberals dispute the military reorganization. Without their financial help the government had fought and won two wars. Concessions on the constitutional issue now had the appearance of a royal benevolence rather than of a government defeat.

In Berlin the issue produced a major cabinet crisis. Even though all the ministers recognized the wisdom of ending the conflict, most thought this could be done by shadow concessions. Only Heydt, the new minister of finance, wished a "bill of indemnity" by which the government would ask par-

---

[35] Although the crown prince had not lost his bitterness over the "fox" in the Wilhelmstrasse, he too was affected by the grandeur of the victory and by Bismarck's efforts after Königgrätz at reconciliation. Friedrich III, *Tagebücher 1848–1866*, xlvii–li.

[36] GW, XV, 294.

[37] Dehio, "Beiträge," 149–155.

liament's approval of expenditures made during the last four years without its consent. The other ministers were surprised and shocked when word came from Bohemia that both Bismarck and Wilhelm agreed with this judgment. They strove to have the decision revoked. Never was Bismarck to forget or forgive the "desertion" of his conservative colleagues on this issue. He had, however, a geographical advantage; they were in Berlin, he at the king's side in Bohemia. During the journey homeward on August 4 he talked Wilhelm into holding to the original decision. The next day, Heydt's draft, with only minor changes, was read from the throne in the speech that opened the special session of the new Prussian Landtag.[38]

The Liberals Divide

On August 5, 1866, the white hall of the palace, so empty on February 23, was crowded with deputies, the political atmosphere completely changed. Popular support, for which the opposition had angled so long, was now overwhelmingly on the side of the monarchy. The army, whose reorganization they had opposed and whose financial support they had denied, was brilliantly victorious. Its officers were the Junkers against whose power they had striven in vain. Its commander-in-chief was the king whose ministers had violated the constitution and frustrated the parliamentary will. Back of the whole conservative order, furthermore, loomed the sentiment of German nationalism. In seven weeks dynasty, ministers, army, and Junkers had taken a mighty step toward the realization of the liberal dream of half a century. Achievement of the rest was assumed to be but a matter of time. Now the government announced its willingness to seek a settlement of the constitutional conflict.

The situation was powerfully persuasive. That liberals were so strongly affected by it, however, cannot be attributed merely to the dramatic events of June and July 1866. Their acquiescence had been prepared for more than a century in the development of the liberal tradition. As we have seen, German moderate liberals had always had an ambivalent attitude toward the state, an attitude that reflected the intermediate character of their position in German society. Their value system was that of the German *Mittelstand*, suspended between the traditional ruling estates (*Adelsstand* and *Beamtenstand*) of the Prussian establishment, which liberals aspired to join rather than replace, and (at this stage in the evolution of Germany's economy and society) the inchoate *Volk*, whose potential for disorder they had learned to fear. As in 1848 they were leery of the masses, and as in 1848 the masses were not behind them. With few exceptions, they had never aimed at full responsibility for the management of public affairs. During the constitutional conflict they had fought a largely defensive action in behalf of the *Rechtsstaat* and against arbi-

---

[38] *Ibid.*, 147ff.; Ritter, "Entstehung der Indemnitätsvorlage," 17ff.

trary government. What Bismarck now offered could be interpreted as victory, not defeat.

In early 1864 many liberals had displayed a hunger for military success and foreign expansion; now they found this but an appetizer for the main course. Theirs had been the illusion that wars for great objectives could be fought only with their active support. But now the unbelievable had happened. The supposed spokesman of reactionary conservatism had not only steered the country into a major war, but had also summoned the nation to accomplish its unity under the protective umbrella of Prussian power. Again the Prussian state had stolen vital planks from the liberal platform. To most there now appeared no other place to stand than upon or under the inviting new structure Bismarck was busily erecting with stolen materials.

For many the conversion was not difficult. Wehrenpfennig concluded, "Bismarck is, except for Stein, the greatest statesman Prussia has ever had; it appears that he is luckier and perhaps even bolder than the latter." Rudolf Ihering, Göttingen professor of law, who earlier had denounced the war as an act of "frightful frivolity," now bowed down before the "genius of a Bismarck," declaring that for such a man of deeds he would give one hundred men of impotent honesty. Almost overnight the Bismarck cult was born. Its devotees began to reinterpret their hero's actions during the preceding four years. They excused his infringements of the constitution in view of what was presumed to have been his hidden purpose. Impatiently the liberal press, so bitterly hostile from March to June, now pressed the deputies not to hinder the government in the fulfillment of its "duty" toward the rest of Germany. In view of the "glorious" work ahead, the issues of the constitutional conflict were declared petty and insignificant.[39]

The classic conversions were those of Gustav Mevissen and Hermann Baumgarten. After watching the victorious columns march down Unter den Linden through the Brandenburger Tor, Mevissen, who had headed the revolutionary cabinet of 1848, described the emotions that gripped him: "I cannot shake off the impression of this hour. I am no devotee of Mars; I feel more attached to the goddess of beauty and the mother of graces than to the mighty god of war, but the trophies of war exercise a magic charm upon the child of peace. One's eyes are involuntarily riveted on, and one's spirit goes along with, the unending rows of men who acclaim the god of the moment—success."[40] Baumgarten—student of Gervinus, press official of the new era, professor of history at Karlsruhe—subjected the attitudes of German liberals to a scorching "self-criticism" in the pages of the Preussische Jahrbücher. Theoretical and doctrinaire, they had placed their faith in words and ideas, not deeds.

---

[39] Duncker, Briefwechsel, 425; Eyck, Bismarck, vol. 2, 318; Spahn, "Entstehung," 405ff.

[40] Quoted in Ziekursch, Politische Geschichte, vol. 1, 189; the translation is from Koppel S. Pinson, Modern Germany (New York, 1955), 139–140.

TE DEUM BEFORE THE ROYAL PALACE IN BERLIN DURING THE VICTORY PARADE ON SEPTEMBER 21, 1866
(BILDARCHIV PREUSSISCHER KULTURBESITZ).

Recent events had shown that the German *Mittelstand* could not dispense with the leadership of a "true aristocracy" for the achievement of national objectives. Liberals must abandon their oppositional posture.[41]

With care Bismarck nourished the plant of liberal capitulation. Soon after the Landtag opened he fed the deputies a series of bills designed to appeal to every segment of the former opposition. For men of principle there was a bill of indemnity, for Prussian chauvinists a bill of annexation, for German na-

---

[41] Hermann Baumgarten, "Der deutsche Liberalismus: Eine Selbstkritik," *Preussische Jahrbücher*, 18 (1866), 455–515, 575–628 (especially 617–628).

tionalists a Reichstag suffrage bill. He appeared in person to defend and explain them before the committees; in private talks he spun the web of personal charm and sweet reason that had snared so many diplomatic opponents. When the situation called for it, the master of scorn and contempt was equally adept at deference and consideration. He enjoyed the game intensely. A visitor reported that his face, while pale and ill, was radiant with laughter. The man was beyond all exaggeration.[42]

After Königgrätz liberal deputies were greatly relieved to learn that the triumphant Junker did not intend a coup against the constitution and that he was still serious about a national parliament. Their first chance to respond to his overtures was in the election of a speaker. Since 1862 Grabow had annually been reelected to that office and his bitter opening speeches had been the first demonstration in each parliamentary session of the continued intransigence of the opposition. But now the deputies chose Forckenbeck, a moderate noted for tact and parliamentary skill. In drafting a reply to the speech from the throne, the moderates allowed amendments that made it acceptable even to conservatives. They argued that the message must demonstrate that the German people were entirely united behind the German policy of the government. Only twenty-five deputies voted against it, including the veteran radical Jacoby, who once more condemned the war as a blow to freedom.[43]

Already there were signs of dissolution in the liberal ranks. In mid-August a left centrist, Karl Kannegiesser, reported to his constituents, "The world-historical events of the last months are having a powerful effect upon men's minds." He detected two currents in both of the major liberal parties: one placed the major emphasis on the German question, the other upon Prussian constitutional law.[44] Relieved of the pressure of the constitutional conflict and presented with the possibility of national unity under authoritarian auspices, liberal deputies began to divide once more into the two traditional segments of moderate right and democratic left. The alliance of 1861 broke apart over the issue of the relative importance of national unity and the rule of law.

Both camps, to be sure, were inclined toward settlement. But moderates considered the constitutional conflict irretrievably lost and wished to get rid of it on the government's terms; democrats were inclined to seek as firm a guarantee as possible for the future respect of parliament's budget rights. The men of the left found it difficult to join the general jubilation. They had not forgotten that the last breach of the constitution—the creation by decree of a system of credit banks—had occurred but months before the indemnity bill.

[42] Spahn, "Entstehung," 404.
[43] Ibid., 413ff.; SBHA (1866–1867), vol. 1, 70–83.
[44] Spahn, "Entstehung," 422.

They noted that even now the minister of interior continued his "disciplinary" measures against liberal officials and his refusal to confirm liberal city councillors; the minister of justice persisted in his prosecution of the liberal press and opposition deputies (including Twesten). Finally, they observed that the government's indemnity bill contained no guarantee against budgetless rule in the future.[45] When Forckenbeck officially presented the chamber's address, Wilhelm responded belligerently, "I had to act that way, and I shall do so again, if the same circumstances recur."[46]

In the great debate on the indemnity bill leaders of the left—Waldeck, Gneist, Ziegler, Virchow, Hoverbeck, Jacoby, Frentzel, and Schulze-Delitzsch—maintained that its passage would legitimize the "gap theory" and pardon four years of unconstitutional behavior on the part of the cabinet. The deputies should postpone the bill pending passage of a legal budget and a law fixing ministerial responsibility. Military victory and respect for law must not be confused with each other. Whatever its successes abroad, the government must stay within the law at home. But leaders of the right—Twesten, Forckenbeck, Lasker, and Michaelis—feared that, if liberals remained in opposition, the flight of the voters to the conservatives would continue. By supporting the Bismarck cabinet, on the other hand, they might sever it from its conservative base and influence the future constitutional structure of Germany. In summing up the moderate position, Twesten declared that two issues were fundamental to every state: those of freedom and power. "No one may be criticized for giving precedence to the issue of power at this time and maintaining that the issues of freedom can wait, provided that nothing happens that can permanently prejudice them." From Bismarck the deputies heard of the dangers of French intervention and Austrian resurgence. Only a united people could succeed in Germany's mission against an injured and envious Europe. On September 3, 1866, the indemnity bill passed by a vote of 230 to 75.[47]

The constitutional conflict was over, but so also was the unity of the liberal movement. During August and September the caucuses of the Progressive party became increasingly heated. The exodus of the moderates began with

---

[45] Schulze-Delitzsch, *Schriften und Reden*, vol. 5, 267; Duncker, *Briefwechsel*, 429; SBHA (1866–1867), I, 149–207.

[46] For both Bismarck and Forckenbeck the utterance was an embarrassment. No minister was present, so the speaker chose to interpret it as unofficial and hence not to be formally reported to the chamber. In a cabinet meeting Bismarck got the ministers to take a similar view. SBHA (1866–1867), I, 115; Martin Philippson, *Max von Forckenbeck: Ein Lebensbild* (Dresden, 1898), 154–155; Eyck, *Bismarck*, vol. 2, 305.

[47] SBHA (1866–1867), I, 149–207; Spahn, "Entstehung," 423ff.; Löwenthal, *Verfassungsstreit*, pp. 302ff. For a review of the discussion concerning the meaning and significance of the indemnity act see Rainer Wahl, "Der preussische Verfassungskonflikt und das konstitutionelle System des Kaiserreichs," in Ernst-Wolfgang Böckenförde, ed., *Moderne deutsche Verfassungsgeschichte (1815–1914)* (2d ed., Königstein/Taunus, 1981), 208–231.

Michaelis, followed by Twesten, Lasker, and many others. By a number of concessions Bismarck gave the secessionists the chance to feel at last the exhilaration of being in harmony with the ruling power. They were permitted to redraft the indemnity bill to make it correspond with the budget clauses of the constitution. Instead of "personal union," Bismarck accepted the actual incorporation of the conquered lands into Prussia, but inauguration of the Prussian constitution was to be delayed one year. A bill presented by Heydt to legalize the government-sponsored credit banks was passed, but only after an amendment that soon put them out of business. A serious clash over the government's request for a credit of 60 million thalers was settled by a compromise that limited the size and purpose of the reserves accumulated by the treasury. Prodded by Lasker and Forckenbeck, the crown issued a general amnesty on September 21, the day of the victory celebration in Berlin. Wilhelm's request for a dotation of one and a half million thalers for victorious generals was voluntarily amended by the chamber to include the name of Bismarck![48]

Originally, the secessionists did not intend to found a new party. Their aim was to convince the majority in the Left Center and Progressive parties of the validity of a new strategy. Some of them saw in Bismarck's foreign policy a significant gain for liberty in Germany. The exclusion of Catholic Austria from a unified Germany under Protestant leadership was itself a liberal deed, a victory for modernity over clerical bigotry. By supporting the Bismarck cabinet in foreign affairs, moreover, they hoped to bring it step by step along the road of domestic compromise; constitutional issues should be postponed issues until they could be fought out on more advantageous terrain. In the expanded Landtag and constituent Reichstag of 1867 the secessionists found many non-Prussian liberals sympathetic to their cause. Never personally involved in the Prussian conflict, the latter were untainted by its passions and less concerned about its issues. They too regarded the struggle as lost and relatively unimportant compared to the great task ahead. Out of this union of forces came the National Liberal party. In numbers non-Prussians predominated, and the leadership fell to two Hanoverians, Bennigsen and Miquel.[49]

The liberal caucus in the Chamber of Deputies had divided between a Progressive party, largely Prussian and preserving the tradition of the conflict years, and a National Liberal party, largely non-Prussian and more national than liberal. Economic issues, such as the recent renewal of the Zollverein on the basis of free trade, appear to have had no influence on the split. And yet the two parties, because of the positions their leaders took on many economic

---

[48] Spahn, "Entstehung," 443ff. Otto Michaelis belonged to a group of free traders, whose liberalism was primarily economic. They were attracted by the free-trade policy of the Prussian government and had always been cool toward the constitutional conflict. See Werner Shunke, *Die preussischen Freihändler und die Entstehung der nationalliberalen Partei* (Leipzig, 1916), 50.

[49] Spahn, "Entstehung," 439ff., 469.

and political issues, did tend to attract different segments of the German *Mittelstand*. The priority given to national unity by the moderate liberals who formed the National Liberal party appealed to many merchants, industrialists, liberal landowners, and their journalistic supporters. They saw in the erection of a political roof over the national marketplace a significant gain for bourgeois interests. But they also found merit in Bismarck's argument that Prussia was compelled to carry too great a military and financial burden for the defense of Germany as a whole; a united Germany under Prussian leadership could be expected to spread the tax burden proportionally to other shoulders and in the long run free capital for more productive purposes. To the small businessmen and artisans of democratic temperament who clung to the Progressive party the financial benefits to be expected of German unity were either less important or not so apparent; hence they were more reluctant than the moderates to surrender or defer the issues of freedom and parliamentary rights for which the constitutional conflict had been fought.[50]

To the democratic left the cleavage was between "opportunists" and "men of principle"; to the moderate right it was between "practical statesmen" and "naive idealists." And yet the formation of two separate caucuses in parliament did not mean that the liberal movement as a whole was vertically cloven apart in 1867. For at least a decade the tradition remained alive that there was but one "liberal party" with a common social and electoral base, the *Mittelstand*. Nor was this mere theory in the Chamber of Deputies (later the Reichstag), where the two caucuses collaborated on many basic issues, and in the provinces and electoral districts, where liberals were often chosen as candidates without regard to parliamentary affiliations. Still, German liberalism had reached a point of divergence. The moderates took the track that ultimately led to unconditional surrender, the democrats that which finally ended in frustration and impotence.

The Conservatives Divide

In the heat of the constitutional conflict most conservatives failed to notice that the pied piper in the Wilhelmstrasse was leading them farther and farther away from the party's principles. The vigor and fearlessness of his struggle against parliament, the Alvensleben convention, and the Austrian alliance seemed convincing evidence of his conservative orthodoxy. Though Ludwig Gerlach was shocked by the "Godless and lawless greed" of the annexation policy, most conservatives soon convinced themselves that the duchies were Prussia's just reward for the glorious deeds of the army. Nevertheless, they welcomed the Gastein treaty, for cooperation with Russia and Austria was

---

[50] Heinrich August Winkler, *Liberalismus und Antiliberalismus: Kritische Studien zur Geschichtswissenschaft*, vol. 38 (Göttingen, 1979), 20–23, 25–26, 33–35.

still a primary tenet of conservative political dogma. For the same reason the renewal of the diplomatic struggle in January 1866 was deeply disturbing. By an intensive campaign in the official and conservative press, however, Bismarck was able to propagate the view that his policy was purely defensive.[51]

By the end of February 1866 conservatives were so unsettled and divided about the course of government policy in foreign affairs that Hans von Kleist-Retzow, among others, doubted that conservatives could any longer claim to be an estate (*Stand*). The group consciousness had dissolved to the point that only individuals were still capable of perceiving and fulfilling what had once been expected of the whole.[52] In April news of the Prussian reform plan, rumors of the Italian alliance, and the general drift toward war threw the conservatives into confusion. Wagener strove to convince the readers of the *Kreuzzeitung* of the virtue of the government's policy. But Ludwig Gerlach, as one of its columnists, severely censured the Bismarckian course. Through his contacts he sought to influence court and cabinet. Finally he ventured into the "lion's den." In a "lacerating interview" the two men severed a lifelong friendship. To Gerlach the attack on Austria was like "the fratricide of Cain, the betrayal of Judas, and the crucifixion of the Lord."[53]

But the elderly Junker was unable to carry the party as a whole. Among cabinet members only Bodelschwingh could not square the Bismarck policy with his conscience. He resigned.[54] Most conservatives were not inclined to take the parliament plan seriously; the violent reaction of the liberals seemed proof of its inconsequence. Furthermore, the prospect of Prussian aggrandizement, nourished by the earlier propaganda for annexation, had its appeal. When the climactic moment came, Prussian patriotism and fear of a "second Olmütz" triumphed over the doubts of conservatives. The astonishing electoral victory of July 3 was their reward for constancy. The "small but mighty party" was no longer small.[55]

In late July the first report of Bismarck's intention to reconcile the opposition exploded in the conservative camp. The ultras, even as they gloated over their triumph and the final reckoning they presumed was to come, suddenly found themselves deserted by their own leader. Beginning on July 25, the *Kreuzzeitung* sounded the alarm. Through the indiscretion of a cabinet min-

---

[51] Gerhard Ritter, *Die preussischen Konservativen und Bismarcks deutsche Politik, 1858–1875* (Heidelberg, 1913), 89ff., 131ff.

[52] Hans von Kleist-Retzow to Ludwig von Gerlach, Mar. 1, 1866. Helmut Diwald, ed., *Von der Revolution zum Norddeutschen Bund: Politik und Ideengut der preussischen Hochkonservativen, 1848–1866; Aus dem Nachlass von Ernst Ludwig von Gerlach* (Göttingen, 1970), vol. 2, 1258.

[53] Ernst Ludwig von Gerlach, *Aufzeichnungen aus seinem Leben und Wirken, 1795–1877* (Schwerin, 1903), vol. 2, 281–293, 300; Diwald, ed., *Politik und Ideengut der preussischen Hochkonservativen*, vol. 1, 455–480; vol. 2, 1265–1311.

[54] The minister of finance had long been concerned over Bismarck's readiness to violate the constitution in the struggle with parliament. Gerlach, *Aufzeichnungen*, vol. 2, 273, 277.

[55] Ritter, *Konservativen*, 131ff.

ister, the reactionary Hans von Kleist-Retzow learned the content of the coming throne speech. Frantically he sought to mobilize a camarilla of influential conservatives. Bismarck was bitter. "The little people don't have enough to do; they see no further than their own noses and like to swim on the stormy sea of phrases. With the enemy one can cope, but the friends!"[56]

The indemnity bill was a divisive wedge that penetrated conservative as well as progressive ranks. Led by Count Bethusy-Huc, about fifteen moderate conservatives caucused at the end of July and agreed to support the policy of reconciliation. At the time it was not their intention to form a new party. They wished merely to find a basis for collaboration with the small remaining faction of old-liberals, without whom the conservatives could not control the chamber. But as the session progressed, the cleavage widened, and the Free Conservative party was born.[57]

Outwardly solid, the monolith of the Conservative party had always had an internal fault. Whereas the "old conservatives" were Prussian particularists, the free conservatives were open-minded on the subject of national unity. In religious matters the former were solidly Lutheran, pietistic, and orthodox; the latter were either Catholic or nonreligious. The cleavage was also geographical and occupational. The strength of the old conservatives lay among the feudal gentry of the Prussian heartland (East Prussia, Pomerania, Brandenburg), whereas the free conservatives were strongest in the annexed regions of Silesia and the Rhineland. A party of *Bildung und Besitz*, its deputies were high-ranking noblemen, officials, generals, professors, and (later) great industrialists. Never was the party to cultivate or attract a mass following. Its strength lay in the favor of the government, which it unconditionally supported at home and abroad. It was the "Bismarck party *sans phrase*."[58]

In the debates on the annexation of Hanover and Hesse-Kassel, the effect of four years of Bismarckian leadership was evident in both conservative parties. In the two houses of the Landtag the conservatives, feudal as well as free, voted solidly for incorporation. "Thou shalt not steal," thundered Gerlach, but even Kleist-Retzow rejoiced at "such a handsome expansion for Prussia."[59] In the society of states successful larceny is legitimized by time. Under Bismarck's tutelage the politics of power triumphed over the doctrinaire idealism of romantic conservatism, the appeal of Prussian patriotism over the sense of universal right. One day he would also succeed in the greater task of convincing the conservatives as a whole that German nationalism was a potential friend, not the irreconcilable foe of the aristocratic-monarchical order.

[56] GW, XIV, 720.

[57] Ritter, *Konservativen*, 179ff.; August Wolfstieg, "Die Anfänge der freikonservativen Partei," in Emil Daniels and others, eds., *Delbrück-Festschrift* (Berlin, 1908), 317ff.; Kurd Viebig, *Die Entstehung und Entwicklung der Freikonservativen und der Reichspartei* (Weimar, 1920), 14ff.

[58] See Siegfried von Kardorff, *Wilhelm von Kardorff* (Berlin, 1936), 32ff.

[59] Ritter, *Konservativen*, 184ff.

The Socialists Emerge

The war of 1866 had yet another consequence of importance for German social and political development. By choosing the path of national reform and conversion of the moderate liberals, Bismarck began the attempt to weld a political union between the old landowning aristocracy and new urban elite of industry and finance. After 1867 he cooperated with the latter in clearing away the reservations toward, and legal restraints on, capitalistic endeavor. By promoting a rapprochement between propertied interests, he left labor little choice but to find a leadership and ideology of its own.

At first Schweitzer, now virtual dictator of the General German Workers Association, saw in the war an opportunity to resume Lassalle's negotiations with the extreme right. His premature release from prison and Bismarck's subsidy of the *Sozialdemokrat* pointed to the possibility of success. In December he sought contact with the minister-president, but no summons came from the Wilhelmstrasse and no help from conservatives in the Reichstag election of February 12, 1867. In Elberfeld Schweitzer polled 4,668 votes, but lost the seat to Bismarck himself. Because the progressives also refused cooperation, his party was unable to elect a single candidate in Germany's first major election under universal, direct, and equal suffrage.[60]

The Lassalleans no longer monopolized the independent labor movement. In Saxony a competing organization had appeared under the formidable leadership of August Bebel and Wilhelm Liebknecht. A disciple of Marx and emissary of the Socialist International, Liebknecht had enjoyed no success as a radical agitator until his expulsion from Prussia in August 1865. Migrating to Leipzig, he found in the young Bebel a ready ally of republican and democratic convictions. A wood turner by profession, Bebel was the most important figure in the chain of Saxon educational associations (*Arbeiterbildungsvereine*) founded under liberal auspices for the educational and cultural elevation of workers. As late as 1865 Bebel had appealed to the Nationalverein for financial aid in combating Lassallean socialists. In 1866 he opposed, with Liebknecht, the civil war produced by Prussian imperialism. Unlike Schweitzer and the Lassalleans, both remained unreconciled to the Prussian, small-German solution of the problem of national unity. They were convinced that Schweitzer had sold out to the Prussian government.[61]

But Bebel was also appalled at the readiness with which liberals came to terms with Hohenzollern autocracy. With Liebknecht he founded in August

[60] Mayer, *Schweitzer*, 180ff.

[61] Ernst Schraepler, "Linksliberalismus und Arbeiterschaft in der preussischen Konfliktszeit," in Richard Dietrich and Gerhard Oestreich, eds., *Forschungen zu Staat und Verfassung: Festgabe für Fritz Hartung* (Berlin, 1958), 398ff.; August Bebel, *Aus Meinem Leben* (Stuttgart, 1910), vol. 1, 89–90, 126ff. Two eminent students of the problem have denied that Schweitzer lost his independence through his dealings with Bismarck. Mehring, *Sozialdemokratie*, vol. 3, 248ff.; Mayer, "Arbeiterverein," 170–171.

1866 the Saxon People's party, which succeeded in electing two deputies (one of whom was Bebel himself) to the constituent Reichstag. The first party program was democratic rather than socialistic, for neither of its founders was yet ready to alienate *Mittelstand* voters. At rallies in Nürnberg in 1868 and Eisenach in 1869, however, they were more moved by class-conscious workers to adopt the radical program of the Socialist International. The outcome was the Social Democratic Labor party founded at Eisenach for "emancipation of the working class."[62]

In February 1867 Schulze-Delitzsch wrote that he was considering retirement from politics to devote his entire energy to the social question. "The agitation among the workers is becoming ever more serious and threatens our political and economic development in a dangerous way. Our political leaders do not yet see it. . . . It often seems to me that I am the only seeing person among the blind!"[63] The refusal of liberals to accept the political equality of labor through universal suffrage, their unwillingness to face the social issue by questioning the dogma of laissez-faire, and, finally, their betrayal in 1866 of their own highest ideals, began to convince proletarians of the validity of the concept of class struggle. The crack that had opened in the German social structure in 1863 began to widen.

[62] Bebel, *Leben*, vol. 1, 164ff.; vol. 2, 86ff.; Gustav Mayer, "Die Trennung der proletarischen von der bürgerlichen Demokratie in Deutschland, 1863–1870," *Archiv für die Geschichte des Sozialismus und der Arbeiterbewegung*, 2 (1912), 24ff.

[63] Schulze-Delitzsch, *Schriften und Reden*, vol. 5, 268.

CHAPTER FIFTEEN

The German Balance of Power

Drafting the Constitution

ONE OF the early myths of the Bismarck cult was that the man of genius, assisted by Lothar Bucher, drafted the north German constitution in two days of intensive effort after his return to Berlin on December 1, 1866. Supporting this assumption was the fact that for two months prior to that date he had convalesced at Putbus on the Baltic from a serious illness brought on by the exertions and frictions of the preceding summer. According to his wife, the very thought of politics made him depressed and irate during much of that time.[1] The archives show, nevertheless, that the December draft had a lengthy ancestry, beginning with the "outline" presented to the Frankfurt Diet on June 10, 1866. From such politically disparate persons as Max Duncker, Reichenbach, Wagener, and Savigny, preliminary drafts were received from which features were taken. The ministries of war and commerce supplied the military and economic clauses. Still, the basic structure of the document was entirely Bismarck's work. Only after more than six months of careful calculation and frequent change did the final version mature. Throughout the complicated process of adoption thereafter it retained the basic imprint he gave it. Seldom in history has a constitution been so clearly the product of the thought and will of a single individual.[2]

The interpretation of this document and the purposes of its author have long been the subject of controversy. For almost a century historians and political scientists debated whether it was the outgrowth of a "German or great-Prussian" policy, whether his intention was to create a German national government or merely a federal mask for Prussian hegemony.[3] The issue, however, is falsely conceived. In all probability Bismarck's chief concern in drafting the constitution was simply the problem of political control. He wished to repeat in the North German Confederation the basic power arrangement of the Prussian state and thereby perpetuate the conservative order in the larger political context created by Prussian conquest. But he also had a personal problem: that of circumventing the collegial structure of the Prussian

---

[1] Robert von Keudell, *Fürst und Fürstin Bismarck: Erinnerungen 1846–1872* (Berlin, 1901), 313ff.

[2] For a detailed study of the evolution of the Bismarck draft see Otto Becker, *Bismarcks Ringen um Deutschlands Gestaltung* (Heidelberg, 1958), 211ff.

[3] For a review of this controversy, see *ibid.*, 17ff., 834ff.

cabinet in order to build up his own authority as the chief minister of the crown.

Bismarck's constitution was often celebrated as a masterpiece of political realism. Not an artificial design based on abstract party doctrine, it was a practical instrument that combined existing forces and sought their harmonious development. It united the forces of German nationalism and particularism, and solved the problem of uniting states of disproportionate size. Planned as the first stage toward small-German unity, its national features were intended to attract southern peoples and its federal ones to reassure their governments. All this is true, but the constitution was also designed to serve a particular social and political interest. The essence of the Bismarckian constitution was its perpetuation, by the use of revolutionary means, of the Prussian aristocratic-monarchical order in a century of increasingly dynamic economic and social change.

The Prussian Crown

With the annexations of 1866 the Prussian state embraced over four-fifths of the population of the North German Confederation and two-thirds of that of the future German Reich. The great majority of the German people were now governed under the constitution that had produced the conflict of 1862–1866 and that the indemnity bill had left unchanged. Bismarck's December draft proposed a similar system for the rest of Germany.[4] Actually it gave even greater powers to the Hohenzollern crown than did the Prussian constitution of 1850.

To preserve the fiction that the new confederation was simply a reformed version of the old, the king of Prussia was granted the "presidency," an office previously held by the Habsburg monarchy. But the presidency of the North German Confederation was a position of real authority. It received full control over foreign affairs, including the right to declare war and make peace and to negotiate treaties and alliances. Furthermore, it might appoint and dismiss the chancellor and any officials of the confederation. It was empowered to publish the laws of the confederation and oversee their execution. Although parliament was to meet yearly, the presidency was authorized to summon, open, prorogue, and close it. On the motion of the upper chamber (Bundesrat) the presidency might also dissolve the lower chamber (Reichstag). No provision was made either for new elections or for reconvening that body within a definite time limit.

Among the most detailed articles were those dealing with military affairs. Here some nominal concessions were made to the states and their rulers. The confederate army was to be composed of state "contingents," whose "chiefs"

---

[4] For the December draft see GW, VI, 187–196.

BISMARCK AT PUTBUS, NOVEMBER 1866 (FROM FÜRST HERBERT VON BISMARCK, ED., *FÜRST BISMARCKS BRIEFE AN SEINE BRAUT UND GATTIN*, J. G. COTTA'SCHE BUCHHANDLUNG NACHFOLGER G.M.B.H., STUTTGART, 1900, P. 481).

were the reigning princes. To the latter belonged the authority to appoint all officers below the rank of contingent commander and to employ for police purposes the troops of the contingent and such confederate troops as were located within the borders of the states. The administration of routine military affairs was also apparently left to the state governments.

Yet these concessions to particularism were largely superficial. The draft provided the king of Prussia with most of the powers of military hegemony for which Wilhelm had so long yearned and striven. It left no doubt that the army was a unitary force under his personal command. Its highest officers, including the contingent commanders, were appointed by him and swore allegiance to his person. All confederate troops swore a similar oath of unconditional obedience. He could mobilize all or any part of the army at will. The provisions dealing with the navy were similar, except that there were no contingents, and officers of all ranks were sworn to the king of Prussia. To quell internal disturbances he could declare martial law. In an emergency the king, as commander-in-chief, could order an "execution" against a rebellious state, even to the point of "sequestering" it. Normally, however, such an action required the approval of the Bundesrat.

Bismarck's draft extended the Prussian military system over the whole of the confederate army and consolidated the government's victory over parliament in the matter of military reform. By establishing the peacetime strength of each contingent at 1 percent of the population and the obligation of every able-bodied citizen to serve three years in the line, four in the reserve, and five in the militia, it placed these matters beyond the reach of both the Reichstag and the Prussian Chamber of Deputies. To the commander-in-chief was given the authority to enforce uniformity in weapons, command, training, organization, and general preparedness. The Prussianization of the lesser contingents, moreover, was assured by a clause that made all Prussian military laws, regulations, instructions, and ordinances valid for the whole army. Such matters were to be beyond the control of the states and the Reichstag.

As though to obscure their import and reduce their vulnerability to attack, the articles dealing with public finance were scattered throughout the draft. They made a mockery of parliamentary budget rights. No provision was made for an annual budget, or a periodic budget of any duration. Though the financial support of the armed forces was transferred to the confederation, the Reichstag did not gain the power lost by the Prussian Chamber of Deputies. The "iron budget," as it was subsequently called, set yearly appropriations for the army at 225 thalers per soldier for the indefinite future. Another clause obviously envisioned the creation, though in agreement with the Reichstag, of a similar "iron budget" for the navy. Only military and naval expenditures in excess of the amounts thus determined were to be subject to regular legislative approval. Even under normal circumstances the armed forces consumed almost the whole of the confederate revenues; in 1868 the army received 88.8 percent and the navy 10.7 percent.[5]

Furthermore, parliamentary control over the sources of this income was to be just as scant. The confederation was given power to levy only indirect taxes. Since their yield would increase with the development of the economy, such taxes would produce a constant growth in confederate income without additional legislative approval. It was obvious, nevertheless, that the needs of the armed forces could not be fully met from such sources. To defray the cost and balance the confederate budget the draft provided for financial assessments (Matrikularbeiträge) levied on the states in ratio to their populations. In the case of the army the amount of these transfers was to be determined by the presidency alone according to its estimate of the "need." Because of the overwhelming size of the military budget, this last provision barred the Reichstag from any effective control over confederate income. Should parliament refuse new taxes, the presidency had only to increase state assessments to make up the difference.

The power of the Reichstag and the freedom of its members was checked in still other ways. The draft made no express provision for the rights of interpellation and petition. Immunity was granted the deputies for speeches made in the chamber, but not to the press that reported them. The article dealing with libel and defamation of the confederation, its institutions and officials, was taken from the Prussian penal code, where it had been used to silence the opposition press during the constitutional conflict. Officials were declared ineligible for election to the Reichstag. The remuneration of deputies for parliamentary service was expressly forbidden. The working man was given the right to vote, but only for his betters. Finally, there was no bill of rights stating the fundamental freedoms of the citizenry.

In Bismarck's draft the fundamental dilemma of his constitutional thinking is again apparent. He hoped to generate mass support for conservative institutions, but he distrusted the lower classes and, despite his recent experiences, saw in men of property the best guarantee of political stability. He believed in the necessity of parliament to criticize and check unwise acts of the crown and bureaucracy, but he was reluctant to invest it with a power adequate to make such control effective.

The Equilibrium

Bismarck's German constitution was not, however, a mere copy of the Prussian. His experiences in the recent conflict had demonstrated the inflexibility of the latter. When crown and parliament were in disagreement there was no

[5] Karl Zuchardt, Die Finanzpolitik Bismarcks und die Parteien im Norddeutschen Bunde: Leipziger historische Abhandlungen, vol. 16 (Leipzig, 1910), 33.

alternative to the sort of deadlock that had occurred during the previous four years. In the multiple forces and institutions of a united Germany he saw the opportunity for a system of checks and balances that would provide the means of escape. Bismarck's system was not derived from the theory of Montesquieu or the constitutional practice of the American or any other government, but from those techniques of political strategy that he had developed in the diplomatic quarrels of the 1850s and applied with devastating success in the coups of the 1860s. The pattern was not one of three coequal, mutually balanced forces, but of an equilibrium controlled from the pivotal position of the fulcrum with its constant possibility of choice between opposed interests.

With this insight the old problem of Bismarck's "Germanism" or "Prussianism" loses its actuality. What interested him was not the supremacy of Germany or Prussia, but their duality and the advantages it offered for political control. Centralistic and particularistic institutions were to be played off against each other. A bid for power by the Prussian Chamber of Deputies could be countered through the Reichstag and vice versa. Based upon different suffrage laws, the two parliaments would very likely have different political compositions. After July 1867 there was still a third parliament, that of the Zollverein, chosen by universal suffrage and embracing the whole of Germany.

The structure of balanced forces in Bismarck's draft is also to be seen in the division of powers between the confederate and state governments. The confederation received legislative authority over customs and commerce; the important means of transportation and communication (navigation, railroads, the post and telegraph); certain financial matters (banking, coinage, and currency); certain types of justice (code of civil procedure, bankruptcy procedure, commercial and exchange law); and several miscellaneous affairs vitally important to the business community (weights, measures, patents, copyrights, the consular services, and the rights of domicile, migration, and choice of occupation). To the confederation were also given the rights to levy tariffs and certain consumption taxes (sugar, spirits, salt, beer, and tobacco) and to receive the surplus income of the post and telegraph systems.

The draft did not specifically say so, but the state governments were apparently to retain the right to legislate on all other matters. The most important of the powers remaining to the states was that of executing most of the laws passed by the central government. The confederation was limited to the right of "supervising" this administration as to its conformity to the law. This applied even to the collection of customs and consumption taxes and to the local administration of the post and telegraph. Judicial matters, furthermore, were left within the jurisdiction of the state courts, even where offenses against confederate law were concerned. Although the constitution established a national citizenship, it permitted concurrent state citizenship. The phrasing of this article actually made the latter appear more important by requiring the states to grant to all residents the same rights enjoyed by their own citizens. The states might retain their consuls where none was stationed by the confederation.

Within the confederate government legislative power was shared by the Reichstag and Bundesrat. Reichstag deputies were to be elected by universal, direct male suffrage for a three-year legislative period and were to be regarded as "representatives of the whole population." The Bundesrat was modeled after the old Frankfurt Diet.[6] Its delegates were representatives of the state governments, which instructed their votes. One clause even obliged the presidency to provide them with "diplomatic protection"! To become law, a bill had to pass by simple majority through both houses. Constitutional amendments required two-thirds majority in the Bundesrat. Both houses possessed the right of legislative initiative.

The two chambers were unequal. As conceived in the draft, the Bundesrat was not the upper house of a bicameral legislature, but a "cabinet" equipped with both legislative and executive power. Its executive functions were to be performed through certain committees that were established in the constitution itself. In accordance with their ministerial status, members of the Bundesrat were given the privilege of being heard at will on the floor of the Reichstag. The Bundesrat might convene without the Reichstag, but never the latter without the former. Finally, the delegates of the Bundesrat were paid officials of the state governments, whereas Reichstag deputies were expressly forbidden remuneration.

Bismarck's draft made no provision for a central judiciary. The only higher court mentioned was the superior court of the Hanseatic cities (Bremen, Hamburg, and Lübeck), which received jurisdiction over cases of treason (*Hochverrat* as well as *Landesverrat*). Disputes between states were to be settled by the Bundesrat and constitutional conflicts within states by way of confederate legislation. In other words, constitutional issues in Prussia might be transferred from the Landtag to the Reichstag, which, having a different political composition, might accept the crown's position. Concerning disagreements over the interpretation of the constitution itself, however, Bismarck's draft was significantly silent. The North German constitution, like the Prussian, was to have its "gap."

Here then was Bismarck's mechanism of the balance. The institutions and powers of the confederation were to be in equilibrium with those of Prussia and the states. The former would receive more legislative, the latter more administrative authority. Within the central government a second division was to take place between two organs, one of which had only legislative, the

---

[6] The draft of Dec. 9 actually preserved the terms "Bundestag" and "Gesandte" from the nomenclature of the old diet. On the insistence of the crown prince, who found them "abhorrent," they were changed to "Bundesrat" and "Bevollmächtigte." Becker, *Bismarcks Ringen*, 287–288.

other both legislative and executive functions. Pressure would be met by counterpressure: the nation against the dynasties, the confederation against Prussia, Reichstag against Bundesrat, parliament against parliament, centralism against particularism, the centripetal against the centrifugal. But how was the balance to be controlled?

The Fulcrum

The privileged position of Prussia in the Bundesrat is usually taken as proof of her hegemony. Of 43 votes she received 17. (The number was derived by adding up the votes of Prussia and the annexed states in the Frankfurt Diet.)[7] In addition, Prussia was given representation on all committees and the right to name the entire membership of those on military and naval affairs. Although small in ratio to her population, seventeen votes gave her an absolute veto over constitutional changes. Theoretically, Prussia could be outvoted on ordinary legislation, because the other states together possessed four more than a majority. But it was not difficult to hold enough of the smaller states in line to stave off revolt. Furthermore, the issue might always be taken to the Reichstag, where members of the Bundesrat had the right to present their views.

But the "hegemony of Prussia" was in Bismarck's draft actually that of the Prussian minister of foreign affairs. Through the fiction that the Bundesrat was but the reformed version of the diet, Bismarck retained the power to instruct the Prussian delegates, including the chancellor. In the original plan the latter was to have been merely the presiding officer of the Bundesrat. The position was consciously modeled after that of the "presidential envoy" in Frankfurt, who had acted only on orders from the Ballplatz. Ostensibly it was destined for Savigny, Berlin's last envoy in the diet. Through the power to instruct the chancellor and Prussian delegates Bismarck would have had, as foreign minister, the decisive voice in the affairs of a government in which he held no official post. Camouflaged by the Bundesrat, he would have presented the least possible target for the attacks of opposition deputies in the Reichstag.

But could he have escaped the restraint of his own colleagues in the Prussian cabinet? During the constitutional conflict they had repeatedly opposed him on domestic issues—sometimes with success. Most recently their opposition on the indemnity bill had excited his wrath and scorn.[8] Like the minister of war, the foreign minister had direct access to the king and was an exception to the collegial rule. But once he commenced to handle internal matters such as finance, commerce, and the like, friction with other ministers

---

[7] GW, VI, 168–169.
[8] Becker, Bismarcks Ringen, 243.

was certain. To assist in coordinating the affairs of Prussia and the confederation, Bismarck planned to appoint high officials (below the ministerial level) as Prussian delegates to the Bundesrat, where they were to head the "different branches" of confederate administration. But obviously this would have created conflicting loyalties. Bismarck admitted to the constituent Reichstag that he would not be able to ignore the wishes of the other cabinet members on matters of confederate policy. In cases of disagreement he would either have to concede or seek new colleagues.[9] Neither choice was attractive.

There are indications that from the beginning Bismarck secretly intended to assume the chancellorship and create under that office an executive organ capable of overshadowing his colleagues in the Prussian cabinet. His substitution of the more exalted title "chancellor" for "presidential envoy" is suspicious. Certainly he did not intend this as a favor to Savigny. In fact, he looked upon this diplomat as a talented, ambitious man with dangerously good connections at court. During October he became alarmed over what his old friend "Charles" wanted to make out of the chancellorship on his own account. He suspected him of intending to demand the right of immediate access to the king. This surmise was enough to put an end, we may be sure, to whatever chance Savigny may still have had of becoming chancellor.[10]

Other signs indicate that Bismarck expected the development on the confederate level of a fairly extensive administrative apparatus. His draft assumed the existence of officials to perform the functions and wield the powers of the presidency in the administration of customs, indirect taxes, the post and telegraph systems, and the regulation of railways. It was not difficult to foresee that use by the Reichstag and Bundesrat of confederate legislative power would soon create the need for numerous officials dealing with other matters. How was this civil service to be organized, and who was to direct it? Upon this subject the draft was suspiciously silent. Passages in his October 30, 1866, "dictation" to Keudell show that he expected the appearance of confederate "ministries" and foresaw the evolution of the Bundesrat into a purely legislative "upper house" chosen by the state governments in ratio to their populations. By "ministries" Bismarck actually meant "departments," for he intended them to develop, as they ultimately did, under his own direct authority as chancellor.[11]

But if this was his intention, why did he not openly say so? Like all that came from his pen, the constitutional draft was a diplomatic document. To have made clear his ultimate purpose would have excited the suspicion and

[9] GW, X, 351–353.

[10] Becker, Bismarcks Ringen, 236ff., 257–264, 274–276, 361–362.

[11] Ibid., 241–242, 255–256, 270–271 (n. 28); GW, VI, 167–169. See also his remarks to Grand Duke Friedrich of Baden in 1870 about the necessity of "simplifying the mechanism for handling affairs in the uppermost regions." Hermann Oncken, ed., Grossherzog Friedrich I. von Baden und die deutsche Politik von 1854–1871 (Stuttgart, 1927), vol. 2, 234.

jealousy of fellow ministers and created a dangerous and time-consuming quarrel within the cabinet. So centralistic a feature, moreover, would have increased the difficulties of gaining the approval of the governments of the medium states, particularly those in the south, which were as yet outside the confederation. For these reasons it was prudent to conceal his aim until the time came for its achievement.[12] To progress by stages, attempting at any one stage only what circumstances would allow, while leaving open the avenue toward the next, was typical of his political procedure.

As in the Schleswig-Holstein and German questions, each preliminary stage was a potential halting place, if the higher one should be unachievable. Had the construction of an independent confederate executive proved impossible, the chancellorship could have been left to a subordinate and its "business" (a word carefully chosen for ambiguity) restricted to presiding over the Bundesrat. In this event his personal force and political capacity would have sufficed to make of the Prussian Foreign Ministry the dominant organ in the constitutional structures of both Prussia and the confederation.[13]

Yet the most secure lever of power was neither the chancellorship nor the Prussian Foreign Ministry alone, but the two in conjunction with each other. That Bismarck later relinquished for a time the minister-presidency shows that he believed this position—inaccurately as it proved—less important than the other two. Only by linking these positions of control was it possible to hold on to the many arms of the balance. Together they provided him with the pivotal point from which were possible the many alternative combinations that were his constant quest in the uncertain game of politics. In possession of them he had some hope of avoiding in the future the kind of head-on clash with parliament that he had experienced during the last four years.

King and Cabinet

Bismarck's virtuosity as a political tactician was never more brilliantly demonstrated than in the process by which he obtained the adoption, without crippling amendments, of his constitutional draft as the basic law of the North German Confederation, ultimately the German Reich. Each of the political forces that he intended to harness to the common chariot through the constitution had a voice in its adoption: the Prussian cabinet, the dynasties and governments of the free cities, the nation (represented by the constituent Reichstag), and the Prussian Landtag. None desired the solution he devised. Using the familiar technique, he proceeded by stages, nullifying each force in turn by the strategy of balanced alternatives. Every attempt to alter the fundamental arrangements of his plan was countered by evoking the opposing

[12] Becker, *Bismarcks Ringen*, 273–274.
[13] *Ibid.*, 276–277.

interest that stood to lose by the change. Again he occupied that strategic middle position between conflicting forces that enabled him to exploit their mutual rivalry. The first obstacles thus surmounted were the king and cabinet.

Bismarck's illness in October–November 1866 was a misfortune from which he, as usual, knew how to squeeze an advantage. It removed him from Berlin and Wilhelm's presence at a critical moment, but at the same time placed him conveniently out of reach of the ministers and Savigny, freeing him from the necessity of dealing with their views. In the seclusion of Putbus he made his decisions, and between December 1 and 8 he completed the draft in Berlin. On the ninth the king, crown prince, and ministers saw it for the first time. They had but five days to consider and amend it (two of which were taken up by a royal hunt) before its presentation on the fifteenth to a council of ministers representing the states.

In so brief an interval nobody was able to grasp the real meaning of this document, with its complicated relationships, or to penetrate the hidden purposes of its author. Undoubtedly Bismarck stressed the features that most appealed to their conservative hearts: the hegemonic authority of the presidency and the commander-in-chief, the limited power of the Reichstag in military and financial matters, and the safeguards against repetition of the constitutional conflict. To increase the prerogatives of Prussia, as the king and other ministers wished, or to accentuate the unitary element, as the crown prince desired, would simply make it more difficult for the lesser dynasties and free cities to accept the plan. Bismarck's arguments and the haste with which the matter was considered sufficed to prevent anything more than peripheral amendments.[14] The fundamental structure of the original draft remained unaltered.

The Council of Ministers

Even in the midst of war the first steps had been taken to bind the states of northern Germany to Prussia. An ultimatum on June 16, 1866, compelled nineteen petty principalities and free cities to ally with her, place their military forces under her command, and agree to a "new, more vital union." On August 4 Prussia demanded that they agree to cooperate with a popularly elected parliament in drafting a federal constitution.[15] By August 18, fifteen had signed. The last, Meiningen, capitulated on October 8 under the duress of Prussian occupation. The two enemy states of the north that escaped annexation, Hesse-Darmstadt and Saxony, were incorporated in the confederation through their peace treaties, September 3 and October 21.

Prussia was the victor and the lesser states were compelled to yield. Nev-

---

[14] See *ibid.*, 284–289 and the footnotes in GW, VI, 187–196.
[15] GW, VI, 1–3, 29–30.

ertheless, they were not utterly powerless to resist the terms of the constitution or to effect its amendment. In the south the remaining medium states were watching the fate of Prussia's new "allies," particularly Saxony, for clues to their own future. Furthermore, Bismarck wished to preserve the states as a vital political force. He needed their support against the demands of the liberal parties in the constituent Reichstag. Thereafter they were to be one of the important weights in the constitutional equilibrium.

The potential leader of the dynastic opposition was Saxony, after Prussia the largest in land, population, and wealth. At Nikolsburg Austria had insisted on the maintenance of Saxony's territorial integrity as a condition of peace. Frustrated in his lust for annexation, Wilhelm was determined to insist upon military terms that would have ended the existence of the Saxon army. When the venerable King Johann resisted Prussia's threats and was supported by France, Bismarck moderated his terms to allow for a Saxon contingent under Prussian command. At this point Bismarck fell ill and withdrew from the negotiation. In October he was "depressed" by the news that Wilhelm, unwilling to accept even this concession, had permitted a peace treaty to be signed that left to a later date the settlement of the military question. Bismarck recognized instantly that Saxony would be able to use Prussia's need of a military convention as a lever with which to attempt constitutional amendments favorable to her interests and damaging to his basic constitutional plan.[16]

On receiving the Prussian draft (December 15), the members of the council of ministers were shocked. It had the appearance of a makeshift plan, a bundle of expedients, without the unity and harmony of a basic conception. Saxony, Hesse, and Braunschweig were alarmed because of its inroads into their military sovereignty, the feudal Mecklenburgs because of the powers granted a popularly elected Reichstag, Hamburg because of the loss of its commercial independence, Lübeck and the petty states because of the heavy financial burden assessed by population rather than wealth. Some Thuringian princes considered abdication and cession of their lands to Prussia. The nationalistic rulers of Oldenburg, Weimar, and Coburg, on the other hand, objected to the Prussian-hegemonic features. Only Bremen, a stronghold of the Nationalverein, and tiny Meiningen, now ruled by a pro-Prussian prince, were relatively satisfied.[17]

Although their motives were disparate, the opposition soon found common ground in the counterproposals of Oldenburg for a hereditary Kaiser, house of princes, and confederate cabinet. Thirteen states were attracted to the plan in the belief that it would weaken Prussia's voice in the confederation and

---

[16] Becker, Bismarcks Ringen, 201–210. See also Fritz Dickmann, Militärpolitische Beziehungen zwischen Preussen und Sachsen, 1866–1870 (Munich, 1929), 12ff.

[17] Becker, Bismarcks Ringen, 292ff.

provide a more effective barrier to the ambitions of the Reichstag. The proposal was a serious threat to Bismarck's whole constitutional scheme. It endangered the duality of Prussia and the confederation. By displacing the Bundesrat, it would have destroyed the finely calculated system of control in the
hands of the Prussian foreign minister. The substitution of "Kaiser" for "presidency" would at this point have given Napoleon obvious grounds to challenge the sincerity of the Prussian commitment to stop at the Main. Such
centralistic features, moreover, were unacceptable to the Prussian cabinet and
would have made more difficult the ultimate adherence of the south.[18]

But Bismarck divided the opposition and quelled the incipient revolt. Delaying the sessions of the council, he won time to conduct private negotiations with individual states. The petty princes were conceded the right to
apply the financial burden of the "iron budget" gradually over a period of
seven years. Bremen was encouraged with financial concessions and a strip of
Hanoverian soil. The Mecklenburgs were led on by the prospect of financial
and military concessions. Hesse was teased with the hope of a special status
for that half of its army that lay inside the confederation. Hamburg was frightened into silence by a harsh note and a heavy barrage from the government
press. But the most serious task was Saxony. Kings Johann and Wilhelm, and
their generals as well, were obstinate about their prerogatives. Finally Bismarck hammered out an agreement under which the Saxon king was left the
right to nominate, the Hohenzoller to appoint, the commander of the Saxon
contingent. For eight years, moreover, the confederation was to compensate
Saxony for the loss of its postal revenues.[19]

Bismarck's most effective weapon, however, was the threat of the approaching Reichstag. Its election had been set for February 12, 1867. The
ministers deliberated with the knowledge that by that date they must reach
agreement with Prussia or suffer the consequences. During the electoral campaign in January, Bismarck ordered Prussian officials, to whom all-out support
of conservative candidates had become a habit, not to oppose the election of
moderate liberals. Without them the Reichstag would not exert "sufficient
pressure against recalcitrant governments."[20]

If abandoned by her "allies," Bismarck warned, Prussia would turn to the
revolutionary forces of liberal nationalism. He was no friend of liberal doctrine, he told the Saxon envoy, and his actual aim was "to overthrow parliamentarianism with parliamentarianism." He preferred to establish the confederation in collaboration with the dynasties. But if they failed to support him,
he would without qualm or hesitation unite with the radical liberals and establish a constitution in accord with their views. "Yes!" he said repeatedly,

[18] GW, VIb, 214–216; Becker, *Bismarcks Ringen*, 320.
[19] Becker, *Bismarcks Ringen*, 326ff.; Dickmann, *Militärpolitische Beziehungen*, 55ff.
[20] GW, VI, 237–238.

"*Flectere si nequeo superos, Acheronta movebo.*"[21] Should the attempt miscarry, he warned Oldenburg, Prussia would have no other recourse than the "currents of the national movement and the combinations of European politics."[22]

His divisive tactics prevented the ministers from making a concerted attack upon the Prussian draft, and his threat of a revolutionary alternative kept them from rejecting it outright. The amendments[23] they achieved were those Bismarck was willing to accept because they did not alter the basic structure of his system. As was to be expected, many were intended to build up the power of the Bundesrat at the expense of the presidency, the commander-in-chief, and the Reichstag. Its approval was now required before the presidency might bring bills before the Reichstag. Should the commander-in-chief exercise his power of "execution" against a member of the confederation, the Bundesrat was to be informed without delay of the grounds for the action. Two of its committees were given consultative power in connection with the right of the presidency to appoint consuls and to oversee the collection of confederate revenues. All treaties affecting matters within the legislative competence of parliament had to be approved by the Bundesrat.

On the insistence of Baron Friesen, the Saxon delegate, the scattered clauses dealing with financial matters were assembled in a single section.[24] A new article was inserted providing for legislative enactment of a three-year budget covering all expenditures except those of the armed forces. Expenditures for all purposes in excess of income from tax revenue were to be covered by assessments (*Matrikularbeiträge*) levied by the presidency alone on the states. The presidency was charged with the necessity of transmitting to the Bundesrat and Reichstag, though at no established interval, a statement of confederate expenditures.

The provision for settlement of disputes between states and of constitutional conflicts within states met serious objection. The judicial power of the Bundesrat in the former instance was limited to questions of public law, and it was stipulated that the Bundesrat might enter the case only on the appeal of one of the disputants. That the confederation could by legislative action interfere in the internal disputes of states was too much for the feudal Mecklenburgs and reactionary Hesse to bear. Instead, it was provided that constitutional conflicts could be settled by a competent authority within the state. If none existed, one of the parties might appeal to the Bundesrat. If that

---

[21] GW, VII, 176. See also Helmut Klocke, "Die sächsische Politik und der Norddeutsche Bund," *Neues Archiv für sächsische Geschichte und Altertumskunde*, 48 (1927), 127–129, 135–136.

[22] GW, VI, 251–252. A similar warning was delivered to Hamburg. GW, VI, 211.

[23] The successive drafts completed by the council of ministers and constituent Reichstag are in Karl Binding, ed., *Deutsche Staatsgrundgesetze in diplomatisch genauem Abdrucke* (2d ed., Leipzig, 1901), vol. 5, 75ff. See also Otto von Völlendorff, ed., "Deutsche Verfassungen und Verfassungsentwürfe," *Annalen des deutschen Reichs*, vol. 23, 241–401.

[24] Becker, *Bismarcks Ringen*, 357–358.

procedure were unsuccessful, the case might be settled by confederate legislation. This still left open for Bismarck the possibility of altering the Prussian constitution through the Reichstag and Bundesrat. Such was the meaning of his threat to conquer parliament through parliament.[25]

Despite their fears of the unitary features of the constitution, the ministers saw the wisdom of widening the legislative competence of the confederation. They included insurance, the condition of interstate waterways, the accreditation of public documents, the reciprocal execution of judicial decisions, and the fulfillment of judicial "requisitions." Though still under Prussian command, the navy was renamed the "confederate navy." Although Wilhelm was adamant in refusing any major concessions in military affairs, other than those granted Saxony, it was agreed that contingent commanders would be permitted to determine uniform insignia. On Wilhelm's insistence, however, the title *Oberfeldherr* was shortened to *Feldherr* to emphasize the point that there was but one commander on the level of the confederation.[26]

Bismarck's difficulties were not limited to the states alone. The Prussian ministers had had some weeks to consider the document they so hurriedly ratified in December. They were alarmed over its invasion of Prussian sovereignty and its potential infringement of their own authority. This was useful to Bismarck in convincing the lesser states that is was impossible to get the cabinet to accept further amendments of a unitary character. But the reverse was also true. The impressive show of opposition in the council enabled him to insist that the states must be appeased by the cabinet on less vital issues. In some cases this enabled him to push through the cabinet changes that he himself evidently desired.[27] One such amendment concerned the chancellorship.

Throughout the sessions of the council Bismarck had evaded all efforts to clarify the status of this office. Defeated in the attempt to create a confederate cabinet, the Hessian Minister Karl von Hofmann had proposed that ordinances issued by the presidency for the execution of confederate laws bear the "countersignature of the confederate chancellor." Such a signature implied assumption of responsibility for the measure concerned. If the chancellor, in other words, was not to be a minister, he at least should have an attribute of one. In conference with Hofmann, Bismarck apparently substituted for *Kontrasignatur* the verb *mitunterzeichnen*. The original had the effect of exalting the chancellorship in relationship to the Prussian cabinet, including the foreign minister. But the substitution enabled him as foreign minister to assume the right of cosignature with the chancellor. If unable to assume that office, he could at least keep its incumbent in check. Savigny had begun to suspect

[25] *Ibid.*, 367–368; Klocke, "Die sächsische Politik," 138–140.
[26] Becker, *Bismarcks Ringen*, 356ff.
[27] *Ibid.*, 348.

the truth. "Bismarck is wrapped in silence. Apparently he wishes himself to be confederate chancellor"[28]

Only Bremen was satisfied with the final draft achieved on February 7, 1867. The more resolute ministers were disheartened by the general scramble, particularly on the part of Saxony, for special concessions. Everyone resented the heavy hand of Savigny, who presided over the body for Prussia. In drawing up the protocol that announced the results of their secret deliberations, the ministers angrily struck out the statement that the draft had been "agreed upon," substituting the phrase "definitively established."[29] But Bismarck was never one to quarrel over phrases when he had secured the substance of what he wanted.

The Constituent Reichstag

On February 12, 1867, the voters of northern Germany went to the polls to elect the constituent Reichstag. Popular interest was high, and in many districts over 70 percent of the eligible voted; in some the percentage was over 90. The results seemed to confirm Bismarck's confidence in the masses. Almost half of the 297 deputies chosen were noblemen and most of the rest were men of means. Among the former were 1 royal prince, 4 nonroyal princes, 2 dukes, 27 counts, and 21 barons. The election of several high officers, including Roon and Moltke, testified to the lingering halo of victory. Bismarck was chosen in two constituencies, one of them with the aid of Schweitzer's socialists. Conservatives conquered 59 seats, free conservatives 39, and old-liberals 27. The National Liberal party was largest with 79 members; the progressives were but 19. The remaining seats were shared by splinter parties, some of which—Danes, Poles, ultramontanists, Schleswig-Holsteiners, and Hanoverian particularists—were bitterly opposed to the new confederation.[30]

Despite the rebellion of the previous summer the conservatives could be depended upon to support the draft against liberal amendments. By February 1867 many had found solace in the fact that the new confederation meant an expansion in Prussian power. Again their Prussian pride triumphed over their sense of legitimist right. The free conservatives and old-liberals were unconditional supporters of Bismarckian policy. On the opposite side of the chamber the progressives were equally adamant in opposition. They decried the general willingness to sacrifice liberty for unity, insisted on full budget rights for the Reichstag, and demanded a cabinet of responsible ministers. Between these extremes the national liberals held the decisive position. By participat-

---

[28] Ibid., 359–363.

[29] Ibid., 349–354. For the protocol see Ludwig Aegidi and Alfred Klauhold, eds., Das Staatsarchiv: Sammlung der officiellen Aktenstücke zur Geschichte der Gegenwart, vol. 12 (1867), 359–366.

[30] Becker, Bismarcks Ringen, 371–372; Fritz Specht, Die Reichstags-Wahlen von 1867 bis 1897 (Berlin, 1898), 104.

ing in the work of national unification, they hoped to influence its political structure. They were out to see how far they could go in adding liberal features to the draft without endangering its acceptance by Bismarck and the state governments.[31]

In one hand Bismarck held a carrot; in the other, a stick. Although pleased by the victory of the moderate liberals, for the effect it would have on the governments, he now mobilized the latter to prevent the Reichstag from upsetting the basic features of his draft. The states were asked to defend jointly with Prussia what they had so reluctantly "established." On the floor of the Reichstag, places were prepared for more than forty "commissars," who were "to present a common front of the allied governments toward the Reichstag." But the states were averse to participating in this comedy. "For us," Bismarck warned Dresden, "there are always these alternatives: either to count completely and forever upon the governments now temporarily allied with us or to face the necessity of seeking our center of gravity in parliament." In the latter case Prussia's conduct in parliament would have to assume a "more German-national character." Saxony, he said, was playing a "dangerous game." Confronted with these threats, King Johann and his ministers capitulated, and after Saxony the other states.[32]

But Bismarck also had to be prepared for the possibility that the Reichstag, despite the impressive array of commissars, might insist upon amendments unacceptable to him. On February 19 he invited the governments of Saxony, Darmstadt, Weimar, Oldenburg, and the two Mecklenburgs to appoint plenipotentiaries empowered to negotiate a secret treaty providing that in such a situation the governments would dissolve the Reichstag and decree their own version of the constitution. When friction with parliament increased in late March, he summoned the governments to sign the prepared text. As the conflict reached a dangerous climax during the second week of April, he secured the necessary ratifications. In this way he used the objections of the Reichstag liberals to force the governments to drop their reservations with regard to the draft of February 7. But he also got them to accept through the treaty some of the liberal amendments that he himself desired or found harmless.[33] Rare was the ill wind that failed to blow Bismarck some good.

In the constituent Reichstag, whose debates began on March 4, he made the deputies in turn feel the pressure of the allied governments. His first

---

[31] Becker, *Bismarcks Ringen*, 373–375; Gerhard Ritter, *Die preussischen Konservativen und Bismarcks deutsche Politik, 1858–1875* (Heidelberg, 1913), 204ff.; Hermann Oncken, *Rudolf von Bennigsen* (Stuttgart, 1910), vol. 2, 13.

[32] GW, VI, 273–274, 289–290; Becker, *Bismarcks Ringen*, 383.

[33] GW, VI, 272–273, 312–315; Becker, *Bismarcks Ringen*, 384–387, 445. The text of the treaty is in Egmont Zechlin, *Staatsstreichpläne Bismarcks und Wilhelms II, 1890–1894* (Stuttgart, 1929), 175–176. Prussia, Saxony, Hesse, and Saxe-Weimar signed the agreement on Mar. 31 and ratified it on Apr. 9 and 11; the two Mecklenburgs, on Apr. 9 and 14.

speech pointed out that the Reichstag (like the council of ministers) must work under a deadline. The treaties of alliance that obligated the states to consider the constitution were scheduled to expire on August 18, 1867. Since the treaties also reserved to the states the right of final approval, the Reichstag must finish its work in time for them to deliberate upon the amended draft. Hence the deputies must make haste, avoid acrimony, and steer clear of amendments unacceptable to the governments. Although the agreement of February 7 remained secret, the deputies were given reason to suspect its existence. In his opening address on February 24, Wilhelm spoke of the "grave responsibility" of the deputies for the "peaceful and lawful execution" of the projected union.[34]

Naturally one of the major objectives of the liberals was to strengthen the unitary and national aspect of the draft by extending the legislative competence of the confederation at the cost of the states. Amendments were passed giving the confederation power to legislate on citizenship, passports, the regulation of aliens, army and navy affairs, the enforcement of medical and veterinary standards, certain aspects of transportation, judicial procedure, and corporation and criminal law. Another new clause empowered parliament to authorize credits and financial guarantees for the confederation.[35]

None of these amendments aroused serious conflict. Apparently Bismarck had deliberately limited the legislative power of the confederate government in order to ease the passage of his draft through the cabinet and council. His positive attitude on the subject of *Kompetenz-Kompetenz* (as it was later called) shows, furthermore, that he anticipated and approved the future growth of central legislative authority. During the debates he took the view that Bundesrat and Reichstag possessed the competence to extend their own competence. Their right of constitutional amendment carried with it the right to increase the range of their own legislative power.[36]

The most centralistic of the amendments offered by the liberals aimed at the creation of an independent executive. Both the progressives and national liberals desired to remove the obscurity that enveloped the executive features of the draft. Waldeck confessed that his goal was a unitary state, headed by a "constitutionally responsible cabinet." Though accepting the federal system, the moderates desired a confederate cabinet whose responsibility would be "regulated" in a future law. In answer to the charges of the conservatives, both factions defined "responsibility" as legal rather than political. Their aim

[34] SBR, I (1867), ii, 41–42.

[35] The amendments introduced by the constituent Reichstag and accepted by the governments are italicized in J. C. Glaser, ed., *Archiv des Norddeutschen Bundes* (Berlin, 1867), vol. 3, 23–38. For the proposed amendments see *ibid.*, vol. 4, 30–115. The official version of the completed constitution may be found in *Bundes-Gesetzblatt des Norddeutschen Bundes* (1867), 1–23.

[36] SBR, I (1867), 316ff., 324; Becker, *Bismarcks Ringen*, 435ff.

was not parliamentary government, but realization of a *Rechtsstaat*, the venerable dream of the moderates, a government of laws rather than men.[37]

Certainly "responsibility" in this form was no hindrance to autocratic government. A similar provision in the Prussian constitution had had no effect upon the recent conflict. No regulatory law had ever been passed, so there was no way to bring ministers to account for illegal actions in Prussia. What Bismarck objected to was not the idea itself, but one of the features of the amendment introduced by Bennigsen and the national liberals. By providing that the "heads of administrative branches," as well as the chancellor, might countersign the "orders and ordinances" of the presidency in execution of confederate laws, "thereby assuming the responsibility," the amendment opened up the prospect of a collegial executive like the Prussian cabinet. Bismarck found this intolerable, for the independence of the Prussian ministers had hampered execution of his domestic policies during the constitutional conflict. Hence he informed the liberals that Bennigsen's amendment was unacceptable to the governments. The liberals capitulated. The final version gave the chancellor the sole right of countersignature bearing a responsibility undivided and undefined. This Bismarck did not oppose, which raises the suspicion that it conformed to his hidden aim of becoming chancellor.[38]

Other amendments had the purpose of strengthening the Reichstag and the principle of parliamentary immunity. No one could be prosecuted for repeating or reprinting a true report of the public proceedings of the Reichstag. During a legislative session, members might not be imprisoned or prosecuted without the Reichstag's consent. Officials were no longer prohibited from election to the chamber. In order to deter the corruption of deputies by the government, it was provided that, on the acceptance of a state office or of a promotion in the bureaucracy, a deputy must resign and seek reelection. In the event of dissolution an election must be held within sixty days, and the new Reichstag must convene within ninety. Without approval from the Reichstag the presidency could prorogue that body for only one period of thirty days in each session. Petitions directed to the Reichstag could be forwarded to the Bundesrat and presidency. Treaties involving matters within the legislative competence of the confederation must be ratified by the Reichstag.

These amendments removed some basic deficiencies in the Bismarck draft and gave the Reichstag many essential attributes of a modern parliamentary body. Two other amendments tampered with conservative safeguards in the election laws. Although opposed to universal suffrage, the national liberals dared not say so publicly. By adding the secret ballot, they hoped to prevent

---

[37] SBR, I (1867), 331ff., 359ff., 374ff., 383ff.

[38] Becker, *Bismarcks Ringen*, 388ff. Becker believed Bismarck may have been in collusion with the old-liberal deputy, Carl von Sänger, who proposed the version of the amendment finally accepted under Bennigsen's name. *Ibid.*, 391.

its exploitation for dictatorial ends in the style of Louis Napoleon.[39] This Bismarck accepted. But he firmly rejected their request for the remuneration of deputies. In his view prohibition of per diem payments was necessary to reduce the dangers of universal suffrage. Only the well-to-do (noblemen, landowners, merchants, and industrialists) could afford to serve. The press of their personal affairs would insure short sessions, and their interests would presumably be more economic than political. He wished to prevent the appearance of professional politicians, who, being dependent upon parliament for livelihood, would have a selfish concern for the extension of its powers. When the vote came on March 30, 1867, he declared that under "no circumstances" would the governments accept the amendment. But it passed by a slim majority of six.[40]

Naturally the liberals subjected the articles dealing with parliament's financial powers to close scrutiny. The clause limiting the confederation to indirect taxes was stricken from the draft. An amendment provided that all revenues and expenditures of the confederation must be established annually "before the beginning of the budget year." Another change permitted the levying of state assessments only until parliament should provide the needed revenue. The amount levied, moreover, was restricted to that established in the budget. Surpluses might not accumulate, but must be used to defray current expenses of the confederation. These amendments plugged serious holes in the financial power of the Reichstag. There remained, nevertheless, the yawning chasm of the iron budget.

As long as the peacetime strength of the army and the amount of its financial support were fixed constitutionally in ratio to population, the budget rights of parliament were fictional. The power lost by the Chamber of Deputies with the transfer of the military budget from Prussia to the confederation would accrue not to the Reichstag but to the crown. Unwilling to accept such a retreat, the progressives and national liberals disagreed on what was to be demanded. The former wanted the right to determine yearly the strength of the army through the budget, but the latter, vitally impressed by recent victories, were willing to accept the iron budget until 1870, when it would be subject to legislative approval for an additional period of years. Even this was unacceptable to Wilhelm and his generals.[41]

The iron budget was the climactic issue that in early April threatened the whole constitutional settlement. In precarious negotiations behind the scenes, Bismarck arrived at a compromise with the national liberals. The peacetime size of the army was fixed at one percent of the population until

[39] Ibid., 437.

[40] SBR, I (1867), 474ff.; Becker, Bismarcks Ringen, 441–442. To make it more difficult for journalists to engage in political careers, Bismarck wanted to locate parliament in a provincial city distant from Berlin. Becker, Bismarcks Ringen, 565.

[41] Becker, Bismarcks Ringen, 439–441.

December 31, 1871. Thereafter the ratio would be subject to legislation. The army's financial support was fixed at 225 thalers per soldier until the same date, but with the additional proviso that the states must continue thereafter to provide money at the same rate until the army's size should be changed by law. It was further stipulated that parliament could not use its power to approve military appropriations (after 1871) to alter the organization of the army as established under the constitution.

From the standpoint of popular liberties the north German constitution represented a retreat from the Prussian. One of the final actions of the constituent Reichstag was to vote down a progressive motion to incorporate the Prussian bill of rights.[42] Bismarck's constitution was the first in the history of European constitutionalism not to include such a bill. Although the grant of control over revenues as well as expenditures was an advance, this concession was largely robbed of significance by the exclusion of the military budget. Only by challenging the constitution itself could the opposition attack the basic structure of the army. For this reason Bismarck judged that the government need not fear renewal of the constitutional conflict in 1871.[43] Even so, the final compromise contained yet another sacrifice for the liberals. They were compelled to surrender the amendment providing for remuneration of deputies.[44]

On April 16 the Reichstag accepted, 230 to 53, the amended constitution. In the negative was the remnant of the progressives, led by Waldeck and Schulze-Delitzsch, supported by the Polish and Catholic factions and the chamber's only socialist, August Bebel. On May 31 the Prussian Landtag likewise accepted it, 227 to 93, with the same determined group in the minority. Democratic liberals clung valiantly to the position they had defended since 1861. Without secure budget rights, a judicially responsible cabinet, remuneration of deputies, and a bill of rights, they could not come to terms with the Hohenzollern monarchy. Obstinately they rejected the argument of the moderates that what was sacrificed today might be regained in the parliamentary battles of tomorrow. Unity they refused at the cost of freedom. From the start, however, their cause was doomed. Had they carried the day, Bismarck would have promulgated the North German constitution even without their approval. If necessary, he would have "thrown the entire Prussian constitution overboard."[45] Unity over freedom and power over law—this was the constellation under which the German Reich was born.

[42] SBR, I (1867), 726.

[43] GW, VIb, 217–218.

[44] Becker, Bismarcks Ringen, 448ff.

[45] SBR, I (1867), 729; SBHA (1867), 167–186. Klocke, "Die sächsische Politik," 132–134, 139. Typically Becker justified Bismarck's intention on the grounds that it stemmed from a national rather than a reactionary purpose. Bismarcks Ringen, 368.

The Dualism of Political and Military Authority

The institutional arrangements that Bismarck designed for Germany contained yet another vital deficiency of which the deputies in the constituent Reichstag were hardly conscious. No barrier was provided against the future growth of an unfortunate dualism in political and military authority.

We have seen that during the constitutional conflict one of the major objectives of Edwin Manteuffel was to depreciate the authority of the minister of war, who was subject to interpellation by parliament, and to exalt that of the military cabinet, which was beyond the range of parliamentary attack. In pursuit of this objective he naturally came into conflict with Roon. The minister of war objected sharply to the attempt of the adjutant general to withhold from his cognizance not only Wilhelm's orders to his commanding generals, but even information on such matters as the selection and promotion of officers that Manteuffel handled as head of the personnel division of the Ministry of War. Both Roon and Bismarck, furthermore, were angered by Manteuffel's success in getting Wilhelm to reject the compromise of 1865,[46] which might have ended the constitutional conflict. Soon afterward they insisted that he was the only person who could be entrusted with the delicate task of governing Schleswig. The "fanatic corporal" was removed from Berlin.[47]

The issue, however, was personal, not constitutional. The absolutistic authority of the Hohenzollern crown in military matters, which was the basis of the military cabinet's power, was far greater under the North German than under the Prussian constitution. Being granted to the king of Prussia rather than the presidency, the authority of the confederate commander-in-chief was outside the constitutional sphere of the chancellor. For the same reason there was no confederate ministry of war. The Prussian Ministry of War assumed the routine functions of confederate military administration, but the military cabinet was the agency that assisted the king in the exercise of his new powers of appointment, promotion, supervision, and command in the confederate army. Even without intrigue on the part of Manteuffel's successor, Hermann von Tresckow, its emancipation from the control of the Prussian ministry proceeded with "giant steps" after 1867.[48]

With the rise of Helmuth von Moltke, yet another military agency, the

---

[46] See pp. 182–183, 277.

[47] Gordon A. Craig, *The Politics of the Prussian Army, 1640–1945* (Oxford, 1955), 172–173; Rudolf Schmidt-Bückeburg, *Das Militärkabinett der preussischen Könige und des deutschen Kaisers* (Berlin, 1933), 84ff.; Heinrich O. Meisner, *Der Kriegsminister, 1815–1914* (Berlin 1940), 21ff.; Bismarck's feud with Manteuffel went back to 1857, when the general in effect ordered him out of Berlin and back to Frankfurt in order to keep him from influencing Friedrich Wilhelm IV. Wilhelm Gradmann, *Die politischen Ideen Edwin von Manteuffels und ihre Auswirkungen in seiner Laufbahn* (Düsseldorf, 1932), 79–80.

[48] Schmidt-Bückeburg, *Militärkabinett*, 96ff.

Prussian general staff, began its escape from the same orbit. Charged with war planning, the general staff was until the 1860s one of the subordinate depart-ments of the Prussian Ministry of War. When the Danish War commenced, Moltke, its chief since 1857, had no direct contact with or authority over Wrangel, the field commander. But he finished the war as chief of staff to Wrangel's successor, Prince Friedrich Karl, and was generally recognized as the architect of victory. Later he participated in the crucial crown councils that led to war against Austria. A few days before the outbreak of war (June 2, 1866) a royal order provided for the communication of commands directly from the general staff to the troops, rather than through the Ministry of War. When peace came, the general staff again became subordinate to the minis-try. Nevertheless, the first step had been taken that would one day lead to its liberation from all ministerial authority.[49]

Behind the scenes two military agencies were quietly gathering in the reins of power left dangling under the Prussian and north German constitutions. Both were beyond the reach of the Landtag and Reichstag. Their chiefs were to be immediate to the king and independent of the civil executive, whether chancellor or minister-president. As long as Bismarck was in office they too failed in the effort to usurp the political function. But even the Titan finally fell from Olympus.

[49] Craig, *Prussian Army*, 193ff.; Meisner, *Kriegsminister*, 47ff.

BOOK FOUR

The Years of Fulfillment,

1867–1871

Bismarck is the one man who can juggle with five balls,
of which at least two are always in the air.

—*Wilhelm I*

I was convinced that the gulf which in the course
of history had opened between north and south in our country,
because of differences in ways of life and dynastic and
tribal loyalties, could not be more effectively
bridged than through a common national war
against the traditionally aggressive neighbor.

—*Bismarck in Gedanken
und Erinnerungen*

✠

CHAPTER SIXTEEN

Bridges over the Main

The Military Alliances

TO MANY German nationalists the peace settlement with Austria was a keen disappointment. The triumph of Königgrätz had reconciled them to the idea of a national union under conservative leadership. But now they read in Article 2 of the preliminary peace signed at Nikolsburg on July 26, 1866, that Germany was to be divided into two spheres along the river Main. The south, like the north, was to be allowed to federate. The "national bond" between them was to be the subject of a "closer understanding." The settlement appeared to create for Germany a new dualism, which would again frustrate the demand for national self-determination.[1]

The reasons for this decision have long been a subject of quandary and dispute. Nationalistic writers have found it difficult to believe that Bismarck willingly accepted such a limitation upon German unity. The original Prussian reform plan, it is pointed out, included the whole of small-Germany. One view has it that the "outline" of June 10 was sheer propaganda, another that the halt at the Main was dictated by the danger of French intervention. Otto Becker even maintained that the Main line was "created" by the refusal of German liberals to cooperate in summoning the "preparliament" proposed to them by Bismarck through Eulenburg. In the crown council of February 26, however, King Wilhelm had already given as Prussia's objective the establishment of a "decisive political preponderance" in northern Germany.[2]

Certainly a major reason for this limitation was diplomatic. From the beginning Napoleon's encouragement of Prussian expansion had been restricted to the region north of the Main. For all his talk of national self-determination as a general principle for the reorganization of Europe, Napoleon was enough of a realist to appreciate that the unification of Germany would produce on the French frontier a powerful competitor. Bismarck, the soul of realism, understood full well that, if his policy toward France was to be successful, it must

[1] Otto Scheel, *Bismarcks Wille zu Deutschland in den Friedensschlüssen 1866: Veröffentlichungen der Schleswig-Holsteinischen Universitätsgesellschaft*, vol. 44 (Breslau, 1934), 1–7, 76. For the text of the treaty see Ludwig Aegidi and Alfred Klauhold, eds., *Das Staatsarchiv: Sammlung der officiellen Aktenstücke zur Geschichte der Gegenwart*, vol. 11 (1866), 166–168.

[2] Otto Becker, *Bismarcks Ringen um Deutschlands Gestaltung* (Heidelberg, 1958), 180; APP, VI, 613. For a review of the older literature on this controversy see Bruno Gebhardt, *Handbuch der deutschen Geschichte* (7th ed., Stuttgart, 1931), vol. 2, 415–416.

be based on the premise that the Main frontier was for Napoleon a vital interest. In Paris he had constantly reiterated that hegemony over northern Germany was Prussia's sole ambition.[3] France's claim for compensation went begging, so the Main frontier was the one visible success of Napoleon's efforts in 1866.

But France was not the only reason for the halt at the Main. In years past Bismarck had regarded northern Germany as the natural area of Prussian domination because of the cultural homogeneity of its population. He had argued against German unification in 1848 on the grounds that southern lassitude would corrupt Prussian virtues of industry and discipline.[4] From Frankfurt he wrote to Leopold Gerlach in 1854 that the struggle against ultramontanism was one of his most difficult tasks: "It is not a Christian creed, but a hypocritical, idolatrous papism full of hate and cunning, which conducts an unrelenting struggle with the most infamous weapons against the Protestant governments, and especially against Prussia, the worldly bulwark of the evangelical faith. The struggle goes on in practical affairs from the cabinets of the princes and their ministers to the feather-bed mysteries of the married set. Here in the city and diet, and at nearby courts, 'Catholic' and 'enemy of Prussia' are identical in meaning."[5] With Catholicism, he wrote, there could be no peace short of complete subjugation. Ultramontanes were more dangerous than democrats.[6]

As it did again in the 1870s, Bismarck's suspicion of a Catholic conspiracy clouded his political judgment. Schwarzenberg's "favorite plan," he told Leopold Gerlach, was a coalition of France, Austria, and Russia "to suppress England and Prussia, and with them Protestantism and political freedom, the 'revolution in church and state.' " To counter it he advocated alliances with the Protestant states of northern Europe (England, the Netherlands, Denmark, and Sweden). "Southern Germany is alien to us and the German interest is without foundation." His proposal for a northern league of armed neutrals during the Crimean War had a confessional as well as a political basis.[7]

Despite these cultural differences, the ultimate completion of German unification became a necessity for Bismarck from the moment that war with Austria was certain. Yet this may not be taken as proof of his "will to Germany,"[8] that is, of his German national sentiment. We have seen that Bismarck's

---

[3] GW, V, 436; RKN, I, 329, 344; OD, VIII, 264–266; X, 70–73.

[4] GW, VII, 13; X, 40; Günther Franz, Bismarcks Nationalgefühl (Leipzig, 1926), 77–78.

[5] GW, XIV, 340.

[6] GW, I, 257–258, 265, 393; II, 54; XIV, 544; Franz, Nationalgefühl, 52.

[7] GW, XIV, 405; Leopold von Gerlach, Denkwürdigkeiten (Berlin, 1891), vol. 2, 642; Egmont Zechlin, Bismarck und die Grundlegung der deutschen Grossmacht (Stuttgart, 1930), 137ff. See also GW, I, 503; II, 42; XIV, 335.

[8] See Scheel, Bismarcks Wille.

political thought was primarily concerned with problems of power rather than ideology or sentiment. In German nationalism he had found the moral force with which to expand and buttress the power of the Hohenzollern monarchy against the hazards of European politics and the pressures of social change. Once the path of its exploitation had been taken in 1866, it was obvious that the Main could not be a permanent frontier. The disappointment of German nationalists would have cost the Prussian throne the halo so recently acquired.

Bismarck's decision to accomplish unification in stages was, however, a requirement of German as well as European politics. It arose as much from the continued strength of particularism in Germany as from the danger of French intervention. In July 1866 he wrote that inclusion of the "south-German, Catholic, Bavarian element" would make it impossible for Prussia to consolidate what she had gained. "For a long time" the south would not willingly consent to be ruled from Berlin. To conquer it would simply create a source of weakness, like Naples in united Italy. At Nikolsburg he remarked to Foreign Minister Varnbüler of Württemberg that Munich and Stuttgart could not "now" be digested by Berlin.[9] During the following months the difficulties encountered in integrating Saxony into the North German Confederation confirmed the wisdom of temporarily excluding the southern medium states. Before they could be added, the confederation had to be made a going concern, its institutional relationships firmly established.

After the expulsion of Austria the south was a political vacuum predestined to be filled by the power of France, Prussia, or a resurgent Austria. Even at Nikolsburg the conflict between French and Prussian interests was evident. A clause in Bismarck's treaty draft allowed for a union between the North German Confederation and the southern states on the basis of the "outline" of June 10, 1866, which provided for a national parliament with extensive authority over economic affairs. But Bavaria refused to cooperate, and Napoleon's mediation plan guaranteed the south "an independent international existence." Bismarck tried to evade the issue by deleting both clauses, leaving the matter open. But Napoleon protested, and the French clause was reinserted in the final peace signed at Prague on August 23.[10] If adhered to, it meant that the "national bond" between north and south could be only diplomatic, not constitutional.

[9] GW, VI, 44; Wilhelm Busch, "Bismarck und die Entstehung des Norddeutschen Bundes," Historische Zeitschrift, 103 (1909), 73–74; Ulrich v. Stosch, ed., Denkwürdigkeiten des Generals und Admirals Albrecht v. Stosch (Stuttgart, 1904), 94–95.

[10] Erich Brandenburg, Untersuchungen und Aktenstücke zur Geschichte der Reichsgründung (Leipzig, 1916), 555–556; Wilhelm Schüssler, Bismarcks Kampf um Süddeutschland 1867 (Berlin, 1929), 16ff.; Scheel, Bismarcks Wille, 45ff.; Johannes Petrich, "Der erste preussische Präliminarentwurf in Nikolsburg 1866," Historische Vierteljahrschrift, 30 (1930), 593–599. For the text of Napoleon's proposal, which Goltz helped draft, see GW, VI, 64.

The possibility that French influence might replace Austria's in southern Germany was by no means remote. During the peace negotiations with Prussia in July and August, Dalwigk, Varnbüler, and Pfordten repeatedly turned to Paris for protection against Bismarck's demands. On August 10 Édouard Lefebvre de Béhaine, a French diplomat, was told by Dalwigk that in the event of war with Prussia French troops would be welcome in southern Germany. Their immediate appearance in the Palatinate would encourage resistance to a Prussian invasion.[11] But French policy foundered on its own inconsistency. The wooing of the southern medium states was not compatible with the demand for German soil. In early August Drouyn's request for the frontier of 1814 and the Palatinate helped Bismarck to build his first bridge across the Main.

During the peace negotiations with the southern states, he sought treaties of alliance placing their railways and troops under Prussian command during wartime. For such a price, he indicated, Prussia would relinquish her demand for large annexations and crushing indemnities. The representatives of Baden and Württemberg quickly agreed (August 9–10). Bavaria was more difficult, but Bismarck handled Pfordten with masterly finesse. In their initial interview he presented voracious demands for money and territory without mentioning an alliance. The shocked Pfordten hurried to the French embassy in search of support, but Paris was silent, for Drouyn had just demanded the Bavarian Palatinate. At the next meeting Bismarck stressed the completeness of Bavaria's isolation. Then, having plunged Pfordten to the depths of despair, he sent down a rope: in return for an alliance Prussia's demands would be sharply reduced. Greatly relieved, Pfordten gave his consent.[12]

The three treaties were identical and were labeled "offensive-defensive alliances." Later Bismarck insisted that this designation was purely "technical" and without aggressive intent. The contracting parties mutually guaranteed their respective territories and agreed in the event of war to accept the su-

---

[11] OD, XI, 367–369, 377–379, 386; XII, 35–36, 49, 61–64. Naturally Dalwigk did not record this advice in his diary or in his report to the grand duke. Wilhelm Schüssler, ed., Die Tagebücher des Freiherrn Reinhard von Dalwigk zu Lichtenfels aus den Jahren 1860–71: Deutsche Geschichtsquellen des 19. Jahrhunderts, vol. 2 (Stuttgart, 1920), 248–249, 293. For years the Hessian statesman had looked to France for protection against Prussian imperialism. Until 1870 he actively encouraged French intervention in German affairs. See Walter Vogel, Die Tagebücher des Freiherrn Reinhard von Dalwigk zu Lichtenfels als Geschichtsquelle: Historische Studien, vol. 234 (Berlin, 1933), and Ernst Götz, Die Stellung Hessen-Darmstadts zur deutschen Einigungsfrage in den Jahren 1866–1871 (Darmstadt, 1914), 12ff.

[12] Johannes Petrich, "Die Friedensverhandlungen mit den Süddeutschen 1866," Forschungen zur brandenburgischen und preussischen Geschichte, 46 (1934), 321–351; Gustav Roloff, "Bismarcks Friedensschlüsse mit den Süddeutschen im Jahre 1866," Historische Zeitschrift, 146 (1932), 1–70. In order to offer these terms Bismarck had to overcome Wilhelm's lust for Bavarian territory by threatening to resign. Prussia took only a small strip of land desired for a railway connection. Roloff, "Friedensschlüsse," 62.

preme command of the king of Prussia. For Bismarck the documents were a significant achievement. At the moment of the expiration of the German Confederation he succeeded in creating the strongest bond that had ever existed between northern and southern Germany. It was the fruit of military victory and French rapacity, of southern isolation and the threat of a Draconian peace. He valued it not only for its military reinforcement, but also for the "national basis" it gave for resistance against France.[13]

France Demands Compensation

The cult of the nation requires devils as well as gods. If Bismarck was the Washington of the German revolution, Napoleon was its George III. Americans regarded the British Stamp Act as villainous, and Germans had a similar view of the compensation demands of Napoleon III. And yet it was customary among the great powers of the "European concert" to expect compensation for any major alteration of the balance of power. The territorial expansion of Prussia and the abolition of the German Confederation was such a change, for it meant a fundamental revision of key provisions in the treaty signed by the European states at Vienna in 1815. Furthermore, the European balance of power was a "system" composed of great powers whose interdependent relationships did not allow for isolated solutions to major issues. In the traditional code of diplomatic behavior, the great chancelleries could expect readjustments that would restabilize the equilibrium on a new level. This was particularly true of France, whose interests were unquestionably damaged by the consolidation of the German Reich on her northern frontier.[14]

The reports of Goltz from Paris show that Prussian success in the war against Austria and the progress of German unification produced in Paris an anxiety bordering on panic. Napoleon had already commenced to doubt the tenability of the Main barrier. Prussia's annexation of all the lesser states, he feared, was but a "matter of time."[15] His ministers and advisers reproached him for having encouraged Prussian preponderance in Germany. From the public arose those murmurs of dissatisfaction for which his ear was ever cocked. Emperor and empress, and those dependent upon them for power and influence, were again besieged, as so often in the past, by apprehension over the future of the dynasty. The unification of Germany would mean a fundamental shift in the European balance, which France dared not permit without

[13] GW, VI, 255. For the texts of the treaties see J. C. Glaser, ed., Archiv des Norddeutschen Bundes (Berlin, 1867), vol. 3, 39–42.

[14] See Josef Becker, "Der Krieg mit Frankreich als Problem der klein-deutschen Einigungspolitik Bismarcks 1866–1871," in Michael Stürmer, ed., Das kaiserliche Deutschland 1870–1918 (Düsseldorf, 1970), 75–77. On the systems character of the European balance of power see p. xxix.

[15] OD, XII, 194. Benedetti and Drouyn were of the same conviction. Ibid., 171; RKN, II, 42.

compensation in the form of land, population, and a better military frontier.[16] This was the compulsion behind the demands that the Tuileries now raised for Prussian aid in annexing Belgium and Luxemburg.

In the past Bismarck had given the French reason to expect Prussian approval. Twice during the previous year he had suggested that France seek compensation in French-speaking Europe. According to Benedetti, he specifically mentioned Belgium in the interview of July 26, 1866. On the same occasion, moreover, the only objection he raised to the acquisition of Luxemburg was the difficulty of finding compensation for its ruler, the king of the Netherlands. In rejecting the demands of August 4, Bismarck told Benedetti that Prussia was willing to make "important sacrifices" in order to preserve good relations with France.[17]

The grand duchy of Luxemburg had been granted to the house of Orange in 1815 as compensation for the loss of Nassau. Its only connection with the Netherlands was that of "personal union" under King–Grand Duke William III. Previously the principality had belonged to the German Confederation, and it possessed a confederate fortress manned by a Prussian garrison. The demise of the confederation had dissolved the link with Germany and placed in question the status of the garrison. French was the predominant language of government, but the populace spoke a German dialect with an admixture of French words. Some were pro-French and some pro-German, but most apparently wanted to preserve their country's independence.[18]

In mid-August Napoleon, acting on Rouher's advice, launched a final attempt at understanding with Prussia. Benedetti was instructed to propose two agreements: a public treaty conceding to France the frontiers of 1814 and the right to Luxemburg; and a secret treaty containing an "offensive and defensive alliance" and granting France the right eventually to annex Belgium. Immediately Bismarck objected to the 1814 frontier, and Benedetti let it drop, as Rouher had authorized. Concerning Belgium and Luxemburg, Bismarck indicated that their annexation by France was consonant with Prussia's interests, if Berlin were granted a "free hand in Germany." On August 29, 1866, Benedetti actually handed over a draft agreement, in which France assented, in return for Belgium and Luxemburg, to a "federal union" between the North German Confederation and the southern states, which would respect "in just measure" the sovereignty of the latter.[19]

Agreement with France on such a basis offered several tempting advantages for Prussia. It would eliminate the possibility of French interference in the

---

[16] RKN, I, 331, 340, 353; II, 72, 93, 173–174; Lynn M. Case, *French Opinion on War and Diplomacy during the Second Empire* (Philadelphia, 1954), 205ff.

[17] OD, XI, 219–225; XII, 24.

[18] Becker, *Bismarcks Ringen*, 400; Alexander Matschoss, *Die Luxemburger Frage von 1867* (Breslau, 1867), 40ff.

[19] RKN, II, 82–83, 87–89, 94–96, 166, 182; OD, XII, 116–117, 170–175.

creation of the North German Confederation, and permit a constitutional union with the south without risk of war. In the future, moreover, the French might be brought to sacrifice their interest in the southern states. Perhaps Bismarck's only purpose in listening to the overture was to prolong French hopes for an agreement.[20] But it is more likely that a delimitation of spheres between Berlin and Paris, as earlier between Berlin and Vienna, was one of the courses that entered for a time into his calculations.[21]

The draft that Benedetti suddenly drew out of his pocket, like that of Rechberg at Schönbrunn, was in any case much too precise and far-reaching. On August 17 Bismarck had told the ambassador that such a treaty would be difficult to obtain from Wilhelm, although he would seek to dispose the king in its favor. On September 7 he informed Paris that the king was not opposed to the growth of the empire "in the area of French nationality," but France must take the initiative. As for the alliance, the two nations should agree to consult for common defense, if dangers arose. This was a circumspect refusal. Bismarck and Wilhelm had no intention of getting involved in war with Britain for a purely French interest.[22]

Concerning Luxemburg he expressed on August 17 his desire to be "obliging." While declining to initiate any action, he did offer to assist the French by giving the Dutch a fright. He promised to make a "peremptory demand" at The Hague for the inclusion of Luxemburg and Limburg in the North German Confederation. Simultaneously France should stimulate "manifestations in her favor" among influential circles in Luxemburg. To save the Dutch population of Limburg, William III would probably let Luxemburg go,[23] a neat finesse by two expert bridge players.

Only one day after Benedetti presented his treaty draft, Bismarck actually raised the "peremptory demand" at The Hague.[24] This may not in itself be proof of his willingness to assist French annexation. But neither can it be assumed that his actual aim was the elevation of Prince Henry, the pro-German governor of the duchy, to the status of an independent ruler closely allied

---

[20] This point of view is supported by Bismarck's comment on a document seized during the campaign of 1870. In a report to Drouyn from Nikolsburg on July 26, Benedetti had written of Bismarck as "the only person in the whole kingdom who understands what an advantage there would be for Prussia in forming with France an intimate and lasting alliance at the price of a territorial sacrifice." In the margin Bismarck commented, "So he honestly believed it." RKN, II, 7.

[21] Later he maintained that, had the French not been so "foolish," they could have had Luxemburg. GW, VII, 199–200, 310.

[22] RKN, II, 88, 100–109, 185–186; OD, XII, 215.

[23] RKN, II, 87–89; OD, XII, 213–214. Like Luxemburg, Limburg had been part of the German Confederation.

[24] From Perponcher, Prussian minister at The Hague, he already knew that neither William III, nor his government, was very interested in retaining Luxemburg. GW, VI, 91–92, 144–145, 154–155; APP, VIII, 44–47, 54.

to Berlin.[25] It is more likely that, as in the Schleswig-Holstein question, he wished to leave open two courses of action. Should the French press with vigor and skill on the Luxemburg issue, the wiser course might be to withdraw the Prussian garrison and permit the duchy's annexation rather than suffer French hostility and interference at a critical time in the reorganization of Germany. But if the matter could be dragged out until after the formation of the North German Confederation, it might become highly useful to Berlin.[26]

French handling of the problem was neither vigorous nor skillful. Benedetti failed even to report Bismarck's suggestion that France incite "manifestations" in the duchy. In quest of the unattainable, Napoleon and Rouher risked the attainable. They pressed for the compensation of William III on Prussian soil, which was refused. Instead of concentrating on Luxemburg, they sought from Berlin a secret agreement on Belgium as well. At the end of August Benedetti determined that his health "imperatively" required a two-week vacation at Karlsbad. When he returned on September 15, Bismarck was reported too ill to receive him; on the twenty-sixth he learned that the minister had left for the country and that nothing could be done during his absence.[27]

Not until December 1 was Bismarck back in Berlin. In an interview he told Benedetti that he still favored the project—but the king had to be "converted." On calling again, the ambassador was informed that the minister-president was too weak and too busy with internal affairs to see him. Acidly Bismarck complained to Paris of Benedetti's importunity in pressing the matter. But his procrastination was deliberate. "The French," he had written on October 22, "must retain hope and especially faith in our good will without our giving them definite commitments." Every delay was an advantage, he instructed Goltz on February 15, 1867, "for we shall win time thereby for the consolidation of our relationships in northern Germany and with southern Germany." In six months Berlin would be in a better position to meet the challenge.[28]

But the vital question concerning the Luxemburg crisis is why he wished to provoke the challenge at all. Certainly he did not regard the grand duchy itself as vital to Germany. "The population of the country is hardly homogeneous with ours," he wrote on July 31, 1866. "In the judgment of military experts, moreover, the fortress is not of such strategic importance that its possession ought to be bought at the cost of other advantages and couldn't be

[25] Becker, *Bismarcks Ringen*, 405ff.

[26] This dual purpose is particularly evident in the instruction to Goltz on Feb. 15, 1867. GW, VI, 264–269.

[27] OD, XII, 172, 193–196, 213–216, 311, 334–335; APP, VIII, 110, 121, 133–135, 139–140. On Benedetti's role in the failure of French policy in the Luxemburg affair see Willard Allen Fletcher, *The Mission of Vincent Benedetti to Berlin, 1864–1870* (The Hague, 1965), 141–183.

[28] OD, XIII, 200–202, 226–227, 281; Becker, *Bismarcks Ringen*, 903; RKN, II, 201.

compensated for by other strategically more important points in our adjacent area." He had no interest in acquiring the duchy for Prussia or the North German Confederation. To the Dutch envoy he even admitted that the population was "anti-Prussian."[29]

Not until his return from Putbus did Bismarck begin to refer to Luxemburg as "German" and to its fate as a matter of national concern.[30] On December 6 he instructed Goltz to express doubt that possession of the duchy would compensate France for the animosity that its seizure would "certainly" arouse "in all Germany." On December 19 and 20 he pointed out that Prussia could hardly be expected to take the initiative in ceding "German land" or accept the "odium" of delivering "Germans against their will and for no apparent cause to France." "If we must purchase the alliance with France by a humiliating injury to German national feeling," he told Goltz, "it is too dearly bought."[31]

Certainly Bismarck feared that involvement in the rape of Luxemburg would compromise his liaison with German nationalists. But he also calculated that to pose as the champion of the nation in the affair would help to consummate that alliance. Goltz assumed that Prussia's next objectives could best be achieved in harmony with France; Bismarck, in conflict with her. "Through the excitement of national feeling" he expected "the quick consolidation of our relationships in Germany."[32] What spontaneous love of nation or trust in Hohenzollern leadership could not accomplish might better be achieved by fear and hatred of a foreign foe.

Crisis over Luxemburg

Week after week Benedetti called at Wilhelmstrasse 76, but in vain. Usually so voluble and available, Bismarck was now "silent and inaccessible." In the past so "fecund of resources and expedients," he could now see nothing but obstacles in the path of a French alliance. Bismarck, however, struck the pose of an injured friend. "From the beginning of my ministry," he complained, "I have regarded and handled this alliance as the natural expression of the enduring harmony of interests of both countries." By their "precipitate urgency" the French were endangering it. They must appreciate the difficulties he faced in persuading Wilhelm, as well as the German public, to accept it. By their

---

[29] GW, VI, 91–92, 155; APP, VIII, 344, 471. The expert opinion was that of the Ministry of War. In mid-January 1867 a judgment was requested of Moltke, who took a contrary view. RKN, II, 188.

[30] On Oct. 26 he even ordered August Brass not to publish "any teutonizing articles concerning Luxemburg." Robert von Keudell, Fürst und Fürstin Bismarck: Erinnerungen 1846–1872 (Berlin, 1901), 325.

[31] RKN, II, 130, 143, 183, 203.

[32] RKN, II, 155; GW, VI, 263–264, 303.

earlier demand for Rhenish territory the French had complicated his task. They wished to gather the fruits of a Prussian victory to which they had contributed nothing.[33] The tone was strikingly similar to that toward Austria in the years before the dénouement of 1866.

At Paris there was mounting anxiety and embarrassment. In a circular published on September 17, 1866, La Valette had alluded to the French demands. Now the suspicion began to spread that the government had been rebuffed. The point of political gravity in Europe appeared to be shifting from Paris to Berlin. The emperor and his ministers feared attacks in the coming session of the corps législatif. In desperation they decided to concentrate on Luxemburg, dropping for the time being demands for Belgium and an alliance.[34] But Bismarck refused either to join in a démarche at The Hague or withdraw Prussia's garrison from Luxemburg without apparent cause. The French, he insisted, could furnish the cause, if they would but stimulate a demand for withdrawal on the part of influential Luxemburgers. But Napoleon feared to excite a popular reaction in Germany by such a move—precisely the reason why Bismarck advised it![35]

On February 14, 1867, Napoleon opened the French parliament with a speech in which he strove to cover up the fiasco of his foreign policy during the past year. His words were boastful, but his delivery was uncertain, his manner melancholic. On St. Helena, he recalled, Napoleon I had predicted the future agglomeration of peoples into national states. Hence the recent developments were only natural and no cause for alarm. Without calling up a single soldier or moving a regiment, France had halted the victorious Prussian army before the gates of Vienna. "Prussia seeks to avoid everything that might irritate our national sensitivity and is in agreement with us on the major European issues." But the opposition was unappeased. In mid-March the feared Adolphe Thiers delivered a devastating attack. Rejecting the concept of national self-determination, he upheld that of the balance of power, which required the restraint of Prussia. With biting sarcasm he contrasted the vision and boldness of Bismarck's operations with the pitiful oscillations of the French. His closing sentence combined threat with accusation: "There is not another single mistake to commit."[36]

The debate was barely over when Bismarck revealed that the roster of Napoleon's failures was even longer than Thiers assumed. On March 19 the texts of the treaties of alliance with the southern states were released to the press with their consent. In the constituent Reichstag the chancellor expected

---

[33] OD, XIII, 273ff., 322–323, 367ff.; RKN, II, 143–150; APP, VIII, 212.

[34] Case, French Opinion on War and Diplomacy, 221ff.; RKN, II, 157–158, 161, 172–178, 188–190, 194–196, 216.

[35] RKN, II, 151, 161, 165–168, 173, 210, 224; APP, VIII, 246–247.

[36] Case, French Opinion on War and Diplomacy, 228–229; Emile Ollivier, l'Empire libéral (Paris, 1895–1912), vol. 9, 231–237, 270ff.; APP, VIII, 397.

A MISUNDERSTANDING. NAPOLEON: "I JUST WANTED TO CONGRATULATE YOU ON THE FINE INHERITANCE AND SEE WHETHER YOU MAY HAVE A LITTLE SOMETHING FOR ME." BISMARCK: "WHAT AN IDEA! HERE NOTHING IS GIVEN AWAY." (WILHELM SCHOLZ, *KLADDERADATSCH*, AUGUST 26, 1866.)

heavy criticism of the decision to stop at the Main. He needed an answer to the reproach that the treaty of Nikolsburg had left open the possibility of alliances between the southern states and foreign powers against the north. In Paris the revelation was the greatest sensation in the public press since Königgrätz. For Napoleon and his ministers it was a bitter blow. Bismarck had already acquired what they proposed to sell. The German nationalists were also impressed. "He is as smart as a snake," wrote Bennigsen, "but hardly lacking in deceit like the dove."[37]

Meanwhile, the French had taken the one path left to them. On March 16, 1867, they opened unilateral negotiations with the Netherlands. In return for Luxemburg, Napoleon offered to guarantee the frontiers of the Netherlands and Limburg. At The Hague neither William III nor his government had much interest in retaining Luxemburg, and they feared that Bismarck's aim was to obtain a frontier on the Meuse including the fortress of Maastricht. Nevertheless, they were leery of entering into an agreement with France without consulting Berlin. On March 19 William III consented to cede Luxemburg for an indemnity of five million gulden, but insisted on the approval of the king of Prussia. Simultaneously he informed Berlin of the proposition and offered to assist in bringing about a Franco-Prussian understanding. Mean-

[37] *GW*, VI, 272, 296; X, 328, 347; *APP*, VIII, 409ff.; *RKN*, II, 235, 240–243, 257–260; Hermann Oncken, *Rudolf von Bennigsen* (Stuttgart, 1910), vol. 2, 33.

while, French agents were active in the city of Luxemburg with petitions and placards. Those wishing to escape the "hated domination of Prussia" were urged to assemble in the Wilhelmsplatz every noon to shout: "*Vive la France! Vive Napoléon!*"[38]

The timing of these actions could hardly have been more convenient for Bismarck. The French maneuver reached fruition just as his constitutional draft entered the crisis stage in the constituent Reichstag. On March 26–27 occurred the crucial debates on ministerial responsibility; on March 30, the vote on the remuneration of deputies; in early April, the critical debates and negotiations over the iron budget. Deliberately Bismarck exploited the Luxemburg issue to speed the deliberations of the constituent Reichstag to a favorable conclusion.

Prussia, he complained to Paris, was badly abused. The conditions he had stipulated for tacit permission in the Luxemburg affair had not been followed. By seeking Prussian approval, William III had involved Berlin in the negotiation and hence in the responsibility for the duchy's loss to Germany. Furthermore, the street demonstrations in Luxemburg were far different from the decorous petitions of bankers and merchants that he had suggested. French clumsiness, he telegraphed to Goltz on March 30, had aroused public animosity throughout Germany. "Stoked by our opponents, the excitement is growing to critical dimensions. . . . Interpellation imminent in the Reichstag from the uttermost left."[39]

On April 1 Bennigsen delivered the interpellation. Did the Prussian government and its allies intend to make secure, "against every danger," the union of Luxemburg ("an old German land") with the "rest of Germany" and "particularly the Prussian right of garrison in the fortress of Luxemburg?" With passion the Hanoverian denounced the prince of "German descent" on the Dutch throne for his willingness to sell to France a land that had "at all times been German" and wished now to remain so. Regardless of party, he declared, the nation would stand united behind the "strong policy" of the government. The applause seemed unending.[40]

The chief "stoker" of this demonstration was Bismarck himself. In all probability he had even agreed with Bennigsen upon the wording of the interpellation.[41] Openly he warned the French that their action would "make it easier to bring about the swift completion of the North German Confederation." Indeed it did. During the following days a sense of urgency pervaded the chamber and committee rooms of the constituent Reichstag. It heightened

[38] *OD*, XV, 80, 99ff.; *RKN*, II, 260; *GW*, VI, 320; *APP*, VIII, 381–382, 441–442, 494–495, 509ff.

[39] *GW*, VI, 320–323; *APP*, VIII, 539–541. For the reaction in southern Germany see *APP*, VIII, 531, 557.

[40] *SBR*, I (1867), 487ff.; II, 62; Oncken, *Bennigsen*, vol. 2, 35–40.

[41] "He gladly lets himself be pressed," the Hanoverian wrote. Oncken, *Bennigsen*, vol. 2, 34.

the spirit of compromise and encouraged the liberals to sacrifice vital powers of parliament over the army and military budget. In this way the momentary crisis over Luxemburg left a permanent mark upon the institutional relationships of the Second Reich.[42]

Meanwhile, Napoleon and Moustier (Drouyn's replacement as foreign minister) were heading down the home stretch in the race for the Luxemburg treaty, scheduled for signing on April 1. But Bismarck shoved one obstacle after another on to the track. On receiving the Dutch king's request for Prussian approval, he replied that Wilhelm wished first to know the opinions of the other treaty powers of 1839, the German governments, and even the north German Reichstag. Had the agnates, moreover, been consulted?[43] Three days later he refused, for Prussia, any responsibility for the treaty. William III must decide what he owed himself and Europe. Prussia would look after her own interests "at the right time." The ominous clamor of public protest, he declared, made it impossible for Prussia to withdraw her garrison from Luxemburg. The man who for four years had contemptuously defied the attacks of press and parliament now pictured himself as helpless before the people's fury. "As things stand in Germany we must in my opinion dare the war rather than yield, despite the fact that the object, Luxemburg, is in itself hardly worth a war." The nation's "sense of honor," he actually declared, was the "decisive" factor. On April 3 he telegraphed to The Hague, "After the incitement of public opinion war would scarcely be avoidable if the affair proceeds."[44]

In Paris there was anger and confusion. Moustier complained that France had held to the procedure suggested by Bismarck himself; it looked as though Berlin had set a "trap" for the French. But then he calmed down and added hastily that he had not meant to be comminatory. Napoleon was indignant and determined to go through with the affair if William III would sign. In talking to Goltz, however, he was careful to keep his manner "hearty" and emphasized that he desired peace, if it could be had with honor.[45] France, he knew, was in no condition to fight. The reorganization and strengthening of the army had barely begun; the infantry was not yet fully armed with breech-loaders; the forces being withdrawn from Mexico had not yet arrived in France; the empire had no dependable allies. Furthermore, Napoleon had just opened in Paris a great international exposition, which he hoped would brighten the tarnished luster of his regime and add to the prosperity of French industry. Both Wilhelm I and Alexander II had accepted invitations. War

[42] GW, VI, 322–323, 356–357; Oncken, *Bennigsen*, vol. 2, 45–46.
[43] RKN, II, 260; APP, VIII, 514–515.
[44] GW, VI, 323–324, 331–333; APP, VIII, 615–617.
[45] RKN, II, 270–281.

would have wrecked the exhibition and the chance for Bonaparte to play host to Romanov and Hohenzoller.[46]

Bismarck likewise had no desire to fight over Luxemburg. His reply to Bennigsen's interpellation was moderate, though firm, and his warning to The Hague on April 3 was intended to keep William III from the final act that would make war almost certain. But if the Dutch should sign, Bismarck had in mind a possible compromise with which to avert the struggle. Even while pushing the crisis to its climax on March 30, he instructed Goltz to inquire "cautiously" whether the French would be willing, in return for Luxemburg, to release Prussia from her Nikolsburg commitment ultimately to divide Schleswig on lines of nationality. After listening to Bennigsen on April 1, he telegraphed the ambassador not to bring the matter up "as yet."[47] The cynicism of such a bargain would have been highly damaging to the national posture of the government. With typical elasticity, however, he held the idea in reserve.

Meanwhile, he had sought to mobilize the support of the European powers. Beginning on March 30, he urged Britain and Russia to intervene at The Hague to prevent the king's signature. Although Gorchakov and the tsar were critical of Napoleon's actions, they chose to let Britain take the lead. In London, the new foreign secretary, Lord Stanley, took the view that "so small a rearrangement of territory" would not disturb the European balance. Nor was he impressed by Bismarck's argument that Luxemburg was covered by the treaty of 1839 guaranteeing Belgian independence.[48] On April 2 Bismarck ordered Bernstorff to find out "how far we may count on England" in the event of war with France. Lacking her support, he bluffed, Prussia had the alternative of "shifting from the alliance with German public opinion to an alliance with France" at the cost of Belgium. But the answer was disappointing. Although disturbed about Belgium, Stanley replied that Britain would not take sides.[49]

On April 5, after days of uncertainty, William III finally declined to sign. This gave both sides the opportunity to find a way out of the affair. Soon Bismarck indicated to the British his willingness to accept an international conference. After some hesitation the French, shocked by the extent of their defeat, also declared their readiness to waive the claim to Luxemburg, if Prus-

[46] RKN, II, 231, 268, 278. It was certainly no accident that during the weeks in which the Luxemburg crisis developed, Bismarck solicited invitations for the simultaneous visit of Wilhelm and Alexander and that Wilhelm's acceptance was dispatched on Mar. 30, the day before Bennigsen's interpellation.

[47] GW, VI, 321; RKN, II, 274; APP, VIII, 549, 693.

[48] RKN, II, 269; GW, VI, 320, 324–325, 330–332; APP, VIII, 550, 627–629; Werner E. Mosse, The European Powers and the German Question, 1848–1871 (Cambridge, Eng., 1958), 263–264.

[49] GW, VI, 330, 332–333; APP, VIII, 575–576, 601, 624–625; Mosse, European Powers, 264.

sia would withdraw her garrison and accept neutralization of the duchy. But Bismarck refused to enter into such an arrangement "now." To break with German national sentiment, he declared, would be more dangerous for the German governments than war with France.[50] He had not yet reaped, in other words, all the benefits he expected for his German policy from the Luxemburg crisis. The constituent Reichstag was still in session and negotiations with the south were still under way.

In Berlin during April some advocated mobilization and war. French military preparations made the generals nervous. Convinced of the inevitability of conflict, Moltke wished to strike before her rearmament was complete. Bismarck was also concerned. He feared that Napoleon, while peacefully inclined, might be pushed into an attack by his more belligerent advisers. Though ready to meet the challenge, he had no intention of precipitating a conflict. "The chance of success," he remarked, "is not a just cause for beginning a great war."[51] Until the path of peace had been fully explored and found without exit, he was not ready to try the more hazardous one of violence. For the time being he hoped that mere friction with France would generate the heat with which to weld the nation together under the Prussian system.[52]

Alternative Plans

The Main line, Bismarck boasted, was not a wall but a fence that could never hold back the national stream. After Königgrätz there actually were signs of movement in the south. At Nikolsburg the governments of Hesse-Darmstadt and Württemberg applied for admission to the North German Confederation. By volunteering, they hoped to exact better terms. In Munich the lower chamber voted (August 30, 1866), 124 to 11, for cooperation with Prussia in the formation of a German union. The next day Prince Hohenlohe-Schillingsfürst judged that, while court and government were opposed, the great majority of the Bavarian people were for "union with Prussia." In Karlsruhe a nationalistic cabinet under Karl Mathy, Rudolf von Freydorf, and Julius Jolly assumed office in July, and in October the Baden parliament voted for unconditional union with the north.[53]

---

[50] Mosse, *European Powers*, 265–267; GW, VI, 349; APP, VIII, 649.

[51] Friedrich von Bernhardi, ed., *Aus dem Leben Theodor von Bernhardis* (Leipzig, 1893–1906), vol. 7, 358, 369ff., 375–378; GW, VI, 362, 366–369, also 333 (fn.).

[52] GW, VI, 303, 322, 333.

[53] GW, VI, 303; APP, VIII, 261–262; Brandenburg, *Untersuchungen*, 699; Adolf Rapp, *Die Württemberger und die nationale Frage, 1863–1871: Darstellungen aus der württembergischen Geschichte*, vol. 4 (Stuttgart, 1910), 219ff.; Friedrich Curtius, ed., *Denkwürdigkeiten des Fürsten Chlodwig zu Hohenlohe-Schillingsfürst* (Stuttgart, 1907), vol. 1, 174–175; Theodor Schieder, *Die kleindeutsche Partei in Bayern: Münchener historische Abhandlungen*, vol. 12 (Munich, 1936), 120ff.; Georg Meyer, "Die Reichsgründung und das Grossherzogtum Baden," *Festgabe für Grossherzog Friedrich von Baden* (Heidelberg, 1896), 147ff., 178ff.

But this mood soon evaporated. Berlin's annexations gave the North German Confederation the appearance of an enlarged Prussia. Southern governments feared domination by the Prussian colossus, and liberal nationalists disliked its political system. They were not reassured by the constitution Bismarck designed and pushed through to adoption. Despite his concessions to federalism, the governments were disappointed by the degree of centralism that remained. His concessions to the constituent Reichstag, moreover, were not sufficient to allay the suspicions of southern liberals. German national feeling in the south was chiefly the property of middle-class liberals who were prejudiced against the aristocratic-authoritarian regime in Berlin. Only in Baden did the sentiment for union still prevail. His anticipation of these reactions was precisely the reason why Bismarck had chosen to halt temporarily at the Main in the first place. The south's "indigestibility" was owing to its liberalism and particularism, as well as its Catholicism.[54]

Bismarck faced these difficulties in typical fashion. As in the Schleswig-Holstein affair he regarded the problem in terms of several possibilities, ranging from the desired maximum to the acceptable minimum. The maximum was simply the extension of the northern constitution over the south with no further concessions of either a liberal or decentralistic nature. For the time being, however, this was impractical both because of southern attitudes and the foreign complications that would arise from open violation of the treaty of Prague. The minimum consisted of the military alliances with the south already achieved, supplemented by a Zollverein parliament with power to legislate in matters of customs and commerce.

Between these extremes lay a medium course, upon which Bismarck evidently placed his greatest immediate hopes: a "wider confederation" or "constitutional alliance." The constitution of the North German Confederation would be extended over the south in all but military and naval affairs. Legislative power would be exercised by an enlarged Bundesrat and Reichstag. The virtue of such an arrangement was that it left the southern governments in possession of the most important attribute of their cherished sovereignty (control over the army and its finances) and at the same time prevented the reinforcement of northern liberals by the liberal south in any future attempts to overthrow the iron budget. The constitutional union, moreover, would have made it virtually impossible for southern states to carry on an independent foreign policy.[55]

As so often in the past, Bismarck's goals were not mutually exclusive. They were steps leading upward from the least to the most desirable outcome. If the Zollverein parliament was immediately attainable, the gradual expansion of

[54] Schüssler, Bismarcks Kampf, 19–20, 35–36; Schieder, Kleindeutsche Partei, 136–139; Karl Alexander von Müller, Bayern im Jahre 1866 und die Berufung des Fürsten Hohenlohe: Historische Bibliothek, vol. 20 (Munich, 1909), 160ff.; Götz, Die Stellung Hessen-Darmstadts, 32ff.

[55] Schüssler, Bismarcks Kampf, 66–69.

its legislative competence might eventually create the "wider confederation." In turn, the latter might evolve into a fully sovereign state. The expansion of the Prussian system over Germany might well be achieved by evolutionary rather than revolutionary means, by the organic development of governmental institutions rather than through war with France.

Failure of the Medium and Maximum

Bismarck's plan for a wider confederation had some support. Grand Duke Friedrich of Baden and his ministers were still intent on union with the north, even under Bismarck's constitution. Though King Karl of Württemberg was jealous of his sovereignty—his Russian wife, Queen Olga, even more so— Foreign Minister Varnbüler was a realist who quickly reconciled himself to the prospect of Prussian supremacy after the defeat of 1866. Although determined to preserve as far as possible Württemberg's independence in military and political affairs, he recognized the necessity of union with the north in economic matters. In Bavaria the replacement (December 31, 1866) of Pfordten by Prince von Hohenlohe-Schillingsfürst as minister-president opened the prospect of a new era of cooperation between Berlin and Munich. Whereas Pfordten had distrusted Prussia and dreamed of a southern union under Bavarian leadership, Prince Hohenlohe believed that Bavaria could escape the dangers of isolation only by joining, under advantageous terms, a federal union led by Prussia. He was one of four members of the upper chamber who had voted in favor of the August resolution for union with the north. Nevertheless, he too was disappointed by the centralistic features of the northern constitution; his cabinet colleagues were particularistic; so likewise was King Ludwig, who eyed suspiciously any proposal that threatened Bavarian sovereignty. Hohenlohe, moreover, was not a strong personality of decisive political will.[56]

With utmost care Bismarck sought to draw the prince, and with him the Bavarian state, into a "constitutional alliance." On January 31, 1867, he outlined his plan to Baron Karl von Spitzemberg, the Württemberg minister at Berlin. After reading the minister's report, Varnbüler was favorable. Through him Bismarck hoped to put pressure on Hohenlohe. But the particularistic current in Munich was swift, and, although personally inclined toward such an arrangement, Hohenlohe was compelled to reject it. Nor did the persua-

---

[56] Ibid., 34ff., 57ff.; Hohenlohe, Denkwürdigkeiten, vol. 1, 171–175, 184ff., 194ff.; Müller, Bayern im Jahre 1866, 89ff., and "Die Tauffkirchensche Mission nach Berlin und Wien," in Karl A. von Müller, ed., Riezler-Festschrift: Beiträge zur bayerischen Geschichte (Gotha, 1913), 352ff.; Ernst Salzer, "Fürst Chlodwig zu Hohenlohe-Schillingfürst und die deutsche Frage," Historische Vierteljahrschrift, 11 (1908), 40–74.

sion of Grand Duke Friedrich have any effect. Hohenlohe did not have the power to commit Bavaria to the wider confederation of Bismarck's hopes.[57]

Thus far the treaties of alliance signed in August–September 1866 were Bismarck's only success in snaring the south. But now, as the Luxemburg crisis reached its peak, even these instruments appeared insecure. Although his main purpose in publishing them (March 19, 1867) was to answer his critics in the constituent Reichstag, he also wished "to make it easier for the southern states to come to an understanding with each other over union with the North German Confederation and to accomplish this union itself." Knowledge of the treaties, however, served only to heighten the tension between pro- and anti-Prussians throughout the south. The latter could now claim that they had been misled and betrayed by their own governments. In Stuttgart Varnbüler consented to publication only under protest and requested a public declaration from Berlin to the effect that the treaty was purely defensive in character. Bismarck's reply was an irritated refusal. He feared what might be transpiring between Stuttgart and Paris.[58]

Instead of furnishing the needed impetus for a national union, the Luxemburg crisis even threatened to destroy what had already been accomplished. Both Varnbüler and Hohenlohe were alarmed over the prospect of being dragged into war. Generally it was feared that the south would be the first victim of a war against France, allied with Austria and Italy. In Stuttgart there was talk of neutrality, and in Munich, according to Werthern, Hohenlohe faced the possibility of being outvoted or dismissed if he stood by the alliance.[59] On April 8 Bismarck warned Bavaria that, if deserted, the north would be compelled to seek its allies elsewhere and to consider only its own interests in any constitutional arrangements. Even above the Main, however, Bismarck apparently had grounds for dissatisfaction. In notes dispatched on April 12 to all German capitals, north and south, he maintained that Prussia's sole interest in the Luxemburg affair was the obligation to satisfy German national pride. "If a people feels its honor injured, then it is injured and must be dealt with accordingly. National feeling and national honor are potencies that do not lend themselves to logical measurement." Were those who refused their support ready to defend their refusal and the loss of Luxemburg before the bar of public opinion?[60]

[57] APP, VIII, 353–357, 373, 428–429; GW, VI, 239–241; Schüssler, Bismarcks Kampf, 62ff., 73ff., 120ff., 297–302; Hohenlohe. Denkwürdigkeiten, vol. 1, 198ff.; Müller, Bayern im Jahre 1866, 183ff.

[58] GW, VI, 301, 316–317; APP, VIII, 460, 507–508, 515–516; George G. Windell, The Catholics and German Unity, 1866–1871 (Minneapolis, 1954), 103ff.

[59] APP, VIII, 567, 574, 581–584, 599, 619, 655–656; IX, 35; Schüssler, Bismarcks Kampf, 151ff.; Veit Valentin, Bismarcks Reichsgründung im Urteil englischer Diplomaten (Amsterdam, 1937), 353ff.

[60] GW, VI, 347–348, 350–352.

This attempt to whip the southern states into line by the threat of the nation's rage had only limited success. Karlsruhe and Darmstadt, to be sure, gave clear declarations of support, but the replies from Munich and Stuttgart were equivocal. In both capitals it was feared that Bismarck's actual aim was to unload on the backs of the southern governments the blame for a coming surrender of Luxemburg. While affirming their loyalty to the alliance, Varnbüler and Hohenlohe stressed their hopes that peace would be maintained. The former refused to take a stand on whether the casus foederis was applicable "at this moment," and the latter pointed to the uncertainty of Austrian policy as an "urgent" reason for peace.[61]

In February Hohenlohe had begun to insist that for Berlin the key to the

BULLDOG BISMARCK SETS A MOUSETRAP FOR THE GERMAN SMALL STATES
(GILL, *LA LANTERNE*, PARIS, APRIL 7, 1867).

[61] APP, VIII, 640–642, 662–664, 707–712, 717–718, 730–731; Hohenlohe, *Denkwürdigkeiten*, vol. 1, 230–231. Later Varnbüler asserted in parliament that Bismarck's question demonstrated that it lay in Württemberg's power to decide whether the casus foederis applied. APP, IX, 375–376, 408–411, 532–533.

south lay in Vienna, both with regard to Bavaria's acceptance of the wider confederation and her support in the Luxemburg crisis. The general fear of Prussian hegemony and of a French-Austrian alliance would be allayed only by an agreement between Habsburg and Hohenzoller. Happily for Bismarck this suggestion coincided with his own intentions. In granting Austria an easy peace in 1866, his aim had been to restore her to the list of Berlin's potential allies.[62]

Immediately on returning from Putbus in December 1866, he stressed to Count Felix von Wimpffen, Károlyi's successor as Austrian envoy in Berlin, the need for an "intimate understanding" with Austria. Such a combination was only natural in view of the German character of the Habsburg dynasty and many of its subjects. The amazed diplomat heard him deplore the failure of the Gablenz mission and regret that the two countries had not formed a common front against France and "shot the deer together." On April 12, 1867, Bismarck outlined the details of his plan to Count Karl von Tauffkirchen, Hohenlohe's intimate adviser and emissary. The "organic" connection he desired was not a "constitutional alliance," but the revival of the German Confederation without a diet. This would guarantee indefinitely the security of the German provinces of Austria. The rest of the Habsburg Empire would be guaranteed in a defensive alliance limited to periods of three years. Russia too was to be brought into the system. He hoped for a revival of the Holy Alliance.[63]

The man to whom fell the duty of responding to these overtures was none other than Baron Beust. By refusing to deal with him in negotiating peace with Saxony, Bismarck had brought about his dismissal in Dresden, only to make him available for a more dangerous post! In October 1866 Franz Joseph chose him to replace Mensdorff as Austrian foreign minister. As his memoirs reveal, Beust was a vain and self-important man, who never forgot a witticism or compliment. He was certain that, had his advice been followed, none of the disasters that Austria had suffered since 1859 would have occurred. Nevertheless, he understood that Bismarck's "cynical" offer of an alliance was actually designed to facilitate Berlin's absorption of the south. He was not deceived by Bismarck's assurance that this would be a "misfortune" for Prussia, nor shaken by his threat that, failing an Austrian alliance, Berlin would have to seek allies in Paris and Petersburg. Beust's refusal made it impossible for Hohenlohe to accept the plan for a wider confederation. Russia was also negative. Gorchakov pointed out that the conflict of Austrian and Russian

[62] Hohenlohe, Denkwürdigkeiten, vol. 1, 202, 206ff., 224ff.; APP, VIII, 428; Stosch, Denkwürdigkeiten, 102.

[63] APP, VIII, 190–191, 505–506, 652ff., 671; Walter Platzhoff, "Die Anfänge des Dreikaiserbundes, 1867–1871," Preussische Jahrbücher, 188 (1922), 283ff.; Müller, "Die Tauffkirchensche Mission," 392ff.

interests in the Balkans made impossible a renewal of the Holy Alliance.[64] But these were not the only disappointments Bismarck suffered in the spring of 1867.

As usual he was attempting to move simultaneously on more than one front. While striving for the constitutional alliance, he sought to make headway toward his higher goal as well. The time had come, he determined, to cross the Main by bringing the southern territory of Hesse into the North German Confederation, to which its northern half already belonged. Baden would surely follow, and Württemberg and Bavaria would eventually find it difficult to stay out. Should the French take up his suggestion for a deal on Luxemburg and northern Schleswig, progress toward German unity would make the bargain more palatable in Germany. Should the French seek to frustrate a seemingly spontaneous Hessian demand for union with the north, Berlin would acquire, in addition to the Luxemburg issue, yet another cause with which to excite the patriotic feelings of the German nation.[65]

Again there was some prospect of success. The desire of the Hessian government for a military convention to end the divided condition of its armed forces provided a convenient lever. But the project had an able and determined foe in the Hessian minister Baron Dalwigk. An old personal enemy of Bismarck, Dalwigk was irreconcilably opposed to a Prussian-dominated Germany. In order to get around him, the chancellor instigated an effort by the Prussian crown prince and his brother-in-law, Prince Ludwig of Hesse, to arouse sentiment in Darmstadt for the inclusion of the southern territory. On Dalwigk's advice, the grand duke replied that he would wait to see what kind of military convention Berlin would grant. In view of the crisis with France, Bismarck agreed to the signing of a convention on April 7, followed by a military alliance on April 11. The lever was lost, and thereafter Dalwigk remained unmoved.[66]

Bismarck's defeat was all the more humiliating in view of the fact that he had meanwhile made public his aim. Through Prince Ludwig he brought about an interpellation in the constituent Reichstag on April 9 by Count Otto zu Solms-Laubach, a nationalist Hessian deputy. After describing the divided condition of the Hessian state as intolerable, the deputy expressed confidence that the union of the southern segment to the north would provide a "bridge" for the completion of German unity. In reply Bismarck also emphasized the evils of Hesse's divided condition and the advantages of An-

---

[64] Friedrich Ferdinand Graf von Beust, *Aus drei Viertel-Jahrhunderten* (2 vols., Stuttgart, 1887); APP, VIII, 683ff., 809; Schüssler, *Bismarcks Kampf*, 180ff.; Becker, *Bismarcks Ringen*, 419ff.; Müller, "Die Tauffkirchensche Mission," 415ff.

[65] Schüssler, *Bismarcks Kampf*, 89ff.

[66] Dalwigk, *Tagebücher*, 315ff., 351ff.; APP, VIII, 416–417, 438–439, 443–444, 463–464, 487–488, 497–498, 599–603, 671–672. For the texts of the military agreements see Glaser, ed., *Archiv*, vol. 3, 53–57.

schluss. Should Darmstadt request such a step, Berlin would consult with the southern governments and with Vienna, whose opposition was not expected. But this obvious appeal to public pressure had no effect upon Dalwigk, who found in Beust, and even Hohenlohe, diplomatic support for the preservation of the status quo. The only lasting mark of Bismarck's effort was a hopeful amendment to article 71 of the northern constitution, which the liberals passed with his approval: "The entry of the south German states or of one of the same into the confederation shall take place on the proposal of the confederate presidency by way of confederate legislation."[67]

The Luxemburg crisis had failed to provide the needed steam for the engine of Bismarck's German policy. Neither the medium nor maximum alternatives had been achieved. In fact, the crisis revealed more glaringly than ever the depth of the fissures that still divided Germany. Having squeezed all possible benefit from the affair, Bismarck gave up the pretense of trembling before the terrors of German public opinion. On April 26 he agreed to an international conference to negotiate a compromise. At the conference, held May 7–11, 1867, in London, the sovereignty of William III was confirmed; the duchy was neutralized under the guarantee of the great powers; the Prussian right of garrison was withdrawn; and the fortress was consigned to demolition.

For Napoleon this compromise was a harsh defeat. Withdrawal of the Prussian garrison was the only achievement to which he could point in a year of disaster. The retreat from Mexico under the threats of the United States, coupled with his failure to derive for France any benefit from the German civil war, starkly revealed the debility of his regime precisely in that area in which a Bonaparte was expected to excel. Many Germans were also dissatisfied. To Wilhelm the settlement was a "slap" from France, an inglorious "sacrifice" on the altar of peace.[68] German nationalists looked upon it as "almost a defeat." But from May to July agents of the Nationalverein reported from Luxemburg that, if compelled to choose between Prussia and France, nine-tenths of the inhabitants would prefer the latter. The pro-German party hardly dared show its face in the grand duchy.[69] Bismarck had known it all along.

Success of the Minimum

In his struggle for a favorable relationship with the south, Bismarck held in reserve a weapon of considerable power. Although the economic unity of northern Germany was assured, the Zollverein was still indispensable to the

---

[67] SBR, I (1867), 638–639; Schüssler, *Bismarcks Kampf*, 138ff.

[68] APP, VIII, 829.

[69] Oncken, *Bennigsen*, vol. 2, 43–45. For those who take the cultural view of the nation, however, popular sentiment is not a factor. To Otto Becker the settlement was "a painful, national loss." *Bismarcks Ringen*, 425.

welfare of the south. But the events of 1866 had rendered the Zollverein treaties obsolete. In the peace treaties Bismarck had provided that they might be
abrogated on six months' notice. This was a sword suspended over the heads
of the southern statesmen. For the time being, however, he made no motion
to cut the thread. If neither the medium nor maximum goals could be
achieved through the national pressure generated by the Luxemburg crisis,
the menace of abrogation would suffice to achieve the minimum.

On February 15, 1867, while mounting his campaign for the higher alternatives, he approached the southern states for an informal exchange of views
on the subject of Zollverein reform. Prussia favored, he declared, either a
Zollparlament or the addition of southern deputies to the Reichstag when
matters of customs and commerce were under consideration. On March 11 he
brought the plan before the public in a speech to the constituent Reichstag.[70]
But even this proposal, more modest than that of the wider confederation,
was opposed by Bavarian particularists. To Bismarck's annoyance, Hohenlohe
was compelled to reject for the time being any kind of parliamentary union
with the north.[71]

In May Bismarck commenced to tighten the screw. He rejected the Bavarian–Württemberg counterproposal for a loose confederation with a Bundesrat
composed of state envoys whose legislation would be subject to the approval
of the northern Reichstag and southern parliaments.[72] While disclaiming any
desire to coerce, he declared that a common parliament was the "indispensable prerequisite" for the Zollverein's renewal. Should no agreement be
reached by July 1, Berlin would serve notice of her intention to abrogate.
Varnbüler fully understood the necessity of the Zollverein, and he feared further opposition would enable Bismarck to increase still further the price of its
renewal. The forthcoming visit of Wilhelm to Paris, furthermore, raised the
prospect of a French-Prussian understanding at the cost of southern Germany.
On May 23 he suggested that Berlin grasp the initiative in summoning the
southern states to a general conference. Bismarck speedily complied.[73]

Assembling in Berlin on June 3, 1867, the southern ministers were presented with a Prussian proposal. Drafted by Rudolf Delbrück, it had been
extensively revised by Bismarck and was essentially his handiwork. Like the
northern constitution, its revolutionary character was concealed by the fiction of continuity with older forms. The existing treaties remained in effect,

---

[70] GW, VI, 269–270; SBR, I (1867), 138; Hohenlohe, Denkwürdigkeiten, vol. 1, 205.

[71] Walter Schübelin, Das Zollparlament und die Politik von Baden, Bayern, und Württemberg 1866–1870 (Berlin, 1935), 18ff.; Schüssler, Bismarcks Kampf, 233ff. Because of the Luxemburg crisis Bismarck failed to dispatch the reply he dictated on Mar. 29. GW, VI, 317–319.

[72] Hohenlohe, Denkwürdigkeiten, vol. 1, 232ff.; APP, IX, 45–48; Schübelin, Zollparlament, 34ff.; Schüssler, Bismarcks Kampf, 212ff.

[73] APP, IX, 59, 69ff., 91–92; GW, VI, 393–394; Schüssler, Bismarcks Kampf, 231, 237ff.; Becker, Bismarcks Ringen, 572–574; Schübelin, Zollparlament, 38ff.

but Zollverein affairs were to be decided in the future by a "common organ of the contracting states" and a "common representation of their peoples." The former was to be organized like the Frankfurt Diet, with Prussia occupying the presidency and authorized to negotiate with foreign powers; the latter was to be composed of the deputies of the northern Reichstag and deputies elected from the southern states. In a subtly worded clause Prussia was granted the right of veto. Varnbüler and Freydorf accepted immediately for Württemberg and Baden; Dalwigk declared his agreement, while reserving the final decision for Darmstadt.[74]

Hohenlohe was also favorable, but at home he faced a formidable task. In messages to Munich he frightened king and ministers with the prospect that refusal would mean dissolution of the Zollverein. First the cabinet and then Ludwig, though painfully reluctant, came around. Nevertheless, the Bavarians exacted concessions. While accepting the titles Bundesrat des Zollvereins and Zollparlament, they saw to it that these bodies were differentiated as clearly as possible from the legislative organs of the North German Confederation. In the Bundesrat they achieved for Bavaria six votes, as against four in the Frankfurt Diet. The legislative competence of the Zollverein, moreover, was expressly limited to tariffs, their collection, and the taxation of domestic sugar, salt, and tobacco. Bismarck, on the other hand, clung to the Prussian veto and the provision that the southern deputies were to be unsalaried and elected on the same basis as those of the Reichstag. In the requirement for renewal at twelve-year intervals he retained a means with which to effect future changes. The final treaty was signed on July 8.[75]

The last word belonged to the southern parliaments. As in the case of the constituent Reichstag, Bismarck had taken care that they should work under pressure of a deadline (October 31). In Baden and Hesse there was no difficulty, and in Munich the lower chamber voted (October 22) for acceptance, 117 to 17. But the great majority of the Bavarian upper chamber was fiercely opposed. Aristocratic particularists, ultramontanes, and pro-Austrian great-Germanists were determined to preserve for Bavaria at least the right of liberum veto. Only after Hohenlohe had personally escorted the speaker, Baron Thüngen, to Berlin for an interview with Bismarck could the members be convinced of its impossibility. Angry editorials in the liberal-nationalist press and swarms of telegrams and petitions from the urban public and commercial interests warned them that the Zollverein was indispensable. Finally, on Oc-

---

[74] Becker, *Bismarcks Ringen,* 576–577; Schübelin, *Zollparlament,* 44ff. Delbrück's draft has never been published. For the agreement signed on June 4 and the protocol ultimately signed by Bavaria see Ludwig Hahn, *Zwei Jahre preussisch-deutscher Politik 1866–1867* (Berlin, 1868), 622–624.

[75] Becker, *Bismarcks Ringen,* 579ff.; Schübelin, *Zollparlament,* 48ff.; Hohenlohe, *Denkwürdigkeiten,* vol. 1, 244ff. For the final treaty see Hahn, *Zwei Jahre,* 624–631.

tober 31, the chamber voted with the greatest reluctance, 35 to 13, for acceptance.[76]

In Württemberg the major opposition developed in the chamber of deputies. Both the Zollverein treaty and military alliance were debated, the latter meeting even more antagonism than the former. The democratic majority feared domination by the autocratic, militaristic north with its greater voting strength. But the commercial interests lobbied for acceptance of the customs parliament, and Bismarck warned that neither treaty was acceptable without the other. To his annoyance, however, Varnbüler eased the alliance through the chamber on October 30 by claiming Prussia's acceptance of Württemberg's right to approve the casus foederis.[77] Even now, however, the deputies hoped that an unfavorable vote in Munich would relieve them of the necessity of accepting the customs parliament. But on the thirty-first the telegraph reported the contrary. With heavy hearts the democratic majority capitulated.[78]

The customs parliament had been achieved, but the degree of opposition it met was inauspicious for Bismarck's further aims. In December 1867 Varnbüler voiced the prevailing mood of the south in a speech to the Württemberg parliament. With the Zollverein and alliance treaties, he asserted, the southern states had fulfilled their duty to the German nation. There would be no further sacrifice. "Württemberg wants to remain Württemberg as long as it has the power."[79]

[76] APP, IX, 310, 322ff.; Schieder, *Kleindeutsche Partei,* 158ff.; Schübelin, *Zollparlament,* 59ff.; GW, VIa, 92–93.

[77] GW, VIa, 69–70, 110–111.

[78] Rapp, *Württemberger,* 247ff.; Schübelin, *Zollparlament,* 62ff. In the event of a negative vote the Prussian ministers in Bavaria and Württemberg were instructed to announce termination of the Zollverein in six months. GW, VIa, 84, 92, 96.

[79] Erich Brandenburg, *Die Reichsgründung* (2d ed., Leipzig, 1922), vol. 2, 307; Schüssler, *Bismarcks Kampf,* 281–282.

❊❋

Failure of the National Movement

The Zollverein Elections

N NOVEMBER 1867 Bismarck repeatedly assured the impatient Badenese that his aim was to find the shortest path to the voluntary entry of all southern states into the North German Confederation. "Direct and immediate pressure" was to be avoided. To admit Baden alone would create a pressure upon Bavaria and Württemberg that would be resented—to the injury of the national cause. The simultaneous admission of Baden and Württemberg, on the other hand, might cause Bavaria to take a "regrettable course." It would supply the "pretext" for disunity at a time when Germany required the greatest solidarity.[1]

Through "patience" he hoped to save what would have to be sacrificed by the use of violence. "Force can be useful against a resistance that is to be broken by a single blow, but it can be justified only by necessity against a resistance that would have to be continually held down." The Badenese should be able to imagine for themselves what conditions would develop in Bavaria and Württemberg, "if in their present mood these two states were brought by force into the North German Confederation."[2] Instead he hoped to rely upon the pressure of common interests eventually to unite both sides of the Main under the northern constitution. "If Germany should attain its national goal in the nineteenth century," he remarked, "that would seem to me something great. Were it in ten or even five years, that would be something extraordinary, an unexpected gift of God."[3]

"Everything depends," he wrote to Karlsruhe, "on the direction and swiftness with which public opinion develops in southern Germany, and a fairly secure judgment about that will first become possible through the customs parliament." The next task was to elect and summon that body as soon as possible and then "to awaken and nourish" a demand for the extension of its powers. He expected it to adopt the laws of the North German Confederation in such matters as citizenship, passports, and civil law. In a few years—perhaps ten, at the most twenty—the organic growth of the Zollverein would create a small-German union on the northern pattern. Eagerly he waited to see what "temperament" the customs parliament would show.[4]

[1] GW, VIa, 112–113, 133–136; also 127–128 and APP, IX, 289–293.
[2] GW, VIa, 329–330.
[3] RKN, I, 68; APP, IX, 474.
[4] GW, VIa, 113, 135, 153–155; Otto Becker, *Bismarcks Ringen um Deutschlands Gestaltung*

Throughout the south, the parties, politicians, and general public were similarly aware that what was being decided in the Zollverein elections was not merely the question of tariffs and taxes, but also that of Germany's future. In August 1867 the leaders of the national parties convened in Stuttgart to agree on a common platform calling for the extension of the powers of the new parliament.[5] At home they entered into the campaign with vigor and confidence, advertising the election as a plebiscite of the national will. For the first time southerners were to vote under direct and equal suffrage. At last German nationalists had the chance to prove at the polls that their yearnings were those of the masses.

In Bavaria an opposition began to form during 1867. Whereas the old great-Germanist party, now defunct, had been bourgeois and aristocratic in composition, the new "Patriot party" was composed of peasants, lower clergy, and petty bourgeoisie, supported by the high aristocracy and the democratic left. Motives were mixed. The democrats had split with the moderates of the Progressive party. They opposed "dancing to Bismarck's fiddle" in a German parliament that appeared to have all the limitations of the northern Reichstag and Prussian Chamber of Deputies. But the bulk of the opposition was confessional and particularistic, rather than political. Catholics, both clergy and laymen, feared domination by the Protestant north. Conservative aristocrats were horrified by the prospect that the Wittelsbach dynasty, Germany's oldest, should be mediatized by a Hohenzoller. Bavarian nationalism, moreover, was a vital force for particularism, especially in "old Bavaria," the kingdom's nucleus.[6] "Because of her material importance, her definite tribal individuality, and the talents of her rulers," Bismarck had written in 1865, "Bavaria is perhaps the only German country that has succeeded in developing a real, harmonious national sentiment."[7] Even today the Bavarian sense of cultural individuality is a factor of importance in German political life.

Despite the activity of the Patriot party, German nationalists of the Progressive and Middle parties went to the polls on February 10, 1868, confident of victory. But the result was devastating. The Patriot party elected twenty-six of the forty-eight deputies, many by overwhelming majorities. In view of its minor strength in the Bavarian lower chamber it had been expected to capture only four or five seats. Together the two liberal parties brought in but twelve. The greatest defeat was suffered by the Middle party, largest in the

---

(Heidelberg, 1958), 583–584. Since 1858, at least, he had calculated on the possibility that a Zollverein parliament would undermine particularistic governments. GW, XIV, 487; IV, 31–32.

[5] Walter Schübelin, *Das Zollparlament und die Politik von Baden, Bayern, und Württemberg 1866–1870* (Berlin, 1935), 71–72.

[6] Theodor Schieder, *Die kleindeutsche Partei in Bayern: Münchener historische Abhandlungen*, vol. 12 (Munich, 1936), 156ff., 173ff.; Schübelin, *Zollparlament*, 98ff.; George G. Windell, *The Catholics and German Unity, 1866–1871* (Minneapolis, 1954), 124ff.

[7] GW, V, 56.

lower chamber, which elected only nine. Formerly the party of liberal great-Germanists, it had lost its following both to the left and the right.[8]

Of all southern states the nationalists had the greatest prospects in Baden. Ruler, ministers, and the dominant Progressive party favored a united Germany. The campaign declaration of December 20, 1867, signed by ministers and deputies, described the customs parliament as but a "preliminary step" to German unity. Only those determined to further the "national union," it declared, should offer themselves as candidates. But the national issue became intertwined with domestic ones, and the opposition swelled to unexpected proportions. Catholic rights, Protestant conservatism, economic protectionism, and particularistic patriotism were the dominant motives. Beginning quietly and rationally, the campaign ended bitter, fanatical, and demagogic on both sides. Nationalist strength lay in the urban middle class; the particularists appealed to workers and peasants. The government intervened for the progressives, and the Catholic clergy did the same for the opposition during the final days of the campaign. On February 18, 1868, the nationalists won but eight of fourteen seats. Their voting strength (86,890) was actually less than that of the opposition (90,078). Throughout Germany the result was seen as a severe setback for the national cause.[9]

In Württemberg the prospects of the nationalists were least. Only the German party supported further unification. At first the People's party, which in October 1866 had provided the core of the opposition to the treaty, voted to boycott the election. But after the defeat of the nationalists in Baden and Bavaria the populists leaped into the campaign. The government itself was their ally. "We want to prove to Germany and Europe," Varnbüler declared, "that . . . the North German Confederation has no appeal whatever for us." Here the issue was more political than confessional. Swabian democrats dreaded the "Caesarism" and "saber government" of the Prussian north. Their ideal was republican Switzerland and its citizen army. The northern constitution, it was joked, had only three clauses: pay taxes; be a soldier; and hold your tongue.[10]

In fighting back Bismarck chose the weapon of conservatism. The Prussian legation in Stuttgart sued the leading democratic journal, *Beobachter*, for slandering the king of Prussia and obtained a judgment. The anti-Prussian deputies replied by introducing a bill to require jury trial in such cases. Bismarck denounced it to Varnbüler as an attack upon the monarchical principle. After the bill passed, he turned to Dresden, Munich, and Karlsruhe for assistance in warning Stuttgart of the "revolutionary movement" being fostered by its

[8] Schübelin, *Zollparlament*, 100–101.

[9] *Ibid.*, 72–86; Windell, *Catholics and German Unity*, 124ff.

[10] Schübelin, *Zollparlament*, 86–97; Adolf Rapp, *Die Württemberger und die nationale Frage, 1863–1871: Darstellungen aus der württembergischen Geschichte*, vol. 4 (Stuttgart, 1910), 258ff.; *APP*, IX, 774, 815.

policy in the Zollverein election. Then he took the matter up with Vienna, expressing fear that the Württemberg government would lose control to a revolutionary republican party whose aim, nourished by contacts with Switzerland and America, was a "united states of Europe." Finally he addressed his forebodings to London, Paris, and Petersburg with the accusation that Beust himself was playing with revolutionary fire by supporting Swabian radicals.[11]

Yet on March 24, 1868, candidates of the People's party and the government polled three-quarters of the total vote and took all seventeen Württemberg seats in the customs parliament. The German party (popularly called the "Prussian party") had pleaded with the Swabians to consider themselves primarily as Germans and to find in German national institutions the objects of their loyalty and patriotism. For most voters, however, the issue was not whether they were German, but whether they were to be "Prussianized." Only in Hesse-Darmstadt, which had but six votes, did the particularists fail to score.

Of eighty-five deputies chosen by voters of the southern states, forty-nine entered the customs parliament pledged to block attempts to extend its authority. Direct and equal suffrage, so successful for Bismarck's purposes in the north, had proved to be the route to disaster in the south.[12]

The Zollparlament

"To attain with one blow a homogeneous structure for Germany," Bismarck wrote to Karlsruhe on February 28, 1868, "is only possible in the event of war. Aside from this eventuality, which we shall neither predict nor precipitate, the development will have to run through one or more transitional stages." He still hoped, despite the sharp rebuff by southern voters, that the customs parliament would provide such a stage. Once its deputies came to grips with practical problems, he told the demoralized government in Baden, they would find "no room for doctrinaire obstinacy, scholastic habits of thought, or religious bias." Their horizons would widen as they dealt with the problems of German and world commerce. "The satisfaction of each common need will make perceptible yet another and render easier its satisfaction." He expected that the elections at the end of each three-year parliamentary term would produce constantly more favorable results for the national cause.[13]

On April 27, 1868, the customs parliament assembled in Berlin. In a brief speech, composed by Bismarck, Wilhelm traced the growth of the Zollverein and credited its success not only to the economic needs of the German people, but also to "the power of the national idea." "Hold the common German

---

[11] GW, VIa, 202–204, 214–215, 227–228, 234–235, 256–257.

[12] E. R. Huber, *Deutsche Verfassungsgeschichte seit 1879* (Stuttgart, 1963), vol. 3, 635–636; Schübelin, *Zollparlament*, 95–102; Windell, *Catholics and German Unity*, 131ff.

[13] GW, VIa, 284–286.

interest firmly in view . . . ," he admonished at the end, "and win the nation's thanks." The German military alliances "can with God's help always count on the united strength of the German people."[14] The Zollverein and military alliances, in other words, were inseparable links in a common chain. By emphasizing the national character of both he sought to soothe the fear of "Prussianization" and overcome resistance to the expansion of the parliament's powers.

Despite an abundance of official hospitality, the southern deputies felt out of place in Berlin. Behind the "studiously polite amiability" of their reception, the Swabian democrats detected "something sly and pedagogical." "In every corner" of the capital they saw the monuments and memorials of the military state they dreaded. They huddled together in common living quarters and longed for the day of departure. In the chamber, particularists of all political views combined in a "South German party" to fight for the common cause. Among the 297 north German deputies they gained some support from Poles, Hanoverian "Guelphs," Prussian conservatives, and socialists August Bebel and Wilhelm Liebknecht. Romantic conservatism made common cause with Swabian radicalism, Bavarian Catholicism, and Saxon socialism.[15]

During the three years of its existence the achievements of the customs parliament were considerable within the competence granted by the treaties. New trade agreements were reached with Austria and Switzerland; many new lands in Latin America and the Pacific opened their doors to German businessmen. Tariff reductions made possible the entry of Lübeck and Mecklenburg into the customs union. A uniform tax on sugar and tobacco was established for the whole of Germany. After some difficulty a general tariff law was finally passed in 1870.[16]

The South German party, nevertheless, zealously guarded the bridges of the Main against every attempt to extend the competence of the assembly. The first foray in 1868 was a motion, introduced by the nationalists of Baden and Hesse, for an address to the king of Prussia expressing the hope that the "power of the national idea" would soon lead to complete unification. Even Bismarck thought it unwise to allow south German nationalists to defeat their particularistic colleagues with the help of northern votes. The address was rejected. During the deliberations that followed, the South German party sought by vigilant interruptions to halt efforts by nationalist speakers to enlarge the scope of the debates to general political matters.[17]

On May 18, however, one of their own number made a mistake that Bismarck exploited with lightning speed. The issue was the wine tariff and whether the parliament had the authority to take up the grievances of Hessian

[14] GW, X, 464–465.
[15] Rapp, Württemberger, 289ff.; Windell, Catholics and German Unity, 135ff.
[16] Becker, Bismarcks Ringen, 590ff.; Schübelin, Zollparlament, 125ff.
[17] Schübelin, Zollparlament, 111ff.; Windell, Catholics and German Unity, 137ff.

producers. In denying it, a Swabian deputy pointed obliquely to the threat of French intervention. "Somewhere on a mountain hangs an avalanche, which the least disturbance can plunge into the chasm." Never, replied Bismarck, would the North German government seek to force its institutions on the south against the will of the majority. As for the avalanche, the deputies should know that "an appeal to fear never finds an echo in German hearts!" An ovation thundered through the hall. Not for nothing had Bismarck been practicing for a decade the vocabulary of national sentiment. In succession the nationalist speakers followed his lead. "Now it is springtime in Germany," cried Josef Völk, deputy for Augsburg. "If some are still throwing snowballs, the advance of spring will soon put an end to the snow."[18]

Three springs came and went, but the frost remained. After May 18, 1868, the customs parliament produced no major political debates. Except for occasional allusions to the greater issue of unity, the deliberations were restricted to tariffs and taxes. Nationalists sought to promote their cause by exercizing to the fullest the parliament's legislative power, but they were deeply discouraged by its limited scope. Southern particularists, on the other hand, felt triumphant. "The Bismarck machine," they reported home, "stands still."[19] It has been asserted, nevertheless, that the customs parliament was psychologically of great value in preparing the German people for unity. Even southern particularists, like Baron Wolfgang von Thüngen, felt compelled to stress to the parliament the depth of their German patriotism. They had no other choice, moreover, than to base their case for preservation of the status quo upon the very treaties they had previously condemned. To oppose further unity they had publicly to argue the adequacy of what had already been achieved. Contrary to their expectations, Bismarck did not seek openly to exploit the parliament for the extension of Prussian hegemony. He held to his avowal that southerners must themselves decide whether they wished to join the north.[20]

Contemporary observers of nationalist viewpoint differed concerning what was taking place in the hidden recesses of the popular mind. Before the parliament's first session, Gustav Freytag wrote that it was an "error" to assume that "time and some kind of peaceful, cultural effort will bring the southern states into the confederation. On the contrary, they are becoming more alien to us every year, despite the Zollverein."[21] After the first adjournment Wilhelm Wehrenpfennig commented in the *Preussische Jahrbücher* that the parlia-

---

[18] *Stenographische Berichte über die Verhandlungen des Deutschen Zoll-Parlaments* (1868), 264–282.

[19] Rapp, *Württemberger*, 327; Schübelin, *Zollparlament*, 124ff.

[20] Rapp, *Württemberger*, 332; Schieder, *Kleindeutsche Partei*, 191; Becker, *Bismarcks Ringen*, 591ff. It is difficult to see how Becker intended to prove his undocumented assertion that "many returned home with changed views even if they didn't dare openly to say so."

[21] *HW*, I, 408.

ment had been "the preparatory school for the entry of the south into the north German state." With Baron Franz von Roggenbach he felt that even the cooperation of northern and southern particularists against the parliament was a gain.[22] But Heinrich von Treitschke judged otherwise. "All of those loyal German words" and "ardent expressions of affection" spoken by southerners, he growled, "cannot change the fact that the majority of cabinets and peoples in the south wish to continue undisturbed in their *vierthalbstaatlich* confusion." From Munich Josef Maria von Radowitz, the Prussian secretary of legation, reported on September 1, 1868, that anti-Prussian forces were daily gaining in zeal and strength throughout the south. Ultramontane circles were openly pro-French, exulted in her growing military strength, and anticipated her coming victory over Prussia.[23]

The vital question, however, is how Bismarck himself judged the Zollparlament, its achievements, and its potentiality. Certainly it is significant that during the session of 1869 he appeared in the chamber only once for a brief speech. To Rudolf Delbrück was left the task of representing the Prussian government. When the nationalists complained of the chancellor's seeming indifference, he referred them to his doctor. But the register of his activities during the three-week period shows that he was not at all incapacitated and spent a good part of the time on an inspection tour of western Germany. Obviously he no longer had much interest in the parliament and its deliberations.[24] His mind was now busy with other options in the German question.

Failure of the Southern Union

A southern confederation was another possible "transitional stage" that Bismarck foresaw on the way to national unity under the northern constitution. We have seen that the treaties of Nikolsburg and Prague provided for such an organization. At the time both Varnbüler and Pfordten believed in the practicality of a *Trias* arrangement as a lasting solution of the German problem. Varnbüler expected that a south German union, if equipped with free institutions, would have sufficient popular appeal to provide a lasting barrier to Prussian domination. But in November 1866 the two statesmen concluded

[22] *Preussische Jahrbücher*, 21 (1868), 700–701; Julius Heyderhoff, ed., *Im Ring der Gegner Bismarcks* (2d ed., Leipzig, 1943), 86–87; Rapp, *Württemberger*, 302; Becker, *Bismarcks Ringen*, 591–592.

[23] Heinrich von Treitschke, *Zehn Jahre deutscher Kämpfe: Schriften zur Tagespolitik* (3d ed., Berlin, 1897), vol. 1, 246–247; APP, X, 157–161.

[24] *Verhandlungen des Zoll-Parlaments* (1869), 220–222. During the short session of May 1870 Bismarck was actually ill in Varzin. Horst Kohl, ed., *Fürst Bismarck: Regesten zu einer wissenschaftlichen Biographie des ersten Reichskanzlers* (Stuttgart, 1981–1892), vol. 1, 374–375, 392. Schübelin (*Zollparlament*, 130–131) believes that in 1868 he had already ceased to regard the customs parliament as important for his aims. Becker (*Bismarcks Ringen*, 592) argues unconvincingly the contrary view.

that Prussia's annexation of Frankfurt and Nassau, the inclusion of upper Hesse in the northern confederation, and the German policy of the Baden government made achievement of a southern union most unlikely. Bavaria and Württemberg alone could not make it viable.[25]

During 1867, however, the project was revived under stimulation from Vienna and Paris. Bismarck's success in negotiating the military treaties and reorganizing the Zollverein showed that something had to be done to shore up the sagging line of the Main. In a south German confederation Beust and Napoleon expected to find the needed reinforcement. Returning from a conference with Franz Joseph at Salzburg in late August, the emperor expressed to Hohenlohe his regret that the southern states had not united. Two months later, after accompanying Franz Joseph to Paris, Beust conferred with Varnbüler and Hohenlohe in a determined effort to launch the project. French concern over Berlin's intentions toward the south, he declared, endangered the peace. Only the creation of a southern union in some form or other would quiet these fears and prevent a conflict. Hohenlohe found the argument convincing. He was still under the illusion, moreover, that the "stream of public opinion" would swamp any government that failed to show some initiative in the German question, even if it were merely a southern union.[26]

On November 9, 1867, he informed Bismarck through Count von Tauffkirchen of his intention to foster a southern confederation. Bismarck judged that such a combination would not "be particularly dangerous for the national cause; national sentiment, once concentrated in a south German parliament, would be more energetic and effective than it was in the parliaments of individual states." He immediately saw in the proposal a help, not a hindrance, to his own policy. What Beust and Napoleon had set in motion might become their undoing. He had written the provision for such a union into the Nikolsburg treaty with the thought that, "should a south German and a north German parliament exist one day, they would soon link hands and find a way to unite." A southern parliament, he told Julius Fröbel, would "break" southern particularism. What mattered was not the transitory stage, but the end. "Everything human is only provisional."[27]

And yet the draft constitution that Hohenlohe forwarded to Varnbüler on November 30 did not provide for a common parliament. It established a "united states of southern Germany," whose governing "authority" was composed of foreign ministers authorized to "regulate common affairs." In this body Bavaria was accorded six votes, Württemberg four, Baden three, and Hesse two. Having no permanent location, the authority was to rotate yearly

[25] APP, VIII, 173–174; Becker, Bismarcks Ringen, 629–630.

[26] Friedrich Curtius, ed., Denkwürdigkeiten des Fürsten Chlodwig zu Hohenlohe-Schillingsfürst (Stuttgart, 1907), vol. 1, 259, 277–281; APP, IX, 188–189, 361–363, 368–369.

[27] APP, IX, 372, 401–405; GW, VIa, 113, 125–126; Julius Fröbel, Ein Lebenslauf (Stuttgart, 1890–1891), vol. 2, 544–546.

among the southern capitals, returning to each with a frequency proportionate to the voting strength of the state. "By way of treaties" it was to seek conformity in the laws of northern and southern Germany. The "common army" was to have no common commander in peacetime; Prussia was to be granted an advisory voice in military matters. Except for common consulates, the states were to retain their own foreign services.[28]

Varnbüler rejected the plan for the very possibilities that Bismarck saw in it. The greatest barrier to the expansion of the northern confederation, he wrote to Hohenlohe on December 15, was the enduring vitality of existing states. But nothing would sap this vitality more rapidly than a south German confederation of "organic" character. Such a development would cause the traditional loyalties to deteriorate and open the way for the growth of a "great national life." Addition of a parliament would greatly accelerate this process and lead either to a republic or the demand for union with the north. The consultative voice of Prussia in the military committee would very likely become a decisive one.[29]

In Karlsruhe, on the other hand, the nationalist government failed to recognize these potentialities. After transmitting the plan to Bismarck, Mathy and Freydorf were surprised by his positive reaction. Back came the advice that Baden should avoid the odium of rejecting it. She should accept "in principle" and insist upon amendments that would either transform the project into "a bridge" for German unity or cause it to collapse.[30] When Hohenlohe revived the plan in February 1868 after the disaster of the Zollverein elections, Bismarck advised the incredulous Badenese to demand a southern parliament as the price of approval: "The most difficult part of the task of national reconstruction is the removal of the existing. If what exists is breached, even though it be through a south German confederation, a healthy national life will grow by itself out of the ruins. But this breach can be achieved only by such a far-reaching reconstruction as a common parliament, not by a mere confederation of governments."[31]

Though he accepted the argument in general, Freydorf still balked at the prospect of a southern parliament. He feared that the multiplication of parliaments and elections would result in voter fatigue and loss of interest. Bismarck

---

[28] *Hohenlohe. Denkwürdigkeiten*, vol. 1, 282ff.; Otto von Völderndorff, "Deutsche Verfassungen und Verfassungsentwürfe," *Annalen des deutschen Reichs*, 23 (1890), 282ff.

[29] APP, IX, 546–549, 584–587. In 1868 the idea of a southern confederation received considerable support in the People's party and its organ, *Der Beobachter*, and Varnbüler was compelled to take a public stand against it. Rapp, *Württemberger*, 304ff. In May thirty-two members of the South German party of the customs parliament signed a declaration favoring such a confederation. Schübelin, *Zollparlament*, 120–121.

[30] GW, VIa, 155–156; APP, IX, 472.

[31] GW, VIa, 284–286.

countered with the sly suggestion that elections to the southern chamber might be synchronized with those to the customs parliament! To Freydorf's further objection that in a south German parliament the nationalists would find themselves confronted by an "ultramontane-democratic-particularistic majority," he replied that such a coalition could not possibly hold together indefinitely. It must soon founder of its own contradictions.[32]

By March 1868 Bismarck was aware that the attitudes that prevailed in Munich and Stuttgart made the realization of Hohenlohe's project most unlikely.[33] In this he was utterly correct. On the insistence of King Ludwig it was presented to the Bavarian cabinet on February 22. All of the prince's colleagues, except the minister of war, were against it. They shared Varnbüler's premonitions. On March 28 Hohenlohe reluctantly told Ludwig that for the time being nothing more could be done. In July he confessed to Baron Georg von Werthern, the Prussian minister, that the plan was unachievable.[34]

Because they had provided the impulse, Hohenlohe's failure looks like another defeat for Beust and Napoleon.[35] In view of the possibilities Bismarck saw in the plan, however, the defeat has to be regarded as chiefly his. To be sure, he had never positively engaged Prussian foreign policy for its achievement and had instructed his envoys to handle the matter as one of "indifference" to Prussia.[36] Its collapse, nevertheless, removed from the scene one more of those "stages" through which he might have advanced toward German unification under the northern constitution. The alternatives of peace were diminishing.

The Progress of Military Assimilation

During the years 1866–1870 the most tangible progress toward the integration of Germany under Prussian leadership came in the area of military affairs. And yet this gain took years and many struggles to accomplish. Although their defeat in the war of 1866 had exposed many weaknesses in the armies of the lesser states, no unanimity existed about what remedial steps to take. Should the necessary reform follow the Prussian model, whose efficiency had been proven in the war against Austria, or the Swiss militia system, whose democratic features were more sympathetic to many southerners? The former course was favored by Baden, whose leadership favored a military convention

[32] APP, IX, 786–788, 828–830; GW, VIa, 328–330, 338–339.

[33] GW, VIa, 330.

[34] Becker, Bismarcks Ringen, 642. See also Wolf D. Gruner, "Bayern, Preussen, und die Süddeutschen Staaten, 1866–1870," Zeitschrift für bayerische Landesgeschichte, 37 (1974), 799–827.

[35] Thus Becker, Bismarcks Ringen, 642.

[36] GW, VIb, 7, 35–36, 46–47.

with Berlin that meant virtual assimilation of its armed forces into the Prussian army. Because of its divided status, half inside and half outside the North German Confederation, Hesse was compelled to seek such a convention if its army was to remain intact as a single fighting force, and one was signed on April 11, 1867. But in Bavaria and Württemberg there was strong resistance to "Prussianization" of their armed forces and much sentiment for a "citizen army" on the Swiss model. [37]

One of Hohenlohe's first acts upon assuming office in January 1867 was to propose a conference to coordinate military reform throughout the south, preferably on the Prussian model. Bismarck readily supported him. To be sure, he would have preferred individual military conventions with each of the southern states. By providing for common weapons, insignia, training, and the like, such conventions would have been a valuable supplement to the military alliances already achieved. One of the purposes of the concessions made to Saxony in the convention that integrated her forces into the north German army was to entice the south into similar agreements. But it was now obvious that for the time being such compacts were impossible in Bavaria and Württemberg. For Berlin to grant Baden's desire for military and political union with the North German Confederation might drive these states to seek support abroad for the maintenance of their independence. In Hohenlohe's proposal, however, Bismarck saw the chance to achieve his end without the direct engagement of Prussian foreign policy. He urged Karlsruhe to participate in the conference and influence its outcome. [38]

Held in Stuttgart (February 3–5, 1867), the conference produced a protocol signed by Hohenlohe, Varnbüler, Freydorf, and Dalwigk. The southern states agreed to increase and reorganize their forces upon the principles of the Prussian system in order to make possible "the defense of the national integrity in common with the rest of Germany." Behind closed doors, however, the ministers disagreed sharply concerning the degree to which the Prussian system was to be adopted. No agreement was reached upon such important matters as length of service, military regulations and training, and types of armament and munitions. [39]

In late April, as reports streamed into the Wilhelmstrasse of the menacing preparations of the French army, Bismarck complained to Munich, Stuttgart, and Karlsruhe that southern states had not improved their military preparedness since the preceding year. He urged the governments to summon their

[37] Hohenlohe, *Denkwürdigkeiten*, vol. 1, 194–195; APP, VIII, 269–271, 279–281; Becker, *Bismarcks Ringen*, 597ff.

[38] GW, VI, 233–234, 239–243, 256–257.

[39] Max Leyh, *Die bayerische Heeresreform unter König Ludwig II.*, 1866–1870: Darstellungen aus der bayerischen Kriegs- und Heeresgeschichte, vol. 23 (Munich, 1923), 32–37. For the text of the agreement see J. C. Glaser, ed., *Archiv des Norddeutschen Bundes* (Berlin, 1867), vol. 3, 42–44.

parliaments and demand cooperation in remedying the "evils" of their military establishments. In this way they could demonstrate the solidarity of the nation in the Luxemburg affair. But the replies were negative and even the Baden government was offended by the criticism. Nor did he have much better luck in exploiting the French threat to get military conventions. On May 2, 1867, he proposed to Hohenlohe that Berlin negotiate such agreements with individual states "on different levels" commencing with Baden. Hohenlohe approved the convention with Baden, provided it remained secret and was limited to the current crisis.[40] Although drafted, it remained unsigned, for the London conference assured the peace. In any case the episode showed that conventions with Württemberg and Bavaria were still unattainable. Kings Karl and Ludwig rejected the idea. It was his duty, the former declared, to demonstrate to Prussia that he was an independent sovereign and would remain so.[41]

The implementation of the Stuttgart agreement met considerable opposition in all three southern states. In Baden even the nationalists disliked the three-year service period, the cost involved in doubling the size of the army, and the importation of Prussian militarism. Ultimately Baden's military reform bill was passed only through compromise and the promise of liberal reforms. Naturally in Bavaria, remote from the French frontier, the antagonism was even greater. Particularists, ultramontanes, and democrats assailed the reform as the first step in Bavaria's domination by Prussia. The Swiss militia system was extolled and standing armies decried as the scourge of freedom and culture. From the press, however, the public learned on March 17 that Pfordten had already committed the Bavarian army to Prussian command in wartime. After an initial failure, the Bavarian military reform bill finally passed at the end of January 1868. But the dissatisfaction was still intense. "We don't want to be Prussian," conscripts yelled at their officers. Firm measures were necessary to establish discipline.[42]

In Württemberg the difficulties were greatest. Minister of War Oskar von Hardegg regarded the Prussian system as "barbaric and un-German." Instead he advocated a citizen militia of twelve months' training distributed over a period of six years. But the officer corps had become increasingly pro-Prussian and nationalistic. When his views were attacked by a leading officer, Major Albert von Suckow, Hardegg resigned and was replaced by Colonel Wagner von Frommenhausen. As the latter's adjutant, Suckow pushed the military laws through parliament over severe opposition. His only major concession was reduction of the length of service from three to two years. In this parlia-

---

[40] GW, VI, 366–369, 374.

[41] APP, IX, 80, 104–105, 150.

[42] Hermann Baumgarten, *Staatsminister Jolly* (Tübingen, 1897), 88ff., 169–170; Schieder, *Kleindeutsche Partei*, 149ff., 168ff.; Leyh, *Bayerische Heeresreform*, 37ff., 52–63.

mentary struggle the government had to abandon its liaison with the radicals of the People's party and accept the support of the German party, which it had helped to defeat in the Zollverein election.[43]

The pace of Prussianization in the south was speeded by an exchange of military personnel. In Karlsruhe two Prussian officers were appointed chief of the general staff and minister of war. Officer candidates of the Baden army were trained in Prussian academies. By treaty, citizens of Baden and Hesse were allowed to discharge their military service in Prussia, and vice versa. Southern armies took over the Prussian system of drilling, communication, command, and battle organization. Except for Bavaria, they adopted the same breechloading "needle-gun" that had slaughtered their troops in 1866. Even in outward appearance—knapsack, uniform, and spiked helmet—their soldiers began to resemble the Prussian. Younger officers began to imitate the speech, gait, and mustache of their Prussian counterparts. For the troops there was more discipline, spit and polish, and physical duress. "Cadaver obedience" had its insidious appeal to the southern military mind, and began through conscription to influence civilian attitudes as well.[44] The school that Roon and Wilhelm designed for Prussia had opened its classrooms to the whole of Germany.

The problem of what to do with the equipment of the old confederate fortresses offered Bismarck still another opportunity to penetrate the military independence of the south. The fortress of Mainz had been acquired by Prussia, but three others (Ulm, Rastatt, and Landau) were located on southern soil. Soon after the conclusion of peace Bismarck directed that Prussia's share in them be upheld as a means with which to develop "new common relationships." Beginning in April 1868 Hohenlohe promoted the creation of an exclusively "south German military committee" to administrate the three southern fortresses and coordinate the southern military effort. But Baden forced a compromise that required a prior settlement with Prussia.[45]

In January 1869 Bismarck explained to Wilhelm how he intended to exploit this opportunity. Prussia's share in the common property gave her the chance to insist upon the principle of joint inspection and control over its use. Once established on even a periodic basis, a commission for this purpose would of necessity become a standing one. Beginning with a "civilian physiognomy," it could gradually be given a military one. Ultimately he expected the growth of a common organ for national defense under Prussian leader-

[43] Becker, *Bismarcks Ringen*, 598–600; Wilhelm Busch, ed., *Rückschau von Albert von Suckow* (Tübingen, 1909), 111ff.

[44] Becker, *Bismarcks Ringen*, 600; Rapp, *Württemberger*, 333–337; Georg Meyer, "Die Reichsgründung und das Grossherzogtum Baden," *Festgabe für Grossherzog Friedrich von Baden* (Heidelberg, 1896), 176–177; Baumgarten, *Jolly*, 83, 121ff.

[45] *APP*, VIII, 104–106; IX, 872, 903; X, 111, 119–120, 179–181, 198–200; Hohenlohe, *Denkwürdigkeiten*, vol. 1, 320ff.; GW, VIa, 413–414.

ship.[46] From the seed would come the sprout, and from the sprout a flourishing plant.

Hohenlohe and Varnbüler, however, were reluctant to enter into the arrangement. They suspected his ulterior aim and were concerned over the possible reaction of France and Austria. Only after vigorous notes from Berlin did the two men agree to a conference, which convened in Munich on April 4, 1869. After much contention an agreement was finally reached (July 6) that conceded the essence of the Prussian program.[47] The seed had been planted, but the squabbling at Munich placed in doubt the fertility of the soil. From his estate in Varzin, whence he had retired with ailing body and frazzled nerves, Bismarck growled at those southern "phrase makers," who deluded themselves by thinking they were more important to the north than the north to them. He would like now, à la Hannibal Fischer, to auction off everything.[48]

Meanwhile, French military preparations had actually enabled the Prussian general staff to commit the south to a common plan of mobilization. In late April 1867, as the Luxemburg affair reached its final and most dangerous stage, Bismarck negotiated an exchange of "military plenipotentiaries" with southern states. Early in 1868 the pace of French armament and the belligerent tone of its press aroused a fresh war scare. Though reports from Paris indicated that no attack was in the offing, it behooved Moltke to confer with Suckow, now chief of the Württemberg general staff, and Freyberg, the Bavarian military plenipotentiary. In these talks (May 1868) he explained his plan for an "indirect defense" of southern Germany. Southern troops were to assemble in the Palatinate to form the left wing of a general assault upon the flank of any force seeking to invade across the upper Rhine. Soon the details, including the use of railways and communications, had been decided upon. For the first time German sovereigns committed themselves during peacetime to a common plan of deployment for the eventuality of war.[49] If ineffective on other levels, the Luxemburg affair at least produced a greater degree of national cohesion in military planning than had ever before existed in Germany.

A Year of Disappointment

Mobilization plans are, of course, state secrets. As far as the public was concerned, the year immediately preceding the outbreak of war in July 1870 was

[46] GW, VIa, 531–533, also 495–496.

[47] GW, VIa, 527–530, 539–542; VIb, 2–5, 8; Leyh, *Bayerische Heeresreform*, 77–86.

[48] GW, VIb, 104, 118; Becker, *Bismarcks Ringen*, 602–603. In 1852 Fischer, an Oldenburg official, was commissioned to auction off the German fleet assembled during the revolution.

[49] GW, VI, 354, 374–375; VIa, 340–342, 362, 383; APP, X, 96–97. Becker, *Bismarcks Ringen*, 603.

one of decay and even retrogression in the cause of national unity. It was marked in Bavaria by electoral victories of the particularists and the fall of the Hohenlohe cabinet, and in Württemberg by a rousing campaign to end the Prussianization of the Swabian army.

During his three years in office Prince Hohenlohe had the uncomfortable task of balancing the mutual hostilities of a particularistic cabinet, the liberal-national majority in the chamber, and a voting public that was rapidly turning conservative and particularistic. The issues concerned the internal reforms of the Hohenlohe regime, as well as its foreign policy. In February 1869 the cabinet, supported by liberal deputies, pushed through the lower chamber a bill that nearly eliminated clerical supervision of the schools. The Bavarian quarrel over clerical influence in education was part of a general conflict between church and state that developed throughout Europe in the 1860s. The steady progress of the autonomous state since the French Revolution, culminating in Italian unification and the loss of Papal sovereignty, had made Catholics everywhere extremely sensitive to any curtailment of the church's authority. To Hohenlohe and his supporters, on the other hand, the school law was a defensive act intended to protect the "cultural state" from an aggressive ultramontanism.[50]

Under the impact of this dispute the Patriot party began in the winter of 1868–1869 to take on form and organization. In the general election of May 1869 the contrasts were even starker than in the Zollverein election of the preceding year: German nationalism against Bavarian particularism, the autonomous state against the international hierarchy of the church, liberalism against Catholic romantic conservatism, the urban middle class against feudal agrarianism. When the votes were counted, the Patriot party had won another significant victory. Although the progressives picked up some seats, the continuing deterioration of the center chiefly benefited the right.[51]

What they had not been able to achieve at the polls, the progressives now sought to attain through political manipulation. By challenging the count in a number of constituencies, they managed to cut back the patriot majority until the house was evenly divided, 71 to 71. This hopeless parliamentary situation required a fresh dissolution on October 6, 1869. In order to improve their chances, the liberals now demanded that the electoral districts be redrawn. The cabinet complied. Given a new issue, the Patriot party entered the campaign with redoubled vigor and on November 25 captured eighty seats to take control of the chamber.[52]

When parliament met after January 17, 1870, the patriots opened their

[50] Schieder, Kleindeutsche Partei, 193ff. On the general issue of church and state see Georg Franz, Kulturkampf: Staat und katholische Kirche in Mitteleuropa von der Säkularisation bis zum Abschluss des preussischen Kulturkampfes (Munich, 1954).

[51] Schieder, Kleindeutsche Partei, 197ff. Windell, Catholics and German Unity, 176ff.

[52] Schieder, Kleindeutsche Partei, 213ff.

attack. Though no one openly denounced the military alliance, its "offensive" feature met heavy criticism. But the most effective assault was upon Hohenlohe's sincerity. Quite accurately the deputies pointed out that, while constantly proclaiming his intention to preserve Bavarian sovereignty, the prince pursued a foreign policy that must end in its destruction. Bavaria had no desire, they averred, to participate in a "great-Prussian" union; never would she enter the "palace of the North German Confederation, whose walls are cemented with blood—fraternal blood." By 77 to 62 the deputies voted their lack of confidence in the government. Technically Hohenlohe was not responsible to the chamber and under no obligation to resign. From Berlin, Bismarck telegraphed to keep him from such a "dangerous political mistake." But on February 18 King Ludwig accepted his resignation.[53]

The consequence of this event, however, was the enhancement of royal authority in Munich, rather than the inauguration of parliamentary government. Because the opposition majority was weak, Ludwig was able to appoint a professional cabinet with no political connections. His choice for minister-president fell on Count Otto von Bray-Steinburg, Bavarian minister at Vienna and a close friend of Beust. Although not a doctrinaire particularist, Bray was a thorough Bavarian with no feeling for the German national cause. He wished to hold fast to the military alliance with Prussia, but recognized it only as a "defensive" instrument.[54]

During the first six months of 1870 agitation increased in the south against the alliance treaties and the "Prussianization" of the armed forces. In the Bavarian parliament an attempt was launched, with the support of the left wings of both the Patriot and Progressive parties, to substitute for the Prussian system adopted in 1868 a militia of eight months' service on the Swiss pattern. In Württemberg popular discontent and parliamentary pressure for a reduction in military expenditures led to the resignation of Wagner as minister of war in late March. During 1869 the People's party had begun a general campaign to liberate the country from the "slavery of the barracks." Mass meetings protested the harshness of the new drill and discipline, which transformed free citizens into automatons. A monster petition was launched demanding repeal of the military service law of 1868. Ultimately the signatures reached 150,000, about three-quarters of the usual Württemberg electorate. By comparison the pilgrimage of 1,400 persons organized by the German party to visit the Zollerburg, ancestral castle of the Hohenzollern, was a minor effort.[55]

[53] Ibid., 223ff.; GW, VIb, 243–245.

[54] Schieder, Kleindeutsche Partei, 234ff.; Becker, Bismarcks Ringen, 607. Bismarck recognized that the Bray cabinet was at least better for his purposes than an ultramontane one and assured the new minister-president of his "complete trust." GW, VIb, 259.

[55] Schieder, Kleindeutsche Partei, 237ff.; Eugen Schneider, "Württembergs Beitritt zum Deutschen Reich 1870," Württembergische Vierteljahrshefte für Landesgeschichte, 29 (1920), 123–

The victory of particularism in the two southern kingdoms had at least one favorable by-product for Bismarck. Their governments would now have to lean increasingly upon Berlin for support against the domestic opposition. Neither was willing to concede to the demands of the democrats that the Prussian military system be abandoned. In late March 1870 Bismarck even offered Stuttgart military assistance in the event of a revolutionary uprising.[56] Nevertheless, his satisfaction over this development could not have been very great. His plans for acquisition of the south depended on the conversion of peoples as well as governments. In 1870 popular resistance appeared to be hardening. Bavaria had a large minority favoring union with the north and Württemberg a small, if growing national party, but the great majority of voters in both countries were increasingly fanatical in their opposition to it.[57]

The Zollverein elections of 1868, the Bavarian elections of 1869, and the Württemberg petition of 1870 constituted a popular referendum whose meaning was plain to the most ardent German nationalists.[58] After the first of these catastrophes Julius Weizsäcker concluded, "The German question will make little progress until the great conflagration." "We aren't allowed to pick unripe fruit," observed Wehrenpfennig, "but a violent storm could dislodge it into our laps." A year later Werthern wrote, "From the short period in early 1867 when it was powerfully agitated and capable of exploitation German national feeling has steadily declined, and I see no end to this process without a new crisis. . . . No one believes any more that Germany can move forward upon the chosen path."[59]

In 1870 Roggenbach, who had earlier been more optimistic, reached a similar opinion: "At the time of the Luxemburg strife there were still signs of a national movement capable of resisting attempts at outside intervention in the struggle for complete independence and free self-determination in German internal questions. At this hour the situation is no longer so favorable. Division and partisanship of every kind have erased the last traces of the movement for national unity and given the upper hand for a long time to

---

124; Rapp, *Württemberger*, 333ff., 361. Suckow was chosen to replace Wagner as the army's chief administrator in spite of his nationalistic sentiments. There was no other suitable candidate. He was denied ministerial rank until the war of 1870 began. Suckow, *Rückschau*, 154ff.; Freiherr von Mittnacht, *Rückblicke* (Stuttgart, 1909), 2ff.

[56] APP, X, 114–116, 125–126; GW, VIb, 317.

[57] The dissertation by Rolf Wilhelm, *Das Verhältnis der süddeutschen Staaten zum Norddeutschen Bund (1867–1870): Historische Studien*, vol. 431 (Husum, 1978), reasserted the old orthodoxy— Bismarck's "will to Germany" and the south German will to national unity—but unconvincingly. The author ignored or minimized contrary evidence and excluded the issue of the Hohenzollern candidacy to the Spanish throne, the surest evidence that Bismarck no longer counted on spontaneous national sentiment to complete German unification.

[58] See Treitschke, *Zehn Jahre*, vol. 1, 266, and Andreas Dorpalen, *Heinrich von Treitschke* (New Haven, 1957), 134ff.

[59] HW, I, 419, 421; APP, X, 553.

come to centrifugal currents." A Prussian initiative in the national question, he concluded, would arouse little support in Germany, even if it involved Prussia in a European war. Only in the event of an "unjustified attack" would Germany rally to Prussia's defense. Speaking to the downcast Rudolf Haym, Treitschke, the most impassioned nationalist of them all, placed his hopes upon "a sudden, unforeseeable upset . . . like that of 1866."[60] In their discouragement German patriots returned, as so often in the past, to the conviction that the German nation could be welded together only by the torch of a great popular war.

[60] Becker, *Bismarcks Ringen*, 591–592; *HW*, I, 450; Hans Rosenberg, ed., *Ausgewählter Briefwechsel Rudolf Hayms* (Stuttgart, 1930), 281. For similar utterances see the Reichstag speeches of Rudolf von Schleiden (*SBR*, 1869, II, 1309) and Nordeck zu Rabenau (*SBR*, 1870, 75). Even a staunch conservative like Heinrich Leo, who feared that German patriotism would not develop swiftly enough to replace a decaying Prussianism, wrote openly in the *Kreuzzeitung* in 1868 of his hopes for a great national war that would bind Germans together. Gerhard Ritter, *Die preussischen Konservativen und Bismarcks deutsche Politik, 1858–1875* (Heidelberg, 1913), 300.

Parliamentary Struggles

TOLD myself," Bismarck wrote in his memoirs, "that the next important goal was independence and security in European politics. . . . Once we had gained our independence from the rest of Europe, we could then move freely in our internal development, organizing our institutions in as liberal or reactionary a manner as seemed just and suitable. . . . I did not doubt the possibility of giving royal power the necessary strength to reset our internal clock once we had won abroad the freedom to live independently as a great nation. Until then I was ready to pay the opposition blackmail as needed in order to be in a position to throw our full power into the scale, to project the impression of our united strength in European diplomacy and, should the need arise, to unleash revolutionary national movements against our foes."[1]

The difficulties in such a policy are as manifest as the advantages. In political terms it required a combination of forces that would include both liberals and conservatives, the former to speed the work of consolidation, the latter to block liberal reforms that would make impossible the eventual resetting of the clock. In social terms this meant collaboration between commercial, industrial, and professional interests that had the most to gain from the completion of German unity and the agrarian and aristocratic interests that had the most to lose from a weakening of royal authority. It was an uneasy combination, composed of social forces and political parties with disparate interests and objectives. That it proved viable for a time was owing to the willingness of the National Liberal party not to insist on more blackmail than Bismarck was willing to pay.

Goals and Gains of the National Liberals

Among 297 deputies elected to the "ordinary" Reichstag in August 1867 were 84 national liberals, 70 conservatives, 36 free conservatives, 30 progressives, 22 federal-constitutionalists (composed mostly of Saxons and annexed Prussians), and 15 old-liberals. The Prussian Chamber of Deputies, expanded to 432 seats to accommodate the annexed populations, was also reelected in 1867. Conservatives repeated their success of the preceding year, electing 125 deputies; free conservatives brought in 48, national liberals 99, and progres-

[1] GW, XV, 285–286.

sives 48. Small parties and uncommitted deputies made up the rest of both chambers. In both parliaments the social and occupational groups most strongly represented were state officials (42 percent of the Chamber of Deputies and 46 percent of the Reichstag) and agrarian landowners (27.5 percent and 25.3 percent). Together they dominated the two conservative parties, whose strength lay in "Transelbia" and Silesia, but they were also a significant presence in both liberal parties. The number of deputies who classified themselves as merchants, industrialists, or simply businessmen (*Gewerbetreibende*) was small in both parliaments (6.5 percent and 5.5 percent), but this is misleading because of the significant number of big landlords in both chambers who were also heavily involved in coal mining and other industrial projects (for example, the Silesian magnate Count Guido Henckel von Donnersmarck).

Whatever their party affiliation, notables (*Honoratioren*) of high status in society and government set the tone for the two chambers—men who liked to think of themselves as above politics, representatives of the nation rather than of any particular constituency (whether geographical or material).[2] Indeed, interest group politics were not rampant in these chambers, whose members conceived of themselves as the "assembled intelligence of the entire nation." Economic development was equated with the general welfare; its engine was industrial capitalism and its fuel the energies released by laissez-faire. The few who spoke in another voice (August Bebel and Wilhelm Liebknecht) were brushed aside as insignificant cranks.[3]

Because of the polarity of the chambers on most issues, no majority could form without the national liberals. Yet they were not strong enough to predominate, either alone or in combination with the progressives, with whom they maintained good relations until 1874. As was shown, the national liberals did not intend to abandon the quest for revision of the constitution when they accepted it in 1867. They were gradualists who, in Forckenbeck's words, saw in parliament the "means by which—through constant struggle, slowly, step by step, from compromise to compromise—ever more freedom and unity" could be gained.[4] The degree of their determination to wage this

---

[2] Klaus Erich Pollmann, *Parlamentarismus im Norddeutschen Bund 1867–1870* (Düsseldorf, 1985), 274–281, 543–545; Fritz Specht and Paul Schwabe, *Die Reichstagswahlen von 1867 bis 1903* (2d ed., Berlin, 1908), 322; Bernhard Vogel, Dieter Nohlen, and Rainer-Olaf Schultze, *Wahlen in Deutschland* (Berlin, 1971), 287–288; Ludwig Rosenbaum, *Beruf und Herkunft der Abgeordneten zu den deutschen und preussischen Parlamenten, 1847–1919* (Frankfurt a. M., 1923), 62–63. The figures on party representation in the Reichstag differ in these sources. Pollmann's figures—acquired from a previously unpublished official document—are used here. The occupational statistics for Reichstag members were compiled from membership lists in SBR (1867), I, x–xxvi, using the categories supplied by Rosenbaum.

[3] Pollmann, *Parlamentarismus*, 395–408.

[4] Martin Philippson, *Max von Forckenbeck: Ein Lebensbild* (Leipzig, 1898), 166, 181ff. See also HW, I, 367, 381; Hermann Oncken, *Rudolf von Bennigsen* (Stuttgart, 1910), vol. 2, 13; Johannes

struggle varied according to their position within the party's political spectrum. The party's expressed aims were completion of German unification, expansion of the legislative competence of the central government, greater budget rights for the Reichstag and the Prussian Landtag, a north German cabinet with "responsible ministers" (in the legal sense of that term), more economic freedom, guarantees of personal freedom, judicial reform, and extension of local "self-administration" (*Selbstverwaltung*) in Prussia at the cost of corporate institutions.[5] Conspicuously missing was any open demand for parliamentary government, although this may have been the unexpressed aspiration of some members.

Another self-imposed limitation was a general conviction that, at least for the time being, Bismarck was indispensable. His virtuoso performance in foreign affairs during 1864–1866 had persuaded national liberals that he must remain in office until German unification was completed and consolidated. Bismarck strengthened this conviction by asserting that, had Wilhelm not stood in the way, even greater concessions to liberalism would have been possible in 1867. The best strategy for liberals, it appeared, was to unseat ultraconservative ministers (Lippe, Heydt, Mühler, and Eulenburg), liberating Wilhelm from their influence and enabling the chancellor to follow more liberal policies. Most were moderates who looked upon parliament as the palladium of the educated *Mittelstand* and as the partner, not the enemy, of executive authority in a dualistic constitutional system, whose success required collaboration rather than conflict.[6]

Bismarck was quick to use the club they put into his hands. In late November 1867, Karl Twesten charged the government with "breach of trust" for having defrayed the cost of settlements with deposed King Georg V of Hanover and Duke Adolf of Nassau from a war credit authorized by the Landtag for other purposes. Bismarck summoned Max von Forckenbeck, speaker of the Chamber of Deputies, and threatened to resign as minister-president if a retraction were not forthcoming. He would, he declared, advise the king to ask Rudolf von Bennigsen and Forckenbeck to form a new government. "Only the National Liberal party, united with the conservatives, can govern. I have been a sick man for two years. I cannot endure being called dishonest. I have

Schultze, ed., *Max Duncker: Politischer Briefwechsel aus seinem Nachlass* (Stuttgart, 1923), 420; Heinrich von Treitschke, *Zehn Jahre deutscher Kämpfe, 1865–1874: Schriften zur Tagespolitik* (3d ed., Berlin, 1897), 84–85; Martin Spahn, "Zur Entstehung der nationalliberalen Partei," *Zeitschrift für Politik*, 1 (1907–1908), 408–409, 441, 451ff.; Eduard W. Mayer, "Aus der Geschichte der national-liberalen Partei in den Jahren 1867 bis 1871," in Paul Wentzcke, ed., *Deutscher Staat und deutsche Parteien* (Munich, 1922), 142–143.

[5] Felix Salomon, *Die deutschen Parteiprogramme* (Leipzig, 1907), vol. 1, 74–82.

[6] Philippson, *Forckenbeck*, 188, 192; Ernst Feder, ed., *Bismarcks grosses Spiel: Die Geheimen Tagebücher Ludwig Bambergers* (Frankfurt, 1933), 90, 366–367; Julius Heyderhoff, ed., *Im Ring der Gegner Bismarcks* (2d ed., Leipzig, 1943), 96–99; HW, I, 425ff.; Pollmann, *Parlamentarismus*, 342–350.

not slept the entire night." Twesten's criticism was "like a hot iron stabbing me in the chest." Forckenbeck and Bennigsen responded by persuading the chamber's budget committee to disavow Twesten; they insisted only on the replacement of Minister of Justice Lippe, whom Bismarck was happy to sacrifice.[7]

Lippe had incurred the wrath of the liberals by continuing after the war of 1866 to prosecute the deputies Twesten and Frentzel for speeches made in the Chamber of Deputies and during the election campaigns of 1865–1866.[8] The minister of justice was undeterred by the end of the constitutional conflict, passage of the indemnity bill, and the general amnesty that followed. Nor was he influenced either by Twesten's status as a leading spokesman of the National Liberal party or his support of the government on the broad issues of unification. During 1867 Lippe succeeded in having Twesten sentenced to two years in prison. Twesten's position as a Prussian judge then made him vulnerable to disciplinary action for "unpatriotic and dishonorable" conduct, for which he was fined one hundred thalers. Lippe's replacement, Gerhard Leonhardt, former Hanoverian minister and president of the Prussian superior court of appeals, stopped the prosecution, and the deputies were eventually amnestied.[9] But the liberals did not let the issue die. In 1868–1869 bills granting parliamentary immunity for all legislative bodies of the North German Confederation passed the Reichstag by great majorities and were rejected by the Bundesrat. Bismarck, who now found the issue inconvenient, referred the deputies to the Prussian Landtag on the grounds that confederate legislation would injure federalism. A bill reinforcing the principle of parliamentary immunity under the Prussian constitution passed the Chamber of Deputies and was rejected in the House of Lords. Finally, in 1870, the deputies gained their objective by incorporating the principle in the confederate penal code.[10]

The legislative achievements of the North German Confederation were considerable. Among the major statutes passed were: in 1867, abolition of internal passports, a unified merchant marine, freedom to relocate (*Freizügigkeit*), and restrictions on usury; in 1868, abolition of restrictions on marriage and of imprisonment for debt, and uniformity in weights and measures; in 1869, the Reichstag election law, codes of commercial and industrial law, right of legal redress, and establishment of a high court for commercial litigation; in 1870, a penal code, freedom to incorporate, and patent and copy-

---

[7] *HW*, I, 396–399, 503–504; Philippson, *Forckenbeck*, 188; *GW*, VIa, 148–150; *GW*, VII, 228–229; Siegfried von Kardorff, *Wilhelm von Kardorff* (Berlin, 1936), 41.

[8] See pp. 283, 319–320, 334.

[9] *SEG* (1868), 70–72; Oskar Klein-Hattingen, *Geschichte des deutschen Liberalismus* (Berlin, 1911), vol. 1, 361–366.

[10] *SBR* (1868), I, 89, 137, and (1869), I, 99–100, 134; Gordon R. Mork, "The National Liberal Party in the German Reichstag and Prussian Landtag, 1866–1874" (dissertation, University of Minnesota, 1966), 189–190.

right protection. All of these statutes contributed to the consolidation of the
federal union; some benefited the development of industrial capitalism,
sweeping away the remaining obstacles to free enterprise in the laws of the
member states. Many bills drafted by the Bismarck government were amended
in significant ways by the Reichstag and Bundesrat.[11] The Reichstag did not
prove to be a docile instrument of government policy. Liberal deputies took
the lead in agitating for repeal of state anticombination laws—finally accomplished in the industry code of 1869. Their repeated efforts to widen the legislative competence of the confederation to include a code of civil law finally
succeeded in 1873. Liberal amendments modernized features of the penal
code, although Bismarck defeated the abolition of capital punishment—"this
sickly sentimentality of our times"—by threatening to jettison the entire code
when it reached the Bundesrat.[12]

Although gains were made in economic freedom and in human and parliamentary rights, liberal deputies were frustrated in their attempts to alter the
basic relationship between the executive and legislative powers. One critical
area in that relationship concerned executive responsibility (*Verantwortlichkeit*). Under the confederate constitution the chancellor and under the Prussian constitution the cabinet ministers were declared "responsible" for acts
they countersigned, but neither constitution stipulated how these officials
were to be held accountable for actions contrary to law. Neither parliament
had the right of impeachment, and no court had jurisdiction.[13] Naturally,
the question of executive responsibility had been a sore point with the Chamber of Deputies during the constitutional conflict. In 1867–1868, Twesten
and Johannes Miquel sought to amend a government bill creating an agency
to administer the confederate debt (*Bundesschuldenverwaltung*) that would
have empowered either the Reichstag or Bundesrat to take officials to court
on charges of misfeasance. Their aim was to begin "the gradual development of the constitution." Privately Forckenbeck exulted that the deputies
were now in a position to coerce Bismarck into yielding "real power and control."[14]

To liberals the issue was whether the North German Confederation was to
be a *Rechtsstaat*—whether its officials were to be subject to the rule of law. To
Bismarck the issue was whether parliament was to be permitted to enlarge its
power and upset the constitutional balance. The deputies would do better, he

---

[11] For the legislative activity of the North German Confederation see A. Koller, *Archiv des
Norddeutschen Bundes und des Zollvereins*, vols. 1–5 (Berlin, 1868–1871).

[12] BR, IV, 365ff.; see also GW, XIV, 777.

[13] Otto Pflanze, "Juridical and Political Responsibility in Nineteenth Century Germany," in
Leonard Krieger and Fritz Stern, eds., *The Responsibility of Power: Historical Essays in Honor of
Hajo Holborn* (New York, 1967), 162–182.

[14] SBR (1868), I, 143; Hans Herzfeld, *Johannes von Miquel* (Detmold, 1938), 85–89; HW, I,
416–418.

declared, to delay the power struggle until the confederation had become con-solidated. When the vote came on April 22, 1868, the liberal ranks held firm, and the amendment passed, 131 to 114 (conservatives and free conservatives in the negative). Bennigsen, Forckenbeck, and Twesten rejoiced at having taught the chancellor a "lesson,"[15] but once again Bismarck was the teacher. He withdrew the bill. As a consequence, a loan to finance naval construction already authorized by the Reichstag could not be placed. Naval construction ceased; shipyards discharged their workers; war vessels were decommissioned; grass grew at dockside.[16]

German liberals, long interested in the navy's welfare, had not anticipated that Bismarck would retaliate in this way. To Lasker it was the "most sinister point in the man's life."[17] Unwilling to let the navy be dismantled, the na-tional liberals were compelled to drop the principle of juridical responsibility. Administration of the confederate debt was placed in the hands of a Prussian agency (*Hauptverwaltung der Staatsschulden*) monitored by a commission with representatives from the Bundesrat and Reichstag.[18] By this "compromise" the national liberals again sacrificed one of their central objectives.

Though unenforceable through the courts the principle of responsibility

BISMARCK IN THE NORTH GERMAN REICHSTAG. "DECISIVE HE IS AND A POWERFUL SPEAKER—THAT HAS
TO BE CONCEDED." (*FIGARO*, VIENNA, MARCH 5, 1870.)

[15] HW, I, 417; Oncken, *Bennigsen*, vol. 2, 163.
[16] SBR (1868), I, 141ff.; BR, IV, 26ff.
[17] Mork, "National Liberal Party," 179.
[18] SBR (1868), I, 430ff.; Mork, "National Liberal Party," 199–200.

was not devoid of meaning. The responsibility of Prussia's ministers meant that, while they formulated general policy collectively, they had to face the Landtag individually to speak on bills that affected their respective ministries. As the sole minister of the North German Confederation, the chancellor had no peers. Technically he alone was responsible for the defense of confederate policies before the Reichstag. During 1867–1870 liberals hammered at the inadequacy of this system. Although Bismarck held the responsibility, bills reaching the chamber in such critical areas as financial and military affairs were actually drafted in the Prussian ministries, whose heads were not legally accountable to the Reichstag. In April 1869, Twesten and Count Georg zu Münster, acting for the national liberals and free conservatives, called for a confederate cabinet of responsible ministers on the Prussian pattern. This motion struck Bismarck's most sensitive nerve, for it directly affected his authority. He interpreted it as an attack on the constitution and a vote of no confidence in himself and the Bundesrat. Yet the motion passed, 111 to 100, with free conservatives, national liberals, and progressives voting in the majority.[19] Naturally the bill died in the Bundesrat. Yet it had revealed general dissatisfaction with the structure of the confederate executive. Even conservatives were open to suggestions for such a reform, if coupled with the creation of an upper house similar to the Prussian House of Lords.[20]

Power over the Purse

Neither the Reichstag nor Prussian Landtag had secure control over state revenues and expenditures. The Prussian constitution provided that taxes, once granted, could be collected "until changed by law." Although no comparable clause was included in the confederate constitution, revenue bills passed by the Reichstag were of indefinite duration. The practice of granting taxes without expiration dates would not in itself have threatened the fiscal power of parliament, had either the Prussian or confederate constitutions provided for secure parliamentary control over expenditures. This was not the case. The Prussian indemnity act of 1866 contained no guarantee that the government would not again attempt to rule without a legal budget. As was shown, the constituent Reichstag of 1867 won for the Reichstag the right to approve the confederate budget annually before the start of the fiscal year. This was a gain over the Prussian constitution. Yet its significance was seriously reduced by the provision that military expenditures, constituting initially about 90 percent of the total budget, were to be beyond parliamentary control until December 31, 1871.[21]

[19] SBR (1869), I, 389–413.
[20] Gerhard Ritter, Die preussischen Konservativen und Bismarcks deutsche Politik, 1858–1875 (Heidelberg, 1913), 257.
[21] See pp. 344–361.

The founding program that Lasker composed for the National Liberal party made "completion of the budgetary power" a principal goal of liberals in both Prussia and the North German Confederation.[22] In pursuing this objective, national liberals could count on support from progressives and sometimes even free conservatives. They were aware that the limited power liberals had gained for the Reichstag in fiscal measures could be further weakened by the manner in which confederate finances were administered. In resolutions presented in September 1867 at the first session of the north German Reichstag, they sought to install safeguards against abuses that had marred the recent history of the Prussian Landtag: budget bills must be presented at least six months in advance of the fiscal year; money bills to cover expenditures in excess of the approved budget must be presented for parliamentary approval during the following legislative year; surpluses must be factored into the budget bill for the next fiscal year; and all new positions and salary increases required prior approval by parliament. Many loose ends needed tying in dealing with a bureaucracy whose traditions and practices had been established in the age of absolutism. Bismarck and Delbrück put up little resistance to these demands, an attitude that appears to have weakened parliament's determination to secure their passage. In the debate, furthermore, technicalities confused the issues. The first resolution failed on a split vote (99 to 99); the second was rejected by five votes, the third was withdrawn, and the fourth passed.[23]

In the constituent Reichstag no one appears to have comprehended the potential importance of the article in the constitution providing for state assessments (Matrikularbeiträge) with which to balance the confederate budget.[24] It was seen as a temporary device that would lapse when the level of confederate expenditures was fixed and taxes voted. Yet it became a permanent feature of public finance. In the late 1860s about one-third of all confederate revenues came from the states in the form of assessments. Because of these payments the central government could not have a deficit, and for that reason the Reichstag was under no pressure to grant new taxes. By denying new taxes to the Reich, the liberals preserved the assessments, which were subject to annual review by the Reichstag in the imperial budget, and drained the Prussian treasury (Prussia's quota was 80 percent of the total assessment), compelling the Prussian government to turn to the Landtag for new revenue.[25] In the Matrikularbeiträge, liberals found an unexpected check on both confederate revenues and Prussian expenditures. Here they had a surrogate

---

[22] Salomon, Parteiprogramme, vol. 1, 80.

[23] SBR (1867), I, 111–128; II (Anlagen), Aktenstück Nr. 20; Pollmann, Parlamentarismus, 410–411.

[24] See pp. 345, 354, 360.

[25] Karl Zuchardt, Die Finanzpolitik Bismarcks und die Parteien im Norddeutschen Bunde: Leipziger historische Abhandlungen, vol. 16 (Leipzig, 1910), 50ff.

for the budgetary power for which they had vainly fought in the Prussian constitutional conflict of 1862–1866 and in the debates of the constituent Reichstag of 1867. Liberal deputies were slow to appreciate the potentiality of the weapon that fell into their hands. Initially they did not dispute their obligation to cover unexpected deficits. What disturbed them was the manner in which the Bismarck government sought to establish the necessary assessments.[26]

If the Zollverein parliament had become the money-granting machine that Bismarck intended, the assessments would have vanished, but the majority in that body was more interested in tax "reforms" than tax increases. In early 1868 Bismarck and Delbrück attempted to circumvent the Reichstag by claiming that the Bundesrat alone had the power to set the assessments. This would have been possible under the constitution as originally worded, but not as amended by the constituent Reichstag. In July the Bundesrat itself refused to sanction such a patent violation of the constitution.[27]

Soon afterward an approaching fiscal crisis in Prussia gave Bismarck another opportunity to wrest from the Reichstag the weapon he had unwittingly granted. Minister of Finance August von der Heydt estimated that in 1868 Prussia's expenditures would exceed revenues by 6 million thalers owing to a depression that began in 1866 coupled with a poor harvest in 1868; the cost of incorporating the annexed regions; loss of revenues from customs, post, and telegraph; and the assessment paid to the confederation. In early October 1868 Bismarck readily accepted the minister's proposal to reduce the Prussian deficit by demanding new taxes and tariffs from the Reichstag and Zollverein parliament sufficient gradually to eliminate the assessment. For the chancellor the issue was much greater than the Prussian deficit. He wanted to consolidate the confederation by making it financially independent and by "penetrating" and weakening the political life of the member states. The prospect of rejection, he declared, was no reason for abandoning the goal. The government must carry out its duty and place upon the parliamentary majority the odium for neglecting the interests of the country.[28]

Here began a quest that was to occupy Bismarck intermittently for the rest of his political career. For more than twenty years he returned repeatedly to this theme, explaining it in similar words to successive ministers of finance and Reichstag deputies. His failure to achieve a fiscal "reform" that would have reversed the financial relationship between the central and state governments, by making the latter dependent upon the former, and weakened the Reichstag, by abolishing the *Matrikularbeiträge*, was his greatest defeat in domestic politics—judged by the magnitude of the issue and length of time that

[26] Pollmann, *Parlamentarismus*, 411–413.

[27] *Ibid.*, 55–57.

[28] Heydt to Bismarck, Oct. 6, 1868, and Eck to Bismarck, Oct. 13, 1868. DZA Potsdam, Reichskanzleramt, no. 407, 3–5v, 11–19v. Bismarck to Eck, Oct. 18, 1868. AWB, I, 128–129.

it absorbed him. By clinging to the toehold that Bismarck had unwittingly given them, liberals gained for the Reichstag an increment of power, upon which, however, they were never able significantly to capitalize.

The financial crisis in Prussia was for Bismarck not an embarrassment, but an opportunity. He proposed that the government create a "coercive situation" by demanding from the Landtag a huge surtax on Prussia's direct taxes (chiefly on property and income).[29] Though sure to reject such an unpopular proposal, the Prussian deputies would be compelled by the prospect of massive reductions in public expenditures to wrestle with the problem later in the Reichstag and customs parliament (many sat in all three chambers). They would prefer, Bismarck apparently reasoned, to spread the tax burden over the whole North German Confederation through excise taxes and German Zollverein through higher tariffs. They would see the wisdom of goring a different ox—not the Prussian landowner or businessman, but the German consumer through indirect taxes on such items as sugar, spirits, tobacco, petroleum, and illuminating gas.

During the autumn of 1868 Bismarck was ill on his new estate at Varzin in Pomerania, remote from the scene of action. His subordinates in the chancellor's office were reluctant to open a struggle with the Reichstag over budget rights. A sharp message from Varzin quelled that revolt. But the Prussian cabinet was not so easily bludgeoned. Rather than face parliament with bad news, Heydt proposed to raise the needed cash by selling more state-owned railway shares. He persuaded the king and ministers to agree. To Bismarck this was like striking the flag before the first shot. Fear, he wrote to Wilhelm, was a poor counselor in politics. To Roon he groused that the king, having at last experienced popularity, was now unwilling to jeopardize it.[30] But Heydt's expedient merely deferred the problem for a year.

In the spring of 1869 the minister forecast a deficit for 1870 of 10,600,000 thalers. Goaded by Bismarck, he showered Bundesrat, Reichstag, and Zollverein parliament with revenue bills (on spirits, brewing, petroleum, illuminating gas, sugar, securities, business receipts, railway tickets, abolition of franking). Prussia was threatened with insolvency, he warned, unless the confederation and Zollverein increased revenues sufficiently to reduce the Prussian assessment.[31] On May 2, 1869, Bismarck informed Forckenbeck that the

---

[29] Bismarck to Roon, Oct. 24, 1868. GW, XIV, 742.

[30] DZA Potsdam, Reichskanzleramt, no. 407, 6–10, 20–22v. Crown council meeting of Oct. 28, 1868. DZA Merseburg, rep. 90a, B, III, 2c, nr. 3, vol. III. GW, VIa, 418–420, 424–428; Horst Kohl, ed., Anhang zu den Gedanken und Erinnerungen von Otto Fürst von Bismarck (Stuttgart, 1901); vol. 1, 174–184; Waldemar von Roon, Denkwürdigkeiten aus dem Leben des General-Feldmarschalls Kriegministers Grafen von Roon (4th ed., Breslau, 1897), vol. 3, 95ff.

[31] AWB, I, 128–129; Heinrich von Poschinger, Bismarck und der Bundesrat (Stuttgart, 1897–1901), vol. 1, 243–245, 259ff. Zuchardt, Finanzpolitik, 66–67. For Heydt's tax program see SBR (1869), III, Drucksachen, no. 206. Of the 11,268,000 thalers he proposed to raise with new

situation was worse than publicly admitted. "We are close to Austrian conditions. Von der Heydt never told me the truth." Forckenbeck replied coolly that the Reichstag would wait until the end of the year to determine whether the deficit would actually be as catastrophic as Heydt predicted. The Prussian Chamber of Deputies, not the Reichstag, furthermore, was the proper body to deal with Prussian finances. If the situation proved to be as bad as predicted, "we would have to help, but not without guarantees for the future": namely, the right of the Landtag to grant the Prussian class and income taxes annually and to restrict their yields to preestablished amounts.[32] Prussia's financial crisis seemed to offer the chance to close the gap in the Landtag's control over revenues that had enabled Bismarck to govern for four years against the will of the parliamentary majority. Bismarck's offensive against the Reichstag had triggered a liberal counteroffensive. The situation with which Bismarck intended to coerce the Reichstag threatened to coerce the government.

On May 21–22, 1869, these rival offensives collided in the Reichstag. Never before had the chamber, which was packed to the walls for the occasion, witnessed such a general assault on government policy. Bismarck diverted the attack from himself by declaring that all financial measures introduced in the confederation had been prepared by the Prussian minister of finance. The liberal bloodhounds tore into Heydt, attacking his inconsistency in estimating the deficit, the uncoordinated and irrational way in which the "tax bouquet" had been presented, the incongruous fact that Heydt, since the confederation had no minister of finance, could only defend himself as an elected member of parliament. Only conservatives spoke in his defense; even Wilhelm von Kardorff of the free conservatives was critical. Weaving through the debate was the constitutional issue: liberals accused the government of demanding permanent taxes for a temporary deficit, with the ulterior purpose of weakening the Reichstag by abolishing state assessments. Bismarck charged that the deputies wanted to upset the constitutional balance in favor of parliament. "We demand bread, and you give us stones." Never, he said, would he bargain away power for revenue. The fate of Heydt's bills was never in doubt. Only the stamp tax on bills of exchange passed the Reichstag; the customs parliament accepted only the sugar tax reform—more because of its free-trade character than its revenue.[33]

Heydt never recovered from the wounds suffered in this encounter. To be sure, he did retain the confidence of the king. For that reason Bismarck chose

---

taxes, 3,260,000 would have come from business stamp taxes (bills of exchange, bourse receipts), the rest from consumption taxes.

[32] Philippson, *Forckenbeck*, 197. The far-reaching objective of the national liberals was not shared by the progressives, who held the existing budget rights of the Landtag to be more basic than those of the Reichstag. Pollmann, *Parlamentarismus*, 421–425.

[33] *SBR*, 1869, II, 998ff.; Zuchardt, *Finanzpolitik*, 71–72.

to let others unseat him. In September 1869 the chancellor wrote to Roon, "Itzenplitz, who does not want to bite the fox himself, has repeatedly demanded that I murder the money uncle by letter; I referred him and my other colleagues to self-help." To Motley he wrote that he was deliberately staying away from Berlin. "I would like to see whether the Landtag will do me the favor of striking down some of my colleagues. When I am present, they benefit from the deference given me. Our circumstances are so peculiar that I have to resort to strange means to loosen bonds, whose violent destruction many considerations forbid."[34] But Heydt dug his own grave. Conservative land and mill owners, already alarmed by his proposed taxes on brewing and spirits in May, were aroused again by his intent to speed up the payment of brandy and sugar taxes. Bismarck criticized the measure as a "palliative" affecting those interests that generally supported the government's financial program. On October 10, 1869, Heydt presented the budget for 1870 to the Prussian Chamber of Deputies, estimating the deficit this time at only 5,400,000 thalers and calling for a single surtax of 25 percent on Prussia's direct taxes to pay for it. Reluctant to face the coming debate and conscious of Bismarck's disfavor, Heydt resigned as of October 25.[35] Bismarck received the good news from Eulenburg ("The bomb has exploded") and immediately denied having given Heydt any "proof" of his displeasure.[36]

Again Bismarck had used parliament to rid himself of an inconvenient colleague. Heydt had bungled the job, and yet the tax program he proposed, if not the procedure he followed, corresponded to Bismarck's wishes. Hence the defeat was also Bismarck's. The pressure tactics he had so often used with success in both domestic and foreign policy had failed to move the liberals. He had not succeeded in his attempt to exploit the multiparliamentary system—the "three battlefields," as he described the Landtag, Reichstag, and Zollparlament—by playing them off against each other.[37] He had not "broken the resistance of the Prussian members of the [Zollverein] parliament by forcing them to face [in the Chamber of Deputies] the consequences for the Prussian budget of the votes they had cast in the other body" against taxes that he

---

[34] Kohl, ed., *Anhang*, vol. 1, 201–202; GW, XIV, 760, 762.

[35] GW, VIb, 145–146; BP, II, 67; AWB, I, 136–138; Horst Kohl, ed., *Bismarck-Jahrbuch* (Leipzig, 1894–1899), vol. 4, 89–90.

[36] Wehrmann to Bismarck, Sept. 23, 1869, and Eulenburg to Bismarck, Oct. 20, 1869. GSA, rep. 94, nr. 1162. Another nail in the coffin was Heydt's sudden decision to oppose governmental approval of a lottery bond issue desired by four Prussian railways. Although the cabinet had given its approval and a bankers' consortium was ready to launch the issue, major opposition had developed in the Reichstag and Prussian Chamber of Deputies. Deputies of all parties objected in principle to this method of raising capital, which offered to investors little or no interest on their investments but big "premiums" if their bond numbers were drawn in the lottery. Eulenburg to Bismarck, Sept. 1, 1869. *Ibid*. See also Pollmann, *Parlamentarismus*, 406–408.

[37] Kohl, ed., *Anhang*, vol. 1, 178.

admitted would "injure many interests."[38] As of October 30 Bismarck still wished to continue the fight in the Chamber of Deputies under a new finance minister; if denied the requested surtax, he said, the government must cut all expenditures in excess of its revenues.[39]

Bismarck chose as Heydt's successor the ablest financier available to him, Otto Camphausen, president of the Prussian *Seehandlung*. Wilhelm was leery of this bourgeois liberal who had opposed the government in the constitutional conflict. He feared that as finance minister Camphausen would concede budget rights to parliament in return for new taxes. But Camphausen revised the forecast deficit downward to 3,300,000 thalers and found the funds by a simple manipulation. He consolidated the state debt and pressed bond holders to forego scheduled amortization payments in return for a sizable premium; henceforth the Ministry of Finance would decide when the bonds would be redeemed, permitting the government to exploit downward fluctuations in the bond market. This dubious transaction ended the Prussian deficit, and the crisis was over.[40]

Neither Bismarck nor the liberals attained their objectives in the conflict of 1869. Yet the end result was a gain for the latter. Bismarck had lost the first of a long series of battles to liquidate state assessments and the power over the purse they gave to the Reichstag. The toughness displayed by the national liberal–progressive coalition in defending its new-found weapon boded ill for the fate of the "iron budget," whose renewal was but two years away.

Rebellion of the Conservatives

The national liberals were not the only faction wrestling for possession of Bismarck and for influence over his policy. Those "realistic" conservatives who formed the Free Conservative party were able to appreciate that Bismarck's revolution of 1866–1867 was essentially conservative, that he had actually rescued the conservative order from the prospect of decay and oblivion. To the "old conservatives," on the other hand, Bismarck's actions were a betrayal of the conservative cause, a surrender of cherished values, and a hazard to traditional institutions. Yet the role of political opposition did not come easily. Conservatives were accustomed to being in harmony with the

[38] Bismarck to Wilhelm I, Oct. 30, 1869. GSA, H. A., rep. 51, nr. 10.

[39] Bismarck to Eulenburg, Sept. 26, 29, and 30, 1869. *Friedrich Eulenburg Papers*, courtesy of the late Wend Graf zu Eulenburg-Hertefeld and John C. G. Röhl. Otto Pflanze, "Die Krise von 1869 in der Innenpolitik Bismarcks," *Historische Zeitschrift*, 201 (1965), 359–364.

[40] Wehrmann to Bismarck, Oct. 24, 1869; Eulenburg to Bismarck, Oct. 23, 27, and 29, 1869; Camphausen to Bismarck, Nov. 1, 1869. GSA, rep. 94, nr. 1162; Bismarck to Wilhelm I, Oct. 22, 29, and 30, 1869. GSA, H. A., rep. 51, nr. 10. Wilhelm I to Bismarck, Oct. 27, 1869. Kohl, ed., *Anhang*, vol. 1, 202–204. Bismarck to Delbrück, Oct. 11, 21, 22, 23, 25, and 27, 1869. GW, XIV, 762–767. Pollmann, *Parlamentarismus*, 427–431.

ruling power, to which they were linked by so many ties of status, ideology, and self-interest. By opposing Bismarck, moreover, they feared to drive him further into the arms of the liberal parties. What position conservatives took between the two poles of cooperation and opposition depended partly on the chamber to which they belonged. Those who sat in the Reichstag were inclined toward grudging cooperation, those in the Prussian House of Lords to outspoken opposition, those in the Chamber of Deputies to uneasy silence alternating with flaming rebellion.[41]

The strong undercurrent of conservative dissatisfaction in the Chamber of Deputies first reached the surface over the issue of the Hanoverian provincial fund. At the time of its annexation the state of Hanover possessed a capital reserve (*Dominialablösungs- und Veräusserungsfond*) of 16,000,000 thalers that yielded about 550,000 thalers annually. One of the first acts of the new Hanoverian provincial diet was to pass a resolution sponsored by Bennigsen petitioning the Prussian government to leave this fund to the disposal of the province. Bismarck was favorable to the proposal. To deny the requests would have strengthened particularistic sentiment in Hanover and made its assimilation more difficult. Recently Prussia's expropriation of the Hessian state treasury had raised such a storm of protest that the king had disavowed the action. In December 1867, the Prussian cabinet, acting on Bismarck's initiative, presented to the Landtag a bill granting to the Hanoverian provincial government control over the domain fund and its annual income. The implications of the bill extended far beyond Hanover, for it was Bismarck's intention that the old provinces should in the future be granted similar funds as part of a general program for decentralizing the Prussian bureaucracy through greater provincial autonomy.[42]

To Bismarck's surprise this proposition precipitated the first open break between himself and the Prussian conservatives. In the budget committee during mid-December Wilhelm von Brauchitsch, a conservative leader and former *Landrat*, joined the progressives Virchow and Hoverbeck in denouncing the bill as "unjustified" partiality toward the defeated Hanoverians. Conservatives did not oppose in principle the larger program of decentralization, so it is difficult to find concrete reasons for their strong opposition on this issue. Obviously they were piqued by their failure in recent Landtag elections to win significant strength in Hanover. Perhaps they feared that Bismarck, instead of Prussianizing the new provinces, intended to liberalize Prussia, using the institutions of the conquered states as a model for reform. What the sudden rebellion of the conservatives on this issue primarily revealed, however, was the degree of alienation produced by Bismarck's collaboration with national

[41] See Robert M. Berdahl, "The Transformation of the Prussian Conservative Party, 1866–1876" (dissertation, University of Minnesota, 1965), 76–130.

[42] GW, VIa, 59–60, 217–218; BR, III, 445ff.

liberals. The recent fall of Lippe and the appointment of Leonhardt seemed to show that conservative ministers in the Prussian cabinet were being sacrificed. How vexed the conservatives were is revealed in a letter written by *Landrat* von Waldow-Steinhöfel, member of the House of Lords, to Bismarck in mid-January 1868. "More or less as an old friend, you demand approval [of the provincial fund] by the Conservative party as an expression of trust in you and your superior insight. I believe we have given adequate proof of our trust. We have repeatedly sacrificed our convictions for you personally, your excellency, not for the cabinet. What has been done for us in return? . . . Every single measure has been directed against big landowners and conservative interests. Painful as it is, the idea has spread more and more that your excellency has abandoned the conservative cause."[43]

Despite their talk of "conscience," the ultras did not look on the issue of the Hanoverian fund as important in itself. Apparently their aim was to impress on Bismarck that they too were due some blackmail—a few apologetic words and a promise that the approaching reform of county government (*Kreisordnung*) would be conservative in character.[44] Bismarck, outraged by this show of independence on the part of conservative friends, refused to plead or bargain. Instead he hinted at resignation (conservatives would have to see whether they could keep the "heterogeneous forces" of the country together without resorting to even more radical measures) and threatened reprisal (unless they yielded, conservatives could expect a county reform bill drafted by the liberals themselves). "You can say that, dear Bismarck," a conservative said, "but you won't do it." "Won't I?" he replied. "You don't know me very well. In 1866, the Austrians also said, 'Bismarck will not shoot—*that* he certainly won't do!' Now did I shoot?"[45]

Opposition to the Hanoverian provincial fund extended throughout the Chamber of Deputies, including free conservatives, national liberals, old-liberals (headed by Georg von Vincke), conservatives, and progressives. Although Bismarck believed the bill was lost, his pressure on the conservatives was unrelenting. Their constituents, he charged in the debate on February 4–7, 1868, had elected them to support the government "unconditionally." Constitutional government was impossible if ministers could not rely on at least one major party. Otherwise he must "maneuver against the constitution," creating an "artificial majority" by resorting to "coalition ministries," whose fluctuations would be highly damaging to conservative principles. For conservatives to accept only part of the government's program was not enough. If accorded only partial support, he might lose his balance. At a palace ball on February 6 the king showed his displeasure "by words and ges-

---

[43] BP, II, 57–59; GW, VIa, 217–219. On the conservatives in general see Ritter, *Die preussischen Konservativen*, 267ff.

[44] GW, VIa, 218–219, 227; XIV, 737; BP, II, 58–65.

[45] GW, VII, 244–246; Kohl, ed., *Anhang*, vol. 2, 422.

tures." These shock tactics cracked the conservative front. Yet the bill was saved only by the intervention of a group of free conservatives and national liberals who backed an amendment by Kardorff and approved by Bismarck. The Kardorff amendment expropriated the Hanoverian domain fund, but compensated the province with an annual grant of five hundred thousand thalers from the Prussian treasury. In the crucial vote on February 6 this amendment, which retained the essence of what Bismarck wanted, passed by a narrow margin (197 to 192). In the House of Lords only a small group of fourteen members (among them, Bismarck's old friends Alexander von Below-Hohendorf and Hans von Kleist-Retzow), dared vote against the bill. Voting affirmative were 127 members; 125 either abstained or were ominously absent.[46]

Bismarck never forgot this "desertion" by *Duz-Brüder*; years later he denounced them again in his memoirs.[47] They, on the other hand, were stunned by their inability to bend Bismarck to their will either by supporting or opposing him. Neither tradition nor temperament had prepared them to heed Roon's call for a "party of conservative progress."[48] Self-interest compelled them to back the government in its struggles with liberals over parliamentary budget rights and similar issues. But when Bismarck and the liberals agreed, as was often the case during these years, conservatives could only watch impotently the passage of statute after statute injurious to their interests and values. One of their deepest concerns was the steady growth of confederate executive and legislative powers at the cost of the Prussian state. Bit by bit, the *Kreuzzeitung* complained, the Prussian state was being sacrificed to the confederation.[49] In October 1869, Count Lippe, the deposed minister of justice, determined to halt the tide by challenging the constitutionality of two confederate laws, one creating a supreme court in Leipzig to hear cases involving commercial law and another providing for the universal validity of judicial decisions. As a member of the House of Lords, he introduced a motion declaring such confederate legislation illegal unless approved by the Prussian Landtag.[50]

Bismarck, waiting at Varzin for news of Heydt's fall, at first dismissed Lippe's action as an "absurdity that costs me no concern." When he learned that the motion had been reported favorably out of committee, contempt

[46] *SBHA* (1867–1868), III, 1465–1467; *SBHH* (1867–1868), I, 198–199; *BR*, III, 436ff.; Kardorff, *Kardorff*, 43ff.; Oncken, *Bennigsen*, vol. 2, 126ff.

[47] *GW*, XV, 343ff. On May 15, 1868, Bismarck urged Minister of Interior Eulenburg to investigate allegations that certain landowners, whose names might "not be without interest politically," had misappropriated advances from the state for seed purchases. *AWB*, I, 117–118.

[48] *GW*, XV, 344–346.

[49] *Neue Preussische Zeitung*, no. 273 (Nov. 21, 1869), quoted in Berdahl, "Prussian Conservative Party," 120–121.

[50] *SBHH* (1869–1870), II, 1.

gave way to rage. Through the press, personal letters, and instructions to subordinates in Berlin, he assaulted the "narrow-minded particularism" that he had thought impossible among "politically educated Prussians." So deep and firm were the tracks that the government had to follow in its German policy that the "wagon of state" could not be diverted without damage. Behind the resistance of the House of Lords loomed "France and Austria, Saxon and south German particularists, ultramontanes and republicans, Hitzing and Stuttgart." The government could not retreat without surrendering the policy of 1867. "It must pick up the gauntlet." He predicted a parliamentary conflict "in which the whole force of German national sentiment would flow, like flood and wind, in favor of the Chamber of Deputies and against the House of Lords." Again ultraconservatives failed to stand fast. So many absented themselves during the voting that the Lippe motion failed (58 to 42).[51]

As long as he retained Wilhelm's trust, Bismarck could blunt the offensives of both liberals and conservatives by playing off one group against the other. But this tactic contributed to his difficulties by arousing and emboldening the victims. Hence the "breach of trust" crisis of late 1867 and the dismissal of Lippe led conservatives to oppose the Hanoverian provincial fund in February 1868. Bennigsen and his followers then tried to "move into the position the conservatives had blithely vacated" by supporting the Kardorff amendment.[52] Their attempt to exploit that position by advancing the principle of juridical responsibility (April 1868) ended in defeat. Friction between Bismarck and the liberals in the budget crises of 1868–1869 encouraged Lippe to undertake his offensive in the House of Lords. These dissensions over basic issues detracted seriously from the image that Bismarck wished to project before Germany and Europe: that of a united confederation strongly supported by all of its major economic, social, and political interest groups. An equally important consequence was the damage inflicted upon Bismarck's psychic and physical health by these challenges to his leadership.

[51] GW, XIV, 761–762, 768; VIa, 149; SBHH (1868–1870), I, 67.
[52] Oncken, Bennigsen, vol. 2, 116.

+

Prelude to War

Impending Internal Crises

B Y HIS own testimony Bismarck suffered after December 1865 an "enduring illness, . . . a condition that expresses itself in changing bodily symptoms, of which the basic cause is nervous exhaustion. It makes difficult, and at times forbids, every sustained intellectual effort."[1] He recovered long enough to endure the military and diplomatic campaign of 1866, but suffered a serious relapse later in the year. His activities during 1867—the critical year for the creation of the North German Confederation and normalization of its relations with the south German states—would have taxed the endurance of even a healthy person. During the first six months Bismarck steered the constitution through the Prussian cabinet, council of ministers, and constituent Reichstag to final acceptance by the north German governments. Afterward he negotiated the Zollverein and military treaties with the southern states. In autumn and fall he participated in the sessions of the newly elected Reichstag, Chamber of Deputies, and Zollverein parliament. The log of his activities during 1867 shows many other events: brief trips to Ems and Paris and many official dinners, receptions, and hunts—some in distant places. The vacation he allowed himself at Varzin, his Pomeranian estate, was comparatively brief: June 22 to August 2.[2]

On April 15, 1867, the day on which the deliberations of the constituent Reichstag ended, the Baroness von Spitzemberg, an intimate friend and frequent guest of the Bismarck family, recorded in her diary: "Bismarck is suffering so badly that he can scarcely hold out any longer."[3] But he did hold out, only to collapse in the following year. In February 1868, his fury over the defection of the conservatives forced him to go into seclusion; he considered asking for an "indefinite leave."[4] When Gustav von Diest, a conservative deputy, remarked that he looked "strong and healthy," the chancellor exploded, "I, healthy? You have no idea how badly off I am and what it's like behind here [pointing to his forehead]. That is not a brain any more, only a

---

[1] Bismarck to Goltz, Mar. 14, 1868. GW, VIa, 308.

[2] Horst Kohl, ed., *Fürst Bismarck: Regesten zu einer wissenschaftlichen Biographie des ersten Reichskanzlers* (Stuttgart, 1891–1892), vol. 1, 340–359. Bismarck made the trip to Paris with some trepidation. Before departing he prepared a new will—to be ready for any eventuality. Rudolf Vierhaus, ed., *Das Tagebuch der Baronin Spitzemberg* (Göttingen, 1960), 78.

[3] Spitzemberg, *Tagebuch*, 77.

[4] *Ibid.*, 81.

gelatinous mass."[5] At a military review in May, George Bancroft, the American minister, heard him complain, "I cannot sleep, I cannot eat, I cannot drink, I cannot laugh, I cannot smoke, I cannot work. . . . My nerves are bankrupt." That day he became so ill that he had to be driven home—an attack of pleurisy that left him exhausted. His request for an extended leave was granted, and on June 16 he departed for Varzin.[6] In August his horse stumbled and fell on him, breaking two ribs. On October 19, he reported to the king that the pains had delayed the "strengthening" of his nerves. "I can again perform every bodily movement and believe that I am essentially more healthy than in the spring; but every attempt at a livelier intercourse with people has until now always robbed me of sleep." The doctors advised a few more weeks of "isolation" in preparation for the "winter campaign." He returned to Berlin on December 1.[7]

Within three months after his return to Berlin, Bismarck felt that he had already expended the physical and emotional capital stored up during the long leave of 1868. Dealing with the king, eight ministers, three parliaments, twenty-two confederate governments, and various foreign powers exhausted his energy and rasped his nerves. He deplored frictions produced by the "artificial wheels of a constitutional state." To decide was easy, to convince difficult. But even ill health had its uses. His condition, he warned Wilhelm in February 1869, would force him to resign if the monarch continued to accept advice from others, to reopen issues presumed to be closed, and to keep in office men whom Bismarck wished to ditch (specifically, the diplomat Count Usedom).[8] In June 1869, the chancellor requested another extended leave for rest and recuperation. On July 1 he was back in Varzin. Not even in bucolic Pomerania was he free from vexation. "A modest annoyance at the stables," he wrote, "costs me one night: a polemical correspondence, two."[9] In early October (during the budget deficit crisis) he was attacked by stomach cramps of uncertain origin. "I don't know whether it is anger, a cold, or general wear-

---

[5] GW, VII, 250.

[6] M. A. DeWolf Howe, *The Life and Letters of George Bancroft* (New York, 1908), vol. 2, 205–206; Spitzemberg, *Tagebuch*, 84; BP, II, 65–66; Kohl, ed., *Bismarck-Regesten*, vol. 2, II, 66.

[7] GW, VIa, 421, and XIV, 743, 752.

[8] Bismarck to Wilhelm I, Feb. 1869. Horst Kohl, ed., *Anhang zu den Gedanken und Erinnerungen von Fürsten Otto von Bismarck* (Stuttgart, 1901), vol. 1, 190–195. This appears to have been the first of Bismarck's many offers to resign. Wilhelm was patently shocked at the minister's reaction to what had seemed to be harmless actions well within his prerogative as ruler. He strove to appease Bismarck, while trying pathetically to maintain his dignity. The episode shows how powerful Bismarck's grip on the monarch had become. Wilhelm to Bismarck, Feb. 22 and 26, 1869. *Ibid.*, 189–190, 195–199; GW, XV, 137–141. Bismarck, on the other hand, lost few good opportunities to assure the Hohenzoller of his *Vasallentreu*, his regret at not having had a career as a royal officer, his desire to serve his sovereign as would a soldier, his gratitude that God had placed Wilhelm on the throne, and the like. GW, VIa, 420–421, 427–428.

[9] Bismarck to Eulenburg, Sept. 24, 1869. GW, VIb, 147.

ing out of the machine." The doctors recommended Biarritz or Torquai, but he could not face "railways, hostelries, foreign courts and people, newspaper articles, loneliness, and bad beds. I must be older than my parents told me."[10] Under the coercion of his doctors, he finally accepted daily doses of imported Karlsbad water. "Physically I feel much stronger than I have for a long time," he reported to Wilhelm in mid-November. "But intellectual exertions arouse and tire me in a way that I attribute to the effect of the Karlsbad water. At any rate I am rid of the despondency that afflicted me during the summer whenever I contemplated returning to business. It has been replaced by some impatience for the day when I can inform your majesty that I am healthy and ready for duty."[11]

On December 4, 1869, Bismarck returned to Berlin, still in uncertain health. During a formal dinner at the palace on March 20, 1870, he fell ill of an acutely irritated stomach, accompanied by vomiting and intermittent pain. A "morphine powder" brought temporary relief, but the pains returned and became more frequent. His pulse slowed from seventy-two to fifty-six and the symptoms of cholemia (bile salts in the blood) appeared. Bismarck medicated himself with another powder and blamed the subsequent attack of diarrhea on his physician, Heinrich Struck. Since Bismarck refused to receive him any more, Struck was compelled to treat the patient at a distance on the basis of Johanna's reports. On April 14, 1870, Bismarck departed "against all advice and entreaties" for Varzin, where he developed a bad case of jaundice. Struck, who was summoned from Berlin, feared complications (peritonitis or pylephlebitis). But on May 24 the chancellor was well enough to return to Berlin and defend the death sentence in the Reichstag debates on the criminal code. After attending Wilhelm on a four-day trip to Bad Ems, where they conferred with Tsar Alexander, Bismarck returned to Varzin on June 8 in the hope of completing his recuperation.[12] While major crises were brewing in both domestic and foreign affairs, Bismarck exacerbated a potentially serious illness by feuding with his physician and mistreating himself with a narcotic.

In this debilitated state Bismarck faced the possibility of a major struggle with the Reichstag over renewal of the iron budget due to expire on December 31, 1871. To be sure, he told Chief of the Admiralty Albrecht von Stosch that this prospect was "nonsense"; such a struggle was impossible under the constitution of 1867.[13] Technically this was true, because the constitution

[10] Bismarck to Josephine von Seydewitz, Sept. 4, 1869, and Bismarck to Oskar von Arnim, Oct. 12, 1869. GW, XIV, 758, 763–764. Bismarck to Wilhelm I, Oct. 22, 1869. GSA, H. A., rep. 51, nr. 10.

[11] Bismarck to Wilhelm I, Nov. 17, 1869. GSA, H. A., rep. 51, nr. 10.

[12] Heinrich Struck to an unknown physician, Apr. 18, 1870. GSA, rep. 94, nr. 238; Kohl, ed., Bismarck-Regesten, vol. 1, 389–393; Spitzemberg, Tagebuch, 91.

[13] Albrecht von Stosch to Gustav Freytag, May 28, 1870. Ulrich von Stosch, ed., Denkwürdigkeiten des Generals und Admirals Albrecht von Stosch (2d ed., Stuttgart, 1904), 182.

provided that the size (1 percent of the population) and financial support (225 thalers per soldier) of the army would remain the same even after the expiration date, in the event that Reichstag and Bundesrat were unable to reach agreement on a new law. Yet Bismarck could hardly have relished, any more than did Stosch, the likelihood of a confrontation between the two chambers over such an issue. A renewed struggle over the army would have given Prussia a bad press in southern Germany, repelling liberals and strengthening particularists.

The opening round of this fight was expected in late 1870 when the Reichstag and Chamber of Deputies were due for reelection. But the Progressive party did not wait that long to fire its first salvos. Since the constitutional conflict progressives had not lost their militancy against militarism. During the Prussian budget debate of 1869 Rudolf Virchow proposed that the government be asked to wipe out the deficit by reducing military expeditures and opening negotiations for general disarmament. The motion lost, 215 to 99, but the progressives incorporated it as one of four points in their election manifesto of April 1870.[14] Although uncommitted to pacifism, the national liberals were also convinced that the burden of military expenditures had to be reduced after 1871. They believed that the coming debates on the iron budget would inevitably raise some of the most important issues of constitutionalism—with regard not only to the budgetary power of the Reichstag, but also to the form of the confederate executive. How was it possible, Miquel asked, to have a budget of 77 million thalers and no minister of finance? How could the debate over the army be resolved without a confederate minister of war? To Miquel, hardly a radical, it did not appear possible to continue the existing form of government in which the chancellor alone was responsible for foreign policy, trade and tariffs, justice, and the naval and military budget.[15] More than anything that had yet occurred the approaching debate threatened to damage the image of internal solidarity that Bismarck wished to project before southern Germany and Europe. As he began to prepare for the coming election, Bismarck judged that renewal of the iron budget had become "the cardinal question of the North German Confederation" and a matter of "European importance."[16]

Liberals were also increasingly impatient over lack of progress toward German unification. On February 24, 1870—not long after the Hohenlohe cabinet fell in Munich—the Reichstag debated a motion by Eduard Lasker calling

[14] SBHA (1869–1870), IV, 366ff.; Felix Salomon, Die deutschen Parteiprogramme (3d ed., Berlin, 1920–1924), vol. 1, 105.

[15] SBR (1869), II, 1014, and (1870), I, 375ff. In mid-May 1870, the Reichstag gave a foretaste of the approaching debate by narrowly rejecting (86 to 82) in a half-full chamber the government's request for retroactive approval of the purchase of a naval administration building with funds unauthorized for the purpose. SBR (1870) II, 923ff., 1045ff.

[16] Bismarck to Eulenburg, Mar. 8, 1870. GW, VIb, 265–66.

for the incorporation of Baden in the North German Confederation with the "least possible delay." The people of Baden, Lasker claimed, were overwhelmingly in favor of national unity; yet no use had been made of the final article in the constitution of 1867, providing for entry of one or all south German states into the confederation "on the motion of the confederate presidency and by way of legislation." Why had no action been taken despite the patent opportunity for it? Surely the man who had uttered those ringing words, "The appeal to fear finds no echo in German hearts," was not deterred by foreign opposition. The answer to this "puzzle," Lasker concluded, lay in the liberal and popular character of Baden's government, a stark contrast to Prussia's. In the same debate Miquel accused the chancellor of not wanting union with the south, of ignoring public opinion, and of doing nothing to encourage German nationalists of the south in their struggle against particularism.

Bismarck was incensed at this attempt by parliament to interfere in foreign policy. Repeatedly he interrupted Miquel, shouting: "No!" "No!" "That is incorrect!" "Stop!" "Stop!" On gaining the rostrum, he asserted that the inclusion of Baden would strengthen particularism and stifle emergent national movements in Bavaria and Württemberg. Rather than use coercion, it was preferable to wait "another generation." Pointing to what had been accomplished thus far—the customs parliament, military treaties, and Prussian command in wartime—he asked, "Have we not attained with regard to the south a valuable piece of national unity? . . . Does not the presidency of the North German Confederation exercise in southern Germany a degree of imperial power such as German Kaisers have not possessed for five hundred years?"[17]

The Kaiser Project

Bismarck's reference to the title "Kaiser" was no mere oratorical arabesque. For nearly two months he had secretly been working to make Wilhelm "Kaiser of Germany" or at least "Kaiser of the North German Confederation." At a royal hunt in Potsdam on January 7, 1870, he had broached the matter to the crown prince. As the future bearer of the title, the prince might be useful in persuading the king. Bismarck pointed to the two elections due in 1870. Majorities favorable to the government were vitally necessary, for after December 31, 1871, the Reichstag would gain the right under the constitution to review the iron budget. The proclamation of a German Kaiser would provide a winning slogan for those supporting the government and avoid a recurrence of the constitutional conflict. The impending transformation of the "Royal Prussian Ministry for Foreign Affairs" into the "Foreign Office of the North German Confederation" (January 10, 1870) provided a plausible excuse for

[17] SBR (1870), I, 58–77. Lasker withdrew the motion, which was an amendment to a treaty with Baden on judicial reciprocity.

the change. In diplomatic intercourse the neuter *Präsidium* was exceedingly awkward.[18]

To succeed, the scheme required not only Wilhelm's approval, but also that of the lesser states (north and south), the European great powers, and the Reichstag. Wilhelm would most certainly object, but he could be managed. The national liberals to whom Bismarck broached the matter showed a disposition to bargain, but there was no reason to doubt that, when actually presented with the proposition, the Reichstag majority would accept.[19] If Bismarck's calculation was correct, the idea might even generate considerable enthusiasm. In 1866–1867 the lesser states of the north had themselves proposed the Kaiser title as a protection against Prussianization. By early 1870, however, some north German rulers had grown restless under Prussian domination. King Johann of Saxony was not sympathetic toward the Kaiser project, nor was Grand Duke Karl Alexander of Saxe-Weimar. When rumors spread that Bismarck intended to by-pass the rulers and inaugurate a north German *Kaisertum* by plebiscite, Baron Richard von Friesen, Saxony's foreign minister, declared he would advise the chancellor "to think twice beforehand, for in Saxony anti-Prussian sentiment was visibly increasing, especially among farmers."[20]

In the south, Baden was expected to give wholehearted support, particularly if the title chosen were "Kaiser of Germany." Their increasing dependence upon Berlin for support against subversion at home might be exploited to get the approval of Stuttgart and Munich. Without knowledge of Bismarck's intentions, leaders of the Bavarian Patriot party had advocated reviving the imperial title. They were even willing to accept a Hohenzollern Kaiser, but insisted on the inclusion of Austria, location of the capital in Frankfurt, and acceptance of the black-red-gold colors of the revolution. Werthern saw a glimmer of hope that southern particularists would find it much easier to subject themselves to a German Kaiser than to the feared and hated Prussia. "A lot lies in a name."[21]

Most important for Bismarck's purposes was the reaction in London and Paris. This came much quicker than expected. Through the indiscretion of

[18] GW, VIb, 212ff. See also his note to Eulenburg, Mar. 8, 1870, 265–266. Gustav Roloff believed the purpose of the Kaiser project was to counteract a French attempt, through a disarmament proposal, to "encircle" and weaken Prussia, but his argument rested on a "timing coincidence." See his "Abrüstung und Kaiserplan vor dem Kriege von 1870," *Preussische Jahrbücher*, 214 (1928), 189ff.

[19] According to one source, the national liberals demanded as quid pro quo the inclusion of Baden and southern Hesse; another has it that the demand was for the creation of "responsible confederate ministries." GW, VIb, 280.

[20] Josef Becker, "Zum Problem der Bismarckschen Politik in der spanischen Thronfrage," *Historische Zeitschrift*, 212 (1971), 541–542.

[21] GW, VIb, 260, 279; Otto Becker, *Bismarcks Ringen um Deutschlands Gestaltung* (Heidelberg, 1958), J. Becker, "Zum Problem," 542–543.

Franz Duncker, a leading progressive, British Ambassador Lord Augustus Loftus was able to report the plan to Lord Clarendon, the new foreign secretary in London, on January 8, 1870. Three days later Clarendon brought up the subject in a talk with Bernstorff. He claimed to be favorable and said that he would even seek to induce Paris to take a similar view. Though pleased at Clarendon's response, Bismarck quickly denied that an expected struggle over the military budget had prompted the idea. The sole purpose of the Kaiser project, he insisted, was to overcome particularism, especially in Prussia. In passing up the title in 1867, he had "underestimated the importance that superficialities have in the opinion of my countrymen."[22]

But his words were wasted in London, for Clarendon had not kept his promise to Bernstorff. Far from intervening at Paris in behalf of the new title, he disparaged it in his talk with La Valette on January 26. On the following day, he informed Bernstorff of his fears that such a coup would excite the French and produce a new crisis. Surely it was not worth risking the peace of Europe to attain that which must come in the natural course of events. For Wilhelm's benefit Bismarck commented in the margin: "right." At the end he remarked that the matter had not gone very far, and there was no need for haste.[23]

In March, nevertheless, the chancellor began to push the project again. On a visit to Berlin Julius Fröbel, an influential Bavarian publicist on the Prussian payroll, heard from Keudell that the chancellor was "busy day and night with the Kaiser idea." The crown prince recorded in his diary, "Bismarck is working together with Roon and Moltke on a project to regulate the national question by taking up seriously the Kaiser question." About this time the chancellor discussed the matter with Grand Duke Friedrich of Baden. From Constantin Rössler, editor of the official *Preussischer Staatsanzeiger*, Fröbel learned of a proposal to offer King Ludwig II of Bavaria a sort of vice-emperorship with the title "German King." No official démarche appears to have been made in Munich, but British informants reported that the two southern kings, on being approached indirectly, reacted negatively and thereby put an end to the matter.[24]

---

[22] GW, VIb, 214–218. Veit Valentin corrected the assumption of Walter Platzhoff that news of the Kaiser plan reached London first through an indiscretion of Friedrich Wilhelm. Veit Valentin, *Bismarcks Reichsgründung im Urteil englischer Diplomaten* (Amsterdam, 1937), 404–405; Walter Platzhoff, "England und der Kaiserplan vom Frühjahr 1870," *Historische Zeitschrift*, 127 (1923), 454–475. A year earlier Clarendon had volunteered the suggestion that it would have been better had Wilhelm taken the title "Kaiser or King of Germany" in 1867. APP, IX, 862.

[23] GW, VIb, 217; OD, XXVI, 233–234.

[24] Julius Fröbel, *Ein Lebenslauf* (Stuttgart, 1890–1891), vol. 2, 546–547; APP, X, 94–96; GW, VIb, 279–281; Hermann Oncken, ed., *Grossherzog Friedrich I. von Baden und die deutsche Politik von 1854–1871* (Stuttgart, 1927), vol. 2, 137, 162; M. Doeberl, *Bayern und die Bismarckische Reichsgründung* (Munich, 1925), 301–302; Schneider, "Württembergs Beitritt," 126–127; Valentin, *Bismarcks Reichsgründung*, 410–413. Political and diplomatic circles were full of rumors

The Kaiser project reveals that during the early months of 1870 Bismarck was on the hunt for a national issue capable of outflanking southern particularism and overcoming liberal opposition to renewal of the iron budget. Albrecht von Stosch, an intimate of the crown prince, detected a certain "restlessness" in his attitude. To avoid further compromise with the liberals he had to make progress in the national question. Southern rulers, Stosch believed, would never accept a Hohenzollern Kaiser, "unless they were coerced by an external pressure."[25] German affairs had reached an impasse from which, as so often in the past, the only possible egress appeared to be a crisis or war with France.

Renewal of the Russo-Prussian Entente

The years following the Luxemburg crisis were marked by mounting tension in Europe. It was generally believed that another war was in the offing. The German military machine was kept well oiled, ready for motion on short notice. Across the Rhine, French rearmament got under way in 1868. The failures of 1866–1867 had revealed a stark imbalance between France's military preparedness and her commitments in foreign policy. On the Danube the Habsburg monarchy strove to arm within the narrow limits of its financial capability. European chancelleries were full of plans, rumors, and anxieties. Where would the conflict break out—on the Rhine or in the Balkans? How would Europe divide?

The potential combinations were many. The Luxemburg affair had ended French speculation on the possibility of agreement with Berlin. But Russia's need for support in the Balkans caused Gorchakov to revive for a time his perennial hope of alliance with France. Both Vienna and Paris were aware of a common interest in preventing further expansion of Prussian power and of undoing the settlement of Prague. Austria required French help in frustrating Russian penetration of the Balkans. Other possible members of their entente were Italy and Britain. What Bismarck feared most was the combination of French land power and British sea power. In each of these potential alliances the common partner was France. Had any one of them materialized, Bismarck's plans for the future would have been gravely jeopardized.

The source of greatest danger was Beust. "From oxen," Bismarck once remarked, "one can expect nothing but beef; from Beust nothing but an ambitious, intriguing Saxon *Hauspolitik*."[26] The success of his old opponent in gaining the confidence of Franz Joseph alarmed and angered him. In February 1867 the Saxon was appointed Austrian minister-president, in June imperial

---

about the plan. See Erich Brandenburg, "Die Verhandlungen über die Gründung des deutschen Reiches 1870," *Historische Vierteljahrschrift*, 15 (1912), 494ff.

[25] Stosch, *Denkwürdigkeiten*, 181–182.
[26] GW, XIV, 332.

COUNT FRIEDRICH FERDINAND VON BEUST (BILDARCHIV PREUSSISCHER KULTURBESITZ).

chancellor; in December 1868 he was dignified with the hereditary title of count. His primary objective was revenge for the defeat of 1866 and restoration of Austrian power in Germany. In preparation for such a move he pushed through the settlement with Hungary that created the "dual monarchy." At whatever cost, the Habsburg house had to be set in order at home for the reassertion of its powers abroad. By granting a constitution, he hoped to outstrip Berlin in attracting the liberals of southern Germany.

In his German policy, however, Beust had a serious handicap. There was no adequate support in the dual monarchy for a policy of direct action. Hungarians were not interested in restoring Habsburg authority in Germany; its loss had been the means of their own advancement. In Austria there was a small war party composed of influential nobles, officers, and clergymen, but the dominant sentiment was against conspiring with France for war on Germany. Instead, Vienna should wait, they believed, for the outbreak of a Franco-Prussian conflict and exploit her neutrality to dictate her desires in Germany. Unable to undertake a bold policy in Germany, Beust hoped to involve Berlin in a European war over eastern issues.[27]

In 1866 a rebellion in Crete had reopened the "eastern question," the most persistent problem in nineteenth-century politics. The success of Prince Karl

[27] Werner E. Mosse, *The European Powers and the German Question, 1848–1871* (Cambridge, Eng., 1958), 253ff.

in Rumania and friction with Serbia had shaken the Turkish regime. Now the Cretan revolt, actively supported by Greece, threatened its collapse. Digging into the archives, the Russian government discovered that in 1829 the Porte had made commitments on the treatment of the Christian population that it had failed to keep. In London and Paris Gorchakov proposed (August 30, 1866) a joint remonstrance in Constantinople.[28]

From Vienna, however, came the depressing news that Petersburg had a new competitor in the game of protecting Balkan Christians. Abandoning the previous Habsburg policy of supporting the Turks, Beust sought to outdistance Gorchakov by organizing the western powers in a common front in the Balkans. His aim was to embroil Europe in an eastern conflict, compelling Berlin to support Russia, her only major ally. For Austria a war of eastern origin had none of the disadvantages of one over western issues. Hungarians would support it with enthusiasm. Germans, accustomed to Austrian leadership in Balkan affairs, would be sympathetic. Out of the eastern embroglio would come the chance for Austria's revenge against Prussia and the restoration of her power in Germany.[29]

The internal limitations on his German policy, nevertheless, compelled Beust to pass up the opportunity for a far-reaching compact with France. In the final days of the Luxemburg crisis Duke de Gramont, the French ambassador at Vienna, arrived from Paris with a "lot of rather indiscreet, but characteristic questions." Would the Hofburg be interested in an "offensive and defensive alliance?" Napoleon wished to acquire the left bank of the Rhine, but he would leave Belgium untouched. Austria might have Silesia and disposition over southern Germany, except for Baden, which would be reserved for France. But Beust had to reply that such a conspiracy would be ill received in the empire by Slavs, Hungarians, and Germans alike. Nothing would be more repugnant to the latter than a war whose avowed end was to bring part of Germany under alien rule. If the main object of the alliance were the eastern question, on the other hand, Beust confessed that he would "not recoil from any of its possible consequences, not even from an aggrandizement of France in Germany." But this could only be the by-product, not the principal purpose, of the conflict.[30]

During the summer Bismarck's success in reorganizing the Zollverein pro-

[28] O. Becker, Bismarcks Ringen, 625ff.

[29] RKN, III, 60–61, 68–70; APP, VIII, 208; Friedrich Ferdinand Graf von Beust, Aus drei Viertel-Jahrhunderten (Stuttgart, 1887), vol. 2, 337ff.; Walter Vogel, Die Tagebücher des Freiherrn Reinhard von Dalwigk zu Lichtenfels als Geschichtsquelle: Historische Studien, vol. 234 (Berlin, 1933), 61–62; Eduard von Wertheimer, "Zur Vorgeschichte des Krieges von 1870," Deutsche Rundschau, 185 (1920), 1–26.

[30] RKN, II, 338, 362–365. Gramont's presentation may have been more blunt than Napoleon intended. At the outset the diplomat admitted that he was authorized only to "sound out the terrain," but added that he preferred to talk "frankly."

duced a fresh wave of alarm on the Seine. On August 18, 1867, Napoleon called upon Franz Joseph in Salzburg. Ostensibly his purpose was to condole the Kaiser over the execution of his brother, Archduke Maximilian, in Mexico. In the secrecy of the archiepiscopal palace, however, there was talk of the future as well as of the past. Gramont presented an ambitious proposal for an ultimatum to Berlin, demanding the dissolution of its ties with southern Germany. But Napoleon himself discarded it and accepted instead a draft submitted by Beust. In Germany the two powers were to impress upon the southern states the necessity of a "reserved and independent attitude" toward the north. But they would avoid any action that could be exploited by Prussia as "menace or provocation" and that might excite a German national reaction. In the east the French agreed to a joint démarche in Petersburg on the Cretan problem, which the British were to be invited to join. Although London refused, Paris and Vienna entered in the fall of 1867 on a period of cooperation in Turkish affairs.[31]

Beust's success was Gorchakov's failure. Following the rejection of his proposal for a joint remonstrance with Britain in the Cretan question, the Russian vice-chancellor had gyrated from one European capital to another in search of support for his Turkish policy. His greatest hopes were placed on Paris. But Napoleon and Moustier refused to be explicit concerning their eastern plans and requested Russian support for their objectives (undefined) in the west. Although his reaction to the French attempt to grab Luxemburg was unfavorable, Gorchakov assisted in bringing about the London conference and hoped for French gratitude. To his annoyance, Napoleon avoided all serious political discussion during the tsar's visit to Paris in early July 1867. Moustier was cold, moreover, to Gorchakov's plan for uniting Crete with Greece. Nor did the unfriendliness of the public and the two shots fired at Alexander by a Pole help matters. Already it was evident that Gorchakov's hopes were vain. In the fall the first signs of Austro-French collaboration in Turkey confirmed their futility.[32]

Depressed in one direction, the rubber ball of international politics inflated in another. After rebuffs in Paris, Vienna, and London, the Russians had no choice but to turn to Berlin. They expected war in the spring, both in western Europe and the Balkans, and dared not be without an ally.[33] Between a concert and hunt on February 4, 1868, Tsar Alexander had a long, intimate talk with Prince Heinrich von Reuss, the Prussian ambassador. Expressing fears

[31] RKN, II, 454–458; APP, IX, 136ff., 342–344; Joseph Redlich, "L'entrevue de l'empereur François-Joseph et de l'empereur Napoléon à Salzbourg le 18 août 1867," Le Monde Slave, Nouvelle Serie, III (1926), 143–151; Mosse, European Powers, 28off.

[32] Mosse, European Powers, 254ff.

[33] Ibid., 280; Walter Platzhoff, "Die Anfänge des Dreikaiserbundes, 1867–1871," Preussische Jahrbücher, 188 (1922), 287ff.; Gerhard Heinze, Bismarck und Russland bis zur Reichsgründung (Würzburg, 1939), 74ff.

that Austria might exploit the Balkan crisis to occupy Bosnia and Herzegovina, the monarch declared: "Let us hope that this will not occur. Let us hope also that France will not attack Germany. But should, contrary to expectations, both events occur, the king can count on me to paralyze Austria, just as I would rely on his aid. In both cases the deployment of an army on the Austrian border would suffice to achieve this end." In March Alexander became more explicit. Should Prussia become involved in war with France, Russia would mobilize one hundred thousand men on the Austrian border, assuming Prussia would do the same in the event of an Austro-Russian conflict.[34]

Bismarck, however, was cautious. Verbally he assured Baron Paul Oubril, the Russian ambassador in Berlin, on March 20: "We believe ourselves equal to a war against France and have no need to expand it into a general conflict, if Russia covers our rear against Austria. We assume the same of Russia, if she should become involved in war with Austria and we granted her security against French support of the latter. But the minute one of us—whether it be Russia or Prussia—is attacked by a coalition of two powers, common interests necessitate that each support the other." By slight shifts in terrain he had established several crucial points. Common interests rather than a written agreement were to be the foundation of the alliance. Unless the European balance were threatened by French participation, Prussia was not committed to go to war to rescue Russia's Balkan interests against Austria. In event of an Austro-Russian conflict, north German troops would be deployed chiefly on the French rather than Austrian frontier.[35]

The tsar was satisfied and Bismarck doubly so. In a Franco-German war the Russians would help to neutralize Austria; without French support Austria was unlikely to move in the Balkans. The vital question was whether Beust would actually succeed in embroiling all four powers in a war over eastern issues. During 1868 rumors of such a plan appeared in the newspaper press, and Bismarck was well aware of the danger. As winter approached, Beust thought his moment had arrived. In Rumania irredentist agitation, led by Minister Ion Bratianu, mounted against Hungary, and the smoldering feud between Greece and Turkey over Crete flared up once more. But Bismarck saw to it that Prince Karl dismissed the troublesome Bratianu, and he promoted an international conference in Paris that ordered Athens to cease her aid to Cretan insurgents. Had his efforts failed, Bismarck was prepared to provoke war with France over the German question. Nothing would be easier than to make France "assume the role of an aggressor."[36]

---

[34] APP, IX, 671, 706–707, 759–760, 844.

[35] GW, VIa, 321. Fearing Gorchakov's jealousy over direct negotiations with the tsar, Bismarck had earlier avoided all but the most general response to Alexander's proposals. GW, VIa, 262, 306–307. On the character of the agreement see Walter Ebel, Bismarck und Russland vom Prager Frieden bis zum Ausbruch des Krieges von 1870 (Gelnhausen, 1936), 48–57.

[36] GW, VIa, 322, 504–505; APP, X, 402, 523; Chester W. Clark, "Bismarck, Russia, and the

Failure of the Austro-French Alliance

Napoleon, complained Metternich in mid-November 1867, was not frank. He would not say what he thought, what he had done, or what he intended to do. Even his own ministers were uninformed. The Austrian ambassador was inclined to see in his silence the sinister aim to come to terms with Berlin.[37] What the mask of silence concealed, however, was simply indecision. Naturally indolent, his mental processes slowed by ill health, Napoleon was uncertain what to do. Previously he had played at the game of international politics—in the Crimea, Italy, and Mexico—without great hazard to himself. But now suddenly he was compelled to gamble for the highest stakes: crown, empire, and the judgment of history. He had to win.

Bismarck believed the emperor personally had no thought of going to war with Germany. "But conditions in France are incalculable."[38] No longer did he think that the conduct of states was governed by self-interest alone: "In the case of alliances, traditions and personalities carry almost more weight

NAPOLEON III, EMPEROR OF FRANCE (FROM DIETRICH SCHÄFER, *BISMARCK: EIN BILD SEINES LEBENS UND WIRKENS*, TWO VOLS., VERLAG VON REIMAR HOBBING, BERLIN, 1917).

Origins of the War of 1870," *Journal of Modern History*, 14 (1942), 198. See also Horst Michael, *Bismarck, England und Europa (vorwiegend von 1866–1870): Forschungen zur mittelalterlichen und neueren Geschichte*, vol. 5 (Munich, 1930), 127ff.

[37] *RKN*, II, 477.

[38] *GW*, VIa, 253. See also *GW*, VI, 369; VIb, 113, 166.

than interests, emotions more than calculation. . . . The conduct of Russia and England in the Crimean War, that of France with regard to Poland, Italy, Mexico, and that of Austria in the Danish affair and during early 1866 hardly corresponded to the interests of these countries. Personalities and opinions took precedence over interests." Napoleon was not in command of the situation in France; he was dependent upon "the streams of partisan passion."[39]

Indeed the currents of dissatisfaction in France were deep and swift. Repeated blunders in foreign policy had provided plenty of ammunition for an antidynastic opposition by Orleanists, legitimists, and republicans. But even those linked to the dynasty by careers and interests were demanding that something be done to halt the decline of imperial prestige. Evidently this was especially true of the officer corps, whose confidence increased as France rearmed her infantry with the new breechloading *chassepots*. The approach of parliamentary elections added to the general nervousness.[40]

From Rouher, his most trusted adviser, Napoleon received a warning in late September 1867 that important circles of opinion, alarmed over the seeming "stagnation" of French policy, wanted an unequivocal decision on the German question. Would the government oppose or consent to the expansion of the North German Confederation to include the south? To declare the crossing of the Main a casus belli would lead precipitously to war with Germany. Was France prepared? On the other hand, a declaration of consent might momentarily appease some interests, but it would anger the army, "of which we have need." It would also excite more of those "perfidious, cruel, and incessant attacks" from journalists who charged that "France has fallen to the third rank."[41]

During the following months Berlin's increasingly proprietary attitude toward the south made it apparent that a policy had to be found. After Salzburg, Bismarck publicly warned that "German national feeling" would not bear the "tutelage of foreign intervention."[42] When Paris proposed a European conference to deal with the status of Rome, he objected not only to the invitation issued to Saxony (indeed an impertinence!), but also to those sent to the sovereign states of southern Germany. In European questions, he made it known, Berlin alone could speak for Germany.[43] Although the results of the Zollverein election were reassuring to France, it was still possible that Bismarck might succeed in converting the customs parliament into an instrument of unification. After visiting Berlin in mid-March 1868, Prince Napoleon reported that the absorption of the south was only a matter of time. Benedetti was of the same opinion.[44]

[39] GW, VIa, 263.
[40] RKN, I, 64–66; II, 511–512.
[41] RKN, II, 468–469.
[42] RKN, II, 459–461.
[43] GW, VIa, 118, 130–131, 136–137, 140–141, 144–146, 177, 192–193.
[44] RKN, II, 542–543, 545, 547–548; APP, IX, 625, 834.

Under these pressures Napoleon turned again to Vienna. On April 7, 1868, he asked Metternich to find out from Beust what would be done, should the peoples of southern Germany "throw themselves into the arms of Prussia"; what would be done, if Prussia resorted to violence and committed "sponta-neously" a serious infraction of the treaty of Prague; what line of conduct was to be followed, if the Rumanian principalities revolted against Turkey and proclaimed their independence contrary to "our advice"; whether another attempt should be made to bring Britain into an entente, despite the poor prospect of success. In the first eventuality (considered unlikely "if prudence is exercised") direct intervention would be difficult. As for the German prob-lem in general, it was up to Austria to take the initiative in any "preventive diplomatic action or eventual protest." France would support her "in the sec-ond line" to avoid offending German national sentiment and precipitating a "cataclysm."[45]

Beust, however, was not to be enticed from his original position. Taking advantage of Napoleon's cautious words, he agreed that the first eventuality was unlikely and lauded the effect of his own "prudence" in building up south-ern resistance. He doubted, furthermore, that Bismarck would place Prussia in the wrong by an "act of despair." Beust praised Napoleon's desire to avoid a cataclysm, but he left undecided whether France or Austria should "take the second line." The eastern question, he believed, was more important and ought to be "the ostensible basis of our entente." Confident of French sup-port, Vienna awaited events on the lower Danube. As for Britain, Vienna was ready to support Paris in any démarche, but doubted that the London cabinet would bind itself in advance.[46]

During the following months rumors spread through the diplomatic corps that the "war party" had gained the upper hand in the Tuileries. On July 20, 1868, Metternich telegraphed to Vienna that the emperor wanted to know about the possibility of an "active alliance" for a "common and determined end." If that were impossible, would Vienna join in a "passive alliance" call-ing for a European congress to consecrate the status quo in Europe? As for the active alliance, France would not demand "a priori" any territorial aggran-dizement for itself, but would seek only the reestablishment of Austria's posi-tion in Germany. Again Beust pointed out that such an alliance with a for-eign power would cost Vienna the sympathy of those Germans without whose

[45] RKN, II, 553–554. Gramont gave Bray, the Bavarian minister, a different account.
[46] See his dispatch to Metternich, Apr. 14, 1868. RKN, II, 554–556. In a preliminary state-ment to Gramont, however, he regarded the second possibility as "the real menace of the future." He would protest Prussian abandonment of the treaty of Prague, but whether he would act to prevent it was less certain. If France did so, Austria would initially be a benevolent neutral, but thereafter do her duty as a "good ally." Warming to the subject, he declared that Prussian "in-trigues and maneuvers" would untimately compel him to "take some initiative in Berlin." An open war was better than a hidden one. OD, XXI, 165–168. See the more colorful vision of the interview that Gramont related to Bray. RKN, II, 556–559.

support the restoration of Austria's power was impossible. Nothing would be more likely to make Prussia popular in Germany.[47]

Napoleon's second idea, however, suggested to Beust a magnificent opportunity. Neither England nor Russia could support a guarantee of the status quo, he argued in late July, and in rejecting it Bismarck would win the applause of all Germany. But why not, he shrewdly submitted, achieve the same end by another route? By calling for general disarmament, the emperor would electrify public opinion throughout Europe. North Germans would welcome the prospect of tax relief and south Germans the prospect of escape from the rigors of the Prussian drill. In France it would influence the voters in the approaching parliamentary elections. By approving, Prussia would accept in effect the status quo in Germany and destroy her alliance with German nationalism. By refusing, she would invite the disfavor and suspicion of public opinion. In event of war, Berlin would bear the moral responsibility.[48]

At first, Napoleon was enamored with Beust's suggestion. But the longer he considered it, the more he began to fear being "duped." Its reserve system would enable Prussia to reassemble an army in three months; France would require a full year. Hence the agreement would have to provide for dissolution of the Prussian reserve organization. What would be done, furthermore, when Prussia refused, as she certainly would? Beust, however, did not have to answer this embarrassing question, which raised precisely the issue he wished to avoid. In mid-October 1868 Lord Clarendon, on the eve of his appointment to the British cabinet, told Napoleon that a disarmament manifesto "would only serve to render war more inevitable." After visiting the military camp at Châlons, moreover, Napoleon concluded that the word "disarmament" was unsuitable for the ears of the French army.[49]

The failure of Napoleon's proposal and Beust's counterproposal did not cool the ardor of either for an alliance. On the contrary, their mutual need to block Prussian expansionism, their mutual ambition to assert themselves in Germany, and the fear of each that the other might come to terms with Berlin now impelled both into serious negotiations.[50] On November 6 Beust launched the effort by instructing Metternich to state frankly what had often been "insinuated"; namely, that the eastern question provided a far more suitable casus belli against Prussia than the German. Although Napoleon's reply accepted the "eastern base as the point of departure of our entente," the prob-

[47] RKN, III, 12–16. For this and subsequent negotiations see Anton Lamberti, Die Bündnisverhandlungen Napoleons III. gegen Preussen in den Jahren vor 1870 (Würzburg, 1939), 26ff.

[48] RKN, III, 14–15, 19–22, 28–31, 33.

[49] RKN, III, 19–24, 33–37, 53, 71–72.

[50] The failure of his attempt at economic penetration of Belgium in the winter of 1868–1869 reinforced Napoleon's desire to come to terms with Austria. See Kurt Rheindorf, "Der belgisch-französische Eisenbahnkonflikt und die grossen Mächte 1868/1869," Deutsche Rundschau, 195 (1923), 113–136.

lem of the relative importance of the two "terrains" remained the most difficult of the entire negotiation. Napoleon had no interest in getting into another Crimean war, while the Ballplatz was compelled to avoid involvement
in a Franco-German war over the issues of German unity and French expansionism.[51]

By February 1869 a compromise suggested itself. Should Austria go to war
against Russia, France would deploy an observation force on the Prussian
frontier, but remain neutral unless Prussia entered the conflict. Should France
go to war against Prussia, on the other hand, Austria would perform a similar
service against Russia.[52] But still both powers were uneasy about the prospect
of facing a major foe without active support from its partner in the alliance.[53]
Finally, Beust admitted that "force of circumstances" would "soon" make impossible Austrian neutrality in a Franco-Prussian war, and Napoleon conceded that France too would find itself "unable" to remain neutral in an Austro-Russian conflict.[54] Despite avowals of peaceful intent with which they
sprinkled the record, both parties foresaw that the likely consequence of the
commitments they were making would be a general European war.

The reconstruction of Germany, naturally, was to be a fundamental purpose of the alliance. It was agreed that the victorious powers would establish
a new German confederation based on states as nearly equal in size as possible.
Concerning territorial gains and compensations, the evidence left in the files
by the negotiators was intentionally scanty. Littera scripta manet! Hungarians,
wrote Metternich, were to find nothing in the treaty about the restoration of
Austrian power in Germany; Austrian Germans, no mention of the Rhine.[55]
None of the preliminary drafts revealed the full intentions of the participants.

Even so, the final draft of May 10, 1869, was less menacing in appearance
than the preliminary ones. Agreeing to follow a common policy in European
affairs, the contracting powers reciprocally guaranteed the integrity of their
respective territories "against every eventuality." Should "symptoms of war"
appear, they would conclude an "offensive and defensive alliance." In event
of war between Austria and Prussia, France would come to the aid of the
former.[56] Of "neutrality" and "observation forces" there was no longer any

[51] RKN, III, 59–62, 71–74, 79. The chief source for the negotiation is the correspondence
between Beust in Vienna and Metternich and Count Vitzthum in Paris. For Napoleon, Rouher
and La Valette were the negotiators. Neither Moustier nor Gramont were brought into the secret.

[52] RKN, III, 111–113.

[53] See Beust's warning to Metternich that a common diplomatic front in the eastern question
was absolutely essential to the agreement and La Valette's objection that Austrian neutrality in
a Franco-Prussian war was unreciprocal in view of France's commitment to aid in an Austro-
Prussian conflict. RKN, III, 76–79, 160.

[54] RKN, III, 158–159, 168–169.

[55] RKN, III, 111–113, 119.

[56] RKN, III, 185–188.

mention. Franz Joseph had decided these clauses were too provocative; they were unlikely, furthermore, to be accepted by Italy.

The Austrians had finally learned the necessity of buying off the government in Florence before undertaking a major war. In negotiations conducted by Paris, King Victor Emmanuel was asked to contribute an army of two hundred thousand men for common defense, to aid France in a war with Prussia, and to assume the same obligations as France in any war involving Austria. After victory Italy was promised a "rectification" of the frontiers of Nice and the Tyrol, possession of the Swiss canton of Tessin (if Switzerland "violated" her neutrality), a naval base in Tunisia, repayment of war costs, and diplomatic support in certain Papal affairs. On May 15 Metternich telegraphed: "Definitive version reached with Italy. Mr. de Vimercati leaving for Florence. Acceptance almost certain."[57]

Metternich's ecstatic optimism proved unjustified. In Florence the price had risen. The Menabrea cabinet determined to exact, in addition to the concessions already promised, the frontier of the Isonzo from Austria and the evacuation of French forces from Rome.[58] In France, moreover, the treaty was delayed by other startling developments. On May 23 a parliamentary election went badly for the government. During June, five days of street rioting in Paris raised doubts about the stability of the regime. At the end of the month Rouher and La Valette were compelled to resign under attack by the strengthened opposition in the new chamber. Napoleon was faced with the choice of either returning to dictatorial methods or advancing on the road to parliamentary government. "The situation is grave," wrote a dejected Metternich. "It is a decisive crisis."[59]

The emperor chose the latter course. The period of transition, however, lasted six months. In the interim cabinet only the foreign minister, Prince de la Tour d'Auvergne, was told of the alliance project, but he refused to take further action because of his temporary status.[60] On August 20, 1869, Napoleon went to bed suffering from his old malady, a bladder ailment, and was incapacitated for a month. During this time all policy-making ceased in a regime still subject to his will. In September rumors of a triple alliance, launched apparently by the Italian government, excited the European press and alarmed the chancelleries. Lord Clarendon hurried off to Paris to learn the truth. Napoleon, pale and feeble, denied everything but *pourparlers* ending without result.[61]

Actually the emperor believed that something had been accomplished. Al-

[57] RKN, III, 171–176, 185–188.

[58] RKN, III, 194–198, 208, 215–216, 228–229. See also F. Engel-Janosi, "The Roman Question in the Diplomatic Negotiations of 1869–70," *Review of Politics*, 3 (1941), 319–349.

[59] RKN, III, 216–218. Official candidates polled 4,467,720 votes; the opposition, 3,258,777.

[60] RKN, III, 245–246, 253–254, 270–271.

[61] RKN, III, 226–227, 233–234, 251.

though the draft of May 10 remained unsigned, all three sovereigns considered themselves "morally" bound by it. From Victor Emmanuel the emperor received a letter in September in which the king adhered "to the idea of a triple alliance" and hoped for its "prompt" conclusion, but insisted that, first, the French must evacuate Rome. Hence Napoleon had reason to believe that the Italian alliance was attainable whenever the recall of French troops from Rome could be made palatable to French Catholic opinion.[62] On September 24 he wrote to his "good brother" Franz Joseph stating that, if Austria were menaced by any aggressor, "I shall not hesitate an instant to place all the forces of France at her side." Without prior agreement with Vienna, furthermore, he would not negotiate with any foreign power.[63]

Franz Joseph's reply has vanished. Apparently it contained a similar commitment to inform Paris prior to negotiations with a third power, but failed to give a reciprocal promise of military aid in event of war.[64] As the fatal year 1870 arrived, nevertheless, Napoleon persisted in the delusion that the Austrian alliance had been "morally" ratified.[65] Beust, however, had not budged from his insistence upon the necessity of neutrality at the beginning of a Franco-Prussian conflict. His strategy was the same as that of Napoleon in 1866 and was to prove just as futile. By intervening at the critical moment, he expected to achieve maximum gain at minimum cost.[66]

Bismarck banked on identity of interests, rather than a contractual agreement, to secure the entente with Russia, but Napoleon chose to believe in the existence of an alliance with Austria secured neither by a signed treaty nor by actual solidarity of interests. Such were the circumstances as the most realistic political strategist of the century entered upon his final match with its most successful romantic adventurer.

[62] Émile Ollivier, *l'Empire libéral* (Paris, 1895–1912), vol. 11, 611–612.

[63] *RKN*, III, 192–193, 224, 235–236.

[64] *RKN*, III, 232, 253, 261.

[65] *RKN*, III, 251, 268.

[66] See his remarks to Dalwigk. *RKN*, III, 225 (n. 2). He regarded Napoleon's letter with satisfaction and informed Vitzthum (Oct. 19, 1869) that it sufficed "for the moment to fix the state of our relations with France." Further negotiations, he feared, would enable the French to press the argument for making violation of the treaty of Prague a casus belli. *RKN*, III, 261.

CHAPTER TWENTY

Origins of the War of 1870–1871

The Problem of "War Guilt"

ON JULY 3, 1870, reports began to spread through the European press that the crown of Spain had been offered to a Hohenzollern prince. Two weeks later France and Germany plunged into the first truly "national war" that Europe had seen since 1815. No more than the participants have historians been able to agree on the responsibility for this conflict, which poisoned the political atmosphere of Europe for generations. German scholars long tended to hold Bismarck guiltless and put the blame on France, which could not tolerate German unification and wanted war in order to consolidate a new and unstable government.[1] But others have maintained that the provocation for the war came from Bismarck, although he would not have succeeded but for the clumsiness and bellicosity of the French response. Once the first step was taken toward national unity in 1866–1867—so this argument goes—the second had to follow. The rise of particularism in southern Germany, the restiveness of Bismarck's national liberal allies, the approach of both Prussian and Reichstag elections, and the prospect of renewed conflict between crown and parliament over the "iron budget" in 1871 left him no choice but to fulfill German aspirations for national unity. He had to swim with the current.[2]

---

[1] For example: Hermann Oncken, ed., *Die Rheinpolitik Kaiser Napoleons III. von 1863 bis 1870 und der Ursprung des Krieges von 1870/71* (3 vols., Berlin, 1926), vol. 1, 1–121, translated as *Napoleon III and the Rhine: The Origin of the War of 1870–1871* (New York, 1928); Erich Marcks, *Der Aufstieg des Reiches 1807–1878* (2 vols., Stuttgart, 1936), vol. 2, 426; Arnold Oskar Meyer, *Bismarck: Der Mensch und der Staatsmann* (Stuttgart, 1949), 390–414; Herbert Geuss, *Bismarck und Napoleon III.: Ein Beitrag zur Geschichte der preussisch-französischen Beziehungen 1851–1871* (Cologne-Graz, 1959), 252–267; Jochen Dittrich, *Bismarck, Frankreich, und die Hohenzollernkandidatur: Die "Kriegsschuldfrage" von 1870* (Munich, 1962), 36–133; Egmont Zechlin, *Die Reichsgründung* (Frankfurt a. M., 1967), 151–155; Leonhard von Muralt, "Der Ausbruch des Krieges von 1870–71" in *Der Historiker und die Geschichte* (Zurich, 1960), 295–318, and "Die Reichsgründung" in Hans Hallmann, ed., *Revision des Bismarckbildes: Die Diskussion der deutschen Fachhistoriker 1945–1955* (Darmstadt, 1972), 34–38; and Eberhard Kolb, *Der Kriegsausbruch 1870: Politische Entscheidungsprozesse und Verantwortlichkeiten in der Julikrise 1870* (Göttingen, 1970).

[2] Lothar Gall, *Bismarck: Der weisse Revolutionär* (Frankfurt a. M., 1980), 414–435; Ernst Engelberg, *Bismarck: Urpreusse und Reichsgründer* (Berlin, 1985), 711–726; Josef Becker, "Zum Problem der Bismarckschen Politik in der spanischen Thronfrage," *Historische Zeitschrift*, 212 (1971), 529–607, "Der Krieg mit Frankreich als Problem der kleindeutschen Einigungspolitik Bismarcks, 1866–1871," in Michael Stürmer, ed., *Das kaiserliche Deutschland, 1870–1918* (Düsseldorf, 1970), 75–88, and "Bismarck, Prim, die Sigmaringer Hohenzollern und die spanische

Bismarck's defenders can point to an impressive array of utterances during 1869–1870 in which he, while admitting the probability of war with France, forswore its provocation. One of the most eloquent is the famous dispatch of February 26, 1869, to Baron Georg von Werthern, Prussia's envoy to Munich. Werthern was deeply discouraged over the downward course of the national cause in southern Germany and critical of his superiors for not having marched on Vienna in 1866. Bismarck's rebuttal was a lesson on politics: "I also hold it probable that violent events would further German unity. To assume the mission of bringing about a violent catastrophe and take responsibility for the timing of it, however, is quite another matter. Arbitrary interference in the course of history, motivated on purely subjective grounds, has never achieved any other result than to shake down unripe fruit. That German unity is not at the moment a ripe fruit is in my opinion obvious. . . . We can put the clocks forward, but time does not on that account move any faster, and the ability to wait while the situation develops is a prerequisite of practical politics." In view of the progress made toward unity since 1740 (especially since 1840), he told Werthern, "we can look forward to the future with repose and leave to our successors what remains to be done."[3]

In the fall of 1869 Wilhelm came home highly disturbed from a visit with his son-in-law in Karlsruhe. Continued frustration of their desire for union with the north, he feared, would alienate Prussia's "friends" in the south.[4] German unity, Bismarck assured him on November 20, was the "further and greater" goal of Prussian policy. "We can with certainty expect its achievement in the course of time through the natural development of the nation, which makes progress every year" (Wilhelm: "Agreed"). His "nearer goal" was to prevent Bavaria from becoming "a base for Austrian-French-ultramontane efforts against us." He feared the prospect of a "calamity" in Munich: the replacement of Hohenlohe by a "Catholic-Austrian minister" and a reverse for the national cause in the Bavarian parliament.[5] In December 1869, Robert von Keudell reported that French businessmen, with whom he had associated on a voyage to a trade conference in Alexandria, believed that war with Prussia was unavoidable. Individually, they had all assured him that the entire business world in France thought that "confidence in the future" could only be restored by a military decision between the two countries. Bismarck re-

---

Thronfrage," in *Francia*, 9 (1981), 436–471; Raymond Poidevin and Jacques Bariéty, *Les relations franco-allemandes 1815–1975* (Paris, 1977), 79–83.

  [3] GW, VIb, 1–2; VII, 235; Johannes Schultze, ed., *Max Duncker: Politischer Briefwechsel aus seinem Nachlass* (Stuttgart, 1923), 436–437. See also Hajo Holborn, "Bismarck und Freiherr Georg von Werthern," *Archiv für Politik und Geschichte*, 5 (1925), 469ff. Some evidence suggests that Werthern was the first to suggest (Feb. 4, 1867) the possibility and value of a Hohenzollern monarchy in Spain. J. Becker, "Bismarck, Prim, die Sigmaringer Hohenzollern," 466–468.

  [4] GW, VIb, 163–164.

  [5] GW, VIb, 166–168; also 180.

sponded that German businessmen shared this opinion—in reaction to the French attitude. Recently his banker, Gerson Bleichröder, had advocated war to "clarify the situation." But Bismarck found this attitude "abominable." "One must continue to remove the possible causes of war and trust to the calming effect of time. No one can assume responsibility for the outbreak of a struggle that would perhaps be but the first of a series of national wars (*Rassenkriegen*)."[6] Even Count Vincent Benedetti, the French ambassador at Berlin, was convinced of the "pacific views" of king and chancellor and their determination not to provoke "any regrettable incident."[7]

On February 18, 1870, however, the "calamity" happened in Munich. The Hohenlohe cabinet resigned, and the particularists assumed power. Outwardly—toward the French and the German public—Bismarck maintained an attitude of complacency. On February 23, he remarked to Benedetti that the forward current of German development was inexorable.[8] In the Reichstag on the following day he spoke against Lasker's motion to unite Baden to the North German Confederation, arguing that the national cause was making "steady, moderate progress" in Bavaria and Württemberg, "despite every-

BLACK SPECTERS IN BERLIN AND PARIS. BISMARCK AND NAPOLEON DEMONIZE EACH OTHER IN ORDER
TO AROUSE PUBLIC SUPPORT FOR MILITARY EXPENDITURES (WILHELM SCHOLZ,
KLADDERADATSCH, JUNE 20, 1869).

[6] Robert von Keudell, *Fürst und Fürstin Bismarck: Erinnerungen 1846–1872* (Berlin, 1901), 414. See also J. Becker, "Zum Problem," 597–598.

[7] Dispatch of Jan. 14, 1870. Le Comte Benedetti, *Ma Mission en Prusse* (Paris, 1871), 284–285; GW, VIb, 203 (fn. 3)

[8] Benedetti, *Ma Mission en Prusse*, 289.

thing we hear from there."[9] A few hours later he told Moritz Busch, his newly appointed press aide, "The German question is making good progress, but it requires time—perhaps one year, five years, possibly ten years. I cannot make it go faster, and neither can these gentlemen [the deputies], but they can't wait."[10] In a dispatch to Karlsruhe on March 12, 1870, his tone was less confident: "I can leave it undecided whether the policy of deference and consideration has furthered the national cause in Bavaria and Württemberg." At a recent conference of national liberal deputies, he pointed out, the Württemberg delegates had stressed that the national cause in their country "is not going backward."[11]

These remarks—to the French ambassador, Reichstag, a press aide, and a pro-Prussian southern government—were hardly candid. They show Bismarck trying to mask his disappointment over the retrogression of the national cause in the south. The Kaiser project, under way since early January, shows that he felt compelled to move forward in the national question during the year 1870. He required a fresh baptism of national sentiment with which to influence the approaching elections for the North German Reichstag and Prussian Chamber of Deputies and to ward off an anticipated liberal attack on the iron budget. And yet Lord Clarendon was probably wrong in assuming that he intended to use the Kaiser project to precipitate war with France.[12] The issue was not well suited for a casus belli. Apparently he believed that the completion of German unification would depend less upon his own initiatives than upon the opportunities, and even necessities, that might emerge from the political situation in France.

Initially Bismarck judged that the French election of May 23, 1869, would provide greater stability for the liberal empire in France and hence peace. The strong showing of the radical opposition, he reasoned, would compel the propertied class to rally to Napoleon's support; the immense majority of the French nation desired peace. Fortified by this support, Napoleon, whose personal disinclination for war Bismarck did not doubt, would be able to resist the pressure of the relatively small war party of "Arcadians" led by Rouher.[13] Within months Bismarck had reason to change his mind. In early November 1869 Napoleon began again to press for fulfillment of article 5 of the treaty of Prague, that is, the return of northern Schleswig to Denmark. He sent a trusted envoy, Count Émile Fleury to Petersburg to enlist Russian assistance. News of this demand revived Bismarck's conviction that "Parisian policy is

[9] GW, XI, 101.

[10] Moritz Busch, *Tagebuchblätter* (Leipzig, 1899), vol. 1, 4.

[11] GW, VIb, 277.

[12] GW, VIb, 260–266. For the influence of the coming struggle over the iron budget on Bismarck's search for a national issue in the spring of 1870, see Rosslyn Wemyss, ed., *Memoirs and Letters of Sir Robert Morier* (London, 1911), vol. 2, 150–153.

[13] GW, VIb, 113, 116–117.

bewildered and hence incalculable." He feared that an exchange of notes on the issue between Berlin and Paris might lead to war. To prevent it he took a "firm and hard" line in Petersburg, and the incident passed.[14]

On December 27, 1869, Napoleon took the final plunge into parliamentary government by summoning Émile Ollivier, leader of the opposition, to form a cabinet. In Bismarck's judgment this development heightened the unpredictability of French foreign policy. At the end of February 1870 he told Busch: "The French Arcadians are watching the course of events in Germany and waiting for their opportunity. Napoleon is now well disposed to us, but he is very changeable. We could now fight France and beat her too, but that war would lead to five or six others; as long as we can gain our ends by peaceful means, war would be foolish, if not criminal. Warlike or revolutionary situations could emerge that would render the presently brittle metal more malleable."[15] The chancellor's Reichstag speech of February 24 was intended to strengthen the new government in Paris, which "signifies peace for us." The constitutional regime, he explained to Karlsruhe, was developing "not unsatisfactorily" for Germany. Should the experiment succeed, it would give a peaceful direction to French development favorable to the independence of her neighbors.[16] And yet in March he confided to Baron Richard von Friesen, the Saxon foreign minister, his suspicion that "early war with France was an unavoidable necessity"—for Napoleon, because his regime was unstable, and for Germany, because the uncertainty of French policy hampered German development.[17]

Once again, what Bismarck was willing to say to a journalist, to the Reichstag, and to a south German government need not have been in accord with the progress of his private judgment. But what he said to Friesen has to be taken more seriously, for Saxony was (after Prussia) the second most important member of the North German Confederation, and its support would be needed if war was in prospect. Still, it would be a mistake to take his words to Friesen literally—as showing a deliberate determination to bring the war about. To do so would be to underestimate the elasticity of Bismarck's mind and judgment. To mobilize German national sentiment, a war with France must appear to be defensive. France must reveal itself as an aggressor, a foe determined to frustrate the exercise of Germany's natural right to national self-determination. Although Ollivier was publicly committed to a peace policy, there was also a chance that the constitutional reforms would sap the

[14] GW, VIb, 163, 166.

[15] Busch, *Tagebuchblätter*, vol. 1, 7, also 10–11. See also H. E. Brockhaus, *Stunden mit Bismarck, 1871–1878* (Leipzig, 1929), 34, 46.

[16] GW, VIb, 262; see also 206.

[17] GW, VII, 301. Thimme dated this interview in early 1870, rather than late 1869. GW, VIb, 203 (n. 3). But Josef Becker determined that the encounter could not have taken place before March 1870, when both participants were in Berlin. J. Becker, "Zum Problem," 591–595.

regime and lead to revolution. Internal chaos would diminish France's external power and distract her attention from Germany. If his hold on the army weakened, furthermore, Napoleon might seek to divert internal dissatisfaction into foreign adventures. Issues elsewhere in Europe might embroil the great powers and give Germany the freedom, even compulsion, to complete its unification.[18]

Bismarck's favorite garment was not the straitjacket, but the reversible overcoat. He was reluctant to commit himself irrevocably to a course of action long in advance of the necessity for decision. On the contrary, it was his custom to approach major problems with more than one potential solution. The year 1870 was no exception. He had not abandoned the prospect of evolutionary unification, a process that might be expedited by internal difficulties in France. At the same time he did not lose sight of the fact that in the past (1813–1815, 1840, 1858, and 1867) fear of France had most effectively aroused the awareness of nationhood among the governments and peoples of Germany. Hatred of a foreign foe, more than spontaneous devotion to Germany, had proved to be the most effective force against separatism. War with France could accomplish with one blow what might normally require a generation.

The Hohenzollern Candidature

Fundamentally the origin of the war of 1870 lay in a collision of interests. For the sake of Prussian expansion Bismarck had taken up the cause of German national self-determination, whose fulfillment was possible only at the cost of France. Since 1866 the French had dreaded the consolidation of a powerful state on their northern frontier, at least without compensation sufficient to preserve their own relative weight in the European balance. These were the ingredients of an explosive compound. The catalyst that brought them together was the abrupt announcement in the summer of 1870 that a Hohenzollern prince was to be king of Spain.

In September 1868 a long-expected revolution had driven Queen Isabella II from the throne in Madrid. A provisional government came to power, headed by Marshals Francisco Serrano y Domínguez and Juan Prim as regent and prime minister. Weary of Bourbon misrule, the two officers began the hunt for a new dynasty. In the interest of Iberian unity they preferred the ruling house of Portugal, but were refused; two Italian princes likewise declined. Next the Spaniards turned to Germany, the prime market for European royalty. Prince Leopold of Hohenzollern-Sigmaringen was an obvious choice, being the son of Prince Karl Anton, head of the southern and Cath-

---

[18] See GW, VIb, 166; Heinrich O. Meisner, ed., *Denkwürdigkeiten des General-Feldmarschalls Alfred Grafen von Waldersee* (Stuttgart, 1923), vol. 1, 49.

olic branch of the Prussian ruling house. His wife was Donha Antonia, sister of King Louis of Portugal. Someday she or her children might inherit the Portuguese crown. Only recently Leopold's brother Karl had been chosen to rule Rumania.[19]

For the French his candidacy could only be a serious concern. Although but distantly related, the two branches of the Hohenzollern family had in recent years been closely associated. Karl Anton had been minister-president of the new-era government in Prussia; even now he was military governor of the Rhineland and Westphalia. In Prussia he was addressed as "royal highness," his sons were treated as royal princes, and he had living quarters in the royal palace. Leopold was a Prussian officer and had served in the war of 1866. The Sigmaringen Hohenzollern were for all practical purposes members of the Prussian ruling house. Under family law Leopold could not accept a crown without Wilhelm's consent. To be sure, the Sigmaringen branch was even more closely related to the Bonapartes. One of Leopold's grandmothers was a Murat, another a Beauharnais! But this did not count. "I am," he wrote to Wilhelm, "to the innermost fiber of my heart a Prussian and a German."[20]

Even before Leopold's candidature arose, Bismarck regarded the Spanish situation with considerable satisfaction. In contrast to Isabella, the provi-

PRINCE KARL ANTON VON HOHENZOLLERN-SIGMARINGEN (BILDARCHIV PREUSSISCHER KULTURBESITZ).

PRINCE LEOPOLD VON HOHENZOLLERN-SIG-MARINGEN (BILDARCHIV PREUSSISCHER KULTURBESITZ).

[19] Robert H. Lord, *The Origins of the War of 1870* (Cambridge Mass., 1924), 13ff.
[20] *Ibid.*, 14–16; Georges Bonnin, ed., *Bismarck and the Hohenzollern Candidature for the Spanish Throne* (London, 1957), 67.

sional government was expected to be anti-French and pro-Prussian. He saw the issue of the succession as a "peace-fontanel" that would distract the French from an attack upon Germany. "A solution agreeable to Napoleon is hardly useful to us."[21] In December 1868 the prince of Putbus and Colonel Karl von Strantz, a general staff officer, were in Madrid, and in May 1869 Theodor von Bernhardi arrived. Apparently their mission was to report, not negotiate.[22] But soon rumors appeared in the European press that Leopold was under consideration. In some alarm Napoleon, recognizing that the French would never tolerate this choice, instructed Benedetti to make inquiries at Berlin. In an interview on May 8, 1869, Bismarck told the ambassador that the Hohenzollern family had indeed been sounded out but that the prince had declined. He evaded the ambassador's attempt to find out if Wilhelm had vetoed the idea, handling the matter "jestingly."[23]

Before the Reichstag subsequently and in his memoirs in later years Bismarck consistently maintained that until July 1870 Leopold's candidacy had been strictly a family affair with which he as chancellor and minister-president had nothing to do.[24] In September 1869, however, Georg von Werthern, Prussian envoy in Munich, had acted as intermediary between the Spanish government and the Sigmaringen Hohenzollern. He not only introduced Spain's emissary to Karl Anton but also advocated the candidature in Sigmaringen.[25] If not impossible, it is unlikely that he acted without Bismarck's knowledge and, at least, tacit approval. Once the Spanish offer to Leopold was actually made in February 1870, the chancellor became deeply involved in the negotiation. At a crucial point he even promoted it without the knowledge and contrary to the desires of the king. Since 1900 a steady trickle of information has revealed this hidden page of his history. But the full extent of his involvement was until the 1950s a closely guarded secret of the German foreign office and certain patriotic German historians.[26]

On February 24, 1870, Eusebio de Salazar y Mazaredo arrived at Karl Anton's residence in Düsseldorf with letters from Marshal Prim addressed to Prince Leopold, King Wilhelm, and Bismarck. They announced the decision of the Madrid government to offer the Spanish crown to the prince ("a glorious era opens before you") subject to election by the Cortes. Karl Anton,

[21] GW, VIa, 412–413, 422–423, 426–427, 429. According to Forckenbeck, he even remarked that "the Spanish revolution rescued us from war." GW, VIa, 474.

[22] Lord, *Origins*, 17. This part of Bernhardi's story was censored from his diary by his son at the request of the German foreign office. Bonnin, ed., *Candidature*, 19.

[23] Benedetti, *Ma Mission en Prusse*, 306ff.; GW, VIb, 78–82; Bonnin, ed., *Candidature*, 286; Willard Allen Fletcher, *The Mission of Vincent Benedetti to Berlin, 1864–1870* (The Hague, 1965), 232–234.

[24] GW, XI, 129ff.; XV, 302ff.

[25] Fletcher, *Mission of Vincent Benedetti*, 235 (fn. 1); Dittrich, *Bismarck, Frankreich*, 351–355.

[26] Bonnin, ed., *Candidature*, 13ff.; also Rudolf Morsey, "Geschichtsschreibung und amtliche Zensur," *Historische Zeitschrift*, 184 (1957), 555–572.

who dominated his son, was dazzled by the prospect: "a dynasty which represents the center of gravity of central Europe and whose scions flourish by the Black Sea and beyond the Pyrenees, . . . a dynasty such as that has not been known to history since Charles V." Nevertheless, he was realistic enough to appreciate the dangers. In response to earlier soundings he had insisted on the approval of both Wilhelm and Napoleon in the interest of European "peace and tranquillity." But now he dropped the requirement for French consent, which was tantamount to refusal. He anticipated that "a Hohenzoller in Spain would give rise to a wild outcry in anti-Prussian Europe and either precipitate or defer the solution of many pending questions." To counteract it, his son would need the full backing of the Prussian government. Apparently he determined to extract from Wilhelm a command that the crown be accepted in the interest of the Prussia state. This tactic was made all the more necessary by Leopold's genuine reluctance to accept the offered throne.[27]

In letters to Wilhelm and Bismarck on February 25, 1870, Karl Anton expressed the hope that the king would "command an unqualified refusal . . . may spare me all that is necessarily inherent in an acceptance so pregnant with consequences." But "should the interests of Prussian power demand" acceptance, he and his son would, as loyal subjects, accede. On March 2 Leopold himself echoed this sentiment in a letter to the monarch. He showed that he was fully aware of the turmoil in Spain and of the difficulties he would face in Madrid. He lacked, he confessed, both the ambition and experience to rule that turbulent land. The prospect was "repugnant." But if "higher political considerations and the expansion of the power and luster of our house as a whole so demand," he would do his duty as a "Hohenzoller, soldier, and subject."[28]

At the end of February the affair appeared to be at a standstill. Karl Anton tarried at his post in Düsseldorf expecting a royal summons; Salazar waited impatiently in Berlin for an answer to the Spanish offer; Leopold was also in Berlin, seeking an audience with Bismarck. But the chancellor, eager to maintain the facade of noninvolvement, kept him at arm's length for a few days, pleading ill health. When they met at a British embassy ball on February 28, Bismarck told him that a Hohenzoller on the throne of Spain would heighten the prestige of the dynasty; his refusal might lead to the election of a Bavarian prince, who would be open to Rome's influence and play into the hands of the ultramontanes. Leopold got the impression that the delay in arriving at a decision on the Spanish question was owed to the government's momentary preoccupation "with the Reichstag and south German circumstances." On March 1, he reported to his father that, while Bismarck favored the candidacy, neither Wilhelm nor the crown prince could make up his

[27] Dittrich, *Bismarck, Frankreich*, 355–362; Bonnin, ed., *Candidature*, 62–65.
[28] Bonnin, ed., *Candidature*, 62–67.

mind.[29] No one in the Wilhelmstrasse wanted to tell him that the king was definitely opposed.

For Wilhelm, Karl Anton's letter of February 25 was a "bolt of lightning out of a clear sky"; he dashed off a note to Bismarck saying that he was "utterly against the affair." On receiving this message, the chancellor closed his door to all visitors and sat down to think the matter through.[30] If we but knew what passed through his mind in that quiet room in early March 1870, many subsequent disputes about his purposes would never have arisen. But we do know that about this time he remarked to Baron Friesen, as noted above, that war with France was an "unavoidable necessity" for both France and Germany.

We have, moreover, a vital document that resulted from his lucubration— a memorial to King Wilhelm, dated March 9, which made an all-out case for supporting the candidature. Wilhelm's incisive marginalia show that he was not at all convinced by the argument. "French peaceableness towards Germany," Bismarck wrote, "will always wax or wane in proportion to the dangers of a war with Germany." A government in Spain sympathetic to Germany would force Napoleon to station one or two army corps on his southern frontier. (Wilhelm: "How long would the sympathy last?" and "What potentate in Spain would be in a position to *guarantee* such a policy?") If Leopold declined, the crown would probably go to the Wittelsbach dynasty, raising the danger that both Madrid and Munich would fall under French, Austrian, and Roman influence. (Wilhelm: "These hypotheses are possible, but equally possible is their nonoccurrence.") There was also a chance that Spain would turn republican and become a source of revolutionary agitation throughout Europe. (Wilhelm: "These *possibilities* cannot be denied, but the pros and cons seem to be equally balanced.") Friendly relations between Spain and Germany would improve trade and revive "our mutual political sympathies." (Wilhelm: "Are great sympathies for Spain noticeable or extant in Prussia?") "The repute of the Hohenzollern dynasty, the justifiable pride with which not only Prussia but also Germany regards its royal house, the glory that Germany tends more and more to attach to that name as a common national possession and as a symbol of German fame and German prestige abroad—all this forms an important element in political self-confidence, the fostering and strengthening of which would be of benefit to national feeling in general and to monarchist sentiment in particular. It is therefore to Germany's political interest that the house of Hohenzollern should gain an esteem and an exalted position in the world analogous only to that of the Habsburgs after Charles V. This element of pride in the dynasty is not to be estimated lightly as a force oper-

[29] Dittrich, *Bismarck, Frankreich*, 362–364.

[30] Horst Kohl, ed., *Anhang zu den Gedanken und Erinnerungen von Otto Fürst von Bismarck* (Stuttgart, 1901), vol. 1, 207; Keudell, *Fürst und Fürstin Bismarck*, 430ff.

ating for the contentment of our people and the consolidation of our relationships."[31]

Yet Wilhelm doubted that unruly Spain would tolerate for long any foreign dynasty, and the fall of a Hohenzollern monarch there would deal a harsh blow to the family prestige generally. He was not seduced by the mirage of a Hohenzollern dynasty in Europe rivaling that of the Habsburgs in the early sixteenth century. On March 15, 1870, Bismarck marshaled Roon, Moltke, Delbrück, and Thile to support his view at a crown council, disguised as a dinner party hosted by Karl Anton in his quarters at the royal palace. But Wilhelm, weakly seconded by the crown prince, persisted in the negative. He had "strong scruples" against acceptance and would consent only if Leopold himself heard the call of duty.[32]

The issue, however, refused to die; there were too many interested parties. In Leopold's place Karl Anton proposed his third son, Friedrich. But "Fritz" was traveling abroad incognito. When located, he declined on the same grounds as Leopold. Again Wilhelm refused to override the rejection. He was still unconvinced that the question came "within the interests of the Prussian state." Meanwhile, Bismarck had sent an aide, Lothar Bucher, and a staff officer, Major von Versen, to Spain to report on conditions affecting the prince's decision. In mid-April the chancellor fell ill of jaundice at Varzin and was out of action for nearly five weeks—an illness complicated by political frustration and boiling anger. Meanwhile, the enthusiastic reports of Bucher and Versen had no effect on Wilhelm. The two envoys were recalled, and a telegram to Madrid on May 4 seemingly ended the matter. "The Spanish affair," Bismarck complained to Delbrück, "has taken a wretched turn." The interest of state was being sacrificed to princely selfishness and "feminine-ultramontane influences." The chancellor was upset; his nerves, frayed.[33]

But again the candidature refused to expire. Prim had staked all on a Hohenzollern king. On Bucher's advice he ignored the telegram and waited anxiously for Bismarck's return to health.[34] Meanwhile, the sanguine Versen painted for the Sigmaringen princes a rosy picture of monarchist sentiment in Spain. On May 24 he could report to Bismarck, who had returned to Berlin, that Karl Anton was willing to reconsider—"in the interest of state." In a letter to the prince on May 28 the chancellor willingly supplied the missing motive. "Today no less than before I feel no doubt that Germany has a vital

[31] GW, VIb, 271–274. The marginalia are from Bonnin, ed., Candidature, 68–73.

[32] Dittrich, Bismarck, Frankreich, 366–368; Bonnin, ed., Candidature, 291–294.

[33] Dittrich, Bismarck, Frankreich, 369–385; Bonnin, ed., Candidature, 8off., 101–150; GW, XIV, 776; Jochen Dittrich, "Ursachen und Ausbruch des deutsch-französischen Krieges 1870–71," in Theodor Schieder and Ernst Deuerlein, eds., Reichsgründung 1870/71: Tatsachen, Kontroversen, Interpretationen (Stuttgart, 1970), 74–80. In this essay Dittrich modified some of the views expressed in his Bismarck, Frankreich, und die Hohenzollernkandidatur.

[34] Bonnin, ed., Candidature, 135–137, 153ff.

interest here, and that at critical moments the pointer on the scales might well register differently according as we know Madrid to be a friend or an enemy." Wilhelm was indignant; he had thought the matter "dead and buried." Consistent with his previous position, nevertheless, he declared he would not oppose the inclination of "any" Hohenzollern prince to accept. This time Leopold heard the call of duty and destiny.[35]

This accomplished, Bismarck withdrew once more (June 8) to Varzin to take a "drastic cure" with bottles of Karlsbad water. To all further appeals he replied that he was without a code book, separated from "all departmental resources," and unable to attend to state business. Completion of the negotiation was up to the participants themselves, for it was a family matter in which the Prussian government had "no say."[36] This was the posture he was soon to assume toward France, Europe, and history.

It was entirely false. From the outset the aim of Karl Anton had been to make sure that the venture had the backing of the Prussian government. He would have preferred a command from Wilhelm to Leopold, but lacking that he accepted Bismarck's assurance that the Prussian interest dictated acceptance. Without that assurance the project would have lapsed. After Bismarck's withdrawal, furthermore, subordinates acting under his orders provided liaison between the negotiating parties. Bucher dashed off once more to Spain and Versen to Leopold in Bad Reichenhall. By telegraph and courier Hermann von Thile, Bismarck's principal aide in the foreign office, held the threads together and periodically reported to his master in Varzin.

Leopold was vexed when Versen appeared. He wanted to enjoy a leisurely cure at the Bavarian spa and a final summer free of royal protocol before assuming his new dignity. But the major insisted that the matter was pressing. In Madrid the new king had to be legally chosen by the Cortes, which could not be held in session much longer. Intrigues were rife in behalf of other candidates. Before the Cortes could act, the terms of acceptance had to be negotiated with the Spaniards. Under Hohenzollern family law, moreover, Wilhelm's approval had to be formally requested and given. On June 16, the two men hastened to Karl Anton in Sigmaringen to draft the letter of request. Here they were soon joined by Bucher and Salazar, who arrived from Spain with word that the situation was critical and no time was to be lost. On June 19, Bucher hurried off with Leopold's letter to Bad Ems, where Wilhelm was taking his summer cure.[37]

That same day Thile had to report to Bismarck that Wilhelm was highly annoyed.[38] The crown prince, now a convert to the candidature, had "let

---

[35] Dittrich, *Bismarck, Frankreich*, 385–387; Bonnin, ed., *Candidature*, 295ff., 158, 162–164, 261ff.; GW, VIb, 321–325.

[36] Bonnin, ed., *Candidature*, 178–180, 201 (n. 6).

[37] Dittrich, *Bismarck, Frankreich*, 388–397; Bonnin, *Candidature*, 191–192, 271ff.

[38] Bonnin, ed., *Candidature*, 190–191.

slip" the fact that Bucher was in Spain, Salazar en route to Germany, and Versen "travelling about," although Wilhelm had ordered him to return to his post in Posen. The king found it "very extraordinary that this sort of thing was going on without his authorization." While anxious not to "irritate your nerves," Thile reported, the king wished to be informed "of everything that Salazar brings either by word of mouth or in writing before any action is taken." The chancellor's nerves were quite irritated. In the margin of the message he exclaimed:

"That beats everything!"

"So his majesty wants the affair treated with official royal interference?!"

"The whole affair is possible only if it remains the limited concern of the Hohenzollern princes, it must not turn into a Prussian concern, the king must be able to say without lying: I know nothing about it."

What transpired at Ems on June 21, however, demonstrates again how great a fiction was the posture of noninvolvement. Bucher succeeded "not without difficulty" in getting the royal assent. But Wilhelm's exasperation is evident in his reply to Leopold: "You have taken a decision that you earlier— in my opinion rightly—deliberately refused to entertain. Now you regard the political views put forward in the winter of this year by Minister Count Bismarck as justified and incontrovertible from the statesman's point of view. Had that been my own view originally, I should not so decidedly have approved of your rejection at that time of the Spanish crown."[39]

Between quaffs of mineral water, meanwhile, Bismarck had written to absolve himself from acting behind Wilhelm's back. Bucher and Versen, he declared, had been instructed to tell Prim and Leopold that the affair was entirely theirs and nothing more could be expected from the Prussian government. In Ems, Heinrich Abeken, counselor of the foreign office, did his best to defend his chief. On June 22, he could report that Wilhelm resented only the "shillyshallying" of his Sigmaringen relatives.[40]

Sheer chance ultimately prevented Leopold from becoming king of Spain. On June 21 the elated Salazar telegraphed through the Prussian foreign service to Manuel Zorrilla, president of the Cortes, the news that he would arrive in Madrid "about the twenty-sixth" bearing Leopold's acceptance and terms. A clerk in the Madrid legation inexplicably decoded it as "about the ninth."[41] The consequence was disastrous. On June 23 Zorrilla prorogued the

[39] *Ibid.*, 197, 201.

[40] GW, XIV, 778–779. This is the letter of June 20, which Bonnin could not locate "in the files." Bonnin, ed., *Candidature*, 201–202, 204–206.

[41] Dittrich, *Bismarck, Frankreich*, 403; Bonnin, ed., *Candidature*, 196. Josef Becker has suggested that the delay may not be credited entirely to the decoding mistake. General Prim's enthusiasm for the Hohenzollern candidature had waned as he considered the possible consequences

Cortes. Madrid was sweltering, the deputies idle and impatient. He sent them home until November. But the secret could not be kept until then. By July 2 it had reached Paris. The fat was in the fire.

The Problem of Motivation

What did Bismarck intend to achieve with the Hohenzollern candidature? The concentric problems of the origin of the war of 1870 lead inward to this central question. The known evidence does not present a conclusive answer. This is true even of the documents that remained secret until found and published after 1945. They contain no direct proof that the chancellor expected war to develop out of the Spanish affair.[42] Nor do the documents show conclusively what he expected to achieve if his end were not war. The answer must be reasoned from the general situation, his actions, and what we know of his political technique.

Those who maintain that his purpose was pacific point out that his first démarche in the question came on March 9, at a time when he apparently expected progress toward national unity through the proclamation of a German Kaiser and the internal destabilization of the French government. Friedrich Thimme maintained that the candidature was but a "detour" toward the goal of the imperial title. Elevation of the prestige of the dynasty would have eased its acceptance by king, crown prince, and German public.[43] Some German scholars still take seriously Bismarck's own argument that the purpose of the candidature was purely defensive. With a hostile power in her rear France would be less likely to risk war with Germany.[44]

These explanations make the lion of European diplomacy look like a house cat. To argue that Bismarck was unable to anticipate the consequences of the candidature in France is to depict the most skillful and realistic tactician of modern diplomacy as a third-rate chess player shoving his pieces guilelessly about the board of European politics. It would place him even behind such an amateur as Karl Anton, who from the outset predicted a "wild outcry in anti-Prussian Europe." At the moment of final decision on June 19, as the letter to Wilhelm was being drafted in Sigmaringen, the prince still could not rid himself of anxiety on this score. Versen has recorded the conversation: "Then came various scruples on Prince Karl Anton's part. What would France

---

for Spain of a violent reaction from France. See his "Bismarck, Prim, die Sigmaringer Hohenzollern," 450–460.

[42] J. Becker, "Bismarck, Prim, die Sigmaringer Hohenzollern," 42. See also Rudolf Morsey, "Die Hohenzollernsche Thronkandidatur in Spanien," *Historische Zeitschrift*, 186 (1958), 573–588.

[43] GW, VIb, 270.

[44] See Dittrich, *Bismarck, Frankreich*, 71–82, and "Ursachen und Ausbruch," 64–94; Geuss, *Bismarck und Napoleon III*, 265–266; Kolb, *Kriegsausbruch 1870*, 19–70.

say about it? Would it not give rise to complications? I said: 'Bismarck says that is just what he is looking for.' Karl Anton: 'Yes, Count Bismarck may want it, but is it really in the interests of the state?' Myself: 'Yes, Bismarck's interests and those of the state are the same thing.' Bucher: 'I can only say what Bismarck has often said to me: If in these last years Napoleon had wanted war, he could have found plenty of grounds for it.' "[45]

Versen was hardly privy to Bismarck's thoughts. Nevertheless, it is evident that he, Bucher, and Karl Anton were fully aware of the possible outcome of their actions. Surely Bismarck understood as much as they.

It has been argued that the severity of the "complication" to which the candidature gave rise was owing not to his design, but to the chance of a code clerk's error. He had expected to present France with a fait accompli beyond the power of public protest and diplomatic intervention to change. In reply to the uproar he would simply have stated that the affair was the sole concern of the Spanish government and a private individual. The French would find no object for their hostility.[46] But did Bismarck really believe in the effectiveness of this subterfuge? For two years reports from France had constantly stressed the excitable state of French opinion, the fears and anxieties arising from the decline in French power and prestige. He himself had often emphasized the "incalculability" of French policy because of these pressures. Clearly he expected a severe reaction in France from the diplomatic coup he was preparing.

Did he, however, expect it to lead to war or merely the collapse of the regime? Again it is safe to say that he had more than one possibility in view.

[45] Bonnin, ed., *Candidature*, 278.

[46] Owing to the initiative of Josef Becker, we now possess the original version of the long lost "letter of instruction," first published in translated and abbreviated form in 1876 by the Spanish historian Antonio Pirala. Becker confirms that the letter, as Lawrence Steefel had deduced, was written in French by Lothar Bucher on Bismarck's instruction and sent to Salazar in Spain. Dated June 25, the letter instructed the Madrid government concerning the tactic Bismarck intended to adopt when Leopold's election became known in France. "It is possible that we may see a passing fermentation in France, and, without doubt, it is necessary to avoid anything that might provoke or increase it." That being the case, he wished as a Prussian minister to avoid all appearance of official involvement in the candidature. "In this way we shall have an unassailable position before the European public. If there is an outburst in France, we shall simply ask: What do you want? Do you wish to dictate the decisions of the Spanish nation and of a German private citizen? . . . Nevertheless, they will cry 'intrigue.' They will become furious against me but without finding a very precise point of attack." Becker has proved what some historians had surmised: that Bismarck's purpose in this document was to calm Spanish fears that the election of a Hohenzoller could trigger a European war. Because of that purpose the letter does not constitute proof that Bismarck actually expected his posture of noninvolvement to be accepted by the French. J. Becker, "Bismarck, Prim, die Sigmaringer Hohenzollern"; Lawrence Steefel, "Bismarck and Bucher: The 'Letter of Instructions' of June 1870," in A. O. Sarkissian, ed., *Studies in Diplomatic History and Historiography in Honour of G. Gooch, C.H.* (London, 1961), 217–224, and *Bismarck, the Hohenzollern Candidacy, and the Origins of the Franco-German War of 1870* (Cambridge Mass., 1962), 85.

Whatever the result, it would bring egress from the impasse of the German question and triumph in the coming debates on the military budget. In the Reichstag on the day after his return from Varzin (May 23, 1870) he had the chance to ascertain once more the effectiveness of German national patriotism for the achievement of his political ends. The newly drafted code of penal law was threatened with defeat. In two forceful speeches during its final reading he called upon the deputies to sacrifice partisanship in the interest of the "holy cause of our national unity" and to accept the code as a "promising pledge" of Germany's future. The bill passed.[47]

Recent events in France may have influenced his decision to press the candidature. On May 8, Napoleon had resorted for the first time in eighteen years to the device of a plebiscite. The result was an impressive vote of approval for the "liberal empire" and a fresh legitimation for the regime. Bismarck's anticipation that internal contradictions would soon bring about its collapse appeared in error. What followed, however, was even more alarming. On May 15, Daru resigned as foreign minister. He was replaced by Gramont, the volatile advocate of alliance with Austria. Bismarck regarded the appointment itself as a "most warlike symptom." On the margins of three reports dealing with the policy of the new minister he penned the awesome comment: "War!"[48] It was during this period that he relaunched the torpedo of Leopold's candidature.

Before it reached its mark, however, his assessment of the French situation apparently changed. At the end of May he persuaded Wilhelm to visit Tsar Alexander, who was vacationing at Ems. On June 5 he returned to Berlin, evidently confident of the continued solidarity of the Russian entente. Two days later in a lengthy reply to a note from Bernstorff, Bismarck denied that Napoleon might soon be driven to discharge the mounting current of domestic discontent down the lightning rod of foreign adventure. For the last time he reiterated his view that the emperor feared a French attack on the Rhine would unite the rest of Europe against him. Failure in war meant revolution at home and the end of his regime. Both Napoleon and France needed peace and maintenance of the status quo. The danger of a French attack was no greater now than at any time since 1866—recognizing "naturally the incalculability of European conditions."[49] With this judgment he returned to Varzin next day to resume his interrupted cure.

Clearly the Hohenzollern candidacy was an offensive, not a defensive act. It is false to assume that his aim in May was to gain in Spain an ally for the coming crisis.[50] Unlike the Italians in 1866, the Spaniards had no grievance against France. Leopold could scarcely commence his rule by insisting upon

[47] SBR (1870), II, 1120ff.
[48] GW, VIb, 321.
[49] GW, VIb, 326–329.
[50] GW, VIb, 324; see J. Becker, "Zum Problem," 571–579.

war for German interests. Still unanswered was Wilhelm's query: "What potentate in Spain would be in a position to guarantee such a policy?" But the best proof is that Bismarck's first promotion of the candidacy predated his alarm of May by many months and that after that alarm subsided in early June he made no effort to extinguish the fuse he had reignited. He departed for Varzin and let it burn.

Bismarck's goal was not an ally, but a crisis with France. He deliberately set sail on a collision course with the intent of provoking either war or a French diplomatic humiliation. The partisans of his innocence ask us to believe a most improbable case: that the shrewdest diplomatic mind of recent history permitted Germany to be drawn into a war that he was eager to avoid. The man who in 1863, 1865, and 1867 had known how to approach the brink and yet save the peace, when it was wise to do so, found it impossible to maneuver his way out of a situation of his own making in the summer of 1870 without resort to violence. We are asked to believe that this tremendous talent, ordinarily so richly inventive, so inexhaustible of resource, suddenly and briefly became barren and impotent to prevent what, it is declared, he did not seek and did not want.[51] The proposition, to be believed, requires an act of faith.

To the Ems Dispatch

The person to whom fell the duty of meeting Bismarck's offensive was unequal to the task. The situation required in the Quai d'Orsay a personality self-possessed, sober in outlook, without illusion concerning the strength of France and its chances in war with Germany. It called for the deft unmasking of the Hohenzollern intrigue and the maintenance of French prestige without peril to the peace. The duke of Gramont was a career diplomat of the high nobility who had lived for years abroad. His image of France was that of another era, that of French dominance in Europe. He was an ardent patriot, inclined to be rash and reckless where the honor of France was at stake. As a diplomat he was often a shrewd and able reporter, but brash in executing instructions. He was without experience in the formulation of high policy and poorly suited for the tasks of a constitutional minister required to lead a volatile parliament along the narrow path of *raison d'état*. During recent years, moreover, he had associated in Vienna with that circle in court and govern-

---

[51] See Otto Becker, *Bismarcks Ringen um Deutschlands Gestaltung* (Heidelberg, 1958), 669, 682, and Muralt, "Ausbruch des Krieges," 295–318; Kolb, *Kriegsausbruch 1870*, 19ff.; Dittrich, *Bismarck, Frankreich*, 74–76; and Geuss, *Bismarck und Napoleon III*, 266. By contrast see J. Becker, "Krieg mit Frankreich," 75–88; "Zum Problem," 529–607, and "Bismarck, Prim, die Sigmaringer Hohenzollern," 436–471. Josef Becker's essays are the most thoroughly researched and cogently argued work yet published on the subject. They confirm what this author only surmised in the first edition of this work.

ment that dreamed of revenge for the humiliation of Sadowa. He arrived in Paris burdened with a belief in the dependability of the Austrian alliance.[52]

On hearing the news from Madrid on the afternoon of July 3, this proud and irritable man reacted according to form. He took no time to reflect or consult. Instead of shrewdly asking for Prussia's good offices in terminating the candidature, he swiftly drafted a comminatory telegram to Berlin. Was the Prussian government, he demanded to know, "a stranger to this intrigue"? As he knew, the Prussian capital was practically empty of responsible officials. It was the time of year for travel and mineral water. Bismarck was in Varzin, Wilhelm in Bad Ems, Benedetti in Wildbad. Hence the first thrust and parry in the great duel were executed by two underlings: Georges Le Sourd, French chargé d'affaires, and Hermann von Thile, under secretary in the foreign office. Showing embarrassment, Thile answered, as Bismarck wished, "that the Prussian government knew absolutely nothing about this affair and that for it the affair did not exist." When their reports arrived in Varzin and Paris, Bismarck found the question "impudent"; Gramont, the reply "derisory."[53]

The position that Thile assumed for Prussia was the one Bismarck had planned and that, if he had had his way, would have been consistently maintained throughout the affair. His intention was simply to refuse to discuss the matter with the French except to refer them to Madrid and Sigmaringen; the candidacy was an affair of the Spanish government and a private individual with which the Prussian government and Wilhelm had nothing to do. Hardly had Thile given his reply, however, when a cleavage appeared in the Prussian front, which, if properly exploited by Gramont, could have brought the affair to a close with a French diplomatic victory. It arose because of Bismarck's failure to instruct Baron Karl von Werther, his ambassador in Paris, and because of his geographical separation from Wilhelm at Ems.

Goltz's successor in Paris had no advance knowledge either of the candidature or of the attitude he was supposed to take toward it. On July 4, he was preparing for a trip to see the king at Ems and called on Gramont. Far from refusing to discuss the matter, Werther listened considerately to the remonstrance of his colleague of Vienna days. News of the candidature, the minister said, had produced a "painful impression" in France and threatened the peace. Werther promised to convey the complaint personally to Wilhelm. Early on the morning of the sixth he arrived in the Hessian spa. To Count Alfred von Waldersee, who met him at the station, he burst out, "The devil is loose at Paris: it looks very much like war."[54]

---

[52] Pierre de la Gorce, *Histoire du Second Empire* (Paris, 1894–1905), vol. 6, 216–217.

[53] Lord, *Origins*, 30–31, 121–122.

[54] *Ibid.*, 32ff. Bismarck's failure to instruct Werther argues, of course, for the innocence of his intentions. The most damaging aspect of the incident, however, he could not have foreseen. It arose from the accident that Werther was, at the moment the crisis broke, on the verge of a trip to Ems and in a position to take the French protest directly to Wilhelm, rather than submit it through Thile and Bismarck. He proved very inept at interpreting his chief's purposes.

Bismarck was highly alarmed. In a flood of messages from Varzin he strove to reestablish his broken front and to prevent Werther from "worrying" Wilhelm. After the ambassador's trip to Ems, however, it was scarcely possible to continue refusing to discuss the matter. But the French should at least be told, he wrote, that Wilhelm, while knowing of the Spanish offer, had exercised no influence on the outcome and until recently had believed Leopold would refuse. Legally he could do no more than advise rejection, which he had in fact already done. Prussia had no primary interest in the matter and was surprised that France wished to intervene in Spain's internal affairs, considering the usual fate of such interventions. The French reaction was also surprising since the prince was by ancestry more Bonaparte than Hohenzoller! Werther should display only "cool astonishment." Above all the impression had to be avoided that Prussia could be intimidated: "The firm and fearless attitude we have always hitherto adopted in the face of every disturbance at Paris is the most essential factor to which we owe the preservation of peace. France, in my opinion, fears a serious breach more than we; but if we give grounds for the belief that we are the more afraid, French insolence will soon leave us no other choice than war."[55]

Bismarck was determined, in brief, to force the issue; France must either bend or be broken. In Paris a like mood prevailed.

After the disaster Ollivier, Gramont, and Napoleon blamed the pressure of public opinion for the bellicose posture they assumed in the Hohenzollern affair. And yet the public reaction was, in part, stimulated by the cabinet itself. On the morning of July 4 the first protests, dictated by Gramont, appeared in progovernment journals. The opposition, however, did not join in the chorus.[56] On the sixth, a deputy sought to restrain the government through an interpellation. But Gramont, with the approval of his colleagues, used the opportunity for an inflammatory challenge. By placing one of its princes on the throne of Charles V, a foreign power threatened the European equilibrium and "interests and honor" of France: "To prevent it, we count both upon the wisdom of the German, and friendship of the Spanish people. But if it should be otherwise, strong in your support, gentlemen, and in that of the nation, we should know how to do our duty without hesitation and without weakness." Frantic applause filled the chamber and next day spilled over into the chauvinistic press. At the Quai d'Orsay Gramont ordered Benedetti to proceed to Ems and induce Wilhelm "if not to order, at least to advise" Leopold to renounce his candidacy. Should he refuse, "c'est la guerre."[57]

At breakfast in Varzin on the morning of the eighth Bismarck received the

[55] *Ibid.*, 129ff.

[56] OD, XXVIII, 22; E. Malcolm Carroll, *French Public Opinion and Foreign Affairs, 1870–1914* (New York, 1931), 25–26.

[57] Lord, *Origins*, 42, 48; Émile Ollivier, *l'Empire libéral* (Paris, 1895–1912), vol. 14, 92–110; Theodore Zeldin, *Émile Ollivier and the Liberal Empire of Napoleon III* (Oxford, 1963), 168–179.

text of Gramont's speech. According to an assistant, he was surprised at its bellicosity. "Gramont could not have spoken so recklessly," he remarked, "if war had not been decided upon." He talked of mobilizing immediately and falling upon the French. But then he reflected that this would hardly do. Before the bar of Wilhelm's conscience and European opinion, France had to appear the aggressor. Instead he ordered mobilization of the German press. "The newspapers . . . must be very rough and as many of them as possible."[58]

At Ems, meanwhile, there was confusion and uncertainty. Honest Wilhelm was not without a sense of guilt, and Werther warned that war would be the consequence of Leopold's failure to withdraw. News of Gramont's speech stiffened the monarch's back, but did not end his hope of peace. He decided to receive Benedetti, but promised Bismarck he would speak "very sternly," using the arguments supplied from Varzin. Subterfuges, however, were contrary to Wilhelm's nature. On July 9 he admitted to the ambassador having approved Leopold's acceptance and even of having informed Bismarck of "these various incidents." While insisting he had no authority to make Leopold withdraw, he revealed that he was even then asking his Sigmaringen relatives to state their intentions. During the next four days, Wilhelm—for once—followed an independent policy. He kept Bismarck in the dark about the extent of his admissions to Benedetti and of his interpellation in Sigmaringen.[59]

The beginning was unpropitious. On July 10 reports arrived from Paris that war fever was raging in the French capital. Military preparations were under way. Should the candidacy continue, the cabinet was determined to strike. That same evening came Karl Anton's letter refusing a renunciation except on Wilhelm's express command. Leopold himself was off on an Alpine excursion and could not be reached. Still Wilhelm did not give up. While he and Werther staved off Benedetti, Colonel Karl von Strantz was dispatched to Sigmaringen. His train missed connections, and he arrived twelve hours late. In a tense audience at noon on the eleventh, Wilhelm again put off the impatient ambassador. At Paris, emperor and ministers wavered on the brink, averse to war, yet fearful of diplomatic humiliation and the public temper. In the Alps Leopold enjoyed the scenery blissfully unaware that the peace of Europe hung by a thread from his name. On the morning of July 12, Karl Anton, under attack from both Paris and Ems, withdrew his son's candidacy on his own authority. Wilhelm felt as though a stone had been lifted from his heart.[60]

Bismarck felt differently. While Wilhelm, unknown to him, had been mediating between Paris and Sigmaringen, the telegrams from Varzin had di-

[58] Keudell, *Fürst und Fürstin Bismarck*, 429; Lord, *Origins*, 46, 155. For Bismarck's instructions to the press in this critical period see Busch, *Tagebuchlätter*, vol. 1, 28ff., and Eduard Schulz, *Bismarcks Einfluss auf die deutsche Presse (Juli 1870)* (Halle, 1910).

[59] Lord, *Origins*, 49ff.

[60] Bonnin, ed., *Candidature*, 242ff.

rected a policy of stern intransigence. He had opposed suggestions from the king that a royal letter be sent to Napoleon and the mediation of neutrals invoked. He advised against Wilhelm's continued dealings with Benedetti. To keep control of the situation he set out on the morning of the twelfth, uncommonly silent, for Berlin en route to Ems. In the late afternoon his carriage halted in the Wilhelmstrasse and a sheaf of telegrams was shoved into his hand. Sitting there in the street, he learned for the first time of Karl Anton's decision and the extent of Wilhelm's involvement in his renunciation. Other messages from Paris told of "vaunts and taunts" in the Paris press. Descending to the sidewalk, he thought of resigning. Prussia, he judged, had suffered a humiliation worse than Olmütz.[61]

Once at his desk in the chancellery, however, he began to grapple with the problem of salvaging as much as possible from the wreckage. He wanted war, but Wilhelm's appeasement had left no way for Prussia to begin it without appearing the aggressor. Hence all he could do for the time being was to minimize and disguise the extent of the catastrophe. With Roon and Eulenburg he sent a telegram to Wilhelm entreating him not to make the mistake of announcing Leopold's renunciation to Benedetti and hence to the world. If the word came from Madrid or Sigmaringen, the tarnished fiction of the government's noninvolvement might still be upheld. A message from Paris helped. Werther reported that the Spanish ambassador had informed Gramont of an "official telegram" from Karl Anton renouncing the throne for his son. Quickly Bismarck transmitted this news to the press and to Prussian legations in Germany and Europe. In conferences with the crown prince, Ambassador Count Edoardo de Launay of Italy, and Prince Gorchakov, who happened to be in Berlin, he spoke of the crisis as settled and of his intention to return to Varzin.[62]

But the truth was that he was even then searching for a way to renew the conflict on more advantageous grounds. Public opinion, he telegraphed to Ems, had been "injured" by Gramont's threats and his demand for satisfaction; the king should react by granting Werther an indefinite leave and making the reason known. His directives to the press, however, reveal that he himself was stirring up public resentment over Gramont's "offensive tone." To Werther in Paris he telegraphed early on the afternoon of July 13 that, if "a completely satisfying statement as to the intentions of France" were not soon received, he would recommend to the king that the Reichstag be convened and consulted upon what course to take. His aim was to keep the affair

---

[61] Lord, *Origins*, 68ff.; GW, XV, 305ff.

[62] Lord, *Origins*, 201–204, 215, 261–262; Heinrich O. Meisner, ed., *Kaiser Friedrich III.: Das Kriegstagebuch von 1870/71* (Berlin, 1926), 2; Chester W. Clark, "Bismarck, Russia, and the Origins of the War of 1870," *Journal of Modern History*, 14 (1942), 200–201; S. William Halperin, "Bismarck and the Italian Envoy in Berlin on the Eve of the Franco-Prussian War," *Journal of Modern History*, 33 (1961), 35–36. For Bismarck's actions on July 12 and 13 see particularly Steefel, *Hohenzollern Candidacy*, 165ff.

alive by demanding an explanation of Gramont's conduct, by chauvinistic demonstrations from the Reichstag, and by the menace of mobilization.[63]

But this plan was quickly made superfluous by Gramont's folly. The duke failed to recognize the extent of his victory. He was disturbed over the delay in receiving from Wilhelm himself word of the Sigmaringen decision, which would associate the king and his government with the candidacy and its withdrawal. Within the parliament and among the public there were ominous rumblings of dissatisfaction over this "insufficient and almost derisible concession."[64] Much had happened in the Spanish affair without the knowledge of the French government. What more was being concealed? Had Leopold, whose whereabouts were still unknown, slipped off, like his brother to Rumania in 1866, to claim a crown in Spain? There was a feeling in Paris that something more was owed—some act of expiation on Wilhelm's part, perhaps an apology—for what appeared to have been a Prussian conspiracy against France. As the clock advanced on July 12, Gramont's attitude stiffened and his communications to Werther in Paris and Benedetti in Bad Ems became more demanding. With Napoleon's assent, but without the knowledge of Ollivier and the rest of the cabinet, he dispatched that evening the fatal telegram to Benedetti demanding that Wilhelm associate himself with Karl Anton's renunciation and "give us assurance that he will not authorize a renewal of the candidacy." Without such a guarantee it was doubtful whether the government could dominate popular unrest.[65]

In the council of ministers on the morning of July 13, Gramont's colleagues waxed critical of his decision to heighten the government's position and resolved that the demand for a guarantee was not to be given the attribute of an ultimatum. But by then the matter was already beyond their control. Even while they deliberated, Benedetti, believing he could not wait for a formal audience scheduled for the afternoon, approached Wilhelm in the Kurgarten by the Lahn River. While promenaders watched from a respectful distance, he made his demand for a guarantee and was refused. Benedetti kept pressing until Wilhelm, aware of the public attention they were attracting, tipped his hat and coldly withdrew, saying that he had nothing further to communicate. Early that afternoon under the urging of Eulenburg and Abeken, the king determined to call off the scheduled audience with the ambassador. In midafternoon the report of these events was telegraphed to Berlin.[66]

Since morning on that fateful day Bismarck had received a number of comforting dispatches. From Vienna Ambassador Lothar von Schweinitz reported

[63] Lord, *Origins*, 205, 219–220; Ernst Walder, *Die Emser Depesche: Quellen zur neueren Geschichte herausgegeben vom Historischen Seminar der Universität Bern*, vols. 27–29 (Bern, 1959), 62–68; Clark, "Bismarck, Russia, and the War of 1870," 201.

[64] Lynn M. Case, *French Opinion on War and Diplomacy during the Second Empire* (Philadelphia, 1954), 251ff.

[65] *OD*, XXVIII, 254–255.

[66] Fletcher, *Mission of Vincent Benedetti*, 244–260; Walder, *Die Emser Depesche*, 49ff.

that Austria, despite French wooing, would probably remain neutral in event of war. From Bavaria, Baden, and finally even Württemberg came assurances of support. Gorchakov appeared sympathetic. English neutrality was fairly certain. The situation favored war. The problem was how to bring it about on favorable grounds. For several hours vague reports trickled in from London, Munich, Stuttgart, and Gorchakov that Gramont had made new demands, but to Bismarck's growing irritation there was no confirmation from Werther. Then suddenly the dispatch from Ems supplied the missing provocation.[67]

When it arrived that evening Bismarck was at dinner with Roon and Moltke. At first sight the message was rather disappointing. Insulted by an outrageous demand, Wilhelm had failed to dramatize his indignation. (As yet there was no word of Gramont's further request for an apology, whose receipt at Ems later in the afternoon terminated the king's last hope of appeasing the French.) Nevertheless, Abeken's dispatch, whose publication the king had authorized, was made to serve. After asking Moltke once more if the army was ready, Bismarck dictated a new version. By subtracting words, he gave the message a terseness that altered its sense. Now it appeared that, in reply to a presumptuous demand, the king had closed the door to Benedetti and to all further negotiation. The generals read the revised version with relief. "Yes," they declared, "that will do."[68]

On the morning of July 14 Gramont, his face livid, rushed into Ollivier's office with news of the publication of the "Ems dispatch." It was, the trembling diplomat declared, a "slap in the face." The premier also recognized that Bismarck's action was openly provocative. That evening, as the news spread through Paris, a howling mob surged through the boulevards shouting, "To Berlin!", "Down with Prussia!", and singing the forbidden "Marseillaise." Within the court and cabinet, nevertheless, there was wavering indecision. Reports from Ems showed that Wilhelm had remained courteous to the end, that even after the meeting in the Kurgarten he had sent Benedetti a message "approving" Leopold's renunciation, and finally that he had received the ambassador again at the railway station before departing for Koblenz. But it was recognized that he had not complied fully with French demands and that the

---

[67] Lord, *Origins*, 194ff. Although Gorchakov dodged the opportunity to reaffirm the Russo-Prussian agreement concerning Austria, an appeal to the tsar through Oubril brought reassurance. Clark, "Bismarck, Russia, and the War of 1870," 199ff.; Walter Platzhoff, "England und der Kaiserplan vom Frühjahr 1870," *Historische Zeitschrift*, 127 (1923), 299.

[68] William L. Langer cut away the embroidery of the tale that Bismarck told in his memoirs and elsewhere about the swift transition from despondency to exultation that the edited dispatch produced in Roon and Moltke. GW, XV, 301–311. See his "Bismarck as a Dramatist," in Sarkissian, ed., *Studies in Diplomatic History*, 199–216. For the original and revised texts of the dispatch see Walder, *Die Emser Depesche*, 13ff. Because the edited original has never been found, Josef Becker has presumed that it never existed and that Caprivi was correct when in the 1890s he described the revised text to the Reichstag as a dictation. See J. Becker, "Zum Problem" 530–531.

ALBRECHT VON ROON IN 1867 (FROM DIETRICH SCHÄFER, *BISMARCK: EIN BILD SEINES LEBENS UND WIRKENS*, TWO VOLS., VERLAG VON REIMAR HOBBING, BERLIN, 1917, VOL. 2).

HELMUTH VON MOLTKE, ABOUT 1875 (FROM DIETRICH SCHÄFER, *BISMARCK: EIN BILD SEINES LEBENS UND WIRKENS*, TWO VOLS., VERLAG VON REIMAR HOBBING, BERLIN, 1917, VOL. 2).

"Ems dispatch" was a deliberate challenge. The excitement in the streets, the impatience of nationalistic deputies in the chamber, and the agitation of the war party at court constituted pressures that the new and uncertain parliamentary regime chose not to ignore. Napoleon too, dreading the consequences, yielded to the force of the hurricane. Gradually, as the hours progressed and one ministerial conference succeeded another on July 14 and 15, the decision congealed.[69]

In the end war came because Bismarck believed it necessary and opportune and because the French cabinet had neither the wisdom nor the firmness of will to avoid it. Thousands died on the battlefields of France because of conscious decisions made in Berlin and Paris by statesmen who could have chosen otherwise. They were not puppets dancing on strings held by abstract, unaccountable "forces" but flesh and blood men who took risks in full knowledge of the possible consequences.

[69] By emphasizing different aspects of the evidence, Malcolm Carroll and Lynn Case came to diametrically opposed views on the origins of the French decision for war. The former believed that Gramont and Ollivier willed it, while the latter accepted their excuse that public anger required it. The truth probably lies somewhere in between. Carroll, *French Opinion*, 25ff.; Case, *French Opinion on War and Diplomacy*, 256ff. For the best account of the events in Paris on July 14 and 15 leading up to the declaration of war see Steefel, *Hohenzollern Candidacy*, 195ff.

CHAPTER TWENTY-ONE

A National War

Strategy and Diplomacy

OOKING backward from the perspective of the twentieth century, some historians have found much to admire in the way Bismarck's wars were conducted. In our day warfare has tended to become absolute under the influence of crusading national ideologies. The quest on moral grounds for total victory has exalted military over political policy. Statesmen and generals have been increasingly inclined to see as their primary objective the utter destruction of the foe rather than attainment of a stable peace. By contrast the conflicts of 1864, 1866, and 1870 appear to have been classic examples of Clausewitz's famous principle that war is properly but a continuation of policy by other means. They were fought for limited objectives on isolated battlefields. They reconstructed, but did not destroy the European balance.[1]

This was achieved, however, only at considerable cost. The dualism of political and military authority in Prussia, which Bismarck himself perpetuated, made it increasingly difficult to establish the supremacy of political purpose over military strategy. During the Danish War he infuriated the generals by insisting that the invasion of Jutland be delayed. They could not accept his view that agreement with Austria and avoidance of foreign intervention took precedence over military expediency. Later Roon, Moltke, and others were distressed over the leniency shown the Danes in the armistice preceding the London conference. The army, wrote Roon, did not regard itself as "purely a political instrument, a lancet for the diplomatic surgeon."[2]

The Austrian war produced frictions of even graver nature. To Moltke's irritation Bismarck meddled in the mobilization and deployment of the Prussian forces in the west during the first days of the conflict. But the great altercation came after Königgrätz, when the generals urged Wilhelm to pursue the retreating forces of Benedek across the Danube and into Vienna. They wanted a conqueror's peace. "In eight days it will be all over," wrote General-

---

[1] The similarity of viewpoint between the chancellor and military philosopher was apparently accidental. In 1889 Bismarck observed, "To my shame I have to confess that I have never read Clausewitz and have known little more about him than that he was a meritorious general." Freiherr Lucius von Ballhausen, *Bismarck-Erinnerungen* (Stuttgart, 1920), 502.

[2] Gordon A. Craig, *The Politics of the Prussian Army, 1640–1945* (Oxford, 1955), 182–192; Anneliese Klein-Wuttig, *Politik und Kriegsführung in den deutschen Einigungskriegen 1864, 1866, und 1870/71: Abhandlungen zur mittleren und neueren Geschichte*, vol. 75 (Berlin, 1934), 5ff.

Adjutant H. von Boyen on July 19, 1866, "if the diplomats, who attach themselves to every honorable war like bugs to a bed, don't destroy the sport for us."[3] Only with great difficulty did Bismarck succeed in limiting the conflict by gaining Wilhelm's acceptance of French mediation. Although the generals were satisfied with the ultimate peace terms, the incident left behind a residue of resentment that influenced the conduct of the war of 1870.

The potentiality of conflict was greatly increased by the rise of Moltke and the general staff. Roon was usually open to Bismarck's arguments and willing to take into account the needs of foreign policy, but Moltke believed it possible to draw a distinct boundary between politics and strategy. Until the outbreak of war, diplomacy was paramount; thereafter, military necessity. Nor did his experiences of 1864 and 1866 convince him of the error in such a division of functions. With the group of devoted "demigods" that surrounded him in the general staff, he entered the campaign against France firm in the conviction that the movement of German forces was the sole concern of the generals, whatever its effect upon the attitudes of European powers and the negotiation of peace.[4]

During the first month of hostilities there was little occasion for conflict between the statesman and military chiefs. The campaign went so quickly that it discouraged outside intervention. The German forces mobilized with machinelike precision; beyond the Rhine all was chaos and confusion. When the German offensive began (August 4, 1870), the French were still unready. On that day Prussian and Bavarian troops struck at Weissenburg; two days later the double victories of Wörth and Spicheren occurred. On the sixteenth and eighteenth came the bloody battles of Mars la Tour and Gravelotte that cut off the main French army under Bazaine and forced it to retire into the fortress of Metz. Unable to succor Bazaine, the remnant of the French forces under MacMahon marched to Sedan, where on September 1, after fierce combat, it surrendered. Napoleon himself was one of the prisoners.

At the outset the French fully expected Austrian and Italian assistance. In March Archduke Albrecht, Austria's foremost general, had been in Paris to confer on military collaboration between the three powers in event of war with Germany. Toward the end of May the French General Lebrun had continued the exchange of views in Vienna. But the alliance remained a "moral" rather than a military commitment. On June 14 Franz Joseph told Lebrun that he would make common cause with France only "when Napoleon stands in south Germany with his army, not as an enemy but as a liberator." Apparently Gramont, informed by Beust of the secret negotiations in Paris during the

[3] Craig, Prussian Army, 202; Oberst von Haeften, "Bismarck und Moltke," Preussische Jahrbücher, 177 (1919), 85ff.; Hermann Gackenholz, "Der Kriegsrat von Czernahora vom 12. Juli 1866," Historische Vierteljahrschrift, 26 (1931), 332–348.

[4] Craig, Prussian Army, 195ff.; Gerhard Ritter, Staatskunst und Kriegshandwerk: Das Problem des "Militarismus" in Deutschland (Munich, 1954), vol. 1, 247ff.

NAPOLEON III AND BISMARCK MEET ON SEPTEMBER 2, 1870, THE MORNING AFTER THE BATTLE OF SEDAN.
PAINTING BY WILHELM CAMPHAUSEN, 1878 (FROM ALFRED FUNKE, *DAS BISMARCK-BUCH DES
DEUTSCHEN VOLKES*, TWO VOLS., W. BOBACH & CO., LEIPZIG, 1921, VOL. 2, P. 473).

preceding year, assumed office in Paris under the impression that the alliance
had practically been achieved. On July 8 he asserted in a cabinet meeting that
Austria would station an observation corps on the frontier and "paralyze" part
of the Prussian forces. But the next day Beust, in response to Napoleon's
inquiry, promised just diplomatic support. Only if Russia joined Prussia would
the Habsburg monarchy enter the conflict.[5]

Beust suspected an understanding between Berlin and Petersburg, and in
this he was absolutely correct. On July 16 Tsar Alexander responded to an
inquiry from Berlin by confirming his commitment of the previous year;
should Austria go to war, Russia would occupy Galicia with three hundred
thousand men. In a crown council on July 18 Beust raised the question
whether, in view of the Russian threat, Austria should continue her "passive
policy." Opinions were divided, but Franz Joseph decided on a declaration of
official neutrality, coupled with some military preparations. In order to buttress this decision, Bismarck disclaimed any intention of detaching German
Austria, and Alexander offered a guarantee of Austrian territorial integrity.[6]

[5] *RKN*, I, 94ff.; III, 376ff., 413ff.
[6] *GW*, VIb, 389, 422–423; Werner E. Mosse, *The European Powers and the German Question*,

Albrecht believed, however, that in early September a decisive battle would occur in Saxony, and Beust was tormented by the thought that Austria might not benefit from a French victory. Hence he let Gramont know sub rosa that neutrality was for the Habsburg monarchy merely a means for gaining time in which to complete Austrian rearmament. He advised France to come to terms meanwhile with Italy by evacuating Rome. Through an agent Napoleon learned that Victor Emmanuel intended to go through with his commitment of the previous year to ally with France. The emperor revealed his intention to recall the Roman garrison, and the king declared that Italy would respect the independence of the Papal States. But again Bonaparte was destined to disappointment, for Victor Emmanuel could not persuade the Italian cabinet to honor his "anterior promises." Throughout the diplomatic crisis Foreign Minister Emilio Visconti-Venosta worked for peace, and, when war came, he kept Italy neutral.[7]

In England the belligerents engaged in a sharp contest for public and official favor. No sooner had Napoleon proclaimed his respect for Belgian neutrality, the point of chief interest in London, than Bismarck produced for British consumption a document of sensational content. It was the treaty draft that Benedetti had so unwisely left in his hands in August 1866. On July 25 it appeared in the London *Times*. The impression was deliberately created that the document was of recent origin and that Prussia's refusal alone had prevented a Franco-Prussian alliance at the cost of Belgium and the German southern states. Although skeptical, the British cabinet resolved to obtain a fresh guarantee of Belgian frontiers from both belligerents. After it was signed on August 9 and 11, the British sat back to watch the struggle in France, comfortable in the thought that, whatever the outcome, their interests were secure.[8]

These actions by the European powers in July and August went as Bismarck had calculated they would and justified his assumption that war with France in the summer of 1870 was possible without outside intervention and hence without triggering a general European conflict. Austria was the critical point, and Bismarck's judgment that Beust, for all his dreams of revenge, would be unable to ally with France proved entirely correct. But after the fall of Sedan difficulties began to appear that greatly complicated Bismarck's task and led

1848–1871 (Cambridge, Eng., 1958), 306–310; Eduard von Wertheimer, *Graf Julius Andrássy* (Stuttgart, 1910), vol. 1, 510–520. See also Ernst Erichsen, *Die deutsche Politik des Grafen Beust im Jahre 1870* (Kiel, 1927), 14ff.

[7] *RKN*, III, 464–467; *OD*, XXIX, 201ff.; Friedrich Ferdinand Graf von Beust, *Aus drei Viertel-Jahrhunderten* (Stuttgart, 1887), vol. 2, 410–411, 437–438; S. William Halperin, "Visconti-Venosta and the Diplomatic Crisis of July 1870," *Journal of Modern History*, 31 (1959), 295–309.

[8] Mosse, *European Powers*, 312–317; Kurt Rheindorf, *England und der Deutsch-Französische Krieg 1870/71* (Bonn, 1923), 47–56; Richard Millman, *British Foreign Policy and the Coming of the Franco-Prussian War* (Oxford, 1965), 199–207.

to serious trouble with the generals over the most fundamental issues of state policy.

Bismarck and Moltke

On August 16, 1870, while the cannon thundered at Mars la Tour, Bismarck wrote to his wife that the campaign was "as good as ended, unless God should manifestly intervene for France, which I trust will not happen."[9] But the war of 1870 went differently than that of 1866. France's reaction to military disaster was not capitulation, but revolution and resistance. When the ominous news of Wörth and Spicheren reached Paris on the sixth, there was general panic. Under attack from the assembly, Gramont and Ollivier resigned. Acting as regent, while her husband was in the field, Eugénie bravely tried to bolster the regime with ringing words of honor and valor. But after Sedan the flood could no longer be held back. The mob was in motion, and the tottering empire collapsed. On September 4, following the traditional ritual of revolution in Paris, the republic was proclaimed at the Hotel de Ville. A "Government of National Defense" was organized, with General Trochu as president and Léon Gambetta as its leading figure. For the revolutionists the war was far from over; it had, in fact, just begun.

Napoleon had been defeated in one month; six more were required to conquer France. On September 18 the victors of Sedan appeared before the ramparts of Paris. Manning the forts and trenches was a motley army of soldiers, sailors, national guardsmen, and volunteers. Within days the city was enclosed in an iron ring. During the following weeks the great sieges of Metz and Paris (Strassburg capitulated on September 27) tied down the bulk of the German forces. Escaping from Paris by balloon, the fiery Gambetta galvanized the population of the south to further effort. While a new army was being formed on the Loire, the irregular francs-tireurs began their attacks upon German detachments and communications in the north.

Continued French resistance created a host of new problems at the Prussian headquarters in Versailles. For the general staff the transformation of the war from a professional into a popular struggle raised strategic problems that the generals had not foreseen. As long as the fighting lasted, moreover, so did the danger of foreign intervention. Bismarck had to find as soon as possible a French government capable of speaking for the nation and willing to accept Germany's terms. The impingement of these problems of strategy and politics upon each other led inevitably, under the dual structure of the Prussian system, to a test of strength between the chancellor and the chief of the general staff.

Apparently Moltke and his "demigods" had firmly determined to exclude

[9] GW, XIV, 785.

Bismarck from the war councils in which crucial issues of strategy were debated and decisions taken. This time, their ears were to be free of his biting sarcasm and his injection of political considerations into strategic calculations. Before Sedan the chancellor does not appear to have objected to his exclusion. The campaign went largely according to plans already known to him. But after Sedan ignorance of the generals' intentions disrupted his efforts to end the war. Most irritating of all, he had no other source for what had taken place on the fighting front than the army communiqués in the German press, received five days after the event. Repeatedly he demanded at least to see these reports as they emanated from headquarters. Not until October 15 was a system set up for this purpose, and even then it was carried out in a grudging and haphazard way. In January 1871 Bismarck was still complaining over the inadequacy of his information.[10] A still more serious clash, however, came over the treatment of Napoleon.

After his surrender Napoleon was handled with the utmost chivalry and

HELMUTH VON MOLTKE WITH HIS STAFF AT VERSAILLES, JANUARY 1871

(BILDARCHIV PREUSSISCHER KULTURBESITZ).

[10] Craig, *Prussian Army*, 204ff.; GW, VIb, 590–592, 637–638, 658–660. Shortly after Sedan he also had a sharp altercation with Moltke over instructions he had issued to Dr. Stieber, chief of the Feldpolizei, who was officially subordinate to the general staff. GW, VIb, 490–491. For the generals' side of the story see Haeften, "Bismarck und Moltke," 87ff., and Paul Bronsart von Schellendorff, *Geheimes Kriegstagebuch, 1870–1871* (Bonn, 1954), 78–79, 82.

sent off to comfortable captivity in the palace of Wilhelmshöhe at Kassel. "Revenge," said Bismarck, "is God's affair." With the beleaguered army at Metz and thousands of prisoners the fallen emperor was a valuable resource— "Tell's second arrow for the Gessler 'republic.' " "The French must remain uncertain whether they will get him again."[11] As usual, Bismarck left open every door and every turning. For months after Sedan he held out to Louis and Eugénie the prospect of a return to power, while threatening the Government of National Defense with the nightmare of a resurgent Bonaparte. "It is a matter of indifference to us who rules France," he telegraphed to London, "whether Napoleon or a white or red republic." What mattered was to find a government that would cede Alsace-Lorraine.[12]

If a restored empire were to be a real possibility, rapport had to be reestablished between Bazaine at Metz, Napoleon at Kassel, and the demoralized Eugénie, who had escaped to England. The unilinear minds of the military could not comprehend this maneuver. Prince Friedrich Karl, who commanded at Metz, regarded its capitulation as a purely military concern. When Bazaine's emissary, General Bourbaki, returned from a mission to emperor and empress, the stubborn prince protested his readmission to the invested fortress, with the consequence that the impatient general made off for Tours and offered his services to the revolutionary government. Grimly Bismarck wrote that the unexpected failure of a single wheel to turn had rendered useless weeks of careful diplomacy. Warfare, he explained, was properly but a means to political ends.[13]

To Bismarck's disgust Louis and Eugénie could not make up their minds; they were reluctant to mortgage their return to France with the cession of French soil. The fall of Metz (October 27, 1870) increased the difficulty of the negotiation. Not even now, however, did Bismarck remove the Napoleonic ace from his deck. As late as January 14, 1871, he regarded Louis's return as "the most advantageous" solution for Germany. In the final negotiations with Favre and Thiers he used the threat of it to pry concessions from the revolutionary government.[14] Moltke was outraged at the prospect and crossed Bismarck by prejudicing Wilhelm against it. He hated France and despised the Napoleonic regime. Peace, he maintained, was inadmissible until the enemy had been utterly crushed.[15] But Bismarck saw that, with every passing day, the danger of foreign intervention increased.

For a time the seeming finality of the victory at Sedan had discouraged the

[11] GW, VIb, 469–470; VII, 344ff.; XIV, 793, 814–815.

[12] GW, VIb, 504; VII, 373. See Joachim Kühn, "Bismarck und der Bonapartismus im Winter 1870/71," Preussische Jahrbücher, 163 (1916), 49–100.

[13] GW, VIb, 551–553. Klein-Wuttig, Politik und Kriegführung, 109ff.

[14] GW, VIb, 666–669; VII, 379, 393, 407; Hermann Oncken, ed., Grossherzog Friedrich I. von Baden und die deutsche Politik von 1854–1871 (Stuttgart, 1927), vol. 2, 333–334.

[15] Craig, Prussian Army, 208–209; Oncken, ed., Grossherzog Friedrich I. vol. 2, 166–167.

European powers from any such thought. Alexander and Gorchakov aban-doned their project for a joint effort by the neutrals to shorten the war and preserve the European balance. Gladstone reaffirmed the principle of nonin-tervention. Queen Victoria actually rejoiced at the triumph "of civilization, of liberty, of order and of unity . . . over despotism, corruption, immorality and aggression."[16] On September 4 Bismarck heard of the revolution in Paris with some satisfaction for the effect it would have on the neutrals. In Vienna and Petersburg he now argued that the best safeguard for "order and civiliza-tion" against "revolutionary and republican interests" was solidarity of the three eastern monarchies—and the cession to Germany of Alsace and Lor-raine![17]

News of the German intention to annex was received with concern in both Russia and Britain. In August 1870 Alexander had expressed to Reuss, the Prussian ambassador, his fears that the lost provinces would become a source of constant friction in the future and urged moderation.[18] Gladstone was "much oppressed" by this "transfer of human beings like chattels." When Granville, who had replaced Clarendon at the foreign office, proposed (Oc-tober 16) joint steps by the neutrals for an acceptable peace, he was rebuffed by Gorchakov.[19]

Very soon the British learned the real reason for Russian disinterest. On October 31, Tsar Alexander issued a circular repudiating the Black Sea clauses of the treaty of Paris. The Russians had decided to exploit Europe's preoccupation with the war in France to rid themselves of the galling restric-tions imposed after their defeat in the Crimea. For years Bismarck had curried favor in Petersburg by urging Gorchakov to take this step, and now he was compelled to support it. Nevertheless, the timing was most unfortunate for Germany. In Britain public indignation threatened to push the cabinet into war. Austria too became "ominously hostile." But Bismarck managed to get agreement on a conference to be held in London. It opened on January 17, 1871, with a joint declaration on the sanctity of treaties and ended on March 13 with a revocation of the neutralization of the Black Sea. By this legerde-main principle was preserved and self-interest satisfied.[20]

The Black Sea issue was a source of anxiety to Bismarck because of its pos-sible repercussions upon the conflict in the west. Had Russia gotten herself involved in war with Britain, the French-German struggle might easily have developed into a European cataclysm. During the conference, moreover,

---

[16] Mosse, European Powers, 324ff.

[17] GW, VIb, 448, 476, 486.

[18] GW, VIb, 456, 458–459, 476.

[19] Mosse, European Powers, 338ff.; Millman, British Policy, 210–218.

[20] Mosse, European Powers, 346. See Heinrich Mertz, Die Schwarze Meerkonferenz von 1871 (Stuttgart, undated) and particularly Kurt Rheindorf, Die Schwarze-Meer-(Pontus) Frage (Berlin, 1925), 75ff.

there was a chance that the neutrals might discuss intervention in France. Hence it was all the more important to end the war as quickly as possible.[21] His agitation upon this score brought him again into bitter conflict with the generals.

After Sedan Bismarck grew increasingly critical of the way the general staff ran the war. He opposed the advance on Paris. It was better to "let the people there fry in their own fat for a time, while we set up house in the conquered provinces before going further." If left alone, he believed, the quarrelsome republic would fall apart of itself. But his advice was ignored. When the German forces reached the capital, he wanted an immediate assault instead of a siege. The investment, he complained, tied down the bulk of the army and left Gambetta free to raise new forces in the south and west. In the occupied regions German troops were so thinly spread that it was difficult to make the conquered population "feel" the war.[22]

During November and December the major issue was the bombardment of Paris. Most of the generals were skeptical about the effectiveness of their artillery and preferred the tedious course of starving out the inhabitants. Lack of conviction, bad planning, and poor transportation delayed the arrival of the siege guns and adequate munitions. Bismarck could not believe that honest disagreement and technical difficulties stood in the way. His letters home alluded darkly to "some kind of intrigue" spun by wives, archbishops, intellectuals, and freemasons; the war was being prolonged by sentimental humanitarianism and fear of foreign reaction. He fell ill from wrath and jangled nerves; his old leg injury returned to plague him; and for days he lay in bed incommunicado.[23]

Finally, on December 27, 1870, the bombardment began. But the effect was not what Bismarck expected. The siege guns hurled three to four hundred shells daily into the city's center, but they did remarkably little damage. Bismarck's psychological warfare merely increased the will of the Parisians to resist, while the idea that noncombatants could be fired upon horrified Europe and left the Germans with a clinging reputation for brutality. Week after week, the Prussian batteries hammered the walls of the perimeter forts into ruins, but not to defenselessness. Increasingly desperate sorties from the beleaguered garrison were beaten back with heavy casualties. And yet it was the approach of starvation that finally forced the capitulation of January 29, 1871.[24]

[21] GW, VIb, 602–606.

[22] GW, VIb, 648–651; XIV, 791, 800.

[23] GW, VIb, 570–571; VII, 390, 395, 409, 416, 419, 424; XIV, 797ff.; Rudolf Stadelmann, *Moltke und der Staat* (Krefeld, 1950), 232ff.

[24] Otto Bihler, *Die Beschiessung von Paris 1870/71 und die Ursachen ihrer Verzögerung* (Tübingen, 1932); Melvin Kranzberg, *The Siege of Paris, 1870–1871* (Ithaca, 1950), 133ff.; Michael Howard, *The Franco-Prussian War* (New York, 1969), 357–368.

The generals were infuriated by Bismarck's "infantile counsels." They sneered at "the civilian in cuirrassier uniform" and his "ill-mannered," "domineering" ways. Having nothing else to do, it seemed, he meddled in their affairs and conspired to take over the military direction of the war. To Bismarck, on the other hand, it appeared that the generals were woefully ignorant of the political import of their decisions. During December and January he used whatever opportunities came his way to limit their influence. Letters sent by Moltke to General Trochu in Paris gave him occasion to demand the right to review such communications. On January 25 two royal orders curbed Moltke's power to communicate with the enemy and gave Bismarck the right to present his views on future military operations. Moltke was outraged. He drafted a sarcastic reply, suggesting that the chancellor be given responsibility for directing the war. But then he thought better of it and wrote a memorial justifying his position on the grounds that chancellor and chief of the general staff were two parallel, "mutually independent agencies under the direct command of your majesty."[25]

The conflict between Moltke and Bismarck is a classic example of the uneasy relationship between political and military leadership in wartime. To the chancellor the fall of Paris meant the possibility of peace on German terms, but to the general it meant the release of troops for further military operations. After a futile attempt to reconcile the two men, Crown Prince Friedrich Wilhelm realized that Moltke was bent upon a "war of extermination." His aim was to extend the iron grip of German military might over the whole of France. But King Wilhelm was wise enough to know whose side to take. To the anger and mortification of the general staff, Bismarck alone conducted the talks with Jules Favre that produced an armistice. Without their advice he determined which Paris forts were to be surrendered. When the new French government in Bordeaux required an extension of the armistice, he decided for it over Moltke's strenuous opposition. The final terms of peace were essentially of his dictation. "Never," wrote General von Stosch, "have I witnessed such bitterness toward an individual as that at the moment toward Bismarck."[26]

Bismarck had won his private struggle with the military at a crucial time in German history. But the institutional dualism of military and political authority that was its cause remained unaltered. One day, long after his death,

[25] Craig, Prussian Army, 210ff.; Klein-Wuttig, Politik und Kriegführung, 135ff. Schellendorff, Kriegstagebuch, 185–186, 208ff., 233–237, 249, 279–281, 303ff.; Haeften, "Bismarck und Moltke," 98–103; GW, VIb, 615–617, 673.

[26] Heinrich O. Meisner, ed., Kaiser Friedrich III.: Tagebücher von 1848–1866 (Leipzig, 1929), 325–326; Oncken, ed., Grossherzog Friedrich I., vol. 2, 260ff., 279, 282, 290ff., 313–315, 363–364; GW, VIb, 665ff., 676ff., 693–694; Ulrich von Stosch, ed., Denkwürdigkeiten des Generals und Admirals Albrecht von Stosch (Stuttgart, 1904), 227.

the problem would rise again to plague his successors in a war of far greater dimensions.

Furor Teutonicus

By great effort Bismarck was able to limit the war of 1870 to the realization of rational political objectives in the tradition of *raison d'état*. Nevertheless, the conflict was not a *Kabinettskrieg* in the style of the eighteenth century, but a *Nationalkrieg* of modern character.[27] In this respect the Franco-German War was a link between the national wars of the French Revolution and those of the twentieth century. In contrast to 1854, 1859,[28] 1864, and 1866, the war of 1870 was one of peoples, more than governments. By a quick peace after Königgrätz, Kaiser Franz Joseph deliberately avoided the hazardous experiment of calling upon the peoples of the Habsburg Empire to resist invasion. After the destruction of the imperial armies and the fall of the Napoleonic regime, however, the war with France continued far beyond the expectations of Bismarck and the Prussian generals. The catastrophe merely opened wider the Pandora's box of national feeling and the spirit of popular sacrifice. A war for the destruction of armies became a conflict for the exhaustion and dismemberment of a nation.

On both sides the war had the characteristics of a national crusade. As he confessed to Metternich on July 8, 1870, Gramont considered the Hohenzollern candidature a safe terrain for a crisis, precisely because it did not involve German national sentiment.[29] But this was a bad miscalculation. In editing the Ems dispatch Bismarck counted on the reality that any crisis with France, whatever the origin, was sufficient to arouse the *furor teutonicus*. The great revival of national feeling in 1840 had begun with a crisis in Egypt, that of 1859 with war in Italy. Germans of 1870 had been raised in the tradition of the war of 1812. Popular suspicion of France was as endemic in Germany as hostility toward Britain in the United States during the same period. In contrast to 1866, Bismarck's effort in 1870 to identify the Prussian cause with that of the German nation was an overwhelming success.

From the outset the war was popular on both sides of the Rhine. While patriotic crowds demonstrated in the streets of Paris, Wilhelm received ovation after ovation on his journey from Ems to Berlin. In the capital thousands gathered spontaneously at the railway station to receive him. Afterward they massed in the square before the royal palace to cheer and applaud. In a Reichstag speech, composed by Bismarck, he stressed the national character

---

[27] This Moltke himself recognized. Ritter, *Staatskunst*, vol. 1, 252; Stadelmann, *Moltke und der Staat*, 173ff.

[28] Only Italy, the weakest of the three participants, regarded the conflict of 1859 as a national war.

[29] *RKN*, III, 405.

of the coming struggle. France's leaders had used the Hohenzollern candidature as a "pretext" for war. In earlier centuries Germans had borne in silence foreign assaults upon their rights and honor. Since 1813, however, they had been bound ever more closely together by spiritual and legal ties. Now they possessed the will and strength to defend themselves. The governments, north and south, called upon the German people to show the patriotism and sacrifice of their forefathers in a struggle for "our freedom and our right against the brutality of foreign conquerors." His words were interrupted frequently by deafening applause.[30]

Addressing the Bundesrat on July 16, 1870, Bismarck gave a highly partial account of the negotiations that led to the "insult" at Ems, contrasting Prussian innocence with French malevolence. France, he declared, had left "Germany" no choice other than war and had committed a grievous sin against humanity. The aroused state of national sentiment in Germany showed that this conviction was shared by the public. On the twentieth he read to the Reichstag his reply to England's offer to mediate. Berlin was willing to negotiate on any basis acceptable to the "honor and national consciousness of Germany." But the government would undertake no initiative to this end, for it "would be misunderstood by the national feelings of the German people," which were deeply wounded and agitated by the French threat. "Our strength lies in the national sentiment of the nation, in its sense of right and honor." Cries of "Bravo!" "Very good!" and "Very right!" echoed through the chamber.[31]

These declarations set the tone for official propaganda throughout the war. In two published diplomatic circulars (July 18–19) Bismarck traced French aggression to "instincts of hatred and jealousy" and the desire to suppress freedom at home through involvement abroad. The size and power of the two countries and their "national embitterment" opened the prospect of a "titanic struggle" hazardous to national welfare and the peaceful development of civilization. France's "criminal" actions compelled Berlin "to take up the struggle for the sake of the national honor and freedom of Germany." For victory he trusted in God and the "support of the entire German nation."[32]

Most of this was propaganda, but it is nevertheless true that Bismarck himself felt in some degree the national character of the war. During the campaign he entertained his guests and associates at dinner with facile comparisons of German and French character: "France is a nation of ciphers—a mere herd. The French are wealthy and elegant, but they have no individuality, no consciousness as individuals, but only as a mass. They are like thirty million obedient Kaffirs, each one of whom is in himself featureless and worth-

[30] Heinrich O. Meisner, ed., *Kaiser Friedrich III.: Das Kriegstagebuch von 1870/71* (Berlin, 1926), 4ff.; GW, XI, 134–135.

[31] GW, XI, 129–133, 135–138.

[32] GW, VIb, 394–397, 401–402.

less, not fit to be compared with Russians and Italians, to say nothing of ourselves. It is easy to recruit out of this impersonal, invertebrate mass a phalanx ready to oppress the remainder of the country so long as it is not united."

By contrast the Germans were individualists, each with his own opinion. "But when once a large number of Germans come to hold the same opinion, great things can be done with them. If they were all agreed they would be all-powerful." In combat, he declared, the Germans were driven by a sense of duty imposed by religious conviction rather than obedience to the state. Unlike the French they were willing to die at lonely posts, unseen and unrewarded, without hope or fear. He believed in "a divine providence that has ordained this German nation to something good and great."[33]

The "nation of ciphers," the "herd" without individual self-reliance, produced after the fall of Sedan a spontaneous popular resistance that surprised and baffled the German leadership. Without an army at the moment of its birth, the republic resorted to a *levée en masse* in the areas under its control. Most indicative of the transformed, popular character of the war were the *francs-tireurs*. In the German-occupied regions partisans began to appear. From behind hedges and buildings they sniped at passing troops; in guerrilla bands they fell upon isolated detachments and sabotaged communications. Though neither universal nor always motivated by patriotism, partisan activity threatened to become a real hazard for the German forces. On the night of October 8 a band of *francs-tireurs* attacked with success a large German unit at Ablis and took away sixty-five prisoners; at Châteaudun on October 18, 1870, an eight-hour battle occurred; on January 23, 1871, a vital bridge in the Vosges was blasted, putting out of commission one of two railway lines to the German frontier.[34]

The German reaction was harsh. Death was decreed for those found with weapons or caught in the act of sabotage. Heavy contributions were levied on communities suspected of sheltering or assisting *francs-tireurs*. Hostages were taken to insure payment. In extreme cases whole communities were pillaged and put to the torch. At Châteaudun this meant a town of seven thousand inhabitants. Gustav Freytag, acting as a journalist at Prussian headquarters, estimated in late October that two months of partisan warfare had cost France about 3 million francs in contributions, twenty to thirty single houses destroyed, twenty to thirty villages burned down, and 150 to 200 persons shot or burned to death (among them women and children guilty or presumed guilty of murderous attacks on German soldiers).[35]

---

[33] Moritz Busch, *Bismarck: Some Secret Pages of His History* (New York, 1898), vol. 1, 138, 162–163.

[34] Bertram Winterhalter, "Die Behandlung der französischen Zivilbevölkerung durch die deutschen Truppen im Kriege 1870/71" (manuscript dissertation on deposit in the library of Freiburg University), 75ff., 128–129, 229.

[35] *Ibid.*, 94ff.

For Bismarck, however, these measures were not severe enough. Repeatedly he complained that German occupation troops were spread so thinly that
they could not make the civilian population "feel" the war by heavy exactions
of money and material. He deplored the tendency of the military government
to shield noncombatants from suffering.[36] One evening at dinner his views
were reinforced by an expert witness, General Philip Sheridan, who summed
up his experience in the American Civil War: "The proper strategy consists,
in the first place, in inflicting as telling blows as possible upon the enemy's
army, and, then, in causing the inhabitants so much suffering that they must
long for peace, and force their government to demand it. The people must be
left nothing but their eyes to weep with over the war."

Even Sheridan must have been impressed by the way his pupil absorbed the
lesson. Concerning "treacherous *francs-tireurs*," Bismarck said a few days
later, "It will come to this: that we will shoot down every male inhabitant."[37]
Such judgments were frequent. His wrath was aroused by reports that guerril-
las were being taken prisoner rather than shot on the spot. This was also his
view of uniformed prisoners taken in regular combat. On hearing of sixteen
hundred captured in an engagement on the Loire, he remarked, "I should
have been better pleased, if they had all been corpses. It is simply a disadvantage to us now to make prisoners." As the months advanced, he repeatedly
deplored that prisoners were still being taken. Toward African troops he was
particularly savage. "There should have been no question of making prisoners
of these blacks. . . . If I had my way, every soldier who made a black man
prisoner should be placed under arrest. They are beasts of prey, and ought to
be shot down." He accused them of torturing German soldiers.[38]

He thoroughly approved of burning villages out of reprisal, for "war is war."
Concerning the incident at Ablis, he remarked that every male inhabitant
ought to be hanged. In cases of sniping and sabotage he thought it would be
a good idea to transport everyone in the area to camps in Germany. He favored firing on "French scamps" who spat at German troops from a bridge.
Persons escaping from Paris by balloon ought to be treated as spies and shot
immediately on capture. Starving women and children who came out of the
beleaguered city to dig for potatoes in the fields between the lines must be
fired upon. Soldiers who refused to press the trigger ought to be executed.
"Brutality," concluded a listener, "is decidedly one of his instincts!"[39] And
yet Bismarck was hardly alone in these sentiments. As the conflict lengthened

---

[36] GW, XIV, 806, 808; VII, 378. See particularly his memorial to Wilhelm of Dec. 14. GW,
VIb, 632–637.

[37] Busch, *Secret Pages*, vol. 1, 128, 167.

[38] GW, VII, 388, 404, 422; Busch, *Secret Pages*, vol. 1, 246, 258.

[39] Busch, *Secret Pages*, vol. 1, 190, 192–193; GW, VII, 396, 405; Ernst Feder, ed., *Bismarcks
grosses Spiel: Die geheimen Tagebücher Ludwig Bambergers* (Frankfurt, 1932), 153, 241.

and tactics changed, the ensuing war of attrition tended to brutalize both sides, civilians as well as soldiers. Chivalry lost its charm.

Most of Bismarck's statements were made, to be sure, in animated conversation. They show his mounting anxiety and frustration over Germany's inability to end the conflict. While capable of saying, "After all, war is, properly speaking, the natural condition of humanity,"[40] this was more in the nature of a psychological observation than moral approbation. Reports of wanton brutality by German troops aroused his ire, and Johanna shocked him by suggesting in a letter that all Frenchmen be "shot and stabbed to death, down to the little babies."[41] The carnage he saw on the battlefields of Bohemia and France intensified his sense of responsibility for decisions that affect the peace. It confirmed his prejudice against preventive war and his conviction that violence was a last resort, to be tried only when unavoidable or when every other means for the attainment of a necessary political objective had failed.

Alsace and Lorraine

The demand for Alsace and Lorraine was another factor that gave to the French-German struggle the character of a national war. The people of Alsace and part of Lorraine spoke a German dialect; both provinces had once belonged to the Holy Roman Empire. During the reigns of Louis XIV and his successors, they had been gradually annexed to France. It was an era of dynastic politics when national feeling was weakly developed and popular wishes of little concern to governments. With the French Revolution the final connection between the provinces and Germany was severed. Politically and economically the area was completely incorporated into the French state; psychologically its citizens became French through participation in the common experience of the revolution and its wars. By raising the demand for its annexation, Bismarck helped to make the war of 1870 a popular national crusade in Germany and inflicted upon the French nation a festering wound that refused to heal.

In Bismarck's defense it is usually pointed out that his motive for claiming the Vosges frontier for Germany was not blood relationship, common language and culture, or any of the usual justifications from the cult of nationalism. He dismissed such arguments contemptuously as "professorial ideas." In private conversation, diplomatic dispatches, and declarations of government policy the one justification that he consistently stressed was that of security. "We must have the two fortresses [Metz and Strassburg] in order to make difficult for France another aggressive war, not in order to bring Alsace and

---

[40] Busch, *Secret Pages*, vol. 1, 210.
[41] Howard, *Franco-Prussian War*, 370–381.

Lorraine back to Germany."[42] This consideration was, in fact, dominant at the Prussian headquarters. The two provinces formed a triangular wedge with the apex at Strassburg pointing toward the heart of Germany. To France they gave the benefit of interior lines of communication; to Germany, the disadvantage of exterior ones. Only the greater speed of German mobilization, Moltke believed, had prevented a French invasion of Baden at the beginning of the war. This belief was shared by Minister of War Roon, King Wilhelm, and Crown Prince Friedrich Wilhelm.[43] Hence there is some support for the view that the annexation of Alsace and Lorraine was an act of *Staatsräson* rather than *Nationalpolitik*. Once again, however, the argument is but part of the truth.

The necessity of justifying annexation compelled Bismarck to alter fundamentally the official German view of the war and reinforce its popular character. In the beginning the words that he placed in Wilhelm's mouth distinguished between the French government, which desired war, and the French people, whom it misled. "I make war against soldiers," Wilhelm proclaimed, "and not against French citizens." But soon after the first successes on the battlefield Bismarck began to shift the burden of culpability. In Petersburg he declared that, while the folly of Napoleon and his advisers was the cause of war, "everyone has recognized that the emperor was but the expression of the senseless and criminal desires of the French people. . . . It is not merely Napoleon. It is France herself whose quest for domination forms a permanent danger for her neighbors, with or without Napoleon at her head." In London he argued that over two centuries Germany had been attacked "twelve or fifteen times" by France. The source of these wars of conquest was "the incurable arrogance and desire to dominate that are peculiar to the character of the French people and are exploited by every ruler of the country." Nor was the new line limited to diplomatic dispatches. When the German press continued to blame Napoleon, he instructed Thile in Berlin to correct this "error." In two circular dispatches, released to the press, Bismarck publicly traced the origins of the conflict to the domineering pride and ambition of the French nation and described annexation as a national demand of the German people.[44]

During the first three weeks of war, there were many allusions in the German press to the justice and necessity of annexations. On July 21, the influential *Augsburger Allgemeine Zeitung* voiced a demand for Alsace and Lorraine. Four days later, *Die Neuesten Nachrichten* of Munich exhorted Germany not

---

[42] Busch, *Secret Pages*, vol. 1, 124; GW, VII, 338–339.

[43] Martin Spahn, *Elsass-Lothringen* (Berlin, 1919), 246–247; Waldemar von Roon, *Denkwürdigkeiten aus dem Leben des General-Feldmarschalls Kriegsministers Grafen von Roon* (4th ed., Breslau, 1897), vol. 2, 442; Erich Brandenburg, ed., *Briefe Kaiser Wilhelms des Ersten* (Leipzig, 1911), vol. 1, 244, 246; Friedrich III, *Kriegstagebuch*, 115–116.

[44] GW, VIb, 443, 454–455, 492–494, 500–502.

to lay down its arms until they were "again German" and the Rhine was "Germany's river, not Germany's frontier." After the victories of August 4, 5, and 18 the trickle became a flood that swept the entire press.[45] The private correspondence of the leaders of German liberal nationalism—Eduard Lasker, Heinrich von Sybel, Hermann Baumgarten, and others—shows the same swift progress of opinion. By August 20 they had agreed upon a program of agitation. Only among the progressives, according to Forckenbeck, were there any doubts about the wisdom of annexing a hostile population on the basis of its German past.[46]

The public pressure, before which Bismarck professed to tremble, was in part his own creation. On August 25 he telegraphed to Berlin: "Since the position of England and Russia on the dismemberment of France has been discussed in the *Indépendence Belge* and the *Journal de St. Petersbourg*, all papers accessible to us—namely, all German ones—are to express the national indignation over the intervention of neutral powers inimical to us and the firm will of the German people to secure the south German frontier through annexations from France and to make easier the defense of our borders against a repetition of predatory attacks like those that have occurred in the last two centuries."[47]

During the following days there was a perceptible increase in chauvinistic agitation throughout Germany. At a Berlin rally on August 30, with the lord mayor presiding, prominent liberals of both the Progressive and National Liberal parties drafted a resolution in favor of annexation; similar meetings followed in other major cities, north and south.[48] From military headquarters in France, Bismarck added more fuel to the flames. At his direction Moritz Busch, a press secretary, wrote an article on annexation for the official *Provinzial-Korrespondenz*, which was quickly seconded by other prominent jour-

---

[45] Georg Hirth and Julius von Gosen, *Tagebuch des deutsch-französischen Krieges, 1870–1871: Eine Sammlung der wichtigeren Quellen* (Berlin, 1871), vol. 1, 93, 399–400; E. Malcolm Carroll, *Germany and the Great Powers, 1866–1914* (New York, 1938), 75; Karl Jacob, *Bismarck und die Erwerbung Elsass-Lothringens 1870–1871* (Strassburg, 1905), 8; Gustav Körner, *Die norddeutsche Publizistik und die Annexionsfrage im Jahre 1870* (Hanover, 1907), 17ff., 38ff. See also the debate between Walter Lipgens, Lothar Gall, and Eberhard Kolb about whether a significant, spontaneous public demand for the "return" of Alsace and Lorraine existed before Bismarck launched his press campaign in favor of it. *Historische Zeitschrift*: 199 (1964), 31–112; 206 (1968), 265–326, 586–617; and 209 (1969), 318–356. Gall and Kolb took the affirmative and were reinforced by Josef Becker, "Baden, Bismarck und die Annexion von Elsass und Lothringen," *Zeitschrift für die Geschichte des Oberrheins*, 115 (1967), 167–204. The accumulated evidence for their position seems conclusive.

[46] HW, I, 475ff.; Johannes Schultze, ed., *Max Duncker: Politischer Briefwechsel aus seinem Nachlass* (Stuttgart, 1923), 589; Ludwig Bamberger, *Gesammelte Schriften* (Berlin, 1894–1897), vol. 2, 123ff.; Körner, *Publizistik und Annexionsfrage*, 9.

[47] GW, VIb, 460; see also 454–455.

[48] Körner, *Publizistik und Annexionsfrage*, 21ff.; Jacob, *Bismarck und Elsass-Lothringen*, 31; Hirth and Gosen, *Tagebuch*, vol. 2, 1619–1623, 1633.

nals. The *Preussische Jahrbücher* provided the climax with a stirring essay by Treitschke: "What do we demand from France?"[49]

By no means was the German case for annexation limited to strategic necessity. Those who participated in the decision were hardly free from the influence of that "professorial idea" that excited Bismarck's contempt. Long ago during the crisis of 1840 Moltke had published an essay proving that Alsace and Lorraine belonged to Germany on grounds of nationality and historical right. "These fine provinces were severed like a sound limb from the living body of Germany." Thirty years later he still regarded the quarrel with France from the national standpoint. Nor was King Wilhelm free of this conception. To Queen Augusta he wrote that for strategic reasons that area must be annexed "that was and is German."[50] Busch's article shows the same mixture of motives. His emphasis was upon military security, and yet he did not neglect the moral and historical arguments. "Besides, it must not be forgotten that this territory that we now demand was originally German and in great part still remains German, and that its inhabitants will perhaps in time learn to feel that they belong to one race with ourselves." Bismarck too defended the annexation as a "return of German soil," of "her old Reichsland," and once he wrote of the "genuine German nationality" of Alsace. In delimiting the frontier, he wished to follow as closely as possible the linguistic boundary, assuming that the German-speaking population would be easier to assimilate. Later he deplored that "the entire pro-French population" had not been deported from the annexed provinces.[51]

In the public mind the national motive was apparently as important as military security. At any rate both motives were stressed about equally in the flood of newspaper editorials and pamphlets over the issue, which, if they did not reflect public opinion, certainly helped to form it. In the past little attention had been given to Alsace-Lorraine as German irredenta, except in the crisis years of 1814–1815, 1840, and 1859. But now the great historical wrong was rediscovered that it might be righted, the German character of the inhabitants reaffirmed that they might be rescued from the contamination of French decadence. Treitschke's inflammatory article, reprinted as a pamphlet, stressed the rights of security and conquest, but his most powerful appeal was that of nationality: "Those lands are ours by the right of the sword and we

---

[49] Hirth and Gosen, *Tagebuch*, vol. 2, 1648–1651; Busch, *Secret Pages*, vol. 1, 91–93; Körner, *Publizistik und Annexionsfrage*, 33–34; *Preussische Jahrbücher*, 26 (1870), 367–409; HW, I, 476–478.

[50] Helmuth von Moltke, *Gesammelte Schriften und Denkwürdigkeiten* (Berlin, 1892–1893), vol. 2, 175–228; Stadelmann, *Moltke und der Staat*, 182ff.; Brandenburg, ed., *Briefe Kaiser Wilhelms*, 244.

[51] Busch, *Secret Pages*, vol. 1, 93; GW, VIb, 453–454, 498; VII, 339; XIV, 816; Oncken, ed., *Grossherzog Friedrich I.*, vol. 2, 392–393; H. E. Brockhaus, *Stunden mit Bismarck, 1871–1878* (Leipzig, 1929), 80–81.

wish to have disposal over them by virtue of a higher right, the right of the German nation, which cannot permit its lost sons to alienate themselves forever from the German Reich. We Germans, since we know Germany and France, understand better what is good for the Alsacians than those unfortunate people themselves. . . . Against their own will we wish to give them back their true selves. . . . The spirit of a people embraces not merely this generation, but also past generations. We invoke the will of those who were once there against the will of those who now live there."[52]

In diplomatic dispatches Bismarck was compelled to deny this viewpoint. He suspected attempts to arouse the anxiety of the Russians over future German demands for the Baltic provinces. On September 16 he telegraphed that such an idea was "laughable"; the case for Alsace and Lorraine was based on military security, rather than the return of an ancient possession. In Vienna and Budapest he repeatedly denied as "absurd" any ambition to dismember the Habsburg Empire through the annexation of "so-called" German Austria.[53] But Treitschke also disclaimed the need to recover "every clod of German soil" in Austria, Switzerland, and the Netherlands. What could not be tolerated was the "destruction of German nationality (Volkstum)" by French cultural imperialism.[54] Although Bismarck disdained this viewpoint, his propaganda made use of it. What mattered to him at the moment was the greatest possible agitation of German opinion, whatever the justification.

The pressure for annexation within Germany was helpful in warding off intervention by the neutral powers. In Petersburg he maintained that a German government that failed to acquire the provinces would fall prey to revolution and republicanism. Annexation, he advised London, was the firm and unanimous will of the German people. When Lord Granville advised moderation, he savagely replied that for the sake of a defensible frontier Germany would not shrink from a battle of extermination at Paris, from ten years of warfare, from the "most daring invocation of the national strength of Germany against neutral intervention," or from agreement with any French government.[55]

The demand for annexation lengthened the war. No other issue proved to be such a stumbling block. Because of it Louis and Eugénie were extremely reluctant to enter into serious negotiations and for months an armistice could not be achieved with the Government of National Defense. At Ferrières on September 20–21 Bismarck conferred with Jules Favre, and at Versailles on November 1–2 with Adolphe Thiers. Although both desired a cease-fire during which to elect a new government, the threat of annexations compelled

[52] Preussische Jahrbücher, 26 (1870), 371. See also Andreas Dorpalen, Heinrich von Treitschke (New Haven, 1957), 164ff.
[53] GW, VIb, 416–417, 422–423, 499.
[54] Preussische Jahrbücher, 26 (1870), 371–372.
[55] GW, VIb, 454–459, 501, 503–504.

them to demand terms that would have permitted a resumption of the fighting. Naturally this was unacceptable to Bismarck. Not until the fall of Paris on January 28, 1871, did the French face the bleak fact that the war was lost and with it Alsace-Lorraine.

When Thiers, chosen "chief of the executive power" by the new parliament at Bordeaux, reappeared at Versailles on February 21, the only questions remaining were the delimitation of the new frontier and the amount of the French indemnity. Bismarck believed that Lorraine, because of its French-speaking inhabitants, was politically undesirable. But back home its acquisition, as Grand Duke Friedrich of Baden observed, had assumed "the character of a national demand." More importantly, Wilhelm and his generals insisted that Metz was militarily indispensable. The officers at Versailles were in a savage mood. They talked of "destroying the enemy, laying waste the country, exhausting all sources of wealth and income."[56] To satisfy the military, Bismarck insisted on Metz, and Thiers had to capitulate. The chancellor consoled him by conceding Belfort and a reduction of the French indemnity from 6 to 5 billion francs.

Since August the warning had been frequently heard that loss of the two provinces would permanently embitter France toward Germany. But Bismarck was unimpressed. The bitterness, he argued, would be just as great even without annexations. France would never forget her humiliation. "An enemy, whose honest friendship can never be won, must at least be rendered somewhat less harmful. Under the circumstances this is the only correct policy."[57] There could scarcely be any better evidence of the national character of the war of 1870 than Bismarck's own admission that it would inaugurate an era of enduring antagonism between France and Germany.

[56] GW, XIV, 816; VIb, 475; Oncken, ed., Grossherzog Friedrich I., vol. 2, 366–367, 387ff.; Johannes Haller, Bismarcks Friedensschlüsse (Munich, 1916), 82–83.

[57] GW, VIb, 454–455, 457–458, 476–478.

❖❖

CHAPTER TWENTY TWO

Winning the South

Negotiating the Treaties

HE LASTING hostility of France was the unavoidable by-product of a war whose necessity arose from the incohesion of the German nation. Bismarck's major war aim was not the conquest of French soil, but the voluntary acceptance by the south of the north German constitution without essential change. The true significance of the Ems dispatch was that, coupled with the war fever in Paris, it converted what would otherwise have been a mere dynastic into a national issue. There was good reason to doubt that the German population could have been aroused to anger and action by the collapse of the Hohenzollern candidacy to the Spanish throne. But a seemingly gratuitous French insult to Germany's leading dynasty was another matter. Through a national crusade against France Bismarck expected to produce a flood of German sentiment that would overflow the barriers of southern particularism. In Germany and Europe he propagated the view that the struggle against France was "a great national war," "a moral and national revolt against foreign attack and arrogance," whose only logical outcome would be the consolidation of "Germany's unity and power" under the northern system.[1]

At the onset of war the vital question was whether the south would recognize the casus foederis. Of Baden's complete loyalty there was never any doubt. Without summoning parliament, the government in Karlsruhe ordered mobilization and destroyed the bridges over the Rhine. Even the most fanatical anti-Prussians in Baden preferred to fight rather than suffer French occupation. In Darmstadt, on the other hand, Dalwigk and Grand Duke Ludwig tried desperately to evade the commitment to Berlin. In recent months the minister had repeatedly sought French and Austrian aid against Prussia's encroachments. Even now he hoped for the appearance of their troops in Germany. Twist and turn as he might, there was no recourse other than fulfillment of the alliance. Despondently he wrote, "We are completely in the talons of the eagle."[2]

---

[1] GW, XIV, 795, 799, 801; VIb, 394–397.

[2] George G. Windell, *The Catholics and German Unity, 1866–1871* (Minneapolis, 1954), 249; Otto Becker, *Bismarcks Ringen um Deutschlands Gestaltung* (Heidelberg, 1958), 691ff.; Ernst Vogt, *Die hessische Politik in der Zeit der Reichsgründung (1863–1871): Historisches Bibliothek*, vol. 34 (Munich, 1914), 188ff.; Walter Vogel, *Die Tagebücher des Freiherrn Reinhard von Dalwigk zu Lichtenfels als Geschichtsquelle: Historische Studien*, vol. 234 (Berlin, 1933), 46ff., 72ff.

When news arrived of the French demands, Württemberg was shaken by a patriotic tremor that abruptly ended agitation by the People's party against the Prussian military system. The sudden surge of popular anger and fear that swept the cities and towns overcame the lingering doubts of the extreme democrats, rural Catholics, and great-Germanists. On July 13, 1870, Varnbüler informed Berlin that Gramont's impudence had "deeply wounded" German national feeling in Württemberg. Four days later, the king ordered mobilization and on July 22 the Landtag voted, with a single dissent, the necessary war credits. But many cast their ballots with heavy hearts. Thirty-nine deputies signed a declaration lamenting that 1866 had made it impossible for "all Germany" to stand against the foe.[3]

Again the major concern was Bavaria. On July 14 Bismarck forced the issue by inquiring of Foreign Minister Count von Bray-Steinburg how Bavaria would act in the event of a French attack. At a cabinet meeting on that same day, the ministers voted for neutrality with but one exception—Baron Sigmund von Pranckh, the minister of war (joined at the end by the minister of commerce). In an audience on the following day King Ludwig sided with Pranckh, who, despite Bavarian-particularistic sympathies, believed that Bavaria had no choice but to join in the war. "We have to cooperate if we wish to remain German Bavaria; however things go, we can never get loose from the other German states." To become a "French Bavaria" or to try to "hang loose in the area" was to invite the ultimate loss of Bavarian sovereignty. "Recent experiences" (obviously, the fate of Hanover) had demonstrated the consequences of such a course. In parliament the sudden crisis interrupted the assault of the patriots and left-progressives upon the "Prussianization" of the Bavarian army. The majority decided to adjourn and await developments. On hearing of the royal order for mobilization, they reconvened to hear a parliamentary committee recommend armed neutrality and a reduction of 80 percent in the government's request for war credits. As war fever mounted in the cities, the particularists felt compelled to yield. In the end the deputies granted, 101 to 47, nearly 70 percent of the sum requested and left the issue of belligerency up to the cabinet. On July 20 Bavaria entered the conflict without a formal declaration of war.[4]

In August German soldiers, north and south, underwent a common bap-

---

[3] GW, VIb, 365; Adolf Rapp, *Die Württemberger und die nationale Frage, 1863–1871: Darstellungen aus der württembergischen Geschichte*, vol. 4 (Stuttgart, 1910), 363–385; Freiherr von Mittnacht, *Rückblicke* (Stuttgart, 1909), 51ff.

[4] Wolf D. Gruner, "Bayern, Preussen und die Süddeutschen Staaten, 1866–1870," *Zeitschrift für bayerische Landesgeschichte*, 37 (1974), 821–825. The official documents recording the cabinet proceedings were destroyed, apparently in 1918 as the Bavarian monarchy neared its end. *Ibid.*, 822. See also M. Doeberl, *Bayern und die Bismarckische Reichsgründung* (Munich, 1925), 30ff.; Windell, *Catholics and German Unity*, 249ff.; Theodor Schieder, *Die kleindeutsche Partei in Bayern: Münchener historische Abhandlungen*, vol. 12 (Munich, 1936), 251ff.

tism of fire on the fields of France. At home every village and town joined in the general jubilation over their triumphs. As Bismarck anticipated, war with France produced an upsurge of German national feeling that helped to fill the chasm of time. In sharing the same dangers, experiences, and hatreds the Germans established a psychological bond, which, if it did not extinguish, at least diminished, the significance of the tribal (*Stamm*) sentiments, dynastic loyalties, traditions of statehood, sectional customs and mores that had previously divided them.

From Karlsruhe came the first overture. On September 2, 1870, Minister-President Jolly forwarded to Bismarck a memorandum proposing the founding of a "German Reich." On the same day Varnbüler was replaced in Stuttgart by Baron Hermann von Mittnacht, former minister of justice. Although in agreement with Varnbüler's policies in recent years, Mittnacht grasped that a turning point had been reached. Over dwindling opposition he launched a national policy in collaboration with Suckow. At Meaux on September 17, Bismarck informed Suckow, as he had Jolly by dispatch on the twelfth, that the southern governments must take the initiative. Berlin would avoid every appearance of pressure, which could only arouse mistrust and antagonism. He was still in the dark, he declared, concerning the views of King Ludwig II of Bavaria.[5]

Both Bray and Ludwig were suspicious of Bismarck's intent to use the war as a lever against southern sovereignty. Somehow the Bavarians had to be induced to volunteer what could not be openly demanded. In August Bismarck hinted through Thile at the possibility of territorial rewards in Alsace and Lorraine. Ultimately he decided that the two provinces should become the common property of Germany, to be called the "Reichsland." But even this solution was intended to precipitate a discussion of Germany's future. On September 1, 1870, Delbrück, Bismarck's trusted aide, was dispatched to Dresden to discuss the matter and urge the Saxons to take the initiative in Munich.[6] Perhaps by this back door a way could be found into the Wittelsbach castle.

On the Isar the mighty victory at Sedan, and the outpouring of German patriotism that it produced, convinced Ludwig and his ministers that the status quo in Germany could not be preserved. The problem was no longer

[5] GW, VIb, 488–489; Hermann Baumgarten, *Staatsminister Jolly* (Tübingen, 1897), 175–176; Hermann Oncken, ed., *Grossherzog Friedrich I. von Baden und die deutsche Politik von 1854–1871* (Stuttgart, 1927), vol. 2, 128ff.; Wilhelm Busch, ed., *Rückschau von Albert von Suckow* (Tübingen, 1909), 167–168; Mittnacht, *Rückblicke*, 64ff. On Mittnacht see Walter Seefried, *Mittnacht und die deutsche Frage bis zur Reichsgründung: Darstellungen aus der württembergischen Geschichte*, vol. 18 (Stuttgart, 1928), 84ff.

[6] Erich Brandenburg, ed., *Briefe und Aktenstücke zur Geschichte der Gründung des deutschen Reiches, 1870–1871* (Leipzig, 1911), vol. 1, 3ff.; Doeberl, *Bayern und Reichsgründung*, 43ff.; Rudolf von Delbrück, *Lebenserinnerungen, 1817–1867* (Berlin, 1905), vol. 2, 409ff.

whether Bavaria would remain out of a German union, but under what conditions she would enter it. What they most desired was to dissolve the North German Confederation and replace it with a "German confederation" of looser structure.[7] This, of course, Bismarck had no intention of conceding. Although conscious of the necessity of concessions, he was fully resolved to preserve the basic structure of the northern constitution. Alterations might be made in the facade and trim, even new windows and doorways added, but the beams and joists that determined the shape and style must remain untouched.

At Bray's request Delbrück took the train for Munich and a series of conferences (September 22–26, 1870) in which the two southern kingdoms made known their views on Germany's future constitution. By evading the issue of dissolution, the Prussian succeeded in making the northern constitution the basis of discussion. But the demands of Bray and Mittnacht for "special" and "reserved" rights in such matters as foreign policy, military affairs, and the veto power were so far-reaching that the cohesion of the proposed Reich was gravely threatened. Delbrück came away, however, feeling that much had been accomplished. Yet it was ominous that in their final audience Ludwig avoided every allusion to the German question and spoke only of Papal affairs. In view of Bismarck's flat opposition to dissolution, Bray had in fact determined upon a final attempt to form with Württemberg a "wider confederation" whose link with the north was to be diplomatic rather than constitutional.[8]

From afar Bismarck strove to influence the deliberations in Munich with his usual mixture of threat, enticement, and blandishment. In early September he let Count Tauffkirchen, now a prominent official of the military government in France, have a quick glimpse at his armory of alternatives. Should Bavaria's demands be too extreme, the German question would simply be regulated without her, the Zollverein treaties might be permitted to lapse, and the Bavarian Palatinate would be included in the North German Confederation. While the conference was in session, however, he hinted at the possibility of generous concessions to bring Bavaria "over the Rubicon." The object was not to produce in six weeks a constitution for all time, but to build the foundation of a structure that might be completed in ten, twenty, or fifty years. Above all, Wilhelm was eager to come to terms with Ludwig, from whose hands he hoped to receive the imperial title.[9]

---

[7] Otto von Bray-Steinburg, *Denkwürdigkeiten aus seinem Leben* (Leipzig, 1901), 136ff.; Doeberl, *Bayern und Reichsgründung*, 69ff., 85ff.; Brandenburg, ed., *Briefe und Aktenstücke*, vol. 1, 29–32.

[8] Becker, *Bismarcks Ringen*, 715–716; Doeberl, *Bayern und Reichsgründung*, 91ff., 256ff.; Delbrück, *Lebenserinnerungen*, vol. 2, 413ff.; Wilhelm Stolze, "Zur Geschichte der Reichsgründung im Jahre 1870," *Preussische Jahrbücher*, 197 (1924), 1–12.

[9] Karl A. von Müller, "Bismarck und Ludwig II. im September 1870," *Historische Zeitschrift*,

On reading Delbrück's report of the Munich negotiations, Bismarck recognized immediately that much less had been achieved than his emissary assumed. Immediately he set in motion the system of pressures by which he hoped to pierce the barrier of southern particularism. On September 30 he dispatched to Karlsruhe the message for which the Badenese had waited so long and impatiently. A formal request for entry into the North German Confederation was "welcome at the moment both as a basis for negotiations with Bavaria and as a means of pressure on the same." The grand ducal government responded quickly, and the cabinet in Stuttgart followed suit. In mid-October 1870 delegations headed by Jolly and Mittnacht arrived in Versailles to negotiate the necessary treaties. Faced by the prospect of isolation, the Bavarians were compelled to treat.[10] On October 20 Bray and his delegation likewise took the train for France; four days later came the representatives of Hesse. The cast was complete and on stage; the final act in the long drama of German unification could begin.

Luckily for Bismarck, the southern delegations were unable to present a common front at Versailles. Their different goals and mutual frictions enabled him to negotiate separately with each and avoid having to grant the same concessions to all. Baden was willing, and Hesse compelled, to accept the northern constitution almost without reservation. The demands raised by Württemberg were not insuperable, and the negotiation with Mittnacht and Suckow proceeded smoothly. But the Bavarians were difficult. Bray and his associates had not surrendered their desire for a "wider confederation." Although willing to accept "Reich and Kaiser," they presented a long list of requirements that jeopardized the sovereignty of the national government. As at Munich they demanded (among other rights) an equal voice in foreign policy, a separate army (except in war), an independent military budget, the right of veto against constitutional changes, and surrender of the right to terminate the Zollverein.[11]

Bismarck pulled every wire in the effort to bring the Wittelsbach puppet into motion. He proposed a congress of princes to be held in Versailles, but King Ludwig could not be enticed from his Alpine retreat. He thought of mobilizing German opinion by summoning the North German Reichstag to convene in Versailles, but even the national liberals found the idea of a parliamentary session in the hall of mirrors too "baroque." Once again he refused to relinquish Berlin's right to terminate the Zollverein. To show the Bavarians their isolation, he accelerated negotiations with the other three states. In Germany his propaganda service worked full blast to build up public pressure

III (1913), 89–132, and "Aktenstücke aus den Papieren des Grafen Karl v. Tauffkirchen," *Forschungen zur brandenburgischen und preussischen Geschichte*, 27 (1914), 572–592; GW, VIb, 516.

[10] GW, VIb, 527–529, 538–540; Baumgarten, *Jolly*, 177ff.; Doeberl, *Bayern und Reichsgründung*, 103ff.

[11] Doeberl, *Bayern und Reichsgründung*, 109ff.; Becker, *Bismarcks Ringen*, 729.

for national unity. By November 8 these measures had their effect. Bray and his associates realized that they dare not return home empty-handed. They determined to surrender the "wider confederation" and seek the best possible terms for Bavarian entry into a federal union. For a few days it appeared as though the separate negotiations might be brought to simultaneous conclusion. Bismarck looked forward to a dramatic ceremony in which the representatives of north and south would sign the treaties and demonstrate to Germany and Europe their unanimity of purpose.[12]

On November 12 his hopes were rudely shattered. At the final conference with the Württemberger, after the last issue had been settled, Mittnacht unexpectedly declared that he had no power to sign. To Bismarck's consternation the delegation returned home for consultation. In Stuttgart King Karl had at the last minute resolved to make no greater concessions than Bavaria in joining the north. Concerned and wrathful, Bismarck saw that the time had come to unleash the forces of popular agitation against the two southern kingdoms. "Unless a German storm intervenes," he wrote, "nothing will be accomplished with these diplomats and bureaucrats of the old school, at least not this year." To Grand Duke Friedrich he announced his intention to mobilize a "pressure from below." "These governments appear to overlook entirely the dangerous elements that surround them." It was not his fault if a movement should now develop that jeopardized their very existence. To Berlin, Koblenz, Hanover, and Munich went instructions to incite the national liberal press against southern particularism.[13]

In Versailles the negotiations with Baden and Hesse were pressed to conclusion and signed on November 15. As usual Bismarck extracted advantage from calamity. No longer did he have to consider Stuttgart in negotiating with Munich. The concessions made to the latter need not be limited to those granted the former. On November 18 the conferences with Bray and his associates were resumed. Roon's illness compelled Bismarck to handle both the military and political negotiations. In hour-long talks the critical points were hammered out. On November 23 the treaty was signed. Meanwhile, Mittnacht and Suckow had succeeded in convincing King Karl of the futility of his position. Even during the final negotiations with Delbrück in Berlin, however, they had to struggle against the particularistic current in Stuttgart. On November 25 the treaty was finally signed.[14]

[12] GW, VIb, 583–584; Doeberl, *Bayern und Reichsgründung*, 113ff.; Becker, *Bismarcks Ringen*, 727ff.

[13] Busch, ed., *Suckow: Rückschau*, 176ff.; Mittnacht, *Rückblicke*, 136–138; Eugen Schneider, "Württembergs Beitritt zum Deutschen Reich 1870," *Württembergische Vierteljahrshefte für Landesgeschichte*, 29 (1920), 138ff.; GW, VIb, 586–587; Hermann Oncken, *Rudolf von Bennigsen* (Stuttgart, 1910), vol. 2, 196ff., and Oncken, ed., *Grossherzog Friedrich I*. vol. 2, 169–172.

[14] Doeberl, *Bayern und Reichsgründung*, 125ff.; Mittnacht, *Rückblicke*, 139ff.; Becker, *Bismarcks Ringen*, 739ff.

Concessions to Particularism

Since 1866 Bismarck had insisted that the south must be won, not conquered. The system of checks and balances in the constitutional system he had designed for Germany depended upon the voluntary cooperation of the remaining German dynasties and governments. By using force, he would have weakened them and upset the balance in favor of the Reichstag and centralism. He was aware, moreover, that the expansion of the north German system over so many millions of people could be successful only if most approved. Coercion was not enough. To endure as the government of Germany, the Prussian system had to be based upon a moral consensus.

At least one important person in the Prussian camp disagreed. During October and November 1870, the crown prince was filled with apprehension and mistrust by the difficulties of the negotiations with Bavaria and Württemberg. Bismarck's moderation made him question the chancellor's German patriotism and his will to national unity. There seemed to be no awareness, he repeatedly complained, of Prussia's power to coerce. "We have them after all in our grasp." Bismarck replied that such tactics would reap a harvest of hate and suspicion that would last for generations. He was confident that in the future the course of organic development would render unimportant whatever concessions were necessary to win the voluntary adhesion of the south.[15]

The list of concessions made in the treaties of November 1870 was long.[16] They fall into two categories: those that heightened the power of the state governments in general, and those "special" and "reserved" rights that benefited only Baden, Bavaria, and Württemberg. The federated states in general gained from the expanded authority of the Bundesrat. The approval of that body was now necessary for declarations of war, except in cases of foreign attack. Furthermore, the commander-in-chief must seek approval of the Bundesrat for an "execution" against a recalcitrant state. The supervisory power of the Kaiser was limited by the necessity of seeking Bundesrat approval before ordering the correction of deficiencies in the administration of imperial laws. The authority of the Kaiser to issue decrees for the execution of imperial laws was likewise made dependent upon Bundesrat approval, unless the law itself provided otherwise. The old rule that a two-thirds vote in the Bundesrat was necessary to pass a constitutional amendment was changed; henceforth, a negative vote of fourteen could block such an amendment. This placed the veto within reach of the combined votes of Bavaria, Saxony, and Württemberg, or of Bavaria, Württemberg, Baden, and Hesse, or of a combination of

---

[15] Becker, *Bismarcks Ringen*, 747–749; Heinrich O. Meisner, ed., *Kaiser Friedrich III.: Das Kriegstagebuch von 1870/71* (Berlin, 1926), 200, 223–225.

[16] For the final version of the German constitution see *Reichs-Gesetzblatt* (1871), 63–85; also Karl Binding, ed., *Deutsche Staatsgrundgesetze in diplomatisch genauem Abdrucke* (2d ed., Leipzig, 1901), vol. 1, 2ff.

the small states. The principle of *itio in partes* was adopted by the provision that in matters not common to the whole of the Reich, only the votes of the affected states would be counted in Bundesrat and Reichstag. Likewise, "reserved" and "special rights" of member states might be altered only with their approval.

The "special rights" granted to Bavaria were fresh evidence of Bismarck's gift for giving the appearance of concessions without the substance. Should a Prussian delegate be unable to preside over the Bundesrat, a Bavarian delegate might substitute for him. Bavaria was to possess a permanent seat on the Bundesrat committee for military affairs and the chairmanship of a new committee on foreign affairs, in which Saxony and Württemberg were likewise to have permanent seats. Although member states surrendered their consular services abroad, they might receive foreign consuls on their own soil. Should an envoy of the Reich be incapacitated, the Bavarian envoy could be authorized to substitute for him. In a special protocol, which remained secret until 1917, Bavaria was granted the right to be represented at peace negotiations.

Time was to show that these rights were purely decorative. They left to the states merely the symbols of sovereignty. As Mittnacht observed, the committee on foreign affairs was "stillborn"; neither Bismarck nor his successors permitted it any important role in the conduct of foreign affairs. The right to maintain a diplomatic corps was empty, since the Reich's envoys were the actual agents of its foreign policy. The right of substitution was seldom used, and the Bavarian delegate to the peace conference at Brest-Litovsk in 1917 was a mere observer. The foreign services of the lesser states withered on the uprooted vine.[17]

The "reserved rights" were of greater importance. Bavaria was given autonomy in matters of domicile and residence within her borders. She could regulate and maintain her own railway system, subject to Reich laws in matters of national defense. Bavaria and Württemberg retained their independent postal and telegraph systems, subject to regulation by the Reich in only a few respects. With Baden they might levy taxes on domestic beer and spirits, although they should "endeavor" to enact uniform legislation. They were to receive no part of the Reich's revenue from such sources.

The military conventions with Württemberg and Bavaria[18] contained a number of reserved rights even more extensive than those granted Saxony in 1867. Whereas the commander of the Saxon contingent was appointed by the commander-in-chief on the nomination of the Saxon king, that of Würt-

---

[17] Heinrich Triepel, *Unitarismus und Föderalismus im Deutschen Reiche* (Tübingen, 1907), 46; Freiherr von Mittnacht, *Erinnerungen an Bismarck* (Stuttgart, 1904), vol. 1, 3off.; Ernst Deuerlein, *Der Bundesratsausschuss für die Auswärtigen Angelegenheiten 1870–1918* (Regensburg, 1955).

[18] Although the agreements on military affairs were generally called "military conventions," only that with Württemberg was specifically designated as such. For the texts see *Bundes-Gesetzblatt des Norddeutschen Bundes* (1870), 658–662 and *Reichs-Gesetzblatt* (1871), 9–26.

temberg was appointed by the Swabian king with the approval of the commander-in-chief. Whereas all general officers in the Saxon army had to be approved by the latter, this was not true in Württemberg. The king of Württemberg retained the right to determine uniforms and insignia. Although his troops were subject to the authority of the commander-in-chief, to whom they swore allegiance, the king kept the ceremonial rights and privileges of a commanding general. To Württemberg it was also guaranteed that during peacetime the organization of the contingent would be undisturbed; none of its troops would be stationed outside Württemberg; and no other German troops would be stationed in the state without the king's approval (except for border garrisons). Unexpended surpluses of the military budget need not be returned to the Reich treasury at the end of the fiscal year.

Even greater concessions were granted Bavaria. Its "army" was to be "a self-contained unit of the German army with an independent administration and under the command of his majesty, the king of Bavaria." In other words, the Kaiser assumed command of the Bavarian army only on the inception of war. The Wittelsbach king retained, furthermore, the power to appoint all officers and the commanders of all fortresses located in Bavaria. Although obligated to follow the standards of the Reich in such matters as organization, formation, training, and mobilization, the king could adopt Reich standards in equipment, armament, and rank insignia at his own discretion. Though the Kaiser was given the power of inspection, it was hedged by numerous restrictions. Bavaria retained a separate military budget, established by its own government, but according to standards set in the Reich constitution. It was not the Reich chancellor's responsibility to see that actual expenditures conformed to this budget, and the accounting was a purely Bavarian concern. Unexpended surpluses of the Bavarian military budget were to stay in the Bavarian treasury.

Although the sacrifice was great, Bismarck had achieved his basic objective. The governmental system that he had devised for northern Germany had been accepted by the southern governments without fundamental change. There were even some gains for its centralistic side. On the proposal of Bavaria and Württemberg the legislative competence of the Reich was enlarged to include the publishing industry and the right of association (*Vereinswesen*). Twenty-four basic laws of the North German Confederation were accepted by the south along with the constitution. Psychologically speaking, however, the greatest gain was adoption of the title "German Kaiser."

Kaiser and Reich

To Bismarck the imperial title was a political necessity. The historical image that it aroused in German minds, he believed, would encourage "unity and centralization." German princes would accept in good grace from a German

Kaiser what they would resent from a king of Prussia. Only the German title conveyed the idea that the rights associated with it had been "freely granted." National institutions must not appear to be mere extensions of the Prussian state.[19]

Wilhelm disliked the idea for the very virtues that Bismarck saw in it. He was not free from the ambition to lord it over his fellow princes. And yet dynastic pride made it difficult for him to accept a crown whose authority had once oppressed the Great Elector and against which Frederick the Great had fought. "What do I want with that?" he asked contemptuously. "Certainly," Bismarck replied, "your majesty does not want to remain forever a neuter— *das Präsidium?*" But the thought of resurrecting "Kaiser and Reich" sent the imagination of the crown prince soaring. Friedrich Wilhelm busied himself with designs for crowns and coats of arms and dreamed of a "free German empire," which would lead civilization by realizing "all noble ideas of the modern world," by "humanizing" mankind and saving it from French frivolity. The German nation would be freed from bureaucratism, despotism, Jesuitry, orthodoxy, and socialism. "The crown prince," sneered Bismarck, "is the dumbest and vainest of men; he's crazed again by the Kaiser madness."[20]

The key to the situation, he realized, was again Bavaria. A Hohenzoller could hardly reject a crown offered by a Wittelsbach. But the strange man in the lonely Alpine castle of Hohenschwangau was likewise proud of his dynasty, which had borne the imperial title when the Hohenzollern were petty Swabian princes. In negotiations with Tauffkirchen in September 1870 and later with Bray, Bismarck indicated that "Kaiser and Reich" were the price demanded for vital concessions to Bavarian particularism. Only these exciting symbols of past and future glory would make possible a general acceptance of the Bavarian treaty. Should Bavaria delay, the Reichstag might repeat the offer of April 1849. In the interest of monarchism, the matter could not be left to popular initiative.[21]

For months Ludwig II had been vexed by the suggestion. Now his own ministers became its advocates. Grand Duke Friedrich of Baden likewise pressed. Although given to dream and fantasy, Ludwig was not without his practical side. He determined to sell what could apparently no longer be withheld. In addition to the special and reserved rights being negotiated in Ver-

[19] GW, VIb, 601–602.

[20] GW, XV, 324–325; Friedrich III, *Kriegstagebuch*, 103, 146–147, 180, 260, 265–266, 452; Ernst Feder, ed., *Bismarcks grosses Spiel: Die geheimen Tagebücher Ludwig Bambergers* (Frankfurt, 1932), 243. In his memoirs Bismarck claimed that before and after Sedan Friedrich Wilhelm desired the title "King of the Germans" and wished to reduce the kings of Saxony, Bavaria, and Württemberg to ducal status. But the crown prince's diary does not substantiate this. According to another source, he entertained this idea at Nikolsburg in 1866, but shifted to the imperial title at the beginning of the following year. Martin Philippson, *Friedrich III. als Kronprinz und Kaiser* (Berlin, 1893), 144.

[21] Doeberl, *Bayern und Reichsgründung*, 151ff.; Bray, *Denkwürdigkeiten*, 172.

CROWN PRINCE FRIEDRICH WILHELM, ABOUT 1875 (LANDESBILDSTELLE, BERLIN).

sailles, he demanded as "compensation" a segment of territory and 2 million gulden (approximately 4 million marks). Twice in November 1870 his equerry, Count Max von Holnstein, traveled to Versailles to discuss this delicate matter. Nothing came of the territorial demand, but the financial claim was successful. Until 1886 Ludwig apparently received a yearly income of about three hundred thousand marks from Bismarck's secret "Guelph fund"; Holnstein collected 10 percent. Not until many years later, after Ludwig's tragic suicide and Bismarck's retirement, was anything publicly known of this transaction. The exact details will probably never be learned, for no records were kept. To himself Ludwig apparently represented these payments as partial repayment of the war indemnity paid by Bavaria in 1866. But the sums went into his personal account, not the public treasury. German historians have called it a "dotation"; but to outsiders it has more the appearance of a bribe.[22]

Bismarck himself was the author of the famous "Kaiser letter" in which Ludwig bid Wilhelm "reestablish a German Reich and the German imperial dignity." On November 27 Holnstein carried the draft to Hohenschwangau and on December 2 he was back with a copy in Ludwig's own hand. When Prince Luitpold of Bavaria formally presented it on the following day, Wil-

[22] Becker, *Bismarcks Ringen*, 790ff.; Oncken, ed., *Grossherzog Friedrich I.*, vol. 2, 141ff., 207; Wilhelm Schüssler, "Das Geheimnis des Kaiserbriefes Ludwigs II.," in Martin Göhring and Alexander Scharff, eds., *Geschichtliche Kräfte und Entscheidungen: Festschrift für Otto Becker* (Wiesbaden, 1954), 206–209.

helm was deeply annoyed. Once again he had been presented with a fait accompli. Only with the greatest reluctance did he consent to bear the "cross" that Bismarck had hewn for him. Immediately the chancellor telegraphed the text of the letter to Delbrück for use against the parliamentary opposition.[23]

On November 25 the Reichstag had convened in Berlin to consider the treaties with the south and the revised constitution. Led by Schulze-Delitzsch, the progressives objected to the whole procedure. They demanded an all-German parliament to draft a new constitution that would make good what had been surrendered in 1867. When this was refused, they introduced amendments to guarantee fundamental civil rights and the remuneration of deputies. Again they failed. But the national liberals were also disgruntled. Like Lasker, many found the concessions to Bavarian particularism "shocking" and "dangerous"; the cohesion of the Reich appeared in jeopardy. August Bebel of the tiny but noisy socialist faction irritated everyone by advocating a republic.[24]

Bismarck had anticipated these complaints. During the negotiations with Bray and Mittnacht he had invited leaders of the National Liberal, Free Conservative, and Conservative parties to Versailles for consultation. Unable to return to Berlin for the session, he dispatched Delbrück to represent the government and mobilized as many emissaries as possible to convince the deputies that the treaties were the best obtainable. Jolly, Freydorf, and Roggenbach made the trip from Baden. Ludwig Bamberger, Hessian publicist and national liberal, was sent well stocked with arguments. The crown prince wrote to Eduard Simson, the speaker of the chamber, in the interest of a favorable vote. When the situation looked critical, all deputies on duty with the armed forces were furloughed to Berlin.[25]

Boiling with wrath, Bismarck sent the deputies a potpourri of threats. Any essential change in the agreements, achieved with such great difficulty, would be equivalent to rejection. In that case there would be little prospect of union with the south in the immediate future. Ludwig was childless and in bad health; his brother and heir was "entirely in ultramontane hands." An outbreak of strife in Germany over such a vital issue would have "incalculable disadvantages for us in our relations with France and the neutrals." Bavarian nationalists would demonstrate; Beust would renew his attempts at intervention; Bismarck, moreover, would tender his resignation; the king would reject it and dissolve the Reichstag.[26]

Perhaps his most effective stroke, however, was the revelation that more

[23] Friedrich III, *Kriegstagebuch*, 253–254; Brandenburg, ed., *Briefe und Aktenstücke*, vol. 1, 112ff.

[24] *SBR* (2d extraordinary session, 1870), 71ff.

[25] Oncken, *Bennigsen*, vol. 2, 189–190; Friedrich III, *Kriegstagebuch*, 258, 468–470; GW, VIb, 607; VII, 431, 433; Oncken, ed., *Grossherzog Friedrich I*. vol. 2, 231, 233.

[26] GW, VIb, 598–601, 607–608, 611–614. Actually Bismarck expected that the expiration of the Zollverein treaties in 1878 would present another opportunity to make good a failure in 1870.

had been achieved than the national liberals themselves originally thought possible. During September Bennigsen, Forckenbeck, and Lasker had visited the southern capitals to confer with political leaders and help galvanize a popular movement for national unity. In Munich, Lasker, impressed by the strength of particularistic sentiment, left behind a memorandum on the constitutional question that conceded much of what the Bavarians wanted. Taking it along to Versailles, Bray produced it when Bismarck, following his usual technique, argued that the northern Reichstag would never yield to Bavarian demands. But again Bismarck converted a handicap on one front into advantage on another. He sent the embarrassing document off to Delbrück for use against the dissatisfied deputies.[27]

Much was also expected of the announcement that the Wittelsbach king had offered Wilhelm the imperial title. But the weapon nearly failed because of Delbrück's ineptitude as a parliamentary régisseur. In response to a staged inquiry during the debate on December 5, he rummaged through his briefcase and produced the letter, reading it in his usual dry manner without oratorical effect. This casual, seemingly accidental, communication of so important a document incited his hearers to amusement rather than enthusiasm. It was, lamented Friedrich Wilhelm, as though he had pulled the "poor German Kaiser crown" out of his pocket wrapped in an old newspaper. Bismarck also reacted in character. "The farce," he said, could have had a better "stage manager." Nevertheless, the deputies realized that they had no other recourse than to accept the despised treaty. "The maid is ugly," Lasker remarked, "but she has to be married anyhow." On December 9 the measure passed, 195 to 32. Even the progressives voted for it; in the minority were socialists, Hanoverian Guelphs, democratic liberals, and members of the Catholic faction. On the following day the necessary changes in the north German constitution were accepted, with only six socialist votes in the negative. Finally the Reichstag resolved to send a delegation to Versailles to bid Wilhelm to accept the imperial crown.[28]

Again Wilhelm was much upset. Even now he was unreconciled to the new dignity his chancellor had so skillfully thrust upon him. The actions of Reichstag and Bundesrat, he complained, were presumptuous. Neither he nor the German princes as a whole had accepted the titles "Kaiser and Reich" that the parliament had inserted in the constitution. Toward Bismarck his manner was frigid. He would not receive the Reichstag delegation until the other sovereigns had been heard from. Among the latter not all were happy

[27] GW, VIb, 594, 598–600; Doeberl, *Bayern und Reichsgründung*, 247–248. Bamberger, *Bismarcks grosses Spiel*, 227ff. On Lasker's trip to southern Germany see HW, I, 457ff., and Oncken, *Bennigsen*, vol. 2, 180ff.

[28] GW, VIb, 609–611; Friedrich III, *Kriegstagebuch*, 264; Moritz Busch, *Bismarck: Some Secret Pages of His History* (New York, 1898), vol. 1, 292; Eduard von Wertheimer, *Bismarck im politischen Kampf* (Berlin, 1930), 444–446.

over Ludwig's commitment. The kings of Saxony and Württemberg were miffed over his failure to consult them beforehand. Once taken, however, the step was irrevocable. In the night of December 17 a telegram from Hohenschwangau reported that all rulers and free cities had given their consent. The next day Wilhelm, flanked by princes and generals, listened to the Reichstag petition presented by the venerable Simson, who on April 3, 1849, had offered the Frankfurt crown to Friedrich Wilhelm IV. Haltingly the elderly Hohenzoller, nearsighted and choked with emotion, read the favorable reply Bismarck had composed for him.[29]

Wilhelm's conduct in the Kaiser question reveals both his psychology and his relationship to Bismarck. About the sincerity of his revulsion there can be no doubt. Although he must have been aware of the web Bismarck was spinning to entrap him, he took no step to rip it asunder. This had also been true of Leopold's candidature, of the decision for war against Austria, and many other situations in preceding years. The minister had long since become completely indispensable. Bowing to his will had become a habit. It was as though a tacit understanding existed between them that, if Bismarck could make the step appear inescapable, Wilhelm would take it—reluctantly, even angrily, but conclusively. Once done, he accepted the new situation completely, for he was not a brooder and his resentments were never lasting. A few days after receiving the Reichstag delegation he awarded his chancellor the Iron Cross, first class.

Even now the matter was not ended, for the last word lay with the southern parliaments. In Baden and Hesse there was no difficulty. In Württemberg the German party, which had scored a great victory at the polls on December 5, 1870, pushed the treaties through the lower chamber over dwindling opposition. But in Bavaria there was intense dissatisfaction. Not until January 11, 1871, did the debate begin. The irreconcilables of the Patriot party denounced the mediatization of Bavaria and her subjection to Prussian autocracy and militarism. And there were also signs that Ludwig himself, disturbed by criticisms from his family, was wavering.[30]

From Versailles Bismarck watched these developments with mounting concern. In Rome he sought to bring Papal pressure to bear upon the ultramontanes. Through Werthern he secured Bray's agreement to dissolve the chamber immediately after an adverse vote. But he also warned that in any case the treaties with Baden, Hesse, and Württemberg would go into effect, as would the new constitution and the imperial title. "A painful tension" would arise in Germany that could only benefit the French. "The German nation would hold Bavaria accountable for the sacrifices made necessary by prolon-

---

[29] Friedrich III, *Kriegstagebuch*, 259, 268ff., 279–281; Oncken, ed., *Grossherzog Friedrich I.* vol. 2, 240ff.

[30] See Kläre Kraus, *Der Kampf in der bayerischen Abgeordnetenkammer um die Versailler-Verträge, 11.–21. Januar 1871* (Cologne, 1935).

gation of the war." A separate peace between Bavaria and France would be equivalent to a declaration of war on Germany.[31] In the final vote on January 21 the division of the Patriot party and the absence of three irreconcilables enabled the proponents of the treaties to achieve the necessary two-thirds majority. The margin of victory was two.

The "German Kaiser"

The final scene in the long drama of German unification, like most that preceded it, was taut with suspense. Once the imperial title had been accepted, a fresh quarrel arose over its phrasing. Wilhelm preferred: "By the grace of God, King of Prussia, chosen Kaiser of Germany." But Bismarck insisted on: "By the grace of God, German Kaiser, King of Prussia." After some discussion the Hohenzoller accepted his view that the word "chosen" would make the title appear elective, like that of the Holy Roman Empire. Reluctantly he also acceded to the argument that the imperial must precede the royal title, if the intended political effect were to be achieved. But he stubbornly insisted upon the form, "Kaiser of Germany." He wanted no "pseudo-emperorship." If he had to bear the title, it must clearly express his authority. In the crown prince and the grand duke of Baden he found support.[32]

To Bismarck the issue was petty in itself. What did it matter in which form the imperial authority was clothed, as long as it existed? He had to point out, nevertheless, that commitments had already been made to the title in its weaker form. To abandon it now would jeopardize his entire work. During the treaty negotiations Bray had insisted upon "German Kaiser" and this was the form used in Ludwig's letter. When the issue came up in the Bundesrat, he had telegraphed to Delbrück, "Kaiser of Germany, if possible, but, if the others don't want it, German Kaiser will do."[33] Hence the constitutional amendments accepted by Bundesrat and Reichstag had used the latter form. If Wilhelm could not be brought to change his mind, the amendments would have to be reworded, the agreement with Bavaria redrafted. All of the hazards so successfully surmounted would have to be faced again.

January 18, 1871, birthday of the Prussian monarchy, was the date set for the ceremony in which the emperorship was to be proclaimed. In a three-hour conference on the preceding day Wilhelm held to his position. With rising temper he insisted upon the more exalted title, yet wept that within a few hours he must "take leave of the old Prussia." Friedrich Wilhelm pointed out to his father that the house of Hohenzollern had repeatedly assumed new and higher titles as it rose in power and responsibility. Finally Wilhelm broke

---

[31] GW, VIb, 643–646, 657, 672.
[32] GW, VIb, 654–656, 662–665; Oncken, ed., *Grossherzog Friedrich I.* vol. 2, 308ff.
[33] Becker, *Bismarcks Ringen*, 811; GW, VIb, 622.

off the discussion in fury, declaring he wanted to hear no more of tomorrow's celebration. He considered abdication; "Fritz" would know better than he how to adjust to the new situation.[34] But the mood passed.

The next day the celebration took place on schedule in the glistening hall of mirrors, where the kings of France once held court. As the prince of highest rank (the kings of Saxony, Bavaria, and Württemberg not being present), Grand Duke Friedrich of Baden had the honor of hailing Wilhelm with the new title. While the company assembled, he conferred hastily with Wilhelm and Bismarck. Neither had changed his mind. When the historic moment came, Friedrich simply evaded the issue by crying out, "Long live his imperial and royal majesty, Kaiser Wilhelm!" Descending from the dais to greet the assembled princes and generals, the indignant old man passed Bismarck by without a word or handshake.[35]

To no one else, however, belonged the credit for what was consummated that wintry day in Versailles. The imperial title, the glittering uniforms and regimental standards, and Wilhelm's sonorous manifesto "To the German People"[36] symbolized the completed union of three traditions: Hohenzollern authoritarianism, Prussian militarism, and German nationalism. This new combination had a powerful influence upon German cultural life for more

PROCLAMATION OF WILHELM I AS KAISER IN THE HALL OF MIRRORS AT VERSAILLES, JANUARY 18, 1871.
TO THE KAISER'S LEFT ON THE DAIS IS GRAND DUKE FRIEDRICH OF BADEN; TO HIS RIGHT, CROWN
PRINCE FRIEDRICH WILHELM; AT THE FOOT OF THE DAIS, BISMARCK AND MOLTKE.
PAINTING BY ANTON VON WERNER.

34 Friedrich III, *Kriegstagebuch*, 334–338, 349 (n. 3).
35 GW, XV, 328–329; Oncken, ed., *Grossherzog Friedrich I.*, vol. 2, 320–329.
36 The document was composed and read by Bismarck. GW, VIb, 671–672.

than half a century thereafter. By embracing the cause of German national unity, the old Prussian "establishment" (crown, cabinet, bureaucracy, Protestant church, officer corps, and gentry) gained a fresh baptism of moral legitimacy. Its leadership in fulfilling the most compelling goal of the revolution of 1848 reaffirmed the establishment's claim to social and political predominance. But that was not all. The Prussian establishment enlarged its reach by becoming the Prussian-German establishment. Its king became German Kaiser; its ruling dynasty, Germany's ruling dynasty; its political and military institutions, the core of a refounded German Empire; its historical tradition, that of the German people as a whole. And yet the results of this revolution from above were still fragile and vulnerable in 1871. What had been accomplished by military prowess and political manipulation was yet to be consolidated and fortified.

✦ INDEX ✦